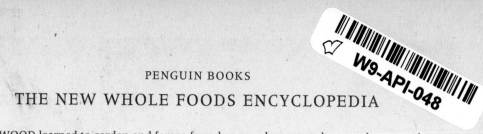

PENGUIN BOOKS

THE NEW WHOLE FOODS ENCYCLOPEDIA

REBECCA WOOD learned to garden and forage from her grandparents, who were homesteaders in northern Utah. She studied with leading experts in traditional Oriental medicine and since 1970 has taught, consulted, and written about the healing properties of whole foods and how to achieve a sustainable and healthy diet. Her book *The Splendid Grain* won both a James Beard Award and a Julia Child/IACP Award. Ms. Wood has appeared on numerous television and radio programs, including Discovery Channel's *Home Matters* program. Her food columns have appeared in *Whole Foods Magazine* and multiple newspapers. Her food articles have appeared in *Martha Stewart Living, Ladies' Home Journal, Family Circle, Cook's Illustrated,* and countless other publications. Wood and Associates, created in 1981, was the educational consultant to numerous organizations in the natural foods industry. Rebecca Wood also cofounded and directed the East-West Center in Boulder, Colorado, and has established cooking schools in London, Oregon, and Colorado. Today Ms. Wood hosts a comprehensive Web site, www.RebeccaWood.com, and is the author of the popular e-books *Detox and Cleanse, Bugs Eating You?* and *The Face Diet.* She continues to consult with people individually to help them implement a diet best suited to their personal needs and time constraints. She resides in the mountains outside Boulder, Colorado.

For the past seventeen years PEGGY MARKEL has traversed the Mediterranean and North Africa, from Elban fishing villages and Moroccan markets to the homes of Tuscan artisans and chefs, furthering her own exploration of culture and cuisine. On these journeys, she saw an opportunity to design and direct her own brand of culinary tours, which she calls Peggy Markel's Culinary Adventures. Ms. Markel is a designer, photographer, and illustrator who lives a grateful life in Florence, Italy, and Boulder, Colorado. You can read more about her at www.peggymarkel.com.

The New
Whole Foods Encyclopedia

*An A to Z of Selection, Preparation, and Storage for More Than 1,000
Common and Uncommon Fruits, Vegetables, Grains, and Herbs—
Including How to Heal with Ayurveda, Western Nutrition, and
Traditional Chinese Medicine*

A COMPREHENSIVE RESOURCE

FOR HEALTHY EATING

Rebecca Wood

Foreword by Paul Pitchford

Illustrations by Peggy Markel

PENGUIN BOOKS

PENGUIN BOOKS
Published by the Penguin Group
Penguin Group (USA) Inc., 375 Hudson Street, New York, New York 10014, U.S.A.
Penguin Group (Canada), 90 Eglinton Avenue East, Suite 700, Toronto, Ontario, Canada M4P 2Y3
(a division of Pearson Penguin Canada Inc.)
Penguin Books Ltd, 80 Strand, London WC2R ORL, England
Penguin Ireland, 25 St Stephen's Green, Dublin 2, Ireland (a division of Penguin Books Ltd)
Penguin Group (Australia), 250 Camberwell Road, Camberwell, Victoria 3124, Australia
(a division of Pearson Australia Group Pty Ltd)
Penguin Books India Pvt Ltd, 11 Community Centre, Panchsheel Park, New Delhi – 110 017 , India
Penguin Group (NZ), 67 Apollo Drive , Rosedale, North Shore 0632, New Zealand
(a division of Pearson New Zealand Ltd)
Penguin Books (South Africa) (Pty) Ltd, 24 Sturdee Avenue, Rosebank, Johannesburg 2196 , South Africa

Penguin Books Ltd, Registered Offices:
80 Strand, London WC2R ORL, England

First published in the United States of America as *The Whole Foods Encyclopedia* by Prentice Hall Press 1988
Revised and updated edition published in Penguin Books 1999
This second revised and updated edition published 2010

1   3   5   7   9   10   8   6   4   2

Copyright © Rebecca Wood, 1988, 1999, 2010
Illustrations copyright © Peggy Markel, 1999
All rights reserved

A NOTE TO THE READER
The New Whole Foods Encyclopedia is a reference volume. Because people differ widely
in their individual responses to foods, this book is not intended to treat, diagnose, or prescribe.
Neither the author nor the publisher shall be liable or responsible for any harm, damage, or illness
allegedly arising from the use of the information contained herein.
If you have a medical concern, consult a qualified health care practitioner. Ideally your practitioner
is knowledgeable about using whole foods as one facet of maintaining (or regaining) well-being.

Grateful acknowledgment is made for permission to reprint the following copyrighted work:
"Green Plum . . ." by Buson from *The Essential Haiku*, edited by Robert Hass. Selection and translation
copyright © 1994 by Robert Hass. Reprinted by permission of The Ecco Press.

LIBRARY OF CONGRESS CATALOGING IN PUBLICATION DATA
Wood, Rebecca Theurer.
The new whole foods encyclopedia : a comprehensive resource for healthy eating/
Rebecca Wood; illustrations by Peggy Markel.—2nd rev. and updated ed.
p.   cm.
Includes bibliographical references and index.
ISBN 978-0-14-311743-8
1. Natural foods—Encyclopedias. I. Title.
TX369.W67 2010
641.5'636—dc22   2009052292
Printed in the United States of America
Set in Meridien Lt Std

This book is dedicated to the long life and well-being of

the Venerable Dzigar Kongtrul Rinpoche

FOREWORD

I first met Rebecca Wood when we were both teaching at a pristine mountain retreat center in the Canadian Rockies. I can still recall her delightful cooking class dishes composed of wild herbs, whole grains, recently harvested vegetables from the garden, and freshly plucked berries.

Meeting Rebecca, I found her attuned to the present and exuding a sense of ease. In speaking with her, I could only begin to plumb the depths of her life experience, which included her natural cure from cancer, and studies with expert cooks, shamans, and master healers. Through the medium of whole foods, she has invested incredible time and effort in bringing a healing message to the world.

A few years later, with her revision of the *Whole Foods Encyclopedia* in hand, I was enthralled by the lore, insights, recipes, properties of foods, and her intuitive awareness that so clearly touches every part of her writing. One senses mastery and integration.

After reviewing the notes on the health properties of foods, and taking a pleasurable read through the rest of the text, I was reminded of a feature essential to our nutritional well-being—*quality*. How to know which foods are the best quality? What does a quality cabbage look like? Which potatoes taste best? When is the best time to buy apricots? *The New Whole Foods Encyclopedia* gives information that enables us to obtain optimum nutrition.

In addition, this massive reference informs us who benefits most from a specific food and, importantly, when a food is not appropriate or is contraindicated. I have never known a food or health product that is good for everyone, even though salespeople may lead us to believe otherwise. Knowing the properties of foods is a valuable tool. For example, if you easily become chilled, you can warm up by emphasizing more warming foods and spices in your diet. Simply changing your thermal nature can help heal afflictions marked with thermal imbalance—as any affliction may be—from arthritis to premenstrual syndrome. Rebecca includes health benefits attributed to foods in Oriental and Western traditions to help us choose the best foods for thermal and other dimensions of balance in our lives.

The New Whole Foods Encyclopedia is a vital work for several reasons, among the first being its focus on unrefined, whole foods. Today, whole foods are greatly lacking in our diet. Most people cannot identify a grain of wheat; most do not know that unrefined oils exist or that unrefined cane sugar actually prevents tooth decay and nerve deterioration instead of causing them as refined sugars do. White rice, white bread, and the other white foods can promote blood sugar imbalances, which in turn can lead to emotional instability and addictions. The denaturing of foods into separated ingredients over the last hundred years or so parallels the movement of our culture into hyperspecialization and societal fragmentation.

Perceiving food solely according to scientific data is a dull experience. Whole foods in particular are immeasurably more than mere nutrients. They are imbued with subtle life energies, colors, aromas, thermal natures, and various healing properties. Food also sustains awareness—our thoughts are influenced by it, as is life itself. To help us understand this gestalt, let's briefly contrast whole food with refined foods.

Whole foods means foods that are in their unrefined edible state, for example, whole wheat and whole grain pasta, whole fruits, and unrefined oils, salt, and sweeteners. After some four million years of evolution, humanity has just recently (ca. 1850) started consuming highly refined foods. Refined foods, such as white flour used in bread, pastry, and pasta, are not just missing a few ingredients that can be replaced by enrichment with three or four vitamins, they lack up to 50 different minerals and trace minerals, a number of vitamins, virtually all the fiber and precious oils, and untold numbers of phytochemicals that support full immune function.

These nutrients are required for complete metabolism to occur. As a result of consuming refined foods, the missing nutrients are extracted from the bones, tissues, and nerves. This is why in a land of great excess and obesity, there is so much underlying deficiency. It is precisely this etiology of deficiency that leads to cravings, addictions, emotional turmoil, and nearly every degenerative disease, including diabetes, cancer, heart disease, and arthritis, to mention the most common. Whole vegetal foods, with fiber and all nutrients intact, can reverse most cases of heart and artery disease in as little time as four weeks.

The nutrients in whole foods clean, build, and maintain the body. Refined foods rob us of our birthright—a vital body and mind during our entire life span. Hence, the great need for this encyclopedic text. It has the potential to awaken the entire food industry, as well as to educate many individuals and families about quality, healthful foods and healthy food practices. In my experience, people want good nutrition; however, they've been misinformed by incomplete or misapplied food sciences that claim refined foods are acceptable.

This pattern contains a message. If we continue with lifeless, denatured, refined food (and the refined medicines that accompany them), we lose our connection with nature. We are led unerringly to degeneration. A lifestyle of wholeness fosters strength and unity. This book helps us to respect food for the gift it is and affirms that we are at the forefront of a quiet, whole foods revolution.

A quintessential factor in our nutritional well-being, once we accept the idea of wholeness, is freshness. Recently prepared whole foods impart this. Nearly everyone can taste the liveliness in a meal of fresh foods. We hear this reminder throughout this text and receive many pointers for gathering, preparing, and locating the best-quality fresh foods.

In summary, what distinguishes *The New Whole Foods Encyclopedia* is the blend of wisdom and wit, the personal stories, the anecdotes as well as the hard science you would expect from such a seasoned researcher as Rebecca Wood. She has studied, grown, written about, sought out, and taught whole foods and their cookery over the last 30 years. I can think of no one else in America with her expertise. No other reference is as complete. This book is a superb resource. May you be inspired to dive in and delight in foods that are elegantly simple.

Paul Pitchford
Author of *Healing with Whole Foods:*
Asian Traditions and Modern Nutrition
January 1999

ACKNOWLEDGMENTS

Sincere thanks to editor Alexis Washam, Leda Scheintaub, and the Penguin team for your excellent help in producing this book.

Deepest gratitude to Bob Flaws, Honora Wolf, Paul Pitchford, Michio Kushi, and the others whose classes, books, and friendship have helped form my understanding of food.

To my students and readers over the past four decades, thank you for your questions, support, and enthusiasm about healing with whole foods.

For the unrivaled kindness of the Mangala Shri Bhuti Sangha, and especially to Elizabeth Mattis Namgyel, Jampal Namgyel, Pema Chodron, Vernon Mizner, Tashi Gonpo, Peggy Markel, Deborah J. Haynes, Nicholas and Natasha Carter, Sasha and Tatjana Meyerowitz, and the home team: Jen Kearn, Greg Maloney, Andrew Shakespeare, and Kelly Smith. For your friendship, thank you Ani Rioh Heigh, Lama Bruce Newman, Lama Jamie Kalfas, Dana Gerhardt, Michele Grace, Barbara Falconer, Carole Summer, and Chris Webster.

To my treasured parents, Mel and Verna Wood, for your countless and unrepayable kindnesses, thank you.

For my beloved children, Elizabeth, Asa, Roanna, and for Marc, Katherine, Avram, Jonah, and Dalia, I rejoice and give thanks for and to you.

CONTENTS

INTRODUCTION

In the pages that follow, you will find an alphabetical listing of available vegetables, fruits, grains, nuts, seeds, seaweeds, fungi, sweeteners, fats, oils, and culinary herbs and spices.

You'll find entries for turnips, turnip greens, and beets—but not beet greens. Turnip tops stand on their own, beet tops don't. Baby beet greens do find their way into mesclun—and I always add them to borscht—but they're not sold or served solo and so do not appear herein as an individual entry.

I've included traditional food products that once were homemade. Most of these, I prepare—or have prepared—from scratch, including umeboshi, masa, koji, bulgur, soy sauce, miso, tempeh, ghee, tofu, barley malt, rice syrup, natto, amasake, seitan, vinegar, and even (in my mother's kitchen) maraschino cherries. These food products are all part of a healthful, plant-based diet and, cherries excepted, most are available in their traditional—versus hi-tech—form.

While culinary herbs are covered in some detail, I have not included strictly medicinal herbs. Even though in the heart of my garden I grow echinacea and St. John's wort for tinctures—and I recommend them to you—they're not included here. Parsley and sage have entries because they're culinary ingredients. Chamomile, too, since it is our most common tisane.

Cornsilk squeaked in because, although my primary use of it is *medicinal* (it's a diuretic and treats kidney stones) rather than culinary, it makes an oh-so-sweet stock. Besides, the next time you're shucking corn, its silk will be right there in your hand—free for the taking—ready to be dried.

You won't find entries for alcoholic beverages, supplements, meat, fish, eggs, dairy products (except butter), or other animal foods (except honey)—the scope is the vegetable realm. Butter and honey are included for their inimitable medicinal and culinary properties. I've included the whole food supplements microalgae and barley grass and wheat grass juice. Unlike other supplements that are isolated food components, these are remarkable foods in their own right, ones that I heartily recommend to you. I will alert you to a few noxious food products, masquerading as healthful, by stating next to their entry "Not Recommended." These highly processed foods have no historical precedent and cannot enhance your health.

I include some information about foraging for freely given foods, but more as a tease. A foraging guide this is not. If, however, you find yourself out in the open spaces with a gathering bucket in hand, so much the better. Food foraging is, after all, humanity's oldest profession. Wild foods offer superior nutrients and medicinal properties, and make you feel—in one word—wild. There are three guidelines for foraging. One, identify plants carefully, since some varieties—especially mushrooms—are toxic. There are numerous regional plant guides available to help with identification. Two, gather only in areas that you are confident are free from chemical contamination. Do not gather along heavily traveled roadsides. And last, do not overforage. Always leave enough healthy plant specimens to assure their propagation.

Wild foods with commercial availability include hand-harvested wild rice, mesquite, ramps, fiddlehead ferns, glasswort, purslane, fat hen, some mushrooms, most seaweeds, some wildflower blossoms, wild blue-green algae, and pine nuts.

WHAT ENTRIES INCLUDE

Entries provide a description of the food, suggestions for its use, buying tips, and its medicinal benefits. When a foodstuff has specific storage needs, they are given within the text. (General storage information is described on pages 404–407.) Last, when a food is contraindicated for health reasons or reasons of quality, there is a "Be Mindful" note.

Entries are cross-referenced. In the case of mushrooms, oranges, grains, and others, refer to the specific food as well as to the family. If an entry does not contain a section on Medicinal Benefits or Buying, you can find its properties by looking up the cross-references.

A PERSONAL NOTE

Where did my interest in food as medicine begin? The foundations were laid at my grandpa's farm in Tremonton, Utah. How I loved being at his side, bursting with pride for both of us that "since that last rain, them sugar beets are leafing out pretty." With him or with Grandma, there was the thrill of the find when foraging pine nuts and mushrooms. And there was feasting upon the find. There was always enough to set some by and to share with friends and those in need.

My mother and her four sisters all delighted in marvelous made-from-scratch foods, from homemade root beer to my mom's signature dish, tender crescent rolls. My father and uncles, avid fishermen and hunters, provided wild game for the table. From an early age, how could I help but favor the energy in a pheasant or sage hen over supermarket chicken, for example, or seek out the pure aliveness of wild asparagus over store-bought?

It was a given that my siblings and I would help with the gardening and canning. We set aside hundreds of quart jars of tomatoes, peaches, apricots, pears, raspberries, tomatoes, and cherries, plus grape juice and assorted jams and jellies—a respectably appointed fruit larder for our Mormon family of six.

Today it's precious to visit home during canning season and help my now-88-year-old parents. I wish you could see the litany of their hands as they prep, scald, peel, pit, jar, and then share the bottled peaches with their family. Such nurture in their kitchen duet!

After college, I ended up in Boston in the home of macrobiotic teachers Michio and Aveline Kushi, who spearheaded the natural foods industry. Macrobiotics is primarily a vegetarian diet of whole (rather than refined) foods. We were a community of 25 living in two large "study houses." Aveline cooked, Michio taught, and I experienced how daily foods affected physical, emotional, and mental health. As a community, we observed and discussed the same, we studied the energetic properties of foods, and we explored the effects of diet on world cultures. We experienced how changing our eating changed our consciousness. It was a fascinating education, which I followed up with studies of Five Elements medicine at the Traditional College of Oriental Medicine in Kenilworth, England.

After 20 years of following a macrobiotic diet, I developed invasive, third-stage cervical cancer. Fortunately, I was able to reverse the cancer by using natural methods, which included adding meat back to my diet and reducing carbohydrates. In all, it was an effective lesson in moderation.

Meanwhile, I was teaching and writing about whole foods cookery. My own study of food energetics deepened as I raised my children, taught countless whole foods cookery classes both privately and in the corporate world, and maintained a diet consultation practice.

Throughout my life, I've focused my spiritual studies and practices on how to transcend limiting views and patterns for egalitarian and healing ways. This book is a meld of my interests. I envision a world where all beings are well nourished.

EARLY EDITIONS OF
THE WHOLE FOODS ENCYCLOPEDIA

The original edition, written in 1983, was entitled *Whole Foods: A Guide for Employees of Natural Food Stores*. It was part of a training program I developed for Alfalfa's Market in Boulder, Colorado, and it became the primary industry reference. I then traveled throughout the United States conducting workshops, seminars, and lectures for natural foods business. This opportunity enabled me to meet many farmers, producers, distributors, and retailers, and to learn even more about our foods, how they're produced and processed, and their quality. Over the years, I've especially enjoyed meeting the people who grow our staple foods. I love walking fields and orchards and talking crops and soil with farmers.

Five years later, this book was revised for Prentice Hall and published as *Whole Foods Encyclopedia: A Shopper's Guide*. The third revision, in 1999, was published by Penguin as *The New Whole Foods Encyclopedia*.

Twenty-six years after the original book, it is my pleasure to serve it up again. I'm heartened by how much stays the same—there are no substantive changes in the nutrient profile or energetic properties of basmati rice or mustard greens, for example. Likewise, and even more so today, we find that our common sense and the authority that tradition carries is more trustworthy than a new market trend, advertising campaign, or scientific study.

I rejoice in our expanded market offerings, especially with the increasing availability of heirloom crops such as tepary beans and agretti. The information we have available on every food is indeed astonishing; I delighted in honing my appreciation and understanding of foods while culling through the data as I revisited the entries herein. One small example: I had never before really paid attention to how an orange segment is sweetest at the stem end. A small detail, yes, but a tasty one.

I am excited to provide more in-depth information than heretofore about how to use each food medicinally. And since food sensitivities have become epidemic in proportion, I've added more information on them. If you happen to have an allergy to a certain food, then you'll find useful cross-references to its family members. For example, if walnuts trigger a reaction, then the same is more apt to be true of their relatives, black walnuts and pecans, than of other nuts. Allergies or not, it's enriching to know that cashews, mangos, mastic, pistachios, and sumac berries are all related.

As I reflect upon our food quality, information, and general health in these past 26 years, I am also sobered. I'm appalled by the corporate self-interest that continues to propagate misinformation and puts out substandard products. I have provided you with guidelines to discern quality.

To a significant degree, the quality of our food determines our health. Let's better understand our daily foods so that we might more fully enjoy and be nourished by them. Foods aren't the whole picture—add exercise, healthy lifestyle, right livelihood, and spiritual practice and you'll have preventative medicine at its best.

Cooking need not be drudgery. Over the years, I've discovered the critical ingredient in food preparation is intention. I have found that how I cultivate, prepare, serve, and eat a food affects how the food will taste and how I will assimilate it. So make your hearth a bright and welcoming place. Enjoy the appearance, touch, and aroma of cabbages and kiwis as you wash and prep. And enjoy the incomparable aromas as you simmer and serve. Then, as we sit to break bread together, may we all be renewed by earth's bounty.

R. W.

Phuntsok Choling, Ward, Colorado, June 2009

MEDICINAL BENEFITS

Foods are more subtle in their action than an aspirin or shot of penicillin, but they undoubtedly act upon us. Nibble a Sichuan pepper or drink an espresso and you experience a physiological reaction. Foods have multiple energetic properties, and discerning and using these properties to enhance well-being are an age-old activity. Hunter-gatherer peoples had a profound understanding of local plant species and knew each one's edibility and medicinal value.

This ancient knowledge helped form Western herbology and traditional Asian medical systems. While much of this wisdom was lost in the West, it has, however, remained vital in India and even more so in China, where written records of a food's medicinal applications for humans extend unbroken for more than 4,000 years. Traditional Chinese medicine has the most sophisticated and time-proven pharmacopoeia in existence.

Reclaiming this wisdom and weaving it in with contemporary knowledge of nutrition enables us—from a biochemical vantage—to select foods that encourage healthful metabolic processes. Using this book as a guide, you can attune to the medicinal effects that foods have on your well-being. What an invaluable key to preventative health care!

Here is an overview of how to determine a food's specific medicinal value. (Refer to the bibliography for sources of more detailed information concerning traditional Chinese medicine and Ayurveda.) If any of these models is too unscientific for you, consider it a poetic device and digest it a bit at a time. Or bypass it entirely. A year from now you might consider reconsidering it. And for any unfamiliar terms in an entry, refer to the Glossary of Terms on page 399.

WHOLE FOODS

A whole food has only one ingredient—itself. Most whole foods have been in our diets for eons. Favoring whole, intact foods builds your health. Fragmented foods, even whole wheat flour as compared to the whole wheat itself, impart less energy. Eating integral foods that are capable of regenerating themselves supports our own regeneration. Nutritionally there's no difference between the whole wheat flour in a bagel and a handful of wheat grains . . . energetically there's a world of difference.

Refined foods have something taken away from them and, therefore, are not as *whole*some. Apple juice is just part of the apple and, as such, is metabolized as a simple sugar. In excess, fruit juice is problematic, though apple juice is far better (closer to being "whole") than a cane-sugar-sweetened soft drink. But then a soft drink sweetened with what once actually grew (cane) is far superior to a drink sweetened with high-fructose corn syrup, chlorine-containing Splenda, or the chemical compound aspartame.

Traditionally refined foods that you can duplicate in your own home kitchen are in a different league than are today's highly processed foods. Simple technologies do not denature a food. At home you can extract extra virgin coconut or olive oil from a coconut or olives, but you cannot produce "lite" olive oil or an aroma-free coconut oil. Likewise, you can make delicious and healthful soymilk or tofu from soybeans, but you cannot make soy isolates, margarine, TVP, soy deli foods, or lecithin.

Highly processed foods resemble nothing you could grow in your garden or produce in your home. They've been stripped, colored, extruded, refined, bleached, injected, hydrogenated, genetically modified, irradiated, gassed, and grown with hormones, fertilizers, pesticides, antifungal agents, and herbicides.

No matter what the FDA claims or what slick marketing strategies exhort, ignore newfangled ingredients and products. Rely on whole foods that for thousands of years have promoted human health.

FRESH FOODS

Fresh produce, in a word, enlivens. It offers more than irradiated, old, overly mature, or past-their-prime fruits and vegetables can. Grains, beans, sea vegetables, and seeds remain fresh for a year or more when properly stored. Due to their higher fat content, nuts—once shelled—quickly become stale. *Unrefined* vegetable oils are fragile and demand special processing, handling, and storage to remain fresh and viable.

The same holds true for freshly cooked foods. They impart more energy the day they're prepared rather than the next day—or in the case of packaged foods, the next month or the next year.

COOKED FOODS

Historically, people have eaten at least 80 percent cooked foods because they are easier to assimilate—and therefore more nourishing and energizing. In addition, cooking offers a greater range of sensory pleasures. As delicious as a fresh peach or carrot is, think how limiting it would be if we could only eat it raw.

Raw foods have great appeal when your diet contains many packaged, refined, leftover, and denatured foods. As you increase your consumption of freshly prepared foods, the craving for raw typically decreases.

Popular dietary advice mistakenly claims that cooking destroys nutrients. That's a partial truth. Yes, prolonged cooking at high temperatures destroys enzymes and water-soluble vitamins. Moderate cooking, however, does *not* destroy carbohydrates, proteins, fatty acids (omega-3s excepted), fat-soluble vitamins, minerals, or micronutrients. Most of our ills today are not from a deficiency of enzymes and water-soluble vitamins.

People with strong digestion and abundant energy better assimilate salads and raw fruit. On the other hand, people suffering from low energy, congestion, allergies, and weak digestion better assimilate cooked foods.

Freshly cooked foods give energy. If you doubt this, try for one week to eat only microwaved, left-over, stale, frozen, or canned foods. Physically, emotionally, and mentally, you'll probably feel lousy.

THERMAL PROPERTIES OF FOODS

When consumed, foods have an overall cooling, neutral, or warming effect. This observation helped form Western herbology and medicine from Persian times until the seventeenth century. It remains a critical tenet in traditional Oriental medicine as well as in Ayurvedic medicine.

While all agree that garlic is heating and watermelon cooling, exceptions arise, as a result of each model's paradigm. For example, in traditional Chinese medicine the overall effect of radishes is considered cooling. But in Ayurvedic medicine, radishes increase *agni*, or digestive fire, and are therefore considered warming. Both are correct within their context. For consistency, I follow the traditional Chinese medical way of evaluating thermal properties.

Here are seven rules of thumb that suggest a food's thermal properties:

1. Foods that take longer to grow, like cabbage and winter squash, are more warming than foods that grow quickly, like lettuce and summer squash.
2. A food is more cooling when eaten raw than when it is cooked.
3. Chilled food is more cooling than warm or room-temperature food.
4. Blue, green, or purple foods are more cooling than similar foods that are red, orange, or yellow; thus a lime cools more than a lemon does.
5. Cooking a food with more time, more oil or fat, less water, greater pressure, or at higher temperatures makes that food more warming.
6. Foods cooked over gas or wood heat impart more warmth than foods cooked with electricity. A microwave-cooked food holds and conveys even less warmth than food cooked on an electric range.
7. Tropical and subtropical foods tend to be more cooling than foods grown in temperate zones.

ORGANIC FOODS

Buying organic is voting with your fork. Favor organic foods whenever possible for their extra flavor and greater nutritional value and energy. Chemically grown foods take their toll on your kidneys and liver (the organs that filter chemicals) as well as on the environment. We're barely four generations into ingesting artificial chemicals, and judging from the results, it's been a disastrous experiment.

Unfortunately, the National Organic Program (NOP) is largely dysfunctional due to inadequate testing and documentation. Additionally, there are problematic loopholes, for example, foods may be labeled organic even when irradiated, grown with domestic sewage sludge as a fertilizer, or genetically engineered. The term "organic" on foods imported from China and elsewhere may be merely a label decoration. Domestically, there are problems as well. Some of our largest organic food companies are often cited for disregarding organic regulations.

Whenever possible, buy from a local and known source or from a reputable manufacturer. For help discerning honest manufacturers, I recommend the Cornucopia Institute (www.cornucopia.org) as a resource. For example, they researched and published the national and various regional manufacturers that fully disclose their soybean sources, do not use hexane-extracted lecithin (as is found in some "organic" products), are in compliance with organic testing, and that perform testing for GMO (genetically modified organism) contamination on every load of incoming soybeans. Cornucopia also names manufacturers who make spurious sustainability claims and actually purchase their raw materials from China while refusing to make public their documentation.

If your budget for organic foods from reliable sources does not cover all of your food purchases, then spend it wisely. As many toxins concentrate in fatty acids, your top dollar is best spent on organic meat and dairy, and then on nuts, seeds, and oils. Hopefully it includes organic produce as well.

Nonorganic strawberries, celery, and apples can contain as many as 80 pesticide residues. At the very least, consider avoiding commercial produce that is highest in pesticide residues. According to Cindy Burke, author of *To Buy or Not to Buy Organic*, vegetables on the top of the list include sweet peppers, spinach, potatoes, and celery. The fruits highest in pesticide residues and therefore best avoided include strawberries, raspberries, apples, peaches, pears, nectarines, and cherries. (Nonorganic vegetables and fruits that are essentially free of pesticides include avocados, bananas, onions, broccoli, blueberries, and cabbage.)

If you are pregnant or nursing or have young children, to the very best of your ability, favor organic and unrefined foods. Toxins in a mother's food can cross the placenta to the growing fetus or wind up in breast milk. Our young are developing organs to last a lifetime. Infants and children are highly vulnerable to health and developmental damage from contaminants because they eat more food relative to their body mass, have fast-growing speedy metabolisms, and eat less varied diets.

SEASONAL AND REGIONAL PRODUCE

Seasonality is not an issue for shelf-stable whole grains and beans. Produce is a different matter. I grow watermelon, grapes, and zucchini in my garden, but not in January. I could purchase these cooling foods fresh in January, shipped in from a different region, but their thermal properties won't support me staying warm in zero temperatures. Besides, a long-distance zucchini has no flavor. It makes sense to eat zucchini in season when it tastes like zucchini.

Prior to the advent of refrigerated trucking in the 1940s, people ate seasonal produce or what they had set by. Period. In cold weather, my grandmother's fresh options were a few cold-loving greens like broccoli and kale from the garden; parsley from the pot on her windowsill; and potatoes, onions, cabbage, turnips, rutabagas, parsnips, carrots, and squash from her root cellar. In addition to dried or preserved fruits, she also stored apples and pears.

Eating seasonally doesn't mean that we must limit ourselves. But at the supermarket, favor local produce as much as possible. The best way to attune to seasonal produce is to garden.

Until very recently, people consumed only regional food staples. Unlike us, most people knew the hands that grew, milled, winnowed, slaughtered, and cooked their staples. Support retailers who clearly label their food sources.

Purchasing regional foods strengthens your local economy—besides offering superior flavor. Also, foods of your region help you to be in balance with and attuned to your specific environment.

DOCTRINE OF SIGNATURE

In natural healing systems worldwide, people have discovered that a food's appearance often indicates its medicinal potential. Thus a beet's color correctly indicates that beets build blood. The milky sap of mature lettuce aptly infers that lettuce supports lactation. Beef and chicken liver supports our liver function. To work with this system, look at the foods you eat with a new and expansive eye, and then notice how specific foods make you feel.

COROLLARY VEGETABLE PARTS

Similar to the doctrine of signature is that each plant part has a propensity to support the corollary body part. From the bottom up, here's a quick sketch:

- **Roots** Vegetable roots correlate to our roots—our intestines, kidneys, and regenerative organs. Roots are the most mineral dense plant part and the most strengthening. Consider the types of roots to further determine their potential. Take a radish, turnip, and carrot, for example—the carrot penetrates the earth more deeply and therefore is, energetically, more strengthening to the kidneys than a radish or turnip.
- **Corms, Rhizomes, and Tubers** Growing belowground, as the thickened, fleshy part of an underground stem, these food storage parts of plants lack the mineral density of true roots. Traditional medical systems recommend tubers for people wishing to gain weight, as is suggested by their amorphous, undifferentiated mass. Other vegetables have a distinct top, bottom, and often a core. A tuber's energy is, nevertheless, more grounding than a stalk or flower. Potatoes and sweet potatoes are tubers; taro and celery root are corms; ginger and lotus are rhizomes.
- **Bulbs** The onion family has an underground vertical shoot with thickened leaf bases that store food for the plant. These bulbs are nutritive and grounding but not as nutrient dense as their true roots, which are at the bulb's base. While our only common edible bulbs are from the onion family, the stamen of the crocus, also a bulb, yields the wondrous colorant and flavorant saffron.

- **Stalks and Stems** The stalk of a vegetable transports. Vegetable stalks are good for moving our energy and may perk up someone whose energy is stuck or who has a limited view. Examples of vegetables with pronounced stalks include asparagus, bok choy, cardoons, celery, Chinese cabbage, chives, fennel, leeks, and scallions.
- **Leaves** Chlorophyll is to a plant what blood is to an animal. Since leaves are richest in chlorophyll, eating leafy greens supports blood formation and liver function. In addition, leaves also breathe by converting carbon dioxide into oxygen, and so eating leafy greens supports our lungs. Greens with greater surface area, like a sprig of parsley, offer more chlorophyll than narrow leaves, like a scallion blade.
- **Flowers** Our eyes are drawn to faces and flowers. It's where the essence is more clearly seen, and temperature-wise it is measurably warmer than the rest of the plant. Eating broccoli and cauliflower brings energy up to the head. Eating actual blossoms revivifies the spirit. It's amazing how a tiny blossom packs so much energy.
- **Seeds** A seed, like an egg, is the self-contained embryonic plant that holds the future. Seeds tonify our regenerative organs. Seeds contain more precious and nutrient-dense fatty acids than other plant parts. Grains, beans, seeds, and nuts are both the seed and the fruit in one.
- **Fruit** A fruit is the ripened ovary of a seed-bearing plant that contains the seed. What we commonly term a fruit also contains soft fleshy tissues high in sugars. These lush and juicy fruits engender softness and a sense of ease or relaxation. However, a diet with excessive sugars—fruit sugars or otherwise—can make one too soft, unfocused, or ungrounded. In general, fruits tend to be cooling and cleansing.

WESTERN NUTRITION

Structural in view, Western nutrition takes things apart and looks at the pieces—literally. Years ago, we learned that carrots are good for the eyes because they're high in vitamin A. Next, we learned of the pre–vitamin A factors, carotenes. Now carotenes have been further subdivided into first alpha and beta, and now more recently into gamma, delta, epsilon, and zeta. We can anticipate that as scientists continually reduce nutrients to smaller parts, termed "phytochemicals," the supplement industry will have an unending supply of newly discovered micronutrients to address specific health problems. This mechanist view treats symptoms rather than causes.

It's a valuable contribution, but not the whole picture.

YIN AND YANG

Asian healing modalities are based on a yin-yang system that promotes health and harmony through balance. Yin refers to the relatively more passive processes that are more like water in substance. Our body's fluids and tissues (hormones, blood, lymph, flesh, bones, and so on) are yin. Conversely, yang processes are relatively more active and tend to be more fiery and energetic. Our energy, mental and spiritual processes, and life essence are yang.

The yin-yang system is useful in describing foods' medicinal action. For instance, according to its thermal nature, a yin food tends to cool us down while a yang food tends to warm us. Imagine eating watermelon on a sizzling-hot summer afternoon. The melon's cooling fluid (yin) helps balance the hot (yang) weather. If you're suffering from the common cold, cooking with fresh ginger helps resolve it. Ginger's hot, ascending, dispersing yang qualities help dry up the yin (watery mucus deposits) and drive out the invading pathogens.

A balance of yin and yang promotes health and harmony. Use this system to understand imbalances within your body, and then choose appropriate foods or herbs to support your overall health.

TRADITIONAL CHINESE MEDICINE

Traditional Chinese medicine assumes that we maintain optimum health through a balanced diet and lifestyle. A diet of wholesome, easy-to-assimilate foods promotes digestion, and whatever promotes digestion supports the health of the entire organism. Health concerns (imbalances) are adjusted with diet and lifestyle modifications. If a problematic condition persists, accelerating levels of intervention are indicated, starting with the least invasive, such as herbal medicines, and progressing as necessary up to more invasive treatments like acupuncture.

The use of foods and herbs as medicine is based upon a science of functional relationships, which considers various properties according to their ability to strengthen and regulate specific body systems. It's termed the Five Elements system, and each element is associated with an organ/meridian system and other attributes, including flavor, color, season, time of day, emotions, and environmental influence.

According to this system, a food has energetic properties of tonifying and regulating, and it influences meridian pathways. Meridians are the route whereby an organ system's energy travels.

Tonifying Foods are strengthening to a specific bodily substance or function.

- **Chi Tonics** improve and maintain the quality and quantity of available energy in the body. Beef, ginseng, and sweet potatoes are examples.
- **Blood Tonics** improve and maintain the quality of immediate nourishment available to the body; examples include beans, beets, and dark leafy greens.
- **Yin Tonics** improve and maintain our deepest reserves of subtle nourishment and soothe our system; examples include apples, honey, and watermelon.
- **Yang Tonics** maintain and improve our ability to generate warmth and stimulate our system; examples include cinnamon, garlic, and quinoa.

Regulating Foods help remove conditions of stagnancy or excess; they act the following seven ways:

- **Chi Circulation** is stimulated by sweet and pungent flavors; examples include basil, cayenne, and mustard greens.
- **Blood Circulation** is also regulated by sweet and pungent flavors, as chi moves the blood; examples include eggplant, peaches, and vinegar.

- **Heat** Excessively hot conditions (like a fever, infection, or menopausal discomfort) are improved with cooling foods, which help moisten and quell the fire. Examples include barley, mint, and sprouts.
- **Cold** Warming foods that increase one's thermal temperature improve cold conditions such as cold extremities and low energy; examples include black pepper, chicken, and winter squash.
- **Damp** When the body doesn't burn off excess moisture, damp conditions of either water or mucus occur. This is exacerbated by overeating; by eating excessive carbohydrates, fruits, sugars, or raw foods; by consuming refined fats or excessive nuts; and from lack of exercise and/or living in a humid environment. Symptoms include overweight, lethargy, edema, skin diseases, cysts, cancer, candidiasis, and tumors. Foods that astringe or burn off damp include aduki beans, green tea, and parsley.
- **Water** Where moisture is retained as water, as in edema, foods that drain water include grapes, lettuce, and seaweed.
- **Mucus** When dampness coagulates it forms as mucus. When mucus occurs in the respiratory system, it's labeled phlegm. Foods that help resolve mucus, and also phlegm, include almonds, daikon, and onions.

Pathways or Meridians The tonifying and regulating actions of foods have a general influence on the whole body. But, via the meridians, they may also have a specific influence on certain organs. Thus, for example, lettuce is not considered a tonifying food; it's not as strengthening as beef. But lettuce is a cooling food that travels the large intestine and stomach meridians and aids chi circulation to help regulate damp, water, and hot conditions. Note: While not all cooling foods reduce hot conditions, lettuce does (but chicory and zucchini do not).

The following chart will help you apply the "Medicinal Benefits" information found throughout the book to your specific health needs.

FIVE ELEMENT CHART

Pull out your mirror, look at your face, and read column 1. Using Five Elements and the ancient Chinese art of face diagnosis, you can match a health symptom (columns 2 and 3) with its correlating element. Take a "before" photo. Refer to that element's diet and lifestyle suggestions (columns 4 to 6) and use the index (beginning on page 420) to find foods that help remedy your symptom. For example, if you have an earth symptom such as chronic fatigue or anxiety, the "earth element" entry in the index refers you to foods especially healing to you. You'll also find that food entries include this invaluable Five Element information.

Make appropriate diet and lifestyle modifications according to the element that your symptoms indicate. Note your facial changes and track how your physical and emotional conditions improve. With a balanced diet suited to your specific condition, your glowing face will clearly mirror your renewed well-being and vitality (column 7). For free support materials, visit my Web page, www.rwood.com. For a comprehensive program, see my e-book, *The Face Diet*.

In the **Medicinal Benefits** entry for most of foods listed herein, you'll see how a specific food supports specific bodily organ functions (one of the Five Elements) and, therefore, its healing

Notes: *Don't expect all symptoms to be present. The same symptom may relate to more than one element (for example, both metal and wood trigger complexion problems). "Irregularities" in column 1 refers to color, shape, texture, size, lumps, veins, and/or lines.*

Element	1. Facial Diagnosis	2. Emotional Clues of Imbalance	3. Common Physical Complaints	4. Foods to Avoid	5. Foods to Favor	6. Action to Support Health	7. Health Indicators
EARTH Organ system: spleen/stomach Flavor: sweet Color: yellow Season: harvest Direction: centering	Dark skin near inner corner of eyes; irregularities of upper lip.	Worried, fretful, nervous, compulsive. Oversympathetic or undersympathetic to others.	Hypoglycemia, chronic fatigue, sinusitis, weak digestion, food sensitivities, bloating. Excess weight, yeast, and menstrual problems.	Excessive sweets, carbohydrates; fruits; cold or raw foods. Artificial sweeteners.	Freshly cooked, easy-to-digest foods. Starchy vegetables. Soups and stews. Moderate use of natural sweeteners.	Regular meals (don't skip meals). Sing and dance. Avoid a damp, humid climate.	Hardworking, practical, creative, responsible, nurturing. Strong, toned muscles. Lips a healthy pink color.
METAL Organ system: lungs/large intestine Flavor: pungent Color: white Season: autumn Direction: descending	Irregularities on cheeks, lower lip, and 1/2 to 1 inch below eyes. Complexion problems.	Unresolved grief, sadness, melancholy. Feel "stuck" or like a victim.	Viral, fungal, bacterial infections. Skin, lung, and bowel infections or problems.	Coffee, allergens, dairy, baked goods, mucus-forming foods.	Pungent foods, root vegetables, moist (not dry) foods like noodles versus pizza crust.	Avoid dry climate (or hydrate home with plants).	Lustrous skin and hair. Strong immune system. Steady, orderly personality. Effective in what you do.
WATER Organ system: kidneys/bladder Flavor: salty Color: dark, black Season: winter Direction: sinking	Irregularities and discoloration directly below eyes; occasionally dark color above the eyes.	Fear, depression, paranoia, insecurity, nervous, emotionally cold.	Weak bones, teeth, legs. Gray hair or balding. Dizziness, emaciation, infertility, menstrual problems. Ear or hearing problems.	Frozen or chilled foods. Stimulants, caffeine, intoxicants, chemicals.	Seaweed, beans, root vegetables, bone stock, meat, animal kidneys. Adequate salt.	Protect yourself from the cold (especially your lower back); walk. Avoid excessive sitting or standing.	Bright eyes, healthy hair. Courageous, strong will, gentle, active, yet calm.
WOOD Organ system: liver/gallbladder Flavor: sour Color: green Season: spring Direction: rising	Line(s) between eyebrows or across nose bridge. Puffy above eyes. Complexion problems or yellow/green pallor. Rigid body.	Anger, impatience, depression, resentful, rude, impulsive, mentally rigid, arrogant, stressed.	Vision problems. Lumps, cysts, tumors, menstrual problems, belching, gas, indigestion, spasms, allergies, headaches. Wakeful between 11 p.m. and 3 a.m.	Refined oils, excess nuts, fried foods, drugs, and intoxicants. Overeating or eating after 6 p.m.	Sour-tasting foods, leafy greens, quality oils and fats, sprouts, onions and garlic, beets, cabbage, chlorophyll-rich foods.	Avoid wind. Exercise regularly. Move and stretch your whole body.	Enjoys adventure. Calm, excellent judgment. Strong and flexible: a natural leader.
FIRE Organ system: heart/small intestine Flavor: bitter Color: red Season: summer Direction: floating	Florid or pallid facial color, no irregularities at nose tip.	Confused, insomnia, memory loss, irrational behavior, depression, mental illness.	Lethargic, tired, seizures, stabbing pain, shortness of breath, speech problems. Aversion to heat.	Stimulants, excessive hot spices, refined oils and sugar.	Mushrooms, whole grains, lettuce, lemons, cucumber. Freshly prepared foods. Some bitter-tasting foods.	Meditate, relax. Avoid strenuous exercise (especially in the heat).	Relaxed, humble, joyous, friendly, active, expansive, clear thinking.

potential. Sorrel, for example, is both green and sour tasting, and so it acts upon the liver. Whereas watercress, also green, acts upon the liver, but its pungent flavor gives it lung/colon action, and as a water plant it influences the kidneys.

In nature, mix too much water with earth and you'll have a sticky environment. Excessive moisture challenges the spleen (earth element), and so living in a humid environment may exacerbate digestive imbalance. Also, eating too many sweets (the earth element flavor) often creates a too-damp, sticky digestive system that is the perfect environment for an overgrowth of fungi, bacteria, and candidiasis. To support balance, minimize the use of foods that promote dampness, such as dairy products, eggs, meat, pineapple, salt, soy products, and sweeteners. Also, use bitter-tasting foods that dry dampness, including amaranth, aduki beans, asparagus, bitter melon, celery, lettuce, garlic, turmeric, turnips, and vinegar. In the index, you'll find foods are listed according to their energetic actions, such as their propensity to be drying, moistening, warming, or cooling.

AYURVEDA

As with Chinese medicine, Indian Ayurvedic medicine was developed by a culture using a plant-based diet of whole, fresh, seasonal, and regional foods. Its purpose was to promote health and to prevent disease. An interesting difference between Ayurvedic and Chinese medicine is the fact that India is predominately a subtropical region and China is predominately a temperate region. Because of this dramatic climatic difference, Ayurvedic cuisine used more sweat-inducing spices and is overall a more cooling and cleansing diet.

The Five Elements in Ayurveda correspond closely to the old European system of the humors. They are earth, water, fire, air, and ether. Depending upon the qualities of these elements, people are described as one of three *doshas*, or types, which are *vata*, *pitta*, and *kapha*. Each human being is a combination of these *doshas*. Additionally, the practitioner looks at a person's constitutional *dosha* as well as their current condition to formulate treatment. Foods described as *tridoshic* are balancing to all conditions.

Vata, a combination of air and ether elements, embodies the very essence of life energy and is considered dry, light, cold, clear, hard, subtle, and mobile. It relates most directly to the nervous system but also rules respiration, movement, will, and sense acuity. Foods that reduce an excessively *vata* condition are nurturing, soft, soothing, warm, and have a sweet flavor.

Pitta, the fire element, governs our internal heat, digestion, circulation, thirst, courage, and intelligence. Foods that reduce excess fire are drying and cooling. They have a bitter, astringing, or sweet flavor.

Kapha, the water and earth element, is cold, wet, heavy, and slow; it builds the body and fosters peacefulness and patience. Foods that reduce excess *kapha* are drying, warm, and cleansing with spicy, bitter, and astringent flavors.

Coffee, for example, overstimulates the already overly mental *vata* type, and it is too exciting for the already excitable *pitta* person. However, for the lethargic *kapha* person, a cup of coffee can provide a useful start-up energy.

See the Ayurvedic Food Guidelines section on pages 411–414 for a more thorough description of the three *dosha*s and recommended dietary guidelines for each *dosha*.

END NOTE

I hope my description of these healing systems helps you decipher a food's medicinal properties. But don't fill your head with too many food facts and figures. Rather, fill your belly with good food. Then notice how it makes you feel.

Knowing is both a cognitive and a carnal process. Thus as you attune yourself to a food's potential, watch your relationship to that food deepen. In any relationship, the more deeply we know the other—be it a neighbor, your pet cat, or an apple—the more that relationship offers. We don't expect depth from a stranger. Anonymous foods provide calories, but they lack succor. May your everyday food choices help ameliorate specific health problems, and may you be deeply nourished and utterly satisfied.

The New
Whole Foods Encyclopedia

AÇAÍ
Amazon Palm Berry
(*Euterpe oleracea Mart*)

Although an açaí (pronounced ah-sah-ee) berry looks like a grape, don't bite hard. It is 90 percent seed encased in a scant layer of flesh and, typically, a thin dark purple skin. These berries grow on the tops of açaí palm trees and are native to central and tropical South America. The very tip of the palm itself is also enjoyed as the vegetable known as heart of palm.

Medicinal Benefits Açaí fruit, a newly popularized "cure-all," has 10 times more antioxidants than red grapes and is traditionally used by Amazonian peoples to boost both stamina and libido.

Açaí fruit scored "the highest of any food reported to date against the peroxyl radical," according to the *Journal of Agricultural and Food Chemistry*. It reports that açaí berries trigger a self-destruct response in up to 86 percent of tested leukemia cells.

This makes açaí an invaluable food-medicine that helps maintain the healthy function of bodily organs and systems—including the immune system—with antiviral, anticancer, antifungal, and antimicrobial properties. The fruit is used to treat anemia, diabetes, and dysmenorrhea. Açaí is rich in B vitamins, minerals, and fiber, and has multiple phytosterols. Among other benefits, phytosterols, also known as plant sterols, help reduce blood plasma cholesterol. Açaí root is used for hepatitis.

Use In South America, açaís are eaten raw, but as the fresh fruits do not ship well, only their juice (powdered or fresh) or frozen fruit pulp is exported. The puree can be served cold or warm as a topping or added to frozen desserts. Açaí juice is featured in nutritional beverages, energy formulas, and supplements. Açaí seed oil is used as an antiaging agent in the cosmetics industry.

See **Fruit; Palm Family.**

ACEROLA
Acerola Cherry, Barbados Cherry, West Indian Cherry
(*Malpighia glabra*)

Famed for its vitamin C content, this bright red, cherrylike acerola is about the size of a grape and contains several hard seeds. Acerola is a common decorative shrub throughout the semitropical Americas and southern Texas and California. Should one grace your yard, by all means enjoy the sweet and sour cherries straight from the bush, and plan to pie or jam the rest. The fruit has a raspberrylike flavor. As acerola declines within a few hours after it is plucked, its primary commercial use is in the supplement industry.

One hundred grams of acerola juice contains 1,600 milligrams of vitamin C; the same amount of orange juice contains 138 milligrams. Purchase acerola powder from the supplement section of natural food stores and stir into energy drinks, desserts, and beverages.

ACHIOTE SEE **ANNATTO.**

ACORN
(*Quercus* spp.)

More than squirrels feast on the fruit of oak trees, acorns. As oak trees thrive in temperate regions worldwide, acorn meal has figured in countless world cuisines. It is currently featured in some Asian foods and Native American recipes and is a favorite food of foragers and survivalists. Like its chestnut relative, an acorn is a thin-shelled starchy seed; the acorn, however, is nestled in a tiny basal cup.

Medicinal Benefits Acorns have antioxidant and antimicrobial properties. Tea from oak bark or acorns makes an astringent, antiseptic beverage used internally for prolapses, hemorrhage, and diarrhea. Externally it may be used for eczema and as an antiseptic for minor abrasions.

Use Nibble a seed and if it is pleasant tasting, roast or boil some more and enjoy as a treat. To leach out their bitter-tasting tannins, chop the seeds and boil in water for 15 minutes. (Acorns from white oak species require little if any leaching, whereas those from red or black oak species are higher in tannins and may require several boiling baths.) Pulverize acorns in a food processor and use the meal in combination with other grains in mush, soups, bread, and quick breads.

ACORN TEA PARTY

My children used to forage acorns, as do my grandchildren today. Since the woody caps make perfect doll-size tea cups, we have a seasonal supply of the nutmeats. We leach out their tannins, roast them to bring up their flavor, and then stir them into muffins or cookies for their excellent flavor—and for the fun of serving acorn treats at our tea parties.

See **Beech Family; Coffee Substitutes; Nuts.**

ACORN SQUASH SEE SQUASH; SQUASH, WINTER.

ADUKI BEAN SEE BEANS AND LEGUMES.

AGAR
Agar Agar, China Grass, Kanten, Vegetable Gelatin
(*Gelidium amansii, G. corneum, G. cartilagineum*)

Contrary to popular belief, gelatin is *not* made from cattle hooves and horns. Commercial gelatin is extracted from the dregs (the cartilage, ligaments, tendons, bones, and hides) of cattle, horses, and swine. This information gives agar—a nutritious seaweed gelling agent—extra appeal.

You may remember agar from school days as the growth medium found in petri dishes. White and semitranslucent, it is processed from several varieties of red marine algae known as agarophytes (agar yielding). These algae grow as deep as 200 feet in stunning purplish red fronds. Their color pigments enable them to absorb what little light penetrates their deeply dark wet and mineral-dense environment.

These seaweed fronds are refined to extract an odorless, tasteless, colorless, and transparent 94 percent complex carbohydrate that gels, retains water, and emulsifies. Typically agar products are a blend of several different agar varieties. Agar is available flaked, powdered, granulated, or extruded into crinkly strands or large (and when purchased from Asian food stores, sometimes colored) bars.

Agar is the base for many famous Asian jelled desserts, including the Japanese jellied dessert *yokan*, Chinese almond bean curd, and Burmese coconut jelly (*kyauk kyaw*). Throughout the world, agar is used as a texture agent in jam, jelly, yogurt, processed meat, beverages, and confections, as well as in many industrial products.

Medicinal Benefits Agar gel not only enhances the flavors of other foods, but it has remarkable medicinal properties. If taken as a supplement, it is a weight-reduction aid, as agar's indigestible fiber absorbs and retains water, resulting in a feeling of fullness. Its remarkable fiber also soothes the digestive tract and chelates with (and then dispels from the body) toxic and radioactive pollutants. Agar is an excellent invalid and infant food, as it is light, nourishing, and easy to digest.

Agar contains absolutely no calories and is mineral rich. It reduces *vata* and *kapha*.

Use Use agar to gel fruit desserts and aspics as well as to thicken soups and jellies. Or simply stir in ½ teaspoon powdered agar into a glass of fruit or vegetable juice. As it requires heat to gel, adding it to a cold beverage will go unnoticed (no need to tell the kids they're drinking seaweed) and it will slow down the absorption of simple sugars, thus helping regulate blood sugar as well as boosting nutrition and flavor. And it will make the juice more filling.

To firmly gel 2 cups of liquid, use 1 teaspoon agar powder as per the accompanying recipe. Some ingredients affect agar's gelling ability. Acidic fruits (such as citrus and strawberries) may require additional agar, and it simply won't gel with highly acidic foods like kiwi and wine. The enzymes in raw pineapple, fresh figs, papaya, mango, and peaches lessen its gel-ability, as does the oxalic acid in chocolate, rhubarb, and spinach.

Be Mindful If you use dry agar powder, granules, or capsules as a weight-reduction aid, stir into (or swallow) with adequate fluid. Should agar become stuck in your throat or esophagus, it can swell rapidly and may cause

BETTER THAN JELL-O DESSERT AND KITCHEN REMEDY

Here's a dessert that takes 3 minutes to cook and—without refrigeration—sets in 30 minutes. As agar enhances other flavors, your dessert tastes more delicious than the fruit juice and fruits themselves. You'll find this unpretentious dessert satisfying for all, and one that especially delights children.

As a kitchen remedy for a nonproductive cough or to ease bronchitis, make the accompanying gelatin recipe as is. For a pleasant dessert, substitute other juices (except citrus) or fruits (except figs, mangos, raw pineapple, figs, papayas, or kiwis, which will not gel well).

Makes 6 cups.

- 4 cups apple juice or fresh apple cider
- 2 teaspoons agar powder (or 4 teaspoons granular agar, or 5 tablespoons kanten flakes)
- 2 cups diced fresh apples or pears

Place the juice, agar, and apples in a medium saucepan. Do not cover. Bring to a boil and watch closely to prevent boiling over. Reduce the heat, stir to blend, and simmer for 3 to 5 minutes, or until the apples soften to desired texture. Pour into individual serving dishes and allow to set on the counter (or, to expedite, refrigerate).

Variations: For a softer (some might say less "rubbery" gel), reduce the agar by one quarter. For a creamier texture, add and cook in 2 tablespoons kudzu or tapioca powder dissolved in 2 tablespoons cold water and stir and cook for an additional minute or two or until the mixture is translucent.

choking. Do *not* take as a dry supplement if you have trouble swallowing.

See **Kanten; Seaweed Family; Vegetable.**

AGAR AGAR SEE AGAR.

AGAVE NECTAR (NOT RECOMMENDED)
Agave Syrup

Imagine a mild-tasting honey that is extra-sweet but not too sticky and you'll have a fair flavor and texture description of agave (pronounced uh-GAH-vay) nectar. This syrup is produced from a large desert plant with spiky leaves. To harvest, the pineapple-shaped agave heart is hollowed out from the top and the plant secretes a milky white liquid into this basin. The liquid is collected and enzymatically processed into tequila or agave nectar. It is primarily produced in the state of Jalisco, Mexico.

Some people, I for one, object to its slightly metallic aftertaste. It is commonly—and erroneously—assumed to be more healthful than honey. Agave is popular with raw food advocates as it's spuriously marketed as raw. It's also regarded as good for diabetics because of its low glycemic value. On the market since the 1990s, agave nectar is produced in different grades and varies in flavor and color. As is true for most foods, the lighter colored syrup is lighter in flavor and the darker product has a richer flavor profile.

Medicinal Benefits Agave syrup does not create a "sugar rush" as do other simple sugars because it is 90 percent fructose and, therefore, does not stimulate digestive insulin secretion. It is higher in minerals than honey.

Use Agave is easier to use than honey in that it pours when cold, readily dissolves (even in chilled beverages), and does not crystallize. Agave syrup can also be dehydrated and is available powdered. Agave nectar is used to sweeten dry and hot cereals, quick breads, baked goods, sauces, and glazes. For baking, its moisture-retention properties are comparable to those of honey. In recipes substitute from ⅔ to ¾ cup agave nectar for 1 cup of sugar, reduce your liquid measurement by as much as one-third, and reduce the oven temperature by 25°F.

Be Mindful Unlike all natural sweeteners, agave syrup is predominately fructose; therefore, I do not endorse it. Fructose corn syrup is a cheaper and comparable product. When a sweetener is 90 percent fructose, it's original food source—be it corn or agave—is not relevant. The numerous health problems associated with high-fructose consumption include obesity, heart disease, diabetes, interference with copper metabolism, and liver cirrhosis.

There's an additional concern with the fructose in agave products: If it is eaten following a large meal that overly raises the blood sugar or if eaten with high glycemic foods, then agave syrup no longer has a low glycemic value. Rather, it mysteriously takes on the value of the higher glycemic food. Use agave syrup in moderation, if at all; preferably on an empty stomach or with other low glycemic foods.

See **Sweeteners.**

AGRETTI
Marsh Grass
(*Salsola soda*)

A small annual salt-tolerant shrub native to the Mediterranean region and a member of the goosefoot family, the mineral-rich ash of agretti was once used in the manufacturing of glass. When very young and tender, it has edible fleshy green leaves. Agretti has a grassy and slightly salty taste with a pleasing crunchy texture.

The stems and leaves, sold in clumps that look rather like a bunch of chives but share one taproot, are enjoyed raw in a salad or boiled—as for spinach—until the leaves just soften. In Italy, agretti is blanched, nested on a plate like pasta, drizzled with extra virgin olive oil, and called "green spaghetti." Agretti has some availability in specialty markets; although it is hard to germinate from seed, it may be grown in a home garden.

See **Goosefoot Family; Vegetable.**

AJOWAN
Ajwain, Bishop's Weed, Carom
(*Trachyspermum copticum*)

If you enjoy the brief sensation of a tingly numbed tongue, munch a few ajowan seeds. These tiny, crescent-shaped seeds are a little-known spice that smells like thyme but tastes more bitter and fiery hot. Ajowan is used primarily in Indian and Middle Eastern dishes, especially flatbreads and curries. It is a member of the carrot family.

Medicinal Benefits Ajowan contains thymol, a germicide and antiseptic, and so is used in the treatment of diarrhea and other bowel problems. It relaxes spasms, soothes tummy upsets and motion sickness, improves digestion, and increases perspiration. It also helps treats colds and arthritis, but it is contraindicated for people with hyperacidity. Because ajowan helps relieve intestinal gas, it's a valued ingredient in bean dishes. It also helps counter the side effects of general anesthetics and chemotherapy.

Use Add toasted or sautéed ajowan to stir-fries, curries, chutney, or pickling spices. It's small enough—half the size of a cumin seed—that it may be used whole or, if you prefer, ground.

Be Mindful I found this out the hard

way . . . raw ajowan overpowers other flavors with a sharp and bitter taste. To mitigate its punch and brighten its flavor, first toast or sauté the seeds in oil and then add them to enliven a savory dish.

See **Carrot Family; Herbs and Spices.**

ALARIA
(*Alaria marginata*)

My friend Shep Erhart, who makes his living foraging seaweed in Maine, reports that alaria "is the most beautiful to look at, the most delicate to the taste, and the most dangerous to harvest." Alaria loves rocky, wind-swept peninsulas, where it curls and crashes with every breaking wave. At the lowest tides of the new and full moon during late spring, Shep hand-cuts these native greens, handful by handful.

Alaria is biologically similar to Japanese wakame (see the Wakame entry for medicinal benefits and uses) but is wilder tasting and requires 20 minutes' cooking time. Alaria

---

IMMERSED IN SENSUALITY

Harvesting alaria, I enter into another time/ space consciousness, mesmerized by the motions of undulating alaria fronds, the ocean's rhythms, and sunlight. Immersed in the sensuality of it all with deep joy, I fill my sacks and then carry them ashore across the slippery, rocky, ocean-washed terrain. . . . As I do this work, I feel thankful and honored from my depths to be able to continue to be with the alaria, remembering that along with it goes the obligation to work for protection of the ocean and her inhabitants.

—John and Eleanor Lewallen,
Sea Vegetable Gourmet Cookbook and Wildcrafter's Guide

contains an impressive 18 percent protein, 1000 mg calcium per 100 grams edible portion, and is high in other minerals and nutrients.

See **Seaweed Family; Vegetable; Wakame.**

ALBI SEE **TARO.**

ALFALFA, LEAVES AND SPROUTS
Buffalo Grass, Lucerne
(*Medicago sativa*)

Alfalfa originated in Arabia and was called *al fasfasah*, meaning "father of all foods." How did such a tiny seed earn such a big name? Look to its roots. This legume's amazing and massive root system penetrates 100 feet into the ground to pull up deeply buried minerals and trace minerals unavailable to common vegetables. By comparison, a little red radish has minimal mineral access. That's why alfalfa is one of the most nutritionally rich foods.

Medicinal Benefits Alfalfa leaves and sprouts have cooling and anti-inflammatory properties that boost the immune system, help cleanse toxins, purify the blood, and dry damp conditions. They treat the kidneys, large intestines, spleen, and stomach and are a blood and yin tonic. One of the most significant dietary sources of phytoestrogens, alfalfa helps increase breast milk and prevent menopausal symptoms, osteoporosis, cancer, and heart disease. Alfalfa controls bleeding, acts as a diuretic and appetizer, and augments the urinary system and the intestines. It aids in the assimilation of protein, fats, and carbohydrates. Alfalfa has been studied recently for its ability to help diabetic patients who do not respond well to insulin.

The natural fluorine in alfalfa helps prevent tooth decay and rebuild damaged teeth. Dried alfalfa leaf contains an impressive 899 mg calcium per 100 grams edible portion and is an excellent source of potassium, manganese, beta-carotene, and niacin. Alfalfa sprouts boast a whopping 42 percent protein and all eight essential amino acids. They are an excellent source of chlorophyll and a good source of trace minerals. Alfalfa sprouts reduce *kapha* and *pitta*.

Use While most of alfalfa grown today is fermented into silage for cattle, we typically sprout it for use in salads and sandwiches or as a garnish. The sprouts have a mild, nutlike flavor. Leaves from a young plant may be used as a salad ingredient.

For their remarkably medicinal properties, I sometimes use mild-flavored dried alfalfa leaves interchangeably with parsley in savory dishes and blender drinks. The leaves are also available as a medicinal tea and in supplements.

Be Mindful While alfalfa leaf is medicinal for autoimmune diseases such as rheumatoid arthritis and lupus, its sprouts and seeds are not. The amino acid canavanine, which is found in the seeds and sprouts of alfalfa, can exacerbate inflammatory conditions.

See **Legume Family; Sprouts.**

ALGAE FAMILY

A primitive large and diverse group of single or multicelled organisms that lack the distinct organs found in land plants, they are therefore, not classified as plants. Seaweed is the largest and most complex subgroup of algae. Microscopic algae (phytoplankton) that live suspended in the ocean provide the food base for most marine food chains. Algae are also found in fresh water and throughout terrestrial environments, including snow and ice.

See **Chlorella; Microalgae; Seaweed Family; Spirulina; Wild Blue-Green Algae.**

ALLSPICE
Jamaica Pepper, Pimiento
(*Pimenta officinalis, P. dioica*)

Apple pie is my first association with allspice, and I don't stop there. Beef stew, sugar cookies, chocolate, sautéed carrots, and more—allspice adds rich flavor to countless savory and sweet dishes. Plus it makes them more warming and easier to digest. That's impressive.

These small berries look rather like large, smooth-skinned, mocha-colored peppercorns. They are the immature, dried fruit of a small evergreen tree native to South America and a relative of cloves and guava. Named *pimienta* (pepper) by early Spanish explorers who, upon finding them in Jamaica, concluded that their quest for East Indian pepper was successful. Wrong. Allspice is not related to pepper, and while it has a peppery accent, its flavor and aroma are an agreeable blend of cinnamon, nutmeg, and cloves with a hint of juniper.

Medicinal Benefits As clove oil applied directly to an aching tooth relieves the pain, so allspice oil, or its crushed berries, is a useful anesthetic for painful teeth and gums. Externally, it is used for chest pain and joint and muscle pain. Internally, allspice is a stimulant and antioxidant. It has antibacterial properties, treats adrenal exhaustion, and is a carminative (it reduces intestinal gas, pain, and distention, promotes peristalsis, and treats diarrhea, flatulence, and indigestion).

Use Whole allspice is used in pickling spices, marinades, and mulled wine. Ground allspice is a common ingredient in sausage, spice blends, and barbecue and mole sauces. Many home spice racks include a bottle of ground allspice to enliven countless sweet and savory dishes as well as a cup of hot chocolate or chai.

See **Myrtle Family; Herbs and Spices.**

ALMOND
(*Prunus dulcis*)

The almond is believed to be one of our oldest cultivated foods. Botanically, it is categorized as a fruit and is a cousin of cherries, peaches, plums, and apricots. It is a member of the prune family. Two types of almonds are grown—sweet and bitter. We primarily use the sweet as a nutmeat, while the bitter is made into an extract used in both foods and cosmetics.

California grows 75 percent of the world's almonds in vast orchards in the fertile Central Valley. As almonds are California's number one agricultural export, this two-billion-dollar industry is highly regulated, and today all almonds are pasteurized.

Medicinal Benefits Almonds are typically regarded as superior to other nuts in terms of their medicinal properties. They restore, tone, and nurture. They support the digestive tract and the nervous system. Almonds are the only nut that helps to beneficially alkalinize an overly acidic body pH.

Like the pits of plums, apricot kernels, and its other relatives, the almond contains cyanidelike substances that—besides giving a feeling of well-being—have strong medicinal properties, including inhibition of cancer. It's phytonutrient and phytosterol, has cholesterol-lowering properties, and also acts in cancer prevention.

Almonds are used to ease a dry cough (but not a productive cough). They relieve constipation, kidney stones, and gallstones. They build mental and spiritual proclivity and strengthen the bones, nerves, and reproductive system according to Ayurvedic medicine. Almonds are *tridoshic* and especially calming to *vata*.

Almonds contain about 72 percent fat (predominately unsaturated) and are an exceptional

SAD ALMONDS

Because almonds have been associated with salmonella outbreaks, the FDA has mandated since 2007 that all almonds be pasteurized, but that they still may be labeled raw. Routine "pasteurization" of commercial almonds is fumigation with the suspected carcinogen propylene oxide. Other sterilization methods are roasting or blanching or flash-pasteurization with steam. Organic almonds are flash-pasteurized, which is the preferred method. The Almond Board maintains that pasteurized almonds "do not differ in any significant way from untreated raw almonds."

That pasteurized and raw almonds are deemed comparable flies in the face of our common sense. We all have firsthand experience of how cooking changes flavor, nutrition, and viability. Plant a raw almond and it grows; plant a pasteurized almond and it rots.

Whenever possible, purchase raw nuts (seeds, beans, and grains) with intact vitality and fatty acids. Then, when cooked, you'll have fresher, more energizing foods that proffer greater nutrition than those precooked in a factory. You can taste the difference between vital and denatured foods.

Yes, this might mean relying less upon almonds and almond products. Try to see it as an opportunity to explore the wonderful array of flavors, textures, and nutrition offered by our many other nuts and seeds, none of which have mandatory pasteurization.

source of vitamin E (alpha-tocopherol). They're also rich in manganese, magnesium, and riboflavin.

Use Almonds are easiest to digest when soaked for a few hours and then eaten as is or toasted. The brown skin is bitter and a mild stomach irritant; remove it by rubbing soaked or blanched almonds between your hands.

Buying/Storing Favor organic almonds, as they are *not* fumigated with a toxin (see sidebar). Due to their high fat content, almonds require protection from rancidity. As the thin brown skin of shelled almonds provides some protection, favor shelled almonds with this skin intact. For important details about buying and storing all nuts, see the Nut entry. Almonds can absorb odors, so store them in a covered container.

Be Mindful In various studies, nuts are listed among the top allergenic foods; in my consulting work, I consistently find that more people are allergic to almonds than to other nuts. Perhaps it is in part because many people have eaten almonds as a daily staple rather than as an occasional treat. Frequent or addictive consumption of a food is one marker of a food sensitivity.

See **Prune Family; Nuts.**

ALMOND BUTTER SEE **NUT AND SEED BUTTERS.**

ALMOND, GREEN

Immature almonds are a seasonal delicacy available only from mid-April to mid-June. These young almonds are encased in a velvety green hull. Using a paring knife, cut along the seam and extract the ivory-colored nutmeat. It is grapelike in texture and has a subtle grassy, herby flavor. Green almonds are featured in Middle Eastern and Mediterranean cuisines. They are an exceptional kidney yin tonic. Enjoy them as a nibble or garnish or added to a salad. Search for them online or in specialty produce shops.

See **Nuts.**

ALMOND MILK SEE **NONDAIRY MILK SUBSTITUTES; NUT MILK.**

ALOE VERA
Medicine Plant
(*Aloe Vera*)

> Nicodemus . . . brought a mixture of
> myrrh and aloes, weighing about a
> hundred pounds. They took the body
> of Jesus and wrapped it with the spices
> in linen cloths, following the Jewish
> burial custom.   —John 19:39–41

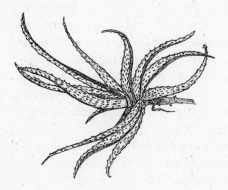

As a handy "first-aid kit," many a kitchen sports a potted aloe plant. Snip a piece of leaf from this easy-to-maintain houseplant, slice it open, and dab its cooling and healing gel directly onto burns, insect bites, and minor skin irritations.

Aloe vera grows in clustering rosettes of stiff, upright leaves. There are many aloe species; aloe vera (which means "true aloe" in Latin) is considered to be the most therapeutic. For more than three centuries, the gel from this succulent tropical plant has been used medicinally and historically it was an embalming agent.

Medicinal Benefits Aloe is an antibiotic, antiviral, astringent, coagulating agent, pain inhibitor, growth stimulator, and antiparasitic. Acemannan, a compound in aloe, enhances the immune system. Aloe vera juice is widely used as a bowel regulator and is nonabrasive and soothing to the intestinal tract; it also relieves ulcers. Aloe is a balancing beverage for summer heat and is a *yin* tonic. It treats premenstrual pain and menopausal heat, and it is good for women who have had hysterectomies. It is *tridoshic*.

Externally, aloe contains a "wound hormone" that accelerates the rate of healing of injured and burned surfaces. The enzymatic activity of aloe reportedly reduces or eliminates scars.

GREAT SLEEPING PARTNERS— ORCHIDS AND ALOE

Most houseplants release oxygen and absorb carbon dioxide during the day. Aloe, orchids, snake plants, and bromeliads, however, do the opposite. By upping the oxygen while you sleep, they make ideal bedroom companions. In addition, they remove toxins.

The noted scientist who created a breathable environment for the NASA lunar habitat, Dr. B. C. Wolverton, pioneered the study of the value of houseplants for our health. In addition to increasing humidity and oxygen, they remove human bioeffluents (substances emitted through normal biological processes) including carbon dioxide, carbon monoxide, hydrogen, methane, alcohol, and others. Houseplants are also superior filters of common environmental pollutants such as ammonia, formaldehyde, and benzene.

"Houseplants," writes Dr. Wolverton, "are no longer luxuries, but essential to health. They are nature's 'eco-friendly' living air purifiers, with years of documented scientific evidence to prove it."

Use As a beverage, scrape off 2 tablespoons of gel from a split leaf, stir it into a glass of water or juice, and drink. As with the fresh gel, you may also apply bottled aloe gel directly to burns and other skin irritations.

Buying/Harvesting Aloe vera is available as a concentrate, drink, powdered extract, gel, and juice. Purchase only *unrefined* aloe vera products; the more bitter flavor reflects a higher percentage of active (medicinal) ingredients.

Be Mindful Powdered aloe gel is intensely purgative—consult with your natural health-care practitioner regarding dosage. Because aloe stimulates the uterus, it is not used during pregnancy.

ALOO METHI SEE **FENUGREEK.**

AMARANTH
**(*Amaranthus cruentus, A. caudatus,
A. hypochondriacus*)**

Even more flamboyant than the dahlias and hibiscus flourishing in my garden is the magenta amaranth. Also known as love-lies-bleeding, amaranth is an astounding plant that can reach a stately six feet in height on sturdy, fuchsia-colored stems.

Amaranth is one of the world's most successful weeds. It includes more than 60 different species—most of which are wild—on five of seven continents. Amaranth seeds are as small as poppy seeds and typically are golden, cream colored, or sometimes pink hued. One plant yields a massive number of seeds, up to 50,000, which is enough to plant two acres. This brings to mind another positive feature of amaranth: It so effectively reseeds itself that I've only ever had to plant it in a garden once.

Amaranth is grown for its grainlike seed, its edible leaves (see **Amaranth Greens** entry), as a dying agent, or as a decorative plant. It was the sacred grain of the Aztecs—they

domesticated amaranth about 7,000 years ago and esteemed it over corn, that is, until the conquering Spaniard Hernando Cortez forbade its cultivation. (It suffered the same fate as did the Inca's revered grain quinoa.) Also an Inca staple, today Peruvian's call it *kiwicha*, and when I traveled there to research grains, I heard many people speak of its energizing properties. Further north, Zuni legends relate that amaranth had been brought up from the underworld as a staple food at the time of their emergence.

Amaranth plants are members of an elite group of photosynthetic super-performers, the C4 group, that make them extraordinarily nutritious. C4 plants utilize a photosynthetic process or "pathway" that has super-normal efficiency in converting soil, sunlight, and water into plant tissue. Thus amaranth has enhanced environmental adaptation and is nutrient dense.

Medicinal Benefits The United Nations Food and Agriculture Organization has fostered amaranth's use since 1967 because wherever amaranth is consumed there is no malnutrition. Compared to milk, cup for cup amaranth is much higher in protein and even has more calcium (including the supporting calcium cofactors magnesium and silicon), making it an especially helpful food for nursing or pregnant women, infants, children, people who do heavy physical labor, and people trying to gain weight. Additionally, it contains two nutrients that help reduce excessive blood cholesterol, tocotrienols (a vitamin E fraction), and the fatty acid squalene.

Indeed, 1 cup cooked amaranth provides over half your daily protein needs. It's also a superior source of magnesium, phosphorus, and iron, and a good source of zinc and calcium.

Amaranth is one of only two dozen other vegetable foods regarded as a chi tonic. Chi tonics maintain and improve the quality and quantity of available energy in the body. A cooling and astringing food, amaranth disperses damp conditions and so is beneficial to congestion, mucus conditions, tumor inhibition, diarrhea, excessive menstruation, and yeast overgrowth. Amaranth reduces *vata* and *kapha*.

Use Various snacks, breakfast cereals, crackers, and packaged health foods contain an insignificant percentage of amaranth flour but are promoted as amaranth products. That's a scam. Likewise, don't look to a cold breakfast cereal, amaranth or otherwise, as healthful; it is too denatured to really nourish.

If you want to benefit from amaranth's vitality, cook it as a grain entrée and expect a bold flavor and sticky texture. Or cook a few tablespoons amaranth with a cup of rice, quinoa, or another grain. It thickens soups and stews and is tasty when popped. A confection sold by street vendors, *alegria* in Mexico and *ladoos* in India, is made of popped amaranth bound with a sweetener.

See **Amaranth Family; Amaranth Flour; Amaranth Greens; Grains.**

ONE POT OF AMARANTH— TWO RECIPES

Perhaps you'll be one of the people who love amaranth's wild and wooly flavor— not everyone does. But I've yet to find a person who doesn't enjoy Amaranth Crispbread as a hearty and novel treat. Here's how to easily make both steamed amaranth and crispbread.

Steamed Amaranth

Makes 1½ cups
1 cup amaranth
1 teaspoon butter or extra virgin olive oil
1 clove garlic, minced
¼ teaspoon unrefined salt

Soak the amaranth overnight in water to cover by several inches. Strain out and discard the soaking water using an extra-fine-mesh strainer.

Place the amaranth, butter, garlic, and salt in a small pot, and add fresh water to just barely cover the amaranth. Bring to a boil over high heat. Cover, lower the heat to a simmer, and cook for 7 to 10 minutes, until the liquid is mostly absorbed. Remove from the heat and allow to steam, covered, for 5 minutes or so. Serve in small portions as a grain entrée and use leftovers for the crispbread below.

Amaranth Crispbread

Makes 1 7-inch diameter flatbread

Scrape ½ cup cooked amaranth into an oiled and warmed sauté pan and press the amaranth into a thin (⅛- to ¼-inch-thick) diameter; I use moistened fingertips, but you may also use a dampened spatula. Cook over medium-low heat for 5 to 8 minutes, until the edges start to dry and slightly curl up and the bottom is browned. Flip over the crispbread. With a butter knife, slice into 4 or 6 pie-shaped wedges and cook for about 5 minutes, or until browned. Serve hot or cold.

AMARANTH FAMILY
(*Amaranthaceae*)

The large and diverse amaranth family is primarily composed of herbs and small shrubs growing worldwide in tropical and temperate regions. Amaranth, a primary edible member of this family, is just one of many amaranth family species.

As an amaranth subfamily, the chenopod, or goosefoot family, is widely distributed throughout the world. Its name is derived from the Greek words for goose (*khen*) and foot (*podium*) because its trilobed leaf looks like the webbed foot of a goose. Beets, chard, quinoa, spinach, and the sugar beet are our most common chenopods.

See **Amaranth; Beet; Chard; Fat Hen; Goosefoot Family; Orach; Spinach; Sugar.**

AMARANTH FLOUR

Amaranth flour has a distinctive flavor and blends well with other flours in muffins, pancakes, and quick breads. As it is gluten-free (and so doesn't leaven well), add only a small percentage to yeast breads to boost their flavor and nutrition.

See **Flour.**

AMARANTH GREENS
En Choy, Chinese Spinach, Pigweed
(*Amaranthus tricolor, A. oleraceus, A. dubius, and A. spinosus*)

Amaranth leaves are available green or magenta red as a sweet and earthy-tasting vegetable that is similar to spinach but with more substance and character. Unlike the amaranth plants grown for their seeds, these varieties are used as a green vegetable.

The slightly sweet-tasting leaves are soft but rough textured and look like extra-large basil leaves, but lack serration. Amaranth leaves may be egg shaped or as narrow as mint. Their immature fleshy seed heads are eaten like broccoli.

Medicinal Benefits Throughout Asia, amaranth greens are enjoyed during the summer to help reduce internal heat and dampness. Amaranth greens effectively treat diarrhea and other gastrointestinal disorders. More nutritious than spinach and kale, amaranth greens are second only to parsley as a superior source

of vitamin K. They have negligible calories and are an excellent source of vitamin C and the B vitamins. When the greens are cooked, their abundant iron is more bioavailable than when they are eaten raw.

Use Add very young amaranth greens to salads or sandwiches. Larger leaves are rather coarse when raw, but cooking quickly softens them. One of my favorite uses of magenta-colored amaranth is with purple potatoes in a spectacularly colored pink soup. You may also stir-fry, sauté, or steam them or add them to a dal or a grain dish. Cook the leaves only until just tender, as overcooking fades their otherwise vivid color.

Buying/Foraging/Storing You can find amaranth greens in Asian grocers and farmers' markets in late spring and early summer. If foraging or harvesting, collect the greens from the plant before it flowers. Or gather their immature seed heads as they bud and prepare them as you would broccoli.

Amaranth is typically sold bunched and with its roots intact. As the roots help extend the leaves' shelf life, remove the roots just prior to use. Buy fresh and sprightly looking bunches and use quickly before they become limp.

See **Amaranth Family; Vegetable.**

AMASAKE

At the Crestone Mountain Zen Center, where I enjoyed many a retreat, amasake is the nightcap. At the end of a long, rigorous silent practice day and while still formally seated in the *zendo*, we'd be served a cup of amasake. Creamy, warm, and sweet, it feels so good in the belly and helps assure a good night's sleep.

Amasake is fermented from a koji inoculant and, typically, sweet white rice. It may be as thick and lush as a malted milk or as thin and sweet as mother's milk. This traditional Japanese food is produced in the first fermentation of sake making; the name literally means "sweet sake."

Medicinal Benefits If I were running a marathon, I'd stash amasake at my aid stations because it is nutrient dense and predigested so it doesn't take energy—it gives it. This fermented rice is broken down into soluble complex carbohydrates and maltose (a grain-malt sugar), and it increases blood sugar slowly rather than rapidly like more simple sugars. It calms *vata* and *pitta*. Nurturing amasake is an excellent food for the very young, the elderly, and invalids.

Use Serve it hot or cold with your favorite seasoning or with ginger, cardamom, and a drop of vanilla.

Buying/Making You'll find thick amasake in the refrigerated section, or thin amasake in shelf-stable Tetra Paks in the dairy section of natural food stores. They come in various flavors. As is usual with fermented products like cheese and wine, brands vary in flavor and texture; experiment with different brands to find your favorite.

Making amasake is as easy as making yogurt. Mix koji with any freshly cooked, unsalted grain and incubate at 130°F for about 12 hours. The koji inoculant is available online from companies such as Miyako Oriental Foods and GEM Cultures.

While it's most typically made with white rice, I enjoy making amasake from other grains; currently posole is my favorite.

See **Fermented Food; Koji.**

AMBARELLA
Golden Apple, Otaheite Apple, Tahitian Apple
(*Spondias dulcis Forst.*)

The tropical ambarella fruit is sour on the outside but becomes sweeter near the seed. This little-known, acidic-tasting fruit has a crunchy texture and a flavor and fragrance like pineapple and mango. While some people enjoy eating it out of hand, most people find it too sour, and so ambarellas are typically used in chutneys and jams or in juice blends.

Shaped rather like a small mango, ambarella fruits are either red or yellow skinned. Their skin is tough, their flesh is yellow, and they contain a single large seed. The seeds are difficult to separate from the flesh. Ambarellas are available from November through May in specialty markets.

See **Cashew Family; Fruit.**

ANAHEIM CHILE SEE **CHILE PEPPER.**

ANASAZI BEAN SEE **BEANS.**

ANCHO CHILE SEE **CHILE PEPPER.**

ANGELICA
(*Angelica archangelica*)

As the medieval story goes, when the Archangel Raphael saw the suffering caused by the Black Plague, he revealed this herb's effectiveness as an antidote, and so it was named on his behalf. In Asia, that angelica ranks second only to ginseng as a tonifying herb makes another strong case for its virtue. Angelica is a member of the carrot family.

Medicinal Benefits Angelica leaves, roots, stems, and seeds are used as an antiseptic (especially of the respiratory system), to support the immune system, to treat nervous disorders and adrenal fatigue, to enhance digestion, and to help prevent flatulence. Its essential oil is an antibacterial and antiviral agent that also treats spasms, fever, flatulence, and indigestion.

Use Despite its remarkable medicinal properties, there's little culinary use of angelica today outside crystallized stems for decorating confections. It is a common, tall, and stately weed that grows rampantly in moist habitats and is easy to grow in a garden. Blanch the young stems as a salad ingredient, or stew the stems and leaves in puddings or stock (then extract and discard as you would a bay leaf), where they add sweetness and a pleasing flavor while boosting the immune system.

For fresh angelica, either forage or grow your own. Crystallized stems are available in import shops, and the root and seeds are available in herb shops, either loose or extracted in tincture.

See **Carrot Family; Herbs and Spices.**

ANISE
Anise Seed
(*Pimpinella anisum*)

Of my mother's vast cookie repertoire, my favorite is an anise cake. One teaspoon of batter per morsel rests on a cookie sheet overnight. When baked the next day, the moist interior batter puffs up under the dried surface to create an iced, double-decker appearance. The cookie's whimsical shape befits the sweet but racy anise seeds sprinkled throughout.

The tiny fruits of this carrot relative have remained popular since ancient Egyptian times. Because its licoricelike aroma is so similar to fennel, in Asian countries the two are used interchangeably; of the two, however, anise has a more round and sweet licorice flavor.

Medicinal Benefits Anise benefits the heart, lungs, liver, stomach, kidneys, and spleen. It is a warming, yang tonic that builds *chi* and energy, supports lactation, aids digestion, clears asthma that has underlying cold symptoms, and relieves bronchitis. Anise also has anticarcinogenic properties and was traditionally considered an aphrodisiac. Anise seed essential oil treats indigestion and respiratory complaints.

Use Figs and anise seeds are particularly delicious together; anise also enhances fish, meat, and vegetable dishes as well as desserts. Use fresh anise leaves in salads or, briefly cooked, as a potherb. The seed is a principal flavoring

of alcoholic beverages such as pernod, absinthe, anisette, and ouzo. Anise tea is a digestive aid with a pleasant and comforting flavor; it's a popular beverage in South America.

Be Mindful Anise has mild abortive properties, so its medicinal use is not recommended during pregnancy.

See **Carrot Family; Herbs and Spices.**

ANISE PEPPER SEE **SICHUAN PEPPER.**

ANNATTO
Achiote, Roucou
(*Bixa orellana*)

The rust-colored seeds of the achiote evergreen are a potent, almost neon orange-red colorant. Annatto's color intensity is comparable to turmeric but salmon-red (rather than yellow). The plant's alternate name, lipstick tree, denotes its cosmetic use; but long before the term "lipstick" was coined, Amazonians used annatto as a body dye and insect repellent. The seeds themselves are small, about the size of a peppercorn, and angular shaped.

Medicinal Benefits Annatto's antibacterial properties are so powerful that adding it to live cultures (such as sauerkraut, kefir, or yogurt cultures) would effectively inhibit their valued microbial populations. Annatto's antioxidant properties can even protect our DNA from mutations induced by ultraviolet light, superoxides, or peroxides. Annatto is mildly bitter and astringent. It is high in carotenoids, which explains its effectiveness as a dye and as a medicinal herb. Annatto's vast ethnobotanical uses include treatment for headaches, cancer, diabetes, inflammation, jaundice, epilepsy, and tumors.

Use Annatto was used in the Aztec chocolate beverage to deepen the brew's color. It continued as a common chocolate ingredient in Europe through the sixteenth century. Since then, annatto's main culinary use is as a tint

FOR COLOR

I love using oil-infused annatto for the beauty of it. A little annatto in the oil gives a golden, sunshiny color, while a lot makes it a vivid scarlet-orange. Simply sauté ½ teaspoon annatto seeds in 1 tablespoon oil or butter over low heat for 4 to 5 minutes, or until the oil turns the color you wish. Strain, discarding the seeds. Stir the seasoned oil into soup, pilafs, glazes, sauces, desserts, and marinades or as a stuffing for tamales. For a glamorous garnish, drizzle the infused oil onto any dish in need of pizzazz.

for butter, margarine, and cheese. Annatto colors Latino, Caribbean, Philippine, and other Asian dishes, including an inauthentic version of Peking duck. A paste of blended spices and annatto, *recado rojo*, is a signature seasoning agent in Yucatán, Mexico. Annatto adds a faint floral perfume to cooked foods and a mild and sweet but peppery flavor.

Buying Look for annatto online, in herb shops, and in Latino and Asian markets. It's also available as a paste or in an infused oil.

Be Mindful People allergic to the preservatives BHA and BHT and artificial red and yellow dyes may also be sensitive to annatto.

APPLE
(*Malus sylvestris, M. pumila*)

Why is the protrusion in your neck called an Adam's apple? Apparently Adam couldn't swallow that bite of forbidden fruit. The apple originated not far from the mythical Eden, in Almaty, Kazakhstan, in Central Asia, where wild apple trees still cover the foothills.

The apple's nearest cousins are Asian pear and pear. It is the most popular temperate-zone fruit, with more than 7,500 apple varieties grown throughout the world today. Domestic consumption of apples and their products is about 120 apples per person per year. While they grow in almost every state, Washington produces nearly half the apple crop, most of it from eastern Washington, where some 12 billion apples are thinned and picked by hand.

Medicinal Benefits A cooling food, apples are a yin and chi tonic that treat the heart, lungs, large intestines, stomach, and spleen. They invigorate and promote vital energy and help dispel toxins. They contain malic and tartaric acid, which inhibit fermentation in the stomach, making apples easier to assimilate than most other fruits. They are moistening and so reduce thirst, reduce fever, and ease dry, hot lungs. In addition, apples, especially green apples, help cleanse the liver and gallbladder and help soften gallstones. Give grated raw apples to children to reduce a fever. To ease a dry cough, steam apples with honey until they're soft and eat. To eliminate phlegm from the lungs, prepare apples with agar (see page 3).

Apples are a rich source of pectin and so can lower cholesterol, promote beneficial intestinal flora, and support normal colon function. They're high in quercetin and other flavonoid antioxidants that help protect against heart disease, cancer, and asthma. They are also an excellent low-calorie source of fiber and vitamin C and other nutrients. Apples reduce *pitta* and *kapha*. When cooked, they reduce *vata*.

Use How to use an apple? Bite into it and savor it. Or slice it for salads, snacks, or a cheese platter; dry it, juice it, bake, stew, sauce, or pie it. Apples are versatile, and the favorite varieties are crisp textured with a sweet—or sweet and tart—flavor. Some apples have a juicy flesh and others less so.

Dried apples and apple juice are ingredients in numerous food products, and they are also brewed into hard (alcoholic) cider. One of the simplest, and often overlooked, desserts is baked apples. Simply put an apple into a preheated 350°F oven (if you wish, first core it and stuff it with raisins and walnuts and a dash of cinnamon) and bake it until it softens, anywhere from 25 to 60 minutes, depending on the apple variety and size. In general, the more tart the apple, the better it retains its shape when cooked. To increase the sweetness or acidity of an apple dish, add sugar or another sweetener or lemon juice to the recipe. Use the following guidelines when selecting apples:

Crisp, juicy, and firm-textured for eating out of hand: Braeburn, Cameo, Cortland, Crispin, Criterion, Empire, Fuji, Gala, Golden Delicious, Granny Smith, Jonagold, Jonathan, McIntosh, Mutsu, Newtown Pippin, Pink Lady, Red Delicious, Stayman, Sundowner, Winesap.

Juicy and holds shape in pies and baking: Braeburn, Cox's Orange Pippin, Fuji, Jonagold, Jonathan, Gala, Granny Smith, Mutsu, Newtown Pippin, Northern Spy, Pink Lady, Suncrisp, Rome Beauty, Stayman-Winesap.

Cooks to a soft texture; good for applesauce: Cortland, Elstar, Fuji, Gala, Gravenstein, McIntosh, Pippin, Rhode Island Greening.

Firm and crisp; a good salad ingredient: Cortland, Criterion, Golden Delicious, Empire, Fuji, Gala, Red Delicious, Pink Lady, Winesap.

Buying/Storing Select bruise-free, firm apples that have a vivid, fresh color and intact stem. Whenever possible, favor old cultivars that may taste less sugary but will have a more diverse flavor profile. They'll often have a mottled skin and unsymmetrical shapes. Look for old cultivars and regional favorites in farmers' markets.

Freshly harvested apples have their own waxy coating that protects them from shriveling and weight loss. Once harvested, apples are washed, and washing removes about half the original apple wax. Apples are waxed with carnauba (from a Brazilian palm tree) or shellac (made from the resinous secretion of various insects of the *Lacciferinae* family; it also includes food additive E904). This coating may not be considered vegetarian, since it may, and probably does, contain crushed insects. Shellac is known to cause allergies on contact, resulting in skin irritations. According to the Washington Apple Commission, it is a thin coat and requires but a few drops to cover each fruit. Organic fruits are not waxed and therefore have a reduced shelf life.

Some apples, including Granny Smith and Fuji, have a longer shelf life than others. Peak season for apples is from September to March. In controlled atmosphere storage, some apples hold as long as 12 months, but their quality does deteriorate with time.

Be Mindful Whenever possible, favor organic apples. Today's commercial apples are genetically uniform, which makes them highly vulnerable to bacteria, fungi, and viruses. Consequently, commercial apples require more pesticides than most other crops. Apples are one of the top eight most chemically contaminated fruits. (The others are strawberries, nectarines, pears, peaches, raspberries, cherries, and imported grapes.)

See **Apple Butter; Apple Cider; Apple Family; Vinegar (Apple Cider).**

APPLE BUTTER

A thick, chocolate-colored paste made by concentrating applesauce. When apple butter contains 100 percent organic apples, it is decidedly the most healthful and natural preserve available—and it is oh-so-sweet and delicious. Other jams, jellies, and conserves have fewer nutrients and a lesser flavor profile as a result of added sweeteners and, typically, texture agents.

See **Apple.**

APPLE CIDER

Unfortunately, it's hard to come by real apple cider today. Until 1998, this raw and effervescent beverage with a 10-day shelf life was a seasonal favorite wherever apples were grown. Since then the FDA requires that cider display a warning label saying it "may contain harmful bacteria that can cause serious illness in children, the elderly, and persons with weakened immune systems." This effectively ended commercial cider availability. The legislation followed a tragic incident when a load of cider apples was hauled in an unsterilized truck that had previously hauled manure, resulting in the death of one child.

If you or a neighbor has access to a cider press—and if you use commonsense cleanliness in pressing—you may still relish a harvest toast of inimitable fresh cider. Such a cider, if allowed to ferment, either turns into vinegar or develops into a "hard" (alcoholic) beverage. As the term "apple cider" is not regulated, some pasteurized apple juice products—especially during harvest time—are labeled "cider."

See **Apple; Fruit Juice.**

APPLE CIDER VINEGAR SEE VINEGAR.

APPLE FAMILY
(*Maloideae*)

A subfamily of the large rose family, the fruits of this family are called pomes. Their core consists of five ovules in a fleshy endocarp that is surrounded by ripened stem tissue.

See **Apple; Asian Pear; Loquat; Pear; Quince.**

APRICOT
(*Prunus armeniaca*)

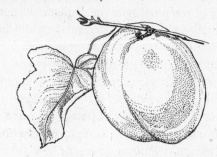

For those who have dallied amid apricot trees bearing fully ripened fruit, it makes perfect sense that nectar was the drink of the gods. Though my *Oxford English Dictionary* does not associate the apricot with nectar, common usage did, and it's an association that I never doubted.

Plump, juicy, and soft, these aromatic, golden-colored fruits originated in Armenia. Their name is derived from Latin, *praecox,* meaning "precocious," as they blossom—and ripen—earlier than their peach, plum, and almond cousins. Smaller than a peach, apricots are oval and contain a single pit that tastes like an almond (see **Apricot Kernels** entry). Apricots are a member of the prune family.

The malic and citric acids in apricots give a lemony, plumlike flavor to this otherwise sweet fruit. Today California produces 90 percent of the domestic apricot crop, with Washington, Colorado, Idaho, and Utah supplying the rest.

Medicinal Benefits Apricots are a blood and yin tonic that treat the lungs, large intestine, and stomach, have a lubricating action, and are medicinal for a dry throat, dry coughs, bronchitis, asthma, emphysema, and dry constipation. The classic Chinese herbal prescription to relieve these conditions is to eat two to three pieces of dry or fresh apricots in the morning and the evening. An easy medicine to take!

Apricots have laxative properties, and as their gold color aptly indicates, they're a superior source of vitamin A (and the carotenes lycopene and lutein) as well as a decent source of iron, something that is unusual in fresh fruit.

The same measure of unsweetened dried apricot halves yields comparable vitamin A and an impressive increase of mineral content, with iron increasing to 19 percent of our daily requirement, copper to 22 percent, calcium 7 percent, and selenium 4 percent.

The vitamin A is predominately beta-carotene (1696 mcg in fresh apricots and 1913 mcg in dried apricots). This antioxidant may reduce the risk of heart disease and cancer and help protect DNA from free radical damage. Apricots are *tridoshic*, unless they are sour, in which case they are not recommended for *pitta*.

Use Fresh apricots are unsurpassed eaten out of hand and lend themselves to fruit salad, chutneys, salsa, fresh fruit soups, smoothies, sorbet, ice cream, salads, yogurt dishes, home canning, juices, preserves, and as a garnish. Enjoy dried apricots as a snack or rehydrate and use in fruit compote or as a sauce or filling. They also make excellent liqueurs, and their sweet but tart flavor complements meat—traditionally pork, veal, and poultry.

Unlike the skin of apples or peaches, which is often peeled, an apricot skin is so tender that it's typically eaten with the fruit. Once pitted, a squeeze of lemon juice prevents the flesh from darkening. Substitute apricots freely for peaches, mangos, papaya, or nectarines.

Buying/Storing For an apricot to have a good flavor it must be fully ripe when picked, and then it keeps no more than a few days. This explains why only 8 percent of the total commercial crop is sold fresh. Look for apricots during June and July. Purchase those that yield to a soft touch and are golden all over with a rosy blush. Avoid firm apricots with traces of green—they'll remain sour. Also avoid those that are overly soft, bruised, wilted, or shriveled, as they quickly decay. If fresh apricots don't meet these criteria, purchase a dried apricot or a different fresh fruit. Tenderly handle apricots because they bruise easily, which causes rapid spoiling.

Refrigerate apricots to prevent overripening and plan to use as quickly as possible. Their flavor and aroma, however, are superior at room temperature.

Be Mindful According to traditional Chinese medicine, large quantities of fresh apricots stress the spleen and stomach. During pregnancy, it is advised to enjoy apricots in moderation.

See **Apricot Kernels; Prune Family.**

APRICOT KERNELS

My mother always puts a few apricot pits (or seeds) into her preserves for, she says, "the flavor." As a child, her logic was beyond my ken, as apricot kernels are nastily bitter. Today I take my hat off to mom and the perennial kitchen wisdom she still serves up.

Medicinal Benefits Apricot kernels are a yin tonic that supports the kidney and stomach function and helps clear excess damp, heat, phlegm, toxins, and water. According to both Oriental and alternative medicine, these kernels are anticarcinogenic. In Chinese pharmacology, the pits are classified as a drug rather than as a food, as they contain cyanide (hydrocyanic acid) and amygdalin. They're used medicinally to combat cancer, stimulate respiration, improve digestion, help reduce blood pressure and arthritic pain, and give a sense of well-being.

Amygdalin, also termed "laetrile," is commercially available as vitamin B_{17}, and it continues to be used in cancer clinics outside the United States. The Food and Drug Administration, however, maintains that there is no scientifically accepted evidence of its efficacy. The amygdalin content in apricots is chemically identical to that in bitter almonds.

Be Mindful Mom also told us kids that we could taste an apricot kernel or two but never eat them in quantity, as they could be poisonous. Of course we tasted them, but they were so bitter we spit them out. When cooked or fermented, apricot kernel toxicity is reduced.

Consumption of 10 or more apricot kernels for children and 40 or more for adults may cause an adverse reaction, even death. Yet bitter almonds or apricot pits are an essential flavoring ingredient in authentic marzipan and amaretto.

APRIUM SEE **PLUOT.**

ARAME
(*Eisenia bicyclis*)

The sea vegetable arame is a brown kelp closely related to wakame and kombu, but in the package or cooked, it looks more like strands of black hijiki. Japan is the only country that is a significant producer of arame, but it has a mild, sweet taste that most Westerners enjoy from the start. Arame blades, which grow in wide leaves up to a foot in length, are sliced into long, stringlike strands, cooked for seven hours, sun-dried, and packaged.

Medicinal Benefits A yin tonic that treats the kidneys and stomach, arame helps disperse toxins, damp conditions, mucus, and heat. In addition to the numerous medicinal properties of sea vegetables in general, arame is noted for treatment of high blood pressure and, because it supports hormone functions, treatment of female disorders, including infertility, scanty lactation, and menstrual pain. A half cup of arame is an excellent source of calcium, iron, and trace minerals.

Use My favorite way to fix arame is sautéed with garlic, onions, and julienned carrots for a richly colored and flavored dish that my cooking students always enjoyed. Serve this—or arame with your choice of vegetables—as a side dish or filling for turnovers, cabbage leaves, baked peppers, or roasted squab. Because arame is precooked, it may also be rehydrated and added directly to a salad for its dramatic color and pleasurable texture.

See **Kelp; Seaweed Family; Vegetable.**

ARBORIO RICE SEE **RICE.**

AREPAS SEE **MASA.**

ARGAN OIL

Healthful, tasty, and truly exotic, argan oil is produced from the seeds of the argan fruit grown only in southwestern Morocco. The argan tree is a sole species in the genus *Argania* and grows wild in semidesert soil, its deep root system helping to protect against the northern advance of the Sahara. UNESCO has designated the 10,000-square-mile argan-growing region near the coastal town of Essaouira a biosphere reserve.

Roasted argan oil has a nutty aroma and flavor—rather like peanuts and walnuts—with a hint of pepper. Unless, that is, it's imbued with a funky billy goat aroma imparted when goats climb the low-branched and sprawling argan trees to feed upon the fleshy fruit. There is only pleasure, though—nothing goaty—in the argan oil that I've savored in Moroccan cuisine.

Raw argan oil is a high-profile ingredient in cosmetics because of its excellent vitamin E and essential fatty acid profile; it's prized for its ability to treat dry skin, acne, psoriasis, eczema, and wrinkles.

Argan oil is expensive, about $30 for

REFUGE AND A BANK ACCOUNT

In the Muslim world of Morocco, a woman's ability to earn income is highly limited. This, unfortunately, has meant that divorced women, with no means of self-support, have become outcasts and burdens to their family of origin. Fortunately, the Women's Argan Collective is upgrading the lives of many women, and divorced women now have more of an opportunity to be self-sufficient. The argan cottage industry is also a great boon to married woman, as a two-family income has obvious benefits and is now becoming more accepted. The Argan Cooperative helps provide women refuge, enhanced esteem, and a bank account.

---

5 ounces. Happily, the purchase of this sustainable product directly supports Berber women according to tradition and—more recently—law, as argan harvest and production is limited to women. The Women's Argan Collective is helping to improve their quality of life, nutrition, and educational opportunities.

ARROWHEAD
Chinese Potato, Swamp Potato
(*Sagittaria sinensis, S. trifolia*)

If you enjoy the crunchy texture of water chestnuts, seek out arrowhead rhizomes in Asian and specialty greengrocers. They look rather like a large shallot but have a dark line or two around their circumference. Select rhizomes with shorter shoots, as they are younger and therefore more sweet and tender. Peel and discard both the skin and shoot. Parboil or sauté to remove any bitterness and then use and enjoy as a potato.

Arrowhead helps stop coughing and bleeding and controls diarrhea. (It is not recommended during pregnancy or for anyone suffering from constipation.) There are several edible arrowhead relatives that are foraged or, primarily in Asia, cultivated.

ARROWROOT
Arrowroot Powder
(*Maranta arundinacea*)

This fine-grained, white starch comes from the root of the tropical arrowroot plant, a member of the arum family; it is a high-gloss natural thickener that is superior to highly refined cornstarch and, unlike flour, not at all grainy. Most of our arrowroot powder comes from St. Vincent Island in the West Indies. The root is ground, sun-dried, and then powdered.

Curiously enough, there are several other tropical powdered starches used as thickening and medicinal agents also termed "arrowroot" but that come from different plant species. East Indian arrowroot, from Curcuma angustifolia and C. leucorrhiza plants, is the second-most common. It is typically pale yellow in color and is considered inferior to West Indies arrowroot.

Medicinal Benefits Arrowroot powder is easily digestible and nutritive. It helps soothe an inflamed gastrointestinal tract and is good for convalescing. For infant care, arrowroot powder is excellent for diaper rash, as it is absorbent, soothing, natural, and nontoxic; it reduces friction and keeps the skin dry. Arrowroot benefits *pitta* and *kapha*.

Use Arrowroot has a distinct advantage over flour in that, once thickened, it is crystal clear. I don't use arrowroot with milk or milk substitutes, however, as it becomes slimy. Overstirring, or letting it stand too long before serving, may cause an arrowroot-thickened sauce to become thin again. As this starch cooks more quickly—and has a more neutral flavor—than flour or cornstarch, it's ideal for lightly cooked fruit sauces.

One tablespoon of arrowroot will thicken 1 cup of liquid. Substitute 2 teaspoons of arrowroot to replace 2 tablespoons of all-purpose flour or 1 tablespoon of cornstarch. Dissolve in cold water, add the slurry to other ingredients, and cook, stirring continuously for a minute or two, until it thickens. Use arrowroot powder to thicken sauces, glazes, soups, pie fillings, icings, and desserts.

Buying/Storing I purchase arrowroot from the bulk herb section of my food co-op at 20 cents per ounce. At the supermarket, a 2-ounce jar costs $5. Store in a tightly covered glass container in a cool, dark cupboard and it will hold for a year or more.

See **Arum Family.**

ARTICHOKE
Globe Artichoke
(*Cynara scolymus*)

Back in 1948, Marilyn Monroe's first claim to fame was being crowned California's first Artichoke Queen. Today artichokes need little endorsement. People love their "buttered popcorn" aroma. Then there is the tiny nibble at the base of each leaf (technically a "scale"), whetting the appetite for the artichoke heart—which is actually the bud of the plant. The smooth, sweet taste of artichokes and the leisurely manner of consuming them make this a popular vegetable.

This edible thistle with silvery green leaves that grows waist high is of Arabian-Mediterranean origin and a close relative of the cardoon and daisy family member. It's an elegant garden plant; I always let a few go to flower for the incomparable electric mauve of their florets. Castroville, a town south of San Francisco that bills itself as the "Artichoke Cen-

ter of the World," produces three-fourths of all California artichokes, and California grows nearly 100 percent of America's domestic crop. The plants are cloned from root stock.

Medicinal Benefits Artichokes are a yin and blood tonic, they support the gallbladder and liver, promote chi circulation, and have a neutralizing effect on some toxic substances. Their most stellar phytochemical is cynarin, which increases bile production and thus may aid digestive disorders marked by poor fat assimilation. In addition, cynarin lowers blood cholesterol levels and improves blood-clotting time.

If, however, your focus is anticarcinogens and antioxidants, then you could argue that an artichoke's glutathione is its primary claim to fame. Among vegetables, artichokes are among the highest in antioxidant activity.

Fresh artichokes are an excellent source of inulin and therefore of use to diabetics. As a blood tonic, artichokes maintain and improve the quality of immediate nourishment available to the body and are therefore excellent for anemia, building overall energy, and as immune support. Artichokes are easy to digest and good for convalescence.

For medicinal purposes, use the fresh or dried leaves and stems as a food or herbal tea.

Artichokes are an excellent source of chromium and fiber; they are a very good source of vitamin C and a fair source of vitamin C. Artichokes are *tridoshic*.

Use Large artichokes are one of the few vegetables that I typically pressure cook: Simmering them in a pot requires 50 minutes, while pressure steaming takes only 15 minutes. Remove all but a half inch or so of the stem and (if you wish) trim the sharp—and sometimes prickly—outer scales. Serve large artichokes, one per person, as a main dish with melted butter, mayonnaise, or aioli.

Trim well, slice, and sauté or fry smaller artichokes for appetizers or a stir-fry ingredient. In all but baby artichokes, a furry "choke" forms under the smallest leaves and covers the heart; it is removed before eating. Artichokes of varying sizes may be stuffed, and artichoke hearts are delicious pickled.

Buying How convenient that in the spring, when the liver and the gallbladder most need support, artichokes are at their peak availability. Their secondary season is October; they are, however, in the markets year-round. Look for compact heads with fresh, vibrant green leaves; and look at the cut end of the stalk, which withers as it ages. Fall and winter artichokes may be darker or bronze-tipped. If they have a whitish, blistered appearance, they were "kissed" by a light frost. Such kisses heighten the flavor of artichokes as well as apples and winter squash.

See **Daisy Family; Vegetable.**

ARTIFICIAL SWEETENERS SEE **SWEETENERS.**

ARUGULA
Rocket, Roquette, Rucola
(*Eruca vesicaria*)

The green vegetable arugula grows as a rosette of deeply lobed leaves. It has a peppery, pungent taste—like a radish— but with an almost musky aroma. Mediterranean in origin, it has been valued as a wild herb from Roman times. Since the 1990s, arugula has become popular in the West and is now widely cultivated. It is a member of the cabbage family.

Medicinal Benefits Arugula is a digestive and chi tonic. It contains antioxidant glucosinolates, which have anticancer properties. Like its mustard relatives, arugula moves stuck energy and reduces *kapha*. It is an excellent source of vitamins A and C, folic acid, and calcium, and a very good source of riboflavin, potassium, copper, and iron. The oil extracted from arugula seeds was long considered an aphrodisiac in Europe.

Use Young arugula leaves are a wake-up note in a salad of otherwise mild-tasting ingredients, a little like dandelion greens. In midsummer when it is larger and more peppery in taste, I cook arugula in soups and stir-fries. It's a great basil substitute in pesto, or mince and strew as a garnish.

Buying You'll find arugula in mesclun salad blends as well as bunched or in packages. Avoid overgrown, yellowing, or wilted leaves or leaves from a plant that has flowered. Once garden arugula goes to flower, though, you can use the blossoms in salads. Arugula is available throughout the year but is at its best in the early summer and fall.

See **Cabbage Family; Vegetable.**

ARUM FAMILY
(Araceae)

A large and diverse family of flowering plants that includes some favorite ornamental plants such as dieffenbachia and aglaonema. The flower is typically enclosed in a leaflike hood. It is found throughout tropical and northern temperate regions. The most common food in this group is taro; it also includes arrowroot and yautia.

See **Arrowroot; Taro; Yautia.**

ASAFETIDA
Asafoetida, Devil's Dung, Hing
(*Ferula assafoetida*)

I don't know what I love most about asafetida—its knock-your-socks-off sulfurous aroma (which explains its scatological name) or, once cooked, its pleasant flavor reminiscent of sautéed onions and garlic. This spice is often, therefore, a signature ingredient for Hindus and people with religious prohibitions against the onion family. I also love the way the word rolls off my tongue. *As'e-FET'E-da.* Its name is from middle Latin and means "fetid-smelling sap."

Asafetida is the resin extracted from the stem and roots of a large, fennel-like perennial plant native to Iran. The resin is grayish white when fresh, but it dries to a dark amber color.

Medicinal Benefits A favorite Ayurvedic herb, hing, as they call it, is used to strengthen and cleanse the liver, to aid digestion, and to help relieve flatulence, constipation, asthma, bronchitis, and intestinal worms. It's one of the best herbs to help ground a high-strung *vata*-type person.

Use As its stink dissipates with cooking, hing is used in cooked dishes, be they meat, vegetable, grain, or bean. Use, however, a minuscule amount, as too much will overpower and spoil a dish, as I know from first-hand experience. Be certain to store asafetida in a tightly closed glass container or its aroma will contaminate other foods and, if you take a deep whiff, can be nauseating.

Buying/Storing If the powdered resin you purchase is merely potent, rather than devilishly potent, it has been blended with powdered fenugreek, gum Arabic, or rice flour. Asafetida is sold in small quantities in tightly closed containers. It is also sold in lumps that need to be crushed before using. Even ground, this powerful spice lasts well over a year if stored away from light and air.

See **Carrot Family; Herbs and Spices.**

FORMER PRESIDENT JIMMY CARTER WORE DEVIL'S DUNG

Until recent times in Asia, Europe, and the Americas, wearing asafetida was a folk remedy against invasive bacteria and viruses. Former president Jimmy Carter noted in his autobiography, *An Hour Before Daylight,* "I think the most obnoxious medical experience I ever had was when someone convinced Daddy that we children could avoid an outbreak of flu or some other prevalent illness by wearing pieces of asafetida, or devil's dung, around our waists. This horrible-smelling extract from some kind of root undoubtedly earned its reputation as a protector by keeping bearers of germs at a healthy distance from the wearer of the stench . . . ."

A POWERFUL ROMAN RECIPE

As did the ancient Romans, I keep asafetida-imbued pine nuts on hand and then use these nether-worldly-smelling seeds to flavor soups, stews, and roasted dishes. The fats in the pine nuts marry with the asafetida, creating a pleasant flavor enhancer.

¼ cup pine nuts
2 teaspoons asafetida powder

Combine the ingredients in a small jar, shake to coat the pine nuts with the asafetida, tightly cover, and store in the refrigerator for up to a year. The imbued pine nuts may be used in a few days but are at their best after a week or more. For a dish serving 4 people, crush and add 1 teaspoon of flavored pine nuts.

ASAFOETIDA SEE ASAFETIDA.

ASH PEPPER SEE SICHUAN PEPPER.

ASH PUMPKIN SEE WINTER MELON.

ASIAN PEAR
Apple Pear, Chinese Pear, Nashi, Sand Pear
(*Pyrus pyrifolia*)

As crunchy as an apple and as juicy as a melon, Asian pears have long been a favorite Asian fruit—where they're often given as a gift—and with good reason. They taste something like a memorable pear. Some are sweet. Some are tart. Flavors run from subtle to unexpected, and they have a slightly floral aroma. Asian pears range in weight from four ounces to a whopping two pounds or more. The European pear's flesh is meltingly soft, but the Asian pear remains firm and has numerous gritty cells, giving it a granular or sandlike texture.

A cousin of the pear, this fruit was introduced to the United States during the Gold Rush by Chinese miners, though it did not become widely available until the 1980s. Like an apple, their flesh remains crisp, and while some are pear shaped, most are spherical. Asian pear colors are like less vivid common pears and range from yellow or green to tan and russet. Their succulent flesh is white. Most of our commercial crop comes from California, Oregon, and Washington.

Use Asian pears are delicious raw, as a snack, or sliced and added to salads or a cheese platter. They can be sliced into paper-thin wedges for a canapé base and topped with, for example, sour cream and a dab of salmon roe or curried crab. Poach, grill, broil, or bake Asian pears. Cooking intensifies their flavor and compromises neither their shape nor their texture, which remains firm and even meaty. Allow longer cooking time than for European pears, though.

Medicinal Benefits As Asian pears are astringing and cooling, they help stop diarrhea and ease indigestion and stomachache. The Chinese recipe is to slice the fruit, add water, simmer until cooked, and then mash to a pulpy sauce and eat the sauce (or express the juice from it and drink) three times a day. The same mixture is applied to leg ulcers, athlete's foot, and ringworm for relief and to speed healing.

Buying Domestic Asian pear harvest is primarily from mid-July through October. They are ready to eat when purchased and, if unbruised, will keep for a week at room temperature or up to three months in the refrigerator. There are more than 25 Asian pear varieties commercially grown in the United States, and their size, appearance, and—most important—flavor varies greatly. I select them by aroma, as those with the most fragrance typically have more flavor. Or better yet, ask your greengrocer for a sample taste because if they were harvested before maturity, they'll never sweeten.

Asian pears are typically more expensive than pears and apples because they require careful handling to minimize bruising, brown marks, and stem punctures, and therefore are not suited to large, fast-moving packinghouse lines.

See **Apple Family; Fruit.**

ASPARAGUS
(*Asparagus officinalis*)

Harvesters claim that asparagus spears grow so fast that when you are astride a row and bending to cut, you either work briskly or get speared from behind. One spear may grow as much as 10 inches in a day.

Compared to modern plants like roses,

grass, and cabbages, this herbaceous perennial plant looks ancient and even phallic; indeed, it dates back to the age of reptiles, when ferns were the dominant vegetation.

Asparagus is a member of the lily family and a distant relative of onions. Botanically, asparagus is unusual in that there are distinct male and female plants; the male spears are skinny and the females plump. Their flavor depends upon freshness, however, and not sex, and only the young green shoots or spears are eaten. If allowed to mature, a beautiful fern develops; the asparagus fern is in fact a popular hanging houseplant.

Medicinal Benefits Asparagus is a slightly cooling yin tonic that energizes the kidneys, lungs, and spleen and helps dispel excess heat, damp, toxins, and water. As the Indian name *shatavari* (she who possesses a hundred husbands) indicates, an Asian asparagus (*Asparagus racemosus*) is the primary Ayurvedic root for strengthening female hormones, promoting fertility, increasing lactation, and relieving menstrual pain. But that's not all—it is *tridoshic*, meaning it's good for everyone.

As a kitchen remedy, our table-variety asparagus reads like a cure-all. Asparagus soothes internal membranes and so reduces phlegm and mucus, eases constipation, cystitis, kidney disease, infectious diseases, liver disorders, gout, rheumatism, and (when heart-related) edema. It is also good for nervous disorders. Asparagus contains asparagine, a diuretic that gives the urine a characteristic odor in people who lack the gene to break it down.

Asparagus contains the bioflavonoids rutin and glutathione, which boast remarkable immune-strengthening and antioxidant and anticarcinogenic properties. They help increase the strength and permeability of capillaries while increasing the oxygen-carrying capacity of the blood and are an antidote against X-rays and other forms of radiation. Asparagus is one of the top five vegetables highest in glutathione. Glutathione helps regulate other antioxidants, such as vitamin A and E.

For a vegetable, asparagus is relatively high in protein. It is an excellent source of potassium, vitamin K, folic acid, vitamins C and A, riboflavin, thiamine, and vitamin B_6.

Use To remove the fibrous stalk end, hold the stalk by each end and bend it until it snaps in two. Use the stalk ends for soup stock; or peel to remove the fibrous skin and use the tender centers in salad or as finger food; or cook as you would the upper stalk. Steam the spears just until tender; you can even find special asparagus steaming pots for this purpose, but, to my sensibilities, it seems like a lot of pot for a seasonal vegetable. If just picked, steaming requires but two minutes; older—and also thicker—stalks require longer time. Serve with hollandaise sauce, butter, or any full-flavored oil. Asparagus, especially when older or less fresh, is delicious sautéed and, when chopped, add to stir-fried dishes and soups. It may also be pickled.

Buying In the store, look for bright green, fresh-looking spears with compact tips. Darker-colored asparagus is typically more nutrient dense. As pesticides are not used on commercial asparagus, I often bypass the more expensive organic asparagus. Use asparagus as soon as possible after purchase or harvest. Avoid angular or flat stalks that are woody. For uniform cooking, select those of similar thickness. White or blanched asparagus is popular in Europe and is grown by mounding earth above the plants, which keeps them dark and, therefore, unable to develop chlorophyll. It has a milder flavor than green asparagus. A variety of purple asparagus, which is higher in sugar and less fibrous, is becoming more available.

STAKE OUT YOUR CLAIM

Hunting for asparagus with my grandparents was one of my favorite spring rituals. Grandma had a favorite knife for just this purpose, but a paring knife or pocketknife will do. The season starts after the first few good warm days and when the soil is still moist from spring rains. Today it's not advisable to forage along country roads because of weed-control spraying. But my children and grandchildren and I have found asparagus along unmaintained creek sides and old farmsteads; I wish the same for you.

Here's how you spot an asparagus stand. In the fall, look for wild, rather stringy "ferns" with bright red, pea-size berries and—this is important—remember the spot. Then, in the spring, you'll see weathered bleached stalks (but no berries) and at their base new asparagus spears poking up through last year's leaves and debris. Harvest and enjoy some on the spot. In a good spring, you'll have enough asparagus to share with friends and neighbors. As long as it's warm and the soil is moist, you can return to the spot every few days to harvest again. The rhizomes will keep producing spears until they dry out or are no longer harvested. Then the spears will mature into fronds and develop fruit.

Once bought, store asparagus loosely covered in the refrigerator. To maintain freshness, wrap a moist paper towel around the stem ends, or stand them upright in two inches of cold water.

See **Vegetable.**

ASPARAGUS BEAN See **LONG BEAN.**

ASPARAGUS PEA See **WINGED BEAN.**

ASPARAGUS LETTUCE See **LETTUCE.**

ASPARTAME (NOT RECOMMENDED)
Candarel, Equal, NutraSweet

The artificial sweetener aspartame is a chemical compound (phenylalanine and aspartic acid) synthesized from petrochemicals. It is 200 times sweeter than sugar and is a popular sugar substitute in soft drinks, breakfast cereals, powdered beverages, and other dry packaged foods. Curiously enough, aspartame does not satisfy hunger; rather, it increases hunger, especially for sweets.

High levels of phenylalanine can have irreversible and toxic effects on the fetal brain and are implicated in liver damage (it breaks down into aldehyde, which damages liver cells). Symptoms include behavioral changes in children, headaches, blindness, dizziness, epilepticlike seizures, menstrual problems, obesity, and an increased risk of cancer.

See **Sweeteners.**

ATEMOYA
(*Annona cherimola* × *A. squamos*)

Cross a cherimoya and a sugar apple and the creamy result is an atemoya. This tough-skinned, pale green hybrid fruit is, by size and appearance, reminiscent of an artichoke. An atemoya's creamy, lush, ivory-colored flesh tastes like mango-flavored custard; but if not well ripened, its flavor is starchy. Atemoyas are grown commercially

in Florida, Hawaii, California, New Zealand, and Australia. The seeds, like those of all *Annona* species, are toxic.

Use Slice or cube atemoya and add to fruit salads or other desserts or pass through a ricer and serve as a fruit sauce. They're also eaten from the "shell" a spoonful at a time. The pulp (be sure to discard the seeds) may be blended and frozen with, for example, coconut milk and lime juice for an iced dessert.

Buying/Storing This West Indies delicacy is available in the fall. Select thin-skinned atemoyas, which are somewhat tender and unblemished. Allow to ripen at room temperature until they are soft. Then consume immediately or refrigerate for a few days. Do not refrigerate until the fruit is ripened. Upon ripening, it may split at the stem end.

See **Cherimoya Family; Fruit.**

AUBERGINE SEE **EGGPLANT.**

AVOCADO
(*Persea americana*)

Super Bowl Sunday is the third-biggest food day for supermarkets (after Christmas and Thanksgiving) and the day that avocado sales peak. It seems that slathering chips with the avocado dip guacamole is a way TV viewers participate in this national ritual. Although technically a fruit, and chemically more like a nut, the avocado is commonly considered a vegetable—albeit a creamy, sensory vegetable. Its pale yellow-green flesh seems to be universally enjoyed.

Native to Central America and Guam, the avocado, a laurel family member, is a relative of bay, cinnamon, and sassafras. There are hundreds of avocado varieties, with 90 percent of our domestic supply coming from California, primarily San Diego County. The Hass variety is, undoubtedly, the most popular. All Hass avocado trees can be traced back to grafts made from a single "mother tree" purchased in 1926 as a seedling by a mail carrier named Rudolph Hass and planted in his La Habra Heights, California front yard.

Medicinal Benefits Avocados are a cooling food and blood and yin tonic that support the large intestine, liver, lung, and spleen meridians. With their high fat content (20 percent), they are an excellent food for people wishing to put on weight, and who need nourishment. They are also an excellent fat source for people who have difficulty assimilating other fatty foods. Avocados are a good "first fruit" for babies.

Avocado is a superior source of monounsaturated fatty acids, vitamin E, B vitamins, and fiber. They are a very good source of the carotenoid lutein, required for healthy eyesight as we age.

Use A versatile food, avocados are enjoyed raw in a variety of dishes, fruit smoothies, dips, gazpacho, and other cold soups, fruit salads, desserts, garnishes, and even ice cream. Avocados are a healthful substitute for sour cream or cream cheese in dressings and spreads.

Buying/Storing The most readily available avocado is a dark, rough-skinned Hass variety from California that blackens as it ripens and is available year-round. It's the creamiest and so favored for guacamole and dips, but you might find it a bit mushy for salads. The Fuerte, or Florida, avocado, is smooth skinned and remains green when ripe. It is available from late fall through the spring and is more firm and less buttery. A Reed avocado is large and roundish; it remains firm even when ripe and so is less suited for dips and spreads. Its skin is easy to remove. The small, black Mexican avocado has an edible skin.

A fruit that yields to gentle pressure in the palm of your hand is ripe and ready to eat. Select avocados that are heavy for their size and free of irregularities. Avoid fruit with dark blemishes or bruises or fruit that is overly soft.

Store at room temperature until ripened, then refrigerate until ready to use. To speed ripening, place the fruit in a brown paper bag at room temperature. To accelerate the process, place an apple or banana in the bag. Once ripened, refrigerate for up to two or three days. To store cut fruit, sprinkle it with lemon or lime juice, place in an airtight container, and refrigerate.

Be Mindful Avocados contain a substance called chitinase, which is associated with the latex-fruit allergy syndrome. If you have a latex allergy, you may very likely be allergic to avocados, as well as papayas and bananas. When ethylene gas is used to speed ripening, this increases these allergenic enzymes; as this treatment is not permitted on organic avocados, they are less apt to cause an allergic reaction.

See **Avocado Oil; Fruit; Laurel Family.**

AVOCADO OIL

Relatively new to the market, it's important to differentiate between refined and unrefined avocado oil. Unrefined avocado oil is pressed from the flesh of the fruit (not the seed) and dark green in color; it smells and tastes like an avocado. At $20 a pound it is primarily used in cosmetics or, uncooked, in salad dressings. Due to its high chlorophyll and omega-3 content, it is unstable, degrades (oxidizes) quickly, and, therefore, is not used in cooking.

The culinary avocado oil advertised with a high smoke point is highly processed and therefore denatured; it has little flavor and is not recommended.

See **Avocado; Fat and Oil.**

GROW YOUR OWN AVOCADO HOUSEPLANT

Here's a project that's fun for children (of all ages) and, in five to thirteen years, may yield the basis for guacamole. In the meantime, however, you can enjoy a beautiful houseplant. Poke three toothpicks into a clean avocado seed to form spokes that will enable you to suspend the seed, broad end down, to the depth of one inch, into a water-filled glass. Place the seed in a warm place out of direct sunlight and replenish the water as needed. Within two to six weeks, rootlets should form and the stem should sprout.

When the stem is six to seven inches long, cut it back to about three inches. When the roots are thick and the stem has leafed out, plant in a rich humus soil in a 10½-inch diameter pot, leaving the seed half exposed. It thrives in sunlight and moist, but not water-saturated, soil.

At a foot high, the plant will be spindly; cut it back to six inches to encourage new shoots. Then be patient. Not all avocado seeds are able to reproduce themselves; some require a second plant for pollination, and if they do flower, the fruit itself may not be delicious. But the plant is a beauty and truly homegrown.

BABY BROCCOLI SEE **BROCCOLINI.**

BAKING POWDER

In use as a yeast substitute since 1850, baking powders are a mixture of various simple chemical substances. When a baking powder is mixed into a batter, carbon dioxide gas is released from sodium (baking soda in our recipe) by the action of an acid or an acid salt (such as cream of tartar). A moisture absorber, such as arrowroot, inhibits a premature reaction.

Commercial baking powder is a leavener that contains unhealthful and acrid-tasting aluminum compounds and, sometimes, corn or gluten. Favor aluminum-free brands, which can be found at natural food stores. Or try homemade baking powder, which takes seconds to make, performs equally well, and leaves no bitter aftertaste.

See **Arrowroot; Cream of Tartar.**

ALUMINUM-FREE BAKING POWDER

Makes 1¼ cups

¼ cup baking soda
½ cup cream of tartar
½ cup arrowroot powder

Mix the ingredients together and store in an airtight container. Substitute equal parts for commercial baking powder in any recipe. Keeps for one year.

BALSAMIC VINEGAR SEE **VINEGAR.**

BAMBOO SHOOTS
(*Bambusa vulgaris, Phyllostachys edulis, P. pubescens*)

Before the world's fastest growing woody plant has a chance to become woody, its tender new asparagus-shaped shoots (culms) may be dug and harvested. Once bamboo shoots are peeled and, if necessary, their cyanide leached out, they are popular in Asian dishes. Varying from slender to stout in shape, shoots have a crisp texture, white color, and—when raw or freshly cooked—they taste rather like immature sweet corn.

Medicinal Benefits Bamboo shoots support the large intestine, lungs, and stomach and help remove excess damp, heat, water, and mucus from the organ systems. Traditionally paired with meat in Asian dishes, bamboo is regarded as invaluable because its "cool" energy balances the "hot" energy of meat. Bamboo shoots are used in Chinese medicine as a tonic for respiratory disease and treating infections. To treat a searing cough, simmer bamboo shoots in water with sugar to taste until tender and eat, preferably on an empty stomach. They are high in silicon and low in calories.

Use When fresh, some bamboo varieties are sweet tasting, delicious, and succulent in salads or as crudités. Carefully peel fresh shoots to remove the entire outer husky leaves that, in some types, may contain needle-sharp hairs that can perforate the gastrointestinal tract. Trim away and discard the base.

If the shoot tastes bitter, it's a variety that contains hydrocyanic acid. Boiling leaches out this toxin. Boil for 10 minutes and taste; if not yet sweet, add the shoots to fresh water and repeat the leaching as necessary.

Bamboo shoots are as versatile as carrots: Serve as a side dish with butter and salt or ferment as a condiment, boil in coconut milk, sauté or fry, or add to soups, stir-fries, casseroles, or stews.

Buying In the winter, you'll find fresh bamboo shoots in Asian markets. They're also available canned, frozen, or refrigerated and vacuum-packed in many supermarkets. Refrigerated fresh shoots will hold for about a week.

In countless "healthy" product ingredient panels you'll see listed "all natural fiber" or "vegetable fiber." Have you ever wondered what this euphemism means? It's typically bamboo. The term may refer to psyllium, guar gum, pectin, or bran; however, as a by-product of the building industry, bamboo is cheaper and, in a word, fibrous.

See **Fiber; Grass Family**.

BANANA
(*Musa* esp. *M. acuminata*)

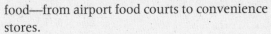

Bananas are one of the most widely consumed foods in the world. Both the sweet and starchy (plantain) bananas are major staples for people in developing countries. The sweet banana is the most popular—and due to price controlling, the cheapest—fresh fruit consumed in the United States. You're apt to find bananas in most every store that sells food—from airport food courts to convenience stores.

Bananas grow in almost every tropical country on a giant herb. This soft, seedless fruit with its thick, inedible peel grows in bunches, technically called a "hand," and each fruit is a "finger." We import most of our bananas from Central and South America.

The ubiquitous, blunt-ended yellow banana is a Cavendish variety that gained popularity in the 1950s when the preceding mono-crop cultivar was stricken with a fungal disease. It's less flavorful than other sweet banana varieties.

Medicinal Benefits More than cooling, bananas are classified as a cold food and a yin tonic that support the large intestine, lung, stomach, and spleen meridians. They help disperse toxins and excess heat. Ripe bananas are sweet tasting, highly nutritive, easily digested, anti-ulcerous, and soothing to the mucous lining of the stomach. They are used to treat constipation, ease thirst, and reduce *vata*. Conversely, underripe or green bananas are astringent and more difficult to digest; they relieve diarrhea and colitis and reduce *pitta* and *kapha*. Bananas contain tryptophan, an amino acid that the body converts into serotonin, which helps one feel more relaxed and happier. To ease swelling and irritation of an insect bite, rub the affected area with the inside of a banana skin.

Bananas are high in potassium and useful in treating high blood pressure. They are high in vitamin B_6 and vitamin C.

Use Peel and enjoy out of hand, or bake, broil, or add to fruit salads and yogurt dishes. Seems that bananas were made for fruit smoothies because, blended, they make the perfect "smoothie" texture. Dip slices in chocolate, split them over ice cream, fire them up for flambé, bake into a comforting banana bread, or fry them as fritters . . . bananas are indeed versatile.

A green-tipped banana may be substituted for a plantain: Sauté and serve as a meal's starchy carbohydrate serving.

Buying/Storing Cavendish bananas are available fresh 365 days of the year. Large and ethnic markets feature other varieties. Dried bananas, fried banana chips, and banana flour have varying availability. Banana leaves are available, fresh or frozen, for wrapping tamales, sweet rice dumplings, and other food morsels. While the food is cooking, the banana leaf keeps it moist and adds a pleasing scent.

Bananas are picked green and (unless organic) gassed with ethylene gas to speed their ripening. Allow them to ripen at home at room temperature to a dull yellow color mottled with numerous black spots. The browner the skin, the higher is the banana's sugar content. Or place them in a closed bag in a warm spot to speed ripening. Do *not* refrigerate green bananas, as they will not ripen. However, once ripe, they can be refrigerated for up to two weeks (this blackens their peel but does not compromise the color or flavor of the fruit itself).

Select bananas that are slightly green, firm, and without bruises. If their peel has a gray tint and a dull appearance, they were refrigerated and will not ripen properly. Green bananas may take up to three weeks to soften and ripen. Avoid bananas with soft spots or black or moldy stems. In addition to the common Cavendish, other varieties include:

- **Baby Banana** (also known as Lady Finger and Manzano) is thick skinned, plump, and finger-size with a pinkish golden peel. In comparison to a Cavendish, a baby banana has a drier texture and sweeter flavor with a hint of apple and strawberry. It's ripe when the peel is freckled with sugar spots and when it gives to a gentle squeeze.

- **Burro Banana**, also called a chunky banana, is shorter and more angular than the common banana and has a tangy lemon-banana flavor. Its flesh is a creamy yellow color with a firm center. When ripe, it's yellow with black spots.

- **Red Banana** is about six inches long and dark green and maroon red. When ripe, its color changes to a dark bronze, even black. It's soft when ripe and slight scars do not affect quality. A red banana has a creamy white to pink flesh with a slight raspberry flavor.

Be Mindful Bananas contain a substance called chitinase that is associated with the latex-fruit allergy syndrome. If you have a latex allergy, you may very likely be allergic to bananas and plantains, as well as papayas and avocados.

See **Plantain; Fruit.**

BANANA FAMILY
(*Musa*)

Bananas and plantains are fruits of treelike herbaceous plants that are native to Southeast Asian tropical regions. Banana fronds are also used, like corn husks or grape leaves, to both flavor and wrap dishes such as tamales and sweet rice dumplings. Plantains look like an oversize banana and are primarily used as a vegetable.

BANANA PASSION FRUIT SEE **PASSION FRUIT.**

BANANA SQUASH SEE **SQUASH; SQUASH, WINTER.**

BARBADOS MOLASSES SEE **MOLASSES.**

BARLEY
(*Hordeum vulgare*)

Barley and wheat, the world's oldest cereal crops, originated in Southwest Asia around

8500 BC. The Roman gladiators were called *hordearii*, or barley men, after their primary crop, barley. It was a staple in Europe through the Middle Ages until higher-yielding wheat varieties replaced it. Until recent times, barley remained the main food of the physically strong peoples of the Himalayan region.

Whole barley is a tan-colored grain and larger and plumper than all other grains except corn. It is a member of the grass family.

Today most people think of barley in connection with soup—it makes a tasty, hearty soup base—but the bulk of barley is drunk in a malted form, otherwise known as beer.

Medicinal Benefits Esteemed as a nutritious and strengthening food, barley helps build the body and muscles. It is strengthening to the spleen, stomach, large intestines, gallbladder, and bladder. It tonifies blood, chi, and yin and helps regulate heat, damp, water, and toxins. Barley stimulates the appetite and helps reduce *pitta* and *kapha*. Barley is used for hepatitis and painful urination, and it helps reduce tumors. The most acidic of the grains, barley is made more alkaline and flavorful by roasting it a shade darker prior to cooking; this also eliminates whole barley's laxative property, but it may exacerbate constipation, as does pearled barley. In England, barley water is used as a traditional convalescing food.

Whole barley is an excellent source of thiamine, but not when it is pearled. Barley's dietary fiber is high in beta-glucan, which helps lower cholesterol.

Use Whole barley cooks into a chewy, sustaining dish. Try it plain, combined with brown rice, cooked with beans, or cooked with extra water to make a breakfast porridge. Barley is especially hearty and delicious cooked risotto-style.

Its tough hull and bran adhere so tightly to the grain's starchy core that milling leaves only a small white "pearl" of barley. Whole barley, which sometimes is available in natural food stores, has only its outer hull removed. Its vitamin and mineral content is intact, and it is significantly higher in protein, potassium, calcium, and iron than is pearled barley.

Buying Barley is available in several different forms:

- **Barley Flakes (Rolled Barley)** Like rolled oats, thin barley flakes are a tasty substitute for rolled oats in hot breakfast cereal and in granola and muesli. They may also be used in baked goods and to thicken soups.
- **Barley Grits** These toasted and coarsely ground whole barley kernels are quick cooking because of their size. Use grits as a hot breakfast cereal or as a grain side dish. The grit size—and therefore its cooking time—varies from manufacturer to manufacturer.
- **Hull-less (Naked) Barley** These heirloom varieties are whole grains. As they easily thresh free from their hull, they are an ideal grain for backyard gardeners and subsistence farmers.
- **Pearled (Pearl) Barley** This form of barley has had its bran polished off and has lost all of its fiber and half of its protein, fat, and minerals. Pearled barley is the most commonly available barley. Oftentimes pearled barley from a natural food store has undergone less pearling than that sold in a supermarket, as is indicated by its larger size.
- **Purple (or Black) Barley** This one is the midnight beauty of grains. Its blackish purple hull retains its gorgeous color when cooked. This older type of barley is more robustly flavored than modern cultivars and regarded as medicinal to the kidneys. In Tibet, it was favored for beer. Prepare and use as you would whole or

hull-less barley; as its color bleeds, do not cook it with white-colored foods.

- **Whole Barley** Also called barley groats, Scotch barley, or pot barley, it is similar to brown rice in that its bran is intact. It is darker, chewier, and more nutritious than its refined counterpart. Like brown rice, whole barley has only had its inedible hull removed and it takes longer to cook than when the bran is also removed in the more processed forms of barley.

Be Mindful Barley, along with the other gluten-containing grains like wheat, is among the top allergens. If you have compulsive eating patterns with gluten-containing products, this may indicate gluten sensitivity. Avoid such foods until you've regained your digestive health.

See **Barley Flour; Grass Family; Grains.**

BARLEY FOR STRENGTH

The Himalayan diet is primarily *tsampa*—roasted ground barley mixed with black tea, salt, and yak butter and formed with your fingers into a bite-size dumpling. Peter Hackett, a high-elevation medical expert who lived in a small Everest region village, told me of this amazing grain diet, where his biggest food treat was an occasional turnip pickle. "They were a strong, healthy, hardworking people," Peter told me, "who subsisted almost entirely on tsampa or sometimes *sen*, a thick gruel made of ground roasted millet and water. . . . It was not unusual for one person to eat two pounds at a sitting! The diet included potatoes but no other vegetables or fruits except when holiday foods were carried up from the lowlands. There was seldom meat."

BARLEY FLOUR

Although, owing to its grayish crumb, barley bread may not look immediately appetizing, those who acquire a taste for it are likely to become addicts. I am one. An addiction which is not always easily satisfied.

—Elizabeth David, *English Bread and Yeast Cookery*

Barley flour is starchy and soft and has a sweet earthy taste. It yields a cakelike crumb and when baked curiously imparts a grayish color. Curious, because both grain and flour are white. Whole barley flour, however, yields a darker crumb than pearled barley flour and a moister quality. In flavor, aroma, texture, and ease of handling, the difference between pearled and whole barley flours compares to the difference between white and whole wheat flour. A traditional staple of Tibet is *tsampa*, or roasted barley flour.

Barley is low in gluten. Therefore, generally no more than 15 percent barley flour is added to a yeast bread, as it imparts a softer and denser texture. In cookies and cakes, it gives a light crumb. When substituting barley flour, bake in an oven that is 25 degrees lower than the recipe calls for. Toasting the flour prior to use heightens its flavor; orange zest and sweet spices provide a complementary flavor.

See **Barley; Flour.**

BARLEY GRASS JUICE

The juice of the chlorophyll-rich grass of young barley plants is nutritionally comparable to wheat grass juice as one of the most remarkable high-chlorophyll foods. Of the two, barley juice is more alkaline and therefore balanced, while wheat grass juice is stronger and faster acting. Both contain a wide spectrum of vitamins, minerals, amino acids, and enzymes. Barley grass juice is particularly rich in beta-carotene, calcium, iron, and vitamin C; it also contains vitamins B_1, B_2, B_6, and B_{12}, pantothenic acid, and folic acid. It contains the antioxidant enzyme superoxide dismutase. In addition, the enzymes in barley grass help resolve toxic substances and slow cellular deterioration and mutation.

Barley grass juice is available at many natural food stores and juice bars, freshly juiced in 1-ounce servings—a little is all it takes—or sold in tablet or powder form.

See **Wheat Grass Juice.**

BARLEY MALT POWDER
Barley Sugar, Malt Powder

Barley malt sugar is a buff-colored, crystalline powder made by evaporating the water out of barley malt syrup. Malt sugar is primarily used for brewing, although it is also available as an alternative sweetener.

Malt sugar absorbs moisture very easily and then becomes rock-hard. To prevent hardening, store sugar in a closed glass jar. Malt sugar is easy to substitute for white sugar, and unlike natural liquid sweeteners, it gives the same tender crumb that sugar does. Substitute measure for measure. The result is a lighter sweetness with a pleasing malt flavor.

See **Sweeteners.**

BARLEY MALT SYRUP

Hop flavored, and therefore intensely bitter, barley malt syrup was sold "strictly as a sweetener" during Prohibition. This "sweetener," however, would have ruined anything but home brew. Sprout whole barley, roast it, and then extract it to a liquid form, and you've got barley malt syrup. Combine the syrup with hops, ferment with yeast, and the result is beer.

Barley malt syrup, compared to honey, is less dense, less sweet, and more intensely flavored.

Medicinal Benefits Like all natural sweeteners, barley malt is mostly carbohydrate, with a high B vitamin profile. One ounce—that's one jiggerful—of barley syrup is a good source of vitamin B_6, niacin, thiamine, and riboflavin.

Buying Favor 100 percent barley malt (rather than an inferior barley-corn blend). Imported pure barley malt is produced for table use and has a richer—but less intense—flavor than domestic malt that gives it wider culinary applications.

Store barley malt syrup in a glass or plastic container in a cool, dark cupboard. If stored a long time (more than 12 months) or in a warm place, the malt may ferment. A sign of fermentation is bubbles percolating up through the malt. Should this occur, refrigerate and use quickly, or discard if it has an unpleasant aroma.

See **Sweeteners.**

BASIL
Holy Basil, Tulsi
(*Ocimum basilicum*)

This tender and pungent herb seems a universal favorite. Its name comes from the Greek, *basileus*, and means "king." The Italians use this herb so copiously you'd think it's a vegetable, and it's almost a staple in Vietnamese cuisine. Basil's taste is reminiscent of its cousin

mint—but with licorice, cinnamon, clove, lemon, and thyme tones. Apparently mosquitoes, houseflies, and cockroaches don't like the scent, as basil repels these bugs when planted around windows and doors. This herb is usually green, but there are also purple varieties.

A native of India, basil comes in multiple varieties with distinct flavors and aromas. The Indians esteem the *tulsi*, or holy basil, variety, which is a popular tea ingredient and memory tonic in the West.

Medicinal Benefits One of the valued yang tonics, basil helps maintain and generate warmth and regulate chi circulation and resolve cold, mucus, and damp conditions. It supports the kidney, liver, stomach, spleen, and large intestine functions. The essential oils in basil oil have potent antioxidant, anticancer, antiviral, and antimicrobial properties, making this a valued kitchen medicine, aromatherapy agent, and cosmetic ingredient. Long considered an aphrodisiac, basil is used to treat mild depression, headache, and menstrual pain. It calms the nerves, aids memory and digestion, and treats fevers, kidney malfunction, whooping cough, constipation, nausea, insomnia, fatigue, colds, and flu.

Basil essential oil treats bronchitis, fatigue, colds, poor concentration, migraine headaches, gout, and aches and pains. Basil reduces *vata* and *kapha*.

Use A favorite in ethnic cuisine from Indonesia to Italy, basil is especially savored as a pesto ingredient and has a great affinity for tomato, fish, bean, and egg dishes. Unlike many herbs, its flavor increases with moderate cooking, so use moderately. Dried basil is an acceptable substitute for the fresh.

Storage Fresh basil is more fragile than most herbs, so plan to use it quickly. Kept in a glass of water on the counter, it holds better than when refrigerated.

See **Herbs and Spices; Mint Family.**

BASMATI RICE SEE **RICE.**

BATATA SEE **JINENJO.**

BAY LAUREL SEE **BAY LEAF.**

BAY LEAF
Bay Laurel, Laurel, Sweet Laurel
(*Laurus nobilis*)

While Westerners "see" a man in the moon, the Chinese "see" a bay laurel tree and accordingly name the laurel "moon-laurel." For the ancient Greeks, bay leaves formed the laurel wreath given as the prize at the Pythian Games (precursor to the Olympic Games), as Apollo decreed that bay leaves would signify honor and glory for those who excelled in accomplishment or courage. The term "poet laureate" refers to being crowned in laurel.

One of our most common culinary herbs, the bay leaf, usually dried, comes from an evergreen shrub native to the Mediterranean called the bay laurel (*daphne* in Greek). The name Lawrence refers to this herb. Turkey is one of the main bay exporters.

Medicinal Benefits Bay helps regulate blood circulation and cold conditions. It is an antioxidant, anti-inflammatory, and anticonvulsant with some analgesic properties. It helps relieve insomnia, hysteria, gas, colic, and indigestion and helps regulate menstruation. Steep bay in water and drink the tea to help promote sweating and break a fever. Strew bay leaves in a hot bath to help relieve rheumatism, sprains, and bruises.

The essential oil of bay is an antiseptic and also treats insomnia, rheumatism, and sprains. Bay reduces *vata* and *kapha*.

Use As it takes a while for bay's sweet balsamic flavor to permeate foods, it's added to dishes at the beginning of cooking. Remove bay leaves prior to serving, as cooking doesn't soften them; use one or two leaves for most dishes of six servings. When finely ground, bay is included in spice combinations such as some blends of Indian garam masala. Bay leaves round the flavor of a wide variety of savory dishes including soups, stews, sauces, pickles, sausage, and meat and fish dishes. Bay is often included in the French bouquet garni.

Bay keeps bugs at bay. To help prevent miller moths from hatching in stored grains, tuck several bay leaves into the grain. Or strew in problematic areas to prevent infestation of fleas and roaches. High-quality bay leaves are aromatic and a bright green color. With time its bitter flavor increases and its color fades; discard bay that lacks a fresh color and aroma.

Be Mindful The larger and darker green California bay (*Umbellularia californica*) is inferior as a culinary spice and lacks the GRAS (generally recognized as safe for human consumption) status by the Food and Drug Administration. A main constituent of California bay, umbellulone, is considered a central nervous system toxin when eaten. And when inhaled, it may cause headache, sinus irritation, and sneezing. California bay has a harsher and more camphorous taste than does sweet laurel.

See **Herbs and Spices; Laurel Family.**

BEAN CURD SEE **TOFU.**

AN EASY KISS

Prior to serving the soup, some cooks remove the bay leaf. I do not. At my table, "Whoever finds the bay leaf gets to kiss the cook." Indeed, bay adds spice!

(Do not, however, leave small or broken bay leaves in a dish as, if undetected and inadvertently swallowed, they can lodge in the throat.)

BEAN FLAKES

Some beans are partially cooked, then dehydrated and rolled like oats to shorten cooking time. Bean flakes are generally found in natural food stores. I leave them there. For full flavor and maximum nutrition and energetic properties, favor intact beans.

See **Beans and Legumes.**

BEAN FLOURS SEE **CHICKPEA FLOUR AND SOY FLOUR.**

BEAN PASTE SEE **MISO.**

BEANS AND LEGUMES
Legumes, Pulses
(*Leguminosus*)

"Beans, beans, the musical fruit . . ." Indeed, beans are technically a fruit, as the childhood rhyme accurately states. A bowl of beans is a more universal image of nurture than is a loaf of bread. Unpretentious, filling, and warming, a pot of beans, peas, or lentils simmering on the back of the stove evokes home cooking at its humble best. Peas, along with grains, have been cultivated since 8500 BC, making them the earliest cultivated crops. Today beans and legumes are grown everywhere that people farm.

They grow on vines and are contained in pods; peanuts, with underground pods, also belong to the legume family. For millennia farmers have dried legumes in the field and shelled, cleaned, and stored them. The same today. Beans (with, typically, the exception of soy) are unrefined—they're not parched, polished, gassed, preserved, or colored. They have no added ingredients and nothing taken away. Their earthy sweetness is utterly unadulterated. No wonder they're so satisfying.

Medicinal Benefits Beans are typically neutral in their thermal properties (however, black beans are warming and soy, lima, and mung beans are cooling). Beans support the stomach and spleen and the kidneys; chickpeas also support the heart. They counteract damp conditions and help reduce blood cholesterol, lower blood pressure, regulate colon function, and prevent constipation.

Because they are slowly digested, beans help people who are diabetic or have low blood sugar, as beans cause only a gradual rise in blood sugar. The phytochemical diosgenin and isoflavones in beans help prevent cancer. They're typically a good source of a lecithin component, choline, which supports fat digestion. Beans strengthen the kidneys and adrenals and promote physical growth and development. As a stick-to-the-ribs filling food, beans are more "grounding" than is a salad, baked potato, or bowl of rice.

A bean's color indicates the organ it most benefits, and so green beans, mung beans, and split peas benefit the liver. Red beans, including aduki and kidney beans, influence the heart. Yellow-colored beans, such as chickpeas and soybeans, support the spleen. Navy beans, limas, and other white beans energize the lungs and colon. Black beans are kidney supportive.

Most legumes range from 17 to 25 percent protein, roughly double the protein of grains and higher than that of eggs and most meats. Beans are a good source of calcium, potassium, iron, zinc, and several B vitamins including folate, and they are low in fat. In general, beans reduce *pitta* and *kapha;* lentils, however, increase *pitta.*

Below you'll find our most common dried beans conveniently grouped according to species. Get to know them by clan, as you'll find each has similar culinary applications and cooking times. Some people find that digestibility varies according to clan.

Soybeans are in a class unto themselves and therefore have their own separate entry. For beans with lesser availability and specific culinary uses, see **Fava Bean; Lupin; Winged Bean.** Also see **Dal; Sprouts.**

Chickpeas (*Cicer arietinum*) A chickpea, or garbanzo bean, is unlike other legumes in two curious ways. First, while beans and lentils are smooth surfaced, a chickpea is not; it's wrinkled and roundish but compressed and flattened at the sides with a projecting nascent radicle that looks like a chick's beak. Second, while most legumes share a pod with half a dozen or so other seeds, a chickpea typically has one mature pea per pod.

Chickpeas originated in and were an early Middle Eastern crop. Today they are a popular legume throughout the temperate world. The most common chickpea in the United States is tan colored, although there are red, white, brown, and black varieties available.

Chickpeas are one of the creamiest and tastiest of beans. Add them whole or mashed to soups, croquettes, and vegetable dishes, or enjoy them plain as a side dish. They form the popular Middle Eastern dishes hummus and falafel. Cooked and then seasoned and roasted, they make a tasty nutlike snack food. (Also see **Chickpea Flour** entry.)

Common Beans (*P. vulgaris*) These popular and versatile beans originated in the Americas but are now worldwide staples. Dried, common beans are available in many colors and also include most of the beans we eat in their green, immature stage: snap, shell, and green beans. Oval or kidney shaped, common beans have a sweet and hearty flavor and a dense texture. While their flavors have subtle variations, for the most part their culinary applications are comparable. The common beans are classified as follows:

Black Beans Also known as black turtle beans, they are a black matte with an ivory flesh. Black beans seem more filling and substantial than the lighter-colored beans. Highly versatile, black beans are a staple throughout much of Latin America and are great refried, in chiles or soups, or in marinated salads. For salads, drain and rinse the beans or they will color the other ingredients black.

Flageolets These tiny, tender beans are light green in color and have an herblike essence because they are harvested and dried before reaching full maturity. The pricey flageolet and a similar variety, the Chevrier, are popular in French cuisine and gaining increased availability in the United States. For a homegrown quasi-flageolet substitute, allow green beans to mature in the pod just beyond their best eating stage, then shuck the beans and let them dry.

Mottled Beans These include anasazi beans, appaloosa beans, borlotti beans, cranberry beans, Jacob's Cattle beans, pinto beans, and rattlesnake beans. The mottled beans with their variable colors and patterns are gorgeous to behold, but once cooked, their color turns a uniform pink. Of this diverse group, pinto beans are the most hybridized and commercial crop and, to my palate, less satisfying than the less utilized common mottled beans. Experiment with them all to discover your personal favorites. Many people find anasazi beans easy to assimilate; compared to a pinto, for example, they contain 75 percent less of the flatulence-causing carbohydrate trisaccharides.

Nuña Popping Beans Native to South America, the nuña, or popping bean, will burst from its seed coat with a bang when heated in a thin layer of oil for two to four minutes, or when cooked in a popcorn popper. The popped beans are soft and taste a bit like roasted peanuts. I enjoyed eating nuñas so much when I was in Peru that I later tried (unsuccessfully) to grow them in my garden. There are current efforts to introduce them to our market.

Pink Beans Bolita beans and pink beans (also known as *Pinquito and Rosada*) are a little smaller than pinto beans and a regional favorite in Mexico and the Southwest. They cook to make a sweet and tender dish and are among my personal favorites.

Red Beans Red beans, also known as kidney beans, are available both large and small. The large variety is typically more tough skinned than are the other common bean varieties and, therefore, yields a more gritty-textured dish. Small red beans are a signature ingredient in Creole cuisine.

Tepary Beans This heirloom bean grows in desert and semidesert conditions in Arizona, New Mexico, and Mexico and has been around for the past 8,000 years. It's so drought resistant that it can set seed and mature on a single irrigation or thunderstorm downpour. Available via mail order, the tepary is smaller than other common beans but similar in flavor; it may be white, reddish brown, purplish brown, or speckled brown.

White Beans Cannellini, great Northern, and small white navy beans (which are also called pea beans or haricot beans) are featured in such dishes as baked beans.

Yellow Beans These small beans are oval in shape, thin skinned, and with a creamy texture. They're also called canary beans.

Yellow-Eye Bean A white bean with a yellowish eye that wraps halfway around the bean, this heirloom New England bean was a staple of the Native Americans in the Northeast.

Lentils (*Lens esculenta*) Judging from the French name for lentil soup, *potage esau*, lentils date back at least to the book of Genesis and the hungry Esau, who sold his birthright to Jacob for a bowl of these legumes. For 8,000 years lentils have remained an important dietary staple in Europe, the Middle East, and India.

As a key vegetarian protein source, lentils are second only to soybeans. They are convenient to use, as they cook more quickly than beans and are more mild in flavor. Most Americans think of lentils in terms of soup. They're also great with walnuts in a vegetarian pâté, or cooked with vegetables or on their own as a side dish. Whole lentils are most commonly available as brown or a smaller blue-green French lentil. When split and hulled, they're either yellow or salmon colored and then are also known as dal.

Unlike beans, lentils have no sulfur and so produce very little wind. Lentils have a mild diuretic action, are neutral in thermal properties, and benefit the heart and circulatory systems.

Lima Beans (*P. lunatus*) Mesoamerican in origin and named for the Peruvian city, lima beans are either large or small and typically white, although there are some red, purple, and black varieties. This starchy bean tastes almost buttery, which explains its alternative name, butter bean. Limas may be oval or kidney shaped and typically are flat, although there are some plump varieties.

Because lima beans contain cyanide compounds, the United States restricts commercially grown varieties to those with very low cyanogen levels. Thorough cooking drives off the hydrogen cyanide gas.

When eaten in their immature green stage, lima beans are lime green or yellow in color and a regional favorite in the South. Look for green limas in farmers' markets.

Pea (*Pisum sativum*) Peas, an ancient legume, were among the first cultivated crops in Europe and Asia. Pea varieties grown for drying are starchier than those we eat in their immature, green stage. This facilitates their drying and, once rehydrated, makes for a creamier cooked dish. As a dried food, peas are available whole, or they may be split and hulled, in which case they're also known as dal. They're typically colored yellow or green; the latter forms the classic split pea soup, which is often prepared with a ham hock. Peas reduce *pitta* and *kapha* and are medicinal for the spleen and stomach.

Vigna (*P. vigna*) Native to Asia, vigna-species beans are small and cylindrically shaped with blunt ends and cook more quickly than common beans. For many people, these beans are easier to assimilate than the common beans. Medicinally they help induce urination and relieve damp conditions such as candidiasis-type yeast overgrowth. They are *tridoshic*.

Long beans are a vigna species and available fresh; they are often found in Asian markets. Dried vigna beans include:

Aduki Aduki beans are typically dark red with a thin white line down the ridge, although there are also varieties ranging from tan to black. The beans are mildly diuretic; to increase this property, drink just their cooking liquid on an empty stomach.

Aduki beans have a pleasant nutty flavor and cook into a creamy texture that imparts a dark pinkish hue to lighter-colored foods. In Japan, aduki beans are cooked with sweet rice and served on auspicious occasions, because the color red denotes good fortune but also, surely, because they're tasty and filling. Throughout East Asian cuisine, aduki beans are typically sweetened and cooked to a uniform paste. This red bean paste, sometimes in combination with other ingredients, is used in moon cakes, ice cream, and many other desserts.

Aduki beans imported from Japan are lightly polished to remove the outer seed coat and have a bright sheen. Domestic and Chinese beans are not polished and, as a result, have a just-noticeable gritty texture and, typically, a lower price.

Black-Eyed Pea (Cowpea) The classic New Year's Day menu in many Southern homes includes black-eyed peas and collards—an excellent start for the new year. This earthy-tasting legume originated in Africa about 5,000 years ago, where it is still found growing wild. It is cream colored with a distinctive black spot. Black-eyed peas are also enjoyed green, in the pod. A variety grown to be eaten in its immature pod stage is the long bean.

Mung Bean This small, khaki green legume is Indian in origin and an important Asian staple. It is split and hulled for dal, sprouted, cooked as a legume, or made into a pasta that looks like cellophane. Of sproutable seeds, mung beans rank at the top with alfalfa seeds as easy to sprout, tasty, and multipurpose. A black mung variety is popular in the West Indies. They cook more quickly than most beans and are served during hot seasons for their ability to disperse body heat.

Pigeon Pea The yellowish brown pigeon pea, which originated in Egypt, is ¼ inch long and plump, with a mildly pungent flavor and a tough outer skin. This is a popular bean throughout the Caribbean and among Latino peoples in semitropical and tropical areas.

Urad This small, plump, and slightly kidney-shaped bean has a white hilum, or eye.

While usually black, the urad bean may also be grayish, dark green, or brownish.

Urad is an extremely popular bean in India. Prepare urad beans whole as a side dish or pureed in soups. Urad is especially complemented by ginger, chiles, turmeric, and fresh cilantro or mint. In India, split and husked urad beans are soaked and fermented with rice, then ground for featherlight steamed dumplings (*idlee*), pancakes (*dosas*), and fried savory breads (*bada*).

Use From dumplings and *dosas* to pies and pasta, for more than 30 years I've cooked with beans or their products on a daily basis. Sometimes it seems there aren't enough meals to match the number of delicious legume dishes that I want to make.

A seasoned pot of beans with a garnish makes an excellent side dish. Add beans sparingly to a soup for their interesting shape and melting texture, or add generously to create a hearty soup, chili, or stew. In Central and South America, beans fill tamales, empanadas, and humitas. In China and Japan, they're sweetened and used as a filling for steamed buns. Or they're fermented into tempeh, miso, soy sauce, or natto. For bean cooking inspiration, peruse any ethnic cuisine cookbook. For cooking instructions, see sidebar, page 41.

MOM AT THE KITCHEN TABLE

As a child, my favorite thing about ham was anticipating the sure-to-follow navy bean soup with the ham hock. I so clearly recall mother sitting at our Formica table before a small mound of white beans culling the rejects. It's such a timeless image. I always enjoy fingering my way through a cup of beans. It takes but a minute, and I feel at one with mother and all cooks, past and future, picking over a pile of beans.

Buying/Storing Canned beans are great to have on hand for quick-fix meal. They're one of the few whole "heat-and-eat" foods. However, you pay for convenience. One cup of canned beans costs around 70 cents, while one pound of dry beans costs $1 and yields twelve cups cooked beans! When buying canned beans, read the ingredient label to know what you're getting besides beans. Also, compare a couple of brands and note the brands that are brimming with the beans (and those which are scrimping on them).

Purchase beans from a bulk bin or packaged in a see-through wrapper. Favor those with a vibrant look, for they'll be the current crop of beans. Dull, faded beans are older and tougher and take longer to cook. Select well-formed legumes with few broken, chipped, or split seeds. Uniformity of shape and color is not desirable, though—it indicates a hybrid, which is less vital than an heirloom variety.

What about the eye-catching packages of mixed beans? Another marketing gimmick. Bean varieties differ in their soaking and cooking time, so jumbling them together targets the uninformed cook.

BEAN COOKING SECRETS

If beans are relatively new to your diet or if you have trouble digesting them, use the following techniques to enhance their digestibility. Also, start by eating small amounts frequently to allow your body to adjust to them. But if beans challenge your digestion no matter how they're prepared, this typically reflects a compromised digestive system. Once mended, beans are then digestible.

1. *Soak beans until hydrated.* Soaking time varies, depending upon their variety and freshness, from 2 to 24 hours or until fully hydrated. Soaking helps tenderize beans and reduces their cooking time. (For a quick soak, cover with triple their volume of water and boil for 5 minutes. Turn off the heat, tightly cover, and leave for 2 hours. Drain and rinse. Soaking and then discarding the soaking water will leach out the indigestible sugars—oligosaccharides—in beans that may cause intestinal gas.)

2. *Soak with lemon juice.* Add a tablespoon of lemon juice per cup of dry beans and soak until hydrated.

3. Add *seasonings to aid digestibility.* Salt aids digestion of all foods and is especially important with harder-to-digest foods like beans. Cook until softened and then add 1 teaspoon salt per cup of dry beans. The herbs asafetida, cumin, epazote, fennel, ginger, and winter savory enhance bean digestion. I also find the seaweed kombu indispensable. It is a natural source of glutamic acid and a flavor enhancer and tenderizer, and kombu adds invaluable vitamins, minerals, and trace minerals.

4. *Cook at a slow simmer.* Boiling toughens beans, so simmer them slowly. (Or, conversely, cook in a pressure cooker, as the addition of pressure makes them velvety soft; pressure cooking is especially useful at high elevations.) At the beginning of cooking, skim off and discard any foam that rises to the top of the pot.

5. *Add fat to reduce flatulence.* There's something about the combination of fat and beans that helps quell wind, and that's why classic bean recipes such as refried beans, falafel, pork and beans, marinated beans, and hummus contain added fat.

6. *Cook beans,* then *add acid ingredients.* If you add an acid medium to partially cooked beans, they will not get any softer, regardless of cooking time. Thus, add citrus, vinegar, tomatoes, or wine to already-soft beans.

7. *Sprout beans.* The oligosaccharides in mature beans challenge normal digestive enzymes, and this, in turn, may result in flatulence. While soaking reduces some of these complex carbohydrates, sprouting—or even partially sprouting—beans activates enzymes that further reduces the oligosaccharides into easier-to-digest starches. In addition, sprouting increases their protein content and reduces cooking time.

8. *Try Beano enzymes.* This dietary supplement helps reduce intestinal gas—it contains enzymes that help digest the otherwise hard-to-digest sugars in beans. It is available in supermarkets in both tablet and liquid form.

I store my beans in airtight glass jars in a dark cupboard. An open shelf with glass jars, each holding beans of a different color, may make a beautiful display, but all seeds—beans included—will best retain vitality away from heat and light. At least two nutrients found in beans, pyridoxine and pyridoxal (the natural forms of vitamin B_6), quickly deteriorate when exposed to light. While you can store whole dried beans for several years or more, their germination rate—and therefore their essential fatty acids, flavor, and viability—decreases with age.

See **Legume Family.**

BEANS AND LEGUMES (DRIED) SEE **DAL; FAVA BEAN; LEGUME FAMILY; LUPIN; PEANUT.**

BEANS AND LEGUMES (FRESH) SEE **GREEN BEAN; LEGUME FAMILY; LONG BEAN; PEA, FRESH; WINGED BEAN.**

BEAN SPROUTS SEE **SPROUTS.**

BEAVERTAIL CACTUS SEE **NOPAL.**

BEECH FAMILY
(*Fagaceae*)

This large family of both evergreen and deciduous trees grows in temperate regions worldwide. It includes two with edible seeds, the acorn and chestnut.

See **Acorn; Chestnut.**

BEEFSTEAK LEAF SEE **PERILLA.**

BEET
(*Beta vulgaris*)

The beet is the most intense of vegetables. The radish, admittedly, is more feverish, but the fire of the radish is a cold fire, the fire of discontent, not of passion. Tomatoes are lusty enough, yet there runs through tomatoes an undercurrent of frivolity. Beets are deadly serious.
—Tom Robbins, *Jitterbug Perfume*

Why is it that one day eating a beet turns your urine pink, whereas another day and another beet produce a magenta stool? According to nutritionist Jeffrey Bland, PhD, pink urine may indicate an iron deficiency, while magenta stool indicates adequate iron. Beets are curious. Red beets get their color from a pigment called betalain. You'll also see this pigment in beet relatives including red-stemmed chard, bougainvillea, and amaranth.

Beets have the highest sugar content of all vegetables. Indeed, one extra-sweet variety is grown for the production of sugar. The beet varieties you'll find at the store are red, gold, or candy cane (with a red-and-white-striped interior). Technically, chard is a beet that's grown strictly for its leaves. Beets originated in the Mediterranean region, and wild beets still grow there in the coastal regions. Beets are a member of the diverse goosefoot family.

Medicinal Benefits Beets support blood and chi circulation and the heart, liver, and large intestine. In Roman times, beet juice was considered an aphrodisiac; perhaps not coincidentally, it's high in boron, a mineral critical for the production of human sex hormones. Betacyanin, the pigment that colors beets, is a potent anticarcinogen. Beets treat anemia, are anti-inflammatory, purify the blood, and help dissolve and eliminate acid crystals from the kidneys that can form into kidney stones. Beets alleviate constipation, aid and cleanse the liver, and promote menstruation. Beets reduce *vata* and *kapha*.

Beet greens are also remarkably nutritious. They are an excellent source of folic acid and vitamin K and a very good source of vitamin A. They contain more calcium and iron than the roots.

SUGARY BEET

You won't find a buff-colored, cantaloupe-size beet in the produce section, but once refined, you'll find it in countless products as sugar. The sugar beet, directly related to our common red beet, accounts for one-third of the world's sugar production, with the remainder coming primarily from cane or corn.

Use To retain most of the nutritious color pigment of beets, cook with their skin intact. Beets are a popular addition to fresh juices. They're also pickled, boiled as a side dish, or sliced into arranged salads; bake a beet, grate it raw into a salad, or feature it in a classic borscht soup—either hot or chilled and with a dollop of sour cream to accentuate its brilliant ruby red color. To brighten their color, add lemon juice or vinegar to their cooking water (or to turn the beets a darker purple, cook with an alkaline substance like baking soda).

Beet greens may be substituted for chard in many recipes and, like red chard stems, beet stems can add a bright color note to a soup or stir-fry. Very small and tender beet greens make a beautiful and tasty salad ingredient.

Buying Although some beets are gold or white, most are identified by their bright red to dark purplish skin and flesh that turn the cooking water red. Select firm, fresh-looking plump beets. Their leafy greens, when intact, should look vibrant. At home, cut the leaves from the roots to extend the freshness of the roots, and store the unwashed greens in a separate perforated plastic bag.

See **Goosefoot Family; Vegetable.**

BEETBERRY
Strawberry Spinach
(*Chenopodium capitatum*)

Although the pulpy beetberry flower looks like a strawberry, one taste and you'll know otherwise. Its bland flavor restricts its use as a color accent in salads; it's also used as a natural red dye. The greens, either braised or in salads, are an excellent spinach substitute. You'll find this native American plant in farmers' markets or as a decorative cover plant in many home gardens.

See **Goosefoot Family; Vegetable.**

BELGIAN ENDIVE SEE CHICORY.

BELL PEPPER SEE SWEET PEPPER.

BERGAMOT SEE BITTER ORANGE; ORANGE.

BERRY SEE BLACKBERRY (ENTRY INCLUDES BLACKBERRY HYBRIDS: BOYSENBERRY, LOGANBERRY, MARIONBERRY, AND YOUNGBERRY); BLUEBERRY; CRANBERRY; CURRANT; DEWBERRY; GOOSEBERRY; GROUND CHERRY; HUCKLEBERRY; RASPBERRY; STRAWBERRY.

BESAN SEE CHICKPEA FLOUR.

BIB LETTUCE SEE LETTUCE.

BILBERRY SEE BLUEBERRY; HUCKLEBERRY.

BIRCH FAMILY
(Betulaceae)
Both birch and hazel are deciduous trees and large shrubs that are native to the temperate Northern Hemisphere.

See **Birch Syrup; Hazelnut.**

BIRCH SYRUP
This excellent and delicious sweetener is similar to maple syrup in flavor and use except that it's concentrated from birch trees. These medium- to small-size trees, also known for yielding the bark traditionally used for canoes and basketry, are a close relative of oaks and chestnuts but unrelated to maples.

Birch syrup is produced in Scandinavia and Alaska and is even more energy intensive—and therefore pricey—than maple syrup. While it takes 40 gallons of maple sap to make 1 gallon of pure syrup, it requires 80 gallons of birch sap to yield 1 gallon of pure syrup.

See **Birch Family; Maple Syrup; Sweeteners.**

BITTER MELON
Balsam Pear, Bitter Gourd, Karela
(*Momordica charantia*)

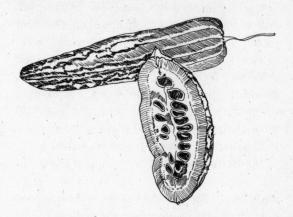

The bitter melon is not a melon but rather a summer squash similar to a cucumber in size and shape. Its lumpy, ridged skin is the color of pale jade, and its dry flesh is a creamy white.

Medicinal Benefits Cooling and astringing, the bitter melon affects heart, liver, and lungs and has detoxifying properties. It is a traditional diabetic remedy throughout Asia. In clinical tests, it inhibits glucose absorption, increases insulin flow, and has insulinlike effects.

The bitter taste of this vegetable is due to its quinine content, which makes it good for reducing fevers, pain, and inflammation. It's an especially good food-medicine for hot flashes, sunstroke, and a common summer cold with a fever. This melon also has diuretic and laxative properties. Nutritionally, it is comparable to summer squash. Bitter melon reduces *pitta* and *kapha*.

Use Bitter melon is available as a supplement; however, for a new culinary pleasure, enjoy it freshly prepared . . . but not raw, as one nibble informs you that some technique must be used to mitigate its bitterness. Cooking, pickling, and salting mellow its bitter flavor. To salt, slice the melon in half lengthwise, remove and discard the brown seeds and the pithy core, salt it generously, and allow to stand for 15 minutes. Then rinse and squeeze out excess liquid before cooking. Taste it, and if the melon is still too bitter for your palate, briefly boil it in salted water, discard the water, and then cook it according to the recipe you're using. Once cooked, it's rather like a zucchini with a bitter tang. Bitter melon may be stir-fried, stewed, stuffed, braised, made into a curry, or pickled and used in chutneys.

Buying Look for bitter melons in Asian markets and farmers' markets and, increasingly, in well-stocked supermarkets. Favor melons that are shiny, firm, plump (not shriveled), and pale green—if dark green, they are immature and extremely bitter. If orange, they're overmature, soft, and bitterly inedible. They will keep refrigerated in a perforated plastic bag for about one week. They're available year-round.

Be Mindful Eat bitter melon moderately, if at all, during pregnancy or if you suffer from low energy with a cold, "empty" feeling in the stomach.

See **Gourd Family; Squash; Squash, Summer.**

BITTER ORANGE
Bergamot, Seville Orange, Sour Orange, Yuzu
(*Citrus aurantium, C. bergamia*)

The grandmother of all oranges, the bitter orange originated in northern India and is too intense to eat out of hand. Its astringency explains its alternative name—sour orange—but its bitterness predominates. This fruit came to Europe via the Moors and Seville, Spain. Bitter oranges are the most hardy citrus and today are grown as ornamentals as far north as Maryland. They're flatter than a sweet orange, with a thick, rough peel that fits loosely over its flesh. The bergamot, a close relative, has an even more aromatic rind.

Medicinal Benefits Considered one of the strongest chi-moving substances, bitter orange is a warming food that treats the liver and kidneys and helps break up hardened masses, including lumps, tumors, and cysts. The peel is used for indigestion, abdominal distention, flatulence, constipation, stubborn coughs, and colic in babies. It reduces *pitta* and *kapha*.

In aromatherapy, the essential oil of bitter orange blossoms, called neroli, is used to soothe the nervous system, reduce anxiety, and increase circulation. Externally it is used in douches for vaginal infections and skin complaints such as thread vein scars.

Use The bitter orange is an indispensable ingredient in orange marmalade. Its juice adds piquancy to sauces, such as the Latin American *mojo*, which is equal parts bitter orange juice and olive oil with minced garlic and onion. Bitter orange complements duck and game. The peel may be candied, used to make orange-blossom water, or added to flavored teas such as Earl Grey and liqueurs such as Grand Marnier.

Buying Winter is the best time to find bitter oranges at specialty greengrocers or Asian markets. Yuzu is a variety of bitter orange with a unique, limelike fragrance that is extracted and used as a flavoring agent in Japanese cuisine. The fruit itself is the size of an orange with an uneven yellow or green skin.

See **Citrus Family; Orange.**

BLACK BARLEY SEE **BARLEY.**

BLACK BEAN SEE **BEANS AND LEGUMES.**

BLACKBERRY
(*Rubus fruticosus, R. laciniatus*)

Plump, sweet blackberries are closely related to raspberries but are larger and juicier and have a grainier texture and a more assertive flavor. Their core does not separate from the fruit as does a raspberry. Although black-berries grow wild in temperate regions of the Northern Hemisphere, they're Asian in or-igin. Oregon is the world's leading blackberry producer.

Blackberries are rather easily hybridized, so if you see the name of a new berry, such as **Kotata, Olallieberry,** or **Tayberry**, odds are that it is part blackberry. Four of the more common *Rubus* hybrids are:

- **Boysenberry**—In 1923 Rudolph Boysen crossed a blackberry and a raspberry and created a namesake. Boysenberries are red and both larger and more acidic than blackberries. They are grown primarily for canning.
- **Loganberry**—This large, lackluster red berry has an intensely acid taste due to its high content of citric acid. Too acidic to eat raw, loganberries are used primarily in wine making and preserves and, with plenty of sugar, as a raspberry substitute.
- **Marionberry**—Named after Marion County, Oregon, where this fruit was de-veloped, it's popular in fruit preserves where the added sweetener helps coun-ter the berry's acidity.
- **Youngberry**—A cross between the blackberry and dewberry, this fruit is often found in preserves, syrup, and juices from South America, Australia, and New Zealand.

Medicinal Benefits Blackberries are a warming and tonifying fruit that nourish the liver and kidneys and act as a blood tonic and a mild diuretic. Their astringency makes them a useful kitchen remedy for diarrhea, dysen-tery, and hemorrhoids. The Romans used them as a gout treatment. Berries are *tridoshic.* They are rich in vitamin C and pectin.

TWO TYPES OF PEDESTRIANS

From late July through the first frost, I've repeatedly observed two types of pedestri-ans along public pathways in the Pacific Northwest. Some are focused on the trail ahead, and others are scanning the sur-rounding bushes for blackberries. Many of the latter carry a pail or bag for their loot, their fingers are stained purple, and their faces sport a smile—especially after finding a really juicy one!

See **Dewberry; Fruit; Blackberry Family.**

BLACKBERRY FAMILY
(*Rubus*)
Raspberries and blackberries are the best known of several hundred *Rubus* fruits. These aggregate fruits are widespread throughout the temperate regions of the Northern Hemi-sphere as well as in South America.
See **Blackberry; Raspberry.**

BLACK CHANTERELLE SEE **CHANTERELLE.**

BLACK CURRANT SEE **CURRANT.**

BLACK CURRANT SEED OIL
(*Ribes nigrum*)
Oil from black currant seeds complements omega-3 fatty acids and is a quality source of gamma-linolenic acid (GLA), an essential fatty acid that contributes to prostaglandin syn-thesis, which has a profound positive effect on health, particularly on ameliorating pre-menstrual symptoms. Mother's milk, spirulina, evening primrose oil, and borage oil are other GLA sources.
See **Currant; Currant Family; Essential Fatty Acids.**

Black-Eyed Pea See **Beans.**

Black Forest Mushroom See **Shiitake.**

Black Pepper See **Pepper.**

Black Quinoa See **Quinoa.**

Black Radish See **Radish.**

Black Rice See **Rice.**

Black Salsify See **Scorzonera.**

Black Sesame Seed See **Sesame Seed.**

Black Soybean See **Soybean.**

Black Trumpet Mushroom See **Chanterelle.**

Black Turtle Bean See **Beans and Legumes.**

BLACK WALNUT
(*Juglans nigra*)

The native American walnut, the black walnut, is related to the more common English walnut and prized for its sweet, robust, and woodsy flavor. These rounded but oblong nuts, about an inch in diameter, grow on an elegant and long-living tree that can reach a height of 150 feet. The black walnut is a member of the hickory family.

The black walnut is extremely difficult to crack, requiring a cement floor, heavy hammer, and a hefty swing. Once split, each morsel of nut meat needs coaxing from the still-unyielding shell. In this process, the black walnut oil leaves an impervious brown stain on fingers, fabric, and even on the cement. The amount of meat per nut is small, but its flavor

> ## SHORT STOP FOR BLACK WALNUTS
>
> One October I was driving near Fruita, Colorado, and happened to see a handmade sign next to a large old Buick: BLACK WALNUTS. A couple sat in the front seat. I stopped short. A farmer in his seventies got out of his car to meet me, a one-pound zip-top bag of black walnuts in hand. Did he crack them himself, I asked, and he held out his brown-stained hands as evidence. We exchanged money, product, and names, and the Mrs. and I exchanged recipes. Michael Springmeyer said that his 36 black walnut trees don't produce uniformly but that there's always a crop to sell. At $12 a pound, they were a steal.

is great. Just a bit of black walnut marvelously flavors quality chocolate and ice cream.

The black walnut is lower in fat and higher in protein and iron than is the English walnut. It contains more vitamin A than any other nut. Black walnuts reduce *vata*.

See **Hickory Family; Nuts; Walnut.**

BLADDER WRACK
Rockweed
(*Fucus vesiculosus*)

Walking along the beach at low tide, you'll often see what looks like a sprig of fir or juniper. This seaweed, bladder wrack, is not a diuretic as its name suggests. *Wraec* is an old English word for "seaweed," and "bladder" refers to its bladderlike, gas-filled pouches that form in pairs along its central midrib.

Medicinal Benefits Bladder wrack is the original source of iodine as a nutritional additive and an effective medicine for obesity, hypothyroid function, rheumatism, and edema. It helps detoxify the system, is cooling, and helps balance conditions of excess heat and damp. Bladder wrack treats the lung, spleen, and stomach pathways.

Along with the other brown seaweeds, bladder wrack is an important source of fucoidan, an anticarcinogen and anticholesterol agent available as a nutraceutical and supplement in two forms, U-Fucoidan and F-Fucoidan.

Use Bladder wrack has a pleasing, sweet flavor, but its slippery gel is a texture most people don't enjoy. It is used primarily in stock or as an ingredient in food supplements.

See **Seaweed Family; Vegetable.**

BLOOD ORANGE SEE **ORANGE.**

BLUEBERRY
Bilberry, Whortleberry
(*Vaccinium corymbosum*)

I once read an account of an explorer who, retracing Mackenzie's route to the Arctic Ocean, found and feasted upon blueberries 10 miles from the Arctic Circle. Imagine that.

Not too juicy and not too sweet, it is no wonder that the delectable blueberry is the second most popular berry after the strawberry. Because of its superior shipping properties, the blueberry is a sizable business in the northeastern states, especially Maine. The United States produces 95 percent of the world's blueberry crop. This native American plant is related to azaleas, rhododendrons, huckleberries, and cranberries.

Medicinal Benefits Supporting the lung, spleen, and stomach meridians, blueberries are a cooling food that helps clear toxins and excessive damp or hot conditions. Of our common fruits, blueberries are the best source of invaluable anthocyanidin compounds, antioxidants that help slow and prevent cell deterioration. Blueberries support eye function and help protect against age-related macular de-

BLUEBERRY SORE THROAT REMEDY

Here's a tasty sore throat remedy that also helps boost your immune system. Plan on making it early in the cold season, as it requires a few weeks to macerate. (If you are coughing now, try this for instant relief: Combine 2 tablespoons honey with 1 tablespoon lemon juice; flavor with 1 teaspoon frozen fruit concentrate if you like.)

As *cooked* honey is mucus-forming, it would be counterproductive in this recipe, so I use sugar. To substitute dried berries for fresh, add ¾ cup water and increase the cooking time if necessary until the fruit is soft. If using dried berries, use those that are 100 percent fruit and additive-free.

Makes ¾ cup syrup

- 1 cup fresh blueberries (or blackberries, cranberries, currants, or elderberries)
- 1 cup sugar
- ¼ cup gin or vodka

Place the berries and sugar in a medium saucepan over medium heat and bring to a simmer. Cook, uncovered, for 5 minutes, stirring as necessary to prevent scorching. Remove from the heat and cool completely. Add the gin, stir to combine, and pour into a sterile glass jar. Cover and let macerate in a cool place for two weeks. Strain and discard the fruit pulp (or spread it on toast), and use the syrup as needed to relieve a sore throat.

generation. They help treat both constipation and diarrhea and are therapeutic for varicose veins, hemorrhoids, and peptic ulcers. They have bacteria-fighting capabilities, and like their cranberry cousins, blueberries are particularly useful in countering urinary tract infections. Blueberries are *tridoshic*. They are a very good source of vitamin C and fiber.

Fresh or frozen, blueberries are a colorful and tasty addition to cakes, shortcakes, pies, cobblers, preserves, and syrup. They dry well and are used in numerous prepared foods. Blueberries darken if stored in a metal container, and if combined with excessive alkaline ingredients (such as baking soda), the berries turn a greenish blue.

Buying/Foraging Wild blueberries, smaller, tarter, and more vibrantly colored than cultivated ones, are prized for their superior nutritional profile. These foraged berries sometimes are available either fresh or dried in regional markets. Since commercial blueberries are boxed with a cellophane covering, it's hard to see their quality. Stains on the carton exterior indicate mashed and moldy berries. To know for sure, slip off the wrapper and look. Avoid withered or green fruits, and favor fresh, plump navy blueberries with a powdery bloom. This bloom is a natural protective waxy coat. Blueberries hold far better than other berries, but are best within 10 days of picking. This lush berry is at its peak in midsummer.

The wild blueberry (huckleberry or bilberry) is still found in many parts of the country and is smaller and more tart than the commercial varieties.

Be Mindful For some allergic individuals, blueberries trigger hives and swelling of the face, lips, and eyes.

See **Blueberry Family; Fruit.**

BLUEBERRY FAMILY
(*Vaccinium*)

Blueberries and their near relatives, bilberries, huckleberries, lingonberries, and cranberries, typically grow in cold climates in the Northern Hemisphere. They are not true berries, as the sepals of their flower remains at the bottom (not stem end) of the fruit. Other false berries include bananas, watermelon, and the whole cucumber/melon family.

See **Blueberry; Cranberry; Fruit; Huckleberry; Lingonberry.**

BLUE CORN See **CORN.**

BLUE-GREEN ALGAE See **WILD BLUE-GREEN ALGAE.**

BOK CHOY
Baby Bok Choy, Chinese Cabbage, Pak Choy, Snow Cabbage, Tai Sai
(*Brassica rapa, Chinensis* group)

Bok choy is a tasty vegetable that grows as a rosette of upright, crinkled green leaves held on large, thick, flat, and crunchy white stalks. Popular in China since at least the fifth century, it is, compared to many of its cabbage relatives, sweet and mild tasting.

Medicinal Benefits More cooling than many of its cabbage relatives, bok choy is a chi tonic that energizes the stomach and large intestine functions and helps clear excess water, mucus, and toxins. It is effective in cases of heat congestion in the lungs which, in the early stages, typically would have symptoms such as fevers, chills, dry cough, shortness of breath, and thick mucus discharge. Bok choy reduces *pitta* and *kapha*.

As indicated by its deep green leaves, bok choy has more beta-carotene than cabbage, and it supplies considerably more calcium. It is also an excellent source of vitamin C as well as the numerous phytonutrients common to its family.

Use To wash, remove the outer stems and clean individually, as sand may be trapped at their base. Enjoy these juicy and sweet stems raw with a dip or in salads or cook it in a stir-fry or any other number of dishes. The stems will require longer cooking than the greens; for the stems to retain their juiciness, cook over a relatively high heat. Bok choy leaves are also used as a vegetable wrap for food morsels that are then cooked. Their outer leaves are a little coarse for use in salads.

Buying Select those with whole (not ragged), vibrant green leaves and crisp, unblemished stems. Store in an unsealed plastic bag. Bok choy keeps well but not as long as cabbage; it is most flavorful when used within five days.

There are several varieties of bok choy, including the more tender baby types about six inches tall up to larger varieties several times that height. The most common have white stalks, but a Shanghai variety is a uniform light green. Another variety, bok choy sum, has small yellow flowers (*sum* is the Chinese word for "flower"), white stems, and dark green leaves.

See **Cabbage Family; Vegetable.**

BOLETE
Cèpe, King Bolete, Porcino
(*Boletus edulis*)

Mushrooms don't get any more delicious than the bolete. Its texture is reminiscent of filet mignon—only more succulent. This large mushroom is spongy (with tubes rather than gills) under the cap and is famed throughout the Northern Hemisphere for its piney, earthy flavor.

Medicinal Benefits In the folk medicine of Bohemia and Bavaria, boletes are accredited with cancer prevention. This folk wisdom is supported by studies at Memorial Sloan-Kettering Cancer Center in New York. The bolete is also an ingredient in the patent Chinese medicine tendon-easing pills, which ease lumbago, leg pain, numbness in limbs, bone and tendon discomfort, and leukorrhea.

Boletes are low in calories and a good vitamin D source. Medicinally they are a cooling food, stimulate the appetite, and are best eaten in moderation. As an occasional food, they reduce *pitta* and *kapha*.

Use Some people discard the tubular spore-bearing part of boletes, but not I. It develops a delicate, oysterlike texture, which I find particularly delicious. You may wish to allow longer cooking time for the more fibrous stem, or cut it into smaller pieces so that it will cook at the same rate as the cap. Bolete mushrooms range in color from whitish through a vivid orange to brick red and may be used in any recipe calling for mushrooms. Lightly sautéed in olive oil with (or without) garlic and parsley is recipe enough. Do not serve raw. To rehydrate when dried, soak in water for about 20 minutes to soften.

Buying/Foraging Boletes are among the most common wild mushrooms and have thus far successfully evaded commercial production. A truly wild food, boletes are an easy mushroom for foragers to find and identify. Occasionally fresh boletes are imported from France and Italy at an exorbitant price. When fresh, this mushroom is highly perishable. Purchase boletes that are firm and bruise-free and show no sign of insect infestation in the stem end. They deteriorate rapidly, so plan to use them immediately. Dried boletes are more readily available in many markets.

See **Mushroom Family; Vegetable.**

BOLITA SEE **BEANS.**

BONIATO SEE **SWEET POTATO.**

BORAGE
(*Borago officinalis*)

Borage is a large, beautiful European herb with velvety leaves and vivid, star-shaped purple flowers. Its nearest relative used medicinally is comfrey, which also has downy leaves. The word probably comes from Arabic *abu araq*, meaning "father of sweat." Borage is the herb used in the popular gin-based British drink Pimm's.

Medicinal Benefits As its Arabic name suggests, borage stimulates sweat; it also helps with lactation. A bland, cooling herb, borage aids digestion and strengthens the heart. It is a natural blood cleanser and so supports the liver and helps treat skin problems like acne and herpes. It is a mild sedative and antidepressant, reduces high fever and catarrh, and is a mild laxative. Borage seeds are an excellent source of the important essential fatty acid gamma-linolenic acid, which regulates hormones and lowers blood pressure. It calms *pitta* and *kapha*.

Use Borage imparts a cucumberlike flavor. The fresh leaves may be stuffed and rolled like grape leaves. When using raw, chop the leaves to minimize their woolly texture. Enjoy the leaves in salads, cold sauces such as mayonnaise, pasta sauces, with cooked vegetables, and as a garnish. When adding the blossoms to a salad, add as a garnish at the last moment; otherwise, the dressing will discolor them. For an especially tasty salad, mix equal portions of watercress with chopped borage leaves.

Buying Borage wilts so rapidly that if not plucked fresh from the garden, it's better to use dried borage.

See **Essential Fatty Acids; Herbs and Spices.**

BOSC PEAR SEE **PEAR.**

BOSTON LETTUCE SEE **LETTUCE.**

BOYSENBERRY SEE **BLACKBERRY.**

BRAN SEE **OAT BRAN; WHEAT BRAN.**

BRAZIL NUT
(*Bertholletia excelsa*)

One of our largest and richest flavored nuts, there's little about the creamy-colored and toe-shaped Brazil nut that is not remarkable. As there are only a few commercial plantations of the gigantic (up to 150 feet high) Brazil tree from the South American tropics, most of our crop is wild harvested. The shell is hard, dark brown, and oblong in length but triangular in diameter. The tree does not grow outside the Amazon basin, so our supply comes from Bolivia, Brazil, and Peru.

Medicinal Benefits The Brazil nut contains the highest level of selenium of any food; this antioxidant helps protect against cancer and heart disease and helps reduce allergies and inflammation. This nut is a superior source of polyunsaturated fats; it is high in flavonoids and the amino acids methionine, cysteine, and arginine, which makes it a good protein source. Brazil nuts reduce *vata*.

Use For an elegant and delicious treat, use

A GENTLE ANTIDEPRESSANT

"Those of our time do use the [borage] floures in sallads to exhilerate and make the minde glad. There be also many things made of them, used for the comfort of the heart, to drive away sorrow, and increase the joy of the minde. The leaves and floures of Borrage put into wine make men and women glad and merry, driving away all sadnesse, dulnesse, and melancholy, as Discorides and Pliny affirme."

—John Gerard, *The Herball, or Generall Historie of Plantes* (1597)

Brazil nuts as a stuffing for dates and serve alongside kumquats. Their creamy texture and rich and delicate flavor make them a prized nut for baking, eating out of hand, or adding to nut mixes and snacks. The high saturated fat content of Brazil nuts makes them interchangeable with macadamia nuts and coconut in recipes.

Buying/Storing If purchasing shelled Brazil nuts, select those with their brown skin intact and that look plump and fresh; avoid those that are yellowed, dark, or bruised. Brazil nuts in the shell should feel heavy when shaken and not rattle. Reddish brown shelled Brazil nuts are dyed for cosmetic purposes. Refrigerate Brazil nuts in a tightly sealed container to prevent them from absorbing food odors. Brazil nuts in the shell may be stored for several months in a cool, dry place.

Be Mindful While selenium is an invaluable antioxidant, an overdose is toxic. Three to four Brazil nuts—about half an ounce—provides the maximum daily selenium intake recommended by the World Health Organization.

See **Nuts.**

PLANTED WITH A BANG

Brazil nuts are collected from the ground, rather than being plucked from their towering trees. The two- to four-pound woody fruits contain up to 24 nuts, which fit together like orange segments. When these heavy fruits break off and come crashing down, they sometimes shatter open, driving (or, perhaps from the seed's perspective, planting) the nuts into the ground. Harvesters use protective shields and, understandably, don't harvest during strong winds.

BREADFRUIT
Ramon Fruit
(*Artocarpus altilis*)

Imagine a baked fruit that has a texture and taste reminiscent of freshly baked bread but is still an acquired taste. The breadfruit is the size of a grapefruit with a green, scaly skin, and it grows on trees natively throughout the Indo-Malayan Archipelago. It is a member of the fig family.

Modern cultivars are seedless, but the older varieties contain edible seeds known as breadnuts. Breadfruit is one of the highest-yielding food plants and used as a starch throughout the tropics. It is prepared as a starch when green, similar to how you would cook white or sweet potatoes; when fully ripened, it is used as a dessert fruit. When dried and ground, it yields a nutritious flour that is high in tryptophan, the amino acid that helps calm stress and anxiety.

See **Breadnut; Fig Family.**

BREADNUT
Ramon Nut
(*Artocarpus altilis, Brosimum alicastrum*)

Two closely related trees, the breadnut tree and the breadfruit tree, produce edible seeds that are known as breadnuts. Similar to chestnuts in flavor and texture, breadnuts are typically roasted, fried, or boiled prior to use; when roasted they develop a flavor reminiscent of cocoa. Ramon nuts were used medicinally by the Maya to detoxify the liver and promote lactation in nursing women.

See **Breadfruit; Fig Family; Nuts.**

BREWER'S YEAST SEE NUTRITIONAL YEAST.

BROAD BEAN SEE FAVA BEAN.

BROCCOLI
(*Brassica oleracea* var. *italica*)

Broccoli, one of the more popular cabbage family members, was developed by the Etruscans and remained primarily an Italian vegetable until it gained widespread use in the 1920s in the United States. It takes its name from the Latin word for branch (*brachium*), as its stalk is indeed like a sturdy branch that divides into smaller stems that are topped by dark green or even blue-green florets, which are immature flower heads. The Salinas Valley in California provides 90 percent of our domestic broccoli crop.

Medicinal Benefits Cooling in nature, broccoli supports the liver, spleen, stomach, and bladder and helps regulate chi circulation, heat, and water. It treats the eyes and helps reduce eye inflammation. It is slightly diuretic in action. Broccoli's anticancer, antifungal, antiviral, and antibacterial properties are due in part to its immune-boosting glucosinolates (specifically indole-3-carbinol and sulforaphane).

Broccoli contains twice the vitamin C as an orange and is a superior source of vitamin A and K. It has almost as much calcium as whole milk—and its calcium is better absorbed. It contains selenium, is a modest source of alpha tocopherol vitamin E, and has value as an antioxidant. Broccoli reduces *pitta* and *kapha*.

Use In addition to the florets, peel and discard the fibrous skin from the stalks and use the tender inner stalk. Use the leaves attached to the stem as you would collards or kale. It is the cabbage family's green leaves (not the white florets, as in cauliflower, or the green florets, as in broccoli) that offer the most nutrients. While steaming is perhaps the most common way to prepare broccoli, it's delicious in countless other dishes, including soups, casseroles, omelets, stir-fries, and pickles. I enjoy blanching broccoli and serving it with a dressing. Broccoli takes well to basil, curry, dill, oregano, tarragon, and thyme.

Buying Select broccoli that has a fresh smell, bright and compact green florets, and firm stalks. Avoid any with a rank smell, yellow florets, or woody or hollowed stalks, as these are overmature. Even though it appears to hold well for a week or more in the refrigerator, for the best flavor, use within a few days of purchase.

Be Mindful The recent trend of serving raw broccoli florets in salads or as crudités is, I believe, a mistake. (Unless, that is, the broccoli is very young and fresh.) Their sulfury taste is one drawback; how hard they are to digest is another. Broccoli steamed al dente is preferable—the steaming renders it easy to digest, brings up its color and flavor, and reduces its otherwise harsh taste.

See **Broccolini; Sprouts (Broccoli); Cabbage Family; Vegetable.**

BROCCOLINI
Baby Broccoli
(*Brassica oleracea Italica group* × *Alboglabra group*)

This trademarked vegetable, a natural hybrid of broccoli and Chinese broccoli, has been available in the United States since 1998. It looks like skinny broccoli, with long and slender stalks that hold clusters of green buds and some yellow flowers and negligible leaves. It is sweeter than broccoli, with a tang of mustard that dissipates with cooking. The stalks, less fibrous than broccoli, do not require peeling. Broccolini is sold in small bunches. Refrigerate, unwashed, in a perforated plastic bag for up to a week. Its use and health benefits are comparable to broccoli.

See **Broccoli; Cabbage Family; Vegetable.**

BROCCOLI RABE
Rapini
(*Brassica rapa* subsp. *parachinensis*)

While the stalks and florets of broccoli rabe look similar to broccolini, the rabe has abun-

INVITING THE RABE IN

When deciding which way to use broccoli rabe—or any other vegetable—consider how it will complement the main dish and help you make balance with the season. If, for example, I'm serving a substantial meaty dish, then I'll make the rabe light by steaming or blanching it and dressing it with nothing but a squeeze of lemon juice and splash of olive oil. If the cooler weather invites a more warming vegetable dish, I'll sauté it with garlic, ginger, or another warming herb. On another day, the soup or stir-fry might invite the rabe into the pot. Rather than religiously following a recipe, let the vegetables—and your energetic needs—help determine how you'll serve them.

dant dark green leaves. Broccoli rabe is pungent and bitter, especially the stems, which you may wish to discard. A nonheading broccoli, it adds zest to bland dishes and can even hold its own with savory ones. Broccoli rabe reduces *kapha*.

Use Rabe is at its best when the leaves are fresh and free from discoloration and when the buds are still tight or just starting to open. The leaf and flower are used primarily. Prepare it as you would broccoli, reducing the cooking time a bit.

See **Broccoli; Cabbage Family; Vegetable.**

BROCCOLI SPROUTS SEE **SPROUTS.**

BROWN RICE SEE **RICE.**

BROWN RICE VINEGAR SEE **VINEGAR.**

BROWN SUGAR SEE **SUGAR.**

BRUSSELS SPROUT
(*Brassica oleracea* var. *gemmifera*)

Of all vegetables growing in a garden, Brussels sprouts look the strangest. From 20 to 40 auxiliary buds (or baby cabbages) grow close together along a tall, single stalk that's topped with small cabbagelike leaves. Brussels sprouts originated in Brussels, Belgium—ergo its name. The Germans more aptly call it *Rosenkohl,* or "rose cabbage."

Medicinal Benefits Brussels sprouts are a warming food that helps disperse cold; they support stomach and large intestine function and mildly stimulate the liver out of stagnancy. They are an excellent source of folic acid, vitamins C and K, and beta-carotene. Nutritionally and energetically, they're comparable to cabbage and contain numerous glucosinolates, which are cancer-fighting phytochemicals.

Use In a traditional British Christmas dinner, Brussels sprouts are a given. Considering that these beauties are then at their peak and, when cooked properly, appropriate fare for the grandest of feasts, it's a custom I readily embrace.

To serve Brussels sprouts whole, trim then cut an ✕ into the base of each one to enable the heat to penetrate their center more quickly and cook through before the outer leaves are overdone. Blanch or steam until just tender but still a vibrant green. Brussels sprouts may also be halved, quartered, or thinly sliced, or, for an elegant but time-consuming dish, separate each leaf. I also add Brussels sprouts to stir-fries and soups or to steamed, braised, and baked dishes.

Brussels sprouts at their prime need to be seasoned only with butter and salt or with extra virgin olive oil and a squeeze of lemon. If they are not sweet, they invite more assertive flavoring such as mustard, capers, or juniper berries.

Buying Brussels sprouts become sweet and

tender after a frost. Unfortunately, since our primary commercial supply of this vegetable comes from California's mild coastal area, Brussels sprouts generally lack sweetness. If your region has frost, seek out local Brussels sprouts.

See **Cabbage Family; Vegetable.**

BUCKWHEAT
(*Fagopyrum esculentum*)

The three-sided buckwheat groat is the shape and rusty color of a beechnut and thus its Middle Dutch name was *boec* (beech) *weite* (wheat). Although not a wheat, or even a cereal grain, buckwheat is grainlike in use. This rhubarb relative was first domesticated in the western Yunnan region of China, possibly as early as 6000 BC, and spread throughout Eurasia. In medieval Russia the word *kasha*, which now means roasted or cooked buckwheat, signified "meal" or "feast" as kasha was an integral food.

Its inedible, durable black hulls are commonly used as a stuffing for pillows and meditation cushions, as they are hypoallergenic and do not readily conduct or reflect heat.

Medicinal Benefits Buckwheat is a cooling grain that supports the large intestine, stomach, and spleen; it helps move chi and disperse heat and damp conditions. Of all the grains, buckwheat has the longest transit time in the gut and therefore is the most filling and stabilizing for blood sugar irregularities including diabetes. In addition, it contains D-chiro-inositol, found

to be deficient in type 2 diabetics. Since it is gluten-free, buckwheat is a favorite of people with allergies and is even brewed into a hypoallergenic beer. It's a good blood-building food, as it neutralizes toxic acidic wastes and reduces cholesterol.

It contains rutin and quercetin, flavonoid glycosides with beneficial effects on the blood vessels that help control bleeding in people with high blood pressure, dilate blood vessels, reduce capillary permeability, increase microcirculation in veins, and lower blood pressure. This makes it a good food to mitigate varicose veins, bruising, frostbite, and radiation damage and to increase circulation to the hands and feet. In Ayurvedic medicine, it reduces *kapha*.

Buckwheat's most outstanding nutritional characteristic is its high proportion of all eight essential amino acids, and it is higher than all other grains in lysine, making it a good protein source. In addition, buckwheat has up to 100 percent more calcium than other grains.

Use Buckwheat has a strong, robust flavor and a soft texture. Use it as a hot breakfast cereal, a side dish, a grain entrée, by itself, or cooked with other vegetables, nuts, or seeds as a grain pilaf. The cooked grains, when formed into croquettes and grilled or pan-fried, make an excellent burger or loaf.

Buying Buckwheat is available in several different forms:

- **Buckwheat or Buckwheat Groats** White-green and a little rusty colored, unroasted buckwheat groats have a mild flavor. For maximum vitality and flavor, I recommend buying unroasted groats and then, if you wish, toasting them before cooking for a fresh roasted flavor. To toast groats, place them in a wok or thin pan over high heat and stir continuously until the groats are aromatic and lightly browned.

- **Kasha** Buckwheat that is factory toasted to a deep amber is called kasha. It has an almost scorched flavor that some people adore (I, however, find it a little stale, and therefore favor buckwheat).
- **Kasha Grits** Available from coarse to fine for "quicker" cooking, I find no advantage to purchasing broken buckwheat, since buckwheat groats are more vital and cook in a quick 10 minutes.
- **Whole Buckwheat** With its inedible black hull intact, whole buckwheat is suitable only for sprouting or for grinding into dark buckwheat flour.

Be Mindful Curiously enough, buckwheat may cause light-sensitive dermatitis. If you have skin cancer or eruptions, it may exacerbate these conditions. In addition, it is not advised should you have extreme heat signs such as high fever, thirst, and high blood pressure.

HOW A HORSE GETS SUNBURNED

A light-colored horse or cow grazing in a buckwheat field on a sunny day may become sunburned and suffer temporary hair loss. Buckwheat inhibits our tanning element, melanin, and judging from farmers' stories about sunburned light-colored livestock, apparently inhibits a horse's as well.

Perhaps this is why buckwheat is a staple of the dark-complexioned Siberian peoples but not of the fair-skinned Scandinavians. If you are dark-skinned, a melanin inhibitor keeps your skin a shade lighter and thus enables you to absorb more of the sun's rays—and therefore more vitamin D—the hard-to-obtain vitamin during long, dark winters.

In our Deep South, buckwheat was an old kitchen remedy for lightening the skin.

See **Grains; Buckwheat Family; Buckwheat Flour.**

BUCKWHEAT FAMILY

This is a family of flowering herbaceous plants, mostly perennial, that grow worldwide but are more prevalent in temperate regions. It's also known as the *Polygonum* family (*poly* means "many" and *goni* means "knee" or "joint") because in many of the species where the stems branch, there are swollen nodes or joints. The primary foods in this family include buckwheat, rhubarb, and sorrel.

See **Buckwheat; Rhubarb; Sorrel.**

BUCKWHEAT FLOUR

Buckwheat flour is made from unroasted buckwheat groats. It is graded light, medium, or dark, depending on the amount of black hull contained in the flour. Since the hull is rich in lysine, an important amino acid, I favor the darker flour. And the tiny black specks add rich color to pancakes and baked goods.

For a soft, aromatic cake or muffin with an earthy flavor and musky aroma, substitute 10 percent buckwheat flour for wheat flour. Add 30 percent or more buckwheat flour to bread and your loaf will have the density of a brick and the moistness of pudding. Buckwheat flour is most familiar in pancakes, waffles, and crêpes. Allspice, ginger, and cinnamon enhance buckwheat products, and a little of it is excellent in gingerbread.

Buckwheat flour, alone or combined with wheat flour, makes superlative pasta. As soba, it's Japan's most famous pasta. Buckwheat noodles, a specialty of Valtellina on the Italian-Swiss border, are combined with potatoes and cabbage in *pizzoccheri*. Throughout northern Italy, buckwheat flour is also made into a hearty black polenta, *polenta nera*.

See **Buckwheat; Flour.**

Buddha's Hand Citron See **Citron.**

Bulgar See **Wheat.**

Bulghur See **Wheat.**

Bullwhip Kelp See **Sea Whip.**

BURDOCK
Gobo
(*Arctium lappa*)

If ever you've strolled through the autumn countryside and collected burrs on your sweater or socks—odds are that they were burdock fruits. One ingenious person examined the burr's minute hooks to see why it so effectively clings to things, went to the drawing board, and invented Velcro. When it comes to eating, though, it's the root—not the fruit—that is a prized vegetable.

Imagine the heady aroma of freshly dug earth . . . that's burdock's aroma. Add sweet, and you've got its flavor, which is similar to artichoke hearts, or salsify, only with a touch of bitter. Burdock skin is brown, while its somewhat fibrous flesh is white. A long favorite of the Japanese, who call it *gobo*, the burdock taproot grows up to two feet in length yet remains as slender as a carrot. Burdock is a member of the daisy family.

Medicinal Benefits Burdock stimulates bile secretions and is an excellent source of blood-sugar-lowering inulin, making it good for diabetic conditions. Burdock is one of the great alterative herbs, restoring the body to normal health by cleansing and purifying the blood, supporting digestion and the elimination of toxins, and helping to restore normal body function.

As an herbal ingredient, burdock appears in both European and Asian formulas as an anti-carcinogen, a treatment for arthritis and liver detoxification, and for general kidney support. Burdock reduces *pitta* and *kapha*.

Burdock has more protein, calcium, and phosphorus than carrots and is an excellent source of potassium.

Use Ignore any recipe instructions that call to peel burdock's comely skin. Give it a light scrub with a vegetable brush, then cut and cook it as you would a carrot, though it requires a longer cooking time. Because of its fibers, it is commonly cooked—rather than served raw. It's hard for me to imagine any cooked vegetable dish that is not enhanced by burdock's sweet, earthy flavor. I especially favor it in soups, stews, and stir-fries or with sea vegetables.

Buying/Foraging Throughout many parts of the world, including the United States, burdock thrives as a common weed. You can identify it by its large, elephant ear–like leaves and its bothersome burrs. If foraging, harvest only the low-lying, first-year plants before they develop tall stocks and set seed. Burdock is an easy plant to grow but is really tough to harvest because it so tenaciously clings to the earth. It's a workout to dig it up. A farmers' market friend of mine uses a backhoe to harvest his. This spring I intend to plant mine alongside a board bordering a raised bed—come harvest I'll remove the board and the burdock will fall into my waiting hands, or so I imagine.

Burdock is available in Asian markets and well-supplied grocery stores throughout the year. Select plump, firm roots. (Limp roots are acceptable if they are not pithy or dehydrated.) Wrap in damp paper towels, refrigerate, and use within a week.

See **Daisy Family; Vegetable.**

BUTTER
For baking at temperatures above 240°F, please use only saturated fats. Of them, butter is

the most versatile, and its superior flavor is undeniable. So, unless you are lactose intolerant, enjoy a bit of butter on—and in—your bread.

Medicinal Benefits Quality butter actually protects against atherosclerosis as long as the overall diet is healthy. Butter is a rich source of vitamin A and also contains vitamin D.

Salted butter is warming, heavy, and hard to digest, whereas unsalted butter is cooling and easier to digest.

Buying Federal standards do not permit butter to contain preservatives or additives except approved food colors (annatto and beta-carotene); nevertheless, cultured, unsalted organic butter is the most healthful butter. In addition to the purchasing guidelines below, rely on your nose and sense of smell. Good butter smells sweet and creamy, but this is not the case with old and rancid butter. Here are your choices.

- **Unsalted Butter** has a more delicate flavor and a shorter life; thus the manufacturer must use fresher cream to make it. If you doubt this, a taste comparison of salted and unsalted butter will convince you. Also, the quantity of added salt varies from manufacturer to manufacturer, so using unsalted butter in a recipe gives you control of the total amount of salt.

- **Cultured Butter** means that the cream was allowed to culture, to sit in a cool place for a day prior to churning it into butter. Our butter-churning grandmothers knew that superior-tasting butter came from cultured milk. They inoculated cream with a splash of buttermilk and let it culture in a cool cellar before making butter. The result, cultured butter, has a richer, more complex flavor and is easier to digest. Because it contains more butterfat and fewer milk solids, it has increased flavor and can be cooked at higher temperatures. Unless the package specifies "cultured" on its label, you may assume that this more time-intensive—and therefore costly—step was omitted. Again, a taste test of cultured versus uncultured butter is telling.

- **European-Style Butter** A *traditional* European-style butter is made from cultured milk with a higher butterfat content and is churned at lower speeds. Its resulting rich taste and smoother texture is notable. Quality European-style butter may have as much as 86 percent butterfat, while standard butter generally contains only 80 percent butterfat. Note that the term "European-style" is not federally regulated. Therefore, some "European-style" butters are not made from cultured milk and their fat content is only negligibly higher than standard butter. Most companies host Web pages about their products that can be quite revealing—read labels carefully and trust your taste.

FRENCH RADISH APPETIZER

Here's how I celebrate the first radishes from my garden, and I invite you to do the same when you happen upon tender radishes. If the radishes are really fresh, any variety will do. The butter's creamy sweetness against the bite of the radishes makes this homey treat a memorable one.

1 bunch French radishes
Unsalted European-style butter
Unrefined salt

Rinse the radishes and trim them. Arrange on a dish with a pat of butter and a little mound of salt. Smear the butter on a radish, dip in salt, and savor.

- **Specialty Butters** While most butter is made from cow's milk, goat's milk butter has some availability in natural food stores and online. Currently in California, you may purchase raw butter online. Elsewhere, there is online information regarding local availability of raw dairy products.
- **Be Mindful** As butter contains lactose it is best avoided by lactose intolerant individuals.

See **Fat and Oil; Ghee.**

BUTTER BEAN SEE BEANS AND LEGUMES.

BUTTERCUP SQUASH SEE SQUASH; SQUASH, WINTER.

BUTTERHEAD LETTUCE SEE LETTUCE.

BUTTERNUT SQUASH SEE SQUASH; WINTER SQUASH.

BUTTER SUBSTITUTE (NOT RECOMMENDED)

No matter how good the package looks or how convincing the advertising, please do not use butter substitutes. They're all made of highly refined oils and are mildly toxic to the liver in that they contribute to the formation of free radicals and thus are carcinogenic.

Healthy options include unrefined oils and butter.

See **Fat and Oil.**

BUTTON MUSHROOM SEE MUSHROOM, COMMON.

CABBAGE
(*Brassica oleracea capitata*)

The word "cabbage" derives from the Latin word *caput*, meaning "head." And a head it is, indeed, and very little else save prerequisite roots.

The cabbage has had more bad press than any other vegetable because when overcooked it emits hydrogen sulfide (the rotten egg smell), ammonia, and other foul aromas. Take a cue and don't boil it to death or your intestinal gas will be similarly sulfurous. Cooked with care, cabbage is sweet, delicious, and remarkably versatile.

Medicinal Benefits Cabbage ranks as one of the healthiest of vegetables, with good reason. It supports chi circulation, clears heat, and tonifies the lungs, large intestine, and stomach. Cabbage is a good source of the anticancer glucosinolates and has antioxidant, antibiotic, and antiviral characteristics; in addition, it mildly helps stimulate the liver out of stagnancy. Cabbage juice is a superior remedy for ulcers and abdominal spasms and pain due to its abundance of glutamine (an amino acid with anti-inflammatory properties). Cabbage helps treat constipation, poor circulation, mental depression, and irritability. It was used by the Romans as a hangover cure. Cabbage reduces *pitta* and *kapha*.

The outer, greener cabbage leaves contain more chlorophyll, vitamin E, and calcium than the inner, pale leaves. Cabbage is higher in vitamin C than oranges. It is a superior source of vitamin B_6 and an ulcer remedy. Phenolic compounds give red cabbage its characteristic color as well as additional antioxidant properties.

Use Cabbage can be eaten raw, as in slaws, or thinly sliced and added to a green salad. When not overcooked, it is delicious and versatile in soups, or in simmered, sautéed, steamed, or baked dishes. The leaves make excellent wrappers for a savory filling. And pickled, in sauerkraut, it's delectable. Outer cabbage leaves are more deeply ribbed, waxy, and more nutrient dense than inner leaves. Trim fibrous parts from the cabbage heart and enjoy the tender core either cooked or uncooked.

To further vivify the ruby of a red cabbage, cook it with a splash of acid like lemon juice, vinegar, or wine. When cooked in alkaline water or with mineral-rich foods such as sea vegetables, it turns blue.

Buying/Storing Purchase cabbages with compact heads that are heavy for their size. Favor those that have their vibrant outer leaves in place; this indicates freshness. Cabbage may be either green or red, with round or pointy leaves, and with smooth or crinkly leaves. The later, savoy cabbage has a looser head, a sweeter, milder flavor, and a buttery smooth texture.

See **Cabbage Family; Vegetable.**

RUBY SAUERKRAUT WITH CARAWAY

"Better than ice cream," says my friend, teacher and author Pema Chodron, about this recipe. Tangy and delicious homemade sauerkraut is a living cultured food that is high in lactic acid and has remarkable healing properties—such as strengthening your immune system! Refrigerated kraut holds well for months and gets sassier as it ages. This recipe takes its color from the beet, but purple cabbage yields a similar ruby color. To make a pale-colored sauerkraut, omit the beet and use green cabbage.

Three things that prevent spoilage are salt, an anaerobic (air-free) environment, and lactic acid fermentation. You'll place a weight on top of the fermenting cabbage to keep it submerged under the brine that forms and thus create an anaerobic environment. Last, as the cabbage ferments, lactic acid develops, which creates an undesirable environment for potential microbial contaminants.

Makes about 3½ cups

- 1   medium-large head cabbage
- 1   small beet
- 2   minced cloves garlic
- 1   tablespoon dried dill leaf
- 1   teaspoon caraway seeds, toasted
- 1   tablespoon unrefined salt

Remove any coarse or dry outer cabbage leaves. Cut the cabbage lengthwise into quarters. Grate the cabbage, core and all, and the beet using the ¼ inch holes of a hand grater or the fine grater of a food processor. Alternatively, shred finely with a knife. Mix the vegetables with the garlic, dill, caraway seeds, and salt. Firmly pack into a glass container such as a wide-mouth quart jar, filling it almost to the brim. Set the jar on a plate to collect any potential overflow.

Apply pressure to the vegetable shreds with a weight that's small enough to nest inside the jar. This weight may be a clean rock, a water-filled glass or bottle, or a partially water-filled zip-top bag.

Rest the weight atop the grated cabbage. Brine will form and rise to the surface, typically within 12 hours. (If the brine fails to rise and/or remain at the top, then dissolve ½ teaspoon salt in ½ cup boiling water; cool and add enough of this brine to cover the cabbage shreds.)

The kraut will be ready in 5 to 7 days, or when it has a pleasant and tangy fermented flavor and the cabbage shreds are translucent rather than opaque. (To heighten the sour flavor, ferment for up to 10 days.) Remove the weight. Discard any bubbly foam or discolored kraut from the top of the jar. Wash and tightly cover the jar. The kraut will keep refrigerated for up to 6 months.

Serve as a condiment, allowing 1 to 2 tablespoons per person. You may also add the kraut to salads or sandwiches or use it as a flavoring agent in dressings and soups.

Variations: Optional ingredients include shredded carrot, turnip, rutabaga, daikon, cumin, seaweed (dulse and arame are good choices), ginger, juniper, or a dried chile.

CABBAGE FAMILY
Brassica, Crucifers, Mustard Family

Historically and nutritionally, the cabbage, or brassica, family is one of the most important—if not *the* most important—vegetable family, and it is certainly one of the most diverse. It's hard to believe that kohlrabi and daikon are related unless you see them gone to seed. The four petals of each flower form a cross, which gives the family its Latin name, *crucifer*.

Medicinal Benefits The vegetables at the pinnacle of phytochemical research are the cabbage family. Their known phytonutrients aid the enzymes that ward off carcinogens and other outside invaders; they also inhibit cancer formation, detoxify carcinogens, and protect against colorectal, stomach, and respiratory cancers. Their leaves—especially their dark green leaves—often contain more phytochemicals than their other parts. Therefore, favor kale, collards, arugula, and Brussels sprouts over cauliflower or a pale cabbage, and even the leaves of broccoli over broccoli heads and stems.

Brassicas contain isothiocyanates, or mustard oil, which is partially responsible for their pungency and which has been used in higher concentrations as a toxic chemical weapon. Those with the highest mustard oil are horseradish, watercress, mustard, and canola (rape). When brassicas are cooked with warming spices and oil and served warm, they are easier for *vata* to digest. Cabbage family members reduce, and therefore are most useful for, *kapha* and *pitta*.

Most dark leafy crucifers are exceptional sources of calcium, vitamins A and C, and beta-carotene.

Be Mindful The cabbage family is goitrogenic, and therefore people with hypothyroidism are advised to use it moderately.

See **Arugula; Bok Choy; Broccoli; Broccolini; Broccoli Rabe; Brussels Sprout; Cabbage; Cauliflower; Chinese Broccoli; Collards, Cress; Daikon; Flowering Cabbage; Horseradish; Kale; Kohlrabi; Mizuna; Mustard Greens; Mustard Oil; Mustard Seed; Nasturtium; Radish; Rutabaga; Tatsoi; Turnip; Turnip Greens; Vegetable; Wasabi; Watercress.**

MUSTARD OIL BURNS

A fiery mustard oil (isothiocyanate) is present in cabbage family members. While it is negligible in mild-tasting ones like Chinese cabbage, mustard oil is abundant enough to give a pungent wallop to horseradish and mustard greens and seeds. Botanists surmise that the plants developed this oil as protection from grazing animals.

Mustard oil is volatile and cooking quickly dissipates it. So if you like it hot, eat it raw—but not when your digestive system is irritated or needs pampering, as in the case of an infant or convalescent. Laboratory-synthesized mustard oil is a chemical weapon used since World War I that burns the skin and mucous membranes.

CACAO See **Chocolate.**

CACTUS FAMILY
(*Cactaceae*)

Native to arid regions in the Americas and distantly related to spinach, beets, and buckwheat, the large cacti family includes several edible members.

See **Dragon Fruit; Nopal; Prickly Pear.**

CACTUS PAD See **Nopal.**

CACTUS PADDLE See **Nopal.**

CACTUS PEAR See **Prickly Pear.**

CALABAZA See **Squash; Squash, Winter.**

CALAMONDIN See **Kumquat.**

CALMATI RICE See **Rice.**

CAMELLIA OIL See **Tea Seed Oil.**

CANDAREL See ASPARTAME.

CANE JUICE See SUGAR.

CANNELLINI See BEANS.

CANOLA OIL (NOT RECOMMENDED)
Prior to the canola oil hype, this plant was used primarily as cattle feed. In the 1980s, a Canadian oil manufacturer saw a profitable market and, concerned that "*rape*seed oil" would be a hard sell, created the acronym "canola," which was derived from "*Can*adian oil, *low ac*id" as his new rape hybrid that indeed contains less erucic acid. Despite multiple government sources that recommend this oil, I do not. Canola oil is highly refined and genetically modified, and it contains 14 percent fragile omega-3 fatty acids, meaning it may not be healthfully heated above 100°F.

For a sobering exercise, look through your pantry and fridge and note how many products contain either canola or cottonseed oil.

See **Essential Fatty Acids; Fat and Oil; Mustard Oil.**

CANTALOUPE See MELON.

CAPE GOOSEBERRY See GROUND CHERRY.

CAPER
(*Capparis spinosa*)
The pickled or brined flower buds of a spiny Mediterranean caper shrub are a pungent condiment. They are harvested from wild or cultivated caper bushes in southern Europe. Nasturtium or purslane buds sometimes are substituted for capers.

Medicinal Benefits Astringent in action, capers are a stimulating digestive tonic useful for treating diarrhea, gout, and coughs.

Use Capers have an intense resiny-tart flavor that vivifies sauces, dressings, and marinades. They're often combined with olives and anchovies and go especially well with fish.

Buying *Nonpareils* are the smallest, most flavorful, and therefore best-quality capers. Capers are available pickled in brine or dried in salt.

CAPSICUM See SWEET PEPPER.

CARAMBOLA See STAR FRUIT.

CARAWAY
(*Carum carvi*)
Shakespeare's Falstaff invited to sup upon "a pippin and a dish of caraways" reminds us that caraway is more than a spice and herb—it's also a vegetable. Pungent and aromatic, this member of the carrot family originated in the Middle East. The small, dark brown seeds have a spicy, aniselike flavor.

Medicinal Benefits Caraway is a warming herb that supports bladder, kidney, and stomach functions. It helps disperse cold and mucus and circulate chi. As a stimulant, caraway reduces spasms in the gastrointestinal tract and uterus. It is used to relieve menstrual cramps, poor circulation, and digestive problems, including hiatus hernia, indigestion, flatulence, stomach ulcer, and some intestinal parasites. Its oil is used in the fragrance industry.

In medieval Europe a love potion called Huile de Vénus made from the oil of caraway was said to also tone the muscles, soften the complexion, and aid digestion.

Use Caraway seeds may be chewed or infused as an herbal tea. The seeds are used to flavor breads, cakes and pastries, sauerkraut, and vegetable and meat dishes, especially in German, Austrian, and Scandinavian cuisine. The feathery, mild-flavored greens are used, before they flower, as an herb. Cook the taproot as you would a carrot.

See **Carrot Family; Herbs and Spices.**

CARDAMOM
(*Elettaria cardamomum*)

Cardamom, an Old World spice that tastes like lemon zest and eucalyptus, is a member of the ginger family. Its papery pods are about the shape, size, and color of a shelled pumpkin seed; they are hand-harvested from a tall shrub that originated in tropical Southeast Asia. After saffron and vanilla, cardamom is the third most expensive spice by weight. Today cardamom is produced in India, Nepal, Sri Lanka, and Mexico.

Medicinal Benefits Cardamom is a sweet, pungent tonic that is warming in its thermal nature. It acts upon the spleen, stomach, lung, and large intestine meridians and helps circulate chi and dispel damp, phlegm, mucus, and cold. Cardamom treats toothaches, gum infections, tuberculosis, and eyelid inflammation. It aids digestion, relaxes spasms, and cuts mucus, making it useful in lung tonics. Cardamom eases coughs, breathlessness, burning urination, incontinence, and hemorrhoids and helps dissolve kidney stones and gallstones. It acts as an antidote to coffee's stress on the adrenal glands. A variety of cardamom known as black cardamom is used in Asian herbal formulas. The essential oil of cardamom is used for nausea, coughs, headaches, tension, and as a digestive tonic. Cardamom reduces *vata* and *kapha*.

Use Use whole cardamom in the pod or the seeds, just shelled and freshly ground. Once the protective pod is removed, cardamom develops an unpleasantly strong, camphorlike aroma and taste. For a subtle flavor, whole cardamom pods may be added to infused drinks or long-simmered dishes; extract the pod prior to serving. For more intensely flavored dishes, use ground seed.

Cardamom is widely used in sweet and savory dishes in Indian and Middle Eastern cuisines—especially in pilafs, curries, and desserts. In the Middle East and North Africa, it is used to flavor coffee; elsewhere in Africa, to flavor tea. In German, Russian, and Scandinavian cuisines, cardamom is used in baked goods, pastries, fruit dishes, and beverages. It is also used as a scent in perfume and incense.

Buying Cardamom is available in small green papery pods. If the pods are white, their flavor will be reduced, as they were sun-dried rather than air-dried. If the pods are black, it's a more strongly flavored medicinal cardamom variety with a smoky aroma that is used in savory, rather than sweet, dishes. This less expensive cardamom is primarily used in Nepal and India.

From 7 to 10 tiny, angular chocolate brown seeds are contained in each pod. When fresh, they're plump and uniform in color. As they age, they shrivel and develop a grayish blue hue.

Cardamom is also available ground but has a short shelf life. If ground cardamom develops a camphorous aroma, discard it.

See **Ginger Family; Herbs and Spices.**

CARDOON
(*Cynara cardunculus*)

A Mediterranean thistle, the cardoon is like a giant artichoke but with smaller, prickly flower heads that are not eaten. It is cultivated, rather, for the leafstalks and roots. This vegetable, a member of the daisy family, grows to heights of four feet and has gray-green leaves; the outer leaves are trimmed away before the plant reaches market.

Properly trimmed, a cardoon yields even more

waste than a globe artichoke—a six-pound bunch yields two pounds of edible stalk.

Medicinal Benefits See **Artichoke** entry.

Use Cardoons taste like artichokes—only more bitter. Very tender, young stalks may be added raw to salads. Larger stalks are blanched and used as you would celery in salads, soups, and stews. The root may also be used as a cooked vegetable. The dried flowers are used to curdle milk or for making the soft curd cheese La Caillebotte à la Chardonette.

To use, separate cardoons into stalks, rinse, and trim all thorns and leaves. With a vegetable peeler, remove the indigestible stringy fibers, chop, and then parboil to reduce their bitterness.

Buying Cardoons are available in specialty markets in the winter and early spring. Because cardoons are blanched (i.e., protected from sunlight while growing), they are an energy-intensive crop, and thus expensive. Look for fresh, crisp heads no larger than one foot long. Avoid heads with wilt or rust.

See **Artichoke; Daisy Family; Vegetable.**

CARNAROLI RICE SEE **RICE.**

CAROB
St. John's Bread
(*Ceratonia siliqua*)

St. John the Baptist lived in the wilderness on locusts and wild honey. In this case, locusts weren't the grasshopper-like critters but the leguminous pods of the locust tree, which we call carob. This explains the alternate name for carob, a chocolate substitute.

Many people enjoy the carob flavor for what it is, namely, carob. To expect a real chocolate flavor from carob is asking too much of any legume. Carob pods are imported from the Mediterranean area and ground and roasted in the United States.

Medicinal Benefits Sweet, light, and dry, carob is warming, astringing, and alkalizing in nature. It nourishes the lungs. Carob contains tannin (as does cocoa), and because tannic acid reduces the absorption of protein through the intestinal wall, it may depress the growth rate of young animals. It is therefore recommended that carob is used in moderation, especially in children's diets.

Carob, an excellent source of calcium, contains more than three times more calcium than milk. It is an extraordinarily rich source of potassium and also has vitamins A and B and other minerals. It has 8 percent protein and contains significantly less fat and calories than chocolate. Unlike chocolate, carob is free of caffeine and oxalic acids, and it is naturally sweet, with 48 percent sugar, including sucrose. Carob reduces *pitta* and *kapha*, and, if moist, reduces *vata*.

Use Carob pods may be eaten fresh out of hand and are a bit like a chewy date. Typically, however, the pods are ground into a powder and used in baking or as an ingredient in energy bars and natural food confections. For baking, flavor unroasted carob, as it will be more flavorful when cooked only once. As a cocoa alternative, substitute equal portions of carob for cocoa but reduce the sweetener.

See **Legume Family; Sweeteners.**

CARRAGEENAN SEE **IRISH MOSS.**

CARROT
(*Daucus carota* L. subsp. *sativus*)

The ancient Greek word for carrot, *philon*, comes from the word "love"—as this root was considered an aphrodisiac. This Afghan native is our most valuable—and favorite—taproot crop. Carrots are derived from a wild carrot with a white root called Queen Anne's lace. Old carrot varieties include yellow, dark red, white, and purple carrots. New red de-

signer carrots contain the pigment lycopene, which also colors tomatoes.

Medicinal Benefits Carrots are a chi tonic that nourish almost every system in the body but especially the liver, lungs, and stomach. As an anticarcinogen, they help clear heat, dispel toxins, and move energy. A carrot is mostly carbohydrate (89 percent), and that explains its sweetness. They also counter intestinal gas and parasites, help prevent constipation, stabilize blood sugar, and treat indigestion. Carrots relieve menstrual pain and premenstrual irritability and improve skin health. Carrots reduce *vata* and *kapha*.

Of our common vegetables, carrots are the best source of the antioxidant vitamin A precursor, beta-carotene, and they improve night vision and help prevent senile cataracts. Carrots are rich in silicon and therefore aid calcium metabolism; in addition, their potassium salts give them diuretic properties.

Use From soups to salads, from juice to cakes, carrots figure so prominently in our daily fare that it is hard to imagine life without them. Because the nutrients in carrots are concentrated in and near their skin, use them unpeeled. If the carrot is so old that the skin looks unappealing, you might want to compost the carrot.

When fresh and young, the nutrient-rich carrot greens may be chopped finely and sautéed for a condiment or added to soups. Remove and discard their more fibrous stem. Dried or fresh, carrot tops may be used like a strong-flavored parsley.

Buying There are several hundred varieties of carrots. Carrots with greens are the

---

PEELED "BABY" CARROTS

I don't get the trend of mini carrots, but then I subscribe to the sentiments of M. F. K. Fisher who, in writing of the value of an intact vegetable, observed:

"All of them, whether tender or hard, thick skinned or thin, die when they are peeled . . . even as you and I."

—M. F. K. Fisher, *The Art of Eating*

---

freshest—and therefore most nutrient dense. Select carrots with the deepest orange color, indicative of the most vitamin A, and a good carrot aroma. The most popular in the United States is the Mediterranean type, which is fairly long, cylindrical, and orange.

See **Carrot Juice, Carrot Family; Vegetable.**

CARROT FAMILY
(*Umbelliferae*)

The umbellifer family is named for its clustered flowers, which resemble an upside-down umbrella. While the most commonly used umbellifer is the carrot, some other staple vegetables are found herein. The most important Chinese tonic after ginseng is angelica, another member of the carrot family.

See **Ajowan; Angelica; Caraway; Carrot; Celery; Celery Root; Chervil; Cilantro; Cumin; Dill; Fennel; Lovage; Nigella; Parsley; Parsley Root; Parsnip.**

CARROT JUICE

A perennial favorite health drink, the fresh juice of carrots is excellent for liver rejuvenation and cleansing. Juice is more medicinal in action when taken on an empty stomach. Carrot juice applied directly to burns aids in their healing.

Enjoy in moderation, as carrot juice is a re-fined food. This surprises people, but consider how many carrots go into one glass of juice and how much pulp is discarded. In a few gulps, the juice is gone. Imagine cramming that many whole carrots into your stomach in the same amount of time it takes to drink their juice. While whole carrots don't raise blood sugar because their fiber slows digestion, car-rot juice is a liquid form of simple sugars, and it does raise blood sugar. So when serving it to children, dilute it first; and the next time you drink it, notice the rush of energy it gives.

See **Carrot.**

CASABA SEE MELON.

CASHEW
(*Anacardium occidentale*)

The cashew, na-tive to Brazil, is one nut, technically a seed, you'll never see it its shell. Its outer shell contains a toxic oil, cardol, which—if touched—burns the skin like its relative poison ivy. Cardol is released from the uncracked nuts by roasting them at 350°F. Cashews are then cracked, roasted a second time to remove an inner shell, and sold "raw."

The sweet-tasting, kidney-shaped nut grows in a curious manner. It hangs at the bottom of a soft, fleshy, pear-shaped orange-colored fruit called a cashew apple. This tasty apple spoils within 24 hours from harvest and so is never exported. It is eaten fresh or made into bever-ages, preserves, or liquor. About 90 percent of our domestic supply of cashews comes from India and East Africa. The remainder come from South America.

Medicinal Benefits Cashews are a nutri-tive and warming food that support lung func-tion. At 47 percent fat, cashews are lower in fat than most other nuts, and most of their fat is unsaturated. They contain 20 percent pro-tein and high amounts of magnesium, phos-phorus, iron, potassium, and zinc. Cashews reduce *vata*. Oil from cashew nuts has antifun-gal properties and is nurturing to dry skin, es-pecially cracked heels.

Use Raw cashews are hard to digest, but roasting will enhance their flavor and digest-ibility. Like almonds, they may be made into a tasty nut milk and even a vegan cheese. They are used as a dessert nut, in stir-fried dishes, and curries or ground to thicken a sauce.

Buying Because they are not shelled do-mestically, cashews frequently are stale. Fresh cashews are crisp, solid, and white. Even though whole cashews are more expensive, they generally are fresher and a better pur-chase than cashew pieces.

See **Cashew Family; Nuts.**

CASHEW BUTTER SEE NUT AND SEED BUTTERS.

CASHEW FAMILY
(*Anacardiaceae*)

Edible members of the cashew family in-clude ambarella, cashews, mangos, mastic, pis-tachios, and sumac berries. Other memorable members include poison oak and poison ivy, and this explains why some people who have suffered from poison ivy may have an intoler-ance to mangos.

See **Ambarella; Cashew; Mango; Mastic; Pistachio; Sumac Berry.**

CASHEW MILK SEE NUT MILK.

CASSAVA
Manioc, Yuca
(*Manihot utilissima, M. esculenta*)

A tuber staple throughout the tropics, cassava is primarily known in temperate regions as the source of tapioca. The cassava, an American native, looks like a sweet potato. It is cylindrical with a brown, bark-covered skin and flesh that is almost white, yellow, or red. Although a cassava can weigh more than 50 pounds, market varieties are harvested at 1 to 3 pounds and are up to four inches in diameter. The cassava's near relative is the popular Christmas ornamental the poinsettia. None of its other relatives are used as a culinary staple.

While tapioca is processed from a bitter cassava (*M. esculenta*), the sweet varieties (*M. utilissima*) are eaten like a potato. Cassava is grown in Central and South America, Africa, and Asia.

Medicinal Benefits Cassava is a soothing, calming food. At 97 percent carbohydrate, even higher than potatoes, it is an excellent source of manganese and vitamin C.

Use Prepare the sweet cassava as a potato or sweet potato, but plan to use it immediately, as it spoils rapidly. When peeled and cooked, its softly fibrous flesh becomes mildly sweet, buttery, chewy, and almost translucent. Remove its central, fibrous core either before or after cooking. Some people love the tapioca-like texture of cassava; for others it's an acquired taste. Cassava absorbs the liquid in soups, stews, or casseroles. It may be deep-fried, baked, simmered, sautéed, or pureed.

Buying You can find cassava fresh in the produce section of some supermarkets and Latino markets or packaged in the form of specialty potato chips. As cassava does not store well, take care to purchase a sound one. Select a cassava that is sweet smelling with no sign of mold, cracks, or sticky patches. The bark on the skin should be intact because if cut or damaged and not used immediately, it becomes toxic. Do not purchase a cassava that is sour or acrid smelling or has blue-gray mottled flesh. Ask your greengrocer to cut into one to assure that its flesh is clear without darkened areas near the skin. Or buy extra, and discard any discolored pieces. Do not refrigerate cassava; store it in a very cool, dry area for up to a day or two.

See **Cassava Flour; Tapioca.**

CASSAVA FLOUR

Throughout the tropics, cassava is ground into a meal and used in porridge, sauces, stews, dumplings, and baked goods. Cassava flour thickens the onion, raisin, and cashew sauce of Brazil's national specialty *feijoada*, a dish of sausage and black beans. In the Caribbean, the flour is made into the unleavened hard bread *cassabe*. Look for cassava flour in Latino and Asian markets as well as an ingredient in gluten-free products.

See **Cassava; Flour.**

CASSIA SEE **CINNAMON.**

CAULIFLOWER
(*Brassica oleracea* var. *botrytis*)

Cauliflower is nothing but a cabbage with a college education.

—Mark Twain, *Pudd'nhead Wilson*

FIRST RECORDED AMERICAN RECIPE

"They serve this [cassava] as a bread, by grating and kneading it, then baking it in the fire." Today this same flatbread remains a dietary staple in the Dominican Republic, where Christopher Columbus, on December 16, 1492, recorded this terse recipe.

The cauliflower is a compact, edible head of thousands of typically whitish undeveloped flower buds, or curd, packed into even larger buds that form multiple florets. The plant's large outer leaves protectively surround the curd, keeping out the light and, therefore, preventing chlorophyll development, which would turn it green. The name means "cabbage flower," and indeed the cauliflower is yet another member of the brassica, or cabbage, family. Cauliflower originated in Crete or Cyprus. Our largest cauliflower supplier is California, followed by Arizona and Colorado.

Medicinal Benefits Sweet in flavor with a slight bitter flavor, especially when old, cauliflower helps tonify and regulate the stomach, spleen, and both the large and small intestines. As with other cabbage family vegetables, it has anticancer, antioxidant, antibiotic, and antiviral characteristics. Nutritionally, cauliflower is similar to broccoli, though it contains lower proportions of vitamins, minerals, and chlorophyll. It is a good source of boron. Cauliflower is a good brain food according to the Doctrine of Signature. It reduces *pitta* and *kapha*.

Use Lime green and purple cauliflower varieties cook more quickly and have a sweeter flavor than white cauliflower. Although raw cauliflower is easier to digest than broccoli, cauliflower still benefits from light cooking and combines well with other vegetables. As with other cabbage family members, it develops a sulfurous aroma if overcooked. Cauliflower greens contain the highest amount of calcium. Use the smaller ones, discarding the overly coarse parts as necessary.

Buying Cauliflower is in peak supply in the fall. Select one with a firm, compact head that is clean and a creamy white color. (Newer varieties may range in color from purple and pink to lime yellow.) Size is no indication of quality. If it is wearing a collar of outer leaves,

those should be fresh. Cauliflower with brown spots or spreading florets is past prime. Refrigerate cauliflower stem side up, loosely wrapped. This prevents moisture from collecting on the cauliflower top and thereby speeding deterioration.

See **Cabbage Family; Vegetable.**

CAULIFLOWER MUSHROOM
(*Sparassis crispa, S. radicata*)

This cream-colored mushroom grows from the roots or bases of trees, primarily hardwoods, throughout North America and Europe. Mild tasting with a pleasing aroma, the cauliflower mushroom has increasing commercial availability. Its tight branches arise from a common base giving it a cauliflowerlike—or some would say brainlike—appearance. With age its color darkens to a pale yellow.

Cauliflower mushrooms contain natural immune strengthening and antitumor properties. Clean thoroughly as its folds can contain debris. It is somewhat more chewy than our more common mushrooms so cooking time should be adjusted accordingly.

See **Mushroom Family; Vegetable.**

CAYENNE SEE CHILE PEPPER.

CELERIAC SEE CELERY ROOT.

CELERY
(*Apium graveolens* var. *dulce*)

If you lived in Kalamazoo, Michigan, in 1874 and wanted to popularize a new celery variety, Pascal, how would you market it? The winning answer was, pass it out free to train passengers traveling through Kalamazoo. Pascal celery soon became—and today remains—our second most important salad crop.

Celery stems are vertical, with distinct grooves and ridges that nest together and are leaf-topped. The whole plant, stalks, leaves, seeds, and roots are edible. Celery and its close relative parsley were once so similar that they were called by the same name in classical times; indeed, celery leaves are flavored and shaped like broad-leafed parsley. Celery is, though, a member of the carrot family. Our domestic celery crop is grown primarily in California, Florida, and Texas, with Michigan providing it in hot weather.

Medicinal Benefits Celery is a cooling vegetable that treats the stomach, liver, kidneys, and bladder. It helps settle an inflamed liver, dispels wind, and helps lubricate or moisten the internal organs. It disperses water, damp, and heat. Since Greek times, celery has been valued as a hangover cure, nerve tonic, and blood cleanser. It contains coumarin compounds, which tone the vascular system and help reduce blood pressure by relaxing the muscle tissue in artery walls and thus enhance blood flow. Coumarin may also be useful in cases of migraines and cancer prevention.

As a kitchen medicine, celery is used for constipation, as a diuretic, to break up gallstones, and to heal wounds. Celery also treats arthritis, rheumatism, and gout. It has one of the highest sodium contents of all vegetables and treats diseases involving chemical imbalances. It is said to help bring energy up so it is good if one is feeling stuck or heavy. Celery is a favorite reducing food, especially for *pitta* and *kapha*.

Use Celery is versatile: Cut it into sticks for a packed lunch, juice it for a tonic, or chop it for a salad or braised dish, or to simmer in a soup. Chop the greens and enjoy them as a parsley substitute—but taste first, as their flavor ranges from mild to bitter. The heart or celery core is crisp, tender, and delicious—trim and enjoy raw or cooked.

Buying Choose a firm, tightly formed bunch with crisp, green leaves. Store celery in a plastic bag in the refrigerator for at least a week.

- **Chinese Celery** has very thin, hollow stocks and a strong flavor that is too intense to use raw but that is delicious used in soups and stir-fries. It is primarily available in Asian markets.
- **Pascal Celery** is our most commonly available celery; it has green ribs (unless it was chemically blanched) and dark green leaves.
- **White Celery,** when grown banked with soil to shade it from the direct sun, is a less nutritious vegetable but has a more delicate flavor.

Be Mindful Whenever possible, favor organic celery. Commercial celery is one of our four most chemically tainted vegetables (along with potatoes, sweet peppers, and spinach). Virtually all supermarket celery is blanched with ethylene gas to reduce its bitter flavor. Organic celery that is a vivid, deep green has not been blanched and will taste stronger, an apt indicator of its superior nutritional and flavor profile.

See **Carrot Family; Celery Root; Vegetable.**

A YOUNG WIFE'S DRUTHERS

Celery . . . "is warm, and has great digestive and generative powers, and for this reason young wives often serve celery to their elderly or impotent husbands," according to a 1614 text by Giacomo Castelvetro, *A Brief Account of the Fruit, Herbs, and Vegetables of Italy.*

Back then, celery was intensely bitter. Its bitterness was bred out several centuries ago, making celery sweet enough to munch on raw—but making it a less effective remedy for young wives. If you had your druthers . . .

CELERY ROOT
Celeriac, Knob Celery
(*Apium graveolens* var. *rapaceum*)

There's nothing tidy about celery root. The swollen stem base, technically a corm, of a type of celery, celery root tastes like a primitive heart of celery—only more so. It's a member of the carrot family. Celery root looks like an irregular brown turnip. Its upper part is covered with leaf scars from old leaves, and its many gnarly roots and rootlets stream from its base and trap dirt and grit in its numerous whorls and crevices. Its roots, if not trimmed away by the grocer, stretch out like octopus tentacles.

Medicinal Benefits Celery root reduces blood pressure, relieves indigestion, and is anti-inflammatory. It is valued for its diuretic properties and helps ameliorate kidney stones and arthritic conditions. A homeopathic remedy made from celery root is used to treat rheumatism and kidney disorders. As a tonic, it stimulates the appetite, aids digestion, and supports the lymphatic, nervous, and urinary systems. It reduces *pitta* and *kapha*.

Use Just prior to use, peel away the mass of roots, rootlets, and skin. Julienne or grate and marinate celery root with a vinaigrette to include in any salad or for *celery remoulade*. If not using immediately, place cut pieces in water acidulated with lemon juice or vinegar to prevent discoloration. Or dice or cut into chunks and cook the knob in soups or purees or braised, sautéed, or baked dishes. I also pickle celery root. It blends beautifully with other foods while retaining its own refreshing celerylike flavor. If overcooked, it may become mushy.

Buying Stems intact on celery root indicate freshness. If you grow this vegetable, or find one with the greens, use the greens to flavor soups and stews—but use them judiciously, as they are more bitter than the root.

Favor small celery roots; the large ones tend to be pithy. Press the stalk end with your thumb and select only those that are firm and heavy for their size. Cut off any stems and refrigerate both. The root will keep up for several weeks. Celery root is primarily available in the fall and winter.

See **Carrot Family; Celery; Vegetable.**

CELTUCE SEE **LETTUCE.**

CÈPE SEE **BOLETE.**

CEREAL GRAINS SEE **GRAINS.**

CERIMAN SEE **MONSTERA.**

CHAMOMILE
(*Chamaemelum nobile, Anthemis nobilis, Matricaria recutita*)

A daisy family member, chamomile is native to the Mediterranean region. Referring to its medicinal properties, the Germans aptly call it *alles zutraut*, which means "capable of anything." But if you've ever seen it growing, you'll appreciate its Greek name, which means "apple" (*melon*) "on the ground" (*khamai*); indeed, the chamomile in my herb garden is a carpet of showy but minuscule white daises with a plump yellow heart and an aroma similar to apples. The Spanish call it *manzanilla*, which means "little apple."

Medicinal Benefits Chamomile is effective for nervousness, anxiety, stress, and insomnia. It strengthens the immune system and soothes the digestive tract, eases headaches and allergies, supports the gallbladder, and helps reduce gallstones. It expels gas and helps quiet spasms and a nervous stomach. It eases stomach ulcers, diverticulitis, and gastritis. Chamomile destroys some intestinal worms. It is *tridoshic.*

Superior to cortisone in speeding skin healing, chamomile is a popular ingredient in herbal skin creams and unguents, where it provides the additional benefit of easing pain and promoting skin growth over a wound. Other external applications include applying it to relieve burns; as an eye wash, gargle, douche, or enema to calm irritated tissues; and as a sitz bath to relieve hemorrhoids. Speaking of baths, strain a pot of chamomile tea into your bath, sink in, and chamomile will not only soften your skin but ease away the day's fears and stresses. A chamomile bath also soothes cranky kids, aids their sleep, and helps protect against nightmares.

Buying Chamomile refers to two botanically unrelated plants of the daisy family with comparable appearance, fragrance, and flavor; and the essential oils of both are the same cobalt blue. Roman chamomile (*C. nobile* or *Anthemis nobilis*) is a perennial plant native to Western Europe that grows close to the ground and is often used as a ground cover. German or Hungarian chamomile (*M. recutita*) is an annual that reaches knee high and is most commonly used, as it is less bitter, less expensive, and a superior source of pharmacological properties.

Only the flowers are used, and as their volatile oils dissipate rapidly, favor chamomile that has a fresh and aromatic aroma. Chamomile is a popular ingredient in many herbal tisanes, and it is found in some desserts and alcoholic beverages such as vermouth.

The essential oil of either German or Roman chamomile treats nerves, migraine headaches, acne, dermatitis, inflammations, insomnia, and menstrual problems. The essential oil of German chamomile also treats a wider variety of skin problems, including eczema, psoriasis, burns, and autoimmune inflammatory diseases.

Be Mindful While chamomile is safe, effective, and nonaddictive, it may be too relaxing to the uterus to consume often during pregnancy, for it might cause a miscarriage.

See **Daisy Family; Herbs and Spices.**

CHANTERELLE
Black Chanterelle, Girolle, Black Trumpet
(*Cantharellus cibarius*)

The uncommonly beautiful and delicious chanterelle mushroom is a sunset orange color and is shaped like a curving trumpet. It has a faint aroma reminiscent of apricots and is a tasty delicacy. The girolle is a lighter-colored winter chanterelle, and a more robustly flavored black variety is known as a black chanterelle.

Medicinal Benefits Chanterelles tonify the blood and support the large intestine, liver, stomach, and spleen functions. They disperse excess heat and help remove toxins.

Use Use immediately. Subtly flavored dishes are enhanced by chanterelles. They are, however, such a rare delicacy that it's a shame to combine them with any other food. For maximum enjoyment, lightly sauté this fungus in olive oil or ghee, with or without garlic, and add a dash of salt.

Buying/Foraging Fresh wild chanterelles appear in some markets in the late summer and, where frost comes late, into the fall. They are also available dried and canned. Select fresh chanterelles that are not withered or bruised.

See **Mushroom Family; Vegetable.**

CHARD
Swiss Chard
(*Beta vulgaris* var. *cicla*)

Chard is a beet relative native to the Mediterranean region that was developed for its broad, fan-shaped leaves and thick crunchy stalks rather than its root. It takes its name from cardoon because of their similarly shaped long—up to two feet—leaf-stalks. These stalks may be white, yellow, orange, pink, or red, and their greens range from a pale green to deep blue-green or even green-red, making them flashy standouts in vegetable displays. The leaf may be either crinkly—savoy-style—or flat. Their flavor is salty and bitter, rather like a combination of spinach and beet greens. Chard is a member of the goosefoot family.

Medicinal Benefits Chard tonifies the blood; treats the large intestine, lungs, stomach, and spleen; detoxifies; and helps cool an overheated condition. It is high in sodium and an excellent source of carotenes, chlorophyll, and vitamins C and E. It has anticarcinogen properties and eases constipation in the elderly, helps regulate the internal organs, helps stop hemorrhage, and supports the liver and lungs. Chard reduces *kapha*, and, in small amounts, it reduces *vata* and *pitta*.

Use Chard greens are nearly as quick cooking as their relative spinach but have a slightly coarser texture. Their more fibrous stems may be prepared as a separate vegetable. Remove them with a knife, or, quicker yet, grasp the stalk end in one hand, hold the greens at their base with the fingertips of your other hand, and pull to strip the leaf from its stalk. Chop the colored stalks and add them to soups, pilafs, or casseroles for their flamboyant color interest and celerylike texture. Note that when the colored stalks are sautéed or fried, their colors become muddied. The greens may be steamed, sautéed, braised, or added to soups, stews, and casseroles. The Italians make a delicious frittata with chard.

Buying Look for clear white or colored stalks that show no discoloration and for intact, crisp leaves. Chard is available throughout the year and, when fresh, will be both sweeter and crunchier. With minimal care and

OXALIC ACID—YEA OR NAY?

Here's a nutritional debate you can ignore. Unless, that is, you consume a lot of high oxalic acid foods (like chard, spinach, chocolate, rhubarb, sorrel, purslane, poppy seeds, fat hen, star fruit, black pepper, and parsley) and are prone to gastrointestinal inflammation, rheumatoid arthritis, gout, kidney stones, or other kidney disorders. Briefly, the oxalic acid found in some foods can bind with calcium, iron, and magnesium, which may be deposited as oxalate crystals that can irritate the gut and kidneys.

While there's agreement on the above, there's no agreement on how much is excessive oxalic acid consumption and whether or not cooking intensifies the problem. Furthermore, the oxalic content of foods varies significantly depending on their growth environment.

Moral of this story: Enjoy chard and spinach several times a week but not as your primary green staples.

a sunny garden spot, a few chard plants in a garden can keep you supplied well into the winter months.

Be Mindful As chard contains oxalic acid (see sidebar), it's advised to enjoy this vegetable in moderation, especially if you have a tendency to form, oxalic-type kidney stones.

See **Beet; Goosefoot Family; Vegetable.**

CHAYOTE
Christophine, Hop Yeung Qwa, Mirliton, Vegetable Pear
(Sechium edule)

The squashlike chayote (cheye-YOH-teh) originated in Central America; there the whole plant—roots, young leaves, fruits, seeds, and shoots—is an important food source. Our supply is produced domestically in the South and also imported.

The chayote is shaped like a somewhat flattened pear, with a thick pale green skin divided by five grooves that run the length of it. One variety has a smooth skin, and another variety is covered with soft spines. It is a member of the gourd family. A chayote is about five inches long and contains a single edible pit. In Asian cuisine, chayote shoots and leaves are a common vegetable used to dissolve kidney stones and to treat arteriosclerosis and hypertension.

Use A fresh chayote has a delicate flavor and texture rather like a blend of cucumber and pattypan squash. When old, it is flavorless. Substitute chayote, skin and all, in any recipe that calls for summer squash, or slice it thinly and add to a salad. Roasting concentrates its flavor. Its large seed has a mild nutty flavor.

Buying Chayote is available year-round, with peak supplies in the winter. Look for a firm chayote with a solid appearance and an unblemished skin from pale green to ivory white in color. For the best flavor, use quickly; refrigerated it will, however, store for several weeks.

See **Gourd Family; Vegetable.**

CHERIMOYA
Custard Apple
(*Annona cherimola*)

Inside a cherimoya's (cheree-MOY-a) rough, armadillo-like green shell is a lush treat. The soft, silky smooth, sweet white flesh has a slightly musky and decidedly tropical taste— part mango, part pineapple, part banana. It is related to the atemoya.

Cherimoya, a Quechua word that means "cold seeds," is native to the tropical Andes. Commercial crops are now growing in Califor-

nia, Australia, and South America, but the fruit is fragile and, despite increasing demand for its custardlike flesh, its availability may remain sketchy.

Use Cherimoya is typically eaten fresh but is also used in salads, sauces, drinks, desserts, and ice cream. Spoon out the inedible black seeds as you would watermelon seeds.

Buying Cherimoyas are most available in the winter and early spring. They are harvested when hard. Purchase cherimoyas that are just beginning to soften, but avoid brown or bruised ones. They may vary in size from half a pound to two pounds; size does not affect flavor. To increase their sweetness, allow these fruits to ripen at room temperature just until they begin to brown but before they become overly soft. Once ripe, they may be refrigerated for up five days. (Do not refrigerate a cherimoya before it softens.)

See **Cherimoya Family; Fruit.**

CHERIMOYA FAMILY

Of the large *Annonaceae* family of tropical plants, only a few produce edible fruits. They include the atemoya, cherimoya, and pawpaw. Only the pawpaw is a temperate region fruit.

See **Atemoya; Cherimoya; Pawpaw.**

CHERRY
(*Prunus avium*)

In New York, Broadway zags west at the East 10th Street intersection because a cherry tree once grew there that was more valued than a tidy crossroads. Of temperate zone stone fruits in the Northern Hemisphere, sweet cherries have, by far, the highest sugar content, but they are not only sweet, they're also lush, juicy, thin-skinned, and, when tree-ripened, delicious enough to zigzag roads for.

Cherries are a stone, or drupe fruit, a member of the prune family and closely related to plums, apricots, almonds, and peaches, but are distinctly different; both the fruit and pit are smaller and more round in shape. Sweet cherries are much more difficult to grow than sour cherries because, not uncommonly, a late frost may devastate the crop. Most cherries are produced in Washington, Colorado, Oregon, Idaho, and Utah.

Medicinal Benefits Unlike most fruits that are cooling, sweet cherries are a warming food; they are a chi and blood tonic and help increase blood circulation. According to traditional Chinese medicine, cherries tone the spleen, stomach, liver, heart, lung, and kidney functions. Cherries remove excess body acids and blood stagnation and, when eaten regularly, are therefore therapeutic for gout, paralysis, numbness in the extremities, and rheumatic pain in the lower half of the body.

A carbohydrate-dense food, cherries are an excellent source of vitamin C and are high in lutein and zeaxanthin, the two compounds that protect vision. The fruit contains several phytonutrients that research suggests may help fight cancer. One such compound, perillyl alcohol, binds to protein molecules to inhibit cancer's growth signals. Also found in cherries are anthocyanins, a class of compounds that act as potent antioxidants, anti-inflammatory compounds, and pain relievers. This makes cherries, especially sour cherries, an excellent antigout remedy.

Buying Because cherries are meltingly tender and juicy, they're not great shippers or keepers. (Even though Southern Hemisphere cherries are air-shipped here in midwinter, in comparison to fresh, their taste is paltry.) Thus, you can feast on local, fresh cherries from approximately mid-June to early August. Afterward, any stored cherries will have a mushy texture and are no fun to eat.

While some fruits get sweeter after harvest, cherries don't. Once picked, a cherry's sugars do not increase. Look for full-colored, soft cherries with a bright, glossy, plump-looking surface and fresh-looking stems. Avoid overmature, dull-looking cherries that have shriveled, dried, brown stems. Examine closely, as cherries easily decay, and decayed areas are often inconspicuous. Soft, leaking flesh, brown discoloration, and/or mold indicate decay.

Bing cherries—almost black-red—are the best known variety, with Lamberts close behind. The golden yellow Rainiers are the most fragile and costly. There are fewer than 10 commercial varieties available fresh.

Refrigerate as soon as possible and use quickly. Wash and remove their stems just prior to use. If cherries must be held more than a few days, keep them in a paper bag.

Use A superior dessert fruit, sweet cherries are most often enjoyed raw and eaten out of hand. They're also great in fruit salads, stirred into yogurt and compotes, blended into fruit soups and smoothies, added to chutneys, and macerated in alcohol. Sweet cherries make a colorful sauce to crown a bowl of ice cream or smear on a slice of cake. Almost anything chocolate welcomes a cherry sauce.

You could put sweet cherries into a pie, cobbler, or turnover. However, sour cherries are the prized pie ingredient because when cooked they have a superior color and flavor.

While I've used both handheld and table-mounted cherry-pitting devices, I prefer a chopstick for poking out cherry pits. Use whatever pointed object works for you. Yes, it's a sticky job, but it's one that kids will gladly volunteer to do. If pitting cherries sounds too tedious, serve them the European way—*with their pits.*

Be Mindful Of fresh fruits, commercial cherries rank among the top dozen of the most highly contaminated with toxic chemical residues. Favor organic cherries and cherry products when possible; it's especially prudent for young children and pregnant and nursing women to do so.

See **Fruit; Prune Family; Sour Cherry.**

CHERVIL
(*Anthriscus cerefolium*)

One of the first herbs to appear in the spring, chervil is a hardy annual of Russian origin used as a seasoning agent or as a potherb. Chervil looks rather like its relative parsley, only its feathery leaves are sweeter with a more delicate flavor that is reminiscent of tarragon or anise. When fresh, it's a common ingredient in Mediterranean cuisine.

Medicinal Benefits Chervil is a mild stimulant and diuretic with cleansing action for the liver and kidneys. As an expectorant, it helps clear mucus and phlegm; it also aids digestion and treats poor memory and depression. For chronic skin ailments and arthritis, the plant may be juiced and consumed or applied topically. As a tea, it makes an excellent wash for inflamed eyes and hemorrhoids. It calms *pitta* and *kapha*.

Use Chervil is a popular herb in Central and Western Europe and one of the four ingredients in the classic French blend *fines herbes* (the others are chives, parsley, and tarragon). It's an essential ingredient in French cuisine. As it withstands neither prolonged heat nor drying, use fresh chervil and add at the last minute.

Freely substitute chervil for parsley and use it in pesto, as a garnish, in salads, and with asparagus, starchy vegetables like beets and potatoes, eggs, or seafood—especially oysters.

Buying Dried chervil lacks flavor and aroma. Because its delicate leaves are poor travelers, it is not always available fresh. Fortunately, chervil flourishes indoors in a pot as easily as it does outside.

See **Carrot Family; Herbs and Spices.**

MOTHER'S MARASCHINO CHERRIES

Every cherry season, my mother made one batch—seven quarts—of maraschino cherries. She first slaked yellow Royal Anne cherries in alum to crisp them, then canned them in a heavy syrup flavored with cherry pits or almond extract, and added red food color. The maraschinos had a delegated shelf spot among more than 300 quarts of peaches, apricots, pears, raspberries, and regular cherries, plus pints of assorted jams and jellies—a common-size fruit larder for our Mormon family of six in the 1940s and 1950s. Relative to commercial maraschinos, mother's were softly colored and tender but crisp—they were delicious and an essential ingredient in my father's favorite cake, Poor Man's Cake.

The original maraschino was fermented in a liqueur made from the juice and crushed pits of *marasca*, a wild sour Italian cherry. Today's maraschino cherry that tops a banana split is tough, sugary (75 percent sugar), and beggarly, and would wreck a Poor Man's Cake. The cake dates from a time when flour was a more prized ingredient than the maraschino cherries and nuts that filled it. The cake is tender (*not* like a holiday fruitcake) and a regal treat.

CHESTNUT
(*Castanea sativa*)

Unlike London, New York, or Boston, where street vendors sell hot roasted chestnuts on nippy days, I'm yet to find the same here in the Rocky Mountains. My friend TuHan Holm remedies this oversight by roasting them at home, pouring them hot into everyone's pockets, and then heading out for a brisk winter walk. There's nothing like a pocketful of toasty chestnuts.

For hunter-gatherers and poor people in times of want, chestnuts were an important staple throughout the Northern Hemisphere. Chestnuts figure prominently in fine cuisine in both Europe and Asia but less in North America after a blight in the early 1900s destroyed all our magnificent chestnut trees. Today a few Japanese chestnuts grow commercially on the West Coast, but our primary chestnut source is Europe. They are a member of the beech family.

Medicinal Benefits As a chi and yang tonic, the chestnut energizes and nurtures the kidney, stomach, and spleen. It is sweet like a fruit, but unlike most fruit, it builds and warms rather than cools and cleanses. A good convalescing food, it has an astringing nature that controls diarrhea, coughing, whooping cough, and rheumatism, and which helps check bleeding (anal bleeding, nosebleeds, vomiting of blood, or bloody sputum). The chestnut is especially calming to *pitta* and *vata*.

By nutritional profile, chestnuts are more like a grain than a nut because of their high—86 percent—carbohydrate content and low oil content. Chestnuts have only 9 percent fat, making them the most easily digested nut. By comparison, walnuts are 83 percent fat.

Use Roasted, boiled, mashed like potatoes, sweetened, candied, or pureed, chestnuts are versatile and nearly always cooked, as they're astringent when raw. Delicious in both sweet and savory recipes, chestnuts can be added to grain, bean, vegetable, and fruit dishes. They're good in soups, stir-fries, casseroles, and even in hot breakfast cereal.

A Roman favorite was to steam chestnuts with bitter greens. A Pakistani dish is roasted, pureed chestnuts topped with fresh walnut or hazelnut oil. The French garnish chestnut puree with crème fraîche for a dessert they call *mont blanc*, after the largest peak in the Alps. Use chestnut puree as a delicious nondairy whipped topping, frosting, or cream sauce.

Buying/Storing Although pricey, seasonal when fresh, and not in major markets when dry, seek chestnuts out. Having chestnuts in your larder is like having silk in your wardrobe. They are primarily available fresh or dried but are also available fresh-frozen, bottled and canned, either whole or pureed. Store fresh chestnuts in a paper bag in the refrigerator and use within a week. Place dried chestnuts in an airtight container, and store in a cool, dark cupboard.

CHESTNUTS AND ROSE PETALS

Reading of traditional food uses often whets my appetite and sometimes inspires me with new ways to work with food. In the seventeenth century in Italy a special covered perforated pan was used for roasting chestnuts. The filled pan was buried under hot ashes, and when roasted the nuts were shelled and served with salt and pepper. An old popcorn popper to hold over embers just might work for fire-roasted chestnuts.

Another old technique is to layer dried chestnuts with fresh rose petals to soften them. As the chestnuts draw moisture from the petals, they are imbued with rose essence. Next rose season, I'll give this a try.

- **Fresh Chestnuts** These are available in the United States during the fall and winter in most supermarkets. Select fresh chestnuts in the shell with clear, silky smooth, brown shells rather than dry or brittle shells. To roast or bake them, first deeply score the shells with a paring knife; otherwise, they may explode. They also may be boiled and then shelled.
- **Dried Chestnuts** These are sweeter and less floury than fresh chestnuts, since in the drying process carbohydrates convert to sugar. Dried chestnuts are always shelled and more expensive than the fresh, but they are a great convenience and are available year-round. They require an hour of rehydration prior to cooking. In replacing dried for fresh chestnuts, one part dried is comparable to three parts fresh. Look for dried chestnuts in specialty food shops and Asian markets and by mail order.

See **Beech Family; Chestnut Flour; Nuts.**

CHESTNUT FLOUR

Fragrant, sweet, and fruity-tasting chestnut flour has a dust-fine and silky texture and ranges from beige to taupe in color. This gluten-free flour sweetens, lightens, and adds creaminess. It is not a thickening agent, but when combined with a grain flour, it makes a delicious pudding, sauce, or "cream" soup. Substitute ¼ cup chestnut flour per cup of flour.

Until this last century, chestnut flour was made into bread and was a staple for European people in mountainous regions where wheat did not grow and flour was a luxury.

See **Chestnut; Flour.**

CHEWING GUM SEE **CHICLE; MASTIC.**

CHIA SEED
(*Salvia columbariae, S. hispanica*)

A relative of garden sage and a member of the mint family, this tiny gray-black or golden tan seed looks like a flat poppy seed and has a mild peppery, nasturtium-like bite. The seeds are slippery to the touch. Chia grows in Mexico and the Southwest and is available in natural food stores or online.

Medicinal Benefits Chia was long prized as an endurance food by Native Americans; today we know that chia is, after flaxseed, the highest source of omega-3 fatty acids. The gray-black (*S. columbariae*) variety is nutritionally superior to the golden chia variety. Chia becomes highly mucilaginous when soaked; it lubricates dryness and relieves constipation, reduces nervousness, treats insomnia, and improves mental focus. Chia reduces *vata* and *kapha* and may be used moderately by *pitta*.

Use Add soaked chia seeds to lemonade or breakfast energy drinks for a sustaining and gelatinous beverage, or sweeten to taste and eat as a rustic tapioca. Chia seeds may be substituted for poppy or sesame seeds as a condiment and garnish.

See **Mint Family; Seeds.**

CHICKPEA SEE **BEANS AND LEGUMES.**

CHIA PETS

While alfalfa, mung, and other seeds easily sprout in a jar, chia does not. Because of its inordinate stickiness, chia requires a special earthenware container. Available in some gift catalogs, these chia pets are often shaped as animals (Chia Pets) or a human head (Hairless Harry). Sprinkle chia seeds on, for example, Harry's pate, water, and, within a few days, he'll sport a lovely head of edible green hair.

CHICKPEA FLOUR
Besan, Gram Flour

The high-protein flour made from hulled and roasted chickpeas is a common ingredient in the East Indian flatbread *papadam,* Indian pasta, and desserts. It is also used in wafers called *pauelle* in southern Italy and *socca* in southern France. It looks dry and powdery, almost chalky, and lends a sweet, rich chickpea flavor. In color, chickpea flour is like corn flour; in performance, it is more like millet flour. Since chickpea flour is gluten-free, it should be used in small quantities in leavened bread.

Chickpea flour is available in Indian, Italian, French, and natural food markets. It is more digestible than is the other common legume flour, soy flour.

See **Beans and Legumes; Chickpea; Flour.**

CHICLE
(*Manilkara zapota*)

Picture yourself unwrapping a stick of spearmint gum, catching its cooling, minty aroma, and munching away on the satisfying familiarity of one of life's simple pleasures. Yum! Let's hear it for petroleum-based synthetic polymers. I'm sorry to pop your bubble, but since the 1950s, chewing gum has been plasticized. "Gum base" on the ingredient list is primarily styrene-butadiene rubber and polyvinyl acetate.

Prior to plastic, chewing gum was made of chicle or mastic. Chicle is the gummy sap or latex of the giant sapodilla tree, which grows in the jungles of Mesoamerica. The ancient Maya chewed chicle as a way to clean their teeth and, presumably, for the fun of it.

The story of chicle chewing gum in North America starts in New York in 1870s when one Thomas Adams experimented with—but did not succeed in—vulcanizing chicle to make an inexpensive rubber substitute. A rubber tire chicle is not. I imagine Adams, in a moment of madness at his umpteenth failure, tearing at a piece of chicle with his teeth and . . . eureka! The rest is history. Adams stirred in some sugar and sassafras and patented Chiclets Chewing Gum. Soon this Central American chewing wonder displaced the North American gum, which was made from the sap of spruce or pine trees.

AUNT ANNA'S CHEWING GUM

My aunt Anna once collected a variety of saps, worked each type separately, then flattened each with her thumb, shaped it into a stick of gum, and wrapped it in a gum wrapper for a multicolored and multiflavored package of decidedly unique home-chewed gum.

If you've never tried chewing wild gum, I recommend it. Select the semihard pitch of a pine or spruce and, in a word, chew. Rather, chew and spit, chew and spit. Spit out the mildly turpentine-flavored saliva that forms, but retain the gummy stuff. After a few chews-and-spits, the flavor mellows and what remains is a wad of pleasantly pine-flavored gum. My favorite chews in the wild are ponderosa, which becomes a beautiful cinnamon color, and piñon, which turns a warm adobe pink. The best way I can describe their flavors is that each tastes like the tree's aroma.

Be sure to collect only almost-hard sap that has oozed from a cut in the trunk or branches of a pine. Fresh pitch is sticky, gooey stuff that wreaks havoc with dentures and sticks in your mouth longer than you'd wish for. Hardened sap crumbles rather than gums up.

Buying Several brands of natural chewing gum made of chicle and natural flavors are available at natural food stores. Chicle, which has a pleasant mouthfeel, comes in various tropical flavors, which all passed my grandchildren's taste test. Besides tasting good and chewing neatly, the important thing about chicle is that it provides a livelihood for indigenous peoples, *chicleros*, who harvest this renewable resource.

See **Mastic; Sapodilla; Sapodilla Family.**

CHICORY
Endive
(*Chicorium endiva, C. intybus*)

Chicory, a member of the daisy family, is closely related to lettuce and the dandelion; it grows wild throughout Europe, Asia, and North America. Its bitter leaves and root have been used from time immemorial for salads and as a medicinal plant. Cultivation has tamed its bitterness and produced numerous varieties, which are adored most by the Italians, who rely upon chicory as a staple cold-weather green that is tender, moist, and crunchy. The family branch used primarily for its leaves is *C. endiva* and includes escarole and frisée.

C. intybus varieties, primarily Magdeburg and Brunswick, are grown for their large, bitter taproots. The roots are dried, roasted, and used to enhance—or, depending upon amount and one's point of view, to adulterate—coffee. Two *C. intybus* varieties used for their greens are radicchio and Belgian endive (witloof).

Today throughout the world common chicories are grown in the absence of light to prevent the sun from opening up the leaves and turning them green and, as a result, more bitter.

Medicinal Benefits Chicory is a cooling food that helps purify the blood and supports the circulatory system. It tonifies the gallbladder and liver and helps regulate water. Chicory's bitter taste comes from intybin, a metabolic stimulant that encourages bile production and aids digestion. Intybin is most highly concentrated in the leaf ribs and root (rather than in the greens). It is traditionally used for insomnia.

Chicory contains inulin, which helps diabetics regulate their blood sugar levels. The root is more active medicinally and is used to treat jaundice, liver enlargement, gout, and rheumatism. As with lettuce, chicory leaves are mostly water and so very low in calories. They are an excellent source of potassium and vitamin A and a good source of calcium. Chicory reduces *pitta* and *kapha*.

Use Add cut, dried, and roasted chicory root—in small amounts—to coffee or blend with other herbs for tea.

The various chicory greens are most commonly thought of as a winter salad green, but their sturdy leaves afford much wider use. Braise, blanch, or grill to reduce their bitter flavor. Individual leaves can be used as cups or wrappers for holding a salad or to wrap food morsels.

Their inner, paler leaves are less bitter than the outer, more green leaves; and the varieties grown without light, like Belgian endive, are even more mild.

My favorite "spring tonic salad" dates to medieval Italy: wild chicory greens, some of the root, and some white shoots seasoned with oil, vinegar, salt, and garlic. Couldn't be simpler, and couldn't be more delicious.

For a great side dish, braise Belgian endive and season with a splash of balsamic vinegar and a dash of salt.

As chicory greens become more bitter with storage, plan to use quickly.

Buying/Foraging Select fresh-looking chicory with a firm white core. Look for fresh, crisp greens and avoid those with wilt or browning; they may be green, red, or variegated. The blanched (grown without light) chicories (Belgian endive, puntarelle, and radicchio) are a labor-intensive crop and therefore more expensive than the green varieties.

Chicory is one of the easiest plants to forage, it is nearly as common as dandelion, sports a perky telltale purple flower, and is readily recognized. Dig new roots in the spring or the fall. Roots more than a year old are extremely bitter. Harvest the new shoots and the leaves before the plant goes to flower.

Chicory root, dried and roasted, is available in the herb section of natural food stores or blended with coffee.

- **Belgian Endive** or **Witloof** The pale yellow Belgian endive, in the shape of a fat cigar, is a chicory with an interesting story. In 1830, a Belgian farmer, Jan Lammers, stored chicory roots in his cellar for use as a coffee substitute. However, before he was able to dry and grind the roots, they sprouted small white leaves. He nibbled a witloof (white leaf) and a new "crop" was born. Belgian endive is a crisp salad green, and its canoe-shaped leaves are attractive as a garnish or on a plate of crudités.

- **Endive** or **Curly Endive** The leaves of this heading chicory are curly, wider than frisée, and more narrow and serrated than escarole.

- **Escarole** This bitter-tasting chicory looks like a loose-leaf lettuce. Its leaves are broader and less curly than endive leaves and more sturdy. In domestic markets, it is one of the more readily available chicory greens.

- **Frisée** This chicory looks like a tangled mop; it has a crisp texture and a bitter-sweet flavor. Frisée is small and loose-heading with slender lime-colored outer leaves and lemon yellow inner leaves. The leaf stalks are white, and the leaf itself is deeply serrated. Frisée is more delicate in flavor than other endives. It is excellent in salad or lightly braised.

- **Puntarelle** or **Catalogna** The dandelion-like serrated leaves of this chicory surround long, hollow, blunt-tipped whitish green shoots. Its flavor is a little peppery and bitter, and the shoots are crisp and crunchy like celery. The shoots and leaves are most often served raw in salad, particularly a salad with a rich, powerful dressing like anchovy. They may also be braised.

- **Radicchio** (Also known as **Red Endive** or **Red Chicory**) Magenta-colored radicchio (rah-DEEK-ee-o) is a heading type of chicory with firm, crisp leaves and an arresting flavor bordering on sweet and bitter. It is enjoyed raw, as a showy garnish, or grilled. Radicchio varieties include:

  Castelfranco Radicchio has mild-tasting, creamy white, red-splashed leaves.

  Radicchio di Treviso has long, narrow leaves and is better than Verona for cooking.

  Radicchio di Verona looks like a little red cabbage, with thick white veins.

- **Sugarloaf** This endive variety looks rather like romaine lettuce with broad and dark green leaves.

See **Coffee Substitute; Daisy Family; Vegetable.**

CHICOS
Dried Sweet Corn, Shaker Dried Corn

Chicos are dried sweet corn kernels; they have a delicious caramel flavor and a chewy texture. This dried vegetable is rehydrated like beans and added to soups, stews, and bean dishes or cooked as a side dish in its own right. In addition to *horno chicos* (see sidebar), the Shakers also sun-dried sweet corn for later reconstitution.

Making chicos is easy. Pull back—but don't remove—the husk from fresh corn on the cob and peg it with a clothespin to a clothesline. The dangling, exposed ears of corn bedeck the line even more promisingly than linen. If you're an apartment dweller, hang them at a sunny window and rotate the ears each day. (The corn is dry and does not attract flies.)

Within a week of sunny weather, they'll dry. A few rain showers will slow the process but cause no harm. Technically, chicos, like beans and grains, are dried to about 12 percent moisture content, but by taste and crunch, you'll know when they're ready.

To shuck the shriveled kernels, hold an ear over a bowl, firmly grasp it with both hands, and twist your hands in opposite directions.

CAR-DRIED SWEET CORN

At an open-air market in New Mexico, I asked the farmer how he dried his sweet corn kernels. If they were *horno chicos,* from a wood-fired, adobe oven, I was ready to put my money down.

"I roast 'em in an old car," he tersely said. Visualizing him torching a car, I asked for more detail.

"I load the car with corn, roll up the windows, the car gets hotter than hell, and dries the corn just fine." I put my money down for car-roasted chicos.

They'll fall, like golden nuggets, into the bowl. Store, tightly covered, in a cupboard for up to a year. To use them, hydrate by soaking in cold water for several hours, or overnight, and then add chicos and their soaking liquid to a stew, soup, pot of beans, or other long-cooking dish.

Buying Chicos are available in Latino sections of supermarkets, many natural food stores, or by mail order. Freeze-dried sweet corn kernels available in supermarkets or the oven-dried Shaker corn are tasty, but they lack the caramel flavor of sun-dried chicos or *horno chicos.*

See **Sweet Corn.**

CHILE PEPPER
Chile, Chili, Hot Pepper, Red Pepper (*Capsicum*)

In a short 400 years, chile peppers, an annual, bushy New World plant, have become the world's most highly consumed spice. This is thanks to a single gene, the incendiary, to-be-respected capsaicin. It's a lack of this gene that keeps sweet peppers cool. Capsaicin is the bitter, acrid, oily alkaloid found in chiles that can literally burn the skin, especially the eyes, nose, lips, and even the gastrointestinal tract. Nearly 90 percent of the capsaicin is concentrated in the white, placental tissues to which the seeds are attached. Depending upon the chile heat you desire, exclude or include these membranes in your cooking.

Although chiles, a night-shade vegetable, are most famous for their heat, behind that heat is their range of earthy sweet flavors. Chiles are popularly believed to be a mood enhancer because they increase the production of endorphins. This proposition lacks clinical data; if you eat a hot chile, however, you'll experience moments of heightened awareness.

Indian summer in the Southwest is chile-roasting time, and the smoky aroma of roasting chiles pervades the air. Many people fire up their home grills to roast their own, and others buy them at roadside stands or in supermarket lots. There, 35 pounds at a clip are roasted over a large gas-fired lattice barrel, a contraption that has a grid rotating over the fire so that the chiles tumble as they roast. People stock up with a year's supply and freeze them.

Medicinal Benefits Capsaicin is a yang tonic and a fast-acting vasodilator that widens the blood vessels and so enhances both blood and chi circulation and increases body temperature. The quick temperature rise causes perspiration, which cools the body back down.

Chiles treat the lungs, stomach, spleen, and heart; they warm the internal organs, invigorate the stomach, aid digestion, diminish swelling, and act as a blood tonic. They stimulate the digestive system and have antioxidant properties, which help preserve and detoxify food. Capsaicin often aids people with chronic bronchial problems. They protect against some chemical carcinogens and mutagens. As chiles disperse cold, dry, overly damp conditions, they help treat colds, fevers, varicose veins, and asthma. Externally, capsaicin in an ointment relieves arthritis, shingles, neuralgia, and pleurisy (even though initially, as the pain is drawn up and out, it may exacerbate the pain).

Chiles are not recommended for anyone with an inflamed colon. Ayurveda considers chiles *rajasic* and uses them primarily as a medicine. Chiles reduce *kapha*.

Red chiles are a superior source of vitamin C, and green chiles are a good source of vitamin A. They are extremely low in calories.

Use Chiles are available fresh or dried and may be used as a spice as well as a vegetable.

- **Dried Chiles** Crushed or powdered dried chiles are ready to use as an ingredient. To prepare whole dried chiles, rehydrate by soaking in hot water for an hour or so. Cut open and remove and discard the seeds, stems, and veins.
- **Fresh Chiles** Cooking reduces the capsicum burn, so if you plan to use fresh, uncooked chiles, dice them finely in consideration of anyone not accustomed to eating chiles. Open and remove and discard the seeds, stems, and veins.
- **Roasted Chiles** Roasted chiles impart a smoky sweetness to savory dishes. Place chiles in a broiler pan (or over coals or directly on a gas or electric burner). Broil, turning frequently with tongs, for about 10 minutes, until skin is blistered and blackened all over. Place in a paper or plastic bag, wrap snuggly, and allow to steam for 10 to 15 minutes. When the skin has loosened and the chiles are cool enough to handle, rub the skin off. Cut in half and remove the core, membrane, and seeds. Hold under running water to rinse off any blackened skin or seeds.

Buying Hundreds of different chile varieties exist and many have more than one name. New varieties are frequently introduced and given a regional name. This issue is compounded, as a fresh chile is called one thing, but when dried it often goes by a different label.

This fruit of the nightshade family ranges in color, size, shape, and pungency. In general, chiles that are small with narrow shoulders and a pointed tip are hotter than larger, chunkier varieties. A hot climate typically produces a hot chile; thus, for example, varieties of the popular California Anaheim now grown in hotter southeastern New Mexico contain more capsicum than the California Anaheim.

A green, immature chile is less fragile, stores longer, and therefore costs less than a mature chile, which may be red, purple, or yellow rather than green. Select fresh chiles that are firm, glossy, and unblemished rather than limp or discolored. Dried chiles are available whole, crushed, or powdered.

The Scoville heat unit, a method for measuring the capsicum in a chile, gives a general guide of its heat. General, because the seed lineage, soil, climate, and growing conditions affect a chile's heat, and even two chiles from the same plant can vary greatly in their hotness. One part capsicum per million is ranked as 15 Scoville units.

Scoville Units (SU)

0–4,000: Mild
4,000–15,000: Medium
15,000–50,000: Hot
Over 50,000: Very Hot

Anaheim (California Long Green, Chile Verde) 500–1,500 SU These slender and long (up to seven inches) peppers are rather flat, often curved, and typically available green; when fully ripe, they're red. One of the most commonly available peppers in the United States, the mild and sweet Anaheim is stuffed for chiles rellenos and typically used in salsas. Odds are that canned "green chiles" are Anaheims. They're also available dried.

Banana Wax (Hungarian Yellow Wax, Sweet Banana) 1,000–3,000 SU Sweetly and gently flavored, this banana-colored pepper is like a smaller (three to five inches) Anaheim. Its flesh is medium-thick and crisp. When fully matured, it turns scarlet. It's difficult to roast.

Cayenne 30,000–50,000 SU The chile most commonly dried as a spice takes its name from Cayenne, the capital of French Guiana. Cayenne is a common ingredient in spice blends, Cajun cooking, and various hot sauces. It is rarely available fresh.

Cherry Bell 500–3,500 SU Aptly named, this deep orange to bright red pepper is the size and approximate shape of a cherry. Flavored either sweet or hot, it makes a great decoration. Too thickly fleshed to be dried, the cherry bell is great in pickles.

Fresno 3,000–15,000 SU Either green or red, glossy, and thickly fleshed, this chile is often mistaken for a red jalapeño, as it is similar in size and shape, but the Fresno has a more pointed end. Too hot for use as a vegetable, the Fresno is primarily used as a seasoning agent.

Habanero 100,000–350,000 SU Small, about two by two inches, and lantern-shaped, habaneros may be green, orange, red, or yellow. One of the hottest of chiles, they are used in salsas, sauces, and condiments.

Hatch 2,500–8,000 Named for the New Mexican town from where they originated, the Hatch is like an Anaheim except that it is more curved and hotter.

Jalapeño (Chipotle, when smoke-dried) 2,500–8,000 SU This bullet-shaped, small pepper, about two to four inches long, is typically available green but will turn red when fully mature. It is, perhaps, the most widely available fresh chile.

Naga Jolokia (Ghost Chile, Naga Morich) 855,000–1,050,000 SU This pepper is renowned as the hottest chile in the world. It grows primarily in northeastern India and is similar in appearance to a habanero chile but with a rough and ridged skin. The Naga Jolokia ranges from two to three inches long, is about an inch wide, and ends in a sharp point.

Pimiento 100–500 SU One of my favorite peppers, the pimiento is heart shaped, richly sweet, and highly aromatic. It is available canned and is the bit of red in stuffed olives. Fresh pimientos are a great addition to many savory dishes and go well in salads.

Poblano (**Ancho,** when dried) 500–2,500 SU Dark, forest green and thickly fleshed, the poblano is shaped rather like a flat bell pepper. It has a rich flavor that enhances soups, sauces, and stews or can be used as a vessel for stuffed dishes.

Scotch Bonnet 100,000–350,000 SU A Scotch bonnet looks rather like a lantern-shaped habanero but is smaller. It may be green, orange, or yellow in color.

Serrano 10,000–23,000 SU Although it's shaped like a small jalapeño, only a little smaller (one to two inches) and thinner, the serrano is fiery hot and boasts a pure chile flavor. It's a staple in Mexican cuisine.

Thai (Bird Chile) 50,000–100,000 SU These tiny chiles, one inch long and one-quarter inch in diameter with a pointed end, are extraordinarily hot.

Storing If you have a good supply of chiles, roast and steam them as instructed, then cool. Pack them, charred skin and all, loosely into small freezer bags and freeze. Remove the chiles from the freezer as needed. Hold under hot running water; the skin, seeds, and veins will quickly and easily separate from the flesh.

Be Mindful Some people suffering from arthritis observe that when they avoid eating chiles and other nightshade family vegetables, their condition improves.

EMADATSE

The national dish of Bhutan, a tiny Himalayan nation, is possibly the most memorable condiment. You don't have to be Bhutanese to enjoy their spicy but creamy *emadatse* (pronounced em'a-dat'se). Yes, 12 serranos is a lot of chiles! But the cheese, butter, and cooking help moderate their heat and deepen their flavor. If you like chiles, it's addicting.

Serve emadatse over rice, meat, or dal, to top a soup, or alongside scrambled eggs. Or go Bhutanese and serve emadatse as a vegetable side dish as you would serve broccoli or carrots. There are many variations; Lama Lodoe Sangpo taught me this one.

12 serrano or Thai chiles
2 jalapeño chiles
3 tablespoons ghee or butter
1 onion, chopped
3 mushrooms, diced
4 cloves garlic, minced
2 plum tomatoes, peeled and diced
2 tablespoons finely minced ginger
2 teaspoons unrefined salt
1 cup crumbled blue cheese, feta cheese, or farmer cheese
1 cup chopped cilantro

Wearing rubber gloves, slice the chiles lengthwise and remove their seeds under running water. Coarsely chop all the chiles. Set aside.

Heat the ghee in a medium skillet over medium heat. Add the onion, mushrooms, and garlic and sauté for about 5 minutes, until the onion is translucent. Add the chiles, tomatoes, ginger, and salt. Stir to blend and cook for 7 to 10 minutes, until the chiles are soft and have lost their vibrant green color. Add the cheese and cilantro and cook, stirring continuously for about 2 minutes or until the cheese is melted. Do not allow the cheese to boil.

Emadatse is best the day it's made. However, leftovers may be refrigerated, tightly covered, and gently warmed before serving.

Wear rubber gloves when you handle chiles, be they fresh or dried. Some people with less sensitive skin may handle chiles directly. If you are one of them, immediately wash your hands thoroughly with soap and water afterward to prevent inadvertent capsaicin burns to more sensitive areas. Should you develop a chile burn, washing with a very mild bleach solution is a good antidote. If capsicum is not well digested, it can burn the anus as it passes in the stool.

See **Herbs and Spices; Nightshade Family; Paprika; Peppers; Sweet Pepper; Vegetable.**

CHILI SEE CHILE.

CHINESE ANISE SEE STAR ANISE.

CHINESE ARTICHOKE SEE CROSNE.

CHINESE BROCCOLI
Chinese Kale, Gai Laan, Kai-Lan
(*Brassica oleracea, Alboglabra* group)

The two most delightful things about Chinese broccoli, a cabbage family member, are its delicate, edible flowers and its sweet flavor, which is like garden-fresh broccoli. Unlike market-variety broccoli stems (stout) and leaves (puny), Chinese broccoli stems are tender, smooth, and slender (about ½ inch thick), and the plant is abundantly bestowed with broad, blue-green, slightly bitter leaves.

Because of its generous leaves and more robust flavor, I favor Chinese broccoli over its patented hybrid, broccolini. Chinese broccoli probably was introduced to China by the Portuguese after 1517; it is a close relative of the Portuguese cabbage Couve Tronchuda.

Medicinal Benefits See **Broccoli** entry.

Use Use as you would broccoli—sautéed, steamed, braised, boiled, and in soup. Chinese broccoli cooks in less time, though, as it's a less dense vegetable. The stems require longer cooking than the leaves, and the leaves longer cooking than the blossoms, so cut and cook the vegetable accordingly.

The yellow blossoms perk up any dish. Fresh,

PASS ON THE KETCHUP, PASS THE SALSA

When I was growing up, Velveeta and cheddar were the cheese options, strawberry ice cream a Sunday treat, and yogurt was an anomaly. Since the 1970s our dairy consumption has increased at about the rate that cheese and ice cream choices have proliferated.

Tangentially, fiery foods have swept north from the Mexican border and east across the Pacific. And therein, I see a correlation. Here's why. For many people—lactose intolerant or not—dairy products are mucus forming and colon congesting.

Back to chiles. The spicy flavor, most remarkable in chiles, tonifies the large intestines. Recall how colon stimulating your early chile experiences were. As more dairy is consumed, Americans gravitate to more pungent foods in an effort to keep things moving.

use them as a garnish on the side of a plate or float them on a steaming bowl of soup. For stir-fried dishes, cook the blossoms for only the last minute so they will retain their color.

Buying Look for Chinese broccoli with solid stems, unblemished leaves, and flower buds that are just starting to open. A year-round feature in Asian markets, this vegetable is becoming increasingly available in super-markets.

See **Broccoli; Broccolini; Cabbage Family; Vegetable.**

CHINESE CABBAGE SEE BOK CHOY; NAPA CABBAGE.

CHINESE CELERY SEE CELERY.

CHINESE CHIVE SEE GARLIC CHIVE.

CHINESE FLOWERING CABBAGE SEE FLOWERING CABBAGE.

CHINESE GOOSEBERRY SEE KIWI.

CHINESE GREENS SEE AMARANTH GREENS; BOK CHOY; CHRYSANTHEMUM GREENS; FLOWERING CABBAGE; LETTUCE; MUSTARD GREENS; TATSOI.

CHINESE KALE SEE CHINESE BROCCOLI.

CHINESE LANTERN SEE GROUND CHERRY.

CHINESE LEEK SEE GARLIC CHIVE.

CHINESE LETTUCE SEE LETTUCE.

CHINESE LONG BEAN SEE LONG BEAN.

CHINESE MUSHROOM SEE SHIITAKE.

CHINESE PARSLEY SEE CILANTRO.

CHINESE PEAR SEE ASIAN PEAR.

CHINESE SPINACH SEE FAT HEN.

CHINESE WINTER MELON SEE WINTER MELON.

CHIVE
(*Allium schoenoprasum*)

The German word for chives is *schnittlauch*, or "cuttable leek," an apt name for the chive, which, like your front lawn, will thrive when the top half is clipped back. This feature is one reason the chive is a common—and rewarding—kitchen window box herb.

The chive grows wild from arctic Russia to Mediterranean climes. A chive looks like a slender scallion, but it's more round, hollow, and lacks the swollen bulb; it grows in dense mats. Only the leaves are used. Its soft spring-time flavor is more delicate than a scallion and also more arresting.

Medicinal Benefits Medicinally, chives are similar to—but more mild in action than—other onion relatives. Nevertheless, chives are a mild tonic that benefit the digestive system and blood circulation. They reduce *kapha*. Garlic chives have potent medicinal properties.

Use The delicate chive flavor is lost when dried at home. However, when industrially dried, more of the flavor is retained. Still, they're best fresh. Long cooking compromises most of their flavor. Chives are most used as a garnish or in subtly flavored dishes. Feature their purple pompom blossoms in flower arrangements or, when young and tender, as a salad ingredient.

Buying This fragile onion family member is available year-round but must be very fresh to be worth the purchase. Avoid yellowed or wilted chives.

See **Garlic Chive; Herbs and Spices; Onion Family.**

CHLORELLA
(*Chlorella*)

Chlorella, the first plant form with a true nucleus, has been on earth since the pre-Cambrian period—more than 2.5 billion years. The single-celled algae grows in freshwater lakes and ponds. At 6 microns (6 millionths of a meter), it is one of the smallest plants we eat—but possibly one of the most useful.

Medicinal Benefits Chlorella is a superior source of assimilable chlorophyll, which helps cleanse and detoxify cells in the body. A clean, healthy cell can better utilize other nutrients. That is why chlorella relieves so many conditions. In addition, chlorella is one of the highest natural sources of DNA and RNA.

Chlorella is useful in a wide variety of maladies and conditions, including chronic gastritis, high blood pressure, some forms of cancer, diabetes, constipation, anemia, and high cholesterol. It helps clear toxic metals from the body. Chlorella has antitumor and anti-inflammatory properties and strengthens the immune system. The microalgae supports normal growth and helps maintain health in old age. It reduces *pitta* and *kapha* and, in moderation, is healing for *vata*.

Paul Pitchford, author of *Healing with Whole Foods*, observes that of the microalgae, chlorella is the "least cooling, the most tonifying, and most gently cleansing. . . . It is the safest to use for children, maintaining health in old age, healing injuries, and initiating growth where it has been stunted from disease or degeneration, including Alzheimer's disease, sciatica, palsy, seizures, multiple sclerosis, nervousness, and other nerve disorders. . . . This microalgae is generally not useful in the treatment of obesity."

Chlorella is similar to spirulina but with less protein and more nucleic acid and chlorophyll. It contains more than 20 different vitamins

---

A DISTASTEFUL—BUT INFORMATIVE—STORY

To stave starvation, pee into a pot, and grow chlorella. In her autobiography, *Wild Swans: Three Daughters of China*, Jung Chang describes an effective cure for edema caused by malnourishment. "Chlorella feeds on human urine and so people peed into spittoons and dropped the chlorella seeds in. They grew into something that looked like green fish roe in a couple of days and were scooped out, washed, and cooked with the rice. They were truly disgusting to eat but they did reduce the swelling."

In the great famine of 1959–61, some 30 million Chinese starved to death. Chlorella, even grown in urine, had observable value. Today chlorella from pristine, mineral-rich spring water and available in easy-to-pop tablets offers formidable nutrition.

---

and minerals, plus 19 amino acids, including all the essential amino and fatty acids. It is particularly rich in lysine and is one of the highest natural sources of chlorophyll. It is 50 to 60 percent protein.

Use Chlorella, like other microalgae, is typically consumed as a dietary supplement. Due to its high processing costs, chlorella is the most expensive microalgae. It is available in pill and powder form.

See **Algae Family; Microalgae.**

CHOCOLATE
Cacao, Cocoa
(*Theobroma cacao*)

Chocolate, a native of tropical and Central America, was called xocoatl by the Maya and Aztecs, which means a bitter drink. It was a favorite beverage for the priests and royalty. The Swedish botanist Linnaeus tagged it *theobroma* meaning, in Greek, "food of the gods"—few would disagree. Cacao beans were so valued that in Mexico they were used as standard currency as late as 1887.

A relative of both cotton and the cola bean, the cacao tree is a tropical plant. Its fruit pods look like small red or gold footballs. Each pod holds from 20 to 70 white beans about the size and shape of almonds. Today Africa and Brazil supply more than 90 percent of the world demand for chocolate, but some of the finest quality chocolate comes from Venezuela and Costa Rica. Shade-grown cocoa has a superior flavor.

Cacao beans are removed from pod, fermented, dried, graded, and delivered to factories. They are then roasted (a process called torrefication), chopped up, and ground into an oily paste called chocolate mass or liquor. This liquor is nut particles suspended in cocoa butter, which is more than 50 percent fatty acids. The liquor gives the chocolate taste and color; the butter imparts a rich, creamy mouthfeel and glossy appearance.

To make cocoa powder used in beverages and baking, most of the cocoa butter is pressed from the liquor. The resulting paste may also be Dutch processed, or further refined to improve its texture and flavor. There are many grades of cocoa powder to choose from—the darkest ones are the most bitter tasting and have the strongest cocoa flavor.

Chocolate for candy is made from the original, fat-rich liquor; fine chocolate is augmented with additional cocoa butter. In addition, superior chocolate undergoes an expensive mechanical conching process of grinding, mixing, and slightly heating the ingredients to enhance its texture and flavor. Lesser-quality chocolate is cut with inexpensive lecithin, vegetable oils, and/or synthetic substances. The taste of chocolate depends upon the variety of the cacao tree, the soil it was grown in, and what it was blended with as well as the processing.

Medicinal Benefits Chocolate is bitter tasting, diuretic, and a stimulant. It gives energy and was historically considered an aphrodisiac. It contains proanthocyanidin flavonoids that help reduce free radicals and phenols that counter artery-clogging plaque and lower blood pressure. It treats the severe chest pain of angina pectoris. Chocolate and cocoa are popularly believed to comfort the brokenhearted and to release the brain chemicals responsible for the feeling of being in love due to their theobromine and phenylethylamine content.

Cocoa butter is used as an unguent for burns and skin irritations and in cosmetics. In moderation, chocolate reduces *vata*.

Buying White chocolate excepted, all chocolate is a blend of cocoa liquor and white cocoa butter. It may or may not contain other flavorings, such as milk, vanilla, or sugar.

Quality chocolate is glossy and shiny. It should smell fresh and, when broken, should break cleanly rather than crumble.

- **Cacao Nibs** Available either raw or roasted, cacao nibs are crunchy, pea-size chunks of husked cocoa beans. Free of any other ingredients, this pure chocolate is bitter but tasty. Eat as a snack, add to trail mix, or use as a baking ingredient.
- **Cocoa Powder** Contains an average of 18 percent total cocoa butter. The dry cake that remains after pressing cocoa butter is pulverized for use as an ingredient in baking, confectionery, and beverages.
- **Couverture** A rich chocolate with a

minimum of 32 percent cocoa butter, it is characterized by an exceptionally shiny finish.

- **Dutch-Process Cocoa Powder (European-Style Cocoa)** Alkali-processed cocoa powder that is darker in color and more mellow in flavor than cocoa powder. The alkali, usually potassium carbonate, is used to neutralize the cocoa's acids and make it easier to dissolve.
- **Milk Chocolate** Contains sugar, added cocoa butter, milk solids, and chocolate liquor.
- **Semisweet (Bittersweet) Chocolate** Contains 35 to 50 percent chocolate liquor, with 15 percent added cocoa butter.
- **Unsweetened (Bitter** or **Baking) Chocolate** Pure, unadulterated chocolate liquor that contains about equal proportions of cocoa solids and cocoa butter. It is used as an ingredient in baked goods and confections.
- **White Chocolate** Contains only cocoa butter, milk solids, sugar, and lecithin (or, historically, chestnuts). It lacks the beneficial flavonoid found in other chocolate products and has a short shelf life, as it easily becomes rancid. In cheap, imitation white chocolate, vegetable oil is substituted for the cocoa butter.

Be Mindful Many women, especially in the West, consider themselves addicted to chocolate. Theobromine is a stimulant and, like caffeine, can trigger various nervous-type symptoms, including hyperactivity in children, anxiety, insomnia or disturbed sleep, heart disease, gastrointestinal complaints, and mood swings. In addition, chocolate and cocoa contain phenylethylamine and oxalic acid, both of which can inhibit calcium absorption. Overall calcium and mineral deficiencies are exacerbated by habitual chocolate consumption. In some individuals, chocolate is implicated in migraine headaches. Some people who wish to reduce their chocolate intake substitute with carob products.

CHOY SUM SEE **FLOWERING CABBAGE**.

CHRISTOPHINE SEE **CHAYOTE**.

CHRYSANTHEMUM GREENS
Edible Chrysanthemum, Garland Chrysanthemum, Shungiku (*Chrysanthemum coronarium*)

Chrysanthemum is one of my favorite garden vegetables; it's easy to grow and keeps producing if you harvest it regularly and before the buds form. This annual Mediterranean herb, a member of the daisy family, is a diminutive variety of the popular decorative chrysanthemum flower. Its sweet and tangy deeply lobed leaves are widely used in Asian cuisine as a vegetable.

Medicinal Benefits These greens treat the liver and kidneys and improve the flow of chi. Like broccoli and kale, chrysanthemum greens are unusually high in protein. Some varieties are grown for their edible flowers. The flower of *C. morifolium,* for example, is a classic Chinese remedy for alleviating migraine headaches and liver discomfort and for treating vision problems. In Ayurvedic medicine, it is used for the treatment of gonorrhea.

Use Chrysanthemum leaves cook as quickly as spinach but don't exude liquid in the same way. Their slightly perfumed taste lends itself to rich dishes as well as salads.

Blanch or stir-fry and add to soups and casseroles. Once they do go to flower, the greens develop a more bitter flavor. Use the buds as you would the greens.

See **Daisy Family; Vegetable.**

CHUÑO
(Solanum tuberosum)

Don't be put off by chuño's appearance. A naturally freeze-dried potato or oca from the Andean altiplano, it looks more like a chunk of pumice than a food, but the earthy flavor and pleasing texture (something like deep-fried tofu) make chuños worth seeking out in a Latino market. The Quechua and Aymara preserve their just-harvested potatoes or ocas in this manner. They're left on the ground for several days, covered with a cloth to keep off the dew; each night they freeze. During the day, they are trampled by foot to express their water. Once freeze-dried in this manner, they'll keep for years. Chuños are an excellent stew ingredient—taking on the other flavors while imparting their own potato goodness.

Papa seca, or dried potato, another preserved Peruvian potato, is boiled but not trampled before being left out to freeze.

See **Nightshade Family; Oca; Potato; Vegetable.**

CILANTRO
Chinese Parsley, Coriander, Mexican Parsley
(Coriandrum sativum)

An ancient and popular herb since Egyptian times, cilantro is in the carrot family. The leaves have an aniselike taste (soapy when

used in excess) and an earthy, fetid aroma. Apparently its distinctive aroma is like a bedbug, and so the Greeks named it *koris*, or bedbug. People either adore or are repulsed by cilantro; for the latter, even a pinch of cilantro spoils a dish. If your first reaction was negative, I urge you to approach it again; odds are, you'll become a convert. Cilantro is similar in appearance to parsley but lightly colored with larger and less curled leaves. Once dried, cilantro loses its heady aroma.

The seed, known as coriander, is tan and the size of a peppercorn. It is sweet and strongly aromatic, with a slight taste of orange peel.

Medicinal Benefits Pungent and sweet in flavor, cilantro supports the spleen, stomach, bladder, and lung meridians. Both the leaf and seed help regulate energy, are diuretic, and specifically treat urinary tract infections. They are diaphoretic (support perspiration) and therefore treat fever. They aid digestion, relieve intestinal gas and pain and distention, and support peristalsis. They treat nausea, soothe inflammation, rheumatic pain, headaches, coughs, and mental stress, and they quench thirst. The seeds and leaves are *tridoshic*. The essential oil of the seed is used to treat indigestion, influenza, fatigue, rheumatism, flatulence, nervousness, and pain.

Cilantro is commonly believed to safely remove toxins, including heavy metals, from the nervous system and body tissues.

Use Cilantro is basic in cuisine the world over; some say it is the most used herb, especially in warm regions such as Mexico, the Middle East, Africa, Southeast Asia, and India. The leaves should not be overcooked.

Cilantro may be used like parsley, as a garnish and a flavoring herb. Use it sparingly with delicate ingredients, or its flavor will overpower. Or use it in large quantities in strongly flavored sauces and salsas. In Southeast Asian dishes, cilantro root is also used.

The slightly sweet, almost caramel-tasting seed acts as a catalyst to bring out the flavors of other ingredients, yet doesn't mask or overpower them. Coriander is an omnipresent ingredient in Indian curries and Ethiopian spice mixtures. Ground coriander quickly looses its pleasantly sweet taste and smell. It is preferable to use the whole seeds or grind them just prior to use. To heighten the flavor of coriander, first toast or sauté the whole or ground seeds.

After a meal, to both freshen your breath and stimulate the flow of gastric juices, chew a few coriander seeds.

Buying Fresh cilantro is available in greengrocers year-round. In Asian markets, it is sold with the root attached, increasing its longevity. Select bunches that look fresh and bright. Cilantro quickly loses its flavor and develops a harsh, unpleasant taste; the leaves rapidly deteriorate, so use it soon after purchase.

Storing Cilantro is highly perishable and stores best when attached to its roots. Place the roots in a container of water, cover the greens with plastic, and refrigerate for up to a week. If purchased without roots, cover cilantro with a damp cloth, refrigerate in a perforated plastic bag, and use within four or five days.

Store whole coriander seeds and ground coriander in a tightly closed container in a dark, cool cupboard. The whole seeds keep a year or more. Once ground, coriander loses its savor less quickly than cardamom but faster than cinnamon. Discard mild, flat-tasting ground coriander.

Be Mindful Excessive coriander seed consumption can have a narcotic action.

See **Carrot Family; Herbs and Spices.**

CINNAMON
Cassia
(*Cinnamomum zeylanicum* syn. *C. verum; also C. cassia, C. burmannii, C. japonicum*)

The strongly aromatic, sweet-tasting dried inner bark of a tree in the laurel family, cinnamon is one of humanity's oldest spices. Its recorded use in China and Egypt dates back to 2500 BC; it was one of the first spices traded to the Mediterranean area. Several cinnamon varieties exist in China, Indonesia, and Vietnam.

In many European languages, names for cinnamon come from the Latin *canella*, which means "small tube, pipe." This refers to how thin strips of the inner bark of the cinnamon tree are sun-dried to form tightly curled semitubular "quills." Cinnamon is related to the avocado and bay.

Medicinal Benefits Sweet and pungent, pleasant tasting and warming, cinnamon is a chi and yang tonic that supports the spleen,

---

THE HEART OF A JAWBREAKER

For the Saturday matinee movie of my childhood, my siblings and I would walk three miles to the Country Club Theater. I don't recall much of the movies I saw. I do recall the manager periodically stopping the film to warn us to quiet down or he'd turn us out (he never did). And I can still almost taste my favorite penny candy, a jawbreaker.

One large, round ball filled a whole cheek plus and lasted the length of the movie. Layer upon layer, each a different color, of sugary candy would slowly dissolve. To give cheek muscles a rest, I'd occasionally pull out the jawbreaker to see if, indeed, there was any progress and to see what color level I was at.

At long last, the sugar all dissolved to reveal the central treasure—one tiny coriander seed. It provided a satisfying crunch and a burst of real flavor.

lung, kidney, heart, and uterus functions. It is one of the most commonly used warming Oriental herbs. As an herb and essential oil it has stimulant, analgesic, and astringent properties. Cinnamon can increase digestive fluid secretion and therefore ameliorate intestinal gas. It raises vitality and stimulates all the vital functions of the body, counteracting congestion and aiding the peripheral circulation of the blood. It is useful for treating diarrhea, nausea and vomiting, influenza, arthritis, menstrual cramps, rheumatism, and candidiasis. Its aroma relieves tension and helps steady the nerves. Cinnamon is *tridoshic* in action, although an excess could imbalance *pitta*.

Use In Western cuisine, cinnamon is commonly used in desserts. But considering that cinnamon aids absorption of nutrients, you might start using it more liberally. Elsewhere in the world, it is a common ingredient in savory dishes and is, for example, an ingredient in Chinese five-spice blend. My favorite way to use a cinnamon quill is to sauté it, along with any other spices, in warm oil until the quill unrolls and then add and cook the remaining ingredients. When using cinnamon powder, add it shortly before serving, as it becomes bitter with prolonged cooking.

Buying Today most ground cinnamon available in the United States is the mahogany red cassia. Its quills are tan and relatively loose. True cinnamon (*C. zeylanicum*) has a more delicate aroma, mahogany-red color, and more tightly curled quills.

Be Mindful True cinnamon (*C. zeylanicum*) is not recommended for pregnant women as it stimulates the uterus.

See **Herbs and Spices; Laurel Family.**

CITRON
(*C. medica*)

Imagine a large, warty or ridged and leathery-skinned lemonlike fruit . . . that's a

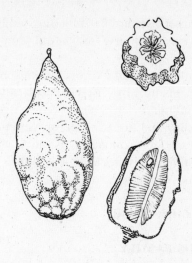

citron. For a treat, soak its aromatic peel in salt brine to pull out its bitter flavor and then candy it in sugar. Nubbins of candied citron abound in fruitcakes—and little else. Citrons are green when immature and turn to yellow or yellow-orange when ripe. Add a citron to your fruit bowl and its pervasive fragrance can linger for weeks at a time. The essential oil of citron peel is used as a flavoring agent.

Medicinal Benefits Citron supports the spleen and helps circulate chi. It clears mucus and phlegm, treats lung and intestinal ailments, alleviates motion sickness, eases coughing, and helps with alcohol detoxification. In aromatherapy, citron is valued for its antibiotic properties.

The most remarkably shaped citron is called Buddha's Hand citron and is composed of a cluster of green, fingerlike lobes. This citrus is considered a symbol of happiness in China, especially when the lobes are closed, as if in prayer. In the Jewish Feast of the Tabernacles, a citron carried on myrtle boughs by celebrants represents abundance. The Corsican liqueur Cedratine is made of citron.

Buying Fresh citrons have some availability in specialty or well-stocked greengrocers. Look for one with a plump, full rind without any signs of discoloration, mold, or softness. To preserve its flavor, use fresh citron promptly.

- Pulpy and acidic citron varieties include Diamante, Etrog, Greek, Balady, and Florentine.
- Pulpy and nonacidic citron varieties include Moroccan and Corsican.
- Pulpless varieties include Buddha's Hand and Yemenite citron.

See **Citrus Family.**

CITRUS FAMILY

From ruby grapefruit to Key limes, the number of citrus fruits is huge. Hundreds of varieties and subspecies grow throughout the tropics and subtropics. Add the endless hybrids for an unwieldy category as well as the largest fruit industry. The extremely hot spice Sichuan pepper is also part of this family.

Citrus plants are small evergreen trees or shrubs with aromatic blossoms that originated in China and Southeast Asia. The primitive citron was the original citrus fruit. Today these fruits grow throughout the world where there's ample moisture and little or no frost. Brazil and the United States are the world's largest citrus producers, most of which is processed rather than eaten out of hand.

Medicinal Benefits In general, citrus are a cooling agent—be the heat from a fever, physical exercise, or a menopausal hot flash. They are a general tonic for weak digestion and poor appetite, clear mucus and phlegm, benefit the lungs and spleen, and help treat coughing. Citrus varieties contain 58 known anticancer agents and are remarkable in their wide range of healing properties. For example, mandarin oranges are specific for breast cancer, whereas grapefruit pits treat candidiasis. For specific medicinal properties, see individual varieties.

Most citrus fruits are high in sugar, although lemons and limes are high in acids. All species are rich sources of vitamin C; they contain potassium and citric acid, and their peel contains valuable aromatic oils. Citrus pith contains bioflavonoids, needed by the body to absorb vitamin C. Citrus seed extract is a natural antibiotic, antiviral, and antifungal.

Buying Citrus fruits are tree ripened and thus ready to eat from the market. Citrons, ugli fruits, and bitter oranges excepted, select heavy fruits with thin skins. As a rough skin indicates a thick skin, it also indicates a fruit with proportionately less flesh. A citrus that's light for its size is an old, dehydrated fruit. Avoid citrus with brown, bruised, or soft spots.

Refrigerate citrus fruit or store in a cool pantry. Do not keep in plastic bags; plastic

---

THE CITRUS RELIGION

Almost religiously, many people consume citrus to ward off whatever ails—from a cold to cancer. I'm not one of those people. Favoring regional fruits best supports our individual and environmental well-being. As right now I can see a snowstorm approaching from the north, a refreshing tangerine is not my typical choice. When I'm building sand castles in Palm Beach, that's another story. This commonsense wisdom of favoring regional foods is, however, a guideline, never a law.

There's a second reason I recommend citrus in moderation. Today a principal cause of chronic illness is due to the consumption of simple sugars, which includes fruits and their juice. You might, therefore, consider citrus as a treat rather than as a staple. Then note if it makes any difference to your overall energy levels and proceed accordingly.

draws moisture from the fruit and quickens spoilage.

Be Mindful For people with food sensitivities, citrus ranks along with the 10 most common allergens.

See **Bitter Orange; Citron; Citrus Peel; Curry Leaf; Fruit; Grapefruit; Kumquat; Lemon; Lime; Orange; Pomelo; Sichuan Pepper; Ugli Fruit; White Sapote.**

CITRUS PEEL
Citrus Zest, Zest

Don't toss organic citrus peels. When finely sliced or grated, the outer part—not the pithy inner white part—is called zest, and, as its name suggests, it gives a lot of flavor. Furthermore, it's remarkably medicinal.

Medicinal Benefits It's curious that while citrus flesh and juice is cooling, its peel is warming. Warming because its high oil concentration makes it a useful medicine for cold and deficient symptoms. Citrus peel supports chi circulation, helps clear phlegm, enhances digestive energy, decongests lungs, and helps relieve intestinal gas, pain, swelling, and constipation. It contains numerous nutraceuticals, such as the antioxidant limonoids, which help combat carcinogens in the liver. As a liver tonic, lime and lemon are more effective than grapefruit peel. *Tridoshic* in nature, citrus peel calms *vata, pitta,* and *kapha.*

Use Zest gives the concentrated flavor of the fruit without adding acid as would the flesh or juice. Use grated orange, lemon, or lime zest, fresh or dried, as a spice in savory and sweet dishes. Cut into julienne strips, zest is an attractive garnish. To make a tea, simmer fresh or dried peel alone or with other herbs for 15 minutes.

Buying Use only organic lemons, oranges, grapefruit, and limes for zest. Despite its pesticide residues and dyes, commercial citrus will up the flavor of a dish, but will not up your

---

ZEST!

With an orange or lemon and a grater in hand, fresh zest is at your fingertips and ready to enliven both savory and sweet dishes as well as tea. Zest is easiest—and least messy—to take from an uncut fruit. Though lemon and orange are the most popular, you may use any citrus variety.

- **Grated Zest** Grate citrus on the smallest opening of a handheld grater, preferably a microplane grater.
- **Sliced Zest** Peel the zest with a sharp knife, zesting tool, or vegetable peeler. Use the strips fresh in bouquets garnis, in medicinal teas, or to flavor a jar of sugar.
- **Julienned Zest** Slice fresh zest strips lengthwise into thin, julienne strips and use as a garnish.
- **Dried Zest** Place zest strips on a saucer and allow to air-dry or sun-dry until brittle (about two to four days). Place the zest in a blender and pulverize. Store, tightly covered.

---

health. Because the rind is not considered a food by the FDA, citrus is treated with toxic chemicals and dyes.

See **Citrus Family; Herbs and Spices.**

CLARIFIED BUTTER SEE **GHEE.**

CLEMENTINE SEE **ORANGE (MANDARIN).**

CLOUD EAR SEE **WOOD EAR.**

CLOVES
(*Szygium aromaticum*)

In ancient China, before an audience with the emperor, people had to chew cloves to freshen their breath. A clove is the dried, unopened bud of an evergreen tree that originated in Moluccas, formerly the Spice Islands, in what is now eastern Indonesia. For more than 2,000 years, Molucca cloves have remained an important spice in Asia and Europe. They have an exceptionally strong aroma. Today Zanzibar and Madagascar are the main clove producers, followed by Indonesia.

The name "clove" comes from the Latin word for nail, *clavus*, for indeed they look like a small, dark nail with a rounded head. Cloves are unusual in that they're the only plant in their genus that is commonly used as a foodstuff.

Medicinal Benefits Strongly aromatic, bitter, and spicy, cloves are a yang tonic that help move chi circulation and tonify the kidney, spleen, and stomach. When there are digestive problems due to "cold" in the stomach, cloves aid digestion and treat nausea, hiccups, and vomiting. They also treat impotence due to kidney deficiency. Cloves reduce *vata* and *kapha*. Oil of cloves is an antiseptic and an effective toothache remedy; it also treats flatulence, bronchitis, arthritis, rheumatism, and diarrhea.

Use Throughout Asia, northern Africa, and many Arab countries, cloves are a favorite spice for meat, grain, and other savory dishes. In Europe and the United States, cloves are primarily used in sweets, especially cold-weather dishes like gingerbread and spice cookies. They're an ingredient in Worcestershire sauce and also a common ingredient in pickling spices. Whole cloves are used to decorate ham. A popular project for grade school children is to make a pomander holiday gift by embedding cloves into an orange or an apple. The cloves preserve the fruit and their perfume is long lasting.

Buying Freshly dried whole cloves are mahogany red, oily, and have a pungent and sweet aroma. If they are black and shriveled, they're old. If ground cloves taste bitter and harsh, they're old and should be discarded.

Be Mindful *Kreteks*, clove-spiked cigarettes, are popular in Indonesia and India and available in the United States. They are equally toxic as regular tobacco; in addition, cloves can numb the throat. Kreteks are not recommended, especially not for people with respiratory infections.

See **Herbs and Spices; Myrtle Family.**

COBNUT See **HAZELNUT.**

COCOA See **CHOCOLATE.**

COCOANUT See **COCONUT.**

COCONUT
Cocoanut
(*Cocos nucifera*)

The tall, tropical coconut palm tree is unusual in that it is so tolerant of salty, sandy soils that it grows right at the beach. This location, coupled with the fact that the fruit's buoyant, protective covering is impervious even to saltwater, has enabled edible coconuts, bobbing along on the Gulf Stream, to float as far as Norway. Unlike other transplanted foods dispersed by colonists and traders, self-sufficient coconuts set sail in their own pods and planted themselves throughout the tropics.

All parts of the plant are used; the fronds for roofing material, the nut's hairy outer fiber for matting, ropes, and clothing; and, of course, the nut meat as an important food and oil source. Although the coconut is popularly considered a nut—and is an exceptional source of lipids and some protein—they are technically a fruit.

Coconut is the most important nut crop in the world in at least 86 countries and most of it coming from small farms. While coconuts are grown domestically in Hawaii and Florida, our commercial supply primarily comes from the Philippines and Indonesia.

Medicinal Benefits Coconut is a warming food that tonifies chi and blood and supports the heart, spleen, stomach, and large intestine. It helps nurture, increase semen, and build energy, blood, and body mass. It soothes internal membranes and has laxative properties. It is especially useful in terms of childhood malnutrition. Coconut milk quenches thirst and is used in the treatment of diabetes and edema and for clearing summer heat.

In addition to being an excellent source of lauric acid, an invaluable medium-chain fatty acid, coconut also contains capric acid, which helps counter sexually transmitted diseases including herpes, gonorrhea, chlamydia, and HIV. Coconut is relatively high in iron, phosphorus, and zinc. Coconut and coconut milk are pacifying to *vata* and *pitta*.

Use The white coconut meat (endosperm) is a popular ingredient. Toasting it caramelizes sugars on the coconut's surface, turning the coconut golden and enhancing its flavor and aroma. Use it with chocolate, fruit desserts, chutneys, cakes, cookies, puddings, pies, and confections. Coconut is also excellent with curries and vegetable, fish, and grain dishes. While it's often coupled with highly flavorful (spicy or sweet) dishes, a little coconut added to a pot of millet or oatmeal elevates an otherwise basic staple. Shredded or flaked, coconut is a common ingredient in trail mixes. My favorite, however, is fresh coconut eaten out of hand as a snack.

Buying Coconuts are available year-round, with a peak supply from October through December.

- **Whole Brown Coconut** Buy a mature, brown coconut that is heavy for its size, has no hairline cracks or soft or moldy spots on any of its "eyes," and that sounds full of liquid when shaken. Some coconuts are sold with a "quick crack" feature—a shallow score around the fruit's equator—for easier opening; these coconuts are wrapped in plastic.

- **White Coconut (Hut)** An immature coconut. Today cultivars are specifically bred to be sold at this stage. The thin flesh is jellylike and exceptionally delicious. The outer white fibrous mesocarp is roughly cut down to form an ⅛ inch

---

COCONUT MACAROONS

Cookies don't get much more healthful—or delicious—than these macaroons. It's with good reason that they're perennial favorites.

Makes about twenty-four 1-inch cookies

- 3 cups unsweetened shredded coconut
- ⅔ cup maple syrup or honey
- 3 tablespoons arrowroot or tapioca flour (or unbleached all-purpose flour)
- ⅛ teaspoon unrefined salt
- 3 egg whites, stiffly beaten

Preheat the oven to 350°F. Grease a cookie sheet or line it with parchment paper.

In a large bowl, mix together the coconut, maple syrup, arrowroot, and salt. Fold in the egg whites.

Drop teaspoons of the batter onto the prepared cookie sheets about 2 inches apart. Place in the oven and bake for 10 minutes, or until the edges are lightly browned. Remove from the oven and allow the cookies to cool on the pan placed on a wire rack. Wrapped tightly, the cookies will keep at room temperature for at least a week.

HOW TO OPEN A COCONUT

To open a mature coconut, use a nut pick, awl, or nail, and first pierce two of the "eyes" (the soft spots on the shell) at the rounded end of the coconut. Drain the coconut water and enjoy it as a refreshing beverage. (If you wish to expedite cracking them open, place in a preheated 350°F oven until the coconut cracks.) Next, place the nut on a hard surface, like cement, and with several sharp blows from a hammer, crack it open. Hammer the halves again to break into smaller pieces. Use a sharp knife to pry out the pieces. (The thin brown seed coat adhering to the white meat is edible and contains nutrients as well as fiber.) Grate, slice, or shred fresh coconut meat, eat out of hand, or use it to prepare coconut milk.

cube. Cut through the cube to get to the delicately flavored flesh within.

- **Shredded or Flaked Coconut** Available sweetened or not; frozen or canned. My choice is organic, nonsweetened coconut from a natural food store that has a quick turnover, as coconut can become rancid. Commercial shredded coconut may contain propylene glycol and sugar. Better yet, "shred" your own in a processor or with a hand grater using freshly shelled coconut for an incomparable flavor and moist richness.
- **Coconut Smiles** The size and shape of a smile, dried coconut slices are available in natural food stores and make a great snack. Fresh coconut slices are available in the produce sections of some supermarkets.

See **Coconut Flour; Coconut Milk, Cream, and Water; Coconut Oil; Fat and Oil; Palm Family; Nuts.**

COCONUT FLOUR

A by-product of oil manufacturing, defatted coconut meal may be added as a flavoring ingredient to baked goods.

COCONUT MILK, CREAM, AND WATER (JUICE)

Coconut water is a thin, sweet liquid that is drained from the center cavity of the coconut fruit. It is available commercially in cans. It's also available if you are on a tropical beach where a vendor with a machete and a straw can present you with coconut water after one thwack of his blade.

Coconut milk and cream are fragrant liquids extracted from fresh coconut meat. The milk is enjoyed as a beverage. Both the milk and cream give body, a silky texture, and sweet flavor to sauces, desserts, and rice pilafs and are featured in Thai, Vietnamese, Indian, and Caribbean cuisine.

Coconut milk is widely available canned. The cream separates from and rises to the top of the milk. To blend the two, shake the can before you open it. Or after opening a can, lift off the cream and use it separately as a garnish or extra-rich ingredient. Cans labeled light coconut milk have had the cream removed. Bypass sugar-sweetened coconut milk intended for beverage use.

Of course, coconut cream and milk are most appealing when freshly made. For milk, place diced white coconut meat from one coconut into a food processor and process until finely chopped. Add ½ cup boiling water and process until fluffy. Line a fine-mesh strainer with a double layer of cheesecloth and pour in the processed coconut. Drain, then twist and squeeze the cheesecloth to express as much milk as possible. To make cream, use ¼ cup water. One coconut yields approximately three cups of milk.

See **Coconut.**

COCONUT OIL

Unrefined coconut oil is remarkable for many reasons besides its nutty flavor and aroma. Since the 1950s, it has been falsely accused of raising blood cholesterol levels. Yes, it is a highly saturated fat—meaning that it is solid at room temperature—but it's an exceptionally healthy fat for all people, and especially for vegans who are often lacking medium-chain fatty acids.

Medicinal Benefits Coconut oil is one of the few significant plant sources of lauric acid, also found in human milk, that enhances brain function and the immune system. Coconut oil is a proven antiviral, antibacterial, and antifungal agent. It's lower in calories than most fats and oils. Moreover, it is more than 50 percent medium-chain fatty acids, the kind that are not stored as fat. Rather, the body metabolizes medium-chain fatty acids into energy. This makes coconut oil a favorite food of dieters and athletes. It does not clog the arteries or cause heart disease. It reduces *pitta* and *vata*.

Use For baking at temperatures above 240°F, coconut and palm oil are the only healthful vegetarian fats available; they may safely be heated to 375°F without becoming denatured. Unlike other oils used for deep-frying, coconut oil is reusable because it remains stable and does not form toxic trans-fatty acids. When heated to high temperatures, however, coconut oil bubbles and froths. To prevent it from bubbling over, deep-fry in a large container and tend carefully.

It's easy to substitute coconut oil for shortening, lard, or butter in pastries. However, reduce the coconut oil measurement by 25 percent because it is almost pure fat. It's more concentrated than shortening, lard, and butter, which contain upward of 20 percent moisture and/or milk solids.

Coconut oil imparts a rich coconut aroma and flavor and adds an almost negligible sweetness—depending upon your dish, this can be a plus or a minus. Coconut oil is also used for massage and cosmetic uses. It reduces *pitta* and *vata*. Coconut oil stores well in a cool, dark place; refrigeration causes it to develop a sweet flavor that is desirable for confections and baked goods.

See **Coconut; Fat and Oil.**

Cocoyam See **Yautia.**

COFFEE
(*Coffee arabica, C. canephora*)

Coffee has been called liquid amphetamine, the devil's brew, or simply "power" by the Arabs, who obtained it from its native Ethiopia a thousand years ago. Everyone is in agreement that it's potent. How much—if any—of this power supports your well-being is an individual question that depends upon your constitution, current health, and individual tolerance. What is undisputed is coffee's popularity. In the United States, 54 percent of adults drink coffee daily, 24 percent drink it occasionally, and coffee is increasingly used as a flavoring ingredient in desserts and confections.

Each small red fruit of the semitropical evergreen shrub contains two white seeds (the beans). These seeds are removed from the berries in one of two methods. The traditional method, which involves fermentation, yields the most flavorful coffee. The second method is mechanical. Most American coffee is imported from Brazil, with Vietnam and Colombia also being key providers. The medicinal plant noni is a coffee relative.

Medicinal Benefits Coffee helps circulate chi and acts upon the liver, kidney, lungs, stomach, and heart. It enhances alertness and is a warming, bitter-tasting stimulant with diuretic and purgative properties. There are numerous and contradictory reports of coffee's healthfulness. It is, however, a known stimulant and therefore best used in moderation, if at all. Coffee, enjoyed judiciously, reduces *kapha*.

Use Coffee is primarily used as a beverage but also to flavor foods and desserts. When combined with chocolate, it is called mocha. Caffeine is used in some medications.

Buying Seventy percent of coffee comes from the superior-flavored *C. arabica*, which is an upland species. An inferior-tasting, less expensive coffee—with double the caffeine—grows on a hardier, larger coffee tree, robusta (*C. canephora*). Cultivated primarily in West Africa, Uganda, and Indonesia, it is typically used in blends and for instant coffee.

Ground coffee oxidizes quickly, becomes rancid, and loses flavor. The best option is to purchase whole beans and grind them prior to use or to purchase small quantities of freshly ground coffee and keep it refrigerated.

- **Deacidified Coffee** When malic acid is removed from coffee, there is a decreased gastric response after ingestion, making this a more healthful product. More healthful, that is, when it is water extracted through ion exchange. Note that deacidified coffee has reduced flavor.
- **Decaffeinated Coffee** The most common way to remove caffeine from coffee is with a solvent, either methylene chloride (a carcinogen) or ethyl acetate; the process leaves chemical residues. Two noncaustic methods are a water extraction method and a method using supercritical carbon dioxide. The problem with these two methods is that it produces

---

HOW TO HAVE YOUR COFFEE AND DRINK IT, TOO

Perhaps to really enjoy coffee, your best bet is to relish a cup as a Sunday or occasional treat rather than as a daily ritual. An Ayurvedic antidote to counter the depleting effect that coffee has on the adrenals and nervous system is to serve it with a pinch of cardamom and ginger. You may also mitigate coffee's acidity—and therefore its damage to the gut—by adding a pinch of salt to your cup.

---

coffee that is far more acidic, making it even more problematic for the small intestine than caffeinated coffee. And decaffeination doesn't remove other strong stimulants in coffee including chlorogenic acid (which raises blood plasma levels), caffeol, and diterpenes.

- **Instant Coffee** Chemically processed and typically higher in caffeine; not recommended.
- **Organic Coffee** Worth the extra price. The chemical residues in commercial coffee include traces of pesticides banned in the United States because they are known carcinogens.

Be Mindful Coffee is an allergen for some people. Coffee—with or without caffeine—stimulates the central nervous system and raises the heart rate and blood pressure. This can leave people feeling bothered, nervous, and anxious. Coffee elevates stress hormones, stresses the adrenals, increases pulse and blood pressure, raises blood sugar levels, suppresses appetite, disturbs sleep, and gives a sense of high energy. Its acids corrode the small intestine's villi and therefore decrease nutrient absorption; heavy coffee drinkers often suffer from B vitamin shortages and have calcium and other mineral deficiencies.

In Oriental medicine, stressed adrenals translate as depleted kidney energy, reduced sexual vitality, and, in the case of pregnancy, increased rate of birth defects. As with any stimulant, coffee aggravates liver function (its acids break down stored fats in the liver) and therefore contributes to irritability and anxiety. In addition, the oils in coffee can increase blood cholesterol.

See **Coffee Family.**

COFFEE FAMILY
(*Rubiaceae*)

This large and widespread family of flowering plants includes one other foodstuff, noni, as well as the flowers gardeia and sweet woodruff.

See **Coffee; Noni.**

COFFEE SUBSTITUTES

Postum, an old-time American hot beverage favorite, is still available, as are another dozen healthful coffee substitutes. Each has a coffeelike aroma and flavor but lacks stimulants and acids. Domestic or imported from Europe, these coffee substitutes are available instant or needing to be brewed. With or without a splash of milk, these beverages are pleasing in their own right. Like coffee, they may be served hot or cold and used as a flavoring ingredient.

Most coffee substitutes, like Roma, Bambu, Cafix, Pero, Inka, and Teeccino, are made of roasted barley or rye. They may contain chicory or other flavorants, beets for coloring, and often malted barley for sweetness. The Belgian-made coffee substitute Yannoh contains acorns. Two grain-free coffee substitutes are Dacopa, which is made from dahlia root, and Raja's Cup, which is a blend of Ayurvedic herbs.

See **Acorn; Chicory; Dahlia.**

COLLARDS
(*Brassica oleracea, Acephala* group)

One of the most venerable of the cabbage family, collards are blue-green with large, smooth, nonheading paddlelike leaves. They're more tender than kale and, typically, sweeter and less bitter.

Medicinal Benefits Collards are a warming food and energetically nourish the blood, lungs, and stomach and help treat liver stagnation. Their flavor is both sweet and bitter. This nutrient-dense green contains multiple nutrients with potent anticancer, antiviral, antibiotic, and antioxidant properties, including diindolylmethane and sulforaphane. Collards contain nearly the same amount of calcium as does milk and are a good source of vitamin C and soluble fiber.

Use Typically, collard stems are separated from the greens and either discarded or chopped and added to soups, stir-fries, or stock. To quickly separate them, grasp a collard by the stem end with one hand and, with the fingertips of your other hand, strip the greens from it. Use the greens in most any recipe calling for cabbage, kale, or potherbs.

Collard greens are a favorite soul food of the American South, where they're well cooked with ham hocks or fatback. To inaugurate the new year with an auspicious beginning, collards, black-eyed peas, and cornbread are traditional Southern New Year's Day fare.

Buying When available, favor small collard leaves, as they're more tender and flavorful than oversize leaves. Select those that are vibrant and with no sign of yellowing. They're available 12 months of the year.

See **Cabbage Family; Kale; Vegetable.**

COMICE PEAR SEE PEAR.

CONFERENCE PEAR SEE PEAR.

CORIANDER SEE CILANTRO.

CORN
Maize
(*Zea mays saccharata*)

What *Zea mays* is to a botanist, and maize to most of the world, is corn in North America. Corn, the most widely used native grain of the Western Hemisphere, originated nearly 6,000 years ago when the Indians of Mexico began selectively breeding a wild grass called teosinte. The early ears ranged in size from a half inch to two inches long.

Columbus returned to Spain with seeds of "Indian Corn" in 1493, and corn quickly spread around the world, following the trade routes of the early Portuguese navigators. With few exceptions, it seemed to adapt to whatever climate it was introduced to.

About 90 percent of domestic corn is fed to livestock. The rest is used for human consumption and in the production of paper, textiles, paints, explosives, and plastics. The United States, primarily in the corn belt, produces nearly 50 percent of the world production of corn. China is the second-largest corn producer.

There are five major types of corn; today they're typically yellow or white, but they may also be blue, red, or variegated. They are:

- **Dent Corn** A deep crease or dent forms on top of each kernel as its soft endosperm dries. Most corn grown today is a hybrid yellow dent.
- **Flint Corn** This corn variety has the hardest, flintlike endosperm, making it difficult to grind. In the United States, colored flint corn is available on the cob primarily as a decoration or as blue cornmeal. Flint corn was introduced to Europe in the 1500s and used in Italy, Romania, and Hungary as polenta, *mamaliga*, and *puliszka*, respectively.
- **Flour Corn** The soft endosperm of this variety makes it easy to grind into flour.
- **Popcorn** This oldest strain of corn has such an impervious hull that moisture trapped within it explodes when heated.
- **Sweet Corn** This corn has a recessive gene, preventing its sugars from turning into starch, and so it is a vegetable, not a grain. (See **Sweet Corn** entry.)

Medicinal Benefits Corn is a chi tonic that strengthens overall energy and supports the kidneys, stomach, and large intestine. Its thermal property is neutral and its flavor is sweet. Corn is used to treat heart disease and loss of appetite, as well as to stimulate bile flow, prevent the formation of urinary stones, lower blood sugar levels, and to treat cases of difficult urination or edema. It reduces *kapha*.

Corn is the only grain that contains vitamin A. Yellow corn is higher in vitamin A than white corn. Relative to other cereal grains, corn is refreshing and an ideal hot-weather grain. As with many other foods, you may assume that the darker and richer the color of a corn kernel, the more flavor it has. What's more, high flavor is an apt indicator of nutrient density.

Use It's primarily popcorn, posole, and sweet corn that are used in their whole form. Corn grits are used as a breakfast cereal. White corn has the blandest flavor, yellow corn has a buttery flavor, and blue corn is earthy sweet with the widest range of flavor components.

Be Mindful Corn, including sweet corn, is often genetically modified (GM) and it is ubiquitous as an ingredient in processed foods. It is tagged "Bt corn," as the gene *Bacillus thuringiensis* has been inserted into the corn, which, when consumed by the European corn borer, perforates the larval digestive tract, causing sepsis and death. Humans have reported adverse reactions to the consumption of Bt corn.

In addition, corn is a common food allergen, and even minute quantities in products as seemingly innocuous as vanilla extract and baking powder can trigger a reaction in sensitive individuals.

If you're eating processed foods, you're eating corn. As an ingredient, corn is found in more than 3,000 grocery food items, including the obvious ones—cornstarch, corn syrup, high fructose corn syrup, and corn oil. But did you know that corn is typically found in baking powder, dextrose, fructose, caramel color, confectioners' sugar, maltodextrin, malt syrup, MSG, sorbitol, food starch, xanthan gum, and much, much more?

See **Chicos; Corn Flour; Corn Oil; Corn Silk; Corn Syrup; Flour; Fructose; Grains; Grass Family; Grits; Hominy; Huitlacoche; Masa; Masa Harina; Popcorn; Sweet Corn.**

CORN FLOUR, CORNMEAL, GRITS, AND PINOLE

> Ma made the cornmeal and water into two thin loaves, each shaped in a half circle. She laid the loaves with their straight sides together in the bake-oven, and she pressed her hand flat on top of each loaf. Pa always said he did not ask for any other sweetening when Ma put the prints of her hands on the loaves.
> —Laura Ingalls Wilder, *Little House on the Prairie*

Grind dried corn and the result is—from coarsest to the finest—grits, meal, flour, and atole or pinole. Different in particle size, these products may be ground from whole or degerminated corn. While the degerminated corn has an indefinite shelf life, it is a vapid-tasting, limp, highly refined product that I don't recommend. Besides, degerminated corn flour is, by law, chemically enriched. Commercial grades of corn flour and cornmeal are usually made from dent corn.

Use Ground corn absorbs more water than do other flours, and yields a drier, more crumbly product. Corn flour imparts a sweet, corny flavor and, when it's yellow corn flour, a beautiful golden color to cakes and cookies. Cornmeal, coarser than flour, is most often used in muffins, cornbread, or corn mush. In Africa and Asia, corn porridge is often fermented.

Pinole, a corn-based dry meal, is made into a sustaining cereal or hot beverage or, roasted, it is used as the primary ingredient in pemmican, the original American trail mix of ground jerky, nuts, fruits, and cornmeal.

Buying Favor stone-ground corn flour for

THE SACRED COLORS OF CORN

Stunning ears of flint corn are available in the fall for decoration. Their colors range—on any one ear—from black, blue, violet, red, and pink to yellow and white. No two ears are alike in pattern or hue.

Traditional Pueblo Indians grow different colored corn for each of the sacred directions and for specific ceremonial uses. Not multicolored corn—rather, the kernels of each ear are one pure color. White corn represents the east, and every morning a pinch of white cornmeal is offered to Sun Father. Blue corn is for the north, red for the south, yellow for the west, and black for above.

its superior flavor and baking properties. Because corn contains fatty acids, whole cornmeal and corn flour quickly become rancid. To avoid rancidity, purchase frequently in small quantities. Refrigerate corn flours in a tightly covered container.

Be Mindful Avoid genetically engineered high-lysine cornmeal. While it does have a superior protein profile, it's not worth the unnecessary risk of consuming bioengineered foods.

See **Corn; Flour.**

CORN OIL (NOT RECOMMENDED)

A popular commercial oil, corn oil is a byproduct of the corn industry. It requires high-tech processing to extract the small (5 percent) amount of oil from corn. Thus it contributes to the formation of free radicals. An additional problem is that commercial corn is genetically modified. To protect your health, avoid corn oil.

See **Corn; Fat and Oil.**

CORN ON THE COB SEE SWEET CORN.

CORN SALAD SEE MÂCHE.

CORN SILK

The silk, or tassel (stylus of female flowers), from any corn variety makes a delicious herbal tea as well as a sweet-tasting stock. Use it as a diuretic to ease edema, reduce high blood pressure, and to help dissolve kidney stones and gallstones. Herbalist Michael Tierra observes that, "Even though it is effective for kidney stones, it is one of the milder and safer diuretics."

Remove the corn husk and then the silk. Use it fresh in season or spread it on a dry surface to dry, which takes about three days. It will be brittle to the touch, look like celery-green silk threads, and taste sweet and corny.

Corn silk is available in the bulk section of herb shops. The commercial silk is brown, matted, and less flavorful than home-dried.

See **Corn; Herbs and Spices.**

CORN SMUT SEE HUITLACOCHE.

CORN SYRUP (NOT RECOMMENDED)

Corn syrup is chemically purified cornstarch, water, and hydrochloric or sulfuric acid. It is available by the bottle as light or dark Karo corn syrup. Dark corn syrup is colored with caramel. This inexpensive sugar-in-solution is widely used as a glaze for meats and vegetables and as an ingredient in marinades, desserts, and candies. Because commercial corn is genetically modified, using it may have unknown consequences to your health.

See **Corn; Fructose; Sweeteners.**

COS LETTUCE SEE LETTUCE.

FUNKY CANDY CANES

Compared to my aunts Rosie and Barbara, who hand-dip chocolates, a candy maker I am not. At holiday time, however, my children—and now my grandchildren—and I open the *Joy of Cooking* and we make candy. When a recipe calls for corn syrup—an ingredient I've never owned—we substitute maple syrup or honey. When it calls for sugar, we use a good dehydrated cane juice. With its chocolate topping, our English toffee looks like the real thing, but to be honest, our taffy that we color, twist, and shape into candy canes doesn't look store-bought. Besides the fun of making quality candies, the best part is their unrivaled flavor.

COTTONSEED OIL (NOT RECOMMENDED)

You can't buy a bottle of cottonseed oil at the store. It is, however, a common ingredient in shoddy salad dressing, margarine, and other processed foods as well as restaurant foods. It's appalling that cottonseed oil is used for human consumption. Here's why.

Cottonseed oil has successfully been used as a male contraceptive because it contains gossypol, a phenol that effectively reduces sperm count. However, it causes numerous toxic side effects and its use has been discontinued in China and other countries. Despite the World Health Organization's strong recommendations to discontinue gossypol research, numerous countries are still looking into its use.

In addition, cotton is a genetically modified (GM) crop, and therefore consuming it puts your health at risk.

But that's not all. Because cotton has a long fruiting period, it is a veritable smorgasbord for the boll weevil and other insects, and so it is one of the most heavily sprayed cultivated crops.

Last, cotton is classified as a nonfood crop and so is treated with chemicals too toxic for food crops (see Be Mindful on page 268). Since many chemical toxins concentrate in the fatty acids, cottonseed oil is the most tainted of oils. I anticipate the day when manufacturers stop using cottonseed oil.

See **Fat** and **Oil.**

Couscous See **Wheat.**

Cowpea See **Beans and Legumes (Black-Eyed Pea).**

Cracked Wheat See **Wheat.**

CRANBERRY
(*Vaccinium oxycoccus, V. macrocarpon*)

A North American native, the cranberry (*V. oxycoccus*) grows in a mat-forming, evergreen shrub in moist woodlands and bogs. It is small, dry, and intensely sour. The larger commercial variety (*V. macrocarpon*) is treated with growth hormones but generally not sprayed with insecticides, as its tart flavor naturally deters bugs. Most commercial cranberry production is in Massachusetts bogs, but cranberries are also produced in Washington, Oregon, New Jersey, Rhode Island, and Wisconsin. Cranberries are relatives of bilberries, blueberries, and huckleberries.

Medicinal Benefits Cranberries are a cold food and dispel heat and damp. They act upon the bladder, kidney, and large intestine. They have a rich source of polyphenol antioxidants, appear to benefit the immune and cardiovascular systems, and have anticancer properties. The tannin in cranberries, a chemical compound called proanthocyanidins, increases urine acidity and inhibits bacteria (especially E. coli) from adhering to the bladder, urinary tract, and teeth. This helps prevent and treat urinary infections and also helps prevent tooth decay and gingivitis. Cranberry consumption also reduces some types of kidney stones. Cranberries reduce *kapha*.

Use While cranberries are primarily associated with Thanksgiving relish, they are also delicious and colorful in cakes, muffins, jellies, and juice. Native Americans pounded them with jerked venison and nuts or fat to make pemmican.

Buying Commercial cranberry juice is usually sweetened; if using this beverage medicinally, consider favoring a cranberry supplement or making your own concentrate. To make your own, simmer the cranberries, covered, in water to cover for 40 minutes. Puree, and sweeten just to taste with a quality sweetener.

THE CRANE'S BERRY

To celebrate spring solstice, I once joined friends to "boil a pot of bush tea" in the deep woods near Lake Athabasca in northeastern Alberta on the Siksika (Cree Nation) Reserve. When clearing snow from the ground to build a fire, we uncovered the previous fall's bright red cranberries. The size of peppercorns and puckery-tart, they were delicious with fresh baked bannock and fire-simmered tea.

Cranberries and their relative blueberries are the only native fruits of the far north—imagine what treasures they were to traditional peoples. Apparently they're also a treat to sandhill and whooping cranes, after whom they are named.

Look for cranberries that are bright red, plump, hard, and shiny. Avoid shriveled, soft, spongy, or browned fruits, which may produce an off flavor. Cranberries will keep up to two months refrigerated. They are at their peak in November.

Dried and sweetened cranberries make a colorful and tangy raisin substitute; you might, however, pay note to what they are sweetened with.

Be Mindful Because cranberries contain oxalic acid, they bind calcium and are best used in moderation, especially by individuals at risk for osteoporosis.

See **Blueberry Family; Fruit.**

CRANBERRY BEAN SEE **BEANS AND LEGUMES.**

CREAM OF TARTAR
Potassium Bitartrate

I remember the time I made grape jelly and tried a shortcut by not straining the juice after it sat overnight. The result was tasty but unexpectedly—and unpleasantly—crunchy with little slivers of tartrate crystals that separated out from the juice.

Cream of tartar is a mildly acidic salt that is a by-product of wine making. Today I keep it on hand for homemade baking powder, and to hold the foam in beaten egg whites for meringues, soufflés, and cakes. Cream of tartar is also used in laxatives.

See **Baking Powder.**

CREAM OF WHEAT SEE **WHEAT.**

CREMINI SEE **MUSHROOM, COMMON.**

CRENSHAW SEE **MELON.**

CRESS
Garden Cress, Peppercress
(*Lepidium sativum*)

Faster than radishes—and sometimes hotter—cress is ready for the table in a mere two weeks after sowing. This diminutive, peppery-pungent salad ingredient originated, and still grows wild, in western Asia.

Medicinal Benefits The mustard oil in cress makes it stimulating and cleansing to the lung and colon meridians. Cress is a tonic herb and diuretic; it stimulates the appetite and is an antianemic. It is also high in vitamin C.

Use Cress is not cooked or dried; its peppery taste is volatile and doesn't withstand heat or moisture. It is interchangeable with watercress in raw dishes and as a sandwich and salad ingredient.

Buying Watch for cress in the sprout section of markets or as one ingredient in a sprout combination.

See **Cabbage Family; Vegetable.**

CROOKNECK SQUASH SEE **SQUASH; SQUASH, SUMMER.**

CROSNE
Chinese Artichoke, Japanese
Artichoke
(*Stachys affinis*)

Here's a small tuber so tender, delicate, and delicious that it is worth seeking out in your farmers' market or, better yet, grow it as a perennial in your home garden. The crosne is, curiously enough, the one root vegetable that is part of the large mint family. This Asian native is related to neither artichokes nor Jerusalem artichokes, but in use and appearance it is similar to the Jerusalem artichoke. In the West, it was first grown near Crosne, France, in 1880s.

Crosnes are small (about two inches long), slender, spiral in shape, with a translucent, pearly white flesh and a thin, buff-colored skin.

Medicinal Benefits Crosnes improve the kidneys, lungs, and spleen and nourish the blood. As they moisten the lungs, this makes them a helpful food for a dry and unproductive cough and for asthma.

Use A crosne tastes rather like a nutty-flavored jicama. Use it as you would the Jerusalem artichoke—served raw in salads, in stir-fries, boiled, in soups, gratinéed, or as a side dish or garnish. Throughout Asia, it is commonly pickled, and in Japan it is an ingredient in *Osechi-ryori*, the traditional New Year's Day celebratory meal.

See **Mint Family.**

CUCUMBER
Gherkin
(*Cucumis sativus*)

The cucumber is one of humanity's earliest food crops; cultivated cucumber seeds carbon dated at 7750 BC were excavated near the Burma-Thailand border. Introduced eventually to India, China, and Europe, the cucumber remains a popular vegetable worldwide. In fact, the Roman emperor Tiberius was so fond of cucumbers that he planted them in carts, and his slaves wheeled them from one sunny spot to the next to catch maximum sunshine. Lacking slave power, I just plant mine and they prosper—even last year's gherkins that climbed up a nearby cornstalk and so were partially shaded.

Medicinal Benefits Cucumber is considered nurturing to the bladder, spleen, large intestine, and lungs. It is considered a cold food that treats hot conditions and helps resolve toxins. A cucumber contains more than 90 percent water (more water than any other food except its relative the melon). This water keeps its internal temperature several degrees cooler than the surrounding atmosphere. No wonder a cucumber clears heat, quenches thirst, relieves edema, and is an effective diuretic.

Cucumbers are considered an *alterative*, a food that tends to restore normal health because of its ability to cleanse and purify the blood and gradually alter the excretory process to restore normal body functions. Cucumbers contain a digestive enzyme, erepsin, that breaks down protein, cleanses the intestines, and helps expel intestinal parasites, especially tapeworms.

Cucumber is used topically for minor burns—simply rub a slice over the burn—and also as a facial ingredient for clearing blemishes and smoothing and softening the skin. Holding a cucumber slice over an itchy, inflamed eye brings relief.

Regarding the USDA's Recommended Daily Allowance of critical nutrients, there's little going for a cucumber except that it contains negligible fat and calories. This, of course, makes it a popular dieting food.

Cucumbers are, however, a superior source of silicon, which is integral for calcium absorption and which is generally lacking in the modern diet. Silicon also helps reduce cholesterol, and it strengthens the nerve and heart tissue. Cucumbers reduce *vata* and *pitta*.

Use Peeled or whole, cucumbers are sliced, diced, or grated for use in salads and slaws or cut into sticks as a finger food. In Asia, cucumbers are typically cooked, but not so in the United States. To make them more digestible, slice in half lengthwise and scoop out and discard the seeds.

The most common cucumber, medium size with a dark green skin, is sold waxed to preserve its shelf life. Peel waxed cucumbers.

Buying Select cucumbers that are plump, firm—almost hard to the touch—and heavy for their size. Avoid those that are pliable, have yellow on the skin or soft spots, or are withered at the stem end. A waxed cucumber has a shiny look and waxy feel, whereas unwaxed its skin is duller.

- **Armenian, Burpless, English, Hothouse, and Japanese Cucumbers** These long—10 inches or more—slender cucumbers are more mildly flavored than the common cucumber. They also have a thinner skin—sometimes with ridges—that doesn't require peeling. Their texture is smoother due to their few and smaller seeds. They may be individually sealed in plastic wrap.
- **Common Cucumber** Dark green, thick-skinned, juicy, and with many larger seeds, our common cucumber is most readily available and—due to its more protective skin—has a better shelf life than the more elongated cucumbers. It ranges from seven to nine inches in length.
- **Lemon Cucumber** As its name suggests, a lemon cucumber is the shape and color of a large lemon but otherwise is similar in texture and flavor to the common cucumber.

A BITTER CUCUMBER? DE-BITTER IT!

If old, or if raised without adequate water, cucumbers develop a bitter-tasting chemical, phenylthiocarbamide. To eliminate bitterness, slice off the stem end and dip it in salt. Now rub this against the exposed cucumber for a few seconds and foam will appear. Discard the end and rinse the bitter-tasting foam from the cucumber.

- **Pickling Cucumber** Harvested at a less mature state so that they'll remain firm once pickled, these small—three to four inches long—cucumbers therefore have a crunchy texture and smaller seeds than the common cucumber. They also have soft spines and a warty skin. Because you can't pickle a waxed cucumber, the pickling cumber is never waxed; it has limited availability in the late summer.

Be Mindful Cucumbers are not advised for someone with a damp condition such as candidiasis or diarrhea. For someone with an excessively cold or sluggish digestion, use cucumber in moderation or favor it seeded and cooked or seasoned with warming herbs such as garlic, onion, and pepper.

See **Gourd Family; Vegetable.**

Cultured Food See **Fermented Food.**

CUMIN
(*Cuminum cyminum*)

Cumin is a parsley family herb with strongly aromatic fruits, commonly called seeds. Popular in India and the Near East since antiquity, today the main countries producing cumin include India, Iran, Indonesia, China, and North Africa.

Medicinal Benefits Cumin is pungent and bitter tasting, with a cooling nature. It benefits the spleen, improves liver function, promotes the assimilation of other foods, and relieves abdominal distention, gas, colic, and digestive-related migraines and headaches. Cumin is *tridoshic.* The essential oil of cumin is a stimulant and is used to treat indigestion, headaches, and liver problems.

Use I use whole cumin seeds and find that, unlike such larger spices as fennel or coriander seeds, whole cumin blends into a long-simmered dish. Ground cumin quickly loses its essence and becomes bitter tasting. When not using the whole seed, use freshly ground cumin powder.

To heighten the cumin aroma, toast it prior to use. A required ingredient in curries and masalas, it's especially popular in Asia, Latin America, and North Africa. I, for one, wouldn't think of cooking a pot of beans or making a jar of pickles without adding a generous pinch of cumin.

Buying Ground cumin has a yellowish hue; it is ground from whole cumin, which is a light tan color. Black or wild cumin, called *kala* in India, is a smaller, darker, more intensely flavored seed; it is often confused with the small black spice nigella.

See **Carrot Family; Herbs and Spices.**

CURLED MUSTARD SEE MUSTARD GREENS.

CURLY CHICORY SEE CHICORY.

CURLY ENDIVE SEE CHICORY.

CURLY KALE SEE KALE.

CURRANT (BLACK AND RED)
(*Ribes nigrum, R. rubrum*)

That currant domestication is recent, a mere 500 years, explains why this small, seedy berry is not very sweet. Red, white, yellow, and black currants grow wild throughout the northern temperate regions of the world, but it is the black currant, followed by the red, that has the most commercial availability.

The currant is a gooseberry relative that grows on shrubs and emits a peculiar, heavy aroma. Its flavor is matchless—not exceptionally sweet, juicy, or tart but decidedly enjoyable. This smooth, small berry, from ¼ to ½ inch wide, is thin skinned.

Medicinal Benefits Currants are remarkably nutritious and, in the United States, most seen as an ingredient in dietary supplements. They are higher in vitamin C than orange juice and an excellent a source of the essential fatty acid gamma-linolenic acid (GLA). Clinical data indicates that this fruit inhibits inflammation and therefore may be of use in treating heart disease, cancer, and other degenerative illnesses.

Use These fruits are widely used in Europe, as their tartness deepens the flavors of savory dishes, desserts, and preserves as well as liqueurs. The white currant is the sweetest; the black is tart and is favored for preserves; while the red is the sourest. You need not remove their stem and blossom remnants, as these soften in cooking.

Buying Wild currants are comparable to domesticated in all respects but size. In well-supplied markets or in farmers' markets, look for currants in August and September. Select those with shiny skins and plump fruits.

See **Black Currant Seed Oil; Fruit; Ribes Family.**

CURRANT (DRIED)
Zante Currant
(*Vitis vinifera*)

Dry the tiny, seedless champagne grape (formerly called zante grape) and you'll have a tiny raisin with a pleasing tart and tangy flavor. It is not to be confused with the fresh fruit known as a currant.

The term "currant" is actually a derivative of Corinth, the Grecian city once known for its small grapes and raisins. Currant cultivation expanded to include the nearby isle of Zante, thus providing the alternative name for currants.

I prefer zante currants over raisins in many baked goods, especially cookies, because their tiny size better holds their shape and is less compromised in mixing.

See **Fruit; Grape; Raisin.**

CURRY LEAF
Sweet Neem Leaf
(*Murraya koenigii*)

"Curry leaves are as important to Asian food as bay leaves are to European food, but never try to substitute one for the other," advises Asian food maven Charmaine Solomon, in her *Encyclopedia of Asian Food*. Curry leaves are similar in shape and size to a bay leaf but impart a mild, slightly currylike flavor. They're a signature ingredient in South Indian, Malaysian, Fijian, and Sri Lankan cuisine. Curry leaves come from a small tropical or subtropical tree that is native to India and in the same family as oranges.

Medicinal Benefits Valued in Ayurvedic cuisine, the curry leaf has antioxidant, antimicrobial, and anti-inflammatory properties. It also helps regulate blood sugar levels and cholesterol.

Use When using curry leaves, either fresh or dried, heighten their flavor by first sautéing them in warm oil (hot oil will cause spattering) and other spices; then add other vegetables or other ingredients. Their aroma and flavor, best when fresh, rapidly declines with dry storage; freezing better preserves their essence. Dried curry leaves are available in Indian or Asian markets; ask when your grocer might have fresh ones, then pull out some coconut milk and plan a celebratory menu accordingly!

See **Citrus Family; Herbs and Spices.**

CUSTARD APPLE SEE **CHERIMOYA.**

Dahl See **D**al.

DAHLIA
(*Dahlia*)

The flashy—even gaudy—dahlia is San Francisco's official flower and popular in backyard gardens across the country. Its tuber is eaten like a potato in central Mexico and, since the mid-1980s, as a natural sweetener and coffee substitute in the United States. Dahlia is a member of the daisy family.

Medicinal Benefits A sweet juice is extracted from the dahlia tuber and cooked at low temperatures to produce a syrup that is 93 percent inulin, a complex carbohydrate that is calorie-free. Since inulin doesn't stress the spleen or result in an increase in sugar in the urine, it is of use for diabetics.

Buying Roasted dahlia extract is marketed in beverage products as a natural brown colorant, and as a chocolate and coffee substitute; the latter is marketed as Dacopa.

See **Coffee Substitutes; Daisy Family.**

DAIKON
Lo Bok
(*Raphanus sativus longipinnatus*)

One of my favorite root vegetables is the giant daikon. I love its flavor, crisp texture, and great versatility. The most readily available daikon in domestic markets are pearly white, carrot shaped, and plump. In Asian markets they're available with green skin and are football shaped; there are also red- or purple-fleshed varieties. Daikon are an easy and rewarding vegetable to grow due to their surprisingly hefty yield.

Medicinal Benefits A sweet and pungent tonic, daikon tonifies the lung, stomach, and liver meridians. It diminishes sluggish feelings, clears feelings of heat and fever, and dispels damp conditions, mucus, and toxins. Fresh daikon contains diuretics, decongestants, and the digestive enzymes diastase, amylase, and esterase. It is effective against many bacterial and fungal infections, and it contains a substance that inhibits the formation of carcinogens in the body. Daikon reduces *vata* and *kapha* and can be eaten in moderation by *pitta*.

Daikon greens help regulate chi and can diminish the appetite.

Use It is not necessary to peel daikon. Wash and grate it to use raw or cut it into the desired shape and cook it as you would a carrot in soups or sautéed, simmered, baked, or braised dishes. Or cut into a fanciful shape and add it to grilled kabobs. Daikon is also a tasty pickle ingredient and condiment. Because daikon aids digestion, in Japanese cuisine it always appears alongside hard-to-digest or fatty foods.

Use the inner, younger daikon greens like turnip greens, but not in lightly sautéed dishes, as their texture is rather coarse. In my garden, I harvest a few leaves from my row of daikon to enjoy the flavor long before I actually harvest the root.

Buying Look for heavy, hard roots with a fresh, vibrant appearance. A withered, flabby,

DAIKON CONDIMENT

This condiment has a bright, fresh taste that clears the palate. Serve it with any meal that contains cheese, a fatty fish, or meat.

Serves 2

- ¼ cup freshly grated raw daikon
- ¼ teaspoon soy sauce
- ¼ teaspoon mirin (optional)
- ¼ teaspoon fresh ginger juice (see pages 154–155) or a pinch of ground ginger powder

In a small bowl, combine all the ingredients, mound on a small condiment plate, and serve immediately.

light-for-its-size, discolored daikon is not worth the purchase price. It will be exceedingly sharp tasting and probably pithy. Refrigerated, the root holds well for up to 10 days but is sweetest when fresh. Daikon may be shipped with its leaves attached but, as the vegetable ages, the greengrocer removes and discards the greens. When available, buy daikon with its tops intact; at home, remove the greens from the root for storage. Some daikon varieties are green skinned at the very top, and in some Chinese varieties the green covers half of the root. Daikon is available year-round. In Asian and natural food markets, both dried and pickled daikon are available.

See **Cabbage Family; Radish; Vegetable.**

DAIRY-FREE MILK SUBSTITUTES SEE **NONDAIRY MILK SUBSTITUTES.**

DAISY FAMILY
(*Compositae Asteraceae*)

Considering that it's the second-largest botanical family of flowering plants, the *composi-* *tae* family actually provides us with relatively few—but important—food plants. Their chief distinguishing characteristic is that each blossom is composed of two kinds of flowers. The center is made up of individual flowers, each of which becomes a seed. Surrounding this flower are the ray petals. Some of this family also has a milky juice called latex. Many roots of this family contain inulin, a complex carbohydrate that helps diabetics lower blood sugar.

See **Artichoke; Burdock; Cardoon; Chamomile; Chicory; Chrysanthemum Greens; Dahlia; Dandelion; Echinacea; Jerusalem Artichoke; Lettuce; Safflower Oil; Salsify; Scorzonera; Stevia; Sunflower Seed; Tarragon; Yacón.**

DAL
Dahl, Dhal

Remove the seed coat of a legume and split it—and you've got dal. Cook it with a full contingent of spices, and this dish, also called dal, is as basic as rice and chapati in Indian, Bangladeshi, and Pakistani cuisine. In fact, dal is a standard accompaniment to both. Since it is typically hull-less and halved, it has the shortest prep time of any dried legume.

Medicinal Benefits Energetically, any split seed is less viable—it can't reproduce itself—and some people contend that therefore dal conveys less energy. It contains decidedly less fiber, which is a plus for those who find fiber hard to digest but, perhaps, a minus for people needing more fiber in their diet.

Buying The most readily available dal in natural food stores is made from red or white lentils. In Indian markets, there's a wide variety—such as *urad, moong, chana, and toovar*—made from peas, beans, or lentils that have been split and decoated; In India dal also refers to any dried legume.

There are two ways to split dal: dry (without soaking) and wet. The more costly mechanical process, dry-split, gives the most delicious dal; it is easily identified because both the flat inside and rounded outer side are smooth. Wet-split dal, on the other hand, is made by soaking, decoating, sun-drying, and then splitting; the legume shrinks on the flat side, leaving a visible depression.

Use Dal is often prepared into a thick, spicy vegetable stew that is a staple in Nepalese and Indian cuisine. Its versatility lends it to other dishes, for example, adding a small amount to a soup to give it body. One of my favorite dal dishes is to cook it as thick as mashed potatoes and then, just before serving, stir in butter-sautéed spices such as cumin, ajawan, black mustard, and chile.

See **Beans and Legumes; Legume Family.**

DANDELION
(*Taraxacum officinale*)

Despite tons of herbicides designed to eliminate it, dandelion reigns indomitable on suburban lawns and byways throughout temperate regions. That gives a clue as to the prowess of this vegetable and good reason to esteem its medicinal properties.

This low-growing weed with its sunny yellow blossoms is Eurasian in origin and today grows wild throughout the temperate world. The dandelion's deeply notched leaves explain its Middle Latin name, *dent leo*, "tooth of the lion."

Medicinal Benefits Dandelion, both root and leaves, is a remarkable bitter tonic for the spleen, stomach, kidneys, and liver. While the greens are cooling, the root is considered cold or very cooling. Dandelion is an effective diuretic (its French nickname, *piss-en-lit*, means "wet the bed"), laxative, and antirheumatic. It stimulates liver function, reduces swelling and inflammation, and improves digestion. Dandelion is antiviral and useful in the treatment

of AIDS and herpes. It treats jaundice, cirrhosis, gout, eczema, acne, and edema due to high blood pressure. It is used to treat (and prevent) breast and lung tumors and to relieve premenstrual bloating. Herbalist Michael Tierra calls it one of the best remedies for the treatment of hepatitis. Dandelion root contains inulin, which lowers blood sugar in diabetics. Dandelion reduces *pitta* and *kapha*.

A cup of dandelion greens provides nearly a day's requirement of vitamin A in the form of the antioxidant carotenoid and a third of the daily vitamin C requirement. It contains double the amount of iron and calcium of broccoli and is an excellent source of potassium.

Use Fresh commercial or foraged dandelion greens (early spring) with a vinaigrette make an excellent salad alone or with other garden greens. If leaves are foraged after the plant blossoms, parboil them to reduce their bitter flavor. From late fall to very early spring, use the bittersweet root as you would a carrot, in stir-fries, soups, or simply sautéed with an onion and garlic. Or use either the root or greens—fresh or dried—in combination with other herbs for medicinal tea.

Buying/Foraging Dandelion cultivars are bred to be more tender and less bitter than the wild plant. Their light green leaves are so large and long that they hardly resemble the darker, small, and jagged-toothed wild dandelion. Cultivated dandelion greens are available throughout the year in many food stores.

I prefer wild dandelions—greens, crowns, and roots—gathered in the spring before they blossom. Their roots and greens are also tasty in the late fall; otherwise, they're too bitter. For mild dandelions, pick those protected by shade or partially mulched over by leaves. Gather dandelions before their buds open and use the whole plant.

Last fall, I dug a dandelion taproot, planted it in a pot of soil, stored it in a dark, cool closet,

AS HOMELY AS A MESS OF TOADS

My season for dandelions begins weeks before the first familiar yellow blossom explodes on the lawn, while the landscape still presents a lifeless monochrome of mud, bark, rock, and dry grass. But the dirt has softened underfoot and the exhalations of soil microbes perfume the air. It's time to harvest dandelions.

I stab down at an angle an inch or so into the cold dirt, trying to sever the root just below its attachment to the leaves to keep the delicate crown, which includes they tiny leaves and tightly folded buds of the blossoms to come, intact.

Lightly steamed, or sautéed with garlic in a little olive oil, dandelion crowns are to me the most succulent vegetable on earth. Buttery soft, with a complex, bittersweet flavor, this venerable dish is not, however, likely to rise to popular status. Dandelion crowns are too much work to harvest and clean. Their sap stains the fingers, and they look as homely as a mess of toads on the plate.

—Peg Boyles, *The Gardener's Companion Newsletter*

watered it as needed, and enjoyed tender, blanched leaves throughout the winter. The idea came from Darcy Williamson, in *The Rocky Mountain Wild Foods Cookbook;* now that I've tried it, I'm going to follow her instructions more explicitly—I'm going to fill a wooden crate.

See **Daisy Family; Vegetable.**

DASHEEN SEE **TARO.**

DATE
(*Phoenix dactylifera*)

The date evokes images of camel caravans plodding through barren sands toward a beckoning oasis shaded by picturesque date palms. These palms provided not only shade and fruit but also a thirst-quenching palm wine made by tapping the trees. The sugary sweet fruit, technically a berry, is one of the most ancient food plants of the Middle East. A tree of dry subtropical areas, the date tree thrives in—and today is planted in—areas like North Africa, Iraq, Iran, and the Coachella Valley in California near Palm Springs. Iraq has long been the primary date producer and currently supplies more than 80 percent of the world's supply.

Virginia Johnson, of Oasis Date Gardens in Thermal, California, recently rattled off a whole list of date varieties that they produce, from "green" fresh dates to pocket dates that dry enough to carry in your pocket but are still moist enough to bite into. Her personal favorite, Halawy, "is what mother used in her fruit cakes."

Medicinal Benefits Dates are sweet, nourishing, and warming and tonify the blood and chi. They help harmonize the liver, lungs, and spleen, and as a result of their astringing tannins, they have cleansing properties for the large intestine and help treat constipation. They build up a person and are used for weakness, symptoms of aging, lack of semen, and impotence. Much like honey is used for sore throats and colds, a date infusion, syrup, or paste helps treat sore throats and chest congestion. Although dates are *tridoshic, kapha* types should use dates in moderation.

As a date dries, its fructose changes to sucrose, and so the drier the date, the sweeter it is. The chief nutritional value of dates is their high sugar content, which varies from 60 to 75 percent. Fresh dates are a premium vitamin C source, but this vitamin is lost when they are dried. Fresh or dried, they're an excellent source of B vitamins, copper, iron, potassium, and magnesium. Their soluble fiber—beta-d-glucan—helps decrease cholesterol and regulate blood sugar levels.

Use The elongated fruits, either dried or fresh, are used as an out-of-hand snack, or chopped and used to sweeten baked goods, puddings, granola, and confections. Dates are often stuffed with almonds or served alongside kumquats. Roasted date pits are used as a coffee substitute.

Buying Dates, today as in antiquity, naturally dry on the tree, making this sweet an unusually "natural" treat, especially when it's organic. Domestic dates may be dusted with sulfur to control a mite. Imported dates are fumigated. By degree of dehydration, they're classified in the following four types:

- **Fresh Dates** While not exactly juicy, fresh dates are higher in moisture content and are lower in sugar than other dates. The yellow Khalal date is hand-harvested before it dries and turns brown. This crisp, fresh date is available in some specialty markets in the fall. Purchase fresh dates that are plump, well colored, and have glossy skins (free from sugar crystals). Refrigerate until use.
- **Soft Dates** Allowed to sun-dry on the tree, soft dates, usually the Medjool and Khadrawy varieties, are then hydrated with steam to plump them back up. The Medjool date, which many regard as the best-tasting date, is Moroccan in origin but also is grown in the United States, Israel, and Jordan.
- **Semidry Dates** With a low moisture content, these dates have a long shelf life and are available year-round. One variety that accounts for 85 percent of domestic production is the Deglet Noor, which translates from the Arabic as "date of light," because when held to the light its center is somewhat translucent.

Other varieties include Bahri, Halawy, and Zahidi.

- **Dry Dates** This driest and least sticky date variety, the Thoory, is often called the Bread date. Its wrinkled skin is firm and colored brown-red with a bluish bloom; its chewy flesh may be hard and brittle, but its flavor is sweet and nutty.

See **Date Sugar; Dried Fruit; Palm Family.**

DATE SUGAR

Date sugar is 100 percent pitted, dehydrated (to 3 to 5 percent moisture) dates that are coarsely ground. Date sugar is about 65 percent fructose and sucrose, and so, if consumed in excess, it upsets the blood sugar balance as does white sugar. Used in moderation, however, date sugar is a quality sweetener, as it contains all the nutrients of dried dates and is certainly more natural and unrefined than most.

Use Date sugar is coarse and is mainly used in two ways: As a sprinkle to top foods like yogurt, breakfast cereals, and baked goods (add after baking to prevent burning). Or dissolve date sugar in hot water to make a syrup, and then use in a similar fashion to honey or maple syrup.

See **Dates Sweeteners.**

DELICATA SQUASH SEE **SQUASH; SQUASH, WINTER.**

DENDÊ SEE **PALM OIL.**

DEVIL'S DUNG SEE **ASAFETIDA.**

DEWBERRY
Trailing Blackberry
(*Rubus procumbens or canadensis*)

A dewberry is similar to its near relative, the blackberry; however, its black fruit is rather squat with a whitish bloom that looks like dew. Because of their less sturdy stems, dewberry vines grow closer to the ground than do the other *Rubus* berries. Dewberries are more delicately—many people say, deliciously—flavored than blackberries, and they fruit earlier in the season.

See **Blackberry; Blackberry Family; Fruit.**

DEXTROSE (NOT RECOMMENDED)

A corn-derived sweetener that is added to granulated cane or beet sugar to create a cheaper sugar. If sugar in the supermarket is not labeled as pure cane or beet sugar, it has been cut with dextrose.

See **Sweeteners.**

DHAL SEE DAL.

DILL
Dillweed
(*Anethum graveolens*)

The most popular American pickle takes its name not from what's pickled—the cucumber—but from the herb that punches up the flavor of this otherwise bland vegetable. Dill is an aromatic herb with delicate lacy leaves similar in appearance to its relative fennel. As with another of its relatives, coriander, both the leaf and seed of dill are used.

Dill's name comes from an old Norse word *dilla*, which means "to lull," because it is a mild soporific; it is used to soothe colicky babies. In the 1800s in America, dill seeds—called "meetin' seeds"—were given to children to chew in church to help keep them quiet. The plant is native to Eurasia.

Medicinal Benefits Dill seed is a pungent, warming, and yang tonic herb that acts upon the stomach, spleen, and kidneys. Dill calms the spirit, aids digestion and insomnia due to indigestion, and relieves hiccups and intestinal gas. It controls infection, is a diuretic, promotes lactation, and alleviates menstrual difficulty. Dill's warming properties help it dry overly moist conditions and therefore helps treat viral conditions. Dill leaf is similar in action but milder and acts more upon the liver than the kidneys. The essential oil of dill is used for flatulence, indigestion, constipation, nervousness, gastric upsets, and headaches. Dill is *tridoshic*.

Use Dill is milder than caraway but sweeter and more aromatic than anise.

It is popular throughout Europe and much of Asia, but it is most prized in Scandinavian, Russian, and Polish cooking, where it appears in breads, sauces, and fish. In the United States, dill is most often used in pickles.

The featherlike greens are added toward the end of cooking because heat diminishes their flavor. Ideally, use fresh dill; or if using dry, use generously, as drying weakens its flavor. Dill seeds are flat and oval and more intensely flavored than the leaf.

Buying In August and September, yard-long stalks of fresh dill are available in supermarkets and roadside vegetable stands. Year-round, its fronds are available fresh or dried.

See **Carrot Family; Herbs and Spices.**

DILLISK SEE DULSE.

DILLWEED SEE DILL.

DINOSAUR KALE SEE KALE.

DIOSCOREA SEE **JINENJO.**

DON QUA SEE **WINTER MELON.**

DRAGON FRUIT
Pitaya
(*Hylocereus*)

The surreal magenta skin of the dragon fruit with its supple, lime green spines makes this fruit a visual standout. Its pink or whitish gray pulp is textured rather like a grainy kiwi and it is filled with tiny black edible seeds. This cactus fruit that is native to Central and South America is favored more for its show than for its flavor.

Medicinal Benefits Dragon fruit is traditionally used to help alleviate constipation, lung congestion, and endocrine problems, and to treat diabetes and high blood pressure and cholesterol. It helps discharge heavy metal toxins through the urine. The fruit—especially the red-skinned varieties—is a good source of vitamin C and contains phytoalbumin antioxidants helpful in preventing the formation of cancer-causing free radicals.

Use Either peel and discard the skin or scoop the pulp out from its skin. Use dragon fruit pulp raw in beverages, salads, or frozen desserts, and it may be candied or made into alcoholic beverages. Some people describe the flavor as being like a bland kiwi and pineapple; others, however, find its flavor offensive. Dragon fruit is available in well-supplied greengrocers, Asian and Latin markets, and online.

See **Cactus Family; Fruit.**

DRAGON'S EYE SEE **LONGAN.**

DRIED FRUIT

As sweet as—and more satisfying than—a candy bar, dried fruit is a natural winner. Drying food is one of the oldest ways of preserving harvest for lean months; and though no longer the necessity it once was, it remains popular. Raisins—not grapes—are essential to an oatmeal cookie, and prunes—not plums—are a morning choice for some people seeking regularity.

Dried fruits are concentrated. Six pounds of fresh apricots, for example, yield one pound dried. A fruit dried without preservatives has enough moisture removed (75 to 95 percent) that it is not subject to decay. Whereas a chemically preserved dried fruit can be 50 percent water.

To dehydrate a food, its moisture is extracted, either naturally or artificially, by air or heat, or both. Some fruit is still sun-dried, which is certainly the most natural method and, where labor is cheap, the most economical method. Fruit dried by passive solar technologies has some commercial availability. Drying by any method darkens the color, changes the texture, eliminates the vitamin C, and concentrates the sugar, minerals, and flavor.

Medicinal Benefits In moderation, dried fruits are nutritive, they tonify the spleen, help build muscle, and nurture body mass. However, dried fruit is a concentrated source of sugar and, if eaten in excess, causes the blood sugar to fluctuate and therefore compromises the spleen. Bushing your teeth after consuming dried fruit helps deter carries.

Dried fruits are easier to digest when rehydrated (especially for *vata* types). If eating dried fruits in their dry state, be sure to consume liquid or they will have a tendency to block the gut.

Use Dried fruits are a healthy sweet snack, delicious on their own, combined with nuts, added to a trail mix, or as a baking ingredient. When hydrated, they're used in fruit salads and compotes, stewed, or pureed for fruit soups and sauces.

If dried fruits are too sticky to cut with a knife, try using kitchen shears—or cleaning the knife blade frequently. To plump fruit, cover with boiling water and allow to soak until softened, gently simmer until soft, or soak overnight. The time varies depending upon the size and thickness of the fruit.

Buying It's prudent to favor organic—and, preferably, domestic—dried fruit. When a fruit is dried, not only its sugars are concentrated, but any chemical contaminants are concentrated as well. Most commercial fruits are grown with chemical herbicides, fungicides, insecticides, and fertilizers. Imported dried fruit is fumigated, and many tropical commercial fruits are adulterated with sugar.

Be Mindful Commercial dried fruits typically contain toxic chemicals and various humectants to retain their moisture and tenderness. Sulfites are especially noxious. In 1986, the FDA banned the use of sulfites on fresh produce but still permits it in many other products, including dried fruits. Your eye can easily spot a sulfured dried fruit, as it will be light—rather than dark—in color and more plump because it retains up to 30 percent more water (making sulfured fruits more profitable to sell). If it's a golden raisin or a pale apple, apricot, or banana, it has been treated with sulfur dioxide, a poison. Bugs won't eat such fruit. It destroys all the B vitamins, retards the formation of red corpuscles, and challenges the kidneys. In sensitive individuals, sulfured foods cause allergic reactions and, in some cases, death. Asthmatics and young children are especially at risk.

See **Apple; Apricot; Banana; Blueberry; Cherry; Cranberry; Currant (Dried); Date; Fig; Goji Berry; Guava; Kiwi; Lychee; Mango; Papaya; Peach; Pear; Persimmon; Pineapple; Prune; Raisin; Sour Cherry; Star Fruit; Strawberry.**

DRIED SWEET CORN SEE **CHICOS.**

THE "HONEY-DIPPING" FIB

Corn syrup or sugar is routinely added to tropical fruits, even though the label may say "honey dipped," "unsweetened," or "fruit-juice sweetened." The fruit is soaked in a sugar water solution until it is saturated to 80 percent sugar. Such fruits often appear in granola, trail mixes, and baked goods.

Tropical fruits that are exceptionally sweet, that have a translucent or glazed quality, or that leave a gritty residue when rubbed between your fingers probably have been sweetened.

DULSE
Dillisk
(*Palmaria palmata*)

Can you imagine seaweed as tavern snack food? Indeed, dulse was served in Boston pubs—especially in Irish neighborhoods—through the 1920s. Today you're not apt to find it in a bar crawl, but do try dulse at your own table. Tear the attractive red-purple fronds into bite-size pieces, mix with a bowl of salted peanuts, set out with some microbrewery beer, and see which goes first.

Dulse grows in smooth, hand-shaped fronds; its Latin name means "palm." It grows from the temperate to the frigid zones of the Atlantic and Pacific, and, oddly enough, it is one of the few seaweeds available in North America that is not eaten in Asia where, in many coastal regions, seaweed is a dietary staple.

Medicinal Benefits Medicinally, dulse is a protein-dense (25 percent) and cooling food with a salty flavor. It's used to strengthen the blood, adrenals, and kidneys and to treat herpes. For temporary relief of irritated gums or a sore tooth, pack a small piece of dulse between the lip and the painful area.

Dulse is a superior source of iron and iodine. Even though it tastes salty, it contains only 122 mg of sodium per serving—that's a fraction of the sodium in potato chips. It is an excellent source of phosphorus, potassium, magnesium, protein, and vitamin A. Dulse is a good source of vitamins E, C, and B complex (including B_{12}) and numerous trace elements. It reduces *vata*.

Use Dulse was a popular food to eat out of hand in Ireland and Alaska. It's chewy at first but tears or cuts easily and has a pleasing slightly tangy, salty flavor. Dulse complements fish, vegetable, and grain dishes, but it is not suited to sweet or delicate dishes or baked beans.

When quickly rinsed under running water, dulse holds its color and is tender and delicious in a green salad or dressing or as a garnish. It makes an excellent bacon substitute in the BLT sandwich. Added to a soup, it gives a seafoodlike flavor, but it is best added at the last minute, as it dissolves after five minutes of cooking. Also add rinsed dulse to stir-fries at the last minute for it to maintain its red color and texture.

Buying Dulse is available packaged in fronds, which are easily torn to the desired size. It's also available as flakes or powder for use as a condiment.

See **Seaweed Family; Vegetable.**

DURIAN
(*Durio zibethinus*)

An equatorial tree native to Southeast Asia, the durian bears a large fruit covered with a semihard green, formidable-looking, spiny shell. Its aroma is so fetid—it's been compared to sewage gas—that some airlines and hotels refuse to admit it. Other people who can get beyond its sulfurous perfume rank the durian supreme of all fruits and regard it as an aphrodisiac. Its flavor is like overripe banana, mango, pineapple, pawpaw, and vanilla. The durian currently has limited availability in the United States.

Use Overripe durians split along seams that are faintly visible among the spines. To open a durian, insert a stout knife into such a line. Durians have about five segments, each containing several seeds surrounded by a rich, juicy custardlike aril, which may be spooned out and eaten as is or used in baking or a milk-based beverage, ice cream, or custard. Frozen and baked preparations diminish the aroma.

The popular Indonesian side dish *tempoya* is fermented durian. Half-ripe fruit is used in soups. Durian seeds are toasted and eaten.

Buying Pick a fruit that is intact, comparatively light, and with a large and solid stem. When you shake a mature durian, you should hear the seeds moving and it should exude a strong—but not sour—aroma. If it passes these tests, insert a knife in the center, and if a sticky knife comes out, it is ripe.

See **Fruit.**

DURUM WHEAT See **WHEAT.**

DUTCH-PROCESS COCOA See **CHOCOLATE.**

ROASTED DULSE

To roast dulse, pick over to remove any foreign material and roast it in the oven (2 to 4 minutes at 350°F) or pan-fry until crisp and the color turns slightly greenish, turning as necessary. Add a squeeze of fresh lemon juice and enjoy as a snack or a side dish. Or crumble it between your fingers and use as a condiment, sprinkle, or an addition to savory nut mixes. Roasted dulse imparts a light sea flavor to breads and casseroles.

E

ECHINACEA
(*Echinacea purpurea*)

Perhaps the most widely used herb used to counter bacterial and viral infections, echinacea is a native North American plant with purple cone-shaped flowers. It is also a popular garden flower and a member of the daisy family. It stimulates the body's immune system against infectious and inflammatory conditions and detoxifies and stimulates digestion. There are no apparent side effects from its use. Echinacea is available as a dry herb and in herbal teas, tinctures, and capsules.

See **Daisy Family; Herbs and Spices.**

EDAMAME
Green Soybean
(*Glycine max*)

Vibrantly green immature soybeans make a fun finger food and a tasty snack. They look like oversize peas in the pod and are available seasoned and cooked. Eating them is rather like shelling peanuts, but you also use your mouth to extract the juicy immature beans. Edamame are also available shucked and freeze-dried to eat like nuts or to add to trail mixes. They are an inexpensive—and nutritious—snack.

Medicinal Benefits Green, immature soybeans are easy to digest (unlike mature, dried soybeans). They're essentially an equal balance of carbohydrates, protein, and fats and an excellent source of vitamin K and folate. They reduce *pitta*.

Use Steamed or boiled in salted water and served as a snack, edamame are seasonally available fresh in Asian markets and farmers' markets. Or you can find them in the frozen food section of supermarkets.

See **Soybean.**

EDDO SEE **TARO.**

EDIBLE BLOSSOMS SEE **FLOWER BLOSSOMS.**

EDIBLE CHRYSANTHEMUM SEE **CHRYSANTHEMUM GREENS.**

EFAS SEE **ESSENTIAL FATTY ACIDS.**

EGGPLANT
Aubergine
(*Solanum melongena*)

The Swedish botanist Linnaeus gave eggplant the Latin name *Solanum insanum*, because Europeans were then convinced that eating eggplant caused—on the spot—insanity. Its name has since been changed to *melongena*, which refers to its dark color. The eggplant was introduced into Europe in the thirteenth century by the Arabs in Catalonia, and its alternate name, aubergine, comes from the Arabic *al-badingan*. The first eggplants were the size and shape of eggs, providing our name for it.

The eggplant is a native of tropical Asia and was first cultivated in India. It is actually a berry and a member of the nightshade family. The most common eggplant in the United States is large, pear shaped, and purple with shiny patent leather–like skin. Smaller, slender Japanese or Chinese varieties, and white, lavender, gold, and green eggplants have increasing availability. They range in size from as large and thin as a cucumber to as small as an olive.

Medicinal Benefits Eggplant is cooling and helps diminish swelling, and it clears heat, feverish conditions, and pain. It has a sweet and astringent flavor, reduces yang energy, and influences the stomach, spleen, and large intestine meridians. It renews arteries, treats dysentery, and is used for bleeding problems and to influence blood in the lower part of the body; for example, eggplant brings energy and blood to the uterus while removing any congealed blood. Because of this, in Asia pregnant women are advised to eat eggplant sparingly if at all, as it can cause miscarriage. Bob Flaws and Honora Wolfe, two Western authorities on Chinese medicine, in their book *Prince Wen Hui's Cook: Chinese Dietary Therapy*, report that these same properties are medicinal in cases of sexually transmitted diseases, ovarian cysts, uterine tumors, and menstrual irregularities (including painful or suppressed menstruation). In moderation, eggplant reduces *kapha*.

Eggplants are mostly water, 90 percent, and therefore low in calories and other minerals, potassium excepted.

Use Eggplant is not eaten raw, but when cooked develops a rich and complex flavor that's featured in cuisines the world over. Moussaka, ratatouille, and baba ghanoush are three favorites from Greece, Italy, and the Middle East, respectively. It's a common ingredient in Indian dishes, and its fleshy, meaty texture makes it a favorite in numerous vegetarian dishes. In fact, eggplant is best when combined with other vegetables—especially strongly flavored vegetables—rather than with meat, fish, or poultry. It may be stuffed and baked or fried, stir-fried, sautéed, baked, or simmered.

Because an eggplant is spongelike in structure with many intracellular air pockets, it soaks up oil like a sponge. When cooked until the eggplant collapses, the absorbed oil is exuded back.

Buying Eggplant is available year-round but is at its peak in summer. Purchase only firm and unblemished eggplants; discoloration or dents indicate a bitter fruit. Avoid spongy-to-the-touch or large eggplants. The smaller varieties generally have a thinner skin, firmer texture, sweeter flavor, and few if any seeds.

Male eggplants have fewer seeds than the female plants, and the seeds of an eggplant are often bitter, according to Sharon Tyler Herbst, author of *The Food Lover's Companion*. The blossom end of a female plant is generally indented, while that of the male fruit is rounded.

DEGORGED EGGPLANT

To improve the flavor and digestibility of large eggplants (which tend to be more bitter than smaller varieties), here's how to degorge, or draw out, their acid and bitter taste. Cut the eggplant into half-inch slices and sprinkle generously with salt. Place on paper towels, cover with additional paper towels, then place a cookie sheet or a cutting board topped with a weight such as full jars or cans, and press for 30 minutes (or, without the weight, press for 45 minutes). Rinse off the salt, drain or pat dry, and cook as directed. A degorged eggplant retains less oil.

This highly perishable fruit should be purchased no more than two days before use. Store in a cool, not cold or hot, area. Summer and fall eggplants are grown commercially in the United States. Those available in the winter and spring are imported from a warmer clime.

Be Mindful Some people find that consumption of eggplant and other nightshade family vegetables exacerbates arthritic-type conditions.

See **Nightshade Family; Vegetable.**

ELDERBERRY
(*Sambucus*)

You won't find elderberries at your nearest convenience store, but you're apt to find their extract in lotions, unguents, and cough drops. Called "the medicine chest of the people," elder is a venerable food and herbal remedy. These tart berries grow wild on large shrubs throughout northern temperate regions.

Our domestic commercial crop comes primarily from Oregon. Elder is in a species to itself and belongs to a small family of flowering plants. It is not related to any other of our foodstuffs.

Medicinal Benefits Elder boosts the immune system and has antiviral properties, which make it effective for relieving colds, flu, fevers, and inflammation. Elder helps clear phlegm and mucus and has diuretic properties. It helps treat skin problems, including acne, boils, rashes, and other forms of dermatitis. It's also used to treat hay fever, rheumatism, neuralgia, and sciatica.

Use According to the diaries of our early American settlers, elderberry pie was a seasonal favorite. The fruits are mildly sweet and may be sauced or juiced or made into jelly. When in season, I sprinkle elderberries over fruit to be grilled or broiled for the beautiful purple specks of color and flavor that they add.

WOODEN WHISTLES AND ELDER BLOSSOM FRITTERS

With his pocketknife and a five-inch length of an elderberry stem (its pithy center lends itself to whistle-making), my favorite uncle, Uncle Grant, used to make a nifty whistle. In short order he could equip a slew of cousins for our own marching band. That's but one reason I'm fond of elderberries.

It's a gorgeous bush that helps hedge my garden. There are plenty of berries for both me and the birds, and then there are their aromatic blossoms. They make elegant fritters. Dip a frond of elder blossoms into a thin batter and cook in a hot oiled skillet until browned on one side, turn, and cook the other side for a lacy fritter bejeweled with countless miniature creamy white elder blossoms.

Their tiny, edible seeds stay crunchy even after cooking, resulting in a slightly gritty taste. So in a pie, combine elderberries with other fruits for a smoother texture. Their blossoms add a muscatel flavor to fruit dishes and beverages.

Buying/Foraging Look for fresh elderberries in farmers' markets in the fall. If foraging, their large, grapelike clusters of purple-black fruits make them easy to spot and identify. There are also several Internet sources for dried and fresh elderberries.

Be Mindful Although the evidence is not conclusive, some sources advise not eating large amounts of raw elderberries. Cooking apparently eliminates a mild toxin.

ELEPHANT GARLIC SEE GARLIC.

EN CHOY SEE AMARANTH GREENS.

ENDIVE SEE CHICORY.

ENGLISH PEA SEE PEA, FRESH.

ENOKI
Enokitake, Snow Puff
(*Flammulina velutipes*)

The creamy white enoki mushroom has a long, threadlike stem with a diminutive round cap; it grows in dense clusters. Its length and color are comparable to a bean sprout, but its gestalt is fairy rings. It is a popular Japanese mushroom.

Medicinal Benefits Enoki inhibits tumor growth and may prevent, as well as cure, liver disease and gastroenteric ulcers.

Use Unlike other mushrooms, the enoki is not earthy but has a delicate fruity flavor. Trim and discard the base. Separate the mushrooms, rinse, and add enoki to any sautéed vegetable, grain, or meat dish. Add them at the end of cooking, or cook them separately and arrange them in the finished dish so they visually stand out, for therein lies their delicate enchantment. A few enoki mushrooms floating in a consommé or clear broth are exquisite.

Buying Enoki mushrooms, packaged with their root section intact, are available in most supermarkets and natural food stores. Purchase those that are firm and white. Refrigerate, in the package, for up to two weeks.

Be Mindful Enoki contains flammutoxin, a protein toxic to the heart, which is rendered harmless when cooked. The trend to serve raw enoki is, unfortunately, misinformed.

See **Mushroom Family; Vegetable.**

ENOKITAKE SEE ENOKI.

EPAZOTE
Mexican Tea, Pazote, Wormseed
(*Chenopodium ambrosioides*)

Epazote is indigenous to the Yucatán peninsula but now grows throughout warm European countries and the United States. Its name is taken from the Aztec words for skunk, *eptal*, and sweat, *tzotl*, which aptly describes its intense, musky-sour aroma. Unlike its assertive smell, its appearance is nondescript. It's a straggly weed that grows several feet high with irregularly toothed green leaves, sometimes splotched with red or purple. Epazote is a very close relative to fat hen.

Medicinal Benefits An acrid and astringent herb with antibacterial properties, epazote increases perspiration and relaxes spasms. Epazote, as its popular name wormseed suggests, is a safe and reliable vermifuge for roundworms. It's used externally for fungal infections, barber's itch, athlete's foot, and ringworm. It reduces *vata*.

Use Epazote has a mild antiseptic flavor that is ingratiating. Foods, typically beans, but also soups, meats, and vegetables, are seasoned with epazote leaves to enhance digestibility, add flavor, and reduce flatus levels. It is commonly used in Mexican bean dishes.

Buying/Foraging Look for fresh epazote in regional Southwestern markets and in Asian and Latino stores. Look for it dried in herb stores, natural food stores, and mail-order suppliers. Or refer to a food foraging book, as odds are it's growing in a nearby vacant lot.

Be Mindful Epazote is not used during pregnancy because it stimulates downward motion in the pelvis. Herbalist Michael Moore in *Medicinal Plants of the Desert and Canyon West* notes that, despite its reputation as an abortifacient or a menstrual stimulant, he doesn't recommend it as such because "there have been many cases of poisoning from taking large amounts of the tea or the distilled oil, and it seldom works."

See **Goosefoot Family; Fat Hen; Herbs and Spices; Vegetable.**

EQUAL SEE **ASPARTAME.**

ESCAROLE SEE **CHICORY.**

ESSENTIAL FATTY ACIDS (EFAS)

The term "essential fatty acids" (EFAs) was coined in 1930 and designates the fragile omega-3 and omega-6 fatty acids that must be obtained through the diet. Unfortunately, this term implies that other fats are less important. Today we know that the more stable omega-9, medium-chain, and saturated fatty acids are also required for optimum health.

The two EFAs are omega-3s (linolenic) and omega-6s; the latter consists of linoleic and gamma-linolenic acid, or GLA. Omega-3s are the most delicate and most lacking in contemporary diets. Unless you eat raw liver, wild (not farmed) fish or game, or the flesh, milk, or eggs of pasture-raised animals on a weekly basis, you'll want to supplement with essential fatty acids. While traditional diets featured these foods, they're lacking in today's menus. As their name suggests, EFAs are an essential nutrient that humans must obtain through diet. The most readily available omega-3 fatty acids come from wild cold-water fish and shellfish. Vegetarian sources are the seeds of flax, hemp, canola, chia, and pumpkin, as well as walnuts, and to a lesser extent dark leafy vegetables; however, vegetarian omega-3s lack two critical derivatives, EPA (eicosapentaenoic acid) and DHA (docosahexaenoic acid), and are, therefore, less absorbable.

The primary omega-6 fatty acid food sources include sesame seeds, sunflower seeds, pumpkin seeds, safflower oil, and many nuts. There are multiple types of omega-6 fatty acids. One of the most lacking in contemporary diets is GLA, available in evening primrose oil, borage oil, and black currant oil. Another omega-6 fatty acid that may be lacking in vegan diets is arachidonic acid, available in meat and other animal products.

Medicinal Benefits When there is an EFA deficiency, the whole body declines and eventually dies. These acids are needed for healthy cell function, brain development,

---

HANGOVER SOUP

Copeland Marks, in *False Tongues and Sunday Bread: A Guatemalan and Mayan Cookbook*, gives an epazote and egg soup recipe traditionally used as a hangover cure, *Caldo de huevo para la goma.* Epazote's ability to increase perspiration would indeed help detoxify, and if you've got the shakes, it would help there as well. Hangover or otherwise, this is a delicious and easy-to-make soup.

Serves 2

- 2 cups water
- ½ teaspoon chile powder
- ¼ cup chopped tomato
- 2 chopped scallions
- ½ cup chopped fresh epazote leaves
- 2 large eggs

In a medium saucepan, combine all the ingredients except the eggs and bring to a boil over medium-high heat. Reduce the heat and simmer for 15 minutes. Drop the eggs into the simmering soup and poach until firm, about 10 minutes. Take care not to break the yolks. Serve hot.

nerve coverings, hormones, bile acids, and prostaglandins. EFAs help maintain healthy blood, circulation, and immune and nervous systems. They transport fat-soluble vitamins, promote normal growth and healthy skin, and contribute to the fatty tissue that surrounds, protects, and holds the organs in place.

EFA deficiency is associated with cardiovascular disease, atherosclerosis, inflammatory bowel disease, cystic fibrosis, brain and behavioral dysfunction, stroke, hypertension, celiac disease, kidney failure, pressure in the eyes and joints, water retention, allergic response, multiple sclerosis, and cancer. By adding EFAs back to the diet, many of these maladies are ameliorated.

Use The good news for omnivores is that if you consume saturated fats, your need for EFAs decreases. If you are able to enjoy wild or pasture-fed animal foods or raw liver, then you do not need to supplement your diet with omega-3s. Most people find it necessary to take EFAs as a supplement or use an unrefined omega-3-rich oil as an uncooked dressing for salads, baked potatoes, or steamed vegetables.

Buying Because EFAs have a limited shelf life and are destroyed by light and heat, take the following precautions. Purchase any oil that contains EFAs in small quantities and purchase only omega-3 oils that list their date of manufacture and a "best if used by" date stamped on the container. Purchase oils bottled in opaque, black, inert plastic bottles and keep refrigerated. When purchasing EFA supplements, favor those that are molecularly distilled.

Be Mindful Because of their fragile nature, oils containing omega-3s should not be heated. Do not use any refined oil containing omega-3 fatty acids (including avocado, canola, pumpkin, soy, or walnut oil), as

the refining will have denatured their heat-sensitive omega-3s.

See **Argan Oil; Avocado Oil; Black Currant Seed Oil; Borage; Canola Oil; Coconut Oil; Corn Oil; Cottonseed Oil; Fat and Oil; Flax Oil; Grapeseed Oil; Hemp Oil; Macadamia Oil, Mustard Oil; Olive Oil; Palm Peanut Oil; Pumpkin Oil, Rice Bran Oil; Safflower Oil; Sesame Oil; Soy Oil; Sunflower Oil; Tea Seed Oil; Walnut Oil.**

Etrog See **Citron.**

Evaporated Cane Juice See **Sugar.**

EVENING PRIMROSE OIL
(*Oenothera biennis*)

Not until dusk in the late spring or early summer does the primrose unfurl its delicate petals. Then to compound the wonder, in the moonlight they glow luminescently to attract moth pollinators. It's always a thrill to come upon the evening primrose, a small plant native to North America that grows throughout northern temperate and subtropical regions. In the West, their four-petaled blossoms are a white-green, whereas in the eastern and central states the blossoms are yellow.

Medicinal Benefits An oil extracted from primrose seeds contains the essential fatty acid gamma-linolenic acid (GLA); it is successful in treating a wide range of medical problems, including arthritis, premenstrual syndrome, obesity, cardiovascular ailments, hyperactivity, diabetes, skin disease, and allergies.

Supplementing the diet with evening primrose oil or other GLA-containing substances may be appropriate for some. Prudent for all would be to avoid those substances that create biochemical obstacles to the body's own formation of GLA. That would include a diet heavy in saturated fats and cholesterol, processed vegetable oil, and alcohol.

Use The primrose root is a long, fleshy taproot with firm, white flesh, rather like salsify. It is a tasty vegetable but one that requires that you forage it or grow it yourself. As with burdock, harvest just the first year's roots.

See **Essential Fatty Acids; Fat and Oil.**

Farina See **Wheat.**

Farro See **Wheat.**

FAT AND OIL

Good fats and oils add pleasure and flavor, as we can quickly verify by recalling the difference between a slice of toast smeared with butter and another with margarine. Also, good fats—called lipids—are essential for our health. Every single living cell in our bodies requires essential fatty acids for construction and maintenance. Shoddy fats accelerate our aging and damage our immune system. We can't live well without fats, and if they are denatured, we can't live well with them. The choice is obvious: Consume quality fats and oils.

In one paragraph, here's a guideline for healthful use of fats and oils: Cook with the stable saturated and monosaturated fats. These fats, which historically are humanity's primary culinary fats, include butter and animal fats and *unrefined* (extra virgin) coconut, palm, olive, and sesame oil. For raw use in salad dressing and such, enjoy *unrefined* polyunsaturated oils, including hemp, avocado, macadamia, walnut and flax oil.

Yes, outdated government and health agencies still warn against consumption of saturated fat from palm oil and coconut oil. Today much lipid (fat) research from independent organizations recommends traditional saturated fats. One excellent resource is Dr. Mary Enig and Sally Fallon's book *Eat Fat, Lose Fat*.

When a fat is liquid at room temperature, it's typically called "oil," but whether solid (saturated) or liquid (unsaturated), it's composed of fatty acids. Every plant and animal requires both kinds of fatty acids.

A plant's fatty acids, found in its reproductive parts, store sunlight energy and contain more flavor and aroma than the rest of the plant. They're precious stuff. Befitting their preciousness, fatty acids require careful handling to protect their integrity. The essential fatty acids are the most fragile and are quickly destroyed by light, oxygen, and heat.

Medicinal Benefits Forget the misinformed "fat-free" craze. We all need both saturated and unsaturated fats. Dietary fats produce body fat needed to insulate and keep us warm and to protect and hold our vital organs in place. The fat-soluble vitamins—vitamins A, D, E, and K—need fat to be bioavailable. Yet another benefit is that fats slow down stomach transit time and so create a feeling of fullness and satisfaction.

Fats help us feel grounded; they impart a sense of feeling soothed and comforted; and they help provide energy and warmth. A food cooked in fat conveys more warmth and energy than does a food cooked in water or steam. That's because fat is denser than water or vapor. Therefore, a sautéed carrot tastes sweeter, has greater flavor range and depth, and is energetically more warming than one that is raw, boiled, or steamed. If you don't have an intuitive sense of this, do side-by-side comparison.

> ### KITCHEN REMEDY TO QUELL JANGLED NERVES
>
> Here's a simple fix to quell hyper nerves from spending too much time at your computer, from being in a strong wind, or from an overly challenging day.
>
> Simply rub coconut or olive oil onto your feet, legs, and forehead—it's so soothing that you might find yourself rubbing it on all the spots in between. Like "pouring oil on troubled water," oiling yourself evokes an involuntary "Ahhhhhhh."

For good health, it's critical to be aware of fat quality: Purchase only unrefined vegetable oils and favor quality animal fats. The fats from pasture-grazed animals and their products (eggs, dairy, and meat) are nutritionally superior to those of factory-farmed animals. They offer more omega-3 fatty acids, a critical nutrient that most Americans are deficient in. They are richer in antioxidants, including vitamin E, beta-carotene, and vitamin C. Furthermore, they do not contain traces of added hormones, antibiotics, or other drugs; nor were they fed the genetically engineered crops corn and soy. The milk of pasture-grazed cows contains 500 percent more of conjugated linoleic acid, an anticarcinogen, than that of grain-fed cows.

Use Important things are worth stating twice: Use only unrefined (sometimes designated extra virgin) oils and fats. Sensually speaking, quality culinary fats enhance eating pleasure because of their own robust flavor and because they carry the flavor of other foods. A guideline is to enjoy one tablespoon of added fat for every meal above and beyond the oils or fats used in cooking. This could include, for example, oil or butter added to bread, potatoes, or grains; oil used to dress a soup or salad; or a generous serving of avo-cado, occasional slice of bacon, or some nut or seed butter as a spread or cooking ingredient.

To skillfully use fats, we need to distinguish between the three primary types of unsaturated fatty acids and saturated fats.

- **Saturated Fats** Our bodies need saturated fats daily, and not just a token amount. Ideally, 50 percent of your dietary fat is saturated. Since saturated fats are molecularly more stable than unsaturated vegetable oils, they are the only fats that can healthfully be used at temperatures between 240 and 375°F. Saturated fats include butter, coconut oil, palm oil, and the animal fats: lard exuded from cooked pork, tallow from beef, and schmaltz from poultry. Lard is the one animal fat commercially available; it is valued for the flavor it imparts as well as for the flaky texture it gives to pastry. Organic lard has limited availability; look for it online or at your farmers' market.
- **Unsaturated Fats** The three unsaturated fats of primary importance are omega-3s, omega-6s, and omega-9s. The first two contain essential fatty acids (EFAs). Any vegetable oil containing omega-3s cannot healthfully be heated above 100°F, omega-6s cannot healthfully be heated above 240°F, and omega-9s can tolerate up to 325°F. It is prudent to avoid refined vegetable oils because they are heated to temperatures exceeding 500°F and therefore are denatured.

Omega-3 fatty acids are important because our common food supply does not provide enough and therefore they are often taken as a supplement. A component of omega-3 fatty acids is gamma-linolenic acid (GLA).

The three quality multipurpose unsaturated

FOOLPROOF TEST OF GOOD OIL

It doesn't take a PhD in chemistry to discern good oils from bad. Simply taste and smell. Compare a superior extra virgin olive oil with any other olive oil, be it labeled pure, virgin, natural, or pomace. If the oil smells and tastes like the food from which it was pressed, that's one indication of quality. If it leaves a fresh, rather than an acrid, burning, or metallic, taste in your mouth, it passes a second test. The third indicator is how the oil feels in your mouth.

Within seconds of swallowing a teaspoon of vital oil, your mouth feels fresh and clean. It's as if your body invites it right in. Conversely, a denatured oil (due to shoddy production or storage) has a greasy taste, coats the mouth, and isn't readily soluble. It's as if your body doesn't want to absorb it. If denatured oil tastes greasy in your mouth, imagine how it gums up arteries and challenges the liver, the organ primarily responsible for fat metabolism.

oils that are a desirable blend of both omega-6s and omega-9s are extra virgin olive oil, sesame oil, and hazelnut oil. They're multipurpose because, lacking the fragile omega-3 fatty acids, they may be used for cooking at moderate temperatures. Of these three, sesame oil and olive oil are superior because they're naturally rich in antioxidants, giving them an excellent shelf life.

Buying/Storing When selecting oils, here's why you may ignore smoke points. An oil reaches its smoke point when it becomes so hot that it releases a bluish smoke and grows close to combusting. Heat damages oil in two ways: It accelerates its rancidity and distorts its molecules. It's crucial to use only oils processed at low temperatures and to not heat them above their safe point, which, typically, is several hundred degrees lower than their smoke point. For example, canola oil's smoke point is 470°F. But its omega-3s are denatured when heated above 100°F.

The best culinary polyunsaturated fats are unrefined olive, macadamia, hazelnut, and sesame oil; for cold applications unrefined hemp, flax, pumpkin, and walnut oil are excellent choices. For cooking at temperatures above 240°F, use butter or ghee or unrefined coconut or palm oil.

I find the best strategy for purchasing quality oils is to do some research and find a trustworthy manufacturer. In my experience, a small or family-owned company or co-op is more apt to be invested in producing a quality product than is a larger corporation.

A quality oil manufacturer presses oil at temperatures under 115°F in the absence of light and oxygen. It's bottled in a dark, opaque glass or inert plastic bottle or a tin can to protect it from light. Because all fresh, vital foods have a limited shelf life, reputable oil manufacturers include a "best if used by" date on the label. Refined vegetable oils, in comparison, are "dead" and have had their flavor and aroma components removed, so it is impossible to detect rancidity with your senses. They'll taste the same today as 25 years from now.

Once you have purchased oil, here's how your senses will inform you as to its quality. Imagine eating sesame seeds, hazelnuts, or olives, and recall their distinctive flavors and aromas. Now, open a bottle of quality oil from that food and it will smell and taste just like food itself. Furthermore, it is delicious and refreshing in your mouth (whereas flavorless refined oil feels greasy, viscous, and unpalatable in your mouth). If what I've purchased doesn't pass my taste test, I cross that producer—and all of his products—off my shopping list.

FAT AND OIL COOKING GUIDELINES

Fatty acids vary in their ability to tolerate heat. Some common sense and the following guidelines will enable you to confidently and skillfully cook with oil at safe temperatures.

- **Sautéing and Stir-Frying**—Add fat to a warm pan, and when it is aromatic, add food. Listen for a subdued "chatter." If the cooking sounds make an angry sputtering, the fat is too hot. Or if the fat starts to ripple or smoke, it is overheated and therefore oxidized. Remove the pan from the heat, allow it to cool, then wipe out all traces of the damaged fat and start over.
- **Baking**—Bake only with saturated fats. Some manufacturers claim that you can healthfully bake with monounsaturated fats because, for example, a muffin's interior temperature remains lower than the oven temperature. Following that marketing "logic," the muffin's interior fatty acids may not be denatured by the heat, but what about the exterior ones? I bake with only butter and palm or coconut oil.
- **Marinating**—A problem with marinades is that if used for grilling or broiling, they're heated above the fat's healthy range. Therefore, in place of an oil-based marinade, consider marinating with only the acid, salt, and other flavoring agents. Then, to protect the heat-sensitive oil, add it after the food is cooked.
- **Deep-Frying**—Consider eliminating, or at least reducing, your consumption of deep-fried foods. Use lard or palm or coconut oil for deep-frying, and do not reuse the oil. When dining out, it's to your advantage to bypass deep-fried foods.

Purchase unsaturated oils in small bottles, refrigerate, and use within six months. Extra virgin olive oil is the exception. It has a longer shelf life and, like saturated coconut and palm oil, does not require refrigeration.

Be Mindful Avoid all refined fats, as they are carcinogenic; they suppress the immune system; they cause gastric distress and irritated lungs and mucous membranes; and they speed aging. Excessive fats and/or poor-quality fats challenge the liver and exacerbate cancer, candidiasis, tumors, cysts, edema, obesity, and some forms of high blood pressure.

Realistically, to favor quality oils requires vigilance. Almost all restaurant foods and baked goods, soups, salad dressings, and prepared foods rely upon cheap, highly refined and, therefore, toxic oils. How astounding that the American Heart Association and government agencies still hype margarine as a healthy food!

Furthermore, be advised that processed foods often contain the genetically modified (GM) canola and cottonseed oils.

Not Recommended Fat and Oil Butter Substitutes, Canola Oil, Corn Oil, Cottonseed Oil, Fractionated Palm Oil, Grapeseed Oil, Hydrogenated Fat, Interesterified (Stearate-Rich) Fat, Margarine, Mustard Oil, Palm Kernel Oil, Rice Bran Oil, Soy Oil, and Tea Seed Oil. These oils lack historical precedent of healthful use by humanity; their manufacturer requires excessive heat and chemical extraction. Some of them (corn, cottonseed, grapeseed, and soy oil) are by-products.

See **Argan Oil; Avocado Oil; Butter; Canola Oil; Coconut Oil; Corn Oil; Cottonseed Oil; Essential Fatty Acids; Flax Oil; Ghee; Grapeseed Oil; Hemp Oil; Macadamia Oil, Margarine; Mustard Oil; Olive Oil; Palm Kernel Oil; Palm Oil; Peanut Oil; Pumpkin Oil, Rice Bran Oil; Safflower Oil; Sesame Oil; Shea**

Butter; Soy Oil; Sunflower Oil; Tea Seed Oil; Walnut Oil.

OIL GLOSSARY

- **Cold Pressed** In theory, this term means that an oil was extracted at temperatures under 115°F. However, the process lacks FDA regulation and shouldn't be relied upon as an indicator of quality because it is often irresponsibly used on highly refined oils. Reputable oil manufacturers state on the label the temperature at which their oil was extracted and may or may not use the term "cold pressed."

- **Expeller Pressed or Pure Pressed** Cooked seeds or grains are mechanically pressed in an expeller (screw) press at such a high speed that high temperatures result. Because of this heat, and the exposure to light and air, the oils begin—from the moment of their pressing—to oxidize and deteriorate. These oils may be termed "unrefined." However, after pressing, they may be deodorized at temperatures exceeding 500°F.

- **Extra Virgin** By FDA regulation, this term refers only to olive oil. If used on another kind of oil, it implies that the oil is not highly refined. But is it? Stating an extraction temperature of 115°F accurately informs the consumer that it is "extra virgin."

- **High Oleic** Seeds that are genetically manipulated to decrease their essential fatty acids yield an oil with a longer shelf life, one that withstands higher heat. I pass on all genetically modified foods (GMs) and strongly encourage you to do the same. Some high oleic oils, however, are derived from hybrid, rather than GM, seeds. Examine the oil label for the manufacturer's stand on GM material.

- **Hydrogenated** Partially hydrogenated oils, typically called shortening, have been in use for more than 100 years and contain trans fats (see below). Avoid all foods containing partially hydrogenated oil. Current legislation mandates their labeling in everything but restaurant food.

- **Interesterified (Stearate-Rich) Oil** Currently hyped as an alternative to trans fat, this process shuffles fat molecules to produce molecules that are rare or nonexistent in nature (as does hydrogenation). Interesterified oils are typically made of fully hydrogenated soy oil. Not recommended.

- **Refined** To increase an oil's shelf life, its color, flavor, and aroma are removed through a multistepped, high-tech refining process that uses toxic solvents, caustic soda, bleaches, and phosphoric acid. In addition, supermarket oils typically contain synthetic antioxidants and chemical defoamers. Sometimes these oils bear a health food label. Buyer beware.

- **Smoke Point** Oil heated to extreme temperatures releases a bluish smoke and is close to bursting into flame; this is termed "smoke point." The toxic smoke vapors turn into acrolein, a varnishlike substance that gums up your kitchen walls and lungs and irritates your throat and eyes. Fats are denatured long before they reach their smoke point. You'll notice that the bottom of a bottle of unrefined sesame or extra virgin olive oil is a little sludgy with specks of sesame or olive debris. These particles will smoke at moderate cooking temperatures and are not to be confused with the extreme heat of an oil's flash point. Likewise, palm oil has an initial "burn off" that is not to be confused with the smoke point.

- **Solvent Extracted or Cold Processed** Mashed seeds are bathed in a petroleum solvent to separate the oil from the meal. It's the most efficient and least healthful method of oil production because not all the solvents may be recovered. If the oil label does not indicate how it was extracted, you may assume that solvents were used.

- **Trans Fats** Any oil that is damaged by heat, light, or air—be it in your own home, a restaurant, or when it was produced—forms toxic trans fats; the trans fats in partially hydrogenated oils are the most harmful. The National Academy of Science advises that there is no safe level of trans fat consumption. The current law enables trans fat levels of less than 0.5 gram per serving to be listed as 0 grams trans fat on the food label. Though this is a small amount, multiple servings can exceed recommended levels. Trans fat content in restaurant and institutional foods need not be listed. However, in Denmark, Switzerland, New York City, Philadelphia, and some other U.S. cities, trans fats are banned from restaurant food. The current substitute for hydrogenated fats, interesterified oil (see above), is *not* a healthy alternative.

FAT HEN
Chinese Spinach, Good King Henry, Lamb's-Quarters, White Goosefoot, Wild Spinach
(*Chenopodium album, C. bonus-henricus*)

Four thousand years ago in North America, cultivated fat hen seeds and greens were staple foods until corn became the dominant crop around 1200 AD. This scraggly green plant remained a valued homegrown vegetable throughout much of the world until refrigerated transportation enabled year-round broccoli. A "mess of greens" often meant a meal of fat hen fried in lard and served with a splash of vinegar. Its name comes from how quickly a chicken plumps up when, after a long winter of only dry meal, these first-of-the-season wild or garden veggies boost her nutrition.

Technically, one variety (*Chenopodium album*) is wild and the other is cultivated; however, garden varieties and wild varieties have long since mixed and merged, and the common names are interchangeable. It may or may not have a purplish stem; at summer's end, the leaves turn a brilliant red. Fat hen is a member of the goosefoot family.

Medicinal Benefits Fat hen, as with other underutilized foods, is more energizing than are our more pampered and cosmetically uniform foods, as you can tell from eating it as well as from comparing nutrient profiles. Fat hen is superior to carrots in vitamin A and has three times the calcium of broccoli. Fat hen has a slightly slippery texture and so is useful in treating constipation, especially in the elderly. Fat hen leaves help cleanse the blood and benefit the liver and lung pathways. The seed is effective in treating dysentery, diarrhea, and eczema. It also acts as a vermifuge.

Use The stems of young fat hen may be used as an asparagus substitute. Enjoy the greens as a mild-tasting potherb, spinach sub-

BEFORE CORN IT WAS "PASS THE FAT HEN, PLEASE"

Fat hen greens and seed remained a food source for some the Tohono O'odham into the twentieth century, as we read in Ruth Underhill's *Autobiography of a Papago Woman*.

> We always kept gruel in our house. It was in a big clay pot that my mother had made. She ground up seeds into flour. Not wheat flour—we had no wheat. But all the wild seeds, the good pigweed (fat hen) and the wild grasses. . . . Oh, good that gruel was! I have never tasted anything like it. Wheat flour makes me sick. I think it has no strength. But when I am weak, when I am tired, my grandchildren make me a gruel out of wild seeds. That is *food*.

> Out of curiosity, I've collected and cooked fat hen seed. The harvesting is easy: With one hand, bend a stalk of mature, dried fat hen over a wide bowl, hold the fingertips of your other hand at the base of the seed heads, and pulling toward the stalk's end, strip the seeds off and into the bowl. The winnowing and cleaning out leaf debris is time-consuming, but your gain is wild and potent seeds. I recommend it to you.

stitute, or salad green. Like spinach, cooking greatly diminishes their volume. From April through September, you're apt to find these tender greens in my salad or soup bowl.

Buying/Foraging This excellent green has increasing availability in farmers' markets. But better than buying it, find a patch of fat hen in early spring while the shoots are just inches high. The leaves are trilobed, like a goose foot, and when young are about the size of a pansy leaf with a silvery cast that looks almost fuzzy. Pinch off the tender green tops for your table. Just like mowing your lawn, repeat this harvest weekly and you'll have abundant greens throughout the growing season. At maturity the stems reach five feet, the seed sets, and the leaves are too bitter to enjoy.

Be Mindful Along with sorrel, fat hen is high in oxalic acids, which, if eaten in excess, are problematic—especially for people with kidney disorders, gout, or rheumatism—because it binds with calcium. Healthy individuals can safely consume fat hen in moderation.

See **Epazote; Goosefoot Family; Vegetable.**

FAVA BEAN
Broad Bean, Horse Bean
(*Vicia faba*)

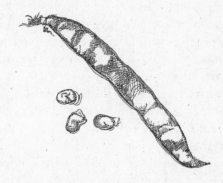

As the words "broad" and "horse" suggest, the fava bean is big—larger even than a lima bean. The pod has a primitive look with a leathery, thick, and downy-covered surface. One of the most ancient cultivated vegetables, it has been found with Iron Age relics in various parts of Europe. Prior to Columbus, and the subsequent introduction of American *vulgaris* bean varieties to the other major continents, fava beans were an Old World mainstay. In the United States, the fava is gaining popularity as a spring and early summer shell bean.

Medicinal Benefits The fava been is neutral in its thermal nature, has a sweet flavor, and tonifies the spleen and kidney meridians. Fava beans are rich in L-dopa, a substance used to increase libido and to treat Parkinson's disease. The bean improves blood circulation and water metabolism. Lui Jilin, in *Chinese Dietary Therapy*, notes two historical Chinese uses of fava beans: For loss of appetite and loose stool owing to weakness in the spleen and stomach meridians, take powdered broad bean mixed with boiling water and brown sugar. For edema and difficult urination due to a deficiency of the spleen function, drink tea made of broad beans. Fava beans reduce *pitta*.

Use Fresh favas have a rich, buttery texture and a sweet, earthy, and slightly bitter flavor. They are available in the spring. Immature pods, up to three inches long, may be cooked and eaten whole like green beans. Mature pods are green with black or brown splotches and down covered with a leathery texture. This pod, which can reach up to 9 or 10 inches long, is shucked to get at the large beans. Each bean is then individually peeled; blanching the beans expedites their peeling.

Buying Fresh favas are increasingly available. Favor small, crisp pods with a bright green color and minimal discoloration. Don't, however, bypass larger and more mature specimens; although the pods aren't edible, the beans themselves are flavorful if slightly less delicate tasting. One pound of pods yields only ½ cup of beans, so purchase accordingly. Although fresh favas may be stored refrigerated (in a paper bag, not plastic) for a few days, plan to use them quickly.

Purchase dried favas, either whole or skinned and split, from a market with a wide selection of dried beans or from a specialty market. Some such markets also may sell fava flour.

Be Mindful In traditional cultures, fava beans are not eaten raw because they can cause constipation and produce jaundicelike symptoms. Furthermore, they cause a small number of people, mostly boys and especially of Mediterranean origin, to develop acute hemolytic anemia, or favism, a potentially fatal disease.

See **Beans and Legumes; Legume Family.**

VIAGRA, BEANS AND THE FATHER OF MATHEMATICS

Pythagoras, a Greek philosopher of the fifth century BC, discovered the numerical relationship of musical tones and is considered the father of mathematics. He's also remembered for founding a religious brotherhood with prohibitions against eating beans because, he maintained, they caused cloudy thinking. Today we know that fava beans—one of the most common beans of Pythagoras's time—contain a natural Viagra-like substance, L-dopa. Perhaps fava beans inclined Pythagoras's brothers to worldly—versus philosophical—concerns.

Or, perhaps, as is believed by some historians, Pythagoras suffered from favism, a congenital adverse reaction to fava beans. It made sense for him and other such sensitive people to avoid this tasty bean, but pity the rest of his buddies.

FEIJOA
Pineapple Guava
(*Feijoa sellowiana*)

Native to southern Brazil and northern Argentina, the feijoa (fay-JOH-ah) is a subtropical evergreen tree that bears egg-size bumpy fruits resembling fuzzless kiwis. The skin ranges from lime to olive green in color and has a tart, tutti-frutti flavor. A feijoa's strong perfume suggests pineapple, strawberry, quince, and a bit of eucalyptus. It has a granular but sweet and creamy whitish flesh that surrounds a jellylike central cavity filled with tiny edible seeds. The feijoa is related to guavas and cloves; the U.S. commercial supply is grown in California and New Zealand.

Medicinal Benefits The most noteworthy property of the feijoa is that it's a rich source of water-soluble iodine compounds. It's also high in vitamin C.

Use The skin is edible, albeit slightly bitter, and in Latin America the whole fruit is often eaten out of hand. When the fruit is slightly soft and ripe, peel or spoon the flesh out of the shell and enjoy it as is or in almost any preparation calling for bananas or apples. The feijoa is tasty in yogurt, fruit salads, compotes, and other desserts. It may be made into jam or jelly. Pureed, it is an excellent flavoring for ice cream, sherbet, flans, and puddings. Note, however, a feijoa's strong fragrance overpowers milder-tasting ingredients.

Buying Once harvested, a feijoa will not become sweeter, so it is imperative to select one with a full fruity aroma. Immature feijoas are bitter, and the seed pulp is white and opaque. A ripe feijoa has clear and jellylike seed pulp; if the jelly is tinged with brown, it is overripe.

If a feijoa is not as tender as a peach, it may be softened at room temperature in a bag with another fruit such as an apple, then refrigerate and use within a day two. Domestic feijoas are available in the fall; imported fruits are available in the spring and early summer.

See **Fruit; Myrtle Family.**

FENNEL
Finocchio, Florence Fennel, Sweet Fennel
(*Foeniculum vulgare* var. *dulce* or *azoricum*)

Fennel is one of our more versatile vegetables as bulb, stalks, flowery greens, and seeds are used. There are two distinct varieties of this Mediterranean carrot relative. Wild fennel (*F. vulgare*) has the small flat seeds, technically the fruits, which are used as a spice; the greens are used as an herb. Sweet or Florence fennel (*F. vulgare* var. *dulce*) is used as a vegetable. This variety has a large, bulblike base, hollow stalks, and threadlike leaves. Sweet fennel has a pleasing licorice flavor.

Medicinal Benefits Sweet and spicy with some bitter tones, fennel is a warming herb that tonifies the bladder, kidneys, spleen, stomach, and liver. It is a yin and chi tonic. Although the whole plant is used medicinally, the seeds are highest in the volatile oil anethole, which treats indigestion, gas, hypertension, and spasms of the digestive tract and increases peristalsis. It helps expel phlegm from the lungs. Fennel is weakly estrogenic and helps stimulate lactation and menstrual periods and facilitate childbirth. It also contains the antioxidant flavonoid quercetin and is therefore anticarcinogenic and of special use for cancer patients following radiation or chemotherapy.

Valued as an eye tonic, fennel tea may be used as eye drops or a compress to reduce eye inflammation. Some evidence suggests that fennel seed extract treats glaucoma. The essential oil of fennel is a diuretic and is used for treating digestive problems, menopause, obesity, constipation, kidney stones, and nausea. Fennel is considered *tridoshic.*

Use Fennel seed is a popular ingredient in curries, breads—especially rye bread—crackers, pickles, vinegar, vegetable and grain dishes, sausage, and liqueur and to season apple pie. In Indian restaurants, a saucer of fennel seeds is served after a meal as a digestive. Wild fennel leaves are also used as an herb.

As a vegetable, enjoy fennel—cooked or raw—in any recipe calling for celery. Its feathery leaves can serve both as a garnish and as a flavoring agent. Cooking softens its licorice flavor. If serving fennel raw, remove the strings from the outer layers of the bulb. Cut or slice as desired. Fennel is great in salads or braised, boiled, sautéed, baked, broiled, or grilled.

Buying Peak season for sweet fennel is fall through spring. Select unblemished bulbs, which look crisp and have soft, fragrant blue-green leaves. The bulb should be medium size, well developed, firm, and pearly white with no sign of browning. Fennel does not store well. Wrap tightly in plastic and keep in the refrigerator for up to four days.

Favor fennel seeds that are green or greenish brown and vibrant-looking; with age, they turn a dull gray. The seeds are similar in size and appearance to anise seeds.

See **Carrot Family; Herbs and Spices; Vegetable.**

FENUGREEK GREENS AND SEED
Aloo Methi, Hilba, Methi
(*Trigonella foenum-graecum*)

Fenugreek is a member of the large legume family, but its seeds are used as a spice and its greens are used as a potherb. One of the oldest known and most valued medicinal plants, it was first mentioned in Egypt's most ancient medical writings, the Ebers papyrus, dating from 1500 BC.

Fenugreek greens are mildly bitter in flavor and similar in appearance to pea or clover greens. Fenugreek seeds are mustard yellow, rhombic (unequal adjacent sides) in shape, and smaller than a grain of wheat. This spice has an aroma like maple syrup and is used in the production of artificial maple syrup.

Medicinal Benefits Fenugreek seed is highly valued in both Chinese and Ayurvedic medicine as a regenerative and aphrodisiac. It is a warming herb and yang tonic that supports the liver, lungs, spleen, and kidneys and the male sexual organs. It increases milk flow, stimulates the uterus (not for use in pregnancy, though it is excellent for postpartum use), enhances digestion, helps treat allergies, and has antiparasitic and antitumor effects. Fenugreek is helpful for wasting diseases, gout, anemia, and debility. In clinical studies, fenugreek reduces cholesterol and is therefore useful for preventing atherosclerosis. It also helps regulate sugar levels of non-

---

PERSIANS AND FENNEL TROMPED UPON AT FIRST MARATHON

In 490 BC, in a fennel field some 26 miles from Athens, the Greeks defeated the Persians. An Athenian runner bearing this welcome news raced back to town. Since then, the length of a marathon race has remained the same as from the fennel field into town, or 26 miles and 385 yards. The Greek name for fennel is *marathon.*

insulin-dependent diabetics—in Ethiopia it is an herbal treatment for diabetes. Today it is an ingredient in some oral contraceptives. Fenugreek balances _vata_.

Use Raw fenugreek seeds have a nasty, uncooked-bean taste. Toasting reduces the bitter taste and gives the seeds a pleasant aroma and flavor. If overtoasted, however, they become bitter, so just lightly toast them until aromatic. If you inadvertently overtoast fenugreek, one taste will tell; from then on, you will have a sense of how much is enough.

Fenugreek seed is featured in Ethiopian, Middle Eastern, and Indian cuisine. It's used in flavored ghee (both Indian and Ethiopian) and in pickled dishes and spice blends. In the West it's a common ingredient in curry blends but is rarely used by itself.

Add fenugreek greens as you would spinach, to curried dishes and other vegetable dishes. In the Middle East and India, dried fenugreek leaves are used to flavor vegetables and baked goods. They have increasing availability in the United States in Indian and other specialty markets. Sprouted fenugreek seeds may be substituted for alfalfa sprouts in salads and sandwiches.

See **Herbs and Spices; Legume Family.**

FERMENTED FOOD

Why do some foods like chocolate, wine, and cheese taste so delicious? Fermenting magically transforms their original ingredients into something more desirable. Besides upping flavor and nutrition, some lactic-acid ferments, such as homemade sauerkraut, actually strengthen your immune system. Pickling, brewing, and culturing are other terms to describe this process by which friendly enzymes, fungi, and bacteria predigest a food. Fermentation increases the flavor, medicinal value, and nutrition of foods. Eating living fermented foods helps you build and maintain your population of digestive enzymes.

As a baby in utero, you had a sterile digestive tract. Within two days of birth, cultures of microorganisms from your mother's milk and the environment established themselves in your gut—by adulthood, you ideally have 400 species of beneficial bacteria in your colon. Unless, that is, you use chlorinated drinking water, which decimates this flora—as do broad-spectrum antibiotics, some medications, meat containing antibiotic residues, alcoholic beverages, and antiseptic soap and mouthwash. In other words, our collective digestion is not optimum.

That's why many health-savvy people eat unpasteurized and naturally fermented foods. You can rebuild and maintain a healthy population of intestinal flora by adding the right pickles to your diet.

Medicinal Benefits Fermentation, in a manner of speaking, is the predigestion of foods before consumption. Molds, yeast, and bacteria break down the complex components of the original ingredients and synergistically create a superior food.

Some ferments create antioxidants (glutathione and superoxide dismutase) that scavenge free radicals, a cancer precursor. Fermentation generates new nutrients, including omega-3 fatty acids, digestive aids, and the trace mineral GTF chromium.

Lactic acid bacteria are among the principal bacteria active in food fermentation; they contribute to the sour flavor and aroma of fermented foods and inhibit the growth of unfavorable organisms. Lactic acid bacteria in fermented foods help the body produce natural antibiotics, natural anticarcinogenic compounds, and even compounds that retard or inactivate toxins and poisons. Lactobacilli help prevent cholesterol formation and completely

---

YOUR 100 TRILLION INTIMATE FRIENDS

No one has done an exact nose count, but your gastrointestinal tract provides room and board to more enzymes, fungi, and bacteria (100 trillion) than there are people in the world. By the pound, that adds up to three and a half pounds of intestinal flora in the healthy adult intestine. The question is: Are these critters doing their job of assimilating food and maintaining your vitality, or are they wreaking havoc?

If you're in robust health, then your numerous colonies of various microorganisms dwell in a balanced, harmonious environment. If, however, you've taken antibiotics, which kill both the good and the bad bacteria, then the odds are that one or more communities of microorganisms is growing out of control. This creates a toxic internal environment.

To rebuild your population of digestive partners, use a quality fermented food daily (you may also wish to use a probiotic supplement). Living fermented foods repopulate the digestive system with healthful microorganisms essential to proper digestion; they thereby strengthen the immune system and inhibit cancer, bowel disease, and pathogens. They also aid in the digestion of protein, fats, and carbohydrates and the assimilation of vitamins.

---

eliminate an antinutritional factor in soybeans. Undesirable phytic acids found in grains, beans, and seeds are totally removed when fermented.

Buying Unfortunately, the fermented foods most often found in markets and restaurants are dead—rather than living—foods. The microorganisms they contained were killed by heat and/or additives to create a consistent product with increased shelf life.

Quality fermented foods available in most natural food stores with entries in this book are listed below. Other fermented foods that may augment intestinal flora—providing they're unpasteurized—include microbrewery beer, traditionally made cheese and yogurt, kefir, wine, and naturally brewed soft drinks (such as specialty brands of root beer or ginger ale). Homemade vegetable pickles such as sauerkraut and *kim chee* (see recipes page 61 and 234, respectively), do the same, providing they're not canned or cooked. In some natural food stores you'll find raw sauerkraut available in their refrigerated section; it is also available online.

See **Amasake; Kombucha; Miso; Olive; Soy Sauce; Tempeh; Umeboshi; Vinegar.**

FIBER

Fiber in a food is a great boon to your health, and it is in abundant supply in all whole foods. It helps bulk up your stool to support bowel regularity, and it helps lower blood cholesterol. As a health-conscious person, however, avoid added fiber, which, today, is typically a cheap by-product of the bamboo and cotton industry.

The U.S. Food and Drug Administration permits the labeling of fiber from bamboo and cottonseed as "vegetable fiber," and that's why it shows up in your shredded cheese. Unfortunately, such by-products are contaminated with chemical residues not allowed on food products. Enjoy the ample fiber from a sumptuous whole foods diet and pass on inert, tasteless bamboo. Or as a supplement, consider the unrefined husks of psyllium seed.

See **Bamboo; Psyllium.**

PLEASE *DON'T* PASS THE BAMBOO

Imagine sitting down to a bowl of high-fiber breakfast cereal. Splash on some milk and spoon up the bamboo. Whoops, unless you're a panda, something is wrong with this picture. Today bamboo and cottonseed fiber are common ingredients in breakfast cereals, pasta, shredded cheese, sauces, mustard, ketchup, beverages, supplements, batters, and bakery goods. It reduces breakage in products such as pretzels, wafers, chips, and ice cream cones. Why are bamboo and cottonseed fiber used? They're cheap industrial by-products.

FIDDLEHEAD FERN
Ostrich Fern
(*Matteuccia struthiopteris*)

Tightly curled fern embryos look like the scrolled end of a violin and taste like asparagus with a woodsy tone. This wild food treat enjoyed in northern climes worldwide includes the new green shoots of ferns in general, but particularly the ostrich fern. This variety grows along stream banks and in moist pastures, woods, and shaded mountain slopes. The fiddlehead is thus far not cultivated. It is a foraged food with limited availability.

Butch Wells Jr. of W. S. Wells and Son in Wilton, Maine, is a fourth-generation fiddlehead processor of canned and freeze-dried local items. A good season for Wells is to process 40 tons of fiddleheads brought to his plant by local foragers in large plastic trash bags. In *Edible Native Plants of the Rocky Mountains*, H. D. Harrington reports that in Japan and Korea fiddleheads are parboiled, sun-dried, and set aside for winter use. In Siberia and Norway, fiddleheads are fermented into a type of beer.

Use Fresh fiddleheads are a remarkable delicacy, likened to asparagus, artichokes, and morels. To cook fiddleheads, first soak them in cold water and then lightly brush or rinse them to remove their brown, flaky casings. Sauté or steam them for 5 minutes, or until tender. Season with salt and a little lemon juice. Because they lose flavor rapidly, use them within a day of picking or purchasing.

Buying/Foraging "When the flocks of geese have flown over and danger of frost is almost past," advises Frances Hamerstrom, author of *Wild Food Cookbook*, "it is time to look for fiddleheads. . . . Often they are one of the dominant ground cover plants in young woods, and they may invade pastures and meadows in abundance." If fiddleheads grow in your area, by all means forage. Collect the tightly coiled plants when they're under four inches in diameter.

Fresh, freeze-dried, and canned fiddleheads are available in specialty markets. Look for small, vital, jade-green young shoots, tightly furled. In the market, avoid any that are wilted, rotted, or more than two inches in diameter.

Be Mindful Food writer Elizabeth Schneider, in *Uncommon Fruits and Vegetables*, warns against the bracken fern (*Pteridium aquilinum*), which may be extremely carcinogenic. There are some reports of illness from eating raw fiddleheads.

FIG
(*Ficus carica*)

> If I had to mention a fruit that descended from paradise I would say this is it because the paradisiacal fruits do not have pits . . . eat from these fruits for they prevent hemorrhoids, prevent piles and help gout.
>
> —The Prophet Muhammad, Qur'an

Part of the fun of biting into a dried fig is crunching into its hundreds of pinpoint-size seeds. The fig's intense sweetness is yet another pleasure. But it's all those seeds—there can be as many as 750—that explain a fig's curious biology. Each seed comes from an individual blossom hidden within the fig itself. These unseen flowers mature into seeds. And then, as the fig dries and its moisture wicks out, the minuscule seeds dry and, as you bite into them, make a satisfying "pop."

Figs are perhaps humankind's oldest cultivated crop, as they predate by 1,000 years agriculture of wheat, barley, and legumes. When fresh, these elegantly shaped fruits are best eaten ripe off their elegant and large-leafed tree. Once picked, figs won't get sweeter. But they quickly soften, and this makes them highly perishable. As a consequence, about 90 percent of the world's fig harvest is sold dried.

The fig originated in southwestern Asia and was one of the first cultivated fruits to come from Asia to the Mediterranean. A species of fig, the bo, is the tree under which Siddhartha Gautama sat when Buddhism was born. Most domestic figs are grown in the orchard country surrounding Fresno, California, which calls itself the fig capital of the world. A claim that, incidentally, Turkey soundly discredits, with its annual fig production at more than 1 million tons.

Medicinal Benefits Figs are neutral in their thermal properties. They increase energy, reinforce the stomach and spleen meridians, and are lubricating to the lung and large intestine meridians (and are therefore useful in the case of a dry cough and as a mild laxative). Figs aid digestion by cleansing and soothing the intestine; they also treat dysentery. In England, Syrup of Figs is a well-known medicinal preparation for constipation; it is included in the British Pharmaceutical Codex. An old Italian kitchen remedy for a lingering cough is lightly roasted dried figs eaten just before bedtime. Figs are *tridoshic*, but dried figs best balance *kapha* and fresh figs best balance *vata*.

Of the common fruits, they contain the highest sugar content. Dried, a fig is about 50 percent sugar; fresh, it is about 10 percent. Dried figs have more dietary fiber than prunes. Of all common fruits, dried figs have the highest overall mineral content—they're high in iron, and ounce for ounce they're higher in calcium than cow's milk. Because figs have edible seeds, they're one of the few fruits that contain the valuable omega-3 and omega-6 essential fatty acids. Figs also contain from 4 to 50 times more bioflavonoid antioxidants than do other fruits.

Use Figs can be enjoyed fresh, dried, or canned. The soft, juicy texture has a sweet, nutlike flavor. Roasted, they make a rich addition to hot beverages. They also make an excellent jam.

Buying Round or pear-shaped fresh figs are available in shades of white, green, purple, and red. Because of their fragility, they're typically harvested when still immature and therefore are lacking in sweetness and flavor. If you're in a fig-growing region, California and a few southern states, the odds of getting a tree-ripened fig are greater. Select plump, soft figs with the skin intact and with a fresh aroma. Figs that are starting to dry are still acceptable. The new crop is available in late August to early September.

Dried figs should be sweet smelling and slightly moist. The two most common domestic dried figs are the light-colored Calimyrna and the dark purple Mission fig. The former was a Turkish native, Smyrna, and was named Calimyrna to acknowledge both its ancestry and its new California homeland; the latter took its name from the Spanish missionaries, who introduced it to California.

See **Dried Fruit; Fig Family; Fruit.**

FIG FAMILY

The common fig is the most commercially valuable of the large *Ficus* genera of predominately woody trees, shrubs, and vines that grow throughout the tropics and in semitropical or warm temperate zones. The common ficus houseplant is of this genera; also included are breadfruit, breadnuts, figs, jackfruit, and mulberries.

See **Breadfruit; Breadnut; Fig; Jackfruit; Mulberry.**

FILBERT See **Hazelnut.**

KITCHEN REMEDY FOR A LINGERING COUGH

This old Italian kitchen remedy for a lingering cough is a tasty cure. Place fresh figs in a shallow, heatproof dish and lightly roast. Eat just before bedtime.

Filé See **Sassafras.**

Finocchio See **Fennel.**

Flageolet See **Beans and Legumes.**

Flat Cabbage See **Tatsoi.**

FLAX OIL

Flax oil readily combines with oxygen, then thickens and hardens, which makes it an excellent varnish; it is available by its industrial name, linseed oil. Stir in pigment and you've got a paint that will dry to a hardened gloss. Our interest in flax oil is, however, culinary.

In northern European countries too cold to produce more stable unsaturated oils, freshly pressed flax oil was a primary polyunsaturated oil until World War II. It was sold by street vendors who made weekly rounds through a neighborhood, assuring a fresh and healthful product. Following the war, fresh flax oil was replaced by cheap refined oils with a long shelf life; the healthfulness of these oils wasn't questioned until recent decades. Since then, unrefined flax oil has, once again, commercial availability.

Medicinal Benefits Unlike flaxseed, the oil doesn't have laxative or expectorant properties. Although it is regarded as less bioavailable than omega-3 fatty acids from fish or algae, flax oil can be used as a source of omega-3 fatty acids. As such, it plays a critical role in healthy brain function and structure. Flax oil helps support proper thyroid, adrenal, and hormone activity. It strengthens the immune system and helps maintain healthy blood, nerves, arteries, skin, and hair. Flax oil helps transport fat-soluble vitamins and cholesterol and also helps to break down cholesterol.

Use Do not heat flax oil, as heating denatures its fatty acids. Use flax oil in dressings and uncooked marinades, or drizzle over steamed vegetables. Some people take flax oil, by the spoonful or in capsules, as a dietary supplement. If flax oil tastes at all acrid, is intensely bitter, or feels scratchy in the throat, it is old and should be discarded.

See **Fat and Oil; Essential Fatty Acids; Flaxseed.**

FLAXSEED
Linseed
(*Linum usitatissimum*)

Flax is a bright plant with small blue flowers topping slender but tough stems—a soothing sight to see. And when the seeds are encased in a small silk eye pillow (available in natural food stores), they soothe tired eyes. The fibrous flax stems are spun into linen and used in papermaking. Linen and linseed oil have culinary and industrial uses. But in terms of health, the tiny, flat, brown seeds are most outstanding, for flax is a superior source of omega-3 fatty acids. There is also a larger yellow or golden flaxseed (Linola) that is very low in omega-3s.

Flax was used by late Stone Age lake dwellers in what is now Switzerland and cultivated in Babylon around 5000 BC, making it one of humankind's earliest food supplies. In the eighth century, Charlemagne considered flax so essential for health that he passed laws requiring its use.

Medicinal Benefits Flaxseeds are a sweet, thermally neutral food that tones the stomach and colon meridians. Flaxseeds contain up to 40 percent oil, primarily linoleic and alpha-linolenic acids, which help strengthen immunity, prevent cancer, clear the heart and arteries, and alleviate rheumatoid arthritis. Flax is a superior source of lignan, a mildly estrogenic compound that helps normalize a woman's menstrual cycle and that has anti-cancer, antibacterial, antifungal, and antiviral properties.

Flaxseeds are highly mucilaginous, and when they come in contact with liquid, they become soft and jellylike. This soothing property makes them highly useful as an intestinal cleanser and bowel regulator for diverticulitis and to soothe coughing, sore throats, and chronic bronchial complaints. In excess, however, they may cause diarrhea.

Flaxseed contains prussic acid, which in small amounts stimulates respiration and improves digestion but in excess causes respiratory failure and death. Flaxseeds reduce *vata* and *kapha* and can be used in moderation for *pitta*.

Use Historically, flaxseeds were cooked or pressed for oil, processes that inactivate their toxins. Use flaxseed as a seasoning in baked goods as the Scandinavians do. Some contemporary health advocates recommend grinding flax fresh for use as a raw condiment or supplement.

Buying/Storing Compared to other culinary seeds, flax is inexpensive. Purchase it in bulk from a natural food store; it keeps well at room temperature for many months. However, if ground and held at room temperature, it can turn rancid within a week. Refrigerate ground flaxseed in a sealed container and use quickly; better yet, grind it fresh for that day's use.

See **Flax Oil; Seeds.**

FLORENCE FENNEL SEE **FENNEL.**

FLOUR
Meal

Most people think that flour means ground wheat. Not so. There is a whole realm of non-wheat flours that offer delicious flavors. Each flour excels in its own way and can transform what might otherwise be a mundane dish into a new or even exotic dish. Although most flour is milled from cereal grains, there are also flours made from other grains (quinoa, amaranth, and buckwheat), legumes (including lupin, chickpea, and soy), starchy vegetables (arrowroot, artichoke, cassava, kudzu, lotus, sweet potato, water chestnut, and yam), and nuts (primarily almonds and chestnuts).

Medicinal Benefits A grain of wheat is an integral, balanced food. When it is broken down into minute flecks of flour, it loses its vitality and its essential fatty acids become denatured. Make these flecks into a dough and bake it, and energetically each speck gets baked solidly into place. Digestive enzymes have a hard time getting at these cemented flecks. Whole wheat grains, on the other hand, demand longer chewing, which means they are more fully mixed with digestive enzymes and therefore easier to assimilate. The same is true for the flours of beans, seeds, and nuts. Therefore, for maximum vitality, favor whole foods.

As a convalescing food, soft flour products, such as noodles, dumplings, and hot breakfast cereals, are easier to digest than baked flour products, especially those that contain eggs, a fat or oil, and/or sweetener.

Buying The type of mill that grinds grains has a surprising effect on the flour's performance, flavor, and nutrition. You can easily verify this for yourself by purchasing different flours and testing them in the same recipe.

The best flour comes from stone mills where layers are flaked off the grain. This is a cool milling process, and essential fatty acids are not damaged. Stone-ground flour is labeled as such at the market. Or purchase a home stone flour mill, either hand-operated or electric. The mills are available in either synthetic or natural stone.

The majority of commercial mills are hammer mills or blade mills. The hammer mill smashes grains into bits. The blade mill is like a gigantic blender, which chops grains into particles. Unless a commercial flour is labeled stone-ground, you can assume that it was milled by the more economical hammer or blade method.

Any whole grain, bean, or nut flour has a limited shelf life. When buying such flour, purchase it from a local retailer who has quick turnover and who refrigerates the flour. Once home, store the flour in a covered container in a cool, dark place or refrigerate it.

If you have the luxury of having your own grain mill or, like the people in Creston, British Columbia, have access to a village mill, grind your own flour 12 hours prior to use. Until then, it is "green," as they say, and performs poorly. Soybeans and nuts, because of their high fat content, may not be ground in a stone grain mill, as their fat adheres to and gums up the stones.

Be Mindful As gluten is one of the most common allergens, many people on healing diets avoid the flour of wheat (including sprouted wheat, Kamut, khorasan, and spelt), rye, and barley.

See **Amaranth Flour; Arrowroot; Barley Flour; Buckwheat Flour; Cassava Flour; Chestnut Flour; Chickpea Flour; Corn Flour; Grits; Cornmeal; Millet Flour; Oat Flour; Quinoa Flour; Rice Flour; Rye Flour; Soy Flour; Tef Flour; Wheat Flour.**

FLOWER BLOSSOMS

Like the faces of children, flower blossoms invite the eye and delight the heart. Their fragrance and essential oils, which are related to warmth, add a magical warming touch to a meal. Indeed, a blossom's inner temperature is higher than the temperature outside, though sometimes only a microthermometer will show this. Blossoms invite a pause and a deeper breath. They uplift the spirit and somehow make the whole meal taste better.

Medicinal Benefits Blossoms, often the brightest and most striking part of the plant, convey the most energy. Sweet-tasting flowers (like honeysuckle) calm *vata* and *pitta*; pungent blossoms (like nasturtium) reduce *kapha*. Bitter and astringent flowers (like marigold) reduce *pitta* and *kapha*.

To sensitive individuals, blossoms may cause allergic reactions. Moreover, some are poisonous. Do not eat Oriental lilies, lily of the valley, sweet pea, or any of the narcissus family (daffodils, narcissus, paper-whites, and jonquils). While the seeds of sunflowers are edible, their petals are not.

Use Flowers often taste similar to how they smell and are mainly used raw in salads or as a garnish. Because flavors differ from variety to variety, always taste blossoms before use. For example, some roses taste alluringly sweet while others are sour, bitter, or metallic. Tasting first also tells you how much—and which parts—to use. The center disk in some flowers, like a daisy or sunflower, is bitter and is not used. Likewise, discard the base or cup of a chrysanthemum, carnation, or dandelion.

Some small- and medium-size blossoms are used whole. Unless stuffed, large blossoms—like the nasturtium or squash—may be sliced or torn. Susan Belsinger, author of *Edible Flowers*, recommends stuffing nasturtiums with guacamole for stellar flavor, color, and texture.

Edible flowers include:

- **Decorative Flowers** Carnation, chrysanthemum, daisy, daylily, fuchsia, geranium (scented), gladiolus, hibiscus, hollyhock, honeysuckle, Johnny-jump-up, lavender, lilac, marigold (taste first, some varieties are very bitter), nasturtium, pansy, pinks, rose, viola, and violet.

FLOWER BLOSSOM PRESERVES

Honey is a preservative and can be flavored with any organic edible blossom. The blossom imbues the honey with its flavor essence and essential oils. Just as blossoms uplift our spirits, eating a blossom concentrate imparts a sense of well-being and uplifted energy.

For flavor and aroma, strawberry blossom spread is my favorite. For color and delight, wild purple violet spread is unbeatable. Dandelion blossom spread has a sunny energy and mellow, pleasing flavor. I often make a blend of whichever edible blossoms are at hand.

I recommend using local unpasteurized honey. (Some health-care experts maintain that consuming local honey may decrease the allergic response for people with pollen allergies.) I prefer dark-colored honey because it is highest in nutrients and flavor, but, for this recipe, flowers look flashier in a light-colored honey.

Makes about 1 cup

2 cups sweet-tasting edible flower blossoms
1 cup honey

Gently rinse the flowers and blot dry. Remove the stems. With large flower heads, such as dandelions, calendula, or apple blossoms, remove the petals and discard the flower heads. For flowers with tiny heads, like lilacs, rosemary, or violets, remove only the stems. Place the honey in a jar and stir in the blossoms. Cover tightly and set aside at room temperature, then stir after 24 hours. The preserves will be ready to use after 3 days. Spread on toast, waffles, or muffins. Do not refrigerate. The preserves will last indefinitely.

The flowers of some bulbs, such as daffodils and tulips, may be toxic, and so it is best to avoid flowers from bulbs.

- **Fruit Blossoms** All blossoms of edible fruits. Orange, cherry, and strawberry blossoms are a special delicacy.
- **Herb Blossoms** Bee balm, borage, calendula, chamomile, chives, dandelion, dill, garlic, marjoram, mint, mustard flowers, oregano, rosemary, savory, and thyme.
- **Vegetable Blossoms** All blossoms of the cabbage, bean, and gourd families are edible.

Buying/Foraging With the exception of squash blossoms and some flowering cabbage family members, edible blossoms are usually not available from the greengrocer. Harvest blossoms from an organic garden or orchard and, when possible, collect just prior to use. Some blossoms—but not all—may be held for a day or more. To enhance storage of some varieties (but not others like squash blossoms or nasturtiums), submerge them in tepid water for five minutes, drain, wrap in plastic, and refrigerate.

Be Mindful Consume only organic blossoms. Do not use flowers from the florist, which are grown and treated with chemicals.

See **Nasturtium; Squash Blossom.**

FLOWERING CABBAGE
Chinese Flowering Cabbage, Choy Sum (*Brassica parachinensis*)

Similar to broccoli rabe, flowering cabbage is a small, nonheading vegetable with white stalks. Like bok choy, the stalks are fleshy, crisp, and sweet, but these are deeply grooved; in addition to dark broad leaves, the central stalk holds beautiful yellow flowers. Flowering cabbage is milder than broccoli rabe, but otherwise its use and properties are similar.

See **Broccoli Rabe; Cabbage Family; Vegetable.**

FOOD YEAST SEE **NUTRITIONAL YEAST.**

FRACTIONATED PALM KERNEL OIL SEE **PALM KERNEL OIL.**

FRENCH BEAN SEE **GREEN BEAN.**

FRENCH SORREL SEE **SORREL.**

FRISÉE SEE **CHICORY.**

FRUCTOSE (NOT RECOMMENDED)

Fructose is a natural monosaccharide that occurs in fruits and honey and, to a lesser extent, in some vegetables. In whole foods, it is an excellent energy source. Pure fructose could be derived from an apple or other fruit, but this is not financially expedient.

Two cheap fructose products that sweeten countless soft drinks are crystalline fructose and high-fructose corn syrup. While there are technical differences between them, both are implicated in the current high rates of diabetes, elevated cholesterol and triglycerides, gastrointestinal distress, and obesity. As with other highly refined substances (fructose is 90 percent pure), the body reacts to it more like a drug than a real food. Some people experience allergic reactions to fructose; others experience loose stools and abdominal cramping.

Food manufacturers who "naturally" sweeten their products with fructose are, to say the least, misinformed.

See **Corn Syrup; Sweeteners.**

FRUIT

Sensory, sweet, saucy, and (when sun-ripened and fresh) utterly irresistible—these are but a few ways to describe fruit. Botanically, a fruit is the ripened ovary of a flowering plant consisting of one or more seeds and surrounding tissue. Grains, legumes, nuts, and seeds are fruits with skins that become hard and dry when mature. The succulent fruits, in contrast, consist of a ripened ovary with soft, fleshy skin; this description includes the gourd family of cucumbers, squash, and melons as well as what fills our fruit bowl. Tomatoes, peppers, and eggplants, which we think of as vegetables, are also fruits, technically speaking.

Herein fruits are categorized by their common usage rather than their botanical category.

It is curious that fruits from temperate regions may be eaten whole (melons, watermelons, and pomegranates excepted) but not tropical and subtropical fruits. Bananas, oranges, pineapples, and most other tropical fruits have a thick, inedible peel.

Medicinal Benefits In general, fruit is an excellent source of many vital antioxidant nutrients and phytochemicals. Regular fruit consumption is associated with good health and protection against many degenerative diseases. Medicinal uses vary according to the fruit; generally, however, they are refreshing and therefore tend to reduce inner heat. For high-energy, "hot-blooded" people who are physically active and who eat many heating foods, such as meat and fried foods, fruit helps bring balance. Conversely, for people with low energy, who tend to feel cold or who suffer from debilitating weakness or wasting diseases including hypoglycemia, diabetes, candidiasis, or gout, all sugary foods, including fruit, are best used in moderation.

Temperate climate fruits, such as apples, plums, and other stone fruit and berries, range from 10 to 12 percent sugar. Tropical and subtropical fruits (citrus excepted) range from 20 to 60 percent sugar, are higher in vitamin C, and are more cooling than fruits that require four seasons to grow to maturity (an exception

is the warming tropical fruit papaya). Cooking a fruit modifies its cooling properties.

Since fruits are digested more quickly than other food, they are best assimilated when eaten alone. Digestion is especially problematic when fruits are eaten with grains and protein food, because the fruit is digested first, and the other foods start to ferment. Fruit makes an ideal between-meal snack. For fruit as a dessert, consider first washing the dinner dishes, then sitting down to dessert.

An excellent source of natural sugar (predominately fructose), fruits provide quick energy, and their fiber aids digestion. They are low in protein and fat. Potassium and vitamin C excepted, most fruits are a negligible source of minerals and vitamins. However, temperate region fruits have more minerals than tropical fruits.

Use Almost all fruits can be enjoyed raw, juiced for a beverage, used in frozen desserts or cooked desserts, preserved, or dried. Apples, plums, berries, and many temperate region fruits are delicious cooked as well as raw. Tropical fruits, however, are more frequently eaten raw, and many collapse when cooked.

Buying Fruit, due to its high sugar and water content, is more perishable than other fresh produce. For maximum flavor and sweetness, most fruits should be picked when fully ripened. Since when fruit reaches its peak of ripeness it starts deteriorating, most commercial fruits are picked before peak maturity. Allow immature fruits to ripen at room temperature, then eat them or refrigerate them and use as soon as possible. If a fruit is picked when too green, it will never become sweet. For the most flavor, serve fruit at room temperature. Some fruits, such as apricots and grapes, do not continue to ripen if picked immature.

When selecting fruit, consider smell, feel, and weight. Ripe fruits smell lightly fruity and fresh; if their aroma is dank or cloyingly sweet, they have started to rot. A gentle press with your thumb will cause ripe fruit to give a bit. Mature fruits are heavy, rather than light, for their size.

On a per-pound basis, smaller fruits contain more nutrients and flavor than larger ones. This is because in most fruits (and vegetables) the nutrient and flavor components are concentrated in the skin or just under it; the smaller the fruit, the more surface there is in relation to total mass.

Be Mindful All fruits may be irradiated unless, that is, they are certified organic. The most commonly irradiated fruits are tropical and imported fruits and highly perishable fruits such as strawberries and raspberries. Therefore, favor underutilized fruits, local fruit from a farmers' market, and organic fruit; as possible, avoid consuming irradiated foods.

The eight fruits highest in pesticide residues are strawberries, cherries, peaches, nectarines, apples, pears, grapes, and raspberries.

See **Açaí; Acerola; Ambarella; Apple; Apricot; Asian Pear; Atemoya; Banana; Blackberry; Black Currant; Blueberry; Boysenberry; Breadfruit; Cherimoya; Cherry; Citrus Family; Cranberry; Currant (Black and Red); Currant (Dried); Dewberry; Dragon Fruit; Dried Fruit; Durian; Elderberry; Feijoa; Fig; Fruit Conserves; Fruit Juice; Fruit Juice Concentrate; Goji Berry; Gooseberry; Grape; Ground Cherry; Guava; Huckleberry; Imbe; Jabuticaba; Jackfruit; Jujube; Kiwano; Kiwi; Kumquat; Lemon; Lime; Longan; Loquat; Lychee; Mamey Sapote; Mango; Mangosteen; Melon; Monstera; Mulberry; Nectarine; Noni; Papaya; Passion Fruit; Pawpaw; Peach; Pear; Pepino; Persimmon; Pineapple; Plantain; Plum; Pluot; Pomegranate; Prickly Pear; Quince;** Rambutan; Raspberry; Rhubarb; Sapodilla; Star Fruit; Sour Cherry; Strawberry; Sunberry; Tamarillo; Ugli Fruit; Watermelon; White Sapote.

HOW TO SWEETEN A PEACH

The starches in some fruits, such as avocados and bananas, the so-called climacteric fruits, become sweeter after harvest. This is not the case with nonclimacteric fruits; if they are picked while immature, they'll remain immature. A peach, for example, that's harvested while still firm lacks flavor, aroma, nutrients, sweetness, and pleasure. The way to turn an immature peach into a sweet dessert is to add honey. Better yet, if the peach isn't tree-ripened, buy a pear.

PURCHASE WHEN FULLY RIPE (After harvest, nonclimacteric fruits do not become sweeter)	PURCHASE WHEN FIRM (Climacteric fruits continue to ripen and sweeten after harvest)
Apple	Asian pear
Apricot	Avocado
Blackberry	Banana
Blueberry	Grapefruit
Cantaloupe	Kiwi
Cherry	Lemon
Fig	Lime
Grape	Mango
Nectarine	Pear
Peach	Persimmon
Pineapple	Tomato
Plum	
Pomegranate	
Raspberry	
Strawberry	
Watermelon	

FRUIT CONSERVES

Life without jam and jelly is hard to imagine. These fruit products embellish bread and toast, plus numerous desserts and entrées, with nutrition, color, flavor, and pizzazz. The FDA, however, requires a high level of sugar concentration for jam, preserves, and jelly. For people seeking more healthful alternatives, apple butter or fruit conserves made from 100 percent fruit are available.

Fruit conserves that are a blend of fruit and fruit juice concentrates bill themselves as a healthful alternative. Read about fruit juice concentrate and then determine for yourself.

See **Fruit.**

FRUIT JUICE

A glass of fruit juice is indeed a fine treat. Unfortunately, some people believe it's a necessary food staple. I respectfully invite you to reconsider that popular myth. Recall that a whole food gives better nutrition than a part of it does. The juice of any fruit is a "refined" food and is predominately fruit sugar and water. Most of the important nutrients and micronutrients remain in the pulp.

In terms of how it impacts your blood sugar, the fruit sugar in a glass of juice is of comparable quantity to the sugar in a candy bar. Excess sugar—no matter its origin—contributes to hypoglycemia or blood sugar imbalance. According to Oriental medicine, hypoglycemia is the first step—and an avoidable one—toward diabetes.

Please enjoy fruit juice as an occasional treat. It adds a boost to many desserts and beverages. When giving it to children, consider diluting it with water.

Be Mindful The image of a healthy, 100 percent natural organic fruit juice on a label doesn't tell all. By FDA law, fruit juice may contain "press aids" and genetically engineered enzymes. The press aids are pellets of compressed scrap wood. These hidden additives are used to extract the maximum amount of juice from the fruit. I support manufacturers who do not use hidden ingredients. I query juice manufacturers and recommend the same to you. I've found one with national distribution that does not use press aids. A second producer reported to me that they use press aids in their organic apple juice but that all their other juices are enzyme-free. I assume that the manufacturers who ignore my queries use enzymes.

In addition, if a fruit juice is reconstituted from a concentrate, the concentrate may contain added sugar.

See **Fruit; Fruit Juice Concentrate.**

FRUIT JUICE CONCENTRATE (NOT RECOMMENDED)

Here's a dishonest practice. Take a cheap, commercial fruit juice and remove most of its flavor, acid, color, and nutrients through deionization. All that remains is sugar water with a trace of minerals and, if the fruit wasn't organic, chemical contaminants. Manufacturers blend this sugar water in a "healthy" product and then label their product as "natural, fruit juice sweetened." It sounds good. And for the manufacturers, it's been a highly profitable scam since 1990. Fruit juice concentrate appears on the ingredient list as the fruit (or fruits) it was derived from followed by the word "concentrate"; or it may be termed "deionized fruit juice concentrate." The two most common are white grape concentrate and pineapple concentrate. There is also mixed fruit juice concentrate.

Medicinal Benefits Jeffrey Bland, PhD, an internationally recognized leader in the nutritional medicine field, observes, "'Fruit juice sweetened' sounds wonderful, so environmentally and physiologically friendly. But, speaking as a nutritional chemist, when we get down to chemical compositions and investigate how these things are processed, they start to look very similar to refined sugars from other sources. They are not a significant source of nutrition and may actually sap the body of minerals." Fruit juice–sweetened baked products often taste acidic and are hard to digest.

Buying Fruit juice concentrate appears in beverages, including juice blends, frozen orange juice, natural sodas, and flavored bottled water. It's a common sweetener in cold breakfast cereals, candy, energy bars, frozen desserts, crackers, fruit conserves, and cookies.

See **Fruit; Fruit Juice; Sweeteners.**

Fuzzy Melon See **Winter Melon.**

G

GAC
(*Momordica cochinchinensis*)

A small round or oblong red-orange fruit from Southeast Asia, this gourd family member grows on a vine and is a relative of bitter melon. Widely used in Vietnam, it's a seasonal and festive ingredient in a sweet rice dish where it colors the rice red and imparts its characteristic flavor.

Medicinal Benefits Gac is the best source of the antioxidant lycopene, containing 70 times more than tomatoes. It supports healthy eyesight and traditionally was used as remedy for arthritis. Gac is also an excellent source of zeaxanthin and vitamin C. Gac seeds are poisonous and are used externally for enlarged lymph nodes, infections, hemorrhoids, and mastitis.

Use Gac is primarily available in the United States in a powder form for use in the supplement and nutritional beverage industry.

See **Gourd Family; Vegetable.**

Gai Laan See **Chinese Broccoli.**

GALANGAL
Greater Galangal, Thai Ginger
(*Alpinia galanga*)

Galangal is a pungent-tasting ginger relative used in Indonesian, Malaysian, Thai, Vietnamese, and Laotian cuisine. It has a camphorlike aroma and a flavor of citrus, pine, and soap. Imported to Europe since the time of Marco Polo, galangal looks rather like an oversize ginger but is denser and harder to cut. It is warming, aids digestion, and helps circulate chi and relieve pain. Considered to be an aphrodisiac, it also treats diarrhea, vomiting, flatulence, and intestinal worms. Its small black fruits are used as a cardamom substitute.

Lesser galangal (*Alpinia officinarum*), a near relative, is used primarily in Chinese medicinal herbal blends.

Galangal is available dried, ground, pickled, and fresh in Asian markets; fresh, it has occasional availability in well-supplied supermarkets.

See **Ginger Family; Herbs and Spices.**

Gamma-Linolenic Acid (GLA) See **Essential Fatty Acids.**

Garbanzo See **Chickpea.**

Garden Cress See **Cress.**

Garden Huckleberry See **Sunberry.**

Garden Pea See **Pea, Fresh.**

Garden Sorrel See **Sorrel.**

Garland Chrysanthemum See **Chrysanthemum Greens.**

GARLIC
(*Allium sativum*)

> Now bolt down these cloves of garlic.
> Well primed with garlic you will
> have greater mettle for the fight.
> —Aristophanes, *The Knights*

The Greeks used garlic for more than fueling the fighting spirit; they also set garlic on stone piles at crossroads to propitiate Hecate, the underworld goddess of magic, charms, and enchantment.

The fleshy bulb of a perennial plant, garlic is a universal pungent and spicy seasoning agent and home remedy. And it's been a favorite from the dawning of Egyptian, Indian, and Chinese civilizations. In fact, it's been cultivated for so long that garlic is no longer found as a wild plant and its seeds are no longer fertile. It's propagated by clove: Plant one clove in the fall or spring and it yields one bulb. Ninety percent of our domestic garlic supply comes from California.

Medicinal Benefits Garlic has a pungent and sweet flavor, is warming in thermal nature, invigorates chi, is a stimulant, and tonifies the spleen, stomach, kidney, and lung meridians. Garlic stimulates metabolism, improves digestion, and is used for both chronic and acute disease. It's antibacterial, anticarcinogenic, and antifungal. It reduces ear troubles, sinusitis, influenza, blood pressure, and cholesterol. Garlic helps stabilize blood sugar levels. Garlic lowers fever by increasing perspiration. It is antiparasitical, and it promotes the growth of healthy intestinal flora. It eliminates toxins from the body, ranging from snake venom to poisonous metals such as lead and cadmium. It increases body heat and thus may act as an aphrodisiac. Garlic reduces *vata* and *kapha*.

Use A primary seasoning agent in nearly every world cuisine, garlic's distinct flavor and aroma whet the appetite and excite the passions. It's this feature that makes it prohibited by the Jain religion and some Buddhist practitioners, and traditionally its use is limited in Indian cuisine.

To quickly remove the papery scales that enclose each garlic clove, place a clove on a hard surface and—using the flat side of a knife blade—crush it. If you use a wooden cutting board and don't want everything else to taste like garlic, then you have two options. Reserve a board for garlic and its kin, or wet the board before cutting strong-smelling foods; the water acts as a buffer and protects the board from absorbing flavors.

Garlic may be mashed, pounded, pressed, diced, sliced, minced, or left whole. "What you *do* to garlic is what you *get* from garlic," according to Lloyd J. Harris, author of *The Book of Garlic*. A whole clove cooked slowly has a mild and nutty flavor because the heat has destroyed the enzyme responsible for the odoriferous sulfur compound. Heat, then, is one factor.

A second is how many garlic cells are exposed to oxygen. Exposed cells release sulfides that oxidize on contact with the air. Therefore, a thoroughly mashed garlic clove is more potent than one sliced or chopped.

When sautéing with garlic, take care not to brown the garlic, or it will become bitter. Garlic has probably been featured in every known savory dish—some people even add it to fruit chutneys and ice cream.

Dried, powdered, or granulated garlic? "Not to be used by anyone truly interested in the flavor of garlic, or in the food value of garlic (including the medicinal properties)," reports Harris.

Buying Select garlic bulbs that are plump and firm—smaller ones tend to be more pungent. Numerous garlic varieties, ranging in color from a pure white to lavender or pink bulbs, are typically available without reference to their variety. Two distinctive varieties are:

- **Elephant Garlic (*Allium ampeloprasum*)** A close relative of the leek, elephant garlic looks like a giant garlic but is milder than garlic and doesn't store as well. Its cloves, the size of an apricot, are used more as a vegetable rather than as a flavoring agent.

- **Rocambole Garlic (*Allium sativum* var. *ophioscorodon*)** The flower stalk of this garlic relative develops an attractive spiral twist that's topped with a cluster of 10 to 40 purple or yellow bulblets (bulbils) or aerial clones the size of a garden pea. The large rocambole garlic cloves are usually rounded and blunt at the tip with a thin and loose skin that is easy to peel but results in a shorter shelf life. It is milder tasting than garlic. The bulbils are eaten when immature and tender. It is an attractive plant used in floral arrangements and available primarily in farmers' markets.

Be Mindful Garlic is not recommended when there are menopausal hot flashes or excessive heat typified by a red face and eyes, thirst, and a sense of feeling too hot. Excessive garlic may damage the stomach and liver. Use moderately during pregnancy, as it mildly stimulates the uterus.

See **Herbs and Spices; Onion Family; Vegetable.**

GARLIC AWAY JET LAG

Garlic and ginger are effective folk remedies for jet lag. Eat generous amounts (or take in capsule form as the bottle recommends) several days before the trip, the day of the trip, and one day after a trip. The day of travel, drink adequate liquid but avoid coffee, carbonated beverages, and alcohol. Favor easy-to-digest, grounding foods, including meat, some good fat, and root vegetables. That night, a hot bath and oil massage—especially of the feet—can help ease jet lag.

GARLIC CHIVE
Chinese Chive, Chinese Leek, Oriental Garlic, Yellow Chive
(*Allium tuberosum*)

The small bulbs of these slowly expanding perennial clumps have a sweet—but mild—garlic flavor. Unlike common tubular chives, garlic chives have larger (up to 10 inches long), flat, bladelike leaves.

Medicinal Benefits Both the bulb and leaf are warming and help regulate chi flow and neutralize poisons. They whet the appetite and tonify the kidney and bladder, stomach, and liver meridians. When raw, garlic chives are more building; when lightly cooked, they are better at dispersing stagnation. The seeds of garlic chives are a traditional remedy for urinary incontinence, male impotence due to kidney weakness, or low back pain. Not recommended for people with fever, ulcers, or eye disorders. Garlic chives reduce *vata* and *kapha*.

Use In the West, garlic chives are used to add a light garlic flavor to any savory dish. In Asia, garlic chives are not used as a garnish but as an important vegetable and a frequent addition to stir-fries; and the buds are a tasty delicacy. Use within a day or two of purchase.

Buying Look for shiny green leaves with plump buds. The stem end should be crisp enough to snap off, as if snapping an asparagus spear; if not crisp, the vegetable is past prime. In the winter, blanched garlic chives, which look like a clump or pale straw, are available in Chinese markets.

See **Chive; Herbs and Spices; Onion Family.**

GHEE
Clarified Butter

Ghee is pure butterfat that looks like liquid gold and is the most soothing and delicious ingredient imaginable. It boosts the flavor of savory and sweet dishes and may be used for baking, sautéing or frying.

This premier Indian Ayurvedic ingredient is butter with everything removed *but* the fat. (In addition to fat, butter contains 18 percent water and 2 percent protein.) In yogic traditions, ghee is regarded as an anti-inflammatory agent and is said to boost memory. Some lactose intolerant people can consume ghee. Commercial ghee is made using a centrifugal separator. At home, you may make ghee by cooking butter until the water evaporates and then strain out the protein solids. Clarified butter, renowned in both French and South American cuisine, is similar to ghee; however, it is cooked a shorter time. Thus,

---

NITER KIBEH

I favor the Ethiopian *niter kibeh* over unflavored ghee because the medicinal properties of the spices become more bioavailable and because it so deliciously enhances the flavor of whatever it is cooked with. It's also an incredible time-saver since your supply of cooking oil is seasoned all at once, rather than with each use. You can also pick and choose the spices you most enjoy. This is one of my favorite cool-weather spice combinations. In hot weather, I eliminate the ginger, nutmeg, and cinnamon. As the remaining spices support digestion, they're good to use year-round.

Makes 1½ cups

- 1 pound cultured unsalted butter
- 1 small onion, chopped
- 2 cloves garlic, chopped
- 1 teaspoon minced ginger
- 1 teaspoon cumin seeds
- 1 teaspoon coriander seeds
- ½ teaspoon asafetida
- ½ teaspoon turmeric
- 1 cinnamon stick piece, about 1 inch long
- 1 bay leaf
- ¼ teaspoon whole cardamom pods
- ⅛ teaspoon ground nutmeg or mace

Place all the ingredients in a saucepan and slowly melt the butter over medium heat. When the butter comes to a boil, reduce the heat to very low and simmer, uncovered and undisturbed, for about 30 minutes. As the temperature reaches the boiling point of water, the butter's water content vaporizes, foaming and making tiny, sharp crackling noises. It will be ready when the crackling noise stops and the sound becomes a rounder, boiling sound; the foaming almost ceases; the butter turns from a cloudy yellow to a lovely, clear golden color; it emits a popcornlike aroma; it develops a thin, light tan crust on the nearly motionless surface; and the white sediment (milk proteins and salts) that forms on the bottom turns a light tan color.

Immediately remove from the heat, as ghee can easily burn. (If it burns, it will begin to foam rapidly again and turn brown instead of golden.) Cool slightly, then pour the hot ghee through a fine stainless-steel mesh strainer or several layers of damp cheesecloth (first wet the cheesecloth, then wring out excess water). When cooled, cover tightly. *Niter kibeh* (and ghee) stores for 4 months or more at a cool room temperature or refrigerated.

---

not all the water and solids are removed, making it less flavorful and giving it a shorter shelf life.

Organic ghee is available in natural food

stores. Organic ghee made from the butter of grass-fed cows is an exceptionally fine product. This ghee, therefore, contains naturally occurring conjugated linoleic acid (CLA) and vitamin K_2.

It's also easy and more economical to make your own, and it will be much more delicious than conventional ghee. In the ghee recipe on page 153, I've used spices to make it the Ethiopian way. If you want to make plain ghee, omit the spices and use only butter.

See **Butter; Fat and Oil.**

GHERKIN SEE **CUCUMBER.**

GIANT MUSTARD SEE **MUSTARD GREENS.**

GINGER
Ginger Root, Stem Ginger
(*Zingiber officinale*)

Ginger ale, ginger beer, candied ginger, gingerbread, ginger snaps, and the pale pink, paper-thin slices of pickled ginger mounded next to sushi—there's no other spice that helps define so many dishes, East and West.

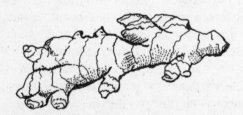

Ginger is a rhizome, or enlarged underground stem. It grows in the shape of a palm with fingers, called a hand of ginger. It's a small plant with slender stalks. Ginger is native to tropical India, and today it grows throughout tropical and subtropical areas and in greenhouses in temperate regions.

Second only to salt as an Asian condiment, as a medicinal, ginger is even more remarkable. Herbalist Deni Brown notes that ginger is found in about half of all Chinese and Ayurvedic prescriptions and in Ayurveda is known as *vishwabhesaj,* or "universal medicine." Equally valued in the West, it was listed as a taxable commodity by the Romans in 200 AD.

Ginger in medieval England was understood to "quycken the remembraunce," writes Lorna Sass in *To the King's Taste: Richard II's Book of Feasts and Recipes*. The medieval kitchen was not limited to one variety as we are but could choose between green, white, columbine, and string ginger.

Medicinal Benefits Ginger has a peppery, pungent taste. It is warming, stimulates digestion, and boosts circulation, respiration, and nervous system function. By increasing circulation, it helps effect a systemic cleansing through the skin, bowels, and kidneys. Ginger treats colds and fevers and is an effective remedy for motion sickness, nausea from chemotherapy, and sometimes morning sickness. It is anti-inflammatory, helps alleviate arthritic pain, and destroys many intestinal parasites. It normalizes blood pressure, helps support the liver, and promotes the release of bile. It eases congestion in the throat and lungs, relieving symptoms of cold and flu, and helps alleviate menstrual discomfort. To relieve a headache, rub a few drops of ginger juice over the affected area. Ginger reduces *vata* and *kapha;* dry or ground ginger is especially not recommended for *pitta*.

Use Ginger gives a clean, fresh taste to foods and is warming. Dried ground ginger is very heating. I use ground ginger in cold-weather stews and in middle-of-the-winter breads, cookies, and pudding but otherwise favor fresh. Fresh ginger can be substituted for ground ginger at a ratio of 6 parts fresh for 1 part ground, although the flavors of fresh and dried ginger are not exactly interchangeable.

An easy way to use ginger is to grate it on a fine grater, then, using your fingertips, press out the juice. A plump, fresh knob of ginger is surprisingly juicy, with 1 tablespoon of finely grated pulp yielding 1 teaspoon of juice. As the root dehydrates, its juice yield decreases. The Japanese make a handy grater especially for ginger called an *oroshigane*, available in porcelain or metal. Even more efficient are microplane graters or zesters.

Young, pink-tinged stem ginger is pickled, candied, and used as a fragrant vegetable in Asian stir-fried dishes. Stem ginger is less spicy than mature ginger.

Buying Stem ginger is available in specialty markets in the spring and fall. It should be used immediately.

Mature ginger is readily available year-round. Look for firm, plump hands or fingers of ginger with clean, smooth skin. The pale yellow flesh is very juicy when fresh, but as it ages it becomes fibrous. Avoid wrinkled, discolored, or moldy ginger. The young, smaller fingers have the most delicate flavor.

Be Mindful Excessive use of ginger, especially powdered ginger, can cause digestive upset and is contraindicated for people suffering with gallstones.

See **Ginger Family; Herbs and Spices.**

GINGER FAMILY
(*Zingiber*)

As a good description of ginger's flavor and action, ginger also means "spirit," "liveliness," and "verve." While the ginger family is named for its most famous member, its other familiar culinary members—cardamom, galangal, and turmeric—are equally distinctive and spirited. The zingiber genus, native to tropical Asia, has reedlike stems and aromatic rhizomes. They make excellent houseplants.

See **Cardamom; Galangal; Ginger; Turmeric.**

Ginger Root See **Ginger.**

Girolle See **Chanterelle.**

GLASSWORT
Marsh Samphire, Samphire, Sea Asparagus, Sea Bean, Sea Pickle
(*Salicornia europaea*)

Glasswort is a name commonly applied to several unrelated succulent, annual plants that thrive in a saline soil. It is one of a handful of delicious wild vegetables with occasional market availability. Buy it when you see it. Or better yet, harvest it from clean Pacific or Atlantic coasts, salt marshes, or alkaline Nevada or Oregon soils. The plant grows about 16 inches high and looks like a leafless, skinny, branch-

---

TO PEEL OR NOT TO PEEL

Some cooks peel ginger and, in the process, waste much of its flesh. Peeling is unnecessary unless you're making candy or pickles, and even then the tough skin is removed only for cosmetic and sensory reasons. Peeling is superfluous when finely grated to express the juice or used by the slice (and later remove it, as you would a bay leaf). As well as when you mince, shred, or cut ginger into matchsticks, as the minuscule bits of skin soften with cooking and are undetected in a finished dish. When a whole knob of ginger needs to be peeled, use the edge of a spoon to scrape the ginger. The skin—and only the skin—almost rolls off.

Refrigerate ginger, unwrapped, in the vegetable drawer (if tightly covered, it becomes moldy). If storing a large quantity, bury it in a bucket of clean sand in a cool spot, and the ginger will keep for several months. Ginger is also available pickled and candied.

ing succulent. Its leaves are like scales, which give the branches a bumpy look. In the spring and summer, it's green, but by fall it turns orange-red.

Elizabeth Schneider tells the charming story of its name. Because this vegetable grows in cliff crevices, the French called it *Saint-Pierre*, for Saint Peter, the rock upon which Christ built his church. Along the way the name became *sampyre* and then samphire (a name shared by an old-fashioned parsley relative that also grows in rocky places). The name "glasswort" comes from the use of the ash in early glass manufacturing.

Use Glasswort has a juicy, salinelike flavor and a pleasing crunch. Use it raw as a trail nibble, an attractive garnish, or salad ingredient, or pickle it, a favorite historical use. When cooking glasswort, trim the roots, then prepare and serve them like asparagus. Take care, however, to cook the greens just until the color brightens, so that their texture is not compromised.

Buying/Foraging Glasswort is occasionally available in specialty markets during the summer and early fall. The plants should be firm, dry, and bright. When foraging, harvest the plant tips from late spring until early summer. The mature plant has a fibrous center, which you may eat around, but glasswort is superior when younger.

GLIADIN

Gliadin, one of the proteins found in wheat, rye, and barley, is commonly referred to as gluten. When people who are allergic to gliadin consume it, an allergic response is triggered and antibodies to the enzyme tissue transglutaminase are formed. This causes the immune system to cross-react with the bowel tissue, and the result is inflammation. If one continues to eat gluten-containing foods, it eventually compromises the villi in the small intestine and leads to malabsorption. The prescription is to avoid all wheat, barley, and rye products.

If a sensitive individual continues to eat wheat, her allergic responses may increase to eventually include other gluten proteins, including glutelin.

See **Glutelin; Wheat.**

GLOBE ARTICHOKE SEE **ARTICHOKE.**

GLOBE ONION SEE **ONION.**

GLUCOSE (NOT RECOMMENDED)

A monosaccharide sugar common in most plant and animal tissue, glucose is the body's major energy source. Honey is primarily composed of glucose and fructose. Commercial glucose is a colorless, syrupy mixture of chemically derived sugars and water.

See **Honey; Sugar; Sweeteners.**

GLUTELIN

All grains, including the pseudo-cereals amaranth, buckwheat, and quinoa, contain glutelin proteins. Many gluten sensitivities start with the gluten protein gliadin; it is common to wheat, rye, and barley.

However, if a person is sensitive to gliadin and continues eating wheat, then the glutelin in other grains can become an irritant and cause allergic reactions. Yes, rice and quinoa used to be hypoallergenic foods, but that's not true for everyone today.

See **Gliadin; Wheat.**

GLUTEN SEE **GLIADIN; GLUTELIN; SEITAN; WHEAT.**

GOA BEAN See WINGED BEAN.

GOBO See BURDOCK.

GOJI BERRY
Wolfberry
(Lycium barbarum, L. chinense)

Goji berries are the small fruits of a common ornamental and woody perennial shrub, the boxwood. When fresh, the small, rather mealy-textured berries are mildly sweet, but otherwise they're not remarkably flavorful; however, their delightful red-orange color perks up the visuals of both sweet and savory dishes, much as does their relative the tomato. Their tiny yellow edible seeds are also similar to those of the tomato. The goji berry is a member of the nightshade family. When dried, goji berries are about the size of a raisin and—depending upon their moisture content—they range from soft and raisinlike to hard and chewy. Although they are often marketed as a Tibetan or Himalayan fruit, this is merely a marketing term. Our commercial goji berries come primarily from plantations in northwestern and western China.

Medicinal Benefits Long valued in Chinese medicine to tonify kidney and liver function and to build energy and strengthen vision, goji berries are a rich source of the carotene zeaxanthin. Their antioxidant properties help protect against cancer and cardiovascular and inflammatory diseases.

Use Due to their recent fame in the West as a superfood and their high price, you'll find goji berries as a showcase ingredient in numerous goods, ranging from trail mixes and muffin mixes to juice and beverage products. They're also available dried in packets or in the bulk bins of natural food stores. I purchase them fresh at my farmers' market in the late summer. Goji shoots and their slightly bitter leaves are added to Asian-style soups.

See **Dried Fruit; Fruit; Nightshade Family.**

GOLDEN NUGGET SQUASH See SQUASH; SQUASH, WINTER.

GOOD KING HENRY See FAT HEN.

GOOSEBERRY
(Ribes uva-crispa, R. grossularia, R. hirtellum)

Tart describes the gooseberry. Very tart. A black currant relative, the gooseberry grows wild in Europe and the Americas; the plant—a straggly bush—was domesticated a short 500 years ago. Most gooseberries are small—the size of a blueberry, but can be as a large as a cherry—with translucent skin that may be smooth or downy. There are a number of soft seeds in their juicy flesh. The color varies from white through shades of green to purple, with the darker colors having a sweeter flavor.

Gooseberries are cold in their thermal properties. They are rich in the essential fatty acid gamma-linolenic acid, and they treat constipation, indigestion, poor complexion, and liver ailments.

Gooseberries may be eaten out of hand but are mostly used in pies, preserves, and sauces for their tart flavor. They are available in specialty markets in late summer. Choose berries that are dry with a bright, unblemished skin.

See **Fruit; Ribes Family.**

GOOSEFOOT FAMILY
(Chenopodiaceae)

The goosefoot, or chenopod, family of plants is found throughout the world. The name is derived from the Greek words for goose (*khen*) and foot (*podium*) because the triangular shape of the leaf looks like the webbed foot of a goose. Goosefoot stems may be green or red; the greens may contain oxalic acid.

See **Agretti; Amaranth; Beet; Beetberry; Chard; Epazote; Fat Hen; Orach; Quinoa; Spinach, Sugar.**

GOURD FAMILY
(*Cucurbitaceae*)

The gourd family is an important food plant family that grows throughout the warm regions of the world. It includes numerous and diversified foods that grow on trailing or climbing plants with tendrils and lobed leaves. The blossoms are edible. Chayote, squash, and pumpkins evolved in the Americas. Cucumbers, gourds, and melons originated in Africa and Eurasia.

See **Bitter Melon; Cantaloupe; Chayote; Cucumber; Gac; Kiwano; Loofah; Melon; Pumpkin; Squash; Squash Blossom; Squash, Summer; Squash, Winter; Watermelon; Winter Melon.**

GRAINS
(*Gramineae*)

Grains, as members of the grass family, are the most complex and highly evolved plant species. Unlike most other plants, which have a separate fruit and seed, the fruit and seed walls of a grain unite in a single unit. By sheer number, the grasses—including bamboo, cane, wild grasses, and even suburban lawns—are the most dominant botanical species; they cover more of the earth's surface than any other plant species. Three seeds that are not members of the grass family are commonly considered along with grains because their use is similar. They are amaranth, buckwheat, and quinoa.

Humankind, the most developed life form of the animal species, coevolved with grains. An examination of the human digestive system and teeth indicates that we evolved eating predominantly a grain-based diet. Almost all peoples have revered a grain as their sacred mother, kept it at the heart of their diet, and made it central to their ritual. Even today grains remain the primary calorie source in most of the temperate world. In terms of alleviating world hunger, grains hold the greatest promise.

Medicinal Benefits Grains are nutritive and sweet, help build body mass, and tonify the spleen. The complex carbohydrate of whole grains is more stabilizing to blood sugar than are refined or milled grain products.

Grain consumption, as Annemarie Colbin notes in her classic book *Food and Healing*, "also has certain nonphysical, psychological, or spiritual effects (that) can foster a holistic worldview. Ancient Central American Indian lore has it that grains facilitate socialization and social intercourse; and in the West, breaking bread with one's neighbor is the ultimate symbol of a spiritually strong social connection. Time and time again I hear from my students that a change of diet (to include more whole grains) has helped dramatically in changing their perception of life—from a fragmented, alienated, self-centered view to one of connection, integration, and oneness."

Grains, along with legumes, are the only foods that contain all the major nutrient groups needed by the body: carbohydrates, protein, fats, vitamins, minerals, and fiber.

Use With the exception of muesli and some grain sprouts, grains are always cooked. Cooking is the first step to making them bioavailable; chewing them is the second. For grains to be well digested, they must be mixed with the digestive enzyme ptyalin, which is found only in the mouth.

The accompanying chart on page 160 lists water proportions and cooking times for one cup of grain. If the grain amount increases to three cups or more, slightly reduce the water. This chart is only a guideline: The level of heat, the type of pot, and your individual preference—some like grain wet; some like it dry—will a make a difference.

I disagree with the many recipes that suggest cooking brown rice 50 minutes or less. To soften the bran of brown rice enough so it is digestible and to bring out the full flavor of the rice requires one hour of cooking time. Like brown rice, whole barley, rye, wheat, and cultivated wild rice require a full hour of cooking. If you prefer a softer texture for these grains, or if you are cooking an especially impervious grain because of its variety or age, add additional water and increase cooking time as necessary.

All whole grains contain hard-to-digest antinutrients: lectins, phytates, and enzyme inhibitors. Presoaking, and discarding the soaking water, enhances the flavor and digestibility of all grains (and sometimes reduces the cooking time of longer-cooking grains). I soak them for several hours or overnight in their measured amount of water in a glass measuring cup. When ready to cook, note the water level of the soaked grain, strain out and discard the soaking water, add fresh water to the same measure, and cook as described. However, I don't soak tef or quinoa because quinoa quickly sprouts, and tef's symbiotic yeast triggers fermentation.

Buying The advantages of purchasing grain from bulk bins are price and quality; doing so also lets you see your purchase. Good-quality grain is whole and contains few broken, scratched, or deteriorated grains.

Be Mindful Gluten (technically, gliadin) and dairy are the top two food allergens; sensitivities to gluten can develop into celiac sprue and can be life-threatening. If you suspect a sensitivity to wheat or other gluten-containing grains (barley, Kamut, khorasan, rye, spelt, or wheat), avoid consuming these products. As all grains and pseudo-grains contain glutenlike proteins (glutelin), some people are sensitive to all cereal grains as well as to amaranth, buckwheat, and quinoa.

SOME GRAINS ARE EASIEST TO DIGEST—AND SWEETEST—WHEN PRESSURE-COOKED

I endorse pressure-cooking the harder grains—whole barley, whole oats, brown rice, sweet brown rice, both types of wild rice, and rye and wheat berries. Pressure-cooking softens their otherwise hard-to-digest bran and yields a sweeter-tasting grain. To pressure-cook these grains, use the accompanying chart but reduce the water level by two tablespoons and the cooking time by five or ten minutes. Place grain, water, salt, and any seasoning into the pressure cooker. Lock the lid in place. Place over high heat and bring to high pressure. Lower the heat just enough to maintain medium pressure. Cook for the designated time. Remove from the heat and allow the pressure to come down naturally for ten minutes. Remove the lid, tilting it away from you to allow any excess steam to escape.

Cooking two cups or less of grain in a large pressure cooker (few pressure cookers are small) often produces grain that's dry on the top and scorched on the bottom. An easy remedy is to use an insert. Put the grain, water, salt, and any seasonings inside a heat-resistant glass bowl and cover it tightly. (A foil-covered ovenproof measuring cup also works fine.) Place the insert inside the pressure cooker. Add two inches of water to the pressure cooker, lock the lid in place, and cook as above.

COOKING WHOLE GRAINS

To cook a grain, combine it with water in a heavy pot, preferably an enameled one. (Sweet rice excepted, I always add ¼ teaspoon unrefined salt for each cup of grain, and I typically add a one- or two-inch strip of kombu. Added oil, ghee, or spices is optional.) Bring the grain to a boil, cover the pot, reduce the heat, and simmer without stirring until the water is absorbed. Remove from the heat and allow the grains to stand, still covered, for 10 minutes before serving. If you are using a thin pot or an electric range, placing a flame distributor (available from hardware and cookware stores) under the pot helps prevent scorching.

1 CUP GRAIN	WATER (*in cups*)	TIME (*in minutes*)	YIELD (*in cups*)
Amaranth	1½	20	2
Barley (pearl)	2½	40	3½
Barley (whole)	3	60 (1 hour)	3½
Buckwheat	2	12	3½
Bulgur (medium)	2	20	3
Millet	2¼	20	4
Oats (whole)	2	45	2½
Quinoa	2	15	3
Rice (brown sweet)	1½	40	3¼
Rice (long brown)	2¼	60 (1 hour)	3½
Rice (long white)	2	20	3
Rye	2¼	60 (1 hour)	3¼
Tef	1½	15	3
Wheat	2½	60 (1 hour)	2½
Wild rice (cultivated)	2½	60 (1 hour)	3½
Wild rice (wild)	1¾	45	3½

See **Amaranth; Barley; Buckwheat; Corn; Flour; Gliadin; Glutelin; Grass Family; Job's Tears; Millet; Oats; Quinoa; Rice; Rye; Sorghum; Sprouted Wheat (or Grain) Products; Tef; Triticale; Wheat; Wild Rice.**

Gram Flour See **Chickpea Flour.**

GRANULAR FRUIT SUGAR (NOT RECOMMENDED)

This is grape juice concentrate mixed with rice syrup—yet another attempt to satisfy the sweet tooth while claiming that a product is more healthful than sugar. Such a case may be made for rice syrup but not for grape juice concentrate.

See **Fruit Juice Concentrate; Sweeteners.**

GRAPE
(*Vitis vinifera*)

Vitus vinifera translates as "the vine that bears wine" and seems to have originated in the southern Caucasus, more or less where Noah, famous as the first of all drunkards, is supposed to have landed his ark after the Flood: a pleasing coincidence," reports French culinary writer Maguelonne Toussaint-Samat.

Grapes are berries that grow on a woody vine. A symbiotic yeast naturally grows on grapes. This makes both a natural choice for fermentation, as their historical use attests. The fermented fruit of Bacchus is associated with not only frivolity but also with fine cuisine, excess, and both Jewish and Christian sacrament.

Wine making, the largest fruit industry in the world, is based on the one and only Eurasian grape, *V. vinifera*, which now has more than 8,000 cultivars. In contrast, there are more than 25 different species native to North America, several of which may be foraged today. American varieties, including the popular Concord, have a softer, juicier flesh and less sugar than Eurasian ones.

Grapes do not tolerate extended periods of freezing or tropical heat, but they grow throughout the world in mild, temperate climates. More than two-thirds of all grapes are produced for wine, with about 20 percent for table use, 10 percent are dried, and 1 percent are used as fruit juice. The volume of U.S. grape production ranks only under that of apples and oranges, with California producing the bulk of our crop. In fact, after almonds, grapes are California's second-largest food export.

Medicinal Benefits Grapes have a sweet and sour flavor and astringent action, they are neutral in thermal properties, and they act upon the kidney, lung, liver, spleen, and stomach meridians. Grapes increase vital energy and are used to build blood and body fluids and to cleanse the glands and the body in general. Grapes are good to treat thirst, constipation, gastritis, menopausal heat symptoms, difficult urination, edema, and dry cough. Grape juice is used to treat liver malfunctions including jaundice and hepatitis. Grapes relieve inflammation of the throat, mouth, gums, and eyes.

The phytochemical resveratrol, found primarily in grape skins and grape seeds, promotes cell health and longevity and inhibits cancer (including breast, colon, stomach, and oral cancers and leukemia), heart disease, Alzheimer's disease, Parkinson's disease, and viral and fungal infections. Their ellagic acid is an anticarcinogen and antimutagen. Red and purple grapes are higher in antioxidants than are green grapes. Grapes reduce *vata* and *pitta* and in moderation can be used by *kapha*.

Use Grapes are a perfect size for tidy, out-of-hand snacking. They are delicious in fruit salads and, poached, add flavor and good texture to compotes, fruit cocktail, and soups. Grape leaves are a tasty vegetable and wrap. Gather the leaves in the spring just when they reach their full size, or purchase brined grape leaves. Use as a wrap for savory food morsels such as stuffed grape leaves.

Whenever available, I favor heirloom grapes that contain their nutrient-rich seeds and enjoy munching on the seeds—or at least some of them—as well as the fruit. Today seedless grapes are primarily available in growers' markets.

Buying Grapes cease ripening when harvested (they're nonclimacteric); therefore, select a mature bunch that are plump with a powdery bloom (a natural waterproofing) on their skins. Examine where the grape attaches to the stem, and if the stem and this area look fresh, the grape will be fresh as well. Gently shake a bunch of grapes and few, if any, should drop. Avoid soft or wrinkled grapes or grapes with stems that are brown and brittle. Unfortunately, grapes—especially South American grapes—are one of the most chemically treated fruits, so favor organic grapes, raisins, and wine. The peak season for domestic grapes is September to November, and when stored under controlled atmospheric conditions they are available until May.

Essentially all seedless table grapes (as opposed to grapes grown for beverages or to dry) are derived from one of three sources: Thompson Seedless, Russian Seedless, and Black Monukka.

- **Green Table Grapes** are seedless and sweetest when their color has a yellow cast with a tinge of amber. They include Calmeria, Perlette, Princess, Pristine, Sugraone, Superior, and Thompson.
- **Purple and Blue Black Table Grapes** include two seeded varieties, Niabell and Concord, and numerous seedless varieties, including Autumn Royal, Exotic, Fantasy, Ribier, and Summer Royal. As with the red varieties, purple grapes are best when one color predominates.
- **Red Table Grapes** are prime when one color predominates on all or most of the berries. They include Champagne, Christmas Rose, Crimson, Emperor, Flame, Red Globe, and Ruby.

Be Mindful Favor organic grapes and avoid all grapes—organic or otherwise—imported from Chile, as they must be fumigated with methyl bromide. Grapes are among the top seven fruits highest in pesticide residues. The same goes for raisins, as toxins are more concentrated in dried fruit.

See **Grapeseed Oil; Raisin.**

GRAPEFRUIT
(*Citrus × paradisi*)

> There's a lot more juice in a grapefruit than meets the eye. —Anonymous

This large citrus fruit was so named because its fruits are borne in clusters, somewhat like grapes. Grapefruit is the most important citrus to have originated outside Asia. It was hybridized in Barbados from an orange and pomelo, and has been cultivated commercially for only 100 years. Our domestic crop comes from Arizona, California, New Mexico, and Texas.

Medicinal Benefits Grapefruit is cold and cleansing in its action. Its sweet and sour flavor acts upon the liver and stomach meridians. It eases constipation, reduces cholesterol, treats poor digestion and jaundice, and is a popular diet food. Its most abundant nutritive property is vitamin C, and the pink varieties contain the antioxidant lycopene. Grapefruit is especially calming to *vata*. Extracts of grapefruit seeds appear to have antioxidant properties. The essential oil of grapefruit treats obesity, kidney and liver problems, migraine headaches, and depression. It is also used to aid drug withdrawal.

Use While grapefruit was once regarded as a breakfast fruit, today it appears in numerous desserts and preserves and as a fruit juice and a mid-meal snack. Try a halved grapefruit sprinkled with maple sugar and broiled. Or even better than sprinkling it with sugar is to add a splash of orange juice, which eliminates the acid and makes the grapefruit sweeter. My personal favorite way of eating it—the way my grandmother did—is to peel it like an orange and then, using a paring knife, extract each segment and savor it on the spot. Once in segments, they're also good in salads or fruit cocktails.

Buying Although there are many varieties, consumers are primarily interested in white, pink, or red is grapefruits, which are available with or without seeds. White grapefruit is the most tart and is red the sweetest. The red or pink varieties have a pink blush to their yellow skin and are generally larger and sweeter than whites.

Select a heavy grapefruit with a thin—rather than puffy and thick—peel, for that means there is more edible fruit. The skin should be firm and smooth to the touch. Surface marks do not affect the fruit's flavor, but avoid bruised or shriveled fruit.

See **Citrus Family; Fruit; Pomelo.**

GRAPEFRUIT ZEST SEE CITRUS PEEL.

GRAPESEED OIL (NOT RECOMMENDED)

A by-product of the wine industry, grapes are the most chemically intensively grown fruit and as toxins are most concentrated in a plant's fatty acids, this oil will be tainted. That's one reason to avoid grapeseed oil. A second excellent reason for not using grapeseed oil is that it's highly refined at high temperatures and therefore its fatty acids are denatured and contribute to the formation of free radicals.

See **Fat and Oil; Grape.**

GRASS FAMILY

This large family of flowering plants is considered one of the most important, as it includes cereal grains, historically a staple food of all peoples in temperate and subtropical regions. Grasses range from our suburban lawns to bamboo forests and from wild oats to sugarcane.

See **Bamboo Shoots; Barley; Corn; Grains; Job's Tears; Lemongrass; Millet; Oats; Rice; Rye; Sorghum; Sugar; Tef; Wild Rice**

GREATER GALANGAL SEE GALANGAL.

GREAT WHITE NORTHERN BEAN SEE BEANS AND LEGUMES.

GREEN ALMOND SEE ALMOND, GREEN.

GREEN BEAN
French Bean, Haricot Vert, Runner Bean, Snap Bean, String Bean, Wax Bean
(*Phaseolus vulgaris*)

Any bean eaten in its pod stage as a vegetable is a green bean; that is, immature as compared to the fully ripened and dried seeds, which are known as beans. The pod of green beans is sweet tasting and usually green, but there are also purple or yellow varieties (the yellow-podded beans are also called wax beans). French beans, sometimes called haricots vert, are straight, very slender beans about seven inches long. Green beans were once known as string beans because of the fibrous string running the length of the pod seam that needed to be removed prior to cooking. Modern cultivars are stringless.

A beautiful crop that either grows in bushes or climbs poles and fences, green beans were once a summertime favorite but now are available year-round. They are delicious fresh and lend themselves to canning and pickling. If there are extras, let them fully mature on the vine and shuck them for succulent, freshly dried beans.

Medicinal Benefits Green beans are neutral in their thermal nature. They are sweet and tone the spleen and kidneys. Green beans increase the yin of the body (its fluids, hormones, and structure), they are diuretic, and help treat diabetes. Dry or poorly cooked green beans irritate *vata;* otherwise, they are *tridoshic.* Fresh beans have ample vitamin A, B-complex vitamins, and calcium and potassium.

Use When beans are green and immature, they are easier to digest than dried beans. Heirloom varieties have strings, which must be removed prior to cooking. It's a time-consuming process; on the other hand, many old varieties have more flavor than modern cultivars.

Compared to most other vegetables, once harvested, green beans age rapidly, so plan to use them quickly. They can be blanched or steamed and served on their own or used in salads, casseroles, soups, and stir-fries—either whole, cut into lengths, or sliced into small rounds. To french beans (cut them into ribbon-thin lengths), trim the beans and, using a vegetable peeler with a frenching end, cut the beans into thin strands. This works best with very fresh beans.

Buying Select green beans that are firm, whole, and crisp, without rust spots. A fresh bean snaps crisply and feels velvety to the touch. Old beans are bulging and leathery. Those with greatest commercial availability include plain green beans, Italian (Romano), long bean, purple podded, yellow (wax), and winged bean.

HUFFING AND PUFFING IN YOUR VEGETABLE CRISPER

Growing plants take in carbon dioxide and give up oxygen, but once picked, fruits and vegetables do the opposite. The technical term is respiration, according to Dr. Robert Shewfelt, one of the world's authorities on postharvest care of fruits and vegetables. While a potato gives off a mere 8 milliliters of carbon dioxide per kilogram per hour, green beans top the vegetable respiration rate by giving off 250 milliliters. The faster the respiration rate, the faster a vegetable expires. To keep vegetables fresher longer, limit their oxygen supply by wrapping them in plastic, recommends Shirley O. Corriher, in *CookWise: The Hows and Whys of Successful Cooking.*

See **Beans and Legumes; Legume Family; Long Bean.**

GREEN ONION SEE **SCALLION.**

GREEN PEA SEE **PEA, FRESH.**

GREEN SOYBEAN SEE **EDAMAME.**

GREEN TEA SEE **TEA.**

GREEN WHEAT BERRIES SEE **WHEAT.**

GRISTLE MOSS SEE **IRISH MOSS.**

GRITS

Grits may refer to any broken cereal grain, most often buckwheat and corn. When a grain is broken, its germ is exposed to light, so it will oxidize and turn rancid. To store grits, refrigerate, tightly covered. Grits made from degerminated corn have an indefinite shelf life.

GROAT

A term referring to any hulled grain, it most often refers to oats and buckwheat.

GROUND CHERRY
Cape Gooseberry, Chinese Lantern, Husk Cherry, Strawberry Tomato
(*Physalis pruinosa, P. alkekengi, P. pubescens*)

At first glance, this small fanciful fruit looks like a tomatillo, but it is not. Neither is it, as its numerous names suggest, a cherry, gooseberry, lantern, strawberry, or tomato, though it is a nightshade family fruit, closely related to the cape gooseberry and tomatillo. The ground cherry is fully encased in its papery husk (calyx), which is thinner than that of a tomatillo, its fruit is small, about a half inch in diameter with a tomato-like skin, and when ripe, a sweet flavor reminiscent of that of a strawberry. Its color may range from yellow or red to purple and even brown. It contains small and soft edible seeds embedded in a soft mealy flesh.

The ground cherry is native to North America, was eaten by most Native Americans, and still grows rampantly as a weed. Ground cherries are also cultivated throughout the world.

Medicinal Benefits The ground cherry supports the digestion of fats and protein. It helps reduce fever, ease rheumatic discomfort, increase urine volume, and is high in pectin and beta-carotene.

Use Green or immature wild ground cherries may be toxic, so be sure to let the fruit ripen in the husk until it's soft and sweet. Remove the husk just prior to eating or, if you are using the fruit as a garnish, pull back the husk and leave it intact. Ground cherries are mild tasting with a distinctive sweet, slightly acidic taste; they are used in compotes, jams, jellies, pies, tarts, sauces, and salsas. They can also be dried.

Buying/Foraging I've yet to find ground cherries in supermarkets, but they are in some farmers' markets.

See **Nightshade Family; Vegetable.**

GROUNDNUT SEE **PEANUT.**

GUAVA
(*Psidium guayava*)

The guava is a relative of cinnamon and feijoas, and its fruit is grainy and pearlike in texture. But what's most memorable is its floral aroma, which fills tropical and subtropical markets when guavas are at their prime. The rounded or ovoid fruits have yellow or chartreuse skin with white, salmon, or crimson-blushed flesh. There are more than a hundred guava species, which range in size from a tangerine to an orange—and like citrus may be loaded with inedible seeds or be seedless.

Originally from Peru and Brazil, the guava grows on a small evergreen tree or large bushy shrub. Today guavas grow throughout the tropical world. Our domestic supply comes from Hawaii, California, and Florida.

Medicinal Benefits The guava is known for its astringent and laxative properties; it tonifies the lymphatic and skeletal systems. It is an excellent source of vitamin C as well as potassium.

Use Remove the skin and the seeds, if any. Guava is delicious raw, in ice cream and sherbet, stewed, and as a sauce or preserve. Guava makes an excellent juice and nectar, by itself or blended with other fruit juice.

Buying Guava is most readily available during the summer. Using your nose is the best way to choose a guava. Select one with a rich aroma, and since the flavor varies considerably from guava to guava, select one with the aroma most enticing to you. A guava with a rank, foul smell is immature and not worth purchasing. To finish ripening a guava, wrap it in a paper bag with a banana and leave out at room temperature until the guava is soft to the touch. Do not refrigerate until it is fully ripe, and then use it within two days.

See **Fruit; Myrtle Family.**

GUMBO SEE **OKRA.**

HABANERO PEPPER SEE **CHILE PEPPER.**

HAMBURG PARSLEY SEE **PARSLEY ROOT.**

HAMLIN ORANGE SEE **ORANGE (TANGOR).**

HARICOT VERT SEE **GREEN BEAN.**

HATO MUGI SEE **JOB'S TEARS.**

HAZELNUT
Cobnut, Filbert, Noisette
(*Corylus avellana, maxima*)

The hazelnut is Oregon's official state nut, with good reason—99 percent of the entire U.S. commercial crop is Oregon grown. The mild Willamette Valley, stretching from Eugene to Portland, provides the perfect econiche for the hazelnut. Long before it arrived in the Willamette, however, it was a favorite European and Middle Eastern nut. The Celts regarded the hazel as the tree of knowledge, and—as water witches know—a forked hazel branch is the best divining rod for finding underground water. The hazelnut is a birch family member that originated in Turkey. It is so closely related to the filbert and cobnut that their names are used interchangeably; they are unrelated to other nuts.

Medicinal Benefits The Greek physician Dioscorides in his book titled *De Materia Medica*, written in the first century AD, observed, "It cures chronic coughing if pounded filbert is eaten with honey. Cooked filbert, mixed with black pepper, cures the cold." Hazelnuts contain antioxidant phenolics and of the various nuts are second only to almonds as a good calcium source. They reduce *vata*.

Use The sweet, somewhat toasty flavor of hazelnuts has been likened to browned butter. Indeed, the French word for browned butter, *noisette*, also means hazelnut. Ground hazelnuts are an old favorite for pastry cooks, who add them to tortes, cookies, and candies. Hazelnuts are particularly delicious with chocolate, and this combination is popular in truffles and products such as the chocolate-hazelnut spread Nutella. They're also good in salads, stuffing, breading, and as a garnish.

Hazelnuts are a popular flavoring for coffee and vodka-based liqueurs such as Frangelico.

For full flavor, roast hazelnuts before using them. To remove the skins, rub the warm nuts with a rough cloth or between your hands, and the skins will flake off.

TRUE OR FALSE: HAZEL BLOSSOMS NEED BEES?

While fruit- and nut-bearing trees rely upon the birds and bees and other flying things for pollination, hazelnuts don't. In the dead of winter, the trees sprout bright yellow male catkins, and with the help of wind and gravity the pollen reaches the inconspicuous red female flowers. This union remains quietly dormant until warm weather. Then, as temperatures rise, the fertilized ovum quickens and the hazelnuts take form.

Buying While all nuts have a fragile shelf life, hazelnuts especially do. Purchase a year's supply in the late fall—ideally in the shell—and wrap the nuts tightly; freeze until use.

See **Beach Family; Hazelnut Oil; Nuts.**

HAZELNUT OIL

Full-flavored hazelnut oil is an excellent culinary oil and is unique among the nut oils, as it lacks omega-3 fatty acids and therefore may be safely heated to moderate temperatures.

See **Fat and Oil; Hazelnut.**

HEADING MUSTARD CABBAGE SEE MUSTARD GREENS.

HEAD LETTUCE SEE LETTUCE.

HEART OF PALM
Palm Heart, Palmito, Swamp Cabbage
(*Bactris gasipaes, Cocos nucifera, Euterpe edulis, E. oleracea, Sabal palmetto*)

Cut off the top of a cabbage palm, Florida's state tree, and the stems' inner portion is a delicately flavored, smooth, firm, ivory-colored vegetable. Removing this veritable heart of the palm effectively kills the tree; thus, historically, this vegetable was an expensive delicacy.

Various palm trees have edible cores, and, fortunately for us, one species, the peach palm, produces up to 40 stems per plant. This makes for a more economical source of heart of palm.

Heart of palm is available fresh in Florida and other palm-growing areas. It's also available canned in water or marinated. Slice, cube, or shred fresh heart of palm and add to fruit salad or make into a slaw-type salad. Or cut and cook it as you would a carrot in any variety of stir-fries, fritters, pot pies, or soup.

See **Palm Family.**

HEDGEHOG MUSHROOM
Sweet Tooth
(*Hydnum repandum*)

A medium-size orange to beige mushroom, the hedgehog mushroom is aptly named, as its small, brittle drooping teeth underneath its cap look like a coat of prickly spines. These spines extend down the stem. If it were not for the spines, the hedgehog might be mistaken for a faded chanterelle. Hedgehog mushrooms are common in wooded areas and a favorite of foragers—both for their excellent flavor and because there are no poisonous look-alikes.

Medicinal Benefits Hedgehog mushrooms have antibiotic and antitumor properties and help clear the system of toxins.

Use Some claim that a pan of sautéing hedgehog mushrooms gives the most enticing of any cooking aromas. A delicate flavored mushroom this is not. It is sweet, nutty, hearty, and meaty, and many people favor it over its near relative, the chanterelle. The hedgehog's flesh is creamy white and remains firm when cooked. It is especially delicious when young; however, its strong characteristic flavor and odor increases with age and especially when the mushroom is dried. The hedgehog mushroom is well suited to long-cooked dishes, where it retains its flavor and enhances the flavor of the other ingredients.

Buying Select hedgehogs that are fresh, firm, free of spots, and well shaped. Store in a paper container, and keep separate from foods with a strong aroma.

See **Mushroom Family; Vegetable.**

HEMP FAMILY
(*Cannabaceae*)

Two members of the hemp family are used for human consumption, hemp and hops. They are annual herbs with distinct male and female plants that twine (hops) or are erect (hemp).

See **Hemp Seeds; Hops.**

HEMP DOUBLESPEAK

Hemp seed is wonderfully nutritious and a great source of protein and the fragile omega-3 and omega-6 fatty acids. But if you want their oils to benefit—rather than be a toxin—then you'll need to use your common sense and disregard marketing dishonesty. Better yet, call the company and demand accountability.

A denatured oil oxidizes and causes the formation of free radical carcinogens. Omega-3 fatty acids are denatured at temperatures above 100°F, and omega-6s are denatured at temperatures above 240°F. (Yes, the smoke point for hemp is much higher, but the oils oxidize long before they start smoking.)

Thus, any hemp product baked, pasteurized, or heated above 100°F, including hemp milk, is one that you want to avoid. What's left to enjoy? Raw hemp oil and seeds.

HEMP MILK
(NOT RECOMMENDED)

You can buy shelf-stable hemp milk; it has, however, been flash-pasteurized at 294°F, and therefore its essential fatty acids are denatured, rancid, and a toxin to your liver.

The good news is that you may make a vital and nutritious nondairy hemp milk. Add ¼ cup hemp seeds to a cup of water, sweeten to taste, and blend until thick for an extraordinarily healthful beverage.

See **Essential Fatty Acids; Hemp Seeds; Nondairy Milk Substitutes.**

HEMP OIL

Oil pressed from hemp seed has a rich flavor and nutrition profile. One tablespoon per day fulfills the daily requirement for essential fatty acids. Dr. Andrew Weil, a hemp oil advocate, notes that it is richer in essential fatty acids than flax oil and provides 1.7 percent gamma-linolenic acid (GLA). He reports, "My experience is that it stimulates growth of hair and nails, improves the health of the skin, and can reduce inflammation." Applied topically, hemp oil ameliorates eczema, psoriasis, and minor skin irritations. In Ayurvedic medicine, it reduces *vata* and is used externally for rheumatism.

Use hemp oil as a dressing for salads or baked potatoes, or add a drizzle to garnish a bowl of soup. Because of its omega-3 fatty acid content, it may not be heated safely and quickly becomes rancid. Purchase only unrefined hemp oil that's refrigerated, packaged in an opaque bottle, and has a "best used by" date.

Due to Drug Enforcement Agency regulations, hemp oil produced in the United States must be made from sterilized or irradiated seeds. Therefore, to obtain vital hemp oil, purchase only imported oil, typically Canadian, that specifies it is made from untreated seeds.

See **Fat and Oil; Hemp Seeds.**

HEMP SEEDS
(*Cannabis sativa*)

The Latin name for marijuana means "useful hemp." And useful it is. Long before flower children smoked it for its psychotropic effects, hemp provided humans with edible greens, seeds, oil, and medicine as well as fiber for clothing, tents, sails, ropes, and paper. Our word for a painter's canvas comes from the word *cannabis*: Mona Lisa smiles from a coarse hemp cloth. In the 1930s, more than 2,500 products were manufactured from hemp. The legislation that put an end to hemp manufacture in the United States is still in place; however, hemp products are in widespread use once again. As per international law, hemp seed used as a food must be sterilized.

Medicinal Benefits Hemp seeds energetically support the kidney meridian. In addition to being a superior source of essential fatty acids, including omega-3s and gamma-linolenic acid, hemp seeds have about 20 percent of a highly digestible protein composed of edestins and albumins. Its amino acid profile is essentially complete when compared to common protein sources such as meat, dairy, soy, and eggs. Hemp seed is an adequate source of calcium and iron and a good source of phosphorus, magnesium, zinc, copper, and manganese. Hemp seed has anti-inflammatory properties.

MARIJUANA GREENS AS A SPRING TONIC

According to Don Wirtshafter, founder of the Ohio Hempery, a company that promotes hemp oil, it is only a small subspecies of the cannabis plant (*cannabis sativa* subsp. *indica*) that produces the psychotropic alkaloid, and since the alkaloid is a recessive gene, it is quickly lost if the plant cross-pollinates with other hemp plants. Other hemp plants abound in rich soil throughout much of the world. In the United States, nonpsychotropic hemp is a common ditch weed. Wirtshafter observes that in the States nobody bothers to pick it because it won't make you high.

Elsewhere in the world—Asia, Europe, and, historically, the Americas—the tender shoots are foraged as a spring green and cooked and eaten like spinach. The seeds are gathered in the fall for culinary purposes. In India, pounded hemp greens are mixed with honey and milk to make *bhang*, a cleansing spring tonic.

Use Hulled and split hemp seeds are available and look and taste rather like hulled sesame seeds. Enjoy them raw, ground into a meal or a seed butter, or sprinkled on salads and soups.

Be Mindful The hemp that appears in numerous food products is a by-product of pressing the seed for oil. These products include breakfast cereals, protein beverages, baked goods, and even ice cream. Any trace fats left in the hemp meal will be denatured when, as an added ingredient, it is heated or processed.

See **Hemp Family; Hemp Milk; Hemp Oil; Seeds.**

HEN-OF-THE-WOODS SEE **MAITAKE.**

HERBS AND SPICES

Herbs and spices are often said in the same breath and may be stored in the same cupboard, but technically they differ. Herbs are the leaves of herbaceous plants. Spices typically grow within 15 degrees of the equator and may be the bark, root, bud, fruit, or berry of a plant. Herbs remain primarily regional in use, depending on local availability. Spices played a significant role in religion and global economics. Spices instigated Marco Polo's travels and turned the small city-state of Venice into a great power. They launched Columbus's voyages, and the wealth from their trade formed the Dutch Empire.

Use The use of herbs and spices to flavor foods and as effective medicinal remedies is as old as cooking itself. Cuisine worldwide is defined more by spices and herbs than by food staples. For example, rice, beans, and vegetables are universal Asian ingredients, but it's the seasoning that identifies a dish as Punjabi, Korean, or Sichuan.

As a cook, it's a great pleasure to use spices and herbs—for a pinch of herbs you gain a large and satisfied "ahhhhh" in return. To season by taste, crush an herb or spice you suspect might go well in the dish you are preparing. Now smell the herb at the same time you taste the dish. If you like the way they meld, then it's a combination worth trying.

Fresh herbs lend a more delicate and refreshing flavor to foods than dried herbs. Take care not to overcook them and, therefore, denature their essential oils and flavor. When substituting dried herbs for fresh herbs, use 1 teaspoon dried herb for 1 tablespoon fresh.

Buying For maximum herb flavor, grow your own and snip them just prior to use. If you don't have a garden, consider a kitchen window herb garden: It requires minimum space and care. Best of all, when fresh herbs are at hand, using them is easy. Snipping at-hand chives is certainly more pleasurable and efficient than this alternative: Write "chives" on a shopping list, purchase them, refrigerate them, remember to use them before they're past prime, find them in the refrigerator, unwrap them, and, finally, dispose of their package.

For maximum spice flavor, buy spices whole and grind them prior to use. "A whole spice," according to herb and spice wholesaler Ann Wilder from Vanns Spices in Baltimore, "is pretty much immortal. Once ground, its oils deteriorate. Cardamom, for example, looses 50 percent of its aroma and flavor in one week."

According to Wilder, price is not an indicator of quality and—with imported product— verifying organic is impossible. A quality spice purveyor lists the country of origin and offers a fresh product that looks vibrant and has a fresh, clean, fragrant, and strong scent. Stale herbs easily crumble between your fingers, have little or an "off" aroma, and taste bitter and flat.

Be Mindful Unless organic, assume that a spice or dried herb has been irradiated or sterilized according to FDA ruling. Ethylene dibromide and ethylene oxide, potentially hazardous treatments banned in Europe, are the principal domestic fumigants. Fumigation reduces the oil and denatures the alkaloids in certain plants. Quality organic purveyors flash-freeze or use a superhot steam process to sterilize imported herbs and spices.

See **Ajowan; Angelica; Anise; Annatto; Asafetida; Basil; Bay Leaf; Borage; Caraway; Cardamom; Chamomile; Chervil; Chile Pepper; Chive; Cilantro; Cinnamon; Citrus Peel; Cloves; Corn Silk; Cumin; Curry Leaf; Dill; Echinacea; Epazote; Fennel; Fenugreek Seed; Galangal; Garlic; Garlic Chive; Ginger; Horseradish; Juniper Berry; Lavender; Lemon Balm; Lemongrass; Licorice Root; Long Pepper; Lovage; Mace; Marjoram; Maté; Mint; Muira Puama; Mustard Seed; Nigella Seed; Nutmeg; Oregano; Paprika; Parsley; Pepper; Perilla; Rosemary; Saffron; Sage; Sassafras; Savory; Sichuan Pepper; Star Anise; Tamarind; Tarragon; Thyme; Turmeric; Vanilla; Wasabi.**

HICKORY FAMILY
(*Juglandaceae*)

Deciduous trees with large nuts, this genus includes species native to North American and Asia. While the walnut and pecan have the largest commercial value, some would argue—I for one—that the black walnut is the most flavorful.

See **Black Walnut; Pecan; Walnut.**

HICKORY NUT SEE **PECAN.**

HIGH-FRUCTOSE CORN SYRUP SEE **CORN SYRUP; FRUCTOSE.**

HIJIKI
Hiziki
(*Hizikia fusiforme*)

The most mineral-rich of all seaweeds are the narrow ribbons of black hijiki. It grows near the low-water mark along the Japanese coast and is harvested in the winter and spring. Hijiki is sun-dried, boiled, and dried again. Hijiki strands are several inches long, slightly bulbous in the middle, and pointed on both ends.

Medicinal Benefits Hijiki has a salty flavor and cooling action and is a superior kidney food. It acts as a diuretic, helps stabilize blood sugar, helps detoxify the body, and supports the thyroid and bones. In Japan, hijiki is valued more than other seaweed as a food that increases one's beauty and strengthens and adds luster to the hair.

An extremely rich source of calcium and iron, one cup cooked hijiki contains calcium and iron—more calcium, in fact, than the same amount of milk. It is high in other trace elements, and a good source of protein, vitamin A, and the B vitamins. Hijiki, like all seaweed, is low in calories. It especially reduces *vata*.

Use Hijiki is black when dried or cooked. It is a deep brown when fresh or hydrated. Soaked hijiki expands to more than four times its original volume, so start with a small quantity. Sautéed or simmered with other vegetables, this seaweed has a unique flavor. If you're new to hijiki, try the accompanying recipe.

Be Mindful Always soak hijiki (preferably in warm or hot water) prior to using it, and discard the soaking water. Unlike other seaweeds, hijiki contains trace amounts of arsenic, which are safely removed with the soaking water.

See **Seaweed Family; Vegetable.**

HILBA SEE FENUGREEK GREENS.

HING SEE ASAFETIDA.

HIZIKI SEE HIJIKI.

HOKKAIDO PUMPKIN SEE SQUASH; SQUASH, WINTER.

GINGER CARROTS AND HIJIKI

I've yet to serve this to students and have leftovers. It seems that when a food is very good for you, quite often it also tastes very good. Bright orange and glistening black, this dish has a deep, mineral-sweet flavor. Hijiki is traditionally served as a small condiment rather than as a substantial side dish.

Serves 2 as a side dish, 4 as a condiment

- ¼ cup loosely packed hijiki
- 1 teaspoon unrefined oil
- 1 clove garlic, pressed or minced
- 1 teaspoon minced ginger
- 1 small onion, sliced
- 1 small carrot, cut into matchstick
- ½ cup water
- 1 tablespoon tamari soy sauce
- 1 tablespoon mirin or sweet white wine (optional)

Rinse the hijiki and soak it in a bowl with ½ cup water for 10 minutes. Drain and discard the soaking water, and chop the hijiki.

Warm the oil in a large skillet over medium heat. Add the garlic, ginger, hijiki, onion, and carrot and sauté for 5 minutes. Add the water and tamari, cover, and simmer for 15 minutes. If any liquid remains, uncover and cook until the liquid evaporates. Add the mirin, if using, adjust the seasoning as necessary, and serve.

HOLY BASIL SEE BASIL.

HOMINY SEE POSOLE.

HONEY

> We had some colonies of bees and I had been keeping track of progress and it was time to take off the apple-blossom honey before the white clover burst. I think the apple-blossom honey flow is the finest kind and look forward all winter to the supremacy of a comb on a pan of hot biscuits.
>
> —John Gould, *The Christian Science Monitor*

A worker bee foraging for flower nectar, a disaccharide, visits up to a hundred blossoms before returning to the hive. There the enzymatic action in the stomachs of the bees processes the nectar to a highly concentrated and refined sugar. One bee's lifetime foraging yields only a twelfth of a teaspoon of honey. What precious stuff. No wonder domesticated beekeeping dates back to the Bronze Age.

Take away the water from honey and it's about as sugary as white sugar. Honey does, however, retain nearly all of the flower nectars' original nutrients. In comparison to table sugar, it is minimally refined.

Some people exalt honey, others disparage it as comparable to white sugar, and vegans won't touch it because it's an animal product. Whatever your stance, savor it for its marvelous flavor and use it in moderation, as with all sweeteners.

Bees are subject to a variety of illnesses and some are treated with antibiotics, traces of which may show up in honey. The FDA periodically monitors honey for drug residues, adulteration (some fraudulent producers cut their product with high-fructose corn syrup or invert sugar), and botulism. A form of botulism (*Clostridium botulinum*) is associated with honey consumption and has caused some infant botulism deaths. Do not give honey to children under the age of two. Most commercial honey is produced in California, the Midwest, and Florida.

Medicinal Benefits Energetically, honey acts upon the stomach, spleen, and lungs. It tonifies, soothes, and nourishes and has laxative properties. It is also useful in cases of fluid retention. Some health-care experts believe that consuming local honey may decrease the allergic response for people with pollen allergies. Ayurvedic medicine has long observed that the beneficial properties of honey are destroyed when it is heated and that, furthermore, it become mucus forming. Raw honey reduces *vata* and *kapha*.

Honey contains up to 60 percent more sugar than white sugar. (There is no industry standard for honey because the composition of each kind varies according to its nectar source.) Seventy-five percent of honey is glucose and fructose. It is thus quickly absorbed and produces hypoglycemic symptoms. Honey is not, however, as empty of nutrients as is sugar because it contains minuscule amounts of enzymes and minerals.

Use Honey can be stirred into herbal tea, spooned on hot cereal, or smeared on toast. Honey is used as an ingredient in spreads, sauces, marinades, and dressings. Since honey absorbs and retains moisture, homemade baked goods made with honey as a sugar substitute stay fresher longer. Honey also reduces crumbliness in cookies and scones.

To use honey as a sugar replacement in baked goods, substitute ⅔ cup honey for 1 cup white sugar, reduce the liquid by ¼ cup, add ¼ teaspoon baking soda per cup of honey, reduce the oven temperature by 25 degrees, and increase baking time as necessary.

Buying Honey is mainly available in liquid form but is also available in the comb or creamed. I favor a local source of unpasteurized wildflower honey. Because of the genetic diversity of wildflowers, honey gathered from wild blossoms is superior in flavor and essence to cultivated crops like clover or orange. The best-quality honey, either dark or light, has not been heated to temperatures over 105°F; it is cloudy because of minimum filtration and clarification. The darker the honey, the more mineral rich it is and the stronger it is in taste.

Most commercial honey is a blend from several different nectar sources. The single most common honey available is from clover; it has a pleasing, mild flavor and varies in color depending upon the clover variety, from very light to amber. Other types include alfalfa, basswood, blackberry, buckwheat, eucalyptus, lavender, orange blossom, tupelo, and wildflower.

ENDLESS HONEY VARIETIES

All edible flowering plants, that's nearly half a million, can potentially, and with the help of a hive of bees, yield honey from their pollen. Just imagine the varieties of pleasure and flavor that you've yet to try! Last year at the Mountain People's Co-op in Nederland, Colorado, I found honey derived from coffee blossoms. It doesn't smell or taste like coffee, but its essence is coffee-like. It's delicious and uplifting and almost has a zing to it.

Another treat comes from Mike Curtis at Wild Bee Honey Farm in Eagle Point, Oregon. His poison oak honey is deeply sweet but leaves a tingle on my tongue reminiscent of immature persimmon. Some say it antidotes a poison oak rash. Rash or otherwise, I say yes to the tingle in a spoonful of honey.

Storage Store honey at room temperature away from direct sunlight. Do not refrigerate honey; refrigeration speeds crystallization, which thickens the honey and turns it cloudy and grainy. To reliquefy, remove the lid, place the honey container in a saucepan with water, and heat slowly until all the crystals are dissolved.

See **Sweeteners.**

HONEYBUSH
(*Cyclopia intermedia*)

The herb honeybush is a member of the large legume family and native to southwest South Africa. It makes a naturally sweet-tasting and aromatic herbal tea that smells like honey. It's similar to rooibos tea regarding family, place of origin, fermentation process, and recent introduction to the West. Honeybush is, however, green rather than red and has a more fruity and floral flavor and aroma.

It contains no caffeine and is very low in tannins. Honeybush phytoestrogens give it antifungal, antiviral, antimicrobial, anti-inflammatory, and antioxidant properties. It helps regulate the menstrual cycle and prevent breast, prostate, and uterus cancer.

See **Legume Family.**

HONEYDEW SEE MELON.

HONEY TANGERINE SEE ORANGE (TANGOR).

HOPS
(*Humulus lupulus*)

Most famous as a beer flavoring ingredient, hops, the fruit of this vine, are a hemp relative. Hops are a common herbal remedy to antidote anxiety, muscle tension, and insomnia. They also improve the appetite and digestion. Hops are readily available as an ingredient in herbal infusions and as a tincture. The essential oil of hops treats neuralgia, bruising, and menstrual and menopausal problems, and is a nerve tonic, diuretic, sedative, and analgesic.

See **Hemp Family; Herbs and Spices.**

HOP YEUNG QWA SEE **CHAYOTE.**

HORN CHESTNUT SEE **HORNED WATER CHESTNUT.**

HORNED CUCUMBER SEE **KIWANO.**

HORNED WATER CHESTNUT
Horn Chestnut, Water Caltrop
(*Trapa bicornis*)

This handsome Asian vegetable, aptly named in Latin "two fruit horns," looks like a play mustache. Each horned point contains a seed, but it's the crisp, starchy central part (16 percent starch) that is cooked and used like a water chestnut and, historically, as a grain substitute. The horned water chestnut is an aquatic plant of the large sedge family that grows in marshes and lakes. Its leaves form a nosegay on the water surface and bear small white flowers; as the plant matures, the chestnuts form under the water surface. A fresh horned water chestnut is plump with firm, creamy colored, unblemished flesh.

This aquatic oddity is new to our markets, but it has been used in both Europe and Asia since the Stone Age. In India, it is called *Singhara* or *paniphal* and when sun-dried and ground its flour is used in batters, flatbreads, and puddings. The European variety (*T. natans*) has four horns rather than two and was called the Jesuit's nut. In Europe, it is still foraged.

To use, shell with a nutcracker. Steam, stir-fry, braise, add to soups, or cook in a honey syrup as a sweetmeat.

See **Vegetable; Water Chestnut.**

HORN MELON SEE **KIWANO.**

HORSE BEAN SEE **FAVA BEAN.**

HORSERADISH
(*Armoracia lapathifolia, A. rusticana*)

What gnarly root vegetable is biting hot, has a cooling aftertaste, and its aficionados equate one taste with rapture? Horseradish. Grate it into shreds and *judiciously* mix it into sauces. If, like most people, you regard horseradish as a food oddity, something your grandmother would have served, think again. Especially, that is, if you're wild about the dab of lurid green wasabi that's served alongside sushi. That's actually horseradish plus green food coloring. (Unless, that is, you're dining at a five-star restaurant serving *real* Japanese wasabi. Compared to horseradish, pale green wasabi is hotter and more aromatic.)

Horseradish gets its wallop from mustard oil (allyl isothiocyanate). This oil, a defining characteristic of the cabbage family, is slight in Chinese cabbage and cauliflower, but it reigns in horseradish. Mustard oil makes horseradish both memorable and medicinal.

Horseradish is one of the five bitter herbs (along with coriander, horehound, lettuce, and nettle) eaten during the Jewish seder, or Passover feast. Still a popular spice in Europe and Western Asia, horseradish was once common in American gardens. (I got a horseradish start for my garden from the original homestead in my neighborhood.)

While a classic accompaniment to corned beef and sauerbraten, a horseradish sauce is a great topping for grain pilafs and adds pizzazz to a homey bowl of beans. It's versatile and adds interest to both mild and strongly flavored foods.

Medicinal Benefits Horseradish is pungent and stimulating to the lung and colon meridians. It inhibits bacterial infection, increases perspiration and circulation, and acts as a diuretic. Its ethnobotanical uses as a medicinal agent are impressive . . . and backed by today's science. Horseradish is an anticancer agent, and it stimulates and cleanses the mucous surfaces throughout the entire body. It increases the appetite and circulation; it aids digestion, inhibits bacterial infection, and is a weight reduction aid. A diuretic, horseradish helps treat edema and kidney stones. Historically, horseradish is also used for rheumatic and arthritic conditions. For instant relief from sinus infections, hold ¼ teaspoon of freshly grated root in your mouth until its taste is gone. This cuts mucus loose, enables drainage, and relieves sinus pressure and infection. It reduces *kapha*.

Use An intact horseradish root is not remarkable in appearance or action. Grate it, however, and your eyes will water and your nose will burn. Horseradish's oil dissipates quickly upon exposure to air, and it is destroyed by heat, so use it raw and freshly grated. To temporarily preserve its intensity, mix it with a sour ingredient like lemon juice, vinegar, or sour cream.

While bottled horseradish sauce is also pungent, I hope you'll try some fresh, as it has a brighter and sweeter taste. Fresh horseradish is easy to use and store. The leaves, when young, make an excellent salad green.

Buying Look for plump, firm, crisp roots, which are often—but not always—available at well-supplied grocery stores. These foot-long, buff-colored, carrot-shaped roots are typically cut into chunks at the market and often plastic wrapped. A piece of horseradish will keep, refrigerated, for months. Horseradish is also available as a dried powder and in prepared condiments.

See **Cabbage Family; Herbs and Spices; Vegetable.**

HOT PEPPER SEE CHILE PEPPER.

HUBBARD SQUASH SEE SQUASH.

HUCKLEBERRY
Bilberry, Whortleberry
(*Gaylussacia baccata*)

The huckleberry is small, wild, and full of seeds, and compared to a strawberry, for example, seems inconsequential. Building on this, Mark Twain named his famous character Huckleberry Finn to indicate a boy "of lower extraction or degree" than Tom Sawyer.

Huckleberry flesh varies from purple to red and its flavor from sweet to tart. Use interchangeably with blueberries. You're most apt to find huckleberries in jams and other preserves rather than as whole berries.

The huckleberry (*Vaccinium parvifolium*) of the Pacific Northwest is a wild blueberry and has soft, hardly noticeable seeds.

See **Blueberry Family.**

HUITLACOCHE
Corn Smut, Cuitlacoche
(*Ustilago maydis*)

This somewhat scarce corn product is a parasitic fungus that attacks corn and other cereal grains. It is found worldwide on corn, wheat, rye, and other grains during the rainy season.

Medicinal Benefits Huitlacoche is cold in thermal properties; it is a tonic for the liver, stomach, and intestines. It has a long tradition in both Asian and Western medicine for enhancing uterine contractions during labor and for postpartum use to control bleeding. It also is used to regulate and tonify the uterus and ovaries.

Use Huitlacoche is a true delicacy that tastes something like wild mushrooms and corn. Slice and sauté for about 15 minutes. Combine with other vegetables, or serve alone as a side dish.

Buying Commercially, huitlacoche is available in Mexico dried, canned, and fresh in the markets. Locally, ask corn growers—especially during a wet season—to watch for it and save you some.

HUNGARIAN PAPRIKA SEE **PAPRIKA.**

HUSK CHERRY SEE **GROUND CHERRY.**

HUSK TOMATO SEE **TOMATILLO.**

ICEBERG LETTUCE SEE **LETTUCE**.

IMBE
(*Garcinia livingstonei*)

A small, Day-Glo orange tropical fruit from East Africa, now also grown in Florida, the imbe is a thin-skinned, juicy fruit with sweet, mildly acidic flesh. More seed than fruit, the imbe is eaten fresh and used in beverages. It is available September through March.

INDIAN FIG SEE **PRICKLY PEAR**.

INDIAN LONG PEPPER SEE **LONG PEPPER**.

INDIAN MULBERRY SEE **NONI**.

INDIAN SAFFRON SEE **TURMERIC**.

IRISH MOSS
Carrageenan, Rock Moss, Sea Moss, Gristle Moss
(*Chondrus crispus*)

Found near the low-tide mark throughout the Atlantic and Pacific coasts, Irish moss is a beautiful, densely tufted, reddish purple to greenish white seaweed. One bushy head grows from a two- to four-inch holdfast, which clings on rocks, shells, and wood pilings. Classified as a red algae, Irish moss has a long culinary history throughout Europe and the United States.

Irish moss is easily foraged. Collect storm-cast greens from a clean beach or rake it by hand at low tide from small boats. It is produced in Massachusetts, the Canadian Maritimes, Hawaii, Ireland, and Brittany.

Medicinal Benefits Long noted for its medicinal properties, Irish moss is used in cough preparations; for digestive disorders (including ulcers), kidney ailments, heart disease, and glandular irregularities; and as a bowel regulator. Irish moss is exceptionally high in vitamin A and iodine. It is highest in vitamin A when harvested in summer. Irish moss also contains iron, sodium, copper, and numerous trace minerals, as well as protein and vitamin B_1. It reduces *vata*.

Use The high sulfur content of Irish moss gives it a sea odor much stronger than that of other seaweeds. Rinsing it several times and soaking it reduces this strong odor. Before adding it to a delicately flavored or sweet dish, soak it for 20 minutes or more. For a savory dish, a 10-minute soak is adequate.

Irish moss provides an excellent gel, softer than agar gel. Its extract, often called carrageenan, has numerous culinary uses. An essential ingredient in blancmange, it is used in beer, ice cream, salad dressings, candy, and puddings or is added to soups and stews as a vegetable. It is an ingredient in a traditional bread of northern France, *pain aux algues.*

Buying Irish moss is occasionally available dried in natural food stores. It is more commonly found as an ingredient in prepared foods.

See **Seaweed Family; Vegetable.**

ISRAELI COUSCOUS SEE **COUSCOUS.**

ITALIAN BROWN MUSHROOM SEE **MUSHROOM, COMMON.**

ITALIAN KALE SEE **KALE.**

ITA WAKAME SEE **WAKAME.**

JABORANDI PEPPER SEE LONG PEPPER.

JABUTICABA
(*Myrciaria cauliflora*)

Not limited to twigs—this subtropical fruit sprouts directly from the tree trunk and large branches of a Brazilian tree. The jabuticaba is like a purple grape in taste, size, shape, and juiciness. Its sugary flesh, however, is milky, and its skin, though edible, is tougher than a grape's and high in tannin. Its small seeds—from one to four per fruit—are edible. Available spring through fall, the fruits are eaten fresh and used in preserves, sauces, and desserts or juiced for beverages and wine. Refrigerated, the jabuticaba stores for up to two weeks; at room temperature, it quickly ferments. Jabuticaba fruits have antioxidant, anti-inflammatory, and anticancer compounds.

See **Myrtle Family.**

JACKFRUIT
(*Artocarpus heterophyllus*)

The jackfruit tree, native to India and Malaysia, currently grows in Florida and most tropical countries. A relative of breadfruit and figs, it is a vegetable staple in many Asian countries; when ripe, it is eaten as fruit and has a banana- and pineapple-like flavor. The jackfruit is among the largest fruits of any tropical plants and can measure up to three feet in length, nearly two feet in diameter, and weigh up to 65 pounds. Its green skin is covered with short, sharp spikes. It is a composite fruit consisting of large bulbs of yellow flesh enclosing a smooth oval seed, surrounding a central pithy core.

Medicinal Benefits Jackfruit pulp and seeds are considered a cooling, nutritious, tonifying food that helps counteract the influence of alcohol. The ripe fruit has laxative properties. Dried seeds contain B-complex vitamins, calcium, iron, and sulfur.

Use When immature, the jackfruit is boiled and used as a vegetable, added to chutneys, or dried and ground into a starchy meal. Its cooked seeds taste something like chestnuts and are added to soups or ground into flour. When mature, jackfruit is eaten raw as a fruit, juiced, added to salads, or served with yogurt. Cooked, it may be pureed for a sauce or preserved in syrups. Jackfruit is also dried. The fruit's skin, core, and the uncooked seed are inedible.

Buying There are two main jackfruit varieties: soft flesh with sweet, juicy pulp, and a crisp variety that is less juicy and sweet. Purchase a fruit that is without bruises or soft spots. Because of its size, jackfruit is often sold precut.

Storing As jackfruit continues to ripen after it is picked, store a whole, immature jackfruit at room temperature for three to ten days. When ripe, its spikes stand clear of one another, its color changes from lime green to yellow or brown, and it has a heavy aroma similar to rotting onions. Its cut flesh, however, has a sweet tropical perfume. Refrigerate when ripe.

See **Fig Family; Fruit.**

JACOB'S CATTLE BEAN SEE **BEANS AND LEGUMES.**

JAGGERY SEE **SUGAR.**

JALAPEÑO SEE **CHILE PEPPER.**

JAPANESE ARTICHOKE SEE **CROSNE.**

JAPANESE HORSERADISH SEE **WASABI.**

JAPANESE MEDLAR SEE **LOQUAT.**

JAPANESE MUSTARD SEE **MUSTARD GREENS.**

JAPANESE PLUM SEE **LOQUAT.**

JAPANESE PUMPKIN SEE **SQUASH.**

JASMINE
(*Jasminum officinale*)

Jasmine blossoms, with their heady, tropical scent, are a favorite perfume and cosmetic ingredient and an important herb in both Chinese and Ayurvedic medicine. Jasmine is used to relieve depression, calm the nerves, and dissolve damp problems such as edema and candidiasis. Its roots and oil, as well as its blossoms, are useful in treating cancer and headaches. Jasmine is also considered an aphrodisiac. It reduces *pitta* and *kapha*.

There are several jasmine varieties including one, Arabian jasmine (*J. sambac*), used primarily to flavor green tea. These sweet blossoms are so aromatic that simply storing them alongside delicate green tea is all that's needed to permeate the tea leaves with the scent of jasmine. Other blends of jasmine tea are predominantly green tea mixed with a few jasmine blossoms.

The essential oil of jasmine treats tension, depression, menstrual problems, laryngitis, anxiety, and lethargy.

See **Olive Family.**

JASMINE RICE SEE **RICE.**

JELLY MELON SEE **KIWANO.**

JERUSALEM ARTICHOKE
Sunchoke
(*Helianthus tuberosus*)

The Spanish named the ubiquitous Native American sunflower *girasol*, because from dawn to dust its blossoms turn from east to west following the sun. Presumably, this word sounded like Jerusalem. That, together with the tuber's sweet, almost artichokelike flavor when cooked, is probably how it earned the unlikely name of Jerusalem artichoke.

Its edible tuber looks like a small, but more knobby and gnarly, ginger root. The flesh is sweet, crisp, and white or yellow. The skin is light tan and sometimes has purplish tinge. The plant, which has narrower leaves and smaller heads than the common sunflower, is widely distributed throughout the United States. This tuber, cultivated by numerous Native American tribes prior to colonization, is frost-hardy and, unlike potatoes, may be harvested year-round.

Medicinal Benefits Jerusalem artichokes are a superior source of inulin, a natural fructose that is medicinal for diabetics. This sweet tuber relieves asthmatic conditions, treats constipation, and nourishes the lungs. Dr K. M Nadkarni, Ayurvedic author of the *Indian Materia Medica*, considers Jerusalem artichokes an aphrodisiac and an enhancer of semen production. They balance *pitta* and *kapha*, and may be used in moderation for *vata*. Jerusalem artichoke also contains vitamins A and B-complex, potassium, iron, calcium, and magnesium. Unlike most root vegetables, it contains no starchy carbohydrates.

Use Jerusalem artichokes are enjoyed raw, they have a crunchy texture and a mild sunflowerlike flavor, and they may be sautéed, braised, steamed, baked, or pickled. If boiling, take care not to overcook, as they toughen and become rubbery Although most people can easily digest Jerusalem artichokes, some people experience digestive discomfort.

Buying The Jerusalem artichoke is at its peak in flavor and availability in fall and winter. Select firm tubers; avoid limp, wilted, wrinkled, or sprouting ones or any that have green blotched areas. Modern cultivars, such as the Fuseau, are less knobby than heirloom varieties.

Be Mindful Some people do not easily digest inulin, and so Jerusalem artichokes may cause flatulence and gastric pain. If this is a new vegetable for you, experiment with a small amount for your first serving.

See **Daisy Family; Sunflower Seed; Vegetable.**

JEUNG QWA SEE CHAYOTE.

JICAMA
Yam Bean, Sa Kot
(*Pachyrhizus erosus*)

A Central American root vegetable, jicama (HEE-kuh-muh) is the underground tuber of a legume; it looks like a beige, oversize turnip. Jicama skin is easily peeled to reveal crisp, slightly sweet flesh that's similar to water chestnuts—only crunchier and with a flavor reminiscent of green beans.

Medicinal Benefits An excellent food for dieters, jicama is up to 90 percent water and the rest is mostly fiber. Its sweet flavor comes from inulin. Jicama balances *pitta* and *kapha* and can be used in moderation for *vata* conditions.

Use Jicama may be eaten as you would water chestnuts, Jerusalem artichokes, or potatoes, and although its flavor diminishes with cooking, it doesn't lose its crunch. Peel the tan outer skin and the fibrous inner layer. Because of its bland flavor, jicama goes with almost any other vegetable. Raw, jicama retains its hint of sweet and lends itself well to both fruit and vegetable salads or as crudités. A popular Latin American preparation is to season raw slices with lime juice, salt, and ground chile to taste, or serve sliced jicama with salsa for dipping.

Buying Select firm, heavy roots that are fresh looking and relatively unblemished. Smaller roots up to three pounds in weight are juicier than the larger ones. Jicama stores best at cool (53 to 60°F) temperatures.

See **Legume Family.**

JINENJO
Batata, Dioscorea, Long Potato, Mountain Yam, Wild Yam, Yamaimo
(*Dioscoreaceae opposita, D. villosa*)

Native Americans and Asians all value the jinenjo as food and as medicine. It's a slightly hairy, buff-colored tuber. Some varieties are skinny as a cucumber and grow to lengths of three feet. Other varieties are fat and yamlike in shape.

Medicinal Benefits Sweet tasting and warming, jinenjo contains hormone precursors that affect the female menstrual cycle and help to reduce pain. In fact, jinenjo extract was the original source for diosgenin in birth control pills; currently it is synthesized. Jinenjo contains allantoin, which is medicinal for stomach ulcers and asthma. It yields the anti-inflammatories steroids and cortisone, which treat rheumatism. It strengthens the lungs, spleen, and kidneys; increases stamina; rejuvenates; supports the liver and gallbladder; and is used for the treatment of various digestive disorders. Jinenjo contains even more starch-digesting enzymes than daikon does. In Ayurvedic medicine, jinenjo is used for sexual and hormonal problems.

Use Grated raw jinenjo is gooey and slimy. Season this goo with a splash of soy sauce and you have a potent digestive aid with a sweet taste. Jinenjo may be cooked like potato chips or potato patties, or used as a binder to hold other ingredients together. When cooked, it loses its mucilaginous quality.

Buying Purchase jinenjo dried for use in medicinal teas. It is also used as a strengthening ingredient in some prepared Japanese foods such as soba noodles. You'll find jinenjo root in Asian markets, often stored in sawdust. Break off as large a section as you wish to purchase. Refrigerate it. Although the cut ends become discolored, the jinenjo will keep for a week or more.

See **Yam; Yam Family**.

JOB'S TEARS
Hato Mugi, Yi Yi Ren
(*Coix lacryma-jobi*)

This heirloom grain has been cultivated in Africa and Asia for centuries. It looks like a large ebony teardrop, and it is strung for rosary beads and other prayer beads. Its black, impervious hull, which makes it a sturdy bead, is inedible. Once hulled, this grain looks like a giant gray pearl barley, and has a sweet flavor.

Medicinal Benefits Job's tears strengthen the stomach and spleen. The grain cools and reduces inflammation and pain and is useful for arthritis and urinary problems. In macrobiotic literature, the grain Job's tears is acclaimed for its anticancer properties; it is considered too strong to consume during pregnancy and menstruation. In Ayurvedic medicine, it is used as a blood purifier.

Use Soak Job's tears prior to use. This grain requires longer cooking than barley and is less sticky than either rice or barley. Combine it with rice or another grain or add it to long-cooking soups.

Buying You can purchase Job's tears from herb stores, Chinese pharmacies, and as a prepared cereal or beverage from Asian markets.

See **Grains; Grass Family**.

JOWAR SEE **SORGHUM**.

JUJUBE
Chinese Date, Red Date
(*Ziziphus zizyphus*)

The jujube, which are "to the Chinese what apples are to Americans," is a fruit about the size of a date that is red, has a fragrant aroma, and tastes like a mildly sweet and sour apple. It grows on small deciduous shrubs or trees, has a single slender pit that is pointed on both ends, and is the only fruit of its species commonly used as a food.

Medicinal benefits When dried, the jujube wrinkles and turns dark red. As such, it is prized throughout Asia as a medicinal ingredient. Jujube builds chi, nourishes the blood, benefits the spleen, helps alleviate stress, and treats the common cold and sore throats.

Buying I've found fresh jujube at farmers' markets in the fall. They're available in Asian markets dried, candied, preserved, juiced, canned, and as a tea or syrup. When smoked, they're known as black jujube.

JUNIPER BERRY
(*Juniperus communis*)

Gin, the alcohol, is flavored with juniper berries, and the names Jenny, Geneviève, and Geneva (Switzerland) all refer to the juniper tree. The small, dusky or dark purple berrylike cones of the common evergreen juniper tree have a sharp pine flavor and are a popular medicinal and culinary agent. They're a relative of the giant redwood trees.

Medicinal Benefits Juniper berries are bitter tasting and antiseptic. They improve digestion and are used for urinary tract cystitis and urethritis, arthritic-type complaints, and neuralgia. They are not to be used for kidney inflammation. Juniper berries reduce *pitta* and *kapha*.

Use Juniper berries are used to season strong-flavored dishes such as meat marinades—especially for game meats—pâté, pork, sauerkraut, and pickles. To use, remove any seeds, crush the berry, and add as a seasoning ingredient. Ten berries season one pound of meat.

Buying/Foraging Juniper trees are among our most common landscape greenery. When foraging, do not harvest berries from red or savin cedars, as their oils are too toxic for internal use. Juniper berries are also available in the spice section of well-stocked natural food stores.

See **Herbs and Spices.**

KABOCHA SQUASH SEE **SQUASH**.

KAFFIR LIME SEE **LIME**.

KAFFIR LIME LEAVES
(*Citrus hystrix*)

The species name for kaffir lime, *hystrix* (Greek for porcupine), refers to the plant's many thorns. The wrinkled, rough, yellow fruit has aggressive lemon aroma and little culinary use. The hourglass-shaped leaves and rind, on the other hand, are popular seasoning ingredients in Thai, Balinese, and Javanese cuisine where the tree originated. When gently rubbed, the richly perfumed leaves release a luscious citrus scent.

Medicinal Benefits In Indonesian medicine the kaffir is used as an insecticide and referred to as "medicine citrus."

Use Kaffir lime leaves are often added to Thai soups, stir-fries, and curries, along with garlic, galangal, ginger, chiles, and fresh Thai basil. Although lime or lemon peel is the nearest approximation, kaffir lime's strong perfume cannot easily be duplicated. The rind, powdered or grated, is available in Asian markets. The fruit's juice, which is intensely sour and has the same fragrance as the leaves, is sometimes added to fish or poultry dishes in Malaysian and Thai cuisine.

For simmering in soups and curries, the leaves are used whole, like a bay leaf. To add to salads or to sprinkle over curries for a burst of flavor, remove the thick mid-rib and finely shred the leaves.

Buying/Storage Look for fresh kaffir leaves in the herb section of large supermarkets or in Asian markets. Because dried kaffir time leaves lose their flavor readily, they are best kept frozen.

See **Herbs and Spices; Lime**.

KAI-LAN SEE **CHINESE BROCCOLI**.

KALE
Dinosaur, Italian, or Tuscan Kale; Ornamental Kale; Scotch or Curly Kale; Siberian or Russian Kale
(*Brassica oleracea acephala*)

Kale is the grandmother of the whole cabbage family. One would expect such an old-timer to be hardy, and indeed kale is. It has a strident flavor, a sturdy appearance, and the pluck to withstand frost and even snow. In fact, kale is sweetest after a good frost or, in mild climates, after it has wintered over. Like a collard green in size and shape, a kale leaf is crisp and tightly curled—like curly parsley. Leaf colors range from light through dark green and violet-green to purple.

Kale has remained a staple vegetable throughout Europe. In Scotland it is so associated with food that the phrase "to be off one's kale" means to be too ill to eat. Over the past few decades, kale has enjoyed increasing popularity in the United States both at the table and as a name for boys.

Medicinal Benefits Kale is warming and when fresh has a sweet and slightly bitter-pungent flavor. When old, its bitter tone increases. Kale eases lung congestion, benefits the stomach, and is a specific healer for the liver and the immune system. Its juice is medicinal for treating stomach and duodenal ulcers. Overall it's a strengthening vegetable. Kale reduces *pitta* and *kapha*.

Kale contains the nutraceuticals lutein and zeaxanthin, which protect the eyes from macular degeneration, and indole-3-carbinol, which may protect against colon cancer. It is an exceptional source of chlorophyll, beta-carotene, vitamins A and C, and a reasonable source of calcium.

Use Substitute kale for cabbage whenever you want a bright green color and additional chlorophyll. Use the very young leaves in salads. Garden-fresh kale may be lightly steamed; if older, it requires longer cooking.

Buying Kale is available year-round but is best in the cold months. Select crisp—not limp—kale with a bright, fresh color and no signs of yellow or decay. The most common kale varieties available today are:

- **Dinosaur, Italian, or Tuscan Kale** is an old variety with narrow, almost black-green savoylike leaves and a sweet, mild flavor.
- **Ornamental Kale** grows like a flat bouquet of ruffly-edged brilliant white, red, pink, or lavender leaves; it is more dramatic than many flowers. Not as flavorful as the more modest varieties, ornamental kale is most typically used as a garnish at food displays, where it holds up for hours, or as a border along a flower bed.
- **Scotch or Curly Kale** is dark green or even blue-green with very curly leaves.
- **Siberian or Russian Kale** has broader, deeply serrated leaves that may or may not be curled. It is available in green or red varieties. This is the largest growing variety.

See **Cabbage; Cabbage Family; Vegetable.**

KALONJI See **NIGELLA.**

PACIFIC HALIBUT STEAMED ON A BED OF KALE AND PIMIENTO

Steaming is the best way to showcase halibut's delicate flavor. Cooked atop onions, kale, and fresh pimiento further enhances halibut's sweet essence, and it provides the meal's freshly cooked—and deliciously flavored—vegetable. Wild Pacific halibut is a lean fish that breaks into large tender flakes when cooked. It's available fresh from May to December. (Atlantic halibut is farmed and not recommended.)

This no-fuss recipe is one of my favorites, as it has but one pot to clean and yields such a colorful and winsome meal served with a side of quinoa or a hunk of bread. You can also substitute salmon or another fish steak. If using sole or a fish fillet, slice the vegetables thinner so they'll cook more quickly.

Serves 2

- 1 bunch kale
- 1 large onion, sliced into thin rounds
- 1 small fresh pimiento or ½ red bell pepper, seeded and sliced into thin rounds
- 2 small 1½-inch-thick wild Pacific halibut steaks
- 1 tablespoon freshly squeezed lemon juice
- Unrefined salt and freshly ground black pepper
- Unrefined hemp or olive oil
- 2 sprigs fresh dill

Strip the stems from kale by grasping the stem in one hand. With the fingers of your other hand, starting at the bottom of the leaf, pull the leaf in one direction and the stem in the other direction. Reserve the stems for stock or another use. Coarsely chop the leaves.

Arrange the onion slices, kale, and half of the pimiento slices in a sauté pan. Add enough water to cover the bottom of the pan by ¼ inch. Place the halibut steaks on top and add the remaining pimiento slices. Add the lemon juice and salt and pepper to taste. Cover tightly and steam for 5 minutes, or until the center of each steak is no longer translucent. Watch closely, adding additional water if necessary; do not overcook.

With a spatula, lift each steak along with its vegetable bed and place on a plate. Dress with oil and garnish with dill. Serve hot.

KAMUT See WHEAT.

KANTEN
(Gelidium amansii)

Kanten is a blend of agar varieties used as a gelling agent in Japan. It is available flaked—in small packets—or in an eight-inch bar that looks and feels like cellophane. Kanten is prepared using a centuries-old traditional method that includes outdoor freeze-drying in the winter. One bar of kanten (or three tablespoons of agar flakes) will gel two cups of liquid. Agar, available in bulk in most natural food stores, is a less pricey gelling agent than kanten.

See **Agar; Seaweed Family; Vegetable.**

KARELA See BITTER MELON.

KASHA See BUCKWHEAT.

KASHI

Contrary to what some people may think, Kashi is not a grain; it is a trademarked blend of grains.

KAVA
(Piper methysticum)

Early Christian missionaries in the South Pacific vilified kava, presumably for its cultural and symbolic valve . . . or was it for the pleasure it brings? Who knows. Despite the missionaries' best efforts, kava drinking couldn't be squelched. Indeed, the peoples of the far-flung Oceania communities—from Australia to Hawaii—remain linked in their kava-drinking customs. Today North Americans value it as a relaxant. Kava is extracted from the pounded roots of a black pepper relative of the same name.

Medicinal Benefits One difficulty in addressing the medicinal properties of kava is that there are at least nine distinct chemotypes (each with different chemical properties). In general, however, kava is recognized by European health authorities as a relatively safe remedy for anxiety. Kava is a muscle relaxant and counters insomnia, fatigue, asthma, and rheumatism. It acts as a diuretic and has some local anesthetic properties. While kava is apparently not addictive, daily use for several months or more may cause skin lesions.

Use To make a kava beverage, place 2 tablespoons powdered kava in a coffee filter or four layers of cheesecloth, pour 1 cup of cold water through the kava, and drink immediately. The flavor of kava is peppery with sour and bitter overtones.

Buying Kava is available in capsules, tinctures, chopped root, and in a powdered form, with or without added flavors.

See **Pepper Family.**

KELP
Brown Algae
(*Laminaria*)

Giant pumpkins weigh more than 800 pounds, and a Douglas fir can reach 400 feet—puny compared to giant kelp, which sprawls up to 1,500 feet in length. No wonder kelp is also called "oar weed."

The kelp family, which includes kombu, sea palm, wakame, and arame, is the largest, most studied, and most widely consumed of the seaweeds. Kelp is also a generic term for seaweed.

Medicinal Benefits Medicinally, kelp is used for blood pressure regulation, weight loss, as a digestive aid and colon cleanser, and to alleviate kidney, reproductive, circulation, and nerve problems. Kelp reduces *vata*.

One serving provides the recommended daily allowance of iodine and has only 15 calories. Kelp is high in calcium, iron, and all the major minerals. It is a plentiful source of trace elements such as copper, zinc, and chromium and contains various vitamins, including A, B_6, B_{12}, C, D, and K.

Use Kelp is most commonly sold as powder or in tablet form. Some people use powdered kelp as a salt replacement in savory dishes. Kelp has numerous commercial uses as a stabilizer, an emulsifier, a suspending agent, and a thickener. When hydrated, its volume increases by almost 40 percent. Kelp does not complement milk, melon, or delicately flavored desserts. It does, however, complement just about everything else, including seafood, vegetables, grains, beans, squash, potatoes, and meat.

Raw, it has a slightly acrid, salty taste. It becomes sweeter with cooking. Check dry fronds for foreign material, and toast until brittle (about 2 minutes at 350°F) to make a tasty snack food. Pan-fry kelp in oil until crisp, and crumble to sprinkle on salads or as a condiment for grains. Or hydrate, cook until tender, about 15 minutes, and season to taste.

See **Arame; Kombu; Sea Palm; Seaweed Family; Vegetable; Wakame.**

KEY LIME SEE LIME.

KHORASAN SEE WHEAT.

KIDNEY BEAN SEE BEANS AND LEGUMES.

KING BOLETE SEE BOLETE.

KIWANO
Horned Cucumber, Horned Melon, Jelly Melon
(*Cucumis metuliferus*)

Kiwano, the African melon that resembles a multispiked spacecraft, is weird-looking. It has a brilliant orange-yellow skin and a seedy flesh that might remind you of lime Jell-O. It's the size of a fist, with a bland, unremarkable flavor vaguely reminiscent of bananas and cucumbers.

Medicinal Benefits The kiwano is a cooling fruit that helps relieve thirst. It is over 90 percent water and is high in vitamin C.

Use The most spectacular use of a kiwano is to halve it, scoop out its flesh, and use its shells to hold individual servings of fruit soup or salad. Or peel the skin and add the flesh to salad, soup, sorbet, or yogurt. When sweetened, its juice makes a tasty summer beverage. A kiwano is best eaten raw.

Buying Select a bright yellow or orange kiwano with firm spikes and firm, undamaged skin. Do not purchase one with dull-colored skin. Today kiwanos are grown in New Zealand and California and are available year-round in specialty sections of supermarkets. When handled with care, kiwanos will store at room temperature or in the refrigerator for several weeks. They are most delicious, however, when used within a week.

See **Fruit; Gourd Family.**

KIWI
Chinese Gooseberry
(*Actinidia deliciosa, syn. A. chinensis*)

A kiwi looks like a furry brown egg, with a sweet but acid-tasting, brilliant green or golden flesh. Tiny edible black seeds are embedded around an edible white core. A native of China, kiwifruit is now grown in temperate regions throughout the world and is available year-round.

Medicinal Benefits Kiwis are cold in nature and therefore clear heat. They help promote the production of fluids and so help induce urination and relieve a dry mouth or throat, or even thirst for those with feverish diseases. They support the stomach and bladder meridians. To aid in the passage of kidney stones, the Chinese recommend eating kiwis or drinking kiwi juice. They help lower fat in the blood and reduce the risk of clots. Kiwis are too cooling for a person with cold or stagnant energy in the spleen and stomach meridians. Kiwi reduces *vata.*

Kiwis are nutrient dense and their seeds contain essential fatty acids. They are an excellent source of vitamin C and potassium. At 45 calories per fruit, kiwis are a low-calorie food.

Use Kiwis are eaten out of hand—peeled or unpeeled. They can also be served juiced, in ice cream, and in fruit salads. They are often used in mixed-fruit tarts. They make a bold garnish and, cooked, are tasty in compotes and preserves. They contain a protein-dissolving enzyme that makes them unsuitable for use in desserts containing dairy or gelatin; unless, that is, the dessert will be served within a few hours, for otherwise the enzyme will start to digest the protein. Cooking, however, deactivates the enzyme. Or put the enzyme to use as a meat tenderizer by rubbing meat with a sliced kiwi; discard the kiwi and let the meat stand for 20 to 30 minutes prior to cooking.

Buying Look for firm, plump, unwrinkled fruit with a fragrant scent. Some kiwis appear to have water stains on their skin; this is normal. Allow to ripen by leaving at room temperature for a few days until the fruit feels like a ripe pear and gives to gentle pressure. A kiwi will also ripen gradually if it is refrigerated for several weeks.

Be Mindful Raw kiwi contains the protein-dissolving enzyme actinidin, which is an allergen for some people, specifically those people allergic to latex, papaya, or pineapple. The fruit also contains calcium oxalate, which may induce an unpleasant itching and soreness in the mouth. It can, however, cause sweating or tingling and swelling of the lips, tongue, and face, and in more extreme cases vomiting, abdominal pain, breathing difficulties, wheezing, and collapse. Severe symptoms are most likely to occur in young children.

See **Fruit.**

KNOB CELERY SEE **CELERY ROOT.**

KOHLRABI
(*Brassica oleracea gongylodes*)

Don't be put off by the kohlrabi's Sputnik-like appearance. A key staple in Eastern Europe until it was deposed by the potato, this delicious bulbous vegetable has a radishlike bite, a crisp turnipy texture, and a sweet cucumber taste. Either pale green or bold purple, kohlrabi grow as a bulbous swelling (or corm) on the plant's stem—one kohlrabi per stem. *Kohl*, which is German for cabbage, aptly indicates which family this vegetable belongs to.

Medicinal Benefits Kohlrabi improves energy circulation and eases stagnancy; it reduces damp conditions and so is effective for edema, candidiasis, and viral conditions. It helps stabilize blood sugar imbalances and is used for hypoglycemia and diabetes. Kohlrabi reduces swelling of the scrotum and balances *kapha*. It is an excellent source of vitamin C and potassium. Kohlrabi is high in fiber and low in calories.

A traditional Chinese recipe to stimulate appetite or to ease indigestion or a stomach or duodenal ulcer uses kohlrabi. Peel and slice a kohlrabi and place it in a glass jar. Add honey to cover; cover the jar and let it rest on the countertop for 48 hours. Eat a slice as desired.

Use Some people first cook kohlrabi and then remove its skin. Using a sharp knife, I peel the vegetable first—but I remove only the tough, fibrous skin at the vegetable's base. Raw and sliced thin, kohlrabi is delicious as crudités served with a vegetable dip. Or grate it or cut it into matchsticks for salads. It can be steamed, stir-fried, baked, braised, added to soups and stews, or—as the Hungarians do it—stuffed. Kohlrabi, unlike cabbage, does not become sulfurous with long cooking. The leaves, when young, are similar in flavor to kale or collards.

Buying Although kohlrabi can grow up to 40 pounds, they're sweetest when smaller, about the size of a tennis ball. Large kohlrabi tend to be pithy or woody. Look for firm, crisp bulbs with no sign of cracking and with fresh, green leaves.

See **Cabbage Family; Vegetable.**

KOHREN SEE **LOTUS TEA.**

KOJI

The "yeast" of Japan, koji is the fermenting catalyst for amasake, miso, sake, soy sauce, and several pickles. To make koji, steamed rice is inoculated with the mold spores of *aspergillus oryzae* and incubated in wooden trays for several days at a carefully controlled temperature and humidity. I've made koji from scratch, and though it's a time-intensive process, it's a most enjoyable one, and its heady fragrance filled my whole home. I can readily appreciate why it's recognized as Japan's national microorganism.

See **Amasake; Miso; Soy Sauce.**

KOMBU
(*Laminaria augustata, L. dentigera, L. japonica*)

To the uninitiated, kombu doesn't *look* like comfort food, but it is. Like a secret bouillon replacement, it enhances the flavor and nutrients of any savory dish that's stewed, simmered, boiled, or baked. I put it in most everything but desserts. Before ladling the soup to someone prejudiced against seaweed, simply remove the spent kombu as you would a bay leaf.

Medicinal Benefits Kombu, like other seaweeds, is cooling and moistening, and it strengthens the kidneys and nervous system. It reduces or softens masses (such as tumors and cysts) in the body, but it is therefore not to be eaten excessively during pregnancy. Kombu reduces *vata* and *pitta*.

Kombu is very high in sugar, potassium, iodine, calcium, and vitamins A and C. It also contains appreciable amounts of B-complex vitamins, glutamic acid, starch, and trace minerals.

Use Kombu is the easiest seaweed to use, and it is versatile. Put it in any soup stock and every pot of beans. Add it to stews, or use it as a wrap for food morsels. It also stands on its own baked, deep-fried, or boiled. Kombu, when rehydrated and cooked with liquid, becomes mucilaginous, and after several hours of cooking it will break into small pieces. When crisped (without hydration) for a few minutes in the oven, it becomes a delicious chip. If the kombu blisters, it was overtoasted and will taste bitter.

Buying Wild-crafted kombu foraged along Mendocino, California, Maine, and Nova Scotia are available in natural food stores and by mail order. It is commercially harvested from South and North American and Asian coastal regions. Store covered, in a cool, dark cupboard, and it will be good for several years. The most commonly used kombu comes in strips several inches wide and of varying lengths. Other forms of kombu include:

- **Natto Kombu** Kombu that's been sliced into very fine strands, natto kombu is used in soups and vegetable dishes.
- **Ne Kombu** The kombu holdfast (or root) is a strengthening food particularly beneficial in treating cancer and dysfunction of the intestines, kidneys, and reproductive organs. Ne kombu is recommended for breaking down fatty acids in the body and reducing cholesterol and high blood pressure. It requires long soaking and cooking.
- **Sweet Kombu** A premier kombu, harvested only from the Pacific during a one-week period, sweet kombu has sporadic availability. It has a deliciously sweet mineral taste.
- **Tororo Kombu** Fine, almost powdery kombu filaments seasoned with rice vinegar, tororo kombu may be used as a condiment or added to soups just before serving. It is tasty and mucilaginous.

See **Kelp; Seaweed Family; Vegetable.**

NATURAL MSG ENHANCES FLAVOR AND HEALTH

In Japan in the 1940s, glutamic acid was extracted from kombu to make monosodium glutamate (MSG). Just as kombu enhances flavor and tenderizes food, so does MSG. However, MSG is now composed of synthetic glutamic acid, and health-conscious people know to avoid it. Laboratory-produced MSG is toxic. The naturally occurring glutamic acid in kombu, on the other hand, improves overall health.

KOMBUCHA
Manchurian Mushroom, Tea Kvass,
Tea Mushroom
(*Fungus japonicus*)

An effervescent, fermented beverage with a winelike taste, kombucha is an old-time folk remedy. Really old-time: Its recorded history dates to 250 BC, when the Chinese called it the immortal health elixir. It is made using a brown culture that looks like a jellied pancake that replicates itself with each new batch. Although the culture is commonly called a mushroom, it is not; rather, it is made of *Acetobacter* (acetic acid bacteria) and several different yeast populations. The culture is also called a SCOBY (symbiotic culture of bacteria and yeast).

Kombucha is easy to make: Brew a jug of black tea, stir in some sugar, add the culture, and let it ferment for about two weeks or until it tastes similar to wine (rather than sugared tea).

Medicinal Benefits This ancient elixir is extolled in popular literature as a cure for everything from cancer to arthritis. It balances the spleen and stomach and aids digestion. Kombucha sounds as good as it tastes. It contains glucaric acid, which makes the liver more efficient and has some B vitamins and antibiotic properties.

In some cases, kombucha supports digestion and may help prevent the common cold. It is used for edema, arteriosclerosis, gout, constipation, mental fatigue, kidney stones, and general convalescence. Some people with candidiasis and yeast-type overgrowths find it medicinal; others, however, advise not to use it.

Use Kombucha may be frequently consumed by the glassful for its uplifting effervescence. However, because it does contain caffeine, you may wish to limit your consumption accordingly. Or brew it yourself with green tea or another acid tisane since the culture requires an acid environment in order to thrive.

Buying Notices for free kombucha cultures are often posted on bulletin boards of natural food stores; you can also find mail-order sources for them online. Prepared kombucha beverages are bottled and available in various flavors in the refrigerated section of markets. Some teas and other supplements contain dry kombucha.

Be Mindful There are reports of contaminated kombucha starters; to prevent contamination, follow basic hygiene when preparing it, and discard a culture that develops pink, green, or black mold. Considering its ancient history, however, as well as the countless hands that have brewed it and passed it on, one can safely assume that a culture cared for with rudimentary hygiene will produce a beneficial elixir. One guideline for fermented foods: If it smells or testes repugnant, don't consume it!

See **Fermented Food.**

KUDZU
Kuzu
(*Pueraria thunbergiana*)

Pronounced *KUD-zoo* between clenched teeth, kudzu was introduced to the southern United States to control soil erosion. It does more than control erosion. According to the locals, turn your back on this green menace and it overgrows your car, barn, and even telephone lines. Officially classified as a noxious weed in 1970, kudzu has been valued on the other side of the globe for 2,000 years as an important food and medicine. Aficionados—myself included—pay top dollar at natural food stores for the powdered, chalklike starchy root extract of this "mile a minute" vine.

Medicinal Benefits In Chinese medicine, kudzu root is a tonifying herb used to relieve acute pain, stiff neck and shoulders, intestinal and digestive disorders, food allergies, headaches, fever, hypertension, type 2 diabetes, colds, tinnitus, vertigo, diarrhea, and hangovers. Kudzu contains the anti-inflammatory and antimicrobial agent daidzein. Its daidzein helps prevent cancer and its genistein helps counter leukemia. Recent research confirms its traditional use for suppressing the desire for alcohol. A cooling, tonic herb, kudzu induces perspiration. It prevents the eruption of rashes and clears the skin. It reduces *pitta*.

Use I use kudzu as a thickener, rather than cornstarch or arrowroot, because of its superior essence. To measure kudzu, crush the lumps with the back of a spoon, then substitute for cornstarch in any recipe requiring a

---

CURE-ALL (UME-SHOYU-KUDZU)

The morning after a birthday party, Halloween, or any good indulgence, my children invariably requested an *ume-shoyu-kudzu*. I'd make servings for all—earned or otherwise—and we'd each savor our portion down to the last sticky drop. This effective kitchen remedy revitalizes energy and relieves colds, flu, headaches, diarrhea, hangovers, and digestive problems. Make it thin and sip from a mug, or thick and spoon it up. Your choice.

1½ tablespoons kudzu powder

1½ cups water

1   teaspoon umeboshi paste or ½ umeboshi plum

1   teaspoon soy sauce, or to taste

½   teaspoon freshly squeezed ginger juice or ¼ teaspoon powdered ginger

Put the kudzu in 1 cup cold water and stir to dissolve. Add the umeboshi paste, soy sauce, and ginger. Bring to a boil over medium heat, stirring constantly, then reduce the heat and simmer for 1 minute, or until the liquid turns from milky to opaque. Thin, if necessary, with the remaining liquid to the desired texture. Drink hot.

FOR ALCOHOLICS, OLD NEWS IS GOOD NEWS

In 1993, Harvard biochemists discovered that a dose of kudzu made alcoholic hamsters cut their imbibing by 50 percent. Apparently the compound *daidzein*, found in the root, leaves, and flowers of kudzu, reduced the rodents' craving and significantly lowered their blood levels of alcohol, even taking into account their lower consumption. Similar studies found that kudzu works on mice in Japan and human alcoholics in China. In fact, after a month of herbal treatment, 80 percent of the Chinese alcoholics in one study reported that they no longer craved alcohol and had no adverse side effects from the withdrawal. This information was published in the *Proceedings* of the National Academy of Sciences, November 1993.

But then, this is not really news. *The Divine Husbandman's Classic of the Materia Medica* from the later Han period (207 BC–AD 220) prescribed kudzu to treat drunkenness and hangovers.

---

thickener. Kudzu enhances the flavor of sauces, desserts, and soups. As it cools, a kudzu sauce thickens; a sauce thickened with arrowroot, on the other hand, thins as it cools.

Buying Currently this starch is available in small packets as an expensive Japanese import. Kudzu is sold in capsules and tablets as an even more expensive dietary supplement, which I find quite unnecessary, as it is such an easy-to-use, and delicious, culinary agent.

Surely one day some industrious individual will harvest and market domestic kudzu.

See **Legume Family**.

KUKICHA SEE **TEA**.

KUMQUAT
Calamondin, Limequat, Meiwa, Nagami
(*Fortunella*)

Kumquats, which look like date-size oranges, are eaten whole, skin and all. The skin

is spicy-sweet (with some bitterness), while the juicy flesh is tart—quite a puckersome tidbit. If you enjoy bold flavors, chances are you'll adore kumquats.

The kumquat is not a true citrus, but its pollen pollinates citrus blossoms, and vice versa, creating crosses, such as limequats, lemonquats, and more.

Kumquats originated in China, and their name in Cantonese translates as "gold orange."

Medicinal Benefits Kumquats are warming and energize the lungs, stomach, and liver. They help alleviate phlegm, relieve coughing, and move energy (chi). A traditional Chinese remedy for cough that has settled in the lungs due to inner cold is to infuse sliced kumquat and fresh ginger in boiling water. When the cold is from a fever, drink an equal mixture of kumquat and turnip juice. Kumquats reduce *vata* and, in moderation, *kapha*.

Use Serve kumquats whole on a fruit-and-cheese platter or to accompany salted nuts. Or slice, quarter, halve, or stuff them as a bold garnish and a welcome flash of color. The seeds are easily removed with a knifepoint.

Cooking releases the full aroma of kumquats, inviting their use in sauces, compotes, ice cream, and preserves. I candy kumquats in a honey syrup and keep a jar in the refrigerator to accompany game or to serve as a sweetmeat. To serve kumquats with greens, grains, or salads, simmer them whole for 10 minutes to tenderize them. Or slice and serve them raw.

Buying Available in the winter months, the best kumquats are firm, not soft and moist. Their thin skin makes this petite fruit more perishable than citrus. Left at room temperature, they will mold, so refrigerate (do not wrap in plastic) and use within two weeks.

See **Citrus Family; Fruit.**

KUZU SEE **KUDZU.**

L

Lactose-Free Milk Substitutes See **Nondairy Milk Substitutes.**

Lady's Finger See **Okra.**

Lamb's Lettuce See **Mâche.**

Lamb's-Quarters See **Fat Hen.**

Laurel See **Bay Leaf.**

LAUREL FAMILY
(*Lauraceae*)

The large laurel family grows worldwide in both tropical and warm regions, typically as evergreen trees or shrubs. Many are valued for their hard wood and some for their essential oils that are used for flavor, herbal remedies, and perfume. Avocados are valued for their high fat content.

See **Avocado; Bay; Cinnamon; Sassafras.**

LAVENDER
(*Lavandula angustifolia*)

The name "lavender" comes from the Latin *lavare*, "to wash." If you love the feminine, floral lavender scent in toiletries, try a pinch of these blossoms in a soup. A color was named for the minuscule blossoms of this mint family member; the aroma takes me back to my grandmother's sachets. Lavender is an occasional culinary herb with potent aromatic and flavoring properties.

Medicinal Benefits Taken internally as a tea or culinary herb or used externally, lavender has both antiseptic and anti-inflammatory properties. It is used for indigestion, depression, anxiety, exhaustion, irritability, headaches (including migraines), and bronchial complaints. Lavender relaxes spasms, benefits digestion, and stimulates peripheral circulation. It also lowers fevers. Lavender essential oil contains a substance called perillyl alcohol, which, in laboratory studies, has antileukemia and antitumor effects for the liver, spleen, and breast. Apply the essential oil directly on burns, sunburn, muscular pains, cold sores, and insect bites. Lavender is *tridoshic*.

Use The spice blend characteristic of southern France, *herbes de Provence*, contains lavender. Its distinctive floral essence can easily overpower, though, so use it sparingly.

Crystallize lavender flowers and use them

LAVENDER POUND CAKE

Hands down, my favorite restaurant is Pangea in Ashland, Oregon. Their use of unexpected combinations, like in this lavender cake, make truly unforgettable and toothsome dishes. Although Pangea's policy is to *not* give out recipes, being the owner's mother has its privileges.

2 teaspoons dried, organic lavender blossoms

1¼ cups unbleached all-purpose flour

¼ teaspoon unrefined salt

1 cup unsalted butter, softened

1 cup plus 1 tablespoon unrefined sugar

2 large eggs

1 teaspoon pure vanilla extract

¼ cup milk

Preheat the oven to 350°F. Either grease an 8½ x 4-inch loaf pan or line it with parchment paper.

Crush lavender flowers gently in your hands to release their fragrance. Combine with flour and salt. Set aside.

Cream the butter and 1 cup of the sugar together in a mixer at medium speed for 4 to 5 minutes, until light in color and fluffy. Add the eggs one at a time, mixing on low speed until they are incorporated.

Still on low speed, add the vanilla, approximately half the flour mixture, and then the milk before adding the remaining flour to create a wet batter. Scrape down the edges as necessary.

Pour the batter into the prepared cake pan and sprinkle the top with the remaining 1 tablespoon sugar. Place in the oven and bake for 30 to 45 minutes, until the top starts to brown and crack slightly and your kitchen smells like fresh lavender. Invert onto a wire rack, remove the pan, and cool completely before serving.

as an elegant decoration or add fresh flowers to jams, ice cream, and vinegar. Or use the flowers, fresh or dried, in an infusion or with an herb tea blend. Lavender blossoms pair well with chocolate or cheese.

Be Mindful Lavender oil is an allergen to some people, and it increases photosensitivity. Many body-care products contain fractionated perfume grade oil (rather than pure essential oil), which is implicated in causing abnormal breast tissue growth in prepubescent boys.

See **Herbs and Spices; Mint Family.**

LAVER
(*Porphyra umbilicalis*)

A variety of red algae, laver is hand-harvested in the northern Atlantic and Pacific from rocky beds at low tide during July and August. The plants are picked over and spread on nets to dry in the sun or in a drying shed. Laver blades may be from an inch to three feet long and are only one to two cells thick. When cultivated, laver is termed "nori."

When I lived in London in the early 1970s, I bought freshly foraged laver from the outdoor market in the small coastal town of Barnstaple. Already marinated with vinegar, it was black, with an unappetizing, sludgelike texture, but its taste was a little like olives with a fresh sea essence and nutty, sweet-and-sour mineral flavor. Traditionally, the Welsh use laver in oat bread, as a seasoning agent, and as a condiment. In Hawaii, coked laver is used as a relish. The California Kashaya Pomo tribe called it *mei bil* (sea leaf) and favor it above other varieties.

Medicinal Benefits Laver is cooling and salty. It helps soften tumors and lumps; it helps eliminate all toxins—from radioactive elements to mucus. Like other seaweeds, laver promotes water passage. As with all wild foods, laver is more energizing than cultivated nori. It contains all the minerals and trace elements required for optimum health. Laver is a superior source of protein, iron, and iodine. It is an excellent source of vitamins B_2, A, D, and C and is high in chlorophyll and enzymes. Laver contains more total dietary fiber and soluble fiber than oat bran. It reduces *vata*.

Use Before using laver, pick it over for occasional small shells or pebbles that may be lodged in the fronds. Roasting tenderizes laver and enhances its nutty flavor. Spread the laver on a cookie sheet and bake at 350°F for 5 to 8 minutes, or toast in a skillet until crisp but not burned. A second way to tenderize laver is to marinate it in vinegar or lemon juice for up to

24 hours. Add marinated laver to salads, sandwiches, or salad dressings. Because laver has not been processed, as is nori, you cannot use it for making sushi.

Buying Wild, hand-harvested laver is available from natural food stores, in coastal region farmers' markets, or online from people who harvest seaweed.

See **Nori; Seaweed Family; Vegetable.**

LEAF LETTUCE SEE LETTUCE.

LECITHIN

A yellowish fatty substance that is an integral part of cell membranes, lecithin occurs in all animals and plants and egg yolks. The term also refers to a pure extraction of phosphatidylcholine that is primarily isolated from soybeans but may also be extracted from egg yolk. This lecithin extraction is used by some home cooks as an emulsifier and is found in countless prepared foods for the same purpose (to, for example, keep cocoa and cocoa butter from separating) and as a texture-enhancing ingredient (to make margarine more spreadable). It's also used as a protective coating on supplements. Studies show that soy lecithin helps lower cholesterol and triglycerides.

Be Mindful Organic lecithin is mechanically extracted from soy. Cheaper lecithin is extracted with hexane, a neurotoxin petrochemical that poses a serious occupational hazard to workers and is an environmental air pollutant. Small amounts of hexane appear in ingredients processed with this toxin. Food products bearing "made with organic ingredients" may contain hexane-extracted lecithin.

See **Soybean.**

LEEK
(Allium ampeloprasum, Porrum group)

The leek, the sweet cousin of the onion, is even more closely related to pearl onions and elephant garlic; its wild progenitor, the ramp, is sometimes available. The leek is the national emblem of Wales and tastes almost like robustly flavored asparagus. It looks like a giant scallion with the dark green tops forming a chevron-patterned crown atop a thick white bulb.

Medicinal Benefits As with onions and garlic, the sulfur compounds in leeks account for some of its healing action. But unlike those cousins, leek greens are an excellent source of the lesser-known carotenoids lutein and zeaxanthin. Because leeks are milder than onions and garlic, they are less stimulating and therefore better suited to young children and people with a fiery, hot temper. Leeks reduce *vata and kapha.*

As a stalklike vegetable, leeks energetically support movement. Next time you're feeling physically, emotionally, or mentally stuck, favor leeks and other such vegetables. They subtly tonify and support energy movement.

Use Trim off the dehydrated tips of the leaves and any large, tough outer leaves. Slice the remaining vegetable in half lengthwise. Wash, taking care to remove any dirt lodged in the leaves. (If a leek is unusually gritty, cut it lengthwise into quarters for more thorough cleaning.)

The bulb and tender greens may be finely sliced and added to a salad. I use rootlets, bulbs, and leaves in soups, sautéed dishes, pilafs, and casseroles. Vichyssoise is a leek-based soup, as is cock-a-leekie, a Scottish soup that contains, as its name suggest, chicken and leeks. In the country of Georgia, they pickle leeks; in Portugal, they grill young leeks.

Buying Look for brightly colored firm (not wilted or flabby), fresh-looking leeks—

ROOTING FOR LEEK ROOTLETS

I also use the leek's many tiny rootlets, which look like a string mop, and recommend them to you. If your greengrocer has not trimmed them off, they'll be up to four inches long. These mineral-dense filaments add valuable flavor and nutrients and are more bioavailable than mineral supplements. Cut them—as a cluster—from the root base. Soak this cluster to loosen any embedded sand, then carefully rinse. Mince the rootlets and use in any soup, sautéed, or simmered vegetable dish or stock; they are too fibrous to add to salads or lightly cooked dishes.

preferably with untrimmed tops and bottoms. Avoid overly mature leeks that are lighter in weight for their size and have developed a fibrous central core that is too tough to use. While large leeks, up to 10 inches or more, are more readily available than small leeks, the smaller ones are more tender and flavorful.

See **Onion Family; Ramp; Vegetable.**

LEEN NGAU SEE LOTUS ROOT.

LEGUME FAMILY
(*Leguminosae*)

A nutritionist names any bean, pea, peanut, or lentil a legume. Botanists consider a leguminous plant as one with a fruit (i.e., seed, like a bean) that splits into two halves. We primarily eat the fruits of this family; however, for rooibos and honeybush we use the leaves, and with jicama, lotus, and licorice, it is the roots.

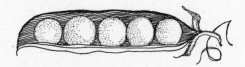

The legume family is the third-largest family of flowering plants behind the orchard and the daisy families.

See **Alfalfa; Beans and Legumes; Dal; Fava; Fenugreek Greens; Fenugreek Seed; Green Bean; Honeybush; Jicama Kudzu; Licorice Root; Long Bean; Lotus Root; Lupin; Mesquite; Pea, Dried; Pea, Fresh; Peanut; Rooibos; Tamarind; Winged Bean.**

LEMON
(*Citrus limon*)

As a world-class seasoning ingredient, the lemon is second only to salt and pepper. Be it a Brazilian prawn soup (*sopa de camarão*) or a Ukrainian yeasted roll (*mandryky*) with a cherry glacé, count on a squeeze of tart lemon to tune your dish's flavor just so. Lemons have less sugar and more acid, primarily citric acid, than do other citrus. The juice and rind of this small citrus are both valued for their refreshing, sour flavor.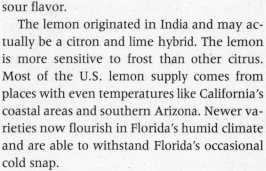

The lemon originated in India and may actually be a citron and lime hybrid. The lemon is more sensitive to frost than other citrus. Most of the U.S. lemon supply comes from places with even temperatures like California's coastal areas and southern Arizona. Newer varieties now flourish in Florida's humid climate and are able to withstand Florida's occasional cold snap.

Medicinal Benefits As a medicinal agent, the lemon is remarkable. It has a cooling effect and so is good for fevers. It constricts body tissues, dries damp conditions, resolves stagnation, and dispels sputum. Lemon aids digestion by stimulating the flow of saliva, thus easing the work of the liver. It acts as a laxative and as a diuretic, and it has important antiseptic and antimicrobial properties. It treats colds, flu, coughs, and parasite infestation. Lemon benefits bile formation and therefore supports liver function; it improves the absorption of minerals, cleanses the blood, and is useful in treating high blood pressure. It relieves sore throats and hiccups, assists with weight loss, and alleviates flatulence. Externally, lemon juice helps heal sores, relieves itching from insect bites and sunburn, and even softens corns. Lemon reduces *vata*.

Like limes, lemons are high in critic acid, making them a good vinegar substitute. They are also used as a remedy for acidosis, as their alkaline content is five times greater than their acidic content. A lemon has less than 1 percent sugar—even a lime has more. It is an outstanding source of vitamin C and is high in potassium and vitamin B_1 as well.

The essential oil of lemon is used as a tonic, astringent, and antiseptic to treat sore throat, nervous conditions, blood pressure, digestive problems, gallstones, debility, fever, and anxiety.

Buying Unlike other citrus fruits, which are tree-ripened, most lemons are picked green in the cold months and then left to ripen and cure in storehouses. Storage mellows the acid, thickens and toughens the skin, and gives the lemon a bright silky yellow finish. Storage also makes it possible to have a year-round lemon supply for ample lemonade and lemon sorbet during hot spells. Lemons with a pale or greenish yellow color are fresh and more acidic than darker lemons.

Organic lemons are available seasonally in some markets. Commercial lemon skins are dyed and waxed. Avoid lemons with a darker

---

MORNING ELIXIR

Gently invite your energy up with this morning elixir. It aids in restoring balance and rehydrates the body, helping you to feel alert without that coffee jolt.

If your body feels stiff and your mind cloudy as you turn off the alarm, then your liver is complaining. It didn't complete its middle-of-the-night task of blood cleansing. In this case, modify your elixir by substituting ¼ teaspoon turmeric for the honey. Better yet, care for your liver by avoiding chemicals, alcohol, refined oils, and too much meat or fried food. Also avoid overeating and, if possible, eat dinner by 6 p.m.

Makes 1 cup

 1 cup boiling water
 2 tablespoons freshly squeezed lemon
    juice
 Honey to taste
 Cayenne to taste (optional)
 In a mug, stir the ingredients together to
    dissolve the honey, and sip away.

---

yellow or dull color or with hardened or shriveled skin, which indicates old age. Soft spots, mold, or broken skin indicate decay.

The main domestic lemon varieties have a long nipple at the blossom end and a thick neck at the stem end—but other varieties are round. Some varieties are seedless, and some are juicier than others.

See **Citrus Family; Fruit.**

LEMON BALM
Melissa
(*Melissa officinalis*)

This easily cultivated perennial herb is a mint family member with a mild lemon scent; it is native to the Mediterranean region.

As a medicinal herb, lemon balm is cooling with a sour and spicy flavor. It supports the lungs and liver and thus aids digestion and treats depression, flatulence, insomnia, and nervousness. Lemon balm has antibacterial and antiviral properties and helps treat herpes. It is often helpful in treating attention deficit disorder (ADD) and Graves' disease. As a natural mosquito repellent, crush the leaves and rub on the skin.

As a culinary herb, it is coming back into fashion for the lemony flavor it gives to vegetable, fish, and poultry dishes. It makes an effective garnish for lemon-flavored dishes by heightening the lemon aroma. Lemon balm may be substituted for some of the basil in pesto. Lemon balm is a relative of mint.

See **Herbs and Spices; Mint Family.**

LEMONGRASS
Sereh, Serei
(*Cymbopogon citratus*)

Twenty years ago, I was walking on an empty beach near Tepiac, Mexico, and developed a hankering for a cup of herbal tea—though I doubted its availability. I eventually came to a makeshift café and was surprised to hear, *"Sí, tengo té de yerba."* The cook took one step off the covered kitchen platform, cut a stalk from a spiky plant, and, that fast, delighted me with a pungent, flowery cup of lemongrass tea.

This reedlike grass, which tastes just as it sounds, is becoming increasingly available as a fresh herb for use in Balinese, Thai, Vietnamese, and Cambodian cuisine. Its pleasing bouquet scents many cosmetics, perfumes, and even Ivory soap.

Medicinal Benefits This tropical grass is rich in citral, the active ingredient found in lemon peel. Lemongrass cools, aids digestion (especially in children), and increases perspiration. It relieves spasms, muscle cramps, rheumatism, and headaches and is also effective against infections. Lemongrass is *tridoshic.*

Use The pleasant flavor of lemongrass is never dominating. Although it can be substituted for lemon balm, it is not a lemon substitute.

The entire stalk is usable. Peel away the fibrous outer layer and use it like a bay leaf, to season but not to eat. The tender center section is also fibrous, but less so, and can be minced and added to sauces, soups, and stews. The lemony flavor increases with cooking, so use it sparingly. The stalk may also be chopped into sections and infused for tea.

Buying In Asian markets, specialty markets, or the specialty produce section of large supermarkets, look for fresh-looking, scallion-shaped stalks about 10 inches long. If not available fresh, look for it in the freezer section. Once dried, lemongrass quickly loses its flavor and aroma, so favor it fresh.

Store any portion that you will use within a week in plastic in the refrigerator, then tightly wrap and freeze the remainder. Slice off a piece as needed and return the unused portion to the refrigerator or freezer.

See **Grass Family; Herbs and Spices.**

LEMON ZEST See **Citrus Peel.**

LENTIL See **Beans and Legumes.**

LETTUCE
(*Lactuca sativa*)

Wild lettuce, the precursor to cultivated lettuce, is found throughout the world as a common weed. It's not a salad bowl weed, however, since wild lettuce, even when young, is intensely bitter. The ancient Egyptians first cultivated lettuce, and it came to America with the early settlers. Today lettuce accounts for almost 25 percent of the fresh vegetable consumption in the United States. It is a member of the daisy family.

Medicinal Benefits Lettuce has healing action for the large intestine and stomach meridian, and it helps circulate chi and alleviate excessive damp, heat, and water conditions. Lettuce leaves secrete a milky latex when the plant bolts or goes to seed; this provides another example of like curing like, as lettuce helps increase mother's milk. Its cooling powers, prized for centuries, are used to tame fevers, liver inflammation, and—in the language of the old texts—lust.

Lettuce with more flavor and color pigments is more medicinal than is the iceberg variety. Long valued for its soporific properties, lettuce contains the sedative lactucarium, which relaxes the nerves. It is also a superior source of magnesium, which contributes to its soothing properties. Lettuce is cooling in its thermal nature. Its flavor is bitter and sweet. It contains antioxidants, acts as a diuretic, and is drying, and so treats edema, candidiasis, and damp conditions. Lettuce contains the highest amount of silicon of the common vegetables, and so it specifically supports pancreatic function.

Lettuce, and salads in general, is balancing for *pitta* and *kapha*. *Vata* people do better with a cooked or warm salad; by combining their lettuce with warming herbs such as arugula, watercress, and nasturtium, or with a more warming salad dressing that might include fennel, garlic, or ginger.

Use Indispensable in salads, garnishes, and on sandwiches, lettuce is primarily used raw; it is valued for its refreshing, crisp nature. Sturdier varieties may be wilted or lightly cooked, and celtuce is primarily cultivated for its stem.

- **Butterhead (Bibb, Buttercrunch, and Tom Thumb)** The small butterhead lettuce has tender leaves bunched almost like rose petals. As its name suggests, butterhead is meltingly delicate. Popular varieties include Boston.
- **Celtuce (Asparagus Lettuce, Chinese Lettuce, and Stem Lettuce)** An Asian lettuce with a taste and texture like celery is called, logically enough, celtuce. Grown primarily for its foot-long, thick stem, it is topped with tender young leaves that may be used like a lettuce. The length of the stem, which is similar in taste to water chestnut, is ridged with brown leaf scars from old leaves. Peel the stem and use it raw or cooked as you would celery—it's tasty by itself or in combination with other vegetables. It is a favorite pickling vegetable of the Chinese and delicious in stir-fries and soups. The leaves may be used in salads.
- **Head Lettuce (Iceberg and Imperial Lettuce)** This lettuce forms tight, dense heads that resemble cabbage. After potatoes, head lettuce is the second most consumed vegetable in the United States. The most mild lettuce, iceberg, has had its bitter properties bred out of it and so has lesser nutrient value; it is 90 percent water and stores longer than other lettuce varieties. It's appreciated for its crisp texture.
- **Loose-Leaf Lettuce** Rather than a com-

pact head, loose-leaf lettuce has tender, delicate, and mildly flavored leaves that are easily separated. This structure makes it ideal for a garden patch since you can pluck the outer leaves as needed, while the plant continues producing throughout the growing season. The more fragile structure of loose-leaf lettuce means it doesn't ship or store as well as other kinds. Plan to use loose-leaf lettuce quickly. An ever-increasing variety of leafy lettuces is becoming available, including:

Lollo Biondo A bright, almost lime-green lettuce with a distinctive frilly edge.

Lollo Rosso Darker green than the Biondo, with red-edged leaves.

Oak Leaf Reminiscent of an oak leaf in shape and comes in green and red varieties.

- **Romaine (Cos) Lettuce** This is the second most popular lettuce after iceberg. This tall lettuce has crisp, dark green outer leaves and is sturdier than other lettuces. Red-leafed romaine is becoming increasingly available. An overly large or mature romaine is unpleasantly tough.
- **Summer Crisp Lettuce** Like a relaxed iceberg, this lettuce forms moderately dense heads and has a crunchy texture.

Buying The best selection of local lettuce greens is in the spring and fall. Look for bright, vibrant lettuce with no signs of rust or dehydration. Many mixed salad greens—organic and otherwise—are available in convenient, prewashed packages with an impressive shelf life of multiple weeks. This unnatural longevity is achieved by dipping the greens in a mild bleach bath. Indeed, the price of a lengthy shelf life is compromised flavor.

WHY DID APHRODITE SLEEP UPON A BED OF LETTUCE?

According to the ancient Greeks, Aphrodite, the goddess of Love, was so distraught over the death of handsome Adonis that, for sedation, she slept upon a bed of lettuce.

Too much sedation, however, is never a good thing. Eating a large quantity of bolted lettuce (that which has gone to seed) has been known to cause comas. Not to worry: You won't find bolted lettuce in the store, and if you find it in your garden, it will taste too bitter to eat.

Experiment with "new" lettuces, which range in color from red and yellow to blue-green. Textures range from buttery soft to crisp and flavors from mildly bitter to distinctly bitter, with some nutty and sweet tastes as well.

Be Mindful Lettuce may be irradiated, unless it is organic. While a crate of irradiated lettuce must be labeled, labeling is not required in supermarket shelves or in deli foods or in meals served in airlines, hotels, restaurants, or other food servicers.

See **Daisy Family; Mesclun; Vegetable.**

LICORICE ROOT
(*Glycyrrhiza glabra*)

Black jelly beans and licorice candy ropes and whips contain a black extract of licorice root. For more than 2,000 years throughout the temperate world, both wild and cultivated licorice have remained a valued medicinal, and sometimes culinary, herb. It is an herbaceous perennial of the legume family.

Medicinal Benefits Licorice is a soothing, moist, sweet root that has a positive action on all organs and so is used as an energy tonic in Chinese medicine. It is a mild sedative, is anti-inflammatory, controls coughing, and has hormonal effects for women. It detoxifies and protects the liver and inhibits breast, colon, and prostate cancer. Licorice treats chronic hepatitis and immune deficiency disease; it is used for arthritis, allergic complaints, asthma, and Addison's disease.

Licorice contains glyceritinic, a neutraceutical that's 50 to 100 times sweeter than sucrose. It's one of the most common ingredients in Chinese herbal formulas, for it moderates the strong effects of other ingredients and makes them more effective. Licorice reduces *vata* and *pitta*.

Use A common flavoring ingredient in candy, tobacco, beer, herbal beverages, soft drinks, and medicines, licorice has an anise- or fennel-like aroma with a strong, dominating sweetness. This taste overwhelms both sweet and spicy dishes, except when minute quantities are blended with other spices—a pinch of powdered licorice added to fruit juices or punch adds an interesting note of flavor.

Buying Licorice root that resembles a brown pencil is available in three- to five-inch lengths or cut into chips. It's also available powdered and in extracts.

Be Mindful At one time licorice was synthesized and used as an effective ulcer-healing medication, but it also caused side effects in some people. Since then, the Western medical community disregards its long record as a safe herb and warns about using the root. Perhaps we might continue to enjoy real licorice and avoid the synthetic.

Licorice, however, is not given to pregnant women or to people with high blood pressure or kidney disease, because, in excess, it may cause water retention and raise blood pressure.

See **Herbs and Spices; Legume Family.**

Lima Bean See **Beans and Legumes.**

LIME
(*Citrus aurantifolia, C. hystrix, C. latifolia*)

All limes are harvested before they ripen. If left to mature on the tree, they lose their acidity, become sweet, and turn yellowish. Unlike most commercial lemons, which are dyed a uniform color, limes are not colored. Limes are the thinnest skinned and most fragile of the citrus fruits.

Medicinal Benefits Limes are just less acidic than lemons and exhibit a more pronounced action on the liver. In other respects, limes are comparable in medicinal action.

Use Limes may be substituted for lemons in most dishes. They are a signature ingredient in tropical marinades, beverages, and, in the case of Key limes, pie. An authentic Key lime pie consists only of Key lime juice, egg yolks, and condensed milk in a graham cracker crust. Refrigeration causes the skin to brown. Select limes that are heavy for their size with a glossy skin. Limes with a dull, dry skin are old and therefore less acidic than fresh limes. These are the common varieties:

- **Kaffir Lime** (*C. hystrix*) With rare exception, only the fragrant leaves and dark rind of kaffir limes are used, where they give incomparable flavor to certain dishes. Their perfume is unlike any other citrus and is indispensable in the wonderfully tangy soups, salads, and curries of Thailand. The fruit has a distinct nipple on the stem end, and its rind is thick, bumpy, and wrinkled.
- **Key Lime** (*C. aurantifolia*) The Key lime is about the size of a golf ball and has a smooth rind that's mottled yellow-green and, because it is so thin, stores less well than a Persian lime. It is heavily seeded, intensely aromatic, and very juicy. Because of its thin rind, it has the shortest shelf life of the limes. The Key

lime is also called a West Indian or Mexican lime.

- **Persian Lime** (*C. latifolia*) This bright green, seedless lime is larger than a Key lime and is the lime most commonly found in U.S. supermarkets. Its juice is sour with subtle peppery overtones.

Buying Unlike most commercial lemons, which are dyed a uniform color, limes are not colored. Limes are the thinnest skinned and most fragile of the citrus fruits; refrigeration causes the skin to brown. Select limes that are heavy for their size with a glossy skin. Limes with a dull, dry skin are old and therefore less acidic than fresh limes.

See **Citrus Family; Fruit.**

LIMEQUAT See **KUMQUAT.**

LIME ZEST See **CITRUS PEEL.**

LINGONBERRY
(*Vaccinium vitis-idaea*)

The lingonberry is bright red, bitter, and tart, and looks similar to its relative the cranberry, but, when sweetened, has a more delicate flavor. These berries are primarily foraged from low growing evergreen shrubs in the temperate to subarctic forests of northern Eurasia and America, including Newfoundland and Cape Breton. They are a signature ingredient in many cold-weather cuisines where the right to forage them on public lands is often protected by law.

Medicinal Benefits Lingonberries are high in vitamin C, beta-carotene, and help treat bladder ailments. Historically, they helped protect against scurvy in the long, dark northern winters.

Use Lingonberries are used in jam, juice, compotes, syrups, baked goods, and liqueur. Due to their high acid content, they're unusual among fruits in that they may be used raw in preserves.

Buying Fresh lingonberries have some seasonal online availability. In large metropolitan areas, or areas with large Swedish populations, they may be found at a specialty greengrocer. Lingonberry products are, however, more widely available in gourmet and import shops.

See **Blueberry Family; Fruit.**

LING ZHI See **REISHI.**

LINOLEIC ACID (OMEGA-6 FATTY ACIDS) See **ESSENTIAL FATTY ACIDS; FAT AND OIL.**

LINSEED See **FLAXSEED.**

LITCHI See **LYCHEE.**

LO BOK See **DAIKON.**

LOGANBERRY See **BLACKBERRY.**

LONGAN
Dragon's Eye
(*Dimocarpus longan*)

Reference to an eye is inevitable with this lychee relative. When peeled, the longan's translucent grayish white flesh feels like a peeled grape and has embedded in its center a large spherical black seed that looks rather like a pupil—presumably a dragon's pupil, but to that I cannot attest. The smooth skin of the longan is brown, thin, and brittle. Native to Southeast Asia, the longan grows on a small evergreen tree.

Medicinal Benefits The longan is a warming food and chi tonic that benefits the spleen, enriches the blood, and has long been valued for its ability to ease tension. It is high in vitamin C. Its seed is used in herbal medicine to arrest bleeding, relieve pain, regulate energy, remove dampness, and treat injuries, hernia, tuberculosis, and eczema.

Use For the best experience of their delicately sweet tropical flavor and evocative musky aroma, eat out of hand. Peel a longan, pop it into your mouth to easily extract the seed, and savor this juicy treat. Or add to a dessert or a fruit soup. Longans may be dried—they turn chocolate brown—or canned with a syrup. Look for fruit without cracks that feel heavy for their size. Longan fruit is now being grown commercially outside Asia and has increasing availability in domestic markets, primarily from October through May.

See **Fruit; Lychee Family.**

LONG BEAN
Asparagus Bean, Chinese Long Bean, Yard-Long Bean
(*Vigna unguiculata*)

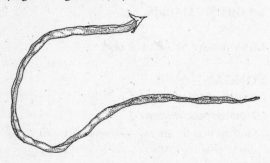

If your children don't eat enough green vegetables, bring home some long beans. Blanch and cool the beans, call in the kids, and let them braid, spiral, and tie them. Their art goes on the dinner table along with a vegetable dip—vitamin A handled for the day. The long bean is a variety of the black-eyed pea and is a vegetable staple throughout Asia and in other semitropical regions.

Use Long beans are a poor substitute for green beans when boiled or steamed (although a zippy dressing helps). Best sautéed or in a stir-fry, a long bean's texture also holds well in stews and braised dishes. Remove the stem end, cut into desired lengths, cook, and serve hot or cold. The beans require no stringing. Long beans are more fragile than green beans and so are best used within a few days.

Buying Long beans are most commonly available in Asian markets. Favor dark green over pale green ones, which are less flavorful. The length—which varies from 1½ to 3 feet—is not important, but choosing pods with undeveloped seeds is critical. Look for pencil-thin, firm long beans that show no sign of rust.

See **Green Bean; Legume Family; Vegetable.**

LONG PEPPER
Indian Long Pepper, Jaborandi Pepper, Pipali
(*Piper longum*)

Long pepper is an invaluable Ayurvedic and Chinese medicinal plant worth getting to know. A relative to black pepper, long pepper is actually a cluster of tiny berries born on a flowering vine that originated in tropical South Asia. These berries merge to a single rodlike fruit about 1½ inches long that, at maturity, turns a mahogany brown. It is typically available ground and is hotter but less aromatic than black pepper.

Medicinal Benefits Hot and warm with sweet overtones, long pepper has a higher content of piperine (the primary micronutrient in black pepper) than black pepper. It aids digestion and has decongestant, antibiotic, and analgesic effects. Long pepper improves absorption in the intestines and helps protect the liver from free radical damage. The Chinese use it externally for toothache. It reduces *kapha* and *vata*.

Use Since long pepper is more pungent than black pepper, add it carefully—unless you like fiery food. Crush the rods before use. Or use the clusters whole as a pickling spice. *Trikatu*, the most important stimulant and digestive tonic in Ayurvedic medicine, is made of equal parts black pepper, long pepper, and ground ginger. Combine ½ teaspoon of this blend with 1 cup of hot water and a teaspoon of honey. It's a great morning wake-up drink that doesn't have the side effects of caffeine.

Buying Long pepper is typically available ground and combined with Asian and North African spice blends.

See **Herbs and Spices; Pepper Family.**

LOOFA SEE LOOFAH.

LOOFAH
Loofa, Lufa
(*Luffa cylindrical*)

While most people imagine a loofah floating in their bath rather than in their soup, it's more delicious in a soup. When immature, this Asian gourd is sweet with a pale green flesh and a slightly spongy texture. When grown to maturity, dried and everything removed but its fibrous network, it makes a pleasingly abrasive bath sponge to stimulate circulation and scrub the skin.

Medicinal Benefits Loofah acts on the lungs, liver, and stomach. It's an astringent, painkilling plant that controls bleeding and promotes circulation. It's used specifically for backache, hemorrhoids, and rheumatism. Loofah reduces *pitta* and *kapha*.

Use If the loofah is ridged, peel only the ridges; if the vegetable is tough, peel the whole thing. Cut it into chunks or slice it, and cook as you would a zucchini in soups, stir-fries, and braised or baked dishes.

Buying There are two types of loofahs: One is slightly curved and ridged; the other is straight, smooth, and slightly thickened at the blossom end, resembling a baseball bat. Select a loofah that is about two to three inches thick, fresh-looking, and pliant rather than brittle. They are available in Asian markets and specialty food stores.

A loofah's flavor is best when it is fresh, so plan on using it within five days. Wrap in perforated plastic; if the loofah becomes too moist, it will soften and may become moldy.

See **Gourd Family; Vegetable.**

LOOSE-LEAF LETTUCE SEE LETTUCE.

LOQUAT
Japanese Medlar, Japanese Plum
(*Eriobotrya japonica*)

Like an apricot in size and color but like a pear in shape, the loquat bruises so easily that you probably won't find it fresh outside California, Hawaii, or Florida, where it grows. It is also available in its native Asia as well as in Mediterranean countries. A loquat tastes something like a dead, ripe (and therefore rather sweet) sour cherry and has a crisp but tender, juicy texture. An apple relative, a loquat contains one or more large seeds.

Medicinal Benefits Loquats are cooling in action and support the lung and stomach functions. They help relieve coughs and ease thirst and a dry throat. Honey Loquat is an effective Chinese patent medicine for this purpose. It is available in Asian markets and health-care sections of most natural food stores, is a syrup of loquat, honey, and fritillaria.

Use Loquats are delicious eaten fresh out of hand or added to fruit salads or made into sauces, jams, or jellies. They are also baked or poached. The seeds and—depending upon its toughness—skin are discarded. In Bermuda, a loquat liqueur is made.

Buying This highly perishable fruit is available early in the spring. Choose smooth-skinned, tender-ripe fruit that may have small brown spots on the skin. Hold at room temperature until completely ripe, then refrigerate. Use within a few days. Loquats are also available canned and dried.

See **Apple Family; Fruit.**

LOTUS ROOT
Leen Ngau; Renkon
(*Nelumbo nucifera*)

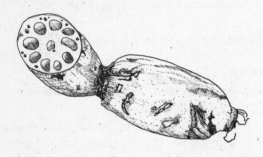

Lotus roots, looking like connected sausage links, grow submerged in the mud of tropical ponds and paddies. From this mire, they send up leaves and exquisite pink or white blossoms that float on top of the water and emit an almost palpable energy. A single lotus blossom can produce 1 watt of energy, and 40 plants can generate the equivalent energy of a 40-watt lightbulb.

The blossom, a Hindu and Buddhist symbol of enlightenment, appears throughout Indian and Asian art. Its Tibetan name, Pema or Padma, is a common given name. The lotus holds the promise that even though we come from muddy, sticky places, we, too, can blossom and become a fully realized, loving person. The lotus blossoms—as well as its leaves, roots, stems, seeds, and the embryonic sprout within the seed—are delicious and valued medicinal foods. The roots and seeds are more readily available.

An individual lotus root (technically, a rhizome) is shaped like a fat cucumber and colored like old ivory with some brown streaks. When it is sliced into rounds, the root's hollow air chambers make a beautiful lacy design.

Medicinal Benefits In Ayurvedic medicine, lotus root is primarily used for cooling function. In Oriental medicine, it is used to support the spleen and stomach, to quell diarrhea, and to nurture the heart. It promotes the production of fluids, is useful for hemorrhages, nosebleeds, and excessive menstruation and enriches the blood. It is prescribed for lung-related ailments, to increase energy, to neutralize toxins, and to treat anorexia. It reduces *pitta* and *vata*.

Use The lotus rhizome is fun to use because of its beautiful shape, its crunchy texture (similar to a jicama), which holds up to cooking, and its mildly sweet flavor. Slice it thin and braise, steam, or stir-fry it, or float it on top of soups. For a dramatic-looking dish, stuff the chambers of a whole root with a brightly colored filling, cook it, and then slice it. Some cooks peel lotus; I never do, as the skin is tender and mild tasting.

Buying Lotus is in season in the fall, winter, and early spring from Asian markets or a well-supplied greengrocer. Select firm, cream-colored roots free of bruises or discoloration. Uncut, the root stores well if refrigerated, in plastic, for up to a week. Once cut, it should be used within three days.

Dried lotus root is available in Asian markets. It is packaged in thin rounds. Reconstitute by soaking in water for two hours prior to use. It may be substituted for fresh lotus in long-simmered dishes.

Be Mindful Although edible raw, it is advised to cook this water- and mud-borne plant to prevent parasitic infection.

See **Legume Family; Lotus Seed; Lotus Tea; Vegetable.**

He drifts on blue water
Under a clear moon,
Picking white lilies on South Lake.
Every lotus blossom
Speaks of love
Until his heart will break.
—Li Po, eighth-century Chinese poet

LOTUS SEED

The cream-colored lotus seed, similar in size and shape to a cooked chickpea, is a tasty food with a pleasant nutty flavor. It can be bought dried from Asian markets. When soaked and split open, notice its unusually large embryonic sprout, which looks like a miniature lotus plant.

Medicinal Benefits Lotus seeds increase kidney energy and overall vitality. They aid digestion, nourish the heart, counter insomnia, and soothe the nervous system. They're used for vaginal discharge, cloudy urine, and seminal emission. They contain 20 percent protein and so are highly nourishing. Lotus seeds reduce *pitta* and *vata*.

Use Lotus seeds require soaking and cooking, like beans. In fact, when I want to give an energy boost to a pot of beans, I'll often add lotus seeds to dry beans, soaking and cooking them together. Use lotus seeds in vegetable, bean, soup, or grain dishes. They're typically available from Asian markets.

See **Lotus Root; Seeds.**

LOTUS TEA
Kohren

Lotus tea, made from fresh or powdered dried lotus, is an excellent medicinal beverage. Regular use of lotus tea builds overall strength and specifically strengthens the heart, lungs, kidneys, and digestive system. When ginger is added to this tea, it treats enteritis, nausea, digestive disorders, and difficulty in swallowing. To quench thirst during a fever, sweeten with honey.

To make lotus tea, mix 2 teaspoons of dried lotus powder (or 2 tablespoons of freshly grated lotus root) into 1 cup of water. Add a pinch of salt and heat over low heat just to the boiling point. Drink hot. The powder is available in Asian markets and some natural food stores.

See **Lotus Root.**

LOVAGE
Love Parsley
(*Levisticum officinale*)

A parsley relative that tastes like strong celery, lovage is a favorite in herb gardens and one of the first to green up in the spring. It is a tall perennial with hollow stems and leaves that resemble celery leaves. As a medicinal and

---

THOUSAND-YEAR-OLD SEED GERMINATED BY UCLA PLANT PHYSIOLOGIST

The viability of most seeds is—depending upon storage conditions—a decade or so, and the percentage of seeds that germinate decreases with each passing year. The scientific world was astounded when an ancient lotus seed not only sprouted but grew to maturity. A lotus seed radiocarbon dated to 1288 BC (give or take 220 years) from a dry lake bed in China was germinated in 1994 by Jane Shen-Miller, as reported in *The American Journal of Botany*, November 1995. According to Shen-Miller, the seed's natural preservative, together with the oxygen-free environment in the lake bed, helped maintain its viability. This enzyme helps repair age-damaged proteins—no wonder lotus seeds are considered an important vitality-building food in Asia.

culinary agent, lovage is popular in southern and central Europe.

Medicinal Benefits Lovage is a bitter-sweet sedative with antiseptic properties; it aids digestion, increases perspiration, and acts as a diuretic and expectorant. It strengthens the immune system and is useful for indigestion and for relieving flatulence, kidney stones, and painful menstruation. It is a good source of quercetin. Lovage reduces *kapha* and *pitta*.

Use In Slavic regions, lovage root is peeled and used as a vegetable. Roots at least three years old are used for extractions and tinctures. Young stalks are eaten as a vegetable and used as a straw for beverages. Its seeds are used as spice; its leaves as an herb. Lovage leaves pep up soups, stews, and pickles; they hold up well to heat and so may be simmered for a long time.

Be Mindful Do not use lovage during pregnancy, as it promotes the onset of menstruation.

See **Carrot Family; Herbs and Spices.**

LOVE PARSLEY SEE LOVAGE.

LUCERNE SEE ALFALFA.

LUFA SEE LOOFAH.

LUPIN
(*Lupini, Lupinus albus, L. luteus, L. varius, L. mutabilis*)

Several hundred varieties of the large yellow legume lupin are dispersed throughout the Americas, Africa, and Europe, and have been an important food crop for both humans and animals. One variety, the bluebonnet, is the state flower of Texas and a popular garden flower, but its seeds may be toxic. Newer cultivars with a higher protein content (up to 40 percent) and fewer bitter-tasting and toxic al-

kaloids are marketed as the next-generation soybean. Because lupin grows in colder regions than soy, it holds promise as a cash crop in northern climates.

Medicinal Benefits Lupins are the largest natural source of the amino acid arginine, which supports heart health. As it contains all the essential amino acids, it is an excellent protein source. Compared to soy, lupin is higher in fiber and lower in fat. It is a low glycemic index food.

Use In Mediterranean and Andean countries, and in Brazil, lupin beans are a common legume; they may also be pickled like olives and eaten as a condiment with or without their skin. As an alternative to soy, lupin is used in some vegan products, like tofu, tempeh, and miso. Lupin flour is used in some nongluten baked goods and pasta products.

Be Mindful For some individuals, lupin is an allergen. People with food sensitivities to other legumes such as peanuts or soy are more likely to have allergic reactions to lupin.

See **Legume Family.**

LUPINI SEE LUPIN.

LYCHEE
Litchi
(*Litchi chinensis*)

The lychee is the size of a small round plum. Peel its strawberry-red, warty, leathery rind and its smooth and milky fruit is as juicy as a muscat grape. The lychee has an uplifting sweetness and an aroma that suggests lavender, jasmine, and rose. It's with good reason that the Chinese have long held it as a revered fruit.

Lychees grow in clusters upon evergreen trees prized for their stately beauty and are native to tropical and semitropical southeastern Asia. Only after a tree is ten years old will it produce fruit, and even then production is erratic. Lychees are now grown in semitropical areas worldwide, including Florida and California.

Medicinal Benefits In Chinese medicine, lychees are an energy tonic and recommended for the spleen, stomach, and liver meridians. They help promote body fluids and ease thirst, reinforce spleen chi, and replenish blood. They are quite cooling. The fruit contains vitamins B and C as well as folic acid, citric acid, malic acid, and arginine.

Use Lychees are easy to eat out of hand. The flesh easily separates from the peel and from its large, mahogany-colored seed. Both peel and pit are inedible. Lychees are at their best eaten fresh and need no accompaniment; they are also excellent combined with other fruits and may be gently stewed. Their sweet acidic flavor makes them a popular last course to a Chinese meal.

Buying Lychees are primarily available in midsummer. The red peel turns brown soon after harvest, but don't pass over brown-skinned fruits as long as they are plump and heavy. Avoid shriveled or cracked fruits. Lychees are best if not chilled; they can be refrigerated for up to two weeks, although this will incur some loss of flavor and texture. Lychees are available canned in syrup in Asian markets. Dried lychee fruits are like raisins in texture; they have a pleasingly nutty flavor.

See **Dried Fruit; Fruit; Lychee Family.**

LYCHEE FAMILY
(*Sapindaceae*)

This large botanical family includes our common maple and horse chestnut trees as well as three delicious semitropical fruits: the lychee, longan, and rambutan.

See **Longan; Lychee; Rambutan.**

MACADAMIA NUT
(*Macadamia integrifolia, M. tetraphylla*)

When I first tasted this most buttery, sweet nut, it evoked for me visions of a lush, tropical macadamia realm. What a laugh on me when I learned that this Australian nut was named for a doctor with the not-so-exotic name of John Macadam.

The texture of a macadamia nut is similar to a Brazil nut but more meltingly tender. This creamy-colored nut is the only native Australian plant that has been domesticated. In the past few decades, Hawaii has become the main producer of the U.S. domestic supply, but the nuts are grown commercially in Florida, California, and other semitropical regions. Availability of the macadamia is increasing.

Medicinal Benefits Oil is the only vegetarian food higher in fat and calories than the macadamia, which contains a whopping 70 percent fat content. They may be aptly termed a "fat bomb." One pound of nuts is over 3,500 calories. They have the highest amount of beneficial monounsaturated fats of any known nut, including 22 percent of the beneficial omega-7 monounsaturated fatty acid.

Use To intensify the sublime flavor of macadamia nuts, oven-roast at 250°F until they turn a shade darker. Enjoy out of hand, in nut mixes, or substitute macadamias for any nutmeat in entrées, desserts, or confections.

Buying Because macadamias are nigh impossible to crack by hand, they're sold shelled. Purchase only if they are a creamy white color; their color yellows and darkens as they become rancid. Macadamia nuts are often available vacuum packed to help preserve their freshness. For storage, refrigerate or freeze and use in a timely fashion.

Be Mindful Don't "treat" your family pet to macadamia nuts. In both cats and dogs, ingestion of macadamia nuts can cause lethargy, vomiting, hyperthermia, tremors, abdominal pain, and temporary lameness. While all nuts are high on the list of potential allergens, for most people macadamia nuts appear to be less problematic than almonds, peanuts, and walnuts.

See **Macadamia Oil; Nuts.**

MACADAMIA OIL

This lush oil contains negligible, up to 3 percent, omega-3 fatty acids and so may be used in cooking as well as for salad dressing. It contains 19 percent palmitoleic acid, a beneficial omega-7 fatty acid, making macadamia oil the principal vegetarian source for this nutrient. It contains up to 85 percent of monounsaturated fats and more than 4½ times the amount of vitamin E as olive oil, which helps preserve its freshness.

Unrefrigerated, unrefined macadamia oil has a shelf life of four months and up to a year refrigerated. Expect the unrefined oil to become cloudy with time; this is normal and not problematic.

See **Macadamia Nut; Fat and Oil.**

MACE
(*Myristica fragrans*)

This spice, quite out of fashion for several decades, is staging a modest comeback. Mace is the yellow-orange aril, or lacy husk, of the nutmeg seed. Like nutmeg, mace has a peppery, cinnamonlike flavor but is more delicate and less sweet; it imbues foods with its rich orange color.

Medicinal Benefits Mace is warming and supports digestive functioning; I tend to favor it during the colder months. Mace essential oil treats indigestion, general weakness, bacterial infections, gout, rheumatism, and arthritis and aids circulation. It reduces *vata* and *kapha*.

Use This pleasing flavoring agent is mostly used in desserts but is also delicious in soups and sauces and with poultry. It beautifully colors and flavors butter.

Buying Mace is sometimes sold in blades but is most often sold ground. Unlike nutmeg and many ground spices, mace holds its flavor well.

See **Herbs and Spices; Nutmeg.**

GRANDMA'S MACE CAKE

Here's my grandma's favorite cake recipe—updated with the more healthful and rich, round flavors of unrefined sugar and whole wheat flour.

- 1 cup unsalted butter, softened
- 1½ cups unrefined cane sugar
- 5 large eggs, separated
- 2 tablespoons milk
- 2 cups whole wheat pastry flour
- ¼ teaspoon unrefined salt
- ½ teaspoon ground mace
- 2 teaspoons freshly squeezed lemon juice
- 1 teaspoon grated lemon zest
- 2 tablespoons finely chopped black walnuts or pecans

Preheat the oven to 325°F. Grease a tube pan or 4 x 10-inch or 5 x 8-inch loaf pan.

In a large bowl, cream together the butter and sugar. Add the egg yolks and milk and beat well.

In a separate bowl, sift the flour, salt, and mace together and stir into the wet ingredients. Add the lemon juice and zest and beat well.

In a third bowl, beat the egg whites to soft peaks and fold them into the batter. Pour the batter into the prepared pan and sprinkle the top with the nuts.

Place in the oven and bake for 1 hour or until lightly browned. Remove from the oven and place on a wire rack right side up to cool, then invert the cake and remove from the pan.

MÂCHE
Corn Salad, Lamb's Lettuce
(*Valerianella locusta*)

What was available at the turn of the century as corn salad is back again as mâche. This attractive blue-green salad green, a valerian family member, has been cultivated since Neolithic times. It has a mild, nutty flavor and a downy texture. It is slightly more chewy and firm than lettuce. The largest of its diminutive leaves are five inches long and about one and a half inches wide. An annual, this hardy vegetable thrives in cold, wet regions and even grows through frost and snow. Mâche is one of my favorite garden plants; for once established, it produces long after and long before other salad greens.

Medicinal Benefits Like other dark leafy greens, mâche is an excellent source of beta-carotene and an excellent liver food. Its ability to survive harsh winters is a good indicator that it is more nutrient dense than lettuce and other fragile salad greens. It contains three times as much vitamin C as lettuce. Mâche reduces *pitta* and *kapha*; in moderation it also reduces *vata*.

Use Mâche is often found in salad mixes or, by itself, prewashed and bagged. It lends itself to arranged salads and is delicious by itself with a simple dressing. Historically it was used as a potherb—a use that I also recommend.

Buying Mâche is available as separate leaves or as a whole plant, roots intact, which is the size of a small nosegay. Select fresh heads with unblemished leaves, and use it immediately.

See **Vegetables.**

MA CHI XIAN SEE PURSLANE.

MAITAKE
Hen-of-the-Woods, Sheep's Head
(*Grifola frondosa*)

The Japanese word *maitake* means "dancing mushroom" because, so tradition tells us, when people found maitake they would dance for joy. What was so joyous about this fungi? For one thing, it was worth its weight in silver.

Maitake clumps grow at the base of stumps in the woods. The stalks of their fan-shaped caps fuse together at the base to form a mass sometimes as large as a football. Maitake grows wild throughout the Northern Hemisphere. Since 1990, it has been successfully cultivated.

Medicinal Benefits The polysaccharide in maitake, Beta 1, 6-glucan, is a unique and potent immunostimulant, apparently helping to neutralize tumors and to ameliorate cancer, AIDS, chronic fatigue, liver function, and problems of obesity. It lowers blood pressure and benefits diabetes sufferers by lowering blood glucose. An adaptogen, this mushroom has long been valued for promoting longevity and optimum weight and maintaining health. As medicine, a standard dosage is 3 to 7 grams daily as a tea, supplement, or cooked vegetable.

Use Maitake is excellent when thinly sliced and sautéed in butter with herbs. It holds its shape well and doesn't absorb as much oil as other mushrooms. Maitake may also be baked, grilled, or added to a casserole or soup. When using it dried, rehydrate in water for at least 30 minutes, or until softened. Substitute about 1 ounce of the dried mushroom for each 8 to 10 ounces of fresh mushrooms.

Buying Fresh from the hothouse, maitake is available year-round in well-supplied food stores for use as a vegetable. It is also available as a medicinal supplement with or without other ingredients.

See **Mushroom Family; Vegetable.**

MAIZE SEE CORN.

MALANGA SEE YAUTIA.

MALLOW FAMILY
(*Malva*)

Species from this large and diverse family are widespread throughout Europe, Africa, and Asia. The leaves of many are edible and used, especially in Asia, as a potherb. The most economically viable mallows are cocoa, cotton, and the cola bean.

See **Cocoa; Cottonseed; Okra.**

MALT SEE BARLEY MALT POWDER; BARLEY MALT SYRUP.

MALTODEXTRIN (NOT RECOMMENDED)

The term "maltodextrin" stands for a family of products that is made by hydrolysis of a starch. The FDA regards maltodextrin as food grade no matter the original source of starch—even cheap plywood industry by-products. Maltodextrins are used in a wide array of foods, from canned fruits to snacks. They also may be an ingredient in the single-serve, table-top packet of some artificial sweeteners.

See **Sweeteners.**

MALT VINEGAR SEE VINEGAR.

MAMEY SAPOTE
(*Pouteria sapota*)

A tropical fruit native to the West Indies, the mamey sapote is just now gaining a market position. It is a fruit to watch for. It's shaped like a large pointed peach with gritty, fibrous skin and striking flesh that ranges from pink to salmon in color. The mamey's memorable tropical flavor is a blend of honeyed sweet potato and almonds. Ripen at room temperature until it is soft to the touch. If underripe, its flesh is astringent. Eat it raw, out of hand, or add it to smoothies, ice cream, or fruit salad. The mamey sapote is grown extensively in semitropical areas.

In the Caribbean region, it is used to treat gastrointestinal maladies and headaches and has historically been used as an antiseptic. The single pit is toxic.

See **Fruit; Sapodilla Family.**

MANCHURIAN MUSHROOM SEE KOMBUCHA.

MANDARIN SEE ORANGE.

MANGO
(*Mangifera indica*)

Sensuously sticky and lush, the mango is the most widely consumed fruit in the world, accounting for 50 percent of the world's trade in tropical fruits. Native to India, where it's the national fruit, the mango is a cashew relative and grows on an evergreen tree. The mango has a smooth, leathery skin colored green, yellow, or red. There are hundreds of mango varieties; they are generally round to oval and vary in weight from six ounces to one and a half pounds. The juicy orange-colored flesh clings to a large, flat pit that is typically fibrous. The U.S. domestic crop, which grows in Florida, California, and Hawaii, is in season during the summer. Out-of-season mangos are imported.

Medicinal Benefits A mango's thermal property is cooling, and it is a yin tonic that travels the lung, stomach, and spleen meridians. It helps circulate chi, disperse water, clear heat, and quench thirst. Ripened mangos are *tridoshic*. This delectable fruit is a superior source of vitamin C, polyphenols, and carotenoids and provides a good source of vitamin B_6, potassium, and antioxidants. It is moderately high in calories.

Use In mango-producing areas, the fruits are often available from sidewalk vendors, peeled and skewered upon a stick, and are better than a lollipop. The stick enables you to tease away the sweet flesh that clings to the pit. Otherwise, removing the flesh from the pit is a slippery affair. The best way is to slice the fruit lengthwise all around the pit. Cut slices and pull them away from the pit, then peel and discard the skin.

A mango (like other fruits) is most flavorful at room temperature. With or without a squeeze of lime, use raw mango, sliced, shredded, or cut into chunks, for vegetable, fruit, and meat salads, fruit kabobs, parfaits, and puddings; or puree mango for ice cream and smoothies. This all-around fruit is equally delicious cooked in tarts, cakes, and cobblers, or even made into jelly. Immature mangos are a classic chutney, relish, and pickle ingredient.

Buying Select mangos that are firm, plump, and fresh-looking and that have a pleasant spicy and sweet aroma at the stem end. If there is no scent, the fruit will be flavorless. Ripen at room temperature in a brown bag until the fruit yields slightly to pressure, like a ripe avocado. As the mango ripens, the skin color intensifies (green-skinned mangos excepted). Once ripe, a mango may be refrigerated for several days. As imported mangos are heat-treated to kill fruit flies or pests, I favor domestic mangos.

EASY MANGO SORBET

Cooling, lush, and effortless to make . . . but prepare yourself for sticky fingers. If there are children at hand, invite their help.

Makes about 3 cups

- 2 ripe mangos (about 1½ pounds)
- 2 tablespoons honey, or to taste
- ¼ cup apple juice or other fruit juice or water
- 1 tablespoon freshly squeezed lime juice
- Fresh mint sprigs

With a sharp knife, cutting lengthwise alongside the pit and cutting as close to the pit as possible, slice the mango from the pit. The mango flesh should be in two large pieces. Scoop the flesh with a spoon from the mango sides. Remove as much flesh from the pit as you can.

Cube the mango flesh, put it into a freezer container, and place in the freezer for about 3 hours, or until partially frozen. Place the mango, honey, apple juice, and lime juice in a blender and pulse until coarsely pureed. Serve immediately, garnished with fresh mint.

Be Mindful Mangos, and their relatives poison ivy, poison oak, and poison sumac, contain urushiol. For people with allergies, this toxic resin can cause contact dermatitis or blistering skin. The peel and juice of a mango seem to be more of a problem than the flesh—especially immature fruits. Eating mangos to excess may cause itching or skin eruptions. Do not eat the pit or skin.

See **Cashew Family; Dried Fruit; Fruit.**

MANGOSTEEN
Purple Mangosteen
(*Garcinia mangostana*)

Many people claim that this Malaysian berry, with its exquisite milky, sweet juice, is the most delicious tropical fruit there is. It is not related to a mango but rather to the medicinal herb St. John's wort. Like a tangerine in size and structure, a mangosteen is covered by a tough, thick, brownish purple rind; it contains from five to six orangelike segments. Carefully cut through and discard the rind.

Mangosteens are readily available as a juice, in nutritional products, canned, frozen, and dried. Since 2007, the USDA has permitted irradiated imports, and so the fresh fruit has some availability; it is, perhaps, the most expensive fruit. Mangosteen juice products typically include the rind, which gives it a purple color; historically, the rind has not been consumed.

Store a ripe mangosteen refrigerated for up to a month, or covered and at room temperatures for up to two weeks.

See **Fruit.**

MANIOC See **CASSAVA.**

MANNITOL (NOT RECOMMENDED)

The powdery dust on sticks of chewing gum is mannitol; it is a synthesized form of corn sugar and similar to xylitol and sorbitol. When used in excess, mannitol has been implicated in kidney and gastrointestinal disturbances. It is used in diabetic foods and breath-freshener candies.

See **Sorbitol; Sweeteners; Xylitol.**

MAPLE SUGAR

Granulated like white sugar but buff in color, maple sugar is made by evaporating the water from maple syrup. This premier sweetener is nearly 100 percent sucrose with a pleasing flavor. Maple sugar is available in fine food stores in packages, as well as in cake, cookie, and icing mixes. It is often found molded into the shape of a small maple leaf for sale as a novelty food or tourist item.

Use Substitute maple sugar for white sugar, cup for cup, in any recipe. It yields a less intensely sweet but more richly flavored dish with a maple perfume.

See **Maple Syrup; Sweeteners.**

MAPLE SYRUP

Using technologies learned long ago from Native Americans in the Northeast, 80 percent of today's maple syrup is still produced by small family operations. As agribusiness encroaches, however, reverse osmosis is now used to process some syrup. By either method, it takes 40 gallons of sap to make 1 gallon of syrup; the sap is collected over three months.

In early February, a small tap hole is drilled into a sugar maple tree trunk, and the seeping sap is collected; at 3 percent sucrose, it is barely sweet. But boiled down to reduce its water content, it turns into a liquid treasure. While Vermont is the largest U.S. producer, the province of Quebec provides more than 75 percent of the world's consumption. A similar syrup with limited availability is extracted from birch trees in Alaska, Russia, and Scandinavia.

Medicinal Benefits Compared to white sugar with its 99 percent sucrose content, maple syrup, at 65 percent sucrose, is obviously a more healthful choice. Like white sugar, however, it may still cause insulin and adrenaline reactions. Maple syrup is damp producing, and so is best used in moderation if at all by people with candidiasis, malignancies, tumors, cysts, or a compromised immune system. It reduces *vata* and *pitta*.

Use Real maple syrup is utterly delicious on so much more than just pancakes and waffles. I use it in place of sugar for some candies and in many baked goods, where it adds a wonderful maple flavor, moisture, and density. It is less intensely sweet than honey or white sugar. To substitute maple syrup in a recipe calling for sugar, replace 1 cup of sugar with ½ to ⅓ cup of maple syrup and reduce the recipe's liquid measurement by ¼ cup for a more flavorful, moister, denser crumb. Easier yet, and to get the same "sugar crumb," use maple sugar.

Buying To the connoisseur, the flavor of maple syrup varies depending upon when the sap is drawn and the maple tree variety. Sap harvested in February yields a light-colored and most delicately flavored syrup—a syrup considered premium (U.S. Grade A Light Amber or Canadian #1 Extra Light) and best suited to dressing pancakes, waffles, or a fine dessert.

As the weather warms, the bacteria content of the maple sap increases, and when it is cooked down, it more readily caramelizes into a darker, more robustly flavored syrup. The darker syrups are typically less expensive in price. They are U.S. Grade B and Canadian #2 and #3 grades.

Because the quality of pure maple syrup varies dramatically, favor certified organic maple syrups. Some syrup producers place a formaldehyde pellet in the tree's tap hole to prolong sap flow. This contaminates the sap. The Canadian government, the state of Vermont, and organic certification codes prohibit use of these pellets.

SNOW CANDY

Grandma stood by the brass kettle and with the big wooden spoon she poured hot [maple] syrup on each plate of snow. It cooled into soft candy, and as fast as it cooled they ate it. . . . There was plenty of syrup in the kettle, and plenty of snow outdoors. As soon as they ate one plateful, they filled their plates with snow again, and Grandma poured more syrup on it.

—Laura Ingalls Wilder, *The Little House in the Big Woods*

Maple syrup may also be contaminated with high levels of lead. This may be from the lead seams in the metal cans it is marketed in or from the evaporating pans used by most producers. Since the FDA limits the lead content of imported maple syrup, Canadian brands can be considered safe, as can certified organic brands.

Maple syrup is the one sweetener that is usually refrigerated. Refrigeration is necessary, however, only in warm temperatures.

See **Sweeteners.**

MARGARINE (NOT RECOMMENDED)

Even if margarine is sold in a natural food store, even if it's made from "good" ingredients, leave it on the shelf. As it is made from highly refined oils and denatured fats, it is rancid, toxic, and contributes to the formation of free radicals. How unfortunate that many people believe that margarine—despite its flavor—is preferable to butter; indeed, this fake butter outsells the real thing by approximately two to one.

Margarine, in use for nearly 200 years, is typically made from animal or vegetable fats, skim milk, salt, and emulsifiers. If you're looking for a vegan or kosher butter substitute, consider nut butter or virgin coconut or palm oil.

See **Fat and Oil.**

MARINE ALGAE SEE **SEAWEED FAMILY.**

MARJORAM
Sweet Marjoram
(*Origanum majorana*)

Related to oregano, marjoram is a perennial herb native to the Mediterranean region; it is the milder of the two herbs, with a citrus and sweet pine aroma and flavor. When dried, its flavor is further reduced, and so this herb is often passed over in favor of its more robust relative. Favored fresh in French, Greek, and Italian cuisine, marjoram is at its best when added just at the end of cooking.

Medicinal Benefits Marjoram is a cooling herb and a yin tonic that helps chi circulation and specifically acts upon the lungs, stomach, and spleen. It is valued for its ability to relieve menstrual cramps and insomnia, calm stressed nerves and muscles, and for bronchial complaints. As a flavoring agent or in tea, it aids digestion. It reduces *vata* and *kapha*.

Use Both the leaves and blossoms of marjoram are used to infuse oils and vinegar and to season pasta and tomatoes and bean and meat dishes.

See **Herbs and Spices; Mint Family; Oregano.**

MARSH SAMPHIRE SEE **GLASSWORT.**

MASA

Masa means "dough" in Spanish; in the Americas, it refers to a wet dough made from posole (hominy or slaked corn). Masa is a base for tortillas, tacos, enchiladas, tamales, and corn chips. Commercially available masa is made from white corn; blue corn masa products, however, have some availability; and yellow masa is usually used for chips and tortillas. Masa is available frozen—and sometimes fresh—from Latino markets. Fresh masa is available in two grades: fine (*masa para tortillas*) and coarse (*masa para tamales*).

Arepas are the Central American and Cuban variety of masa that are slaked from a very large, starchy corn variety. Arepas signify both the meal used to make flatbread and the flatbread itself. They are available in Cuban markets in the United States.

See **Corn; Masa Harina; Posole.**

A TASTE TEST FOR CORN CHIP CONNOISSEURS

Taste a Cheerio, Wheat Chex, or Fritos corn chip. It's hard to find the flavor of, respectively, oats, wheat, or corn. When extruded under high heat and pressure, a grain's subtle flavors are lost, and its heat-vulnerable nutrients and essential fatty acids are denatured. This high-tech process forms the O of a Cheerio, the weave of a Chex, and the curl of a Frito, but about all you can taste is the seasoning agents—not the grain.

In the case of corn chips, however, there are tasty and healthful options to extruded products. Traditional corn chips are made of masa harina and not extruded. Their giveaway triangular shape with sharp angles marks them as wedges cut from tortillas. Their real masa flavor is the best giveaway. The rounded corners on some triangle-shaped corn chips reveal extrusion.

MASA HARINA

Harina means "flour" in Spanish. Masa harina is ground dried masa. It is readily available in supermarkets as well as in specialty food stores.

See **Corn; Masa; Posole.**

MASTIC
(*Pistacia lentiscus*)

The aromatic resin collected from an evergreen shrub on—by law—only the Greek island of Chios is known as mastic. Although the mastic tree grows throughout the Mediterranean region, it's only on the southern part of Chios that the tree, when scored, exudes sap. This production is controlled by a cooperative of villagers known as the *Mastichochoria*. Mastic is a relative of the pistachio and a member of the cashew family. Like chicle, mastic was an original ingredient in the production of chewing gum.

Medicinal Benefits Mastic soothes the stomach and helps reduce blood cholesterol. Mastic has antibacterial and antifungal properties, and is used in ointments for skin disorders and afflictions.

Use As a culinary ingredient, mastic is used to flavor liquors, desserts, cakes, pastries, and candies. It's also used for its gummy texture in gum and candies such as Turkish delight.

See **Cashew Family.**

MATÉ
Yerba Maté
(*Ilex para*)

Maté comes from a Quechua word meaning a gourd vessel used for brewing and drinking a type of holly tea—but it has come to mean the tea itself. It tastes rather like an herby green tea with coffee and tobacco overtones. This holly, a relative of our common holiday greenery, is called yerba maté and grows as an evergreen shrub or tree. It originated in Paraguay, and the tea remains a popular beverage there as well as in Uruguay, Argentina, Chile, Brazil, and more recently in Lebanon, Syria, and Turkey.

Medicinal Benefits Maté is a mildly caffeinated beverage. It reduces feelings of fatigue and hunger. Maté acts as a diuretic, relaxes spasms, clears toxins, and is mildly analgesic. It is said to help relieve headaches, arthritic pain, mild depression, and neuralgia. Maté reduces *kapha*.

Use Maté is traditionally both brewed in and sipped from a dried gourd vessel; additional brewing details vary from region to region and source to source. Agreement is unanimous, however, that maté is best infused in hot—never boiling—water to preserve its delicate essence and flavor.

Buying Maté is available packaged and loose in the tea section of markets; it is also an ingredient in tea blends. You're apt to find the brewing supplies—be they the traditional gourd and metal straw or a traveling mug container—in coffee and tea shops and in stores well supplied with tea selections.

MATSUTAKE
Pine Mushroom
(*Armillaria ponderosa, A. edodes*)

One of the most appealing edible mushrooms, the matsutake has such a superb and spicy flavor that even a few slivers of it can elevate a soup to sublimity. Its aroma, according to David Arora in *Mushrooms Demystified*, "is a provocative compromise between Red Hots and smelly socks." The stems are thick and meaty and the slightly pointed, unopened caps are enclosed in a veil, making them look distinctively phallic. As the caps flare open, the market price declines.

Medicinal Benefits Matsutake mushrooms thin blood and thus lower cholesterol and help prevent stroke and heart attack. By stimulating the immune system, they help prevent cancer and other degenerative conditions. Matsutake contain germanium, which increases oxygen efficiency and counters the effects of environmental pollutants.

Use In Asia, matsutake mushrooms are traditionally broken into pieces rather than sliced. To best reveal their spicy aroma, they are simmered in broth. While they can flavor many savory dishes, they are usually showcased alone or in a simple preparation. To reconstitute dried matsutake mushrooms, soak in water or an unsalted, seasoned broth for 20 minutes, or until softened.

LA BOMBILLA

There's an elaborate culture—some would say it approaches the level of a High Mass—for maté brewing. In the precision of detail, it is similar to a Japanese tea ceremony.

I'm a maté-brewing novice, but it sure is satisfying to slurp maté the traditional way—from a dried gourd and through a *bombilla*. The *bombilla* is a metal straw that ends in a spoon-shaped sieve. The sound made while sucking the dregs to savor one last sip is deliciously barbarous. The irregular-shaped gourd—which is both brew pot and drinking cup—is soft in the hand and adds ambiance. Encounter a true maté aficionado and the odds are that her gourd, *bombilla*, and maté stash are close at hand.

I find my *bombilla* indispensable for my daily herbal brew. Into my tea mug goes whatever herbs I'm in need of and/or delight in. Today's brew, for example, includes eye bright for computer-tired eyes and rooibos and licorice for satisfaction and pleasure. Thanks to the *bombilla*, brewing is a one-step process.

Buying/Foraging Matsutake mushrooms are foraged near stands of red pine in China, Japan, and the Pacific Northwest. They are recently under limited cultivation; this factor, plus their short foraging season, makes them extremely expensive. Dried matsutake are sometimes available; drying diminishes their flavor.

See **Mushroom Family; Vegetable.**

Maui Onion See **Onion.**

Meal See **Flour.**

Meat Analog See **Textured Soy Protein.**

Meat Extender See **Textured Soy Protein.**

Medicine Plant See **Aloe Vera.**

Meiwa See **Kumquat.**

Mekabu Wakame See **Wakame.**

Melissa See **Lemon Balm.**

MELON
(*Cucumis melo*)

Melons do their share to usher in—and give relief from—the dog days of summer. They have come a long way from their original state. Wild melons the size of oranges and bland tasting still grow in Africa. In Roman times, melons were eaten as part of green vegetable salad. During the Renaissance, the monks at the pope's summer residence, Cantalupo, coaxed this watery food into the sugary, flavorful fruit we know today.

As the seed structure indicates, melons are members of the gourd family, relatives of cucumber and squash. There are two types of melons: the muskmelon and the watermelon.

The latter has its seeds embedded in its juicy flesh like a squash or a pumpkin.

The muskmelons so readily interbreed among themselves that there are many varieties, with many more likely to be developed—and endless confusion about nomenclature as a result. Muskmelon's flesh color ranges from a honeydew's lime green to a Crenshaw's pink salmon hue.

Medicinal Benefits Melons have specific healing action upon the lung meridian. They are a cooling food and help disperse hot conditions and treat fevers accompanied by chills or dry coughs. They also have diuretic properties and may relieve mental depression. Melons are best avoided when there is abdominal swelling or watery stools. Melons in general reduce *vata* and *pitta*, though watermelon increases *vata*.

Of late, melons, especially the orange-fleshed varieties, have received much press for their excellent beta-carotene content, which puts them high on the list of anticarcinogenic foods. Melons are also an excellent potassium source, and since they have a negligible amount of fat, are perfect for those concerned with high blood pressure. In addition, they have an anticoagulant ingredient, adenosine, which offers support for those with heart disease and may help bring on menstruation.

Use Melons, with a water content of about 94 percent, are digested very rapidly. It is therefore best to eat melon alone. If melon is combined with another food, digestion is slowed, and fermentation—rather than assimilation—results. Melons do not withstand cooking but are delicious in fruit salads, fruit soups, ices, and sorbet. They may be juiced or served standing on their own, with or without a squeeze of lime. Melon may also be dried for fruit leather.

Buying A melon's sugar content does not

increase after picking, so avoid immature fruits. A ripe melon is heavy for its size with a firm rind, a slight softening, and a sweet aroma at the blossom end (casaba excepted). Avoid an overly ripe melon or one with dark, soft, or sunken spots. The flavor of a fresh local melon far exceeds that of an out-of-season melon, which, of necessity, was picked immaturely. These are the most common varieties:

- **Cantaloupe** Most available of the melons. Cantaloupe is usually sold when mature but not dead ripe. Purchase a cantaloupe with no stem or stem fragment. Hold it at room temperature until it has a pleasant cantaloupe aroma and yields slightly to light thumb pressure on the blossom end, and when the rind's netting has a dull yellowish cast. Avoid purchasing an overripe melon, which is soft with a pronounced yellow rind.
- **Casaba** Round like a pumpkin but pointed slightly at the blossom end. The rind has shallow, irregular furrows running from blossom end to stem end. Some have a pale green rind and pale yellow flesh; others have a light orange to dark green rind with gold flesh. When ripe, it has a slight softening at the blossom end. A ripe casaba has no aroma until cut.
- **Crenshaw** Easy to identify because of its large, ovoid size and pointed stem end. The rind of the Crenshaw melon is smooth, golden, and slightly corrugated. The thick flesh is a bright salmon color. A Crenshaw is ripe when it has a sweet aroma and the rind is a deep golden yellow, yielding slightly to moderate pressure at the blossom end. When ripe, the flesh has a spicy-sweet taste.
- **Honeyball** Similar to the honeydew but smaller.
- **Honeydew** Large with a smooth, very pale green skin and sweet light green flesh. A slight bloom, faint netting, and a slightly sticky feeling on the skin indicate a ripe honeydew. If it is hard with a white or green-white rind, the honeydew was picked prematurely and will not become sweet. It is more subtle and sweeter than a cantaloupe.
- **Persian** Similar to cantaloupe but more nearly round, with a finer netting. The flesh is thick, finely textured, and orange.

See **Fruit; Gourd Family; Watermelon.**

Melon Pear See **Pepino.**

MESCLUN
Misticanza

Mesclun is a mix of salad greens consisting of young, tender lettuces, baby greens like spinach or beet greens, herbs, and sometimes edible blossoms. It is available prewashed. To preserve their freshness, the producer rinses the greens in a mild bleach solution.

See **Lettuce.**

MESQUITE
(*Prosopis veluntina*)

Aromatic mesquite meal is an ingredient I enjoy for more than its malty sweet flavor and many energy properties. Its taste evokes for me the fresh, clean smell of the desert in blossom. It's ground from the small yellow seeds of the leguminous, drought-resistant mesquite shrub. Mesquite has been perhaps the single most important plant food of Southwest native peoples. Today most people associate mesquite with a novelty charcoal for grilling or a honey with a desert bouquet.

Medicinal Benefits Regarded as a high-energy food, mesquite meal is a key ingredient in *pinole*, the dietary staple of the world-famous

Tarahumara runners, who ate pinole to sustain them in their legendary hundred-mile mountain marathons.

Mesquite flour helps stabilize blood sugar; it is high in lysine and rich in calcium, magnesium, potassium, iron, and zinc. It reduces *vata*.

Mesquite pods, as well as their leaves, twigs, and bark, make a strong disinfectant wash for broken-skin injuries. Decoct in boiling water. Or drink this tea for its astringent, antimicrobial action. Mesquite inhibits diarrhea and intestinal inflammations including ulcers, colitis, and hemorrhoids. For pinkeye or conjunctivitis, infuse five washed and crushed pods and half a teaspoon salt in two cups of boiling water.

Use The meal ground from mesquite pods is so sweet that I sometimes use it as a sweetener replacement in cornbread, muffins, puddings, sauces, and even pie crust. Mesquite meal does not contain gluten, so it is best when combined with wheat in a ratio of 1 to 5 in baked goods, pancakes, and waffles. If you have whole pods, you may make, as do some Native Americans, a thin syrup of the pods by simmering them covered in water for a day, then straining out the pods and reducing the liquid.

Buying/Foraging According to Michael Moore, author and herbalist who specializes in plants of the Southwest, if you are in any part of the Colorado, Mojave, Sonora, or Chihuahua desert, then mesquite, the most common shrub in all the Southwest, is nearby. Mesquite meal is available in some specialty shops and by mail order. Mature mesquite pods are foraged in the fall directly from the tree or from the ground below.

See **Legume Family.**

METHI SEE FENUGREEK GREENS.

MEXICAN BREADFRUIT SEE MONSTERA.

MEXICAN LIME SEE LIME.

MEXICAN PARSLEY SEE CILANTRO.

MEXICAN TEA SEE EPAZOTE.

MICROALGAE

The most intense concentrations of chlorophyll are found in freshwater algae. These algae exist on the edge between the plant and animal kingdoms and are not in the same family as seaweed. Thanks to their photosynthetic ability, a strong case can be made for microalgae as the ultimate superfood. Here's why:

Photosynthesis, the conversion of sunlight into food, is possible because of chlorophyll. With this miraculous substance, the plant kingdom manufactures its food from basic elements and sunlight. All life is dependent on the chemical reactions made possible by chlorophyll, which is often referred to as the "blood of plants." Given that the molecular structure between hemoglobin (red blood cells) and chlorophyll is similar, it is not surprising that chlorophyll enriches our blood.

Freshwater microalgae is thus remarkable because of its high chlorophyll content, but that's not all. They are higher in protein, beta-carotene, and nucleic acids than any other food. Their nucleic acids benefit the renewal of human cells and help to reverse aging. Three exceptionally nutritious algae widely available in natural food stores are chlorella, spirulina, and wild blue-green algae. These cooling foods have cleansing, detoxifying, and healing effects upon our bodies.

They are typically available as supplements, in energy drinks, and energy products. Well-supplied natural food stores carry them in bulk; they're typically stirred into a beverage and drunk.

See **Algae Family; Chlorella; Spirulina; Wild Blue-Green Algae.**

Milk Substitutes See **Nondairy Milk Substitutes.**

MILLET
(*Panicum miliaceum*)

Most corn is fed to cattle; most barley is brewed for beer; and most millet is used as birdseed. The claim to fame of the eastern Colorado town of Otis (population 700) is as Birdseed Capital of America.

Elsewhere in the world, millet is a generic term for at least five different small and unrelated cereal grains. In the United States, the word "millet" refers to proso millet, and it is this strain that we find in natural food stores, in some progressive supermarkets, and in parakeet feed.

Proso was among the earliest cultivated cereals and a member of the grass family. The first written reference to this millet is dated at about 2800 BC and lists the five sacred crops of China as rice, soybeans, barley, wheat, and millet. Millet seems to have been brought overland by the Mongols into the Middle East and the Mediterranean basin. Frequently noted in the New Testament, millet flourished throughout the Roman Empire and into the Middle Ages, during which time it was a dominant food crop before being supplanted by modern wheat.

Medicinal Benefits Millet is a cooling grain and yin tonic that supports the kidney, stomach, and spleen meridians. It is used for gastrointestinal irregularities; cooking it with winter squash increases its medicinal value to the earth element organs. Millet is the preferred grain in the treatment of blood sugar imbalances and one of the best grains for those suffering from thrush. A European remedy for relieving rheumatic and some arthritic pains is to apply a poultice of hot (but not so hot as to burn the skin) millet porridge to the affected area. Millet reduces *kapha*.

Of all the true cereal grains, millet has the richest amino acid protein profile and the highest iron content. It is very rich in phosphorus and the B vitamins. It is gluten-free, and because of its high alkaline ash content, the easiest grain to digest. This unusual makeup allows millet to be cooked without salt and yet be alkaline rather than acidic.

Use If millet is cooked with little liquid (1 cup millet to 2¼ cups liquid), it makes a light, dry, fluffy pilaf. Increase the liquid to 3 cups, and it has a smooth texture like mashed potatoes or polenta. Millet can be eaten alone as a cereal or side dish or cooked in combination with other grains in breads, soups, stews, stuffings, and even desserts.

Buying As millet has a more fragile shelf life than the other grains, purchase it in small quantities from a natural food store that has a high turnover and store it in a cool pantry or refrigerate. Millet has a mild, nutty flavor. If it has an acrid, harsh aftertaste, it is rancid and should be discarded.

See **Grains; Grass Family; Millet Flour.**

THE BEST WAFFLE

This recipe has become a favorite—even a staple—of so many people who try it. And it's as delicious as it is easy to make. Soak whole grains overnight, then season, blend, and pour into a waffle iron. Refrigerated, the batter holds for five days, which enables you to bake a fresh waffle in a moment's notice in about as much time as it takes to fry an egg.

Here's the secret to this waffle's outstanding flavor: Soaking whole grains develops their flavor. It also makes the grains more digestible and their nutrients more bioavailable. While this waffle is more substantial and hearty than a flour waffle, it still welcomes a smear of honey or maple syrup. Many people also enjoy it dry as a bread substitute, served alongside a bowl of soup. Do not add fruit, though, as it makes the waffles too acidic and heavy.

Makes four 5-inch-diameter waffles

- 1 cup millet
- 1 cup untoasted buckwheat (not kasha)
- ¼ cup shredded unsweetened coconut
- 2 tablespoons melted unsalted butter or unrefined coconut or palm oil
- 2 tablespoons honey or blackstrap molasses
- ½ teaspoon unrefined salt
- 1 to 3 teaspoons ground cinnamon
- 1 to 3 teaspoons orange zest
- ¼ cup sunflower seeds

Place the millet and buckwheat in a blender or processor (not a Vita-Mixer), add water to cover by an inch, cover with a kitchen towel, and let stand on the counter or refrigerate overnight.

Strain and discard the soaking water, which will have become slightly gooey. Return the grains to the blender and add enough fresh water (or milk if you like) to just reach the top of the grains (about 1½ cups). Add the coconut, butter, honey, salt, cinnamon, and orange zest and blend into a thick batter. Some millet will remain whole and provide crunch.

Pour some of the batter onto a hot waffle iron, sprinkle the top with sunflower seeds, close, and bake according to the manufacturer's directions. Serve with or without your favorite toppings.

MILLET FLOUR

Millet flour lends a dry, delicate, cakelike crumb and a pale yellow color to baked goods. Fresh millet flour has a distinctive sweet flavor. The flour is sold in natural food stores, but since it turns rancid and bitter quite rapidly, it is best to grind it as needed in a spice grinder or grain mill.

Because millet has no gluten, the flour is best combined with wheat flour for cookies, cakes, and bread. For sauces and some cookies and flatbreads, it may be used alone.

See **Flour; Millet.**

MINEOLA SEE **TANGELO.**

MINERAL WATER SEE **WATER.**

MINT
Peppermint, Spearmint
(*Mentha*)

Even if you were blindfolded in a garden, your nose would draw you right to mint. Mint is a fragrant presence not only in the garden but in the kitchen and medicine cabinet as well. This herbaceous perennial plant has a pleasant warm, fresh, aromatic, sweet flavor with a cool aftertaste. There are more than 500 known mint varieties; the two most common culinary mints are peppermint and spearmint. Although used interchangeably, peppermint is the more cooling and stimulating of the two; spearmint is slightly warming.

Medicinal Benefits The pungent menthol flavor of mint makes it a cooling herb that circulates chi and supports the lung and liver meridians. Mint helps disperse pathogens such as viruses or bacteria, and invigorates by promoting circulation of energy, blood, and lymph. These properties make mint a useful ingredient in many herbal remedies, especially where there is excessive heat, such as in mastitis, painful menstruation, and hives. Peppermint relieves spasms, increases perspiration, and tones the digestive system, especially the colon. It is not, according to herbalists, to be used for infants at any time. Spearmint, on the other hand, is a common remedy for feverish childhood illnesses as well as for hiccups, indigestion, and flatulence.

The essential oil of mint treats inflammation, nausea, indigestion, fevers, flatulence, headaches, migraines, liver problems, and arthritis and is a stimulant. Both peppermint and spearmint are *tridoshic*, though they are considered especially calming to *pitta*.

Use As available, favor fresh mint over dried. Mint's menthol is too intense an aroma and taste to go with subtly flavored savory dishes. But it's a great addition to tea, beverages, syrups, ice cream, sugary foods, chocolate, and candy. Because of its cooling properties, in hot weather I strew it in teas and boldly flavored chilled soups and in rice, tabbouleh, and couscous salads. Mint jelly or sauce is a traditional accompaniment to lamb.

Be Mindful In cases of painful menstruation due to uterine fibroids, cysts, or endometriosis, mint is not recommended.

See **Herbs and Spices; Mint Family.**

MINT FAMILY
(*Lamiaceae*)

A single family provides the majority of our culinary herbs, plus a tasty tuber, crosone; a highly energizing seed, chia; and a garden ornamental, coleus. The mint family relatives are easy-to-grow perennials throughout temperate regions.

See **Basil; Chia Seed; Crosne; Lavender; Lemon Balm; Marjoram; Mint; Oregano; Perilla; Rosemary; Sage; Savory; Thyme.**

MIRIN

Quality mirin is an ambrosial cooking wine. Like sake, it is naturally brewed and fermented from sweet brown rice, koji, and water. The 13 to 14 percent alcohol in mirin evaporates quickly when heated—but not before it has imparted a mild sweetness. Mirin rounds out and gives a signature Japanese flavor to many dishes.

Inexpensive, commercial-quality mirin, available in Asian markets, is chemically brewed to quicken production time and is sweetened with sugar or corn syrup. Look for a traditionally brewed sweet rice wine found in natural food stores. Use mirin for a glaze on pie crusts, pastries, and barbecued dishes. It is excellent in vinaigrettes, fish or vegetable dishes, and sauces and dips.

MIRLITON SEE CHAYOTE.

MISO

Miso is a fermented paste with a texture like peanut butter. It is made of soybeans, a koji inoculant, salt, and a grain—most commonly rice or barley. Just as grapes may be fermented into a wide range of differently flavored wines, soybeans may be fermented into a vast range of differently flavored misos, from meaty and savory to delicate and sweet.

Prior to the 1970s, *miso* was an unknown word—and taste experience—to most Americans. Today this traditional Japanese seasoning agent has become an important staple in haute cuisine as well as in healthy diets.

Medicinal Benefits Miso is a warming food that travels the stomach, spleen, and kidney meridians. An anticarcinogen, it tonifies the blood and reduces the effects of radiation, smoking, air pollution, and other environmental toxins. While all naturally fermented foods are invaluable digestive aids, miso is one of the most remarkable—probably because soybeans, already a nutritive food, are further enhanced through fermentation.

Miso is a concentrated protein source that contains a rich amino acid profile of the eight essential amino acids. Miso reduces *vata*.

Use Miso may be used in place of Worcestershire sauce, salt, or soy sauce as a flavoring agent. Miso's most typical use is in soup, where it serves as a rich and flavorful bouillon, but it is also used in sauces and dressings and even some desserts.

Before adding miso to a soup, thin it with soup stock. Add this thinned puree to the soup, and then allow it to simmer very lightly for one minute. Longer cooking or boiling destroys miso's beneficial microorganisms.

Buying The more expensive, traditionally made miso—which is aged for up to 18 months—is superior to high-tech miso with chemically induced, and therefore shortened, fermentation periods. Domestic, unpasteurized, and naturally fermented (rather than chemically processed) miso is available in the refrigerated section of natural food stores. The lighter-flavored misos are yellow or creamy beige in color, whereas the stronger-tasting misos are red, dark amber, and brown in color.

Kept in an airtight container, refrigerated, miso will last for a year or more. As a convenience item, packets of additive-free, freeze-dried instant miso soup are available in natural food stores; they do, however, lack living cultures.

Be Mindful Miso is typically made of soy and therefore an allergen for many people. Such people can usually enjoy soy-free chickpea miso.

See **Fermented Food; Soybean.**

MISTICANZA SEE **MESCLUN.**

MIXED FRUIT JUICE CONCENTRATE SEE **FRUIT JUICE CONCENTRATE.**

MIZUNA
Siu Cai
(*Brassica rapa, Japonica* group)

Mizuna is a variety of mustard greens, but, unlike them, it is eaten in a more tender and mild immature stage and is as often eaten raw as cooked. Mizuna has deeply serrated, almost lacy leaves. It is less sulfurous and warming than mustard greens but energetically is otherwise similar. It reduces *kapha.*

Mizuna is an excellent potherb or salad or sandwich green. It makes an exceptionally beautiful garnish. Mizuna is interchangeable with spinach in any recipe. The stalks, more fibrous than the leaves, need to be coarsely chopped before serving.

See **Cabbage Family; Mustard Greens; Vegetable.**

MISO, THE RADIOPROTECTIVE FOOD PAR EXCELLENCE

A remarkable and widely reported account comes from the Japanese medical doctor Shinichiro Akizuki, director of Nagasaki's St. Francis Hospital, which was located only a mile from the center of the atomic bomb blast in 1945. This report comes from *Fighting Radiation with Foods, Herbs, and Vitamins* by Steven R. Schechter, N.D.

The staff at St. Francis treated hundreds of people for radiation sickness in the aftermath of the explosion. He [Dr. Akizuki] and his hospital staff remained at St. Francis; however, none of his staff members became ill—a remarkable occurrence since they were so close to the epicenter of the explosion and were exposed to enormous doses of radioactivity. Akizuki hypothesized that it was the daily consumption of miso soup taken by him and his staff that protected them from the effects of radiation.

MOCHI

When Japanese children look at the full moon, they don't see the man in the moon; rather, they see a rabbit pounding mochi. Look and you'll see the rabbit's ears at the top right as she faces left with a long pestle in hand, pounding cooked sweet rice until it becomes glutinous. Mochi is such a favorite Japanese food that New Year's Day feasting includes mochi as a harbinger of good in the coming year.

Medicinal Benefits Mochi is beneficial for pregnant and lactating women and for children. It becomes so elastic with the pounding that, as my macrobiotic teacher Aveline Kushi used to say, "it supports our being flexible." Mochi strengthens the kidneys, builds blood, and helps regulate blood sugar. Mochi also reduces *vata*.

Use Mochi is my favorite "instant" natural food on the market. Flavored or otherwise, it may be baked, broiled, or fried until it puffs. I like it best sliced into thin (¼ inch) pieces and baked in a waffle iron. It puffs up into an airy, crunchy but moist, satisfying waffle. Serve hot with a sweet or savory dipping sauce. To make mochi from scratch, pound cooked sweet rice with a pestle or beat it in a heavy-duty mixer until it becomes glutinous. Enjoy it fresh or form it into a flat cake, dust with arrowroot flour, and refrigerate until use.

Buying Richly flavored whole grain mochi is available in the refrigerated or frozen section of natural food stores. The white rice mochi available in Asian food markets puffs beautifully but lacks flavor.

See **Rice.**

MOLASSES

This thick, strong-flavored syrup (56 to 76 percent sucrose) is used most often as an old-fashioned sweetener in traditional recipes. Several different kinds and grades are available. So-called table syrup may be placed on the table and poured directly over a stack of pancakes. Other molasses grades are used as an ingredient.

Medicinal Benefits Molasses is a warming food and a chi and blood tonic that acts upon the kidney, liver, stomach, spleen, and lung meridians. It eases coughing and lubricates the lungs. Molasses reduces *vata*. For a mellowing *vata* tonic, stir a teaspoon of molasses and a few drops of vanilla into a cup of yogurt or kefir and savor slowly.

Most sweeteners have negligible mineral content, but molasses—especially dark molasses—is an exception. Blackstrap molasses is rich in calcium, iron, and potassium. Medium molasses and light molasses are considerably less rich in minerals.

Use Use molasses for its heat-resistant flavor—rather than its sweetness—in gingerbread, baked beans, spice cookies, and other strongly flavored dishes. Dark molasses is used commercially in baked beans, licorice, soy

---

MOCHI POUNDING PARTY

In my community, a pregnant woman is cause to pound mochi. Mochi is especially good for pregnant women. I cook up a pot of sweet rice, call in women friends, and pull out a wooden baseball bat. Then we take turns pounding the hot rice to a sticky, gooey consistency. Next, with moistened fingers, we tear off bite-size pieces, roll them in a savory condiment or in chopped nuts, and then feast. At such a feast, we include a Blessing Way, borrowed from Navajo tradition, in which we offer wishes and a small talisman for good birthing and a healthy baby.

sauce, and chewing tobacco. Molasses with lighter flavor and color is used in toppings, syrups, and baked goods. Health enthusiasts in the 1950s and 1960s liberally used dark molasses in baking and health beverages because of its high mineral content.

Buying Organic, unsulfured molasses is made without the use of synthetic chemicals. The more concentrated and darker a syrup is, the higher the percentage of minerals, the stronger the flavor, and the lower the percentage of sugar.

- **Barbados Molasses** Made from the first press of sugarcane. Lighter in color and more delicate in flavor than blackstrap molasses. One tablespoon of Barbados molasses is about 70 percent sugar and has 2 percent of the RDA of iron.
- **Blackstrap or Unsulfured Molasses** Made from the last pressing of the sugarcane. The darkest, most nutritious, and most intensely flavored. One tablespoon of blackstrap molasses contains about 46 percent sugar and is an exceptional source of iron.
- **Commercial-Quality Molasses** A by-product of cane or sugar beet manufacturing; it is processed with sulfur dioxide. I do not recommend it. As a concentrated product, the chemical contaminants (including pesticides, industrial toxins, and sulfur) are also concentrated.

See **Sorghum Molasses; Sweeteners.**

MONSTERA
Ceriman, Mexican Breadfruit
(*Monstera deliciosa*)

The monstera plant, a biological curiosity, belongs to the only plant family that has natural holes in its large, elegantly lacy leaves. It is a common houseplant. Far more curious than the leaves, its conelike fruit resembles a huge primeval green banana covered by hexagonal scales. These scales, or platelets, conveniently fall off as the fruit ripens to indicate which part to eat. With a knife, scrape the creamy flesh away from the core. Wait for more scales to fall off before harvesting the next portion, since underripe monstera contains irritating acidic crystals and a nasty flavor. A Mexican native, monstera is eaten fresh or in fruit desserts.

See **Fruit.**

MONTMORENCY S EE **SOUR CHERRY.**

MONUKKA RAISIN S EE **RAISIN.**

MOREL
(*Morchella esculenta*)

The morel is a small, conical mushroom crisscrossed with irregular pale brown ridges that produce a spongelike appearance. When fresh, the stalk is whitish; it darkens when old. The flavor of the morel is hard to pinpoint. Food writer Elizabeth Schneider comes close: "It may suggest warm autumn leaves, hazelnuts, or even nutmeg. As with truffles and caviar, tasting is believing."

Medicinal Benefits Considered a tonic to the digestive system, morels reduce mucus, regulate the flow of energy, and inhibit the formation and growth of tumors. The Ayurvedic *Indian Materia Medica* by A. K. Nadkarni considers morels an "aphrodisiac and narcotic."

Use Roasting concentrates their flavor and they are especially elegant when cooked in parchment paper with pine nuts and butter. They're also tasty sautéed, marinated, broiled, or used in stuffings. Compared to shiitake or other dried fungi, dried morels quickly rehydrate because of their hollow center and airy structure.

Buying Terry Farms Technology Division in Auburn, Alabama, was the first farm in the United States to produce morels. According to vice president Rod Sorensen, their weekly morel harvest of 3,000 pounds is air-freighted to high-end restaurants, resorts, and signature stores in destination cities around the globe. Select fresh morels that have a sweet, earthy smell and are firm but not slimy. They are available fresh or dried through numerous online mail-order sources.

Be Mindful As with all edible mushrooms, morels contain small amounts of toxins, which are neutralized with thorough cooking. Cases of mild toxic reactions have been reported when cooked morels and alcohol are consumed together.

See **Mushroom Family; Vegetable.**

MOUNTAIN SPINACH SEE **ORACH.**

MOUNTAIN YAM SEE **JINENJO.**

MUIRA PUAMA
(*Ptychopetalum*)

Muira puama, or potency wood, has historically been used to enhance libido and sexual function. Currently dubbed the "Viagra of the Amazon," the root and bark of this small shrubby tree increase blood flow to the reproductive organs and thus help ease menstrual cramps and PMS. Muira puama also builds energy and tonifies and calms the nervous system. It is primarily available as a supplement.

See **Herbs and Spices.**

MULBERRY
(*Morus*)

A native of western Asia, the mulberry is a stately tree best known because the leaves of the white mulberry (*M. alba*) are the sole food source of the silkworm. The inexplicably refreshing, delicately perfumed purple berries of the black mulberry (*M. nigra*), a fig family member, look somewhat like a blackberry but more narrow and with a tubular shape. It's a composite fruit. Their vivid purplish red juice stains everything—fingers, lips, clothing, and the top of your car if you park under a tree with ripe fruits. Berries of the white mulberry are white or pinkish purple when ripe but lack the sweetness of the black mulberry.

Medicinal Benefits Mulberries are a cold food and a chi, yin, and blood tonic that dispel excessive heat and water. They act upon the kidney, liver, lung, and spleen meridians. They are one of the few fruits that strengthen and replenish constitutional kidney energy. In addition, mulberries quench thirst, have detoxifying properties, and are said to nourish the blood, calm the spirit, and relieve constipation in the elderly. For medicinal purposes, white mulberries are harvested just before they are fully ripe. Fresh mulberries reduce *pitta* and *vata* and, in moderation, *kapha*.

Use For culinary purposes, use fully ripened mulberries. Eaten out of hand, black mulberries are irresistible. Sweet but never cloying, these berries are excellent in jam or wine; they can be substituted for other berries in any dessert or salad recipe. The dried fruits may be substituted for raisins.

Buying/Foraging In recent years, mulberries have become somewhat available in natural food stores and specialty food markets. Fresh mulberries are too fragile to have commercial availability, so count yourself lucky if there's mulberry tree in your neighborhood.

See **Fig Family; Fruit.**

MUNG BEAN SEE BEANS AND LEGUMES; SPROUTS.

MURCOTT HONEY ORANGE SEE ORANGE (TANGOR).

MUSCAT RAISIN SEE RAISIN.

MUSHROOM, COMMON
Button Mushroom, Cremini, Italian Brown Mushroom, Portobello, White Mushroom
(*Agaricus bisporus, A. campestris*)

Worldwide, the most frequently consumed mushroom, and one that's found fresh and canned in every domestic supermarket, is the common or white mushroom. It descended from the wild field or meadow mushroom. You'll almost as frequently find it fresh in two different sizes and guises as cremini and portobello.

- **Cremini** Also known as a baby portobello, Italian brown, or Swiss brown. The size and flavor of the cremini are similar to the common white mushroom, though it is tan to brown in color.
- **Portobello** Let a cremini grow for an additional few days and its cap opens and flattens out, its gills turn chocolate brown, its aroma becomes musky, its sweet and "meaty" flavor intensifies, and it's known as a portobello. Because of their substantial size, they hold, refrigerated, for up to a week.
- **White Mushroom** Also known as a button mushroom, it is mild flavored with a large, thick cap and ranges in color from tan to white.

Medicinal Benefits The common mushroom is a cooling food that helps circulate chi, disperse heat, and discharge toxins and mucus. It acts upon the large and small intestine, lungs, and stomach. Fresh *Agaricus* mushrooms are nearly 90 percent water, low in calories, and high in B vitamins. Their nutritional profile is similar to other mushroom varieties; however, energetically they are less potent or medicinal than the varieties that are newer to our market.

Use Once cut, mushrooms quickly oxidize, turn brown, and soften, and their flavor is compromised. Cut just prior to use. Do not consume raw mushrooms (see **Mushroom Family** for more details). The portobello's large size makes it ideal for grilling, broiling, or stuffing. As its dark gills will color a dish, they may be removed prior to cooking. For a petite stuffed dish, white and cremini mushrooms may be used.

Buying/Storing Purchase white or cremini mushrooms with closed—or slightly open—caps. Purchase white, cremini, and portobello mushrooms with smooth (rather than pitted) surfaces and that are firm and evenly colored. Store mushrooms in a paper or cloth bag, as they become slimy when stored in plastic.

Be Mindful The common mushroom contains trace quantities of a suspected carcinogen, hydrazine agaritine, which cooking helps to mitigate.

See **Mushroom Family; Vegetable.**

MUSHROOM FAMILY
(*Agaricus campestris, A. bisporus,* et al.)

What we recognize as a mushroom is actually the fruit of the fungus. This may not sound appetizing, but it sure tastes good. These savory fruits are indeed among the most costly, delectable, and medicinal of foods. In popular usage, the common mushroom (*A. campestris*) is termed "cultivated," while the other varieties—which today are also cultivated—are termed "wild."

Medicinal Benefits Other vegetables contain chlorophyll and convert sunlight into food; mushrooms do not. These primitive fungi scavenge upon other organic matter. That's why in nature they are found growing or decaying on wood or even out in the pasture under cow patties. Rather than cringing at this image, use it to understand why mushrooms so effectively detoxify: In nature, mushrooms draw upon that which is decaying; in the human body, mushrooms are said to absorb and then safely eliminate toxins. These toxins include undesirable fat in the blood, pathogens, and excess phlegm in the respiratory system.

In general, mushrooms are a blood and chi tonic and help resolve mucus and toxins. The common button mushroom is milder in action than other varieties. In Asia, some mushrooms, such as the reishi, are regarded as increasing longevity. Because of how and where they grow, mushrooms are disparaged in traditional Ayurvedic medicine. They reduce *pitta* and *kapha*.

Mushrooms are a rich source of glutamic acid (the natural version of the flavor enhancer monosodium glutamate) and so enhance the flavor of any savory food that they are cooked with. They are high in protein and a good source of vitamin B_2 and zinc.

Use Just before use, clean fresh mushrooms with a damp paper towel. Dried mushrooms may be rehydrated and used in most applications (grilling excepted) like fresh mushrooms. Use about 1 ounce of dried mushrooms for each 8 to 10 ounces of fresh mushrooms called for in a recipe. To reconstitute dried mushrooms, soak in water or wine diluted with water until softened, 20 minutes or longer, depending upon variety. Mushrooms soak up the essence of whatever they are cooked in; the more finely they are sliced, the more flavor they absorb. Mushrooms are excellent simply prepared, and they add a rich flavor to sauces, soups, stuffings, and stir-fried dishes. The larger varieties have a meaty texture when sliced and grilled. Roasting concentrates their flavors.

Buying/Foraging As with other life forms, the quality of a mushroom is greatly determined by the quality of its nourishment. Foraged mushrooms have a flavor superior to commercial varieties grown in a sterile medium of organic fungicide-treated waste (straw, corncobs, sawdust, bark, gypsum, and potassium) in windowless, controlled-atmosphere sheds. Many mushrooms are available dried.

Except for morels and chanterelles, select smooth, plump, and uniformly colored mushrooms that are firm and not slimy and that have a sweet earthy smell. For medicinal purposes, favor button mushrooms with tightly closed caps that hide the gills. (Exposed gills indicate a mature mushroom and dispersed spore.) For taste alone, mushrooms with exposed gills are more intensely flavored but have a shorter shelf life.

You can grow your own mushrooms indoors with the purchase of a small kit containing mushroom spores.

Be Mindful The contemporary Western practice of eating raw mushrooms lacks historical precedence—and with good reason. Carcinogenic compounds found in raw common mushrooms are destroyed in cooking. Do not consume foraged mushrooms unless you are *positive* of their identity. Several varieties are lethal.

See **Bolete; Cauliflower Mushroom; Chanterelle; Enoki; Hedgehog; Maitake; Matsutake; Morel; Mushroom, Common; Oyster Mushroom; Reishi; Shiitake; Truffle; Wood Ear.**

MUSKMELON SEE **MELON.**

MUSTARD FAMILY SEE **CABBAGE FAMILY.**

MUSTARD GREENS
(*Brassica juncea*)

The most pungent leafy vegetables of the cabbage family are referred to as mustard greens. Seed companies and some Asian markets have mustard varieties that make a jalapeño chile seem mild. Unlike a chile's capsicum that burns the mouth, mustard oil also burns the nasal passages. Mustard greens need ample moisture when growing or their mustard oil content increases to the point that they're inedible. The condiment mustard comes from the seeds of this branch of the cabbage family.

There are numerous mustard varieties that vary according to heat, flavor, and appearance. Their color ranges from lime green to burgundy and their bite from mild to fiery. Although mizuna and bok choy are technically mustards, they are eaten in an immature stage, have little mustard oil, and different culinary applications and so are treated in separate entries.

Medicinal Benefits Mustard greens are a warming food that support the lungs, stomach, and spleen; they help with both blood and chi circulation and disperse damp, water, cold, and mucus. Like other dark leafy greens from the cabbage family, mustard greens are a superior anticancer vegetable. As their bite indicates, they help move stuck energy and so are beneficial for people with colds, arthritis, or depression. Mustard greens reduce *kapha.*

Use For most people, the flavor of mustard greens is too strong when they are raw or steamed, but it quickly mellows with parboiling or sautéing. The longer they are cooked, the softer the flavor becomes. Mustard greens are especially good when sautéed with garlic and also may be added to soups and stews. In Asia, mustards are pickled. Their blossoms are edible. Wash just prior to use. Baby mustard greens may be eaten raw in salads or sandwiches or used as a wrapper for a morsel of rice.

Buying Mustard greens are available all year long. Select young, fresh-looking greens. They fade more quickly than collards or broccoli, so plan to use them within several days. These are common varieties:

- **Mustard Greens (Curled Mustard)** This relatively mild mustard is most readily available at greengrocers throughout the United States. It looks like a delicate version of kale, having jade green leaves that are crinkled or ruffled, but it is more tender and moist than kale.
- **Purple Mustard (Giant Mustard, Japanese Mustard)** This large-leafed mustard, like a collard in size, is a dramatic purple when grown outdoors in cold climates (when grown in greenhouses or in warm climates, it is green). Despite its size, it remains tender.
- **Wrapped Heart Mustard Cabbage**

(Swatow Mustard, Heading Mustard) Wrapped heart mustard cabbage has large outer leaves similar to romaine lettuce that swirl around a heart-shaped head of smaller leaves. The younger leaves are less fiery than older leaves and can be used in salads.

See **Bok Choy; Cabbage Family; Mizuna; Vegetable.**

MUSTARD OIL

Pressed from mustard seed, this polyunsaturated oil has an intense cabbagelike aroma and a hot, nutty taste. It contains 6 percent omega-3 fatty acids and so, ideally, would not be heated. However, where this oil is a staple, in South India and Bangladesh, it is typically used at extreme temperatures, perhaps to reduce the flavor and aroma. The oil is used topically as it is antibacterial and increases circulation. It is similar to canola oil, though it has higher levels of erucic acid. In India, mustard oil is available unrefined and freshly pressed.

See **Cabbage Family; Canola Oil; Fat and Oil.**

MUSTARD SEED
(*Brassica*)

Mustard seeds are cabbage family members, be they black (*B. nigra*), brown (*B. juncea*), or white (*B. hirta*) in color. The most common use of mustard seed is in the prepared condiment, indispensable for slathering on a hot dog, which has remained popular since Egyptian times and is still comprised of the same ingredients: ground mustard seed, vinegar, oil, and salt to taste. Both ground and whole, mustard seed as a culinary ingredient is popular in pickles and dressings in Western and Asian cuisine.

Medicinal Benefits Mustard seed acts as a diuretic, a blood purifier, and a stimulant for body energy, circulation, and heat. Ground mustard seed is also used as a topical plaster to increase blood flow to the skin and draw out deep-set inflammation and congestion—as in the case of rheumatism, sprains, colds that have settled in the chest, and arthritis. Mustard seed reduces *vata* and *kapha*.

Use One of my most commonly used spices for soups, curries, and stir-fries is brown mustard seed. I first warm some oil, add mustard seed and cumin, and sauté until they're aromatic and the mustard seeds turn gray, and before the oil has a chance to smoke, I quickly add an onion and proceed accordingly. When prepared in this way, there's something about the pleasing bite of mustard seeds that brightens many a dish.

See **Cabbage Family; Herbs and Spices.**

MYRTLE FAMILY
(*Myrtaceae*)

The large myrtle family is primarily composed of evergreen trees growing in tropical or warm temperate regions. Foodstuffs from this family include the spices allspice and clove, and the fruits feijoa and guava. While eucalyptus is a myrtle, both the biblical myrtlewood and that of the Oregon coast belong to the magnolia family.

See **Allspice; Clove; Feijoa; Guava; Jabuticaba.**

NAGAMI SEE **KUMQUAT.**

NAME SEE **YAM.**

NAPA CABBAGE
Chinese Cabbage

Napa cabbage has been described as a cabbage that even cabbage haters love. It is crisper, juicier, sweeter, and more tender than common cabbage. There are several varieties of napa cabbage. All form a head, but the head varies from round, like cabbage, to elongated, like romaine lettuce. In addition, the crinkly leaves may curl inward or outward.

Medicinal Benefits Napa cabbage is cooling and beneficial to the lungs, stomach, and liver channel. It is an anti-inflammatory, useful in cases of yellow phlegm discharge and other heat symptoms, including fever. Napa cabbage has but a fraction of cabbage's sulfur compounds. For people with chronic low energy, use napa cabbage moderately. It reduces *pitta* and *kapha*.

Napa cabbage is very low in calories and in sodium. It is an excellent source of folic acid and vitamin A.

Use Long simmering enhances napa cabbage's sweet flavor, and the leaves become silky soft but still hold their form. Try it in soups and stews, baked or braised. It is also delicious when lightly cooked (stir-fried, steamed, blanched) and even raw in a salad. Its thick, crispy-crunchy leaves add great texture to a garden salad, and it makes an excellent salad base on its own. The blanched leaf makes a flexible and excellent wrapper that is, compared to common cabbage, easier to work with and, to my eye, more beautiful and delicate.

Pickled napa cabbage, *kim chee*, the signature dish of Korea, is as easy to make as sauerkraut, the pickled cabbage of equal prominence in German cuisine.

KIM CHEE

As with other naturally fermented and unpasteurized pickles, *kim chee* is a rich source of enzymes and flora. A small serving of this easy-to-make Korean pickle aids digestion.

- 1 head napa cabbage
- 3 small dried chiles
- 3 garlic cloves, slivered
- 2 tablespoons minced ginger
- 1 tablespoon sesame seeds, toasted
- 1 tablespoon unrefined salt

Quarter the cabbage lengthwise, then cut cabbage and its core into julienne. Toss with the remaining ingredients. Pack into a widemouthed quart jar. (If the cabbage is extra large, pack the overflow into a smaller jar. It is not necessary to adjust the seasoning.)

Place the jar on a plate to collect the liquid that will form and seep out. Place a weight, such as a smaller water-filled jar, on top of the mixture so that it rests solidly upon the vegetable. This weight presses the vegetable down and keeps it submerged in the brine that will form.

> Let stand for four to five days, or until the cabbage looks cooked and has lost its bright chlorophyll color. If you enjoy a more sour flavor, allow to stand for an additional day or two. Wash the sides of the jar, cover tightly, and refrigerate the *kim chee* for up to six weeks.

Buying In most markets, at least one form of napa cabbage is available year-round. Select fresh, light-colored greens with plump ribs. Squeeze the heads and select one that is firm and heavy. Avoid those that have wilted leaves with any rot spots. Small dark specks, however, are naturally occurring. Napa cabbage stores exceptionally well (but not as long as cabbage), and the flavor even improves when slightly wilted.

See **Cabbage; Cabbage Family.**

NASTURTIUM
(*Tropaeolum majus*)

A favorite edible blossom because of its brilliant orange, red, or yellow color and its peppery, cresslike bite, the nasturtium is native to South America and a near relative of watercress. As beautiful in the garden as in the salad bowl, nasturtiums are enjoying increasing commercial availability. These pungent blossoms are fragile and best used the same day they are purchased or plucked. More warming than lettuce, nasturtium blossoms enhance salad digestion for people with cold or deficient digestive energy.

See **Cabbage Family; Flower Blossoms.**

NATTO

Powerful-tasting natto—soybeans fermented with *Bacillus subtilis*—is an unusual food that I fondly call the Limburger of soy. This traditional Japanese condiment looks like innocuous brown soybeans until you dip a spoon in and out; hundreds of hair-fine fermented strands will stretch from the bowl to your spoon—up to ten inches in length. These strands contain countless beneficial enzymes, bacteria, and fungi. For some people, natto is an acquired taste. Others love it from the first encounter, including my children who often asked for "string beans."

Similar soy products also fermented with *Bacillus subtilis* are found throughout Asia, including Chinese *shuǐdòuchǐ*, Korean *cheong-gukjang*, Thai *thua nao*, and from the Himalayan regions, *kinema*. In West Africa, the same inoculant is used to ferment other beans and seeds.

Medicinal Benefits Natto is the source of vitamin K_2 and is available as a supplement that is said to help prevent—and even reverse—osteoporosis, and is used to treat varicose veins, heart disease, and blood sugar irregularities including diabetes. Energetically, it is considered medicinal for the regenerative organs and is an excellent source of protein.

Use When serving natto as its own dish, mix it with mustard, soy sauce, and chopped scallions to taste. Allow one tablespoon per serving as a condiment for rice or other grains. Natto is also tasty stirred into soups and noodles.

Buying Frozen natto is available in Asian markets. Or buy the culture (search online for "natto culture") and make it from scratch by inoculating and incubating cooked soybeans.

NAVEL ORANGE SEE **ORANGE.**

NAVY BEAN SEE **BEANS AND LEGUMES.**

NECTARINE
(*Prunus persica*)

The drink of the gods—at least the Greek gods—was *nektar*, and indeed the nectarine tastes divine. It is a kind of smooth-skinned peach, only it's more of everything—sweeter, richer, more distinctively flavored, stronger smelling, and more brightly colored. The flesh of a nectarine is also firmer than that of a peach, and it is often smaller in size. The leaves, trees, and seeds of peaches and nectarines are indistinguishable; the fruit may be either freestone or clingstone—that is, loose from the stone or attached to it.

In Mesa County, the peach heaven of Colorado, nectarines are outlawed because their rootstock has disease potential that could harm peach trees. Nectarines are mostly produced in California. They are in season from late summer through September; out-of-season nectarines are imported from South America.

Medicinal Benefits See **Peach** entry.

Use Nectarines are enjoyed raw, cooked, or dried. They can be used interchangeably with peaches and apricots in fruit salads and other desserts. Because of the fuzzless skin, a nectarine doesn't need peeling. The flesh of a nectarine will discolor after being cut, so slice just prior to serving or toss with lemon juice.

Buying A ripe nectarine is too fragile to be shipped, so nectarines are harvested when immature. Once picked, a nectarine does not increase in sweetness. This surely explains why buying nectarines directly from the farmer's roadside stand is the only guarantee for getting good ones. If only everyone had such a stand in the neighborhood! Unfortunately, nectarines do not grow in moist climates. All things considered, it's understandable that nectarines are costlier and generally less available than peaches.

Look for a plump nectarine with a rich (rather than a bright) color, and a slight softening along the "seam" of the fruit. Russeting or staining of the skin does not affect the fruit's quality.

Like the stone fruits cherries and peaches, nectarines are one of our most chemically contaminated fruits. As a kindness to yourself, whenever possible favor organic nectarines and, perhaps, consider passing on commercial nectarines.

See **Fruit; Peach; Prune Family.**

NELIS SEE **PEAR.**

NETTLE
Stinging Nettle
(*Urtica dioica*)

As I write this, the aspens are turning gold and it has snowed once here at my cabin at 1,000 feet in Colorado—and still I feasted on steamed fresh nettles for lunch. They are growing in a protected corner. With luck, the weather will hold for a few more days, so that I can enjoy another mess of this delicious wild green. Used throughout the world to build vitality, nettles are delicious and—if you're in a moist area—free for the grabbing. But do grab carefully!

Although nettles at first glance look similar to spearmint, they're not related and are essentially the best-known plant of their genus. An herbaceous perennial that can reach waist high, nettles are distributed widely throughout the Northern Hemisphere.

Medicinal Benefits Stiff, bristly hairs protrude from the leaves and stems of nettles; if they penetrate the skin, they inject a stinging fluid, which causes temporary burning and irritation. This injection, which, like an ant's bite, contains formic acid, increases circulation and provides external treatment for arthritic pain, gout, sciatica, neuralgia, hemorrhoids, and scalp and hair problems.

Internally, nettles are a yin and blood tonic

that support the bladder, kidney, spleen, and liver. They help regulate damp and water conditions, dispel toxins, and have diuretic properties. They afford allergy relief, enrich the blood, and thicken the hair. Nettles are good for hypoglycemia, as they help reduce blood sugar levels, and they also ameliorate high blood pressure. Nettles are used for anemia and excessive menstruation. Nettles reduce *pitta* and *kapha* and can be used, in moderation, by *vata*.

Use Prepare nettles as you would spinach. Nettles are delicious sautéed alone or with other vegetables such as onions and carrots. Add to soups or casseroles or parboil them. Nettles may also be made into a tea to drink hot or cold. Do not, as some old texts indicate, use nettles raw in salads. Heat and drying destroy nettles' sting.

Buying/Foraging Dried nettles and nettle extracts are available in natural food stores. Bottled nettle-flavored teas and beverages are appearing in specialty food markets. If you want to enjoy nettles as a vegetable, however, head for a sunlight-dappled stream bank or a wooded rural area. Collect young shoots before they flower, or harvest the tender stem tops. Older leaves contain gritty deposits of calcium oxalate and are bitter in taste.

Although rare, nettles may cause stomach upset in some people. If this occurs to you, don't eat nettles.

SHOW NO FEAR AND THEY WON'T STING

Ideally, you'll have gloves along to protect yourself from stinging nettles' pricks when harvesting. Many a time I've glovelessly happened upon a stand of nettles and gladly endured burning fingertips for the treasure at hand. Next time, however, I'll try talking to them, as did Tom Brown's Apache grandfather, as reported in *Tom Brown's Guide to Wild Edible and Medicinal Plants*.

"To my amazement, Grandfather carefully began to gather some of the smaller plants, grabbing them at the base and plucking them from the ground with his fingers. In astonishment, I asked him how he could touch those damn plants without getting stung and why the hell would he want to pick the little monsters. He simply said, 'If you talk to them and show no fear, they won't sting.' He also informed me that they were not little monsters but would soon be his supper."

NEW ZEALAND SPINACH
(*Tetragonia expansa*)

This native New Zealand green is not related to spinach, although it does have a similar—but more intense—taste. New Zealand spinach leaves are tougher, coarser, and smaller than spinach leaves. When the hot summer sun wilts garden spinach, lettuce, and other delicate greens, this vegetable thrives and so it has endeared itself to home gardeners.

It's an excellent source of beta-carotene and a good source of vitamin C and potassium.

As does spinach, it contains medium to low levels of oxalates, which need to be removed by blanching the leaves in boiling water prior to use.

Several decades ago, New Zealand spinach was available in food stores; hopefully it will resurface. In the meantime, look for New Zealand spinach in farmers' markets.

NEW ZEALAND YAM SEE OCA.

NIGARI

Nigari is the traditional coagulant used in making tofu. It is what's left over when you extract sodium and water from seawater—magnesium chloride with additional trace minerals. This residue makes the most delicately sweet tofu. Today commercial tofu is also made with calcium sulfate and Epsom salts or calcium chloride.

NIGELLA SEED
Kalonji
(*Nigella sativa*)

According to the prophet Muhammad, nigella seed can cure everything but death. A popular spice in India and the Middle East, nigella seed is as small as a sesame seed, ebony black, with a triangular shape and an aroma rather like oregano. It is a member of the carrot family. In ancient Rome, it was used as a pepper-type condiment long before the introduction of pepper. It is often mistakenly called black cumin.

Medicinal Benefits Nigella is pungent tasting; it aids digestion, reduces inflammation, soothes bronchial complaints, stimulates lactation, and eases painful menstruation and postpartum contractions. It has laxative properties and helps expel intestinal parasites. It contains an antitumor sterol, beta-sitosterol, which helps explain why traditionally it has been used to treat abscesses and tumors of the abdomen, eyes, and liver. Nigella oil is a topical treatment for eczema and boils.

Use The seeds are used, ground or whole, to season beans, vegetable dishes, baked goods, curries, chutneys, and meat dishes. They impart exotic flavor and, when whole, a pleasant crunch. Nigella is an ingredient in the Indian spice mixture *panch phoron*. I like to use nigella to punch up the flavor of beans and in spice mixes like garam masala.

Be Mindful Nigella contains two mild toxins, melanthin and nigelline; use in moderation.

See **Carrot Family; Herbs and Spices.**

NIGHTSHADE FAMILY
(*Solanaceae*)

Nightshade plants are so named because they grow in the shade of the night rather than, like other plants, in the light of the sun. (Corn, a remarkable evolutionary exception, grows during both day and night.) Most nightshades originated in the fertile altiplano region of South America and were introduced to the rest of the world in the fifteenth century. They include four primary crops: peppers, potatoes, tomatoes, and tobacco.

Be Mindful Although nightshades provide many important nutrients, they also contain a toxic alkaloid, solanine. This alkaloid seems to adversely affect human calcium balance and may be implicated in health complaints ranging from headaches to arthritis. Both macrobiotic and Ayurvedic medicine recommend using the nightshades with moderation.

In his book *The Nightshades and Health*, Norman F. Childers, PhD, professor of horticulture at Rutgers University, reveals a correlation between rheumatoid arthritis and nightshade consumption. According to his studies, when some people eliminate these foods from their diet, their arthritic symptoms are alleviated or even disappear.

See **Chile Pepper; Eggplant; Goji Berry; Ground Cherry; Pepino; Peppers; Potato; Sunberry; Sweet Pepper; Tamarillo; Tomatillo; Tomato.**

Nixtamal See **Posole.**

Noisette See **Hazelnut.**

NONDAIRY MILK SUBSTITUTES

As lactose intolerance increases, milk substitutes multiply. Soymilk was the first to gain popularity in the 1980s; now as ready-to-use milk substitutes we have rice milk, oat milk, hazelnut milk, and almond milk. These beverages come plain and flavored with different degrees of enrichment. Found in shelf-stable packaging, each product varies in quality. Some are available in the refrigerated section or in a powder form for reconstitution.

I regard all packaged nondairy beverages as an acceptable product for a treat or as a transition food for someone weaning herself from dairy. As a staple, however, remember that they're highly processed and therefore their essential fatty acids are denatured and their overall energetic, or chi, properties are diminished. Rice milk is essentially a diluted rice syrup.

Soymilk is the most nutritive; I urge you to purchase a reputable brand that clearly states it is made from whole, non genetically modified soybeans. Such a milk is healthful; do not purchase if it contains soy isolate. Soymilk contains the same amount of protein as cow's milk and 15 times as much iron. It reduces *pitta*, and, when warm, it reduces *kapha*. Soymilk adds flavor and body to casseroles, soups, puddings, pancakes, and quick breads.

You can clabber soymilk (that is, allow it to become sour and separate) to make a buttermilk substitute. To 1 cup of soymilk add 1 tablespoon lemon juice and let stand for 5 to 10 minutes, or until it thickens.

For a fresh—and therefore most healthful—milk substitute, considering making your own nut milk (See recipe on page 243).

Nondairy products that are not certified organic often contain one or more of the following genetically modified (GM) ingredients: soy, canola oil, or corn sweeteners such as fructose, dextrose, or glucose.

See **Nut Milk.**

NONCALORIC SWEETENERS SEE **SWEETENERS.**

NONI
Indian Mulberry
(*Morinda citrifolia*)

A warming herb valued in Chinese and Indian medicine as a kidney tonic, noni is a relative of the coffee family that originated in Southeast Asia. The fruit, which looks like a large mulberry, has a strong smell (some call it "vomit fruit") and a bitter taste but is nevertheless eaten either raw or cooked, often as a starvation food. It is white when ripe and its seeds, when roasted, are edible.

Noni has astringent and antiseptic properties. Its fruits are used for dysentery, gum disease, and hemorrhage; its roots are used to treat constipation and its leaves for tuberculosis.

Noni juice and supplements are currently marketed as a superfood for treating cancer and the immune system; however, the research is controversial and there are several cases of the products causing liver damage.

See **Coffee Family.**

NOPAL
Beavertail Cactus, Cactus Pad, Cactus Paddle
(*Opuntia ficus-indica* and other *O.* species)

The prickly pear cactus stem, shaped like a beaver tail, is a popular Mexican vegetable called nopal or nopalito. Its soft, pulpy texture and pleasant flavor make this vegetable worth experimenting with, especially given its splendid medicinal properties. Its brilliant colored fruit, the prickly pear, is sweet, juicy, and enjoyed worldwide. Nopales may be harvested from various members of the cacti family that originated in the Americas but now grow worldwide in arid regions.

Medicinal Benefits A skinned nopal pad may be substituted for aloe vera as a drawing poultice for contusions, bruises, and burns. It is also an anti-inflammatory and a diuretic, and it soothes the digestive system. Its most remarkable use, however, is as a hypoglycemic tonic. Recent clinical studies confirm the oral tradition that nopales are effective for type 2 diabetes and hypoglycemia, as well as for lowering both total cholesterol and LDL cholesterol levels. The pads are high in vitamins A and C, as well as B-complex vitamins and iron. They reduce *pitta*.

Use Most cultivated nopales are without spines and may be easily peeled with a vegetable peeler or a sharp knife. Wild nopales still have their spines. Grasp such a nopal with tongs, pare off the outer edges, cut off the prickers with a sharp knife, then peel and discard the skin. Nopal enhances egg, tomato, and cheese dishes (with scrambled eggs, they're a favorite Mexican food for Lent) and are used as a taco filling. Add narrow strips of nopales to soups and stews 20 minutes prior to serving, and cook until tender. Like okra, nopales serve as a thickener, in addition to imparting a pleasing flavor. Nopales can also be cut into strips, batter-dipped, and rolled in breadcrumbs, cornmeal, or flour and fried like french fries.

Buying/Foraging Look for nopales that are stiff, firm, fresh-looking (never droopy), and are around eight inches long and four inches wide. Larger ones are available but tend to be fibrous. Nopales are available in some supermarkets and in Latino markets. Unlike most green vegetables, nopales may be refrigerated in plastic for several weeks. I do not recommend canned nopalitos; they have little flavor and a compromised texture. If you live west of the Appalachians and south of British Columbia, you can forage this common desert food.

See **Cactus Family; Prickly Pear.**

GRILLED NOPALITOS

Nopales are easy to grill and they taste great served with salsa on the side. Or you can dice them and add to pilafs, casseroles, or other dishes. You can scale up the recipe as needed.

Makes about 12 finger-size strips

1 nopal
Extra virgin olive oil or vegetable oil
Salt
Lime juice

Preheat a grill to medium-low.

Place the nopal on a cutting board, hold with a fork or tongs, and use a sharp knife to peel its coarse skin and any spines. Make approximately 10 wedge-shaped cuts from the nopal's periphery toward the narrow base—but do not cut all the way to the base so each wedge can remain connected. Fan out the cuts so that the paddles look fringed. Brush with oil, and sprinkle with salt and lime juice. Place on the grill and heat for about 10 minutes, or until soft and slightly charred, turning as necessary.

Alternatively, oven-roast the nopal for 25 minutes at 350°F. Cool, cut into strips, and serve as is or dice and add to casseroles, pilafs, or vegetable dishes.

NORI
(*Porphyra tenera*)

Nori, dried seaweed, is ebony colored, paper-thin, and crisp. A sheet of nori makes an excellent first finger food. Fascinated by its crinkly texture, toddlers gum it until it softens, besmearing fingers and face—a visible and healthy food experience. Nori also has more elegant applications. It's indispensable for sushi and can be made into dramatic garnishes.

Nori is actually several varieties of cultivated laver. Nori spores are scattered over shallow inlets where nets have been sunk on bamboo poles—a contraption something like an underwater volleyball net. Months later, mature nori is hand-harvested, washed, chopped, and spread over bamboo mats to dry into sheets. Nori is also available in flakes.

Medicinal Benefits Like all seaweed, nori is a yin tonic that is medicinal for the kidneys and stomach. It clears heat, damp, mucus, toxins, and water. Nori strengthens the nervous system, and it contributes to a sense of groundedness because it is so mineral rich. Nori is a natural complement to fried foods, as it emulsifies fat and aids digestion.

Nori contains more vitamin A than carrots. It is very rich in protein, higher than soybeans, milk, meat, fish, or poultry. It is also high in B vitamins and vitamins C and D, and it is a good source of calcium, iron, potassium, iodine, and many trace elements. Nori reduces *vata*.

Use Sheets of nori are used to wrap sushi and rice balls; they can be cut or torn and used as a garnish or in soups. Nori may be used as is or lightly toasted by slowly waving it over an open flame or the burner of an electric stove. It has a tasty, delicate, nutlike flavor. Nori flakes can be sprinkled over salads, popcorn, grains, and vegetable dishes.

Buying The price of nori varies greatly and directly reflects quality. Superior-quality nori is almost black; lesser-quality nori is green. Chemical fertilizers are used on inexpensive qualities. Wild North American laver is sometimes marketed as wild nori.

See **Laver; Seaweed Family; Vegetable.**

NUÑA POPPING BEAN SEE BEANS AND LEGUMES.

NUT AND SEED BUTTERS

Many seeds and nuts are ground into paste as a culinary ingredient. The all-American favorite, peanut butter, is also the most economical. Other butters include almond, cashew, macadamia, hazelnut, pumpkin, sunflower, and sesame. Sesame is unique in its duality: Hulled sesame seeds yield sesame butter; unhulled sesame seeds yield tahini. Soy nut butter is available, but I cannot recommend this by-product of soy oil manufacturing, which was chemically extracted but still contains antinutrients.

Medicinal Benefits Freshly ground natural nut and seed butters have the same nutritional value as the foods from which they were ground. But that's not the whole story. They're also harder to digest. Therefore, people with

---

HOMEMADE NUT BUTTER

Really fresh—and therefore the most delicious and healthful—nut butter is an easy treat to make. Use your favorite roasted nut in this recipe, or a blend of them. If using raw nuts, roast them first. For a flavor boost, and to increase digestibility, add ¼ teaspoon ground cinnamon to your nut butter.

Makes about ¾ cup

1 cup roasted almonds, cashews, macadamias, pecans, or peanuts
¼ teaspoon unrefined salt
About 1 tablespoon unrefined vegetable oil

Place the nuts and salt in a food processor, blender, meat grinder, or nut butter machine and process until the nuts are finely ground. Add the oil and continue processing until the nut butter reaches your desired degree of smoothness, adding more oil if necessary. For chunky nut butter, stir in ¼ cup roasted chopped nuts.

Store, tightly covered, in the refrigerator.

digestive or liver complaints or in a weakened condition are advised to moderately enjoy nut butters; as seed butters are less fatty, they are easier to digest. Most nut and seed butters are calming to *vata*.

Use Nut and seed butters make for nutritious additions to sauces, dips, spreads, salad dressings, cookies, icings, and candies.

Buying Because nut butters quickly become rancid, buy them in small quantities or make your own (see accompanying recipe on page 241). Most commercial peanut butter contains sugar and other additives and lacks the flavor of natural peanut butter, which is made only from peanuts and maybe a pinch of unrefined salt. Some food stores have grinders for customers to grind peanut butter fresh. Note that the oil of natural butters separates to the top but can be stirred back in.

See **Nuts; Peanut Butter; Seeds; Sesame Butter; Tahini.**

NUTMEG
(*Myristica fragrans*)

A popular and pleasant spice, nutmeg evokes images of a warm hearth with just-baked spice cookies on a cooling rack. The nutmeg is not a nut but the brown seed of an Indonesian evergreen tree. This one tree produces two separate spices: nutmeg and mace; mace is more strongly flavored than nutmeg.

Medicinal Benefits Nutmeg is a warming yang tonic that acts upon the large intestine, stomach, and spleen. It helps circulate both blood and chi, dispels cold, and aids digestion. It can help relieve coughs, reduce pain, and even relieve flatulence, acting as a carminative. The essential oil of nutmeg is added to hot bedtime drinks or toddies as a sedative. The oil may also be rubbed into an arthritic joint to ease pain. Nutmeg reduces *vata* and *kapha*.

Use Irish I'm not, but like the Irish I love the way one sprinkle of nutmeg enlivens a whole

---

BRING YOUR OWN NUTMEG

It was once used as an embalming ingredient in ancient Egypt, as a perfume in Arabia, and as a medicine in the West. It was also a culinary "security blanket" in the seventeenth century. The fashionable French carried their own nutmeg and grater when going out to dine. Better to be prepared than to take the chance of a dinner short on nutmeg.

---

bowl of hot oatmeal. Heat diminishes nutmeg's flavor and so, if possible, add this spice at the end of cooking. Its pungent and slightly astringent flavor complements other warming spices such as allspice, cardamom, cinnamon, cloves, ginger, and black or white pepper. Sprinkle nutmeg over casseroles, boiled potatoes, spinach, cauliflower, fruit, pasta, or any whole grain dish.

Buying Once ground, nutmeg's volatile essential oils dissipate and therefore so does its flavor and aroma. If you purchase ground nutmeg, buy it in small quantities and replace it often. Better yet, invest in a nutmeg grater or mill and enjoy its full fresh flavor on demand.

See **Herbs and Spices; Mace.**

NUT MILK

As a nondairy milk substitute, you currently can purchase almond or hazelnut milk. Better yet, you can easily, and far more inexpensively, make your own using your favorite nuts. Its better flavor will attest to it being energetically and nutritionally superior to any commercially available nut milk.

See **Nondairy Milk Substitutes.**

NUT MILK

This is a truly refreshing and delicious beverage. Just as with cow's milk, nut milk enhances both sweet and savory dishes or is delicious as is as a rich beverage. Presoaking the nuts enhances their digestibility.

Makes 1 cup

- 3 tablespoons almonds (or cashews or hazelnuts)
- 1 cup water
- 1 teaspoon honey or maple syrup (optional)
- Pinch of unrefined salt

Soak the nuts overnight in water to cover. Strain and discard the soaking water.

Rub the nuts between your hands to remove the skins; discard the skins. Place in a blender and add the water and honey, if using. Blend at high speed until very smooth. Pour through a fine-mesh strainer for a smooth consistency. Rather than discarding the dregs, try using them creatively in cookie dough or waffle batter.

NUTRASWEET SEE ASPARTAME.

NUTRITIONAL YEAST
Brewer's Yeast, Food Yeast, Primary-Grown Yeast

A popular "health" ingredient, nutritional yeast does have an impressive vitamin B profile as well as an extremely rich protein content. It's grown on mineral-rich molasses or wood pulp and pasteurized; then many varieties are blended with a wide range of artificial flavors. Nutritional yeast can challenge a weak or yeast-infected digestive system. Although it's not a natural food, it is a nutritional food and many people—as well as the family pet— seem to benefit from it. Nutritional yeast makes a tasty seasoning agent for popcorn.

NUTS

It's easy for me to sense why nuts are such a powerful food when I'm in my father's garden, standing under the wide canopy of his hundred-foot-tall English walnut tree. A smattering of nuts in almost any dish kicks up its flavor, interest, and overall satisfaction. Be it a curried pilaf with cashews or a quinoa-hazelnut pudding, nuts impart energy. And they do it with style—a rich flavor and a creamy, meaty texture. Hmm, sprinkle in some more.

A nut, popularly speaking, is any oily kernel within a hard-shelled fruit. Technically speaking, not everything we call a nut is a nut: Almonds and pistachios are fruits, peanuts are legumes; and pine nuts and Brazil nuts are seeds.

Medicinal Benefits Valued as a restorative and warming food in both Ayurvedic and Chinese medicine, nuts help build body mass and strength. Nuts energize. Traditional folk medicine associates this burst with sexual energy—a kind of energy not associated with rational behavior; *nutty*, in a word. That's the excessive side of nuts.

Nuts are a superior source of vitamin E and essential fatty acids, which are critical for human health. Moreover, nuts are high in protein, with some nearly as protein rich as meat. Most nuts are good sources of calcium, phosphorus, magnesium, and potassium.

In moderate quantities, and especially for high-strung and nervous people, the fats in nuts make them a calming food. In the Ayurvedic system, nuts reduce *vata*.

Use Nuts contain hard-to-digest antinutrients: lectins, phytates, and enzyme inhibitors. This explains why nuts are a digestive challenge for some people with a delicate digestive system. To reduce these antinutrients, you may either roast the nuts or soak them. Roasting nuts also brings up their flavor but denatures their heat-sensitive fatty acids. Soaking nuts is time intensive but not labor intensive. To soak nuts, place them in water to cover and soak for 4 to 10 hours. Rinse well and then, if you wish them to have a crunchy texture, oven dry at 200 degrees until they reach the desired texture. Redistribute on the pan as needed to achieve the preferred result.

Before chopping nuts, carefully pick them over. A hollow-centered almond, Brazil nut, or other nut is rancid. Toss it. Rancid nuts are too toxic to feed to the dog.

Not too often found in soups but in everything else, from salads to tortes to beverages, nuts enhance many traditional and contemporary recipes. Nuts and some seeds are often interchangeable in recipes.

For full flavor—and to heighten digestibility—toast nuts and seeds just prior to use. I prefer to toast them in a hot, dry (unoiled) wok while stirring constantly. This takes only a few minutes and I can control the degree of toasting, taking care not to denature their oils by letting them scorch or smoke. To oven roast, spread the nuts in a shallow pan and roast at 275°F for 15 to 20 minutes.

Soaking nuts overnight initiates the sprouting process, making them even easier to digest. Once they've been soaked, drain the nuts and use as is or toast and roast them.

Buying Because of their high oil content, nuts are prone to rancidity. The most healthful—and tasty—purchase is nuts in their protective shell. In addition to offering protection from light, shells shield the kernel against fumigants and other chemical treatments. Nuts in the shell keep for about a year if stored in a cool, dry place.

When purchasing shelled nuts, buy them whole and refrigerate or freeze them in airtight containers. Nuts exposed to light and sliced, broken, roasted, or blanched are rancid. Nuts completely contained in their protective skin, such as almonds and hazelnuts, are better protected than are other nuts.

Be Mindful Nuts are the most concentrated vegetable source of oils and, if eaten in excess, challenge the liver. They are one of the most common food allergens.

See **Acorn; Almond; Almond, Green; Black Walnut; Brazil Nut; Breadnut; Cashew; Chestnut; Coconut; Hazelnut; Macadamia Nut; Nut Milk; Nut and Seed Butters; Peanut; Pecan; Pine Nut; Pistachio; Walnut.**

WHEN YOU WANT NUTS—BUT NOT FAT—CHOOSE CHESTNUTS

NUT	PERCENTAGE FAT
Macadamia	88
Pecan	87
Pine Nut	85
English Walnut	83
Coconut	82
Hazelnut	81
Black Walnut	80
Almond	73
Pistachio	67
Cashew	66
Peanut	49
Chestnut	2

OAT BRAN

The fibrous outer layers of oats—the bran—is what makes cooked oatmeal sticky, and it's this sticky stuff that reduces serum cholesterol levels. Studies vary in their conclusions as to whether oat bran or oatmeal is the more effective cleanser. I prefer the whole food over the refined because it is filling, warming, and energizing.

See **Oats.**

OAT FLOUR

Oat flour yields a sweet, cakelike crumb that retains its freshness far longer than wheat flour products because oats contain a natural antioxidant. Substitute up to 20 percent oat flour for corn, wheat, or rice flour in quick breads, cakes, and muffins. To my taste, a waffle containing oat flour is unsurpassable. For a dairy-free but milklike base, use oat flour in sauces and roux. (Rolled oats, rather than oat flour, best enhance yeast breads.)

When purchasing oat flour, favor stone-ground flour. Or to mill 1 cup fresh oat flour, grind ⅔ cup oat groats in a flour mill. For coarser flour, you may use a spice or coffee grinder or a blender. Or substitute 1½ cups rolled oats for the ⅔ cup oat groats for the same yield of flour; note, however, that flour made from an already flaked or cut grain will be less flavorful and nutritious than that made from whole grain.

See **Flour; Oats.**

Oak Leaf Lettuce See **Lettuce.**

Oat Milk See **Nondairy Milk Substitutes.**

OATS
(*Avena sativa*)

> There is great healing power in the sight of oats, the faintly blue color of their stems, the knack of each seed head to hold a single, radiant drop of moisture after rain.
> —Tom Ireland, *Birds of Sorrow*

Cultivated oats are native to northern Central Asia but found a permanent home in the British Isles as well as in other cold, damp climates. That the Celts' staple grain, or daily bread, was oats is reflected by the number of oat dishes that have been handed down, including bannock, brose, and farl. The U.S. domestic supply of oats is grown primarily in the northern Midwest.

Medicinal Benefits

Oats are a blood and chi tonic that act upon the kidney, stomach, heart, lung, and large intestine meridians. They support chi circulation, and because of their high fat content, they impart stamina and warmth, which makes them excellent cold-water fare. Oats are the one adaptogen grain, meaning that they improve resistance to stress and thus support the system being in a healthy state of balance. Oats help stabilize blood sugar, regulate the thyroid, soothe the nervous and digestive systems, reduce the craving for cigarettes, and reduce cholesterol. Medicinally, they're an amazing food. Cooked oats reduce *vata* and *pitta*; dry oats, as in granola or energy bars, calm *kapha*.

Oats contain the highest percentage of sodium and fat (unsaturated) of any grain. High in protein, they have an amino acid content similar to that of wheat. Only the outer husk is removed during milling, so oat products retain more of their original nutrients than refined wheat products.

Use Whole oats may be used in pilafs, stuffings, and casseroles, as well as in porridge. Steel-cut oats are less gummy than whole or rolled oats and are a tasty addition to a grain salad in place of bulgur, rice, couscous, or pasta.

Besides the obvious hot cereal dish, rolled oats are the base of oatmeal cookies, muesli, and granola, and are the secret ingredient in Mrs. Field's chocolate chip cookies.

Buying Unlike other grains, oats must be steamed before their two inedible outer hulls can be removed. As with other grains, the more processed oats are, the more their flavor and nutrients are compromised. Oats are available in four basic forms.

- **Instant Oats or Quick Oats** This form of oats has been precooked in water, dried, and rolled super-thin. This results in reduced nutrition and flavor due to the additional processing and greater vulnerability to rancidity.
- **Rolled Oats** These are made by pressing whole oats between two rollers. Rolled oats vary from old-fashioned to thick flakes, each of which is one flattened oat groat.
- **Steel-Cut Oats (Scotch or Irish Oats)** Cut an oat groat into two or three pieces and you've got a steel-cut oat. Steel-cut oats require less cooking time than whole oats and have a pleasing texture.
- **Whole Oats (Oat Groats)** About the size of long-grain rice, whole oat groats retain the beneficial bran and germ and store well. Whole oats take as long to cook as does brown rice and are richly flavored.

A GREAT ENERGY BAR

The nutrients and flavor in this bar far exceed the typical commercial energy bar that's made of highly processed—and, most likely, stale—ingredients. The eggs and nuts make it protein rich, and the other quality ingredients provide nutrients and satisfaction.

Makes eight 3½ x 1¼-inch bars

- 4 tablespoons unsalted butter, plus more for greasing the pan
- 1 cup dried currants or raisins
- ¼ cup milk or apple juice
- 2 teaspoons pure vanilla extract
- 2¼ cups rolled oats
- 1 cup chopped walnuts or hazelnuts
- 2 teaspoons ground cinnamon
- ¼ teaspoon unrefined salt
- 2 large eggs, lightly beaten
- ¼ cup honey

Preheat the oven to 350°F. Lightly butter an 8 x 8-inch baking pan.

Place the currants in a small bowl and stir in the milk and vanilla. Set aside for 20 minutes for the fruit to plump.

Melt the butter in a large sauté pan over medium heat. Add the oats and nuts and sauté, stirring constantly, for 4 to 5 minutes, until aromatic and a shade darker. Stir in the cinnamon and salt and cook for an additional minute. Pour into a large bowl and cool.

Stir the eggs and honey into the currant mixture. Pour the wet ingredients into the dry ingredients and stir until uniformly blended.

Spread the mixture evenly into the prepared pan, place in the oven, and bake for 30 minutes, or until golden and pulling away from the edges of the pan. Invert onto a wire rack to cool, then transfer to a cutting board and cut into eight bars. Tightly wrapped, they will keep for two or more weeks.

Be Mindful Oats are a common allergen. While they do not contain the same gluten protein (gliadin) as does wheat, barley, and rye, they do, however, contain glutelin, which causes allergic reactions in some people.

See **Glutelin; Grains; Grass Family; Oat Bran; Oat Flour.**

OCA
New Zealand Yam, Papa Roja
(*Oxalis tuberosa*)

In Bolivian Indian markets, I marveled at the ocas, boldly colored tubers. Small and cylindrical with multiple bulges and deep grooves, they look like a stubby carrot. Among root crops, they're second only to potatoes in the altiplano, the place of their origin. Ocas are the only food crop of their widespread family, and they are no longer found in the wild.

Today ocas are also grown in Mexico, where they're called *papa roja*, or "red potato," and in New Zealand, where they're called a yam.

Use Some ocas have a slightly acidic taste due to the presence of oxalic acid; others are so sweet that they're sometimes sold as fruits. Boiled, baked, fried, candied, or used as a salad ingredient, ocas are more versatile than potatoes. Raw or lightly cooked, their texture is crunchy, like a carrot, but when cooked the oca becomes starchy. Like jicama, it is also marinated with salt, lime, and cayenne and served as crudités. Oca leaves and young shoots are eaten as a green vegetable.

See **Chuño; Vegetable.**

OIL See **F**AT AND **O**IL.

OIL **P**ALM See **P**ALM **K**ERNEL **O**IL; **P**ALM **O**IL.

OKARA

When cooked soybeans are pressed to extract soymilk, the remaining fibrous mass, or dregs, are called okara. Okara has a mild, almost neutral flavor, and it is used in second-generation soy products such as soy sausage or soy burgers. It is available frozen in some Japanese food stores.

See **Soybean; Tofu.**

OKRA
Gumbo, Lady's Finger
(*Hibiscus esculentus*)

The size and shape of okra suggest their alternative name, lady's finger, a description that doesn't consider their lime green color. In Louisiana, it's called gumbo. Like cotton, okra originated in Ethiopia and its seeds are pressed for oil.

Medicinal Benefits Okra is high in carotene and contains B-complex vitamins and vitamin C. Its slippery gel effectively lubricates the intestines and thus helps to ease constipation. Okra is *tridoshic,* balancing to all Ayurvedic types.

Use Sliced into rounds, okra looks like fanciful little wheels. Nevertheless, some people are put off by the sticky, mucilaginous texture of okra. Garden-fresh okra can be lightly steamed, seasoned, and eaten like green beans; or it can be pickled, broiled, fried, or baked. Okra goes well with tomatoes and highly seasoned vegetable dishes; it serves as an excellent thickener in soups and stews. Do not cook in aluminum or cast iron, as the vegetable readily absorbs metallic ions from reactive cookware, which compromises okra's color and flavor. Just before preparing, trim the woody stem ends.

Buying Okra, a hot-weather food, is available from midsummer into Indian summer. Select small, crisp okra, preferably under three inches long. Okra longer than seven inches is tough and fibrous. This mildly sweet vegetable does not store swell. Refrigerate okra and use it within a few days.

See **Mallow Family; Vegetable.**

OLIVE
(*Olea europaea*)

And the dove came in to him in the evening; and, lo, in her mouth was an olive leaf plucked off. So Noah knew that the waters were abated from off the earth.

—Genesis 8:11

The fruit of the slow-growing, picturesque olive tree, with its leathery leaves and fragrant blossoms, has been valued since the Neolithic age. Most people adore the soothing and pleasurable experience of eating a good olive—or two or three. Olives are related to the popular and aromatic ornamental plants lilac, jasmine, and forsythia, but are the only food plant of their group.

As a fruit, olives are never eaten raw because of a bitter and inedible glycoside, *oleuropein,* which is concentrated in their skin and which must first be processed out. Some olives are picked green and unripe, while others are allowed to fully ripen on the tree to a black color. In addition to the original color of the olive, the resulting color is affected by fermentation and/or curing in oil, water, brine, or salt. These processing methods vary with the olive variety, cultivation region, and the desired taste, texture, and color. Cured olives may be yellow, green, black, or purple in color and smooth skinned or shiny or wrinkled.

Medicinal Benefits Olives are neutral in temperature and support the lungs and stomach. They help regulate hot conditions and dispel toxins. As with any fatty food, they tend to slow down body functions and processes, making them medicinal for a person with high-strung, nervous energy or for someone with diarrhea. A slow-moving person with blocked or stuck energy patterns or one who has a tendency for cysts and tumors might use olives more moderately. They reduce *vata*; in moderation, black olives can be used by *pitta*. Of the primary nutrients, olives are rich in only two: fat and, when preserved, sodium. Their micronutrients include valuable glycosides (see **Olive Leaf Extract** entry).

Use There are few foods that olives, a signature ingredient in Mediterranean fare, do not enhance. Their flavor ranges from sour to smoky to bitter to acidic. American cuisine has come a long way from the 1950s, when olives were little more than a pimiento-stuffed cocktail snack. Today many kinds of olives enhance spreads, breads, and meat, grain, and vegetable dishes.

Buying The flavor of an olive depends upon the variety, climate, soil, time of harvest (green olives are picked unripe), and curing method and whether it was processed whole, cracked, or pitted. Experiment with Spanish, Greek, French, Italian, Moroccan, South American, and California olives to discover your favorites.

Green olives are soaked in a lye solution and then cured in a salt solution. They may or may not be pitted and stuffed. Ripe, or black, olives are cured directly in salt or in a salt brine. Once cured—be they green or black—they may be packed in olive oil. To enhance the flavor of brined or salted olives, rinse them, pat dry, pack into a sterile jar, and cover with a quality extra virgin olive oil.

WHAT NUTRIENT MAKES OLIVES OUTSTANDING?

Fat. Yes, fat is the nutritional reason that olives are so adored. Olives contain 88 percent fat, and fat spells flavor. Fats also soothe and impart a feeling of ease and well-being. Please pass the tapenade.

Olives are second only to nuts and seeds as an abundant source of fatty acids. Avocados and soybeans are close contenders; a few other foods (mostly grains and beans) contain 1 or 2 percent fat, but the vast majority of all other vegetables and fruits contain less than 1 percent fat.

The common black canned California olive is made by dipping immature olives in ferrous gluconate, soaking them in lye, and then canning in a brine solution. Because they are not allowed to ferment and because it is heat (rather than salt and fermentation) that preserves them, they are bland tasting.

There are many olive varieties including amfissa, arbequina, kalamata, lucques manzanilla, niçoise, and picholine. While whole olives are very common, you may also find ones that have been pitted, as well as olives that have been stuffed with either peppers, garlic, or almonds. If you purchase olives in bulk, make sure that the store has a good turnover and keeps their olives immersed in brine for freshness.

Olives store best in an airtight container in the refrigerator.

See **Fat and Oil; Fermented Food; Olive Leaf Extract; Olive Family; Olive Oil.**

OLIVE FAMILY
(*Oleaceae*)

This family of shrubs, small trees, and sometimes vines grows throughout temperate and tropical zones. The olive is the most commercially important member for its fruits as well as for its wood. Better-known olive relatives include the popular flowering bushes forsythia, lilac, and jasmine.

See **Jasmine; Olive.**

OLIVE LEAF EXTRACT

Available as a supplement, the oleuropein found in olive leaves and bark (as well as in olive oil and olives) is an invaluable nutraceutical. This and other olive glycosides have antioxidant properties and help to strengthen the immune system. Olive leaf extract is an antiseptic and astringent herb that lowers fever and blood pressure, has a calming effect, and is reputed to have antiaging properties. It is used for hard-to-treat viral infections, including Epstein-Barr and shingles, and is reported to help treat liver, prostate, and breast cancer.

The more bitter and pungent tasting an olive or olive oil is, the higher the percentage of oleuropeins it contains. The extract is available as a liquid concentrate, dried leaf tea, powder, or capsule. The liquid concentrate is preferred for its broader range of nutrients.

See **Olive.**

OLIVE OIL

For 25 centuries olive oil has remained the "fat" of Mediterranean peoples. The flavor depends upon the variety of olive, how and where it was cultivated, where it was picked, and—most important—how it was processed. Oils pressed from ripe olives have a more "fruity" flavor, whereas those pressed from green olives have a more "grassy" flavor, but you may also find nutty, woodsy, and peppery tastes. The more assertive, rich, and bright its aroma and flavor, the better quality the oil.

Medicinal Benefits Olive oil's most remarkable property is that, after coconut and palm oil, it's the most stable vegetable oil, which is due in part to its high vitamin E content.

Nearly three-quarters of its fat content is monosaturated fat, which lowers the so-called bad cholesterol (LDL or low-density lipoprotein) and leaves the good cholesterol (HDL or high-density lipoprotein) undisturbed.

Extra virgin olive oil is highly regarded for its ability to support liver and gallbladder functions. Olive oil reduces *vata* and can be enjoyed, in moderation, by *pitta* and *kapha.*

Use Extra virgin olive is a great choice to drizzle on steamed vegetables, a baked potato, or delicate fish. Blend it with herbs for fine vinaigrettes and marinades, or use it for low-temperature stir-frying and sautéing. This is contrary to the popular advice to cook with the less expensive refined, and therefore denatured, olive oil. By not heating extra virgin olive oil above 325°F, you can enjoy its greater health and flavor benefits.

Buying Since extra virgin oil costs from $10 to $100 per quart, it pays to be an informed consumer. There are international olive oil standards determining grade of olive oil (see below) and USDA standards, both of which use different terminology. Unfortunately, there are numerous cases of fraudulent labeling. In purchasing olive oil, it's prudent to go with a manufacturer you trust, and also to trust your own sense of taste. Again, the more character an oil has, the better quality it is.

- **Extra Virgin Olive Oil** The first cold pressing of olives yields the best-tasting and most healthful oil. It may contain up to 0.8 percent free oleic acid.
- **Virgin Olive Oil** The second pressing of olives yields a more acidic product that is up to 2 percent free oleic acid.
- **Semi-Fine Virgin Olive Oil** This oil is ex-

tracted with even greater pressure and may contain up to 3 percent free oleic acid.

- **Pomace** This is made from the acidic dregs of olive pulp from which virgin olive oil was pressed. These dregs, as well as olive seeds, are heated to temperatures exceeding 450°F, and the oil is chemically extracted. This process removes all trace nutrients, flavor, and aroma and denatures the fatty acids.

- **"Natural," "Pure," and "Light" Olive Oil** These are unregulated marketing terms for bland and flavorless pomace olive oil; the manufacturer may blend them with some virgin olive oil to give some flavor.

Storing Extra virgin olive oil is quite stable and may be stored for up to a year in a cool cupboard in a tightly closed container that keeps out all light. Refrigeration is not necessary; in fact, it causes the oil to solidify, and the frequent warming and chilling brought on by pulling it in and out of the fridge instigate ran-

---

ALMOST AS IMPORTANT AS YOUR HOME, OX, AND CAMEL

After the ox *Aleph*, the house *Beta*, and the camel *Gamma*, the olive, or *Zai*, was the symbol denoting the fourth letter of the most ancient alphabets. Flocks and herds, housing, transport, and agriculture were the four poles of a thriving civilization. And out of all cultivated plants, the olive tree was chosen as a symbol . . . and olive oil was the backbone of the import-export trade in the ancient world.

—Maguelonne Toussaint-Samat, *History of Food*

---

cidity. Olive oil's remarkable storage properties lend itself to bulk purchase and thus significant savings.

See **Fat and Oil**; **Olive**.

OMEGA-3, OMEGA-6, AND OMEGA-9 FATTY ACIDS SEE **ESSENTIAL FATTY ACIDS**.

ONION
(*Allium cepa*)

Called the "rose of the roots," the onion is actually not a root vegetable—it's a bulb, but its sulfurous perfume is as distinctive as the rose's. A relative of asparagus, the onion originated in Central Asia and is one of humanity's oldest vegetables.

Its sulfur compound (propanthial S-oxide), concentrated in the base or root end, makes an onion hot and irritates the eyes. Onions grown in regions where the soil and water are low in sulfur produce a sweeter onion. The Vidalia onion, for example, is as sweet as a fruit—with a sugar content of 12.5 percent versus about 7 percent sugar in a generic onion.

Medicinal Benefits Onions are warming and act upon the lung, large intestine, stomach, and liver meridians. They improve blood and chi circulation, disperse cold, damp, and mucus from the system, and help detoxify. Their bioflavonoid quercetin, a potent anticancer agent, is not destroyed by cooking. Onions have antioxidant, anti-inflammatory, antibiotic, and antiviral properties and help remove parasites and heavy metals from the system. They help treat the common cold, constipation, heart disease, and diabetes.

The onion and its relatives are prohibited in yogic diets because they increase sexual appetite and body heat. Raw onions reduce *kapha*, and when cooked they balance *pitta* and *kapha*. Well-cooked, sweeter onions calm *vata*.

Use Most people add onions to any conceivable cooked savory dish, and some people love them raw in salads and on sandwiches. But one question to consider is the type of onion. Are the new sweet varieties interchangeable with the standard yellow? Not according to Madeline Kamman, author of *The New Making of a Cook,* who states that the sweeter onions "will taint anything with their sugars." I agree. Just because a food is sweet doesn't make it better. The red onion has a more spicy flavor. Cook several types of onions separately in a bit of oil or butter and note their flavor. From then on, match the onion variety to the dish you are making to achieve the flavor result you wish.

Buying Select firm onions that have a papery, dry skin with little or no neck and no soot. Avoid onions that are light for their weight or are beginning to sprout. These are the common types of onions:

- **Cipolline** Small, 1 to 1½ inches in diameter, with flattened ends and a mild, sweet flavor. They are delicious grilled or used on kabobs.
- **Globe Onion** Also called yellow or white onion depending upon skin color. Globes are a good all-purpose onion. Small and medium-size globes are pungent; larger globes tend to be sweeter. The more expensive white onion is milder than the yellow onion, and its shelf life is not as long.
- **Pearl Onion** Also called pickling onion, this radish-size miniature onion affords great eye appeal in fancy dishes. You can expedite peeling by parboiling first.
- **Spanish and Bermuda Onions** Purple-red in color and sweeter and milder tasting than the globe, these onions are flavored in pickles and condiments and are excellent grilled. With long cooking,

---

NOT CRYING OVER ONIONS

Unless you have purchased a genetically modified "tearless" onion, then the sulfur in an onion may make your eyes tear as you cut it. (Of course, GM onions also have reduced nutrients and flavor.) Techniques for preventing tears while peeling onions are as numerous as cures for hiccups. Some people cry just looking at a raw onion; others can chop onions for hours and stay dry. Freshly harvested onions and those past their prime are the most sulfurous and therefore the most irritating. To reduce tearing, try any—or all—of the following:

Cut with a sharp knife.

Chill the onion and then peel it.

Burn a candle, and the flame will consume the sulfur.

Wear contact lenses or goggles.

Hold the nonstriking end of a wooden matchstick between your teeth.

---

they turn gray in color as they alkalinize. To maintain or even intensify their red color, keep them in an acid base (use lemon juice or vinegar). These onions are higher in moisture and do not store as well as globes.

- **Sweet Onion** Types of sweet-tasting yellow onions, such as the Vidalia, Walla Walla, Maui, Sweet Imperial, and the Texas Sweet, are sweet and juicy—and therefore don't store well. Their lower sulfur content makes them ideal for salads and sandwiches.

See Onion Family; Vegetable.

ONION FAMILY

Unequivocally the most outstanding characteristic of the onion clan is a strong taste and sulfurous odor. This small family of annual and perennial bulbous plants has been used by humanity for more than 6,000 years and probably originated in Asia Minor. Onions grow throughout the world and are the most universally used vegetable and flavoring agent. Although many cuisines and individuals find the onion family indispensable, others disdain the whole clan or specific members as a matter of personal taste or religious preference; the Jains and some Buddhists and Hindus, for example, refrain from eating onion family members because they excite the passions. Onions and garlic are the most potent of this group.

See **Chive; Garlic; Garlic Chive; Leek; Onion; Ramp; Scallion; Shallot; Vegetable.**

ORACH
Mountain Spinach
(*Atriplex hortensis*)

Orach, one of the earliest cultivated Eurasian vegetables and a member of the goosefoot family, was a standard vegetable in North America from Colonial times until the previous century when its relative spinach displaced it. Today orach is resurfacing among home gardeners as an enjoyable and tasty heirloom crop that is hardier than spinach.

Medicinal Benefits Orach is valued historically in Europe for its ability to soothe sore throats, ease indigestion, treat gout, and cure jaundice. It stimulates the metabolism and is used internally to dispel sluggishness. Orach reduces *kapha*.

Use Less acid than spinach, tender young orach shoots are used like spinach, sorrel, or its relative lamb's-quarters. Add raw orach to salads or sandwiches. Steam it as a side dish or combine it with other ingredients in soups and vegetable, grain, and pasta dishes. Do not use older shoots, as they contain excessive saponin, a mild irritant.

Buying There are three main types of orach, divided according to color: purple, white (actually pale green), and green. White orach is the sweetest and most tender. Look for orach at a farmers' market or purchase the seed from an heirloom seed supplier.

See **Goosefoot Family; Vegetable.**

ORANGE
(*Citrus sinensis*)

An orange is a berry—originally a bitter berry. But after 3,000 years of cultivation, sweet varieties now predominate. This fruit of a subtropical evergreen tree, Malaysian in origin, has blossoms with a hauntingly sweet perfume. It is this perfume that makes the ornamental orange tree popular in landscapes in our southern states; the fruit of such trees is, however, too bitter to eat out of hand but may be used in marmalade (see **Bitter Orange**).

What makes an orange orange is temperature. In Thailand and other tropical zones, the temperature is never cool enough for an orange to turn color and so, even when ripe, it remains green.

Medicinal Benefits Oranges are a cooling food and a sour and sweet yin tonic that help circulate chi, clear heat, and quench thirst. They act upon the lung, spleen, stomach, and liver organ systems and help aid digestion, reduce intestinal gas, pain, and bloating, and promote peristalsis. Oranges are a helpful treatment for those with hot, inflammatory diseases, chest congestion, vomiting, diabetes, and hiccuping. Oranges have medicinal properties for those with liver weakness; they help cleanse the blood and liver. For frail people, those who have low energy, who tend to be cold, who have arthritic-type problems, and/ or who live in cold climates, consider using oranges in moderation rather than as a dietary staple. Mandarins are used for mastitis and breast cancer and pain in the liver, chest, or breasts. Oranges balance *vata* and, if sweet and eaten in moderation, are good for *pitta*.

The aromatic peel of an orange aids digestion and transforms mucus; the peel from an immature fruit treats liver congestion. Oranges are famed for their high vitamin C content. They also contain potassium and some calcium and are a good source of pectin. The interior white orange membrane is a superior source of bioflavonoids, which enhance the absorption of iron from plant foods, defend against cancer, and have antioxidant properties.

The essential oil of orange blossom is known as neroli oil; orange essential oil is extracted from the orange rind. Be it a rind or blossom extraction, orange essential oil treats depression, anxiety, nervous conditions, and muscular spasms and is tonic, sedative, and antiseptic. They differ, however, in the following ways: Essential oil made from orange blossoms treats diarrhea, and the rind treats constipation. In addition, neroli oil also treats menopausal problems and dermatitis and is a cardiac tonic.

Use Nearly 80 percent of sweet oranges are grown for juice; the remainder are eaten fresh. Oranges are easiest to digest when eaten alone or with other tropical or subtropical fruits. They challenge the digestive system when eaten with carbohydrates, sweets, or dried fruits. A fully ripened orange contains as much as 10 percent fruit sugar. Because an orange oxidizes rapidly, it is best used within 15 minutes after its peeled and cut.

Buying Skin color, be it green or orange, is not a reliable index for quality, as all oranges are tree ripened. A greenish cast or green spots indicate that the orange was not colored or gassed for a cosmetic, uniform orange color. Some fully ripened oranges even turn greenish late in the marketing season. Do avoid oranges with dark brown spots, soft spots, or a puffy-looking peel.

Select oranges that are heavy for their size, have a fragrant aroma, and have smooth, shiny skins. Store loose in a dry and cool but not cold place and they'll hold well for about a month. Do not wrap in plastic. Navel and Valencia oranges are the two most popular orange varieties grown in the United States.

Typically, oranges from Florida and other humid climates have a thin and tightly fitting skin and are heavy with juice. Whereas in an arid climate, like California, oranges develop a substantial white albedo (pith), which makes them lighter in weight and easier to peel because their thick rind easily breaks into large pieces. These are the common orange varieties:

- **Bitter Orange** (also **Bergamot** or **Seville**) In terms of use, this orange variety is distinct from other oranges and so is listed separately. See **Bitter Orange**.
- **Blood Orange** An exceptionally sweet and juicy orange with dramatic red-orange flesh. The flesh color may be spotted or totally colored with a flamboyant red. The skin color may be uniformly orange or a combination of orange and red.
- **Mandarin** Fruits from this large citrus group may be termed "mandarin" or "clementine." All mandarins have fibrous strands located under their thin, loose-fitting peel, which easily detaches from the fruit. Most mandarins are low in acid and many are seedless. Mandarins are often crossed with other citrus varieties.

  Clementine This popular mandarin has a smooth, glossy, and deep orange peel. It is small and almost always seedless.

Satsuma This large Japanese seedless mandarin is less round than an orange, has less acid than other mandarins, peels very easily, and has a slight green tint to its otherwise deep red-orange peel. Some satsumas are sold on the stem with intact leaves, which makes a comely presentation.

Tangerine The smallest orange was named for the Moroccan port Tangier, where it was first marketed. Popular varieties include the **Dancy, Honey (Murcott), Fairchild, and Sunburst.** Tangerines typically have many seeds.

- **Navel Orange** This seedless orange is named for the belly-button-like spot at the blossom end. Native to Brazil and favored for eating rather than for juicing, the navel's bumpy skin indicates a thick, easy-to-peel rind. Peak season is from November to May.
- **Page Mandarin** This medium-size citrus fruit has a medium-thin, reddish orange, and leathery rind that is easy to peel. Its flesh is tender, juicy, and sweet. It is a Mineola tangelo and clementine mandarin cross that ripens early and is especially juicy.
- **Tangor** As its name suggestions, a tangor is a cross between the tangerine and the sweet orange. Like a tangerine, this fruit is loosely skinned. The most readily available tangors are the **Hamlin, honey** tangerine (also called the **Murcott honey** orange), **pineapple** orange, and **temple** orange.
- **Tangelo** Cross a mandarin and a grapefruit and you get a tangelo, an easy-to-peel fruit that tastes like an orange and mandarin.

The **Mineola** tangelo contains few seeds, is sweet, and has a nipple at the stem end.

The **Orlando** variety is smaller, rounder, and without an enlarged neck; it has more of a grapefruit's tang.

- **Temple** A medium-large cross between an orange and a tangerine with a pebbly skin that easily peels off, the temple orange is juicy and has a snappy, sweet flavor.
- **Ugli Fruit** See **Ugli Fruit** entry.
- **Valencia Orange** Favored for juicing, with numerous pits, a sweet and juicy pulp, and thin and smooth skin. Valencias are at their peak from late March through June.

WHICH END OF AN ORANGE IS SWEETEST?

If you're near an orange tree with mature fruit, for the fun of it, determine by tasting which part of the tree yields the sweetest—and therefore the most nutritive—fruit. You'll find that the oranges with the greatest exposure to sun (i.e., the tree top and the south side) are substantially sweeter than are oranges growing on more shaded branches.

If you lack a tree but have an orange at hand, note that there are subtle flavor differentiations from one segment to another due to which part was sunny-side out.

Now, be it the stem or blossom end, which part of an orange is sweetest? Taste and you'll be able to determine for yourself.

Hint: If you need a clue, consider which end of the orange the nutrients and flavor first pour into and are, therefore, more concentrated.

FRESH MINEOLA JAM

The bright alive flavor and color of this instant "jam" make it an irresistible spread for toast, a filling for cake, or a topping for cheesecake or ice cream. Unlike most citrus rinds, Mineola tangelos, Meyer lemons, and some tangerines have a thin and sweet-flavored rind, so any of these would work in this recipe. The Meyer lemon, however, is juicier and so yields a creamy sauce rather than a jam.

It's wise to favor organic citrus here, as the peels of commercial citrus are high in pesticide residues. I've adapted this recipe from Sally Schneider's award-winning book *The Improvisational Cook.*

> 2 organic Mineola tangelos (about ½ pound)
>
> ½ cup honey
>
> Pinch of unrefined salt
>
> ¼ cup unrefined walnut, palm, or coconut oil

Wash the tangelos and trim and discard their stem end to remove the thick nubbin of pith. Cut each fruit lengthwise into eights, removing any seeds as you go, then cut each slice into several small chunks. Transfer to a food processor, add the honey and salt, and process to a coarse puree. With the motor running add the oil; let the motor run a minute or two, until you have a thick "jam."

Adjust the salt and sugar until you get the right balance, and serve immediately. The sauce naturally thickens about 30 minutes after it's made—to thin, beat in a few teaspoons of orange juice or water.

Be Mindful Oranges and other citrus fruits are among the most common allergens. If you're one of those people who can't imagine a morning without it, this craving is a potential indicator of an allergy.

See **Bitter Orange; Citrus Family; Fruit Juice.**

ORANGE ZEST SEE CITRUS PEEL.

OREGANO
(*Origanum vulgare*)

A hardy perennial herb, oregano is a mint relative that is native to Europe. Its name derives from the Greek "joy of the mountains," and it is indeed uplifting with a punchy, almost peppery and slightly bitter flavor. Some varieties are so intense that they make your tongue tingle. It's used in countless Greek and Italian dishes, especially tomato-based ones.

Medicinal Benefits Oregano is a chi tonic that supports chi circulation and treats the liver, heart, spleen, kidney, and bladder pathways. It has antioxidant and antimicrobial properties, it aids digestion, and helps prevent gas. Oregano stimulates blood flow in the uterus and so helps treat menstrual pain and irregularities. It supports healthy liver function and perspiration.

Supplements of oregano essential oil are a popular treatment for colds, fevers, fungal infections, indigestion, parasites, and menstrual problems. Use topically as an antiseptic or as a liniment for its warming qualities. It is a well-known kitchen remedy for a toothache.

The oil is strongly sedative, so use moderately.

Use One of our most commonly used herbs, oregano is ubiquitous in pizza and pasta dishes. Use fresh when available. Unlike more delicately flavored herbs, which lose much of their flavor when dried, drying oregano actually intensifies its flavor.

There are many oregano varieties with divergent flavors. Greek and Spanish oregano are typically more strongly flavored than an undesignated variety.

See **Herbs and Spices; Marjoram; Mint Family.**

ORIENTAL GARLIC SEE GARLIC CHIVE.

ORNAMENTAL KALE SEE KALE.

OSTRICH FERN SEE FIDDLEHEAD FERN.

OYSTER MUSHROOM
Pleurotte, Trumpet Mushroom
(*Pleurotus ostreatus, P. cornucopioides, P. eryngii*)

This velvety fawn or gray mushroom has a cap shaped like the bivalve oyster and (when wild) is nearly stemless. The larger commercial variety has a thick, dense stem topped by a convex cap that gives an overall (stem and cap) trumpetlike appearance. Oyster mushrooms are among the more commonly consumed mushrooms throughout the world and are valued for their excellent aroma, thick, sweet flesh, and medicinal properties.

Among mushrooms, the oyster is unusual as it is carnivorous and its root system (mycelia) can kill and digest roundworms.

Medicinal Benefits The protein profile of the oyster mushroom is remarkably high, nearly comparable to protein from milk or meat. It is an excellent blood builder due to its significant percentage of iron. In Oriental medicine, this fungus is used in the treatment of numbness, carpal tunnel syndrome, and tendinitis.

Oyster mushrooms are a natural source of statin, a cholesterol-reducing compound. Clinical studies show the oyster mushroom's effectiveness in inhibiting tumors, lowering cholesterol, and protecting the liver from alco-

hol consumption. This tasty food also binds with and removes heavy metals from the digestive system.

Use The flavor and texture of the oyster mushroom is vastly improved when cooked. When sautéed, alone or with other ingredients, it's at its perfection.

Buying/Foraging Watch for cultivated fresh oyster mushrooms in your market or cultivate them from home kits. If you're *positive* of their identification, forage them in the fall. A wild oyster is mostly cap and grows in shelf-like clusters on poplars, aspens, and elms.

As with other mushrooms, refrigerate until use, stored in their original container or in a paper or cloth bag covered with a damp paper towel. Do not store mushrooms in plastic. Dried oyster mushrooms are not commercially available, but you can dry your own.

See **Mushroom Family; Vegetable.**

OYSTER PLANT SEE SALSIFY.

STRING A STRING OF OYSTER GEMS

If you're fortunate enough to find a large clump of oyster mushrooms (be absolutely positive of their identification), odds are you'll have more than you and your friends can eat fresh. Trim the mushrooms, cut into ¼ inch slices, and, using a needle and thread, string the rest. Regular sewing thread will hold several dozen mushroom slices. For longer strands, use heavier thread or unflavored dental floss. Hang the string indoors and out of the sun to dry. Once dry, store in a covered jar in a cupboard. To reconstitute, soak the mushrooms in water, or water and wine, for about 20 minutes or until hydrated.

PACKHAM PEAR See **PEAR.**

PAK CHOY See **BOK CHOY.**

PALM FAMILY

This picturesque and diverse family grows in tropical, subtropical, and warm temperate climates and typically has large evergreen leaves at the top of an unbranched stem. Palm habitats range from rain forests to deserts.

See **Açaí; Coconut; Date; Heart of Palm; Palm Kernel Oil; Palm Oil.**

PALMITO See **HEART OF PALM.**

PALM KERNEL OIL (NOT RECOMMENDED)

Fractionated Palm Kernel Oil; Oil Palm

The African oil palm tree, which looks like a coconut tree, is unique in that its fruit contains two types of oil—palm oil and palm kernel oil. The oil palm produces more oil per acre than any other vegetable crop. In volume of worldwide oil production, palm oil is the highest. Although this palm originated in West Africa, it is now grown throughout the tropics, with Malaysia and Indonesia producing the most for export.

Oil pressed from the palm kernel constitutes 10 percent of the plant's oil (the fruit, see below, is the richest oil source). Virgin palm kernel oil is primarily used for soap, as in the brand Palmolive and other commercial uses, including fuel and the tactical weapon napalm.

Refined palm kernel is used as a cheap fat filler in nondairy coffee creamers, margarine, vegetable shortenings, dressings, dips, whipped toppings, candy, and baked goods.

Likewise, avoid fractionated palm kernel oil. This low-priced addition to chocolate prevents candy coatings from melting at room temperature or in your fingers.

See **Fat and Oil; Palm Family; Palm Oil.**

PALM OIL
Dendê, Red Palm Oil
(*Elaeis guineensis*)

The rich orange-red color, unmistakable aroma, and flavor of palm oil are as integral to Brazilian cuisine as olive oil is for the Italians. This superior culinary oil imparts a beautiful golden color to soups, fried dishes, and baked goods. While other unrefined fats add their distinctive flavor to a dish, palm oil's mild flavor doesn't stand out. Rather, it supports and boosts the other ingredients' flavors.

Palm oil, like palm kernel oil, comes from the African oil palm tree. Both are liquid when warm and solid at room temperature, but the oil from the seed is not, historically, used as a food.

The oil palm produces more oil per acre than any other vegetable crop. In volume of worldwide production, palm outproduces even soy oil. It is currently used to create biodiesel.

Medicinal Benefits The most remarkable nutritional property of palm oil is that it's the richest natural source of beta-carotene, which, incidentally, is what gives it its vivid red-orange color. Palm oil has 15 times more beta-carotene than carrots. It is also the richest source of tocotrienol and tocopherol, vitamin E components, which helps retard oxidation, making it a naturally stable oil. It provides two valuable anticancer and antioxidant nutraceuticals, coenzyme Q10 and squalene.

Palm oil contains 71 percent of the important medium-chain fatty acids and 47 percent of the invaluable lauric acid. It reduces the tendency for blood to clot, which may lessen the risk of heart disease. It does not raise blood cholesterol; rather, it increases the level of "good" HDL cholesterol and lowers the "bad" LDL cholesterol.

Palm oil has antimicrobial effects and is applied topically to wounds.

Use I'm a great fan of palm oil. As it can withstand normal baking temperatures (unlike liquid vegetable oils), I use it frequently for the way it so beautifully colors sweet and savory dishes. How a golden finish gives allure! I brush palm oil on a chicken about to be baked and use it for truly golden oven fries and for any sautéed dish (unless I don't want it colored). Imagine how quickly you can transform raw cashews into an irresistible treat by sautéing them in palm oil.

Buying Purchase only unrefined, virgin palm oil that is red-orange in color and is produced by environmentally sustainable methods (as commercially produced palm oil causes irreversible environmental damage). If your market does not yet carry it, purchase it online. Store it at room temperature for a year or more.

See **Fat and Oil; Palm Family; Palm Kernel Oil.**

PANOCHA SEE **WHEAT FLOUR.**

PAPA ROJA SEE **OCA.**

PAPAYA
(*Carica papaya*)

A native of Central America, the papaya tree, which looks like a palm tree, bears pendulous fruits weighing from one to twenty

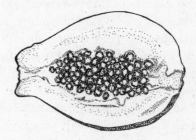

pounds. Columbus called it a melon tree, and it is indeed melonlike in shape and taste. This fruit offers the luscious taste and sunlit color of the tropics. Papayas have a dense, silky texture and a rich and sweetly refreshing taste. Its pink to orange flesh contains many black seeds in a central womblike cavity; the edible seeds look like oversize caviar and have a peppery flavor. Domestic papayas are grown in Hawaii and, to a lesser extent, southern Florida. Papayas also come from Puerto Rico and Mexico.

Medicinal Benefits Papayas are a chi tonic that energize the lung, stomach, and spleen meridians, support blood circulation, and help dispel conditions of excessive damp and mucus. Ripe papayas moisten and lubricate the lungs and so are generally helpful to relieve coughs and asthma. This fruit may be applied topically to treat wounds and is also considered beneficial for easing stomach ulcers and rheumatism, for strengthening vision, and as anticarcinogen. They contain an antitumor compound, carpine. Papaya seeds are an effective vermicide. Papayas reduce *vata*.

Papayas are an excellent source of antioxidant nutrients such as carotenes, vitamin C, and flavonoids. They contain the B vitamins folate and pantothenic acid, vitamins A, C, and E, and calcium, iron, potassium, and phosphorus. They are low in calories and, when ripe, contain about 8 percent sugar.

Medicinally, papayas are remarkably different from other fruits, as they contain—especially when unripe—several unique protein-digesting enzymes, including papain and chymopapain. They support digestion by breaking down proteins, aid with healing sports injuries, and offer allergy relief.

Use Green, immature papayas are used throughout the tropics as a squashlike vegetable. Enjoy it as a melon—cut lengthwise, remove the seeds, add a squeeze of lime juice, and tuck in with a spoon. Or add to fruit salads, kabobs, and frozen desserts. If adding papaya to a fruit salad, do so just before serving; otherwise it will soften the other fruits. Do not use raw papaya in a gelatin or agar dish, as papain prevents gelling. Cooking, however, deactivates the enzyme.

Dried papaya is *not* sweet unless it has been sugar-treated. If the label contains the term "honey-dipped," this means the fruit is saturated with 80 percent added sugar (see page 118).

Buying If you want to eat a papaya within a day of purchase, choose one that has a reddish orange skin and is slightly soft to the touch. While a few black spots on the surface will not affect the papaya's taste, avoid those that are bruised or overly soft. Those that have patches of yellow color will take a few more days to ripen. Ripen at room temperature and then refrigerate them.

Papayas that are partially yellow should be

SAVE ON YOUR SUPPLEMENT BILL

Don't toss papaya seeds. Set them aside and next time you are blending up something that could use a nutritious and peppery addition—like a salad dressing, sorbet, or leafy green energy drink—blend them in. Or dry the seeds on a sunny counter for a few days, then put them in an empty pepper mill for a seasoning agent. The dried seeds could also go into a small recycled supplement bottle; label it "Digestive Enzyme—Papain" and munch on a few seeds with each meal. Not only will these seeds support digestion; they also act as a vermifuge against intestinal parasites.

---

left at room temperature, where they will ripen in a few days. If you want to speed this process, place them in a paper bag with a banana.

Don't purchase a papaya that is totally green or overly hard unless you are planning on cooking it, as it will not develop flavor.

Papayas are more available during the summer and fall; however, you can usually purchase them throughout the year.

Be Mindful About 50 percent of Hawaiian papayas are genetically modified (GM). By definition, certified organic products are not genetically modified; likewise, products that are not genetically modified may indicate this on their label. Papayas contain a substance called chitinase that is associated with the latex-fruit allergy syndrome. If you have a latex allergy, you may very likely be allergic to papaya as well as avocados and bananas.

See **Dried Fruit; Fruit.**

PAPRIKA
Hungarian Paprika, Pimiento

Pulverize a chile or pepper and the resulting bright red powder is known as paprika. Back when the American pepper came to Europe in the 1500s, the Hungarians figured a way to sun-dry and grind them; ever since then, paprika has helped define Hungarian national cuisine and has become a universal seasoning agent.

Paprika may be made of any chile or pepper variety. Sweet paprika is typically made from pimientos, whereas hot paprika is made from a blend of hot chiles.

Medicinal Benefits See **Chile Pepper** and **Sweet Pepper** entries.

Use To heighten paprika's flavor, lightly toast it in a dry skillet for a few minutes until it is aromatic. Use it as a primary ingredient (see the accompanying recipe) or as a finishing herb for color and flavor. It seems that a sprinkle of paprika is a prerequisite for potato salad, deviled eggs, and other dishes wanting an uplift of color.

BUFFALO *GULYÁS* (GOULASH)

You don't have to be Hungarian to appreciate the rich aroma and flavor of gulyás. Its hallmark ingredients are meat with the bone to yield a rich, thick, and gelatinous broth and paprika. Yes, the amount of paprika seems inordinate, but if you use less, expect a less wonderful result. If you're buying paprika in those little bottles, then you're paying more for the jar than the spice. Bulk paprika, online or at your natural food store, costs under a dollar an ounce.

This no-fuss stew requires a long simmer—but that's what transforms inexpensive meat into tender morsels. In a slow-cooker, it can simmer overnight or all day while you're at work. Serve with a side of buckwheat and sauerkraut.

Serves 4

- 2 tablespoons unrefined olive, sesame, or palm oil
- 4 pounds buffalo (bison), beef, lamb shanks, or short ribs, cut into chunks
- 6 cloves garlic, minced
- 1 large onion, diced
- ¼ cup sweet Hungarian paprika
- Hot paprika to taste
- 2 teaspoons unrefined salt
- 4 medium yellow potatoes, diced
- 5 cups water
- ¼ cup chopped parsley or cilantro

In a large skillet, heat the oil over medium-high heat. Add the meat and brown for about 5 minutes, turning as necessary. Transfer the meat to a 3-quart stew pot.

In the same skillet, add remaining oil and heat over medium heat. Add the garlic and onion and sauté for 5 minutes, or until translucent. Add the paprika and salt and cook, stirring continuously, until the paprika is aromatic, 2 to 3 minutes.

Scrape the onion mixture into the stew pot and add the potatoes and water. Bring to a simmer and cook for 5 minutes, skimming off and discarding any brown foam or excess paprika-colored fat.

Cover tightly, reduce the heat to low, and simmer for 3 to 4 hours, adding more water as necessary to just cover the ingredients at all times.

Before serving, remove the meat from the stew with a slotted spoon. Discard the bone, trim the meat, and cut it into bite-size pieces. Skim off any excess fat and adjust the seasonings. Serve garnished with the parsley.

Buying Too often the paprika in the United States is a bland red pepper powder. For rich-tasting paprika that gives an appealing flavor and a warm accent to foods, purchase imported Hungarian paprika, which is so labeled.

See **Chile Pepper; Herbs and Spices; Nightshade Family.**

PARSLEY
(*Petroselinum crispum*)

The world's most popular herb and a carrot family member, parsley originated in Sardinia, and Sardinian coins, until recent times, were minted with a parsley imprint. The name "parsley" comes from the Greek, meaning "rock celery" (parsley is a celery relative); banqueting Greeks wore parsley crowns to stimulate the appetite and promote good humor.

A biennial plant, once established in your garden, parsley will come back year after year.

Medicinal Benefits When Peter Rabbit had overeaten Mr. McGregor's vegetables and was "feeling rather sick, he went to look for some parsley." Parsley, as certainly Beatrix Potter knew, is a digestive aid.

Parsley is a warming food and a blood tonic that specifically supports the bladder, kidney, and stomach meridians. It helps regulate water imbalances and eliminate toxins. Parsley helps stimulate the bowels and treat kidney stones and gallstones, deafness, and ear infections. Parsley is an anticarcinogen and antioxidant. A sprig of it also freshens the breath.

Apigenin, a flavonoid found in parsley, reduces allergic reactions. Dried parsley tea is a diuretic and ameliorates kidney function (do not use for inflamed kidneys, though) and strengthens the teeth. Used after childbirth, parsley helps contract the uterus and encourages milk flow. Parsley reduces *pitta* and *kapha*.

Parsley is a superior source of vitamin A and has three times as much vitamin C as oranges and twice as much iron as spinach.

The essential oil of parsley, made from parsley seed, is a sedative and diuretic that treats nervous problems, kidney weakness, and menstrual irregularities.

Use Do more with parsley than garnish. Its tangy-sweet flavor helps bring out the flavors of other foods and it stands up well to heat. Serve it as a vibrant ingredient in steamed and blanched vegetable dishes, as a base for salad dressings, as a sauce ingredient, or generously strewn in soups and casseroles. Unlike the tops, cooked parsley stems do not color a dish, so chopped fine, they are good for a white sauce.

Buying There are two main types of parsley: the strongly flavored flat-leaf parsley (also known as Italian parsley), which stands up well to heat, and the mildly flavored curly parsley, which is a better keeper. Flat-leaf parsley is a deep blue-green; curly parsley is a lighter green. Select parsley with no signs of wilting. Dried parsley offers little flavor and less color.

Be Mindful Parsley stimulates the uterus and so is used in moderation by pregnant women. In excess, parsley—and especially the essential oil of parsley—is toxic.

See **Carrot Family; Herbs and Spices.**

PARSLEY ROOT
Hamburg Parsley
(*Petroselinum crispum* var. *tuberosum*)

It's a red-letter day when I find parsley roots at the supermarket. This Old World vegetable, still popular in Germany and enjoying increased availability in the United States, is a parsley variety grown for its root. Parsley root looks like a dwarf parsnip and is usually sold bunched with its rather coarse, broad-leaf parsley greens attached. It tastes similar to celery root or like a combination of celery heart and parsley.

Medicinal Benefits Parsley root is medicinal for the stomach; it treats anemia and rheumatism, promotes lactation, and helps contract the uterus. It is a good source of vitamin C and is rather high in sodium. It reduces *pitta* and *kapha*.

Use I like parsley root in almost any soup that invites an onion; it's also delicious cooked with hijiki and onions. Germans often steam the root until tender and serve it with butter or a cream sauce. Russians and Poles use it in borscht.

Buying Parsley root is a fall and winter crop. Select parsley roots that are firm and preferably have the greens attached. Remove the greens and use in soup stock or, moderately, in place of parsley.

See **Carrot Family; Parsley.**

PARSNIP
(*Pastinaca sativa*)

When I was a high schooler, the Russian who filled my daydreams was the poet and author of *Dr. Zhivago*, Boris Pasternak. When I discovered that parsnip is *pasternak* in Russian, that further endeared both the author and vegetable to me. The parsnip is a carrot relative that looks like an oversize albino carrot, but its flavor is much sweeter and nuttier—some would even say banana-like. Wild parsnip is still abundant in Europe and the Caucasus, where it originated. In Europe, the parsnip was an important staple until it was replaced by the blander and more versatile potato.

Medicinal Benefits Parsnips are a warming food that support liver, lung, stomach, and spleen functions. They help resolve damp conditions. They are high in silicon and insoluble fiber and offer some vitamin A and C, calcium, and potassium. Ounce for ounce, boiled parsnips have about 31 percent as much calcium as milk. Parsnips reduce *vata* and *pitta*.

Use Unless it is fresh, a parsnip can dominate other flavors, so use accordingly in soups and stews. Parsnips may be boiled, simmered, steamed, baked, used in puddings, or used in making wine. A young and tender parsnip doesn't require peeling and may be grated or julienned into a salad. With older vegetables, peel as necessary. Steam, rice, or mash them as you would potatoes, and serve with a pat of butter and freshly grated black pepper.

Buying Except in the fall, the parsnips typically available in supermarkets may be too old and flabby to be worth purchasing. No wonder so few people use them today. A parsnip that is allowed to remain in the ground at least two weeks past the first frost is unbelievably sweet and satisfying. Look for straight, smooth-skinned roots that are a tan or creamy white color, firm and fresh-looking, and without gray, dark, or soft spots. Large roots tend to be woody.

See **Carrot Family; Vegetable.**

PASSION FRUIT
Banana Passion Fruit, Purple Passion Fruit, Vanilla Passion Fruit
(*Passiflora edulis*)

If the name of the heavenly scented, intensely sweet passion fruit evokes erotic images, you're off track—at least, off the official track. Named for the passion of Christ, the blossoms' twelve white petals are for the Apostles, its bright red stamens look like the five wounds, and the disk floret holds three nails and crown of thorns. A native of Brazil, passion fruit is now widely planted in the tropics and is hardy enough to grow in California and some Mediterranean countries. It comes from a perennial climbing plant.

The passion fruit is the size and shape of an egg with, most typically, a brown-purple skin that is wrinkled when ripe. Inside are multiple edible seeds—rather like tomato seeds—embedded in a golden-chartreuse-colored jellylike pulp. Its flavor is like a spicy blend of banana, guava, lime, and honey.

Use Passion fruit may be eaten like a canta-loupe from its sliced-open shell; made into juice; or pureed and used as a sauce to decorate and flavor desserts, sorbets, and ice cream. To remove the seeds from the pulpy flesh, force the pulp through a strainer or puree. Bottled and frozen passion fruit juice makes a delicious beverage base and is often found in fruit juice blends.

Buying Look for passion fruit that is heavy for its size, with a firm, smooth shell. Keep at room temperature until it becomes wrinkled, appears old, and sounds liquidy when shaken next to your ear. It is then ready to eat—or it may be refrigerated for up to a week.

In addition to the purple passion fruit, a vanilla (or banana) passion fruit that is the size, shape, and color of a banana has some availability. It is less flavorful, more seedy, and has a stronger vanilla flavor. Currently it is not grown in the United States.

See **Fruit**.

PATTYPAN See **Squash; Squash, Summer**.

PAWPAW
(Asimina triloba)

The pawpaw is the largest indigenous North American fruit; in size it is like a fat and lumpy banana but with a lima bean shape, and it can weigh up to a pound. The pawpaw grows on small trees in the Mississippi basin and is the only temperate region relative of the tropical cherimoya. Its flavor evokes mango, vanilla, and banana, but its aroma is heavy and sweet—some would say cloying. The thick peel and dozen or more dark seeds are inedible. Paw-paw flesh is soft and smooth and ranges in color from creamy yellow to orange—the lat-ter are more flavorful.

Pawpaws contain more protein than most fruit and are currently popular as an antican-cer supplement because of its acetogenin content.

Fresh pawpaws hold only for two or three days, but refrigerated they will store a week or more. They are primarily eaten raw—halve the fruit and scoop out the flesh with a spoon. The frozen pulp has some availability.

See **Cherimoya Family; Fruit**.

PAZOTE See **Epazote**.

PEA, DRIED See **Beans and Legumes**.

PEA, FRESH
English Pea, Garden Pea, Green Pea
(Pisum sativum)

I eat my peas with honey,
I've done it all my life.
It makes the peas taste funny
But it keeps them on my knife.
—Anonymous

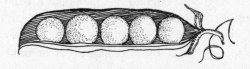

Tiny round green peas encased in a pod are a favorite and ancient food. Pea seeds found in archaeological digs in Anatolia (Turkey) date from 5700 BC, making this legume one of humanity's original staples. When brought straight from the garden to the table, peas are a vegetable unsurpassed in delicacy of flavor. Frozen peas are a mean substitute for fresh, as once the peas are picked and shucked, the sugar content starts converting to starch and their flavor fades. This conversion is delayed in edible-podded peas, which are protected by the pod.

As peas are a cold-weather crop, you'll find

seasonal peas in either the late spring or early fall. My father always plants his peas on Saint Patrick's Day, which is a good four or more weeks ahead of other crops.

Medicinal Benefits Peas are a yin tonic that travel the kidney and spleen meridian. With or without their pods, they reduce *pitta* and *kapha*. Green peas are high in vitamins A and B-complex and are a good source of calcium and potassium.

Use The flavor of fresh peas is distinctive, elusive, rich, and aromatic. Even the blossoms are edible and make a beautiful garnish for or addition to salads. Some golden yellow peas are available as fresh peas. Neither the snow pea nor the sugar snap pea are shucked; rather, the pod itself is used as a vegetable. The green shoots can also be cooked and served as a vegetable, as is done in Chinese cooking.

Buying In the market, look for small, crisp, shiny pods that squeak when rubbed together. When withered at the tips or when the peas are large and round, the vegetable is past its prime. Refrigerate and use immediately. These are the common pea varieties:

- **Pea** Shuck green peas just prior to cooking and save the pods for soup stock. Or, if very fresh, enjoy out of hand.
- **Snow Pea** This cultivar has a tender-crisp, jade green pod that is as succulent as the peas it contains. Snow peas need only to have their tips removed. They're used in soups, salads, stir-fries, and more and are a classic ingredient in Asian cuisine.
- **Sugar Snap Pea** This new cultivar (1970) is the hybrid cross between a snow pea and a green pea that offers the best of both. Its tender but crisp pod is edible, as are the sugary, plump little peas. Their pod is a deeper green than

A SURFEIT OF PEAS

A favorite childhood memory of mine is pea harvesttime in rural northern Utah. As farmhands pitchforked green peas, vines and all, onto trucks for transport to the canneries, my father would bounce our car down dirt lanes to the harvest site and ask for a forkful. Two scoops and the backseat of our old Dodge Coupe was brimming with a mountain of green pea vines and filled with their heady aroma. Back home, my family would loll under a shady tree, pulling pods from the vines, shucking and eating peas, and setting some by for Mom to freeze.

the snow pea and its peas are well formed but smaller than peas. The sugar snap pea is available primarily in the fall and spring.

See **Beans and Legumes; Legume Family.**

PEACH
(*Prunus persica*)

"She's a peach!" describes someone who's remarkable. Indeed, of the various fruits, the peach's fleshy juiciness—that's both sweet and yet mildly tart—makes it an outstanding treat. Fruit of a deciduous tree, the peach originated in China, and the fact that the emperor's royal scepter was made of peach wood bespeaks its great esteem. Indeed, the Chinese associate it with immortality and fertility and considered the peach tree—rather than apple—as the Tree of Life.

From China, peach cultivation moved along caravan routes to Persia and eventually to Europe and the Americas. Originally called Persian apple in the West, the name "peach" comes from the Latin word for Persian. Unlike its near relatives—plums, cherries, apricots, and nectarines—peach skin is velvety.

Unlike many fruits, peaches are produced in most of the states, 36 to be exact, Georgia claims the title of the Peach State because it was one of the first states in the commercial peach industry in the 1800s, but California produces 99 percent of all cling peaches.

Medicinal Benefits Peaches—as well as nectarines—have a sweet and sour flavor, are cooling in thermal nature, and help with blood circulation. They help to build body fluids, making them an expectorant in the case of dry coughs and lubricating for intestines in the case of constipation. They have a cleansing action for the bladder (diuretic) and kidneys. Peaches are sedative in action, they stimulate digestion, and improve the health of the skin. Peaches and nectarines reduce *vata* and are recommended in moderation for *pitta*.

The peach kernel, which contains amygdalin, a naturally occurring cyanide-sugar compound, in minute quantities is used in Oriental medicine to strengthen the blood. However, cases of poisoning after eating peach pits in quantity have been reported. Peach leaves and bark are used as a medicinal tea for chronic bronchitis, coughs, and gastritis. Peach leaf tea is used for morning sickness, to purge intestinal worms, and to cleanse the kidneys.

Both peaches and nectarines are subacid fruits and low in calories. They contain fewer calories than apples or pears, and they aid in elimination. They are high in vitamin A (especially the darker-colored peaches) and vitamin C and, unlike most fruits, contain calcium.

Use For an elegant and irresistible appetizer, pair ripe peaches with a quality cheese and a selection of crackers. Add peach slices to yogurt or use to top ice cream . . . or better yet, turn them into peach ice cream or sorbet.

BOOK CLIFFS ESPALIER

Renaissance gardeners, like Chinese gardeners, used to plant peach trees against a wall with southern exposure, painted white to cast back the warmth and light of the sun, and trained the trees to grow flat. This espalier technique protects the trees from frost, hastens their ripening, and, according to gardeners, produces a superior-tasting fruit.

The peach capital of Colorado, Palisade, abuts the towering Book Cliffs, a sheer 1,000-foot escarpment, which, though too steep for vegetation, absorbs heat from the sun and beams it out to warm the orchards. I can attest to the sweetness of Palisade peaches.

Use peaches as a garnish for salads or breakfast cereal or a filling for tarts, cobblers, strudels, empanadas, or pies. Peaches are great juiced, jammed, dried, canned, or turned into jelly. Distill them into a brandy or liqueur or simply eat out of hand. There's little that beats the pleasure of a ripe peach.

For easiest peeling, blanch peaches in boiling water for a few seconds, then plunge into cold water until cool enough to handle; the skin will slip right off. To keep sliced peaches from discoloring, mix them with a little lemon juice or ascorbic acid.

Buying Select peaches that have a fragrant and warm peachy aroma. The fruit's perfume directly correlates to its ripeness. A ripe peach "gives" to a *gentle* squeeze at its shoulder (adjacent to the stem end) and, overall, has a "fresh" appearance.

Since peaches are seasonal, buying locally grown fruit is the best way to get a tender, ripened-on-the-tree peach that was hand-plucked and packed. Store-bought peaches are picked while hard, dumped into huge bins, and poured onto a processing line. They're mechanically washed, defuzzed, dried, and sorted by size. It takes a tough unripened peach to come off the conveyer belt intact. Unlike some fruits, an immature peach never ripens. It will eventually soften, but it will always be short of flavor, aroma, nutrients, and sweetness.

You can refrigerate a tree-ripened peach for a week to 10 days. If a tree-ripened peach is still a little firm, refrigerate it until a day or so before you need it. Then place the fruit in a bowl and keep it at room temperature until the desired softness is achieved. With ultrasoft peaches, plan on eating or processing them the same day.

There are two main types of peaches, determined by whether the flesh clings to the pit (clingstone) or breaks free of it (freestone). Freestones are preferred for eating fresh; most clingstones are commercially processed and not available fresh in retail markets.

There are hundreds of both red and golden-colored peach varieties and even some more delicately perfumed and fragile (and, therefore, more expensive) white peaches. The white peach is low in acid but high in sugar and, I find, it lacks the personality that the acid-sugar balance gives to more robustly colored fruit. Also new to our markets are a flat, donut-shaped peach with a sweet flavor and low acid known as a Saturn or donut peach.

Bugs also find peaches irresistible and, therefore, commercial crops are sprayed with assorted pesticides and fungicides on a weekly basis for the five-plus months they are growing. According to organic expert Cindy Burke in her excellent book *To Buy or Not to Buy Organic*, if at all possible, avoid consuming commercial peaches, as they are one of our most chemically contaminated foods.

See **Fruit; Prune Family.**

BROILED PEACHES AND BLUEBERRIES

Broiling peaches heightens their flavor and almost crisps their outside while juicing up their interior to create this elegant and deceptively easy-to-prepare dish. You can use peaches on their own or in combination with nectarines, plums, pears, and apples.

Serves 4

1 cup apple juice or apple cider
¼ teaspoon grated orange or lemon zest
2 peaches, pitted and cut into ½-inch wedges
½ cup blueberries
Nutmeg

Preheat the broiler.

Place the apple juice in a small saucepan over medium heat. Bring to a simmer and cook, uncovered, for about 7 minutes, until reduced by half. Stir in the zest and set aside.

Meanwhile, arrange the peach wedges on a shallow baking pan and broil for about 3 minutes. Add the blueberries and broil for another 2 to 3 minutes, until peach juice starts bubbling and the fruit starts to brown.

Divide the peaches, blueberries, and cider among 4 small saucers. Garnish with a grating of nutmeg and serve.

PEANUT
Groundnut
(*Arachis hypogaea*)

The peanut was cultivated by the Aztecs and the Maya, then introduced to Africa, Europe, Asia, and North America. Like many other legumes, peanuts are an inexpensive protein source and an important food for many people throughout the world. China and India together grow more than 50 percent of the world's supply. Peanuts are a nutritious, all-American favorite snack food.

In the early 1900s, botanist George Washington Carver mechanized peanut cultivation and developed more than 300 ways to use peanuts in food. Since his pioneering work, peanuts have become an important crop in the United States.

Technically a legume, the peanut is unusual in two ways. After the flower is pollinated, the flower-bearing stalk elongates, forcing the young pod down into the soil, where it matures. This explains the English name for peanuts, groundnuts. Its second curious feature is that while other legumes store starch, peanuts store fat and so are more like a nut than a bean.

Medicinal Benefits Peanuts are a chi and blood tonic that support the lung and spleen functions and help to eliminate excess mucus and regulate water conditions. They are a grounding food and excellent for people with a fast metabolism. They are also useful for increasing the milk supply of nursing mothers. They have a laxative effect and may cause gas in *vata* types. Peanuts reduce *pitta* and are unfavorably regarded in Ayurvedic medicine for all body types.

A kitchen remedy to strengthen the kidneys is to simmer raw peanuts (preferably in the shell) and salt; eat while still moist and warm.

Like other legumes, the peanut is a good source of protein, but unlike other legumes, it is high in fat, of which a small percentage is saturated. Peanuts are the second-highest source of pantothenic acid. They are high in the B vitamins (thiamine, riboflavin, and niacin), vitamin E, and iron.

Use Unlike nuts and seeds, which may be eaten raw, peanuts—a legume—require cooking to be digestible and to remove their antinutrients. To roast peanuts, spread in a thin layer and bake at 350°F for about 15 to 20 minutes for shelled peanuts, or about 25 minutes for unshelled peanuts, stirring as necessary to ensure even roasting. Or toast shelled nuts in a dry skillet over high heat, stirring constantly until the peanuts start to brown. Reduce the heat to low and continue stirring until the peanuts are uniformly colored a shade darker.

In African and Thai cuisine, ground peanuts form the bases of sauces, curries, and stews. Substitute peanuts for nuts or seeds in both savory and sweet desserts.

Buying It's critical to purchase only organic peanuts from arid regions (see below). Select in-the-shell peanuts with clean, unbroken shells that don't rattle when shaken; they will hold for six months when stored in a cool, dry place. One and a half pounds of unshelled peanuts yield about one pound of shelled nuts. If purchasing shelled peanuts, choose those with no additives and refrigerate until use.

The most popular domestic varieties are the small Spanish, the Valencia, which is primarily used for peanut butter, and the larger, more oval Virginia, which is mostly used whole in roasted nut blends.

Be Mindful Peanuts are among the most common food allergens. They're especially challenging for people with delicate liver conditions, cancer, gout, or candidiasis-type yeast infections. However, considering the following, all people would do best to limit their peanut consumption to only organic peanuts grown in an arid region.

Unfortunately, peanuts are one of the most chemically adulterated crops because Southern peanut fields are typically crop-rotated with cotton. Plagued by the boll weevil, cotton, a nonfood crop, is treated with chemicals too toxic to be permitted on food crops. A field of cotton may receive up to 16 applications of various pesticides annually. These chemical residues affect the following year's peanut crop.

Furthermore, the USDA allows a low percentage of the carcinogenic mold aflatoxin in peanut products. Peanuts grown in the humid Southeast invariably develop some mold while drying in the field. Peanuts grown in arid areas, like eastern New Mexico, are free of aflatoxins because mold cannot form in desert-like conditions.

Last, peanuts sold salted in their shell are best avoided because of how the salt is applied. As it would take too long a soak for the salt in a saline solution to penetrate the peanut shell, a detergent is added to expedite the process. Yuck!

See **Legume Family; Nut and Seed Butter; Nuts; Peanut Butter; Peanut Oil.**

PEANUT BUTTER

A PB & J sandwich is almost synonymous with childhood—and some of us have a delayed childhood. I hope yours is made with the real thing. One taste comparison of natural peanut butter with a commercial variety provides ample argument. Most commercial peanut butter contains 10 percent poor-quality sweeteners, added poor-quality oil, and refined salt. It tastes bland and sugary compared to the rich peanut flavor of natural peanut butter.

Natural peanut butter contains only ground nuts and sometimes salt. Its oil may separate to the top but is easily stirred back in. Some natural brands of peanut butter now add lecithin, which prevents oil separation.

Medicinal Benefits Though nutritious, peanut butter is hard to digest, especially for people with a delicate digestive system or a congested gallbladder or liver. It is grounding and good for persons wishing to gain weight.

Use According to the National Peanut Council, adults actually eat more peanut butter than children do. In fact, it is one of the most commonly purchased food items in supermarkets. Peanut butter, one of the least expensive protein sources, also finds its way into candy and onto celery sticks as a quick snack.

Buying Multiple circumstances make it prudent to be an informed consumer of peanut products. See "Be Mindful" in the **Peanut** entry.

Due to its fat content, peanut butter becomes rancid when exposed to light and heat or with long storage. Refrigeration retards rancidity but firms the butter, making spreading a challenge that's only measured in proportion to the bread's fragility.

See **Nut and Seed Butters; Peanut.**

PEANUT OIL

Peanut oil has a high smoke point and so is mistakenly regarded as good for using at high temperatures; this is unfounded because its omega-6 fatty acids are destroyed at temperatures above 240°F. Peanut oil is low in linoleic acid and vitamin E and high in monounsaturated fats.

Be Mindful Use only organic peanut oil, as commercial peanuts are heavily contaminated with chemical pesticide residues and may contain aflatoxins.

See **Fat and Oil; Peanut.**

PEAR
(*Pyrus communis*)

There once was a duke who, according to a sixteenth-century Italian manuscript, was into pears—and more than just Bartlett or Anjou. During a one-year period, 209 different pear varieties were served to the Grand Duke Cosmo III.

The pear is a fall fruit and is similar to its apple relative in its seeds and core, though with a richer aroma and a texture that is both more melting and grittier. Due to this melting quality, it was once called butter fruit. The pear is native to the Middle East and the sub-alpine zones of Kashmir. Some pears are the distinctive pear shape, while others are elongated, and still others are round. Today 95 percent of American-produced commercial pears are grown in Washington, Oregon, and California.

Medicinal Benefits Pears are a yin tonic that clear heat and mucus and energize the stomach, spleen, and lungs. The pear is used in the treatment of diabetes, hot cough, gall-bladder obstruction, and constipation. Because they are cooling, do not consume pears when feeling cold internally or if suffering from diarrhea. Freshly squeezed pear juice is a kitchen remedy for a hangover. Pears reduce *pitta* and *kapha*, though a dry pear best reduces *kapha*.

Pears are a good source of fiber, particularly pectin, as well as potassium and boron. They are low in sodium and have small amounts of phosphorus and vitamin A. The pectin in pears reduces serum cholesterol and cleanses the body of environmental and radioactive toxins.

Use Sweet, melting, and juicy describe pears preferred for eating out of hand. Varieties that are firmer and crisp are canned and pickled. Pears may also be juiced, pureed, used in salads, brandied, frozen, dried, made into preserves, or distilled into liqueur or wine. To prevent cut pears from browning, sprinkle with lemon juice.

The two main categories of pears are those that change color when ripe, like a Bartlett, and a winter pear in which color change when ripe is negligible. The latter ripen later and store better through the winter.

Buying Unlike most tree fruits, pears are best ripened off the tree. Select firm—not hard—pears with a noticeable pear aroma. Ripen at room temperature in a closed paper bag until the flesh at the stem end yields to gentle thumb pressure. Because pears soften from the inside out, a pear that is really soft on the outside is overripe. Domestic pears are available from the fall into the spring, and pears imported from South America or Australia are available from the spring and through the summer. These are the common varieties:

- **Anjou (d'Anjou) Pear** Egg shaped, with almost no neck, green, spicy-sweet, and juicy. A red Anjou remains maroon-red when ripe. The Anjou is good fresh and better baked or poached—it will not lose its shape—than in a pie.
- **Bartlett Pear** Red or yellow; juicy and with a definite aromatic flavor. Bartletts are bell shaped, medium to large, and often have a red blush when fully ripe. There are two types of red-skinned Bartletts: those that turn bright red when ripe and those that remain dark red. An all-around pear, the Bartlett is good for eating fresh, cooking, and canning.
- **Bosc Pear** Long with a long, narrow neck; dark yellow with brown-russet skin; firm but buttery, highly aromatic, nutty, and flavorful. The Bosc is unsurpassed in pies, muffins, and quick breads and baked or poached.
- **Comice Pear** This superlative winter pear is often featured is gift boxes of fine fruit. The Comice is mild flavored and buttery textured with a round shape and a short neck. When ripe, it is incredibly juicy. It is a medium yellow with pink or brown tinges. A red Comice pear is also available. The Comice is delicious with cheese, in fruit salads, and baked. As an out-of-hand variation, cut it open and eat with a spoon.

- **Conference Pear** Very similar in texture, color, and flavor to the Bosc pear, the Conference pear has a juicy, sweet flesh that is creamy white and granular.
- **Nelis Pear** A russet pear with a squat shape, dull green skin, and a firm, crisp flesh that has a spicy, rich flavor. Good out of hand and in quick breads.
- **Packham Pear** An Australian variety that is a Bartlett cross, the Packham is a large pear with a small neck and green skin that becomes pale yellow as the fruit matures. Its flesh is white, juicy, and sweet.
- **Rocha Pear** A medium-size Portuguese pear that is round with a short, brownish neck. When ripe, the Rocha is buttery soft.
- **Seckel Pear** Green to russet, small, often bite-size; ultrasweet, mildly spicy, and dense flesh. Pickled whole, Seckels are an eye-catcher. They are best eaten fresh or in salads.

Never store a pear sealed in plastic. Without freely circulating oxygen, the core will turn brown and brown spots will develop under the skin.

Be Mindful Pear orchards typically receive nine applications of pesticides per season as well as routine fungicides and herbicides, making them one of our most toxic commercial fruits. Favor organic pears when possible.

See **Apple Family; Dried Fruit; Fruit.**

PEARL ONION SEE ONION.

PECAN
Hickory Nut
(*Carya illinoenis*)

Our most important native American nut crop, the pecan, was an important staple for Native Americans, known to the Algonquian, Cree, Ojibwa, and Abenaki peoples. Pecans are a relative of walnuts and a member of the hickory genus. Of the 11 hickory species native to North America, only the pecan has commercial availability. All nuts of the hickory family are, however, edible, and are an important food for wildlife, from bears to blue jays.

The state tree of Texas, the pecan is indigenous to the Mississippi River basin; pecans are an essential ingredient in Southern cookery. A mature tree produces about 500 pounds of nuts a year.

Medicinal Benefits Second only to macadamia nuts in fat, pecans are a yin tonic and a warming food that help counter cold conditions. One of the highest sources of vitamin B_6 (pyridoxine), they support the nervous system and heart health. Pecans are an excellent source of thiamine, a good source of iron, and they contain the antioxidant ellagic acid. Ellagic acid is an anticarcinogen. Pecans decrease *vata*.

GIFT OF THE WILDS

At a graduation party of my cooking school, Jayme Gregley brought some native pecans. On the counter, an assortment of cakes, cookies, and treats overshadowed her bowl of pecans, which were smaller and darker than commercial pecans. Until, that is, we tasted—as Jayme calls them— the wilds. Their sweet, meaty, robust flavor bursts in the mouth, turning the taste memory of thin-shelled, commercial pecans into cardboard.

On her visit home to Tulsa, Oklahoma, Jayme gathered these from a stand of scrubby wild pecans, cracked them with a hammer, and lightly toasted and salted them. When she was a girl, she told us, the money she earned from foraging "the wilds" paid for her first pony.

Buying These oblong nuts have a smooth light brown, sometimes mottled brown, shell. If the shells are red, they've been dyed. Because of the high fat content, shelled pecans have a shorter shelf life than other nuts. Consume them, ideally, shortly after they are shelled; if this is not possible, refrigerate shelled nuts in a tightly sealed plastic container for a month or two. Freezing holds them in top condition for six months or longer.

See **Hickory Family; Nuts.**

PECAN RICE SEE RICE.

PEPINO
Melon Pear
(*Solanum muricatum*)

My first morning in Lima, Peru, I sat at the breakfast table facing a large bowl filled with fruits I'd never seen before. Which to choose? And then, how to eat it? A pepino drew me—it's neatly contained in the palm of the hand, and its bright yellow, glossy skin with jagged eggplant-purple streaks gives it allure. I found its aromatic, gold flesh similar to honeydew melon—watery, subtly flavored, and not overly sweet.

This native Andean fruit that grows on a bushy evergreen shrub is now produced in New Zealand and California. It's a trendy fruit in Japan.

Medicinal Benefits Pepinos, a subacid fruit, are as good a source of vitamin C as many citrus fruits. They have a fair source of vitamin A and are low in calories.

Use A pepino's many seeds contained in a central cavity are inedible but are easily removed. Its tough skin is slightly bitter and is easily peeled from the fruit. Enjoy out of hand. South Americans and the Japanese eat pepinos almost exclusively as a fresh dessert. Its versatility in New Zealand is compared to a tomato; it goes into soups, juices, or sauces or alongside fish and meat. It will be interesting to see how its use in North America develops.

Buying Pepinos are available in winter and spring. Select a fruit that has a light, sweet aroma, yields to the touch but is not soft, and has a golden pink undercolor. Use immediately or refrigerate, unwrapped, for up to four days. If it is tinged with green, ripen at room temperature.

See **Nightshade Family; Fruit.**

PEPITO SEE PUMPKIN SEED.

PEPPER
Peppercorn
(*Piper nigrum*)

Elias Derby, the first U.S. millionaire, made his fortune importing black peppercorns—a fortune that endowed Yale University. Long before Yale, pepper was the most important spice in world trade; indeed, it was the single most important factor that brought Columbus to America. Pepper, native to India's Ganges River Valley, is the small fruit of a climbing and flowering vine. Like grape vines, they are cultivated on props. Today India remains the primary producer, but pepper is also cultivated in Indonesia, Malaysia, and Brazil.

Medicinal Benefits Historically in Eurasia, pepper was valued to aid digestion, ease pain, cause sneezing, and relieve gas. It stimulates the flow of energy and blood to the body and, because it opens the pores for sweating, it is good at the onset of a common cold.

While black pepper is heating, white pepper is cooling. Both have antifertility effects, depress the central nervous system, act as anti-inflammatories, protect the liver against solvents like tetrachloride, and act as parasite inhibitors. Pepper is a good source of chromium and, in action, reduces *kapha*.

Use Preferably grind pepper to taste; once ground, its flavor rapidly deteriorates. Preground pepper, furthermore, is toasted, and once toasted, it acts as an irritant. Store ground pepper in a dark-colored glass container and use within three months.

At its best, pepper is hot and pungent with sweet or gingery flavor notes. Pepper has more taste than aroma. Once ground, its pungent flavor becomes bitter with long cooking—so add it at the end of cooking. Or place whole peppercorns in a cheesecloth bag, add to a long-simmering dish, and remove prior to serving. Today we use pepper to enhance the flavor of savory dishes. A newer trend, which actually is an old Roman practice, is to use pepper in sweet dishes. It adds zing to herbal teas.

Pepper connoisseurs select their pepper by region. Tellicherry, Lampong, and Sarawak produce the finest-quality pepper; Malabar and Brazilian pepper are overly hot and sharp.

- **Black Peppercorns** Picked when mature but still green in color and sun-dried. The flavor is hot with a hint of sweetness and spice.
- **Green Peppercorns** Picked when mature but still green, cleaned, and packed in brine or dried.
- **Red Peppercorns** Tiny red fruits from the South American tree *Schinus terebinthifolius* are added to peppercorn mixes for eye appeal, but they're effective for both eye and taste bud. These red berries taste sweet and mildly bitter with a resinous flavor.
- **White Peppercorns** All white pepper is picked when red and fully mature; then it's soaked in brine to remove its red outer skin. Because much of pepper's pungency is in its skin, all forms of white pepper are milder than black pepper. Aroma, however, is a different matter,

with the fragrance of white pepper excelling over that of black pepper.

Whole white pepper is available packed in brine or vacuum packed. It is most commonly available when, following the brining step, it is sun-dried. Sun-drying intensifies white pepper's pungency.

See **Herbs and Spices; Pepper Family.**

PEPPERCORN SEE **PEPPER.**

PEPPERCRESS SEE **CRESS.**

PEPPER FAMILY
(*Piperaceae*)

Black pepper is by far the most widely used member of this large botanical family of tropical flowering plants that are Indian and South Asian in origin. Long pepper and kava are other family members.

See **Kava; Long Pepper; Pepper.**

PEPPERMINT SEE **MINT.**

PEPPERS
(*Capsicum*)

Columbus voyaged, unsuccessfully, to find black pepper, and rather than acknowledge his failure, he named the most pungent New World food "pepper." Capsicum peppers are a nightshade vegetable and not related to black pepper.

Even though pepper varieties are legion, they neatly fall into two categories. Chile peppers and sweet peppers are both members of the capsicum family, which is Latin for "box," aptly describing their hollow, boxlike form. The difference between chiles and sweet peppers is that chiles contain fiery capsaicin and are used primarily as a spice; sweet peppers lack capsaicin—and therefore heat—and are used primarily as a vegetable.

The penchant of peppers to cross-pollinate and develop new varieties is matched by our penchant for new and exotic foods. We are apt to see more new pepper varieties as time goes by.

See **Chile Pepper; Nightshade Family; Sweet Pepper; Vegetable.**

PERILLA
Beefsteak Leaf, Shiso
(Perilla frutescens crispa)

Used by the Koreans, Vietnamese, and Japanese, this light green or reddish purple leaf looks like a large basil leaf. A mint relative, it tastes like a tart, minty cinnamon and it has crinkly, sometimes serrated, leaves.

Medicinal Benefits Perilla leaves are a warming herb that act on the lung and spleen meridians and support chi circulation. They are used to treat colds, nausea, abdominal pain, constipation, food poisoning, and allergic reactions. The red leaves are exceptionally high in iron and help build blood hemoglobin. Perilla seeds are used medicinally in Asian medicine.

Use Red perilla both colors and flavors pickled ginger and *umeboshi*, the Japanese pickled plum. Green perilla, which is more strongly flavored, is favored as a fresh herb to season fish, meat, or vegetable dishes. Perilla sprouts, tiny and spicy, often accompany sushi dishes.

Buying Fresh perilla leaves are available in Asian markets; they should be used within two days of purchase. They're also available salted and dried as a condiment. Perilla is easy to grow and makes an attractive border plant.

See **Herbs and Spices; Mint Family; Umeboshi.**

PERSIAN LIME SEE **LIME.**

PERSIAN MELON SEE **MELON.**

PERSIMMON
(Diospyros kaki, D. virginiana)

I liken eating an unripe persimmon to having the business end of a vacuum cleaner in my mouth—and the sensation lingers even after spitting out the fruit. Ah, but eating a ripened persimmon is as pleasurable as eating an unripened one is horrible.

—Lee Reich, *The New York Times*

The persimmon, a glossy, bright red-orange fruit that looks like a plastic tomato, is native both to North America (*D. virginiana*) and Asia (*D. kaki*). When it is mature, its flavor is a blend of apricots, plums, and honey. Immature, its astringent tannins cause one big pucker. The word "persimmon" comes from Algonquian *pessemin;* dried and ground, it was mixed with wild nuts and jerked game as pemmican.

Persimmon is one of the few trees of the ebony family that grow in a temperate region, and its hard and durable wood is highly valued for golf club heads and weavers' shuttles. Native persimmons are not commercially available but may be found growing wild. Food historian Raymond Sokolov reports that the "powerfully fragrant" wild persimmon is superior in taste to the Japanese fruit and about the size of a small lemon.

Medicinal Benefits A ripe persimmon is cooling and moistening and a yin tonic that treats the heart, large intestine, lung, stomach, and spleen and helps reduce excessive heat and mucus. It helps counter dry weather or dry conditions in the body, such as thirst or a dry, hacking, or unproductive cough. It also relieves bleeding, including bleeding hemorrhoids and constipation. An astringent, or underripe, persimmon, cooked, treats diarrhea. Chinese medicine advises against combining persimmon and crab at the same meal, as it can produce extreme diarrhea.

Persimmons are an excellent source of vitamin C. Ayurvedic cuisine notes that the persimmon helps promote clarity but in excess can create pain and stiffness. It reduces *pitta* and *kapha.*

Use Eat a persimmon as you would eat a ripe mango—out of hand. Cut the persimmon in half and spoon out the meltingly jellylike flesh, add it to a fruit salad, or puree it for beverages and fresh fruit sauces. Cooked, it is tasty in compotes, sorbets, puddings, and quick breads. Or, like the Algonquian Indians, dry your persimmons; they are a delicious and versatile dried fruit and, unlike most other dried fruits, hold their brilliant gold color without the assistance of a sulfur treatment.

For no-fuss persimmon "sherbet," halve a persimmon, wrap it tightly in plastic, and freeze it for at least four hours, then eat it out of the shell with a spoon. Freezing is not recommended for other applications, because it reduces the pulp to mush.

Buying The Asian persimmon originated in China. It is widely cultivated by the Japanese, who consider it their national fruit. Japanese cultivars, now grown in California and some southern states, are pointed like an acorn at their base. They become very soft and squishy when ripe. The smaller, tomato-shaped Fuyu is nonastringent and remains firm when ripe.

Select plump fruits that have a smooth skin and an intact green cap. Persimmons are mainly available in the late fall and early winter. These common varieties are:

- **Cinnamon Persimmon** A lighter yellow Fuyu-type persimmon, the flesh of which has a rust-color speckling, making it look as if it's been sprinkled with cinnamon. It has a sweet and rich flavor with spicy notes and is excellent in any fresh application.
- **Fuyu (Fuji) Persimmon** Orange or orange-yellow in color and tomato shaped, the Fuyu is not as astringent and may be eaten when it is as firm as an apple.
- **Hachiya Persimmon** Heart shaped and vivid orange. When ripe it feels like a balloon full of water. If purchased when still firm, store upside down to ripen, turning it occasionally.
- **Hyakume Chocolate Persimmon** A Fuyu variety that has an exceptionally dark-colored flesh and skin.
- **Sharon Fruit** (also called **Israeli Persimmon**) A nonastringent persimmon, this round and sweet fruit may be enjoyed when it is firm.

See **Dried Fruit; Fruit.**

PICKLING ONION SEE **ONION.**

PIE CHERRY SEE **SOUR CHERRY.**

PIGEON PEA SEE **BEANS AND LEGUMES.**

PIGNOLI SEE **PINE NUT.**

PIGWEED SEE **AMARANTH GREENS; FAT HEN.**

PIMIENTO SEE **PAPRIKA.**

PINEAPPLE
(*Ananas comosus*)

The pineapple, which originated in Brazil, is not a fruit in the ordinary sense of the word. It is a multiple organ that forms when the fruits or berries, the indented "eyes" of a hundred or more separate flowers, coalesce together. Its high sugar content and lush flavor make it one of the most popular tropical fruits. Early Spanish explorers named this fruit *piña* because it is shaped like a pinecone.

The pineapple is a perennial herbaceous plant that grows nearly five feet high. It has a stout stem on top of which grows the fruit, which is rather like the crowning ornament on a Christmas tree. Some miniature pineapple plants are available as houseplants. It is the only fruit of its family that is in widespread cultivation. The pineapple is a symbol of hospitality and often appears in household art motifs. Start noticing these pineapples and you'll soon see them on everything from brass door knockers to light fixtures.

Medicinal Benefits The pineapple is a yin tonic that supports the spleen, stomach, and bladder meridians and helps regulate water and heat. It contains an anti-inflammatory enzyme, bromelain, which not only aids digestion of starches and protein but literally digests foreign microbes, diseased cells in the bronchial tissues, and intestinal parasites. Pineapple juice relieves chronic bronchitis and has a soothing effect on a sore throat. Pineapple reduces *vata* and *pitta*.

Unlike most fruit, pineapple contains negligible amounts of vitamins A and C. It is remarkable for its high percentage of the important trace mineral manganese, which is an essential component of digestive enzymes for proteins and carbohydrates.

Use Ripe pineapple is pleasingly sweet for a day or two. (Immature pineapple is overly acidic and lacking flavor; if overly ripe, it rapidly deteriorates.) To improve its overall flavor, store a pineapple upside down for a day or two before cutting it. As its sugar is more concentrated at its base, inversion enables the sugars in the stem end to develop. Once cut, or if purchased cut, use within a day or two.

Bromelain in fresh pineapple lowers a food's capacity to retain water. It is therefore an effective meat tenderizer, but it turns milk sour and prevents gelatin or agar from gelling. Fresh pineapple has no effect on yogurt or ice cream but, if allowed to sit in a fruit salad, the salad will become soggy. Since bromelain is neutralized by cooking, cooked or canned pineapple may be used freely in salads and gelatins.

Thickly peel a pineapple to eliminate its eyes and slice it into desired sizes. Remove the fibrous core of a pineapple—unless it's a coreless miniature or baby pineapple. Add to salads or eat by the slice. Use as a garnish or puree and use as a topping. Broiling heightens pineapple's flavor.

Buying A sweet, fragrant aroma is the single most important key to selecting a ripe pineapple; so take a good sniff at its base where it's most aromatic. Once picked, a pineapple will not become sweeter, so if it lacks a scent, don't buy it. A ripe pineapple feels firm when squeezed. Also look for glossy, golden orange skin; a small, compact, and fresh-looking (rather than dried) leafy crown; a fruit that is heavy for its size; and eyes that are flat and almost hollow. An overmature pineapple is soft and mushy.

Pineapple is available throughout the year, with peak supplies in the springtime.

See **Dried Fruit; Fruit.**

PINEAPPLE GUAVA SEE **FEIJOA.**

PINE MUSHROOM SEE **MATSUTAKE.**

PINE NUT
Pignoli, Piñon
(*Piñus pinea, P. koraiensis, P. edulis, P. gerardiana, and others*)

In rural northern New Mexican cafés, my favorite purchase is pine nuts by the shot glass. The thin shell is easily removed by cracking it between your teeth. Pine nuts are rich, both in taste and in price. As the name suggests, they come from pine trees, specifically those that have seeds large enough to be edible. Such varieties grow in various parts of the world. The U.S. domestic supply comes mainly from the Mediterranean stone pine and a Chinese pine. The piñon of the Southwest is foraged and available locally at roadside stands and in regional markets.

Medicinal Benefits Pine nuts are a chi and yin tonic that stimulate blood circulation and support the lungs, liver, and large intestines. They are warming and have a lubricative action that helps alleviate coughs and constipation. Like all fatty nuts, they aggravate all conditions when eaten in excess. Pine nuts reduce *vata*.

The Mediterranean stone pine nut is much higher in protein than any other nut or seed and lower in vitamins and fat than the domestic piñon. The piñon is richer in vitamin A and the B vitamins and minerals, and it contains 14 percent protein.

Use Whole pine nuts are eaten as a snack, either raw or roasted and salted. They are a main ingredient in pesto and are tasty in cakes, crackers, candies, casseroles, and, when ground, in soups. Because of their high price and limited availability, pine nuts are used sparingly. I follow and recommend to you the old Roman custom of seasoning pine nuts in asafetida (see page 23).

Buying When purchasing pine seeds in the shell, look for dark-colored shells—the light-colored shells contain undeveloped seeds.

WASH UP WITH MAYONNAISE

Since childhood, piñon foraging has been one of my favorite fall expeditions. Watch the pine jays—when they cluster in the piñon and start pecking at cones, don't delay. Wearing old clothes, shake piñon branches with a rake or long stick until the cones fall to the ground. Collect the cones in something disposable, such as burlap bags or boxes (plastic doesn't work because the gum tars it stuck). At home, place the tightly closed cones on a foil-lined cookie sheet and bake at 350°F for 10 minutes, or until the cones open and the house is filled with a heady pine fragrance. Allow to cool. Shake or pick out the pine seeds from each cone, crack them individually, and savor.

To clean your clothing and hands of the pine pitch that gums up everything it touches, wash with salad oil or mayonnaise, and then soap and water. Once the cones bake, the sap hardens to a varnish-like sheen and is no longer sticky.

When purchasing shelled nuts, look for creamy white, plump kernels; refrigerate until use to retard rancidity.

See **Nuts.**

PINK BEAN SEE **BEANS AND LEGUMES.**

PIÑON SEE **PINE NUT.**

PINQUITO SEE **BEANS AND LEGUMES.**

PINTO SEE **BEANS AND LEGUMES.**

PIPALI SEE **LONG PEPPER.**

PISTACHIO
(*Pistacia vera*)

The fruit of a small evergreen tree and a cashew relative, the pistachio originated in Asia Minor before recorded time. The nut grows in clumps similar to grape clusters. It is prized for its pleasant, mild flavor and fetching green color. Iran, Turkey, and Afghanistan are the largest producers of pistachios, and Americans consume nearly 90 percent of the world's supply. Commercial crops were planted in California in 1968, and today California is the world's second-largest pistachio producer.

Medicinal Benefits Pistachio is a chi and yin tonic that supports the liver and kidneys and eases constipation. The pistachio is remarkably nutritious. It contains antioxidants and is an excellent source of vitamin B_6, phosphorus, and zinc. Like most nuts, it reduces *vata*.

Use A favorite way of eating pistachios is out of hand or as a cocktail nut. They are also an ingredient in pistachio ice cream, Turkish delight, nougat, and halvah. Pistachios may be substituted for other nuts in recipes. One cup of unshelled pistachios yields about ½ cup of nutmeats.

Buying Most pistachios are sold roasted and salted. Because the shell of pistachios splits open as the nut matures, they do not have as lengthy a shelf life as other whole nuts do. Don't bother to crack unsplit nuts, as the kernel is immature.

California pistachios are generally larger than those from the Middle East. An Afghan pistachio shell has a natural pink tint; other varieties are tan. Some pistachio growers and importers dye the nut red, which exposes the kernels to the chemical dyes. Favor plain Jane pistachios over Day-Glo reds. By law, imported pistachios are fumigated with methyl bromide or Phostoxin. The fresh crop is available in the fall.

See **Cashew Family; Nuts.**

PITAYA SEE **DRAGON FRUIT.**

PLANTAIN
(*Musa paradisiaca*)

The astringent, oversize banana called the plantain figures prominently in Latin American and Asian cookery, where it is used as a starchy vegetable. Unlike the ubiquitous sweet banana, the plantain is never eaten raw.

Medicinal Benefits Plantains are cold in action; they support the large intestine, liver, stomach, and spleen functions and help regulate heat, water, and mucus. Those with yellow skins are high in vitamin A. They contain a fair amount of vitamin C, are an excellent source of potassium, and are high in calories. Plantains are cooling, reduce *pitta*, and soothe the intestines. When astringent in flavor, they also calm *kapha;* when sweet, they reduce *vata*.

Use As with a banana, peel just prior to use, unless, of course, you wish to bake or grill it in its skin. To peel a plantain, cut off both ends, slit the peel along one side, and remove. The fresh color is creamy yellow or bright pink. The starchy, bland green plantain may be used as a potato—fried, baked, simmered, sautéed, or mashed.

A yellow-ripe plantain may be prepared like the green plantain or with apples or sweet potatoes as a sweet dish. A black-ripe plantain may be cooked as you would a ripe banana; unlike the banana, a plantain will hold its shape and texture.

Buying Do not be intimidated by a black or brown peel: As the plantain ripens, it darkens. A ripe plantain is not hard; it has give like a banana and a sweet flavor. Avoid any that are cracked or overly soft. They are available in Asian and Latino markets and, increasingly, in supermarkets, natural food stores, and greengrocers.

Store plantains at room temperature and do not refrigerate unless absolutely soft (refrigeration stops their ripening). Plantains are available year-round.

Be Mindful Plantains contain a substance called chitinase that is associated with the latex-fruit allergy syndrome. If you have a latex allergy, you may very likely be allergic to bananas as well as papayas and avocados.

See **Banana; Fruit.**

PLEUROTE See **OYSTER MUSHROOM.**

PLUM
(*Prunus domestica*)

> Green plum—
> It draws her eyebrows
> together.
> —Buson

The juicy, sweet-tart plum is a cousin to the peach and the cherry and grows on every continent except Antarctica. The plum has been used by man since prehistoric times, and there are numerous varieties that range in size, shape, and color—from yellow, green, and black to every shade between red and purple. Today there are hybrids of plums and apricots (see **Pluot** entry). California supplies 90 percent of the U.S. commercial crop.

Medicinal Benefits Plums are a yin tonic and support the bladder, liver, large intestine, stomach, and spleen functions. They circulate chi and help regulate heat and water. Plums aid digestion, relieve dehydration, constipation, and thirst, and help stabilize energy flow. According to Chinese texts, they relieve the feeling of "steaming bones" and build body fluids.

Purple plums are more cooling and better for nervous disorders than are yellow plums, which are slightly warming. An acid fruit, plums are not recommended for people with stomach ulcers or inflammation. Plums, sweet or sour, reduce *vata*. Sweet plums reduce *pitta*.

Due to their high content of oxalic acid, eat plums in moderation; otherwise they may deplete calcium from the body. Plums provide sugar but no starch, some potassium, vitamins A and C, and a fair amount of silicon.

Use Plums' sweet-tart bite makes them especially delicious in pies and tarts; sweet they are also eaten fresh, stewed, and made into preserves, wines, and liqueurs. Sloe, a wild plum (*P. spinosa*), is used to make sloe gin. A prune is a dried plum. Cooking plums in an acid base like lemon juice intensifies their color; cooking them with an alkaline base like baking powder reduces their color.

Buying/Foraging Of the thousands of plum varieties in existence, about 20 are grown commercially, most classified as European or Japanese. Purple or blue European plums are small and firm. Red, yellow, or green Japanese varieties are generally larger and juicer.

In the market, the test for a good plum is temperature. Pass your hand over a bin of fresh plums, and they emit a perceptible coolness. If not, they're old and will taste insipid. A ripe plum should be plump and yield to soft pressure. When immature the skin is shiny but turns a dull matte when ripe.

Purchase plums that are plump, slightly soft to the touch, especially at the tip, and with a dull matte skin (if the skin is shiny, it's not ripe). Some ripe plums, especially the "prune" plum, have a powdery white bloom when ripe. Avoid shriveled, split, overly soft, leaky, or bruised fruit. If not fully ripened, leave plums out at room temperature for a few days (they

CHILDREN KNOW BEST

"Don't eat those sour plums," parents admonish, "they'll give you a bellyache." And children go right on eating them.

Immature plums (and apples) stimulate the production of digestive enzymes that support the function of the stomach, liver, and gallbladder. Immature plums are pickled in salt and sold throughout Mexico and Asia. They're sold fresh in Greece and other Balkan countries. In the country of Georgia, sour plums are made into a highly flavored sauce, *tkemali*.

Unripe plums and apples are rich in citric, malic, and succinic acids, and contain phenolic compounds and hydrolyzable tannins, which help increase hydrochloric acid levels.

won't become sweeter but will soften), then refrigerate for up to three to five days.

Wild plums proliferate throughout temperate regions and may be found in abandoned lots, wooded land, or open spaces. If you ever come across a thicket of plums—wild trees are scrubby, not stately—with ripe fruit, sample fruits from more than one tree. The flavor varies dramatically from one to another, and though most will be tart, odds are you'll find a tree or two with remarkably sweet fruit.

See **Fruit; Pluot; Prune; Prune Family; Umeboshi.**

PLUMCOT See PLUOT.

PLUOT
Aprium; Plumcot

A plum-apricot hybrid is rather like apple pie à la mode—either is good by itself, but when combined it is better. While apricots are a superior fruit in terms of flavor, aroma, and texture, they are so fragile that it's hard to get a good one; plums are more sturdy. So take the best that each has to offer, up its sugar content, and you've got a smooth-skinned, firm but juicy fruit that is exceptionally sweet and aromatic. Pluots are often trademarked and have increasing availability in our markets, from late spring to early fall. Their skin and flesh colors vary widely between yellow, orange, and purple.

Generally a plumcot is a 50-50 cross between an apricot and a plum while a pluot is typically 75 percent plum and an aprium is 75 percent apricot. Individual varieties are often trademarked.

See both **Apricot** and **Plum** entries for comparable Medicinal Properties, Use, and Buying details.

See **Chile Pepper; Fruit; Poblano; Prune Family.**

POI See TARO.

POLENTA See CORN.

POMEGRANATE
(*Punica granatum*)

Eat the pomegranate, for it purges the system of hatred and envy. —Muhammad

When I lived in New Mexico, a pomegranate tree grew by the backyard fishpond, and the hummingbirds could not get their fill of the brilliant, salmon-red blossoms. It likewise seems hard to get a fill of the fruit's edible seeds (arils), which have little pulp but lots of juicy, ruby red juice.

The word "pomegranate" means "many-grained apple." From China to the Mediterranean, the many-seeded pomegranate symbolizes fecundity. A Turkish bride throws the fruits to the ground, and the number of seeds that pop out predicts how many children she will bear. This unique fruit, a Persian native, is now widely cultivated in the tropics, subtropics, the Mediterranean region, and Southern California.

Medicinal Benefits Pomegranates are a yin tonic that disperse heat and treat the bladder, spleen, stomach, liver, and large intestine. They promote the production of red blood cells, expel tapeworms (due to their alkaloid, pelletierine), strengthen the bladder (especially for the elderly) and the gums, and soothe ulcers in the mouth and throat.

Punicalagins, the tannins in pomegranates, have free radical activity and therefore treat heart disease and help protect against cancer. Clinical data shows the effectiveness of pomegranates in treating breast, lung, and prostate cancer. Pomegranates are high in pantothenic acid and therefore help with the assimilation of fats, protein, and carbohydrates. The peel treats chronic diarrhea and dysentery. Pomegranates reduce *pitta* and *kapha*.

Use Pulling pomegranate seeds from the fruit is a sticky task but a sweet one—and best if not hurried; but as the juice makes a permanent stain, protect your clothing. The speedy way is to quarter the fruit then submerge a piece in a bowl of water and use your fingers to separate the seeds, which will sink from the bitter white membrane that will float. The juice is easier to extract: Bruise the fruit by rolling it with the palm of your hand on a hard surface until it is soft and you no longer hear the seeds popping, then puncture it in one place and either squeeze out the juice or insert a straw and drink.

The fruit is primarily eaten raw and is a

GRENADINE

Today's commercial grenadine is a synthetic concoction. The real thing is easy to make. Here are two ways to make it—the quick way and the traditional method.

Quick Grenadine: Bring pomegranate juice to a boil in a nonreactive pot. Reduce the heat and simmer, uncovered, for 15 minutes to concentrate the juice. Sweeten to taste. Pour into a sterile jar and refrigerate for up to 6 months.

Traditional Grenadine: Briefly process 2 cups of pomegranate seeds (first remove the bitter-tasting white membrane from around the seeds) with 2 cups sugar. The mixture need not be a smooth consistency. Place in a glass jar or bowl and allow to sit for 24 hours. Bring to a boil in a nonreactive pot, then reduce the heat and simmer for 2 minutes, stirring constantly. Strain out the seeds and press the pulp to extract all the juice. Pour into a sterile jar and refrigerate for up to 6 months.

---

common ingredient in Spanish, Italian, Middle Eastern, and Latin American cuisines. It may be used in jelled desserts, sauces, conserves, and syrups. As a garnish, a few of its ruby red seeds sprinkled in a fruit cup or even risotto add dramatic flair.

Pomegranate juice adds a sweet tang to sauces, marinades, and dressings, and its red color looks great in sorbet and ice cream. It makes an excellent marinade for lamb. Pomegranate molasses, made by boiling down and concentrating only the juice, is used in Persian cuisine. Grenadine (see sidebar) is a popular nonalcoholic sweet liqueur used in many beverages and desserts.

Buying Look for fresh-looking, plump, heavy fruit with a leathery skin. The early fall crop has a pink skin, and the later maturing varieties have a red to red-brown skin color. Domestic pomegranates are at peak supply in the fall. Store in a cool, dark place for up to a week, or refrigerate for up to two weeks.

See **Fruit.**

POMELO
Pummelo, Shaddock
(*Citrus maxima*)

Grandmother of—and double, or even triple the size of—the grapefruit, the pomelo is teardrop in shape with a very thick—up to two inches—and coarse peel and weighing up to 22 pounds. Like a grapefruit, its skin and segmented flesh varies from yellow to pink, and from seedless to full of seeds. Pomelo flesh ranges from tangy and tart to spicy and sweet and is typically less juicy, acid, and bitter than a grapefruit. Its drier flesh enables the sections to better hold their shape in salads and desserts.

See **Citrus Family; Grapefruit.**

POPCORN
(*Zea mays praecox*)

[E]ach Grain burst and threw out a white substance of twice its bigness.
—Benjamin Franklin

Many things American—from pop music to Levi's—are popular elsewhere in the world, but popcorn isn't one of them. Munching popcorn at the movies and at home remains primarily an American pastime. Popcorn is not only native to the Americas, but it is the original grandmother of all corn. In her book *The Story of Corn,* Betty Fussell described the remarkable 1948 discovery that established corn's origins. In Bat Cave, Catron Country, New Mexico, Harvard anthropologists dug through layers of more than 2,000 years of accumulated trash, garbage, and excrement.

"The deeper they dug," writes Fussell, "the smaller and more primitive the cobs, until they reached bottom and found tiny cobs of popcorn in which each kernel was enclosed in its own husk, the 'pod popcorn' . . . identified as the genetic ancestor" of modern corn.

The husk of the first corn was just like the husk or hull that encloses each grain of wheat, rice, and all other grains. Early farmers' development of corn varieties in which the husk covered several kernels was an amazing advancement. It also makes corn dependent upon farmers to remove the husk and plant the seed. All other grains can reseed themselves.

Popcorn, a corn variety unto itself, is typified by a hard hull and endosperm that seals in moisture content. About 14 percent of the kernel is water. When popcorn is heated, the trapped moisture becomes steam, which builds up until the kernel explodes.

Medicinal Benefits Popcorn is light and dry, and its thermal property is hot. The Doctrine of Signature suggests that while it's good for moving stuck energy, it may be best used moderately by someone with an explosive temperament.

One cup of popped corn has 54 calories and 2 grams of protein. Its nutritional value can be greatly enhanced by sprinkling it with kelp, nutritional yeast, and herbs. Popcorn reduces excess in a person and therefore aids *kapha.*

Use Place popcorn in a heated, covered pan over high heat for 3 minutes, or until the kernels pop, shaking the pan as necessary to prevent burning. Or pop in a hot air popper according to the manufacturer's directions. One cup of popcorn yields one quart of popped corn. It is traditionally served salted and buttered or sweetened (see accompanying recipe), but today's flavor variations include cheese and chocolate.

If popcorn kernels are dehydrated, they will

not pop; to rehydrate, place popcorn and ¼ teaspoon water per cup of corn in a sealed jar. Set aside for several days, then pop.

Buying Most popcorn kernels are yellow, but red, blue, and white kernels are also available. No matter the kernel's exterior color, the popped corn is always white. Today's hybrid popcorn is bred to expand up to 40 times the kernel's original size and to have a high percentage of kernels that pop.

Be Mindful I cannot recommend microwaveable popcorn or ready-to-eat popcorn, as most brands contain artificial flavorants and refined fat. One of these common artificial butter flavorants, diacetyl, is implicated in causing respiratory ailments.

See **Corn; Grains; Grass Family.**

POPPING BEAN SEE **BEANS AND LEGUMES (NUÑA).**

POPPY SEED
(*Papaver rhoeas*)

The minuscule poppy seed (900,000 per pound) is slate blue and kidney shaped. This favorite seasoning agent has a mildly spicy aroma, a distinctive nutty-sweet, pungent flavor, and a crunchy texture. The milk sap from the unripe seed pods of a different variety, the opium poppy, yields opium and its derivatives, morphine and codeine. Poppies originated in the Middle East, although today most culinary poppy seeds come from Holland.

Medicinal Benefits Poppy seeds are soporific, which means that they sedate and calm the nervous system. They also relieve coughs and are considered medicinal for the colon. In India, they're valued as a fertility agent and are recommended for pregnant women and new mothers. Poppy seeds help reduce *vata* and *kapha*.

Use The seeds have a long culinary tradition, especially in Middle Eastern, Central European, Slavic, and Balkan cooking. Whole poppy seeds top breads and bagels and are mixed into cake, muffin, and bread batters and dough. Ground poppy seeds are mixed with a sweetener and other ingredients and used as a filling for croissants, strudels, and cookies such as hamantaschen. In Middle Eastern and Indian cuisine, poppy seeds are featured in pudding and vegetable dishes.

Buying Store poppy seeds tightly covered in a cool, dark cupboard for up to a year. If they develop an acrid, sharp, bitter, or unpleasant flavor, they've become rancid. Toss them. In addition to slate blue poppy seeds,

---

CARAMEL CORN

For those times when you're hungry for a quick and satisfying snack, here's a fantastic one. It will bring out the kid in you.

Makes 4 quarts

  1 cup honey or maple syrup
  4 quarts unsalted popped corn
  1 cup toasted almonds or peanuts (optional)

Place the honey in a medium saucepan over medium-high heat and bring to a boil. Lower heat to medium and simmer without stirring for about 5 minutes, until the syrup reaches 270°F on a candy thermometer. (The syrup's appearance as it cooks also indicates readiness—initially it is frothy, then as the froth recedes, the syrup becomes thicker and denser. When it's a shade darker, it's ready.)

Pour the hot syrup over the popped corn and nuts, if using. Quickly stir to coat, taking care to not touch the burning hot syrup. To make popcorn balls, butter your hands and quickly form the warm candied corn into desired size.

AS SOOTHING AS MOTHER'S MILK

A slice of poppy seed cake today can cause tomorrow's urine analysis to test positive for opium or an opium derivative. No wonder poppy seed cake soothes. The seeds are so soothing, in fact, that they used to be given to infants and young children to quiet them. Thus the Latin name for poppy comes from the word *pap,* or "teat," which also explains our word for infant cereal, "pabulum."

---

there are yellow and brown varieties with some limited availability.

See **Poppy Seed Oil; Seeds.**

POPPY SEED OIL

A culinary oil made from poppy seeds has been used since antiquity and is an ingredient in Turkish cuisine. Look for unrefined poppy seed oil online or in specialty food shops.

PORCINO SEE **BOLETE.**

PORTOBELLO SEE **MUSHROOM, COMMON.**

PORTULACA SEE **PURSLANE.**

POSOLE
Hominy, Nixtamal, Pozole, Samp, Slaked Corn

In New Mexico, posole refers to soup cooked for traditional feast days, and it also refers to the slaked corn that goes into the soup. This corn is possibly the most amazing Native American food.

Throughout the Americas, most corn was processed into posole, enhancing the flavor, shortening preparation time, and increasing its mineral and vitamin content. To make posole, whole dried corn is boiled with wood ash or slaked lime until the hull is softened and washed off. It is this hull, the same one that gets stuck in your teeth when eating popcorn, that makes cooking whole dry corn nigh impossible.

Medicinal Benefits Posole is 20 to 300 percent higher in calcium than dried corn, depending upon what it was slaked with. In one study, a half cup of blue corn contains 1 mg calcium; when slaked in juniper wood ash, it contains 334 mg calcium. Slaking dramatically increases both calcium and niacin. The niacin in posole is also more bioavailable than from dried corn. Posole and posole products support the heart and also the kidneys due to their mineral concentration. They reduce *kapha.*

Use Soak dried posole overnight or for several hours, drain it, and cook it for an hour, or until the kernels "butterfly" or splay open. Use this as the base for a grain pilaf or salad, or turn it into a soup using your favorite soup ingredients, with or without meat or beans. It makes a very satisfying soup, to which I usually add onion, winter squash, celery, and a strip of kombu.

Buying Posole, made from white corn, is available dried and often frozen in supermarkets, natural food markets, and Latino markets. It is also available canned as hominy, but this usually tastes bland.

See **Corn; Masa; Masa Harina.**

POTATO
(*Solanum tuberosum*)

The potato is a starchy tuber, a swollen underground stem of the nightshade family and the world's fourth-largest food crop after rice, wheat, and corn. Americans eat about a potato a day, according to USDA figures, and one in every three restaurant meals includes potatoes.

The potato originated in Peru and was introduced into Europe in 1536. As an acre of potatoes outproduces wheat by three times, the potato is valued as a cheap and plentiful crop. Unlike grains, potatoes are not an export crop, as they are more perishable.

Medicinal Benefits Potatoes nurture the kidney, spleen, and stomach functions and are a chi and yin tonic that help cool overheated conditions and inflammations (except some arthritic conditions). They treat acidosis and neutralize body acids. Their juice has antibiotic properties, helps lower blood pressure, and treats stomach or duodenal ulcers. An Asian kitchen remedy to ease acid reflux, gastro-esophageal reflux disease (GERD), or heart-burn is to drink a cup of fresh potato juice every morning before breakfast.

The primary nutritional value of potatoes is as a complex carbohydrate food; they have negligible protein and fat. Their phytochemicals include carotenoids and polyphenols. Potatoes are a good source of vitamin C, and a fair source of vitamin B_6 and iron. Potatoes reduce *pitta* and *kapha*.

Use I find almost every potato preparation, from mashed potatoes to potato salad to hash browns, works well with the skin intact. And the skin provides important nutrients and fiber. From 10 to 50 percent of a potato's potassium may be lost during boiling (so save and use their cooking water); whereas steaming, baking, and frying do not significantly reduce potassium. Potatoes are cooked to make their starch more digestible; they may be prepared whole, chopped, or shredded. Most potato dishes are served warm, with the notable exceptions of potato chips and potato salad.

Buying/Storing Select firm potatoes that are clean, smooth, and free from soft spots or darkened areas. New potatoes may be refrigerated for up to a week. Mature potatoes are best stored in a dry, ventilated, dark area between 41 and 48°F. If refrigerated, some of their starches turn into sugars, develop more of the toxin solanine (see "Be Mindful," below), and they become discolored when fried.

There are multiple potato varieties and more expected. They typically, however, fall into the following classifications, each of which is better suited to certain types of cooking than to others.

- **Fingerlings** Shaped like long, chubby fingers, these yellow, pinkish, purple, or white potatoes are superlative. An heirloom Peruvian crop, fingerlings have a silky fine texture and a creamy, pleasing flavor.
- **New Potato** Not a specific variety but, rather, any freshly harvested potato with thin, flaking skins and a sweet flavor. New potatoes require less cooking than mature potatoes; they hold their shape better after cooking, and are best boiled or steamed within one week of purchase. Typically a boiled potato is started in cold water, but new potatoes should be cooked in boiling water (if brought to boil starting in cold water, they toughen).
- **Purple Potato** They are similar in flavor and shape to the russet with an indigo skin and a lighter purple flesh. When fried, purple potatoes turn a dingy gray color, so boiling, steaming, or baking is recommended.
- **Red Potato** Characterized by a thin, reddish skin, ranging from pink to dark red in color. Moister than a russet or long white potato with a waxy, white, crisp flesh, the red potato is best boiled, but it can also be roasted or fried.
- **Russet Potato** Also called Idaho potato or baking potato. It has an elongated cylinder with yellowish brown skin. Its dry, floury, or mealy texture suits it to baking, frying, and making potato pancakes or dumplings.

CREAMY (DAIRY-FREE) MASHED POTATOES

For rich and delicious mashed potatoes, add avocado. As you take a forkful, just imagine your teeth slipping through a nibble of avocado that is even more velvety than the potatoes—what a lovely texture and flavor surprise. My daughter rolled her eyes when she imagined the combination—but on a recent visit, she and the kids cleaned up every last bit.

You may peel the potatoes if you wish, or keep them intact for the extra nutrients.

Serves 2

> 2 to 3 fist-size yellow potatoes, quartered
> 1 tablespoon unrefined salt, plus more as needed
> 1 small avocado, diced
> ¼ cup extra virgin olive oil or hemp oil
> 1 tablespoon dried dill or 2 tablespoons chopped fresh dill
> Freshly ground black pepper
> Squeeze of lemon juice

Place the potatoes in a medium pot and add cold water to cover. Add the salt and bring to a boil over high heat. Reduce the heat slightly and cook at a steady simmer until the potatoes are very tender and easily pierced with a fork, 15 to 20 minutes.

Drain the potatoes, reserving the liquid. Pass through a ricer into a bowl or mash with a potato masher or fork. Fold in the avocado, oil, dill, pepper to taste, and lemon juice. Season with salt if needed. If necessary, gently mix in 1 to 2 tablespoons reserved potato cooking water for desired consistency. Serve immediately.

- **White Potato** Round or long with a smooth, tan-colored skin and a firm texture. The white potato is an all-purpose potato for baking, steaming, mashing, and frying.
- **Yellow Potato** Also called Yukon Gold or Yellow Finn. A waxy, yellow-fleshed potato that is multipurpose; it's excellent baked, fried, or boiled.

Be Mindful Commercial potatoes are among the top four vegetables with the highest pesticide residues; as possible, favor organic potatoes.

Since 1995, genetically modified (GM) potatoes have been marketed in the United States. They contain DNA from the bacterial toxin *Bacillus thuringiensis*, commonly known as Bt. Simply put, when beetles munch the leaves of bioengineered potatoes, they die. Although any nonorganic potato may be GM, at this time they are primarily russet-type potatoes.

Do not eat the potato sprouts ("eyes") or any green-colored flesh or greenish skin; they contain the poisonous alkaloid solanine. This alkaloid, a nerve poison, can cause drowsiness, itching, diarrhea, headaches, and vomiting. A potato that causes a sharp, burning sensation on the tongue has excessive alkaloid levels. Cooking at over 340°F partly destroys the alkaloid.

Last, for some people there appears to be a positive correlation between consumption of potatoes and other nightshade vegetables and the aggravation of arthritic symptoms.

See **Chuño; Nightshade Family; Vegetable.**

POTATO STARCH

Soak cooked, dried, and ground potato in water and its starch precipitates out from the cell walls. When dried, this potato starch yields a fine powder. Potato starch is used as a thickener for sauces, soups, and stews or for dusting bread prior to baking. If added to bread dough in a ratio of ¼ cup potato starch to 8 cups flour, the bread remains fresh longer. It tolerates higher temperatures than cornstarch or wheat flour when used as a thickener; for such use, it is first dissolved in cold water. Potato starch is a finer and lighter product that potato flour made from whole ground potatoes. Both are used primarily in gluten-free products.

POZOLE SEE **POSOLE.**

PRICKLY PEAR
Cactus Pear, Indian Fig, Tuna
(*Opuntia ficus-indica*)

The sweet and juicy fruits of the opuntia cactus are popular in local cuisines worldwide. As its name suggests, the fruit is shaped like a pear and perches atop a cactus pad; both are covered with glasslike prickles (glochids). Remove from the fruit these little spines, along with their coarse skin—which is colored green, orange, red, or mauve. The tangy pulp, which contains many hard edible seeds, is often an iridescent ruby red.

Medicinal Benefits Prickly pears are astringent and tonifying to the colon and lungs and treat diabetes and diarrhea. They contain a metabolite of dopamine and therefore are medicinal for people with diseases of the nervous system such as Parkinson's. Prickly pears are high in ascorbic acid, magnesium, and bioflavonoids. For *pitta*, they are powerfully cooling and reducing.

Use Although the spines are mechanically removed before the fruits are marketed, inevitably a few hard-to-see ones remain. Skewer a fruit on a fork and lightly singe the skin (like singing pinfeathers from poultry) to permit handling. Or skewer the fruit, and holding it firmly on a cutting board, peel the skin and spines.

To serve prickly pear, slice and serve raw in a salad or fruit cup, as a garnish, or as the base for an unusual salad dressing. Or puree the pulp and sieve it to make a dramatically colored jam, syrup, ice, or beverage from the juice.

Buying Prickly pears are available in Latino markets, the specialty produce section of some supermarkets, and specialty food markets, except during the summer. Some new varieties are seedless. Select those that are tender and fresh-looking. Refrigerate for up to a week.

See **Cactus Family**; **Fruit**; **Nopal.**

PRIMARY-GROWN YEAST SEE **NUTRITIONAL YEAST.**

PRUNE
(*Prunus domestica*)

All prunes are plums, but not every plum can become a prune. The deciding factor is moisture content. Try drying a juicy plum, one that still contains the pit, and fermentation will spoil it before it can dry; a drier plum, like a damson or the French d'Agen, will dry without fermenting. Traditionally, ripe plums were sun-dried for several days and finished in bakers' ovens. Today they are dehydrated to 21 percent moisture in special ovens immediately after harvest.

Valued from ancient times, the premier prune was produced mainly in southwestern France until this century. California now supplies 70 percent of the world's supply. Almost all the crop is the California French prune (originally from the Agen area).

Medicinal Benefits Prunes are an excellent tonic for a sluggish liver. They are a high-fiber food; ounce for ounce, they contain more food fiber than dried beans. The fiber in prunes, together with its oxalic acid, stimulates the colon. To relieve constipation, prunes are most effective simmered in water until plump rather than eaten dried. Prunes are an excellent source of vitamin A and are a B-complex vitamin source. They are also an excellent source of iron (nonheme or vegetable quality), providing more than a third as much iron as an equal serving of liver. Prune fiber lowers blood cholesterol. Prunes reduce *pitta* and *kapha*.

Use Besides being stewed and eaten as a breakfast side dish, prunes are added to savory dishes like salads, soups, the Jewish carrot dish *tzimmes*, and Moroccan *tagines*. They're used in desserts as stuffing, cakes, and confections. In several cultures, a salt-preserved sour plum is popular (see **Umeboshi**).

Buying Choose prunes that are slightly soft and somewhat flexible, with a black skin that is blemish-free. Purchase tightly sealed packages. Prunes are available whole, with or without the pit, dried in paste form, or as a juice. Size varies from 20 prunes per pound to 80 per pound, and is a factor only of size, not variety.

Commercial prunes are preserved with potassium sorbate (the potassium salt of sorbic acid) to protect against mold and yeast spoilage. Organic prunes contain no additives.

See **Plum; Prune Family; Umeboshi.**

PRUNE FAMILY

In early spring, prune family white or pink blossoms rival all other blossoms for their beauty and fragrance. This family (sometimes considered a subdivision of the rose family) is Eurasian in origin and its small shrubs or trees are widespread throughout northern temperate regions. Their fruits (technically almonds are a fruit) are among our most popular foodstuffs. Unfortunately, they're also a favorite food of insects, and some of the prune family members are among our most intensively chemically cultivated crops.

See **Almond; Apricot; Cherry; Nectarine; Peach; Plum; Prune; Sour Cherry.**

PSYLLIUM
(*Plantago psyllium*)

Plantain—no relation to the banana-like plantain—is a small, low-to-the-ground leafy weed widely dispersed in temperate regions and found growing in most lawns throughout the United States. It's one of the most important greens to forage because of its versatility both in the salad bowl and in herbal blends, poultices, and infusions. The seed of one plantain variety, psyllium, and sometimes just its husk, is the most popular herb for people suffering from bowel irregularities. Not only do countless colon support products contain psyllium, but it is often the only active ingredient.

Medicinal Benefits Psyllium seed and its husk are highly demulcent; they swell when mixed with liquid and stimulate normal bowel elimination. This gives a mucilaginous coating to the intestines and provides bulk to the stool, making it useful for both constipation and mild cases of diarrhea. By moistening membranes, psyllium soothes irritation and absorbs digestive toxins. Psyllium reduces *pitta*.

Use Psyllium husks are available in bulk as well as in capsules and numerous colon health products. The products often contain artificial colors and flavors. For constipation, stir 2 tablespoons flaked (or whisk 1 teaspoon powdered) psyllium seed husk into 1 cup of water or juice. Drink immediately as it quickly thickens into an applesauce-like consistency. For diarrhea, stir or whisk into buttermilk or water with lemon juice.

See **Fiber; Seeds.**

PUMMELO SEE POMELO.

PUMPKIN SEE SQUASH; SQUASH, WINTER.

PUMPKIN SEED
Pepito
(*Cucurbita pepo*)

The pumpkin seed, or pepito, is the largest and costliest of seeds; it is not from the jack-o'-lantern pumpkin variety. They are from a South and Central American squash that is grown specifically for its seeds. These seeds are hulled and often sold salted or seasoned. You may harvest seeds from domestic pumpkins or any wither squash, but they have their fibrous hulls intact.

Medicinal Benefits Pumpkin seeds are medicinal for liver, colon, and spleen functions. They are higher in protein (29 percent) than many other seeds and nuts, and they are a valuable source of the important omega-3 fatty acids. An excellent source of iron, zinc,

phosphorus, and vitamin A, they also contain calcium and some of the B vitamins. Chewing raw pumpkin seeds with their hulls is a popular home remedy to expel pinworms or other intestinal parasites. Pumpkin seeds are *tridoshic*, or balancing to all body types, when used in moderation. They are most calming to *vata*.

Use Pumpkin seeds have a slight crunch, an interesting green color, and a mildly nutty flavor. Pumpkin seeds are available roasted and salted or raw. Light roasting improves their flavor and digestibility (see accompanying recipe).

See **Pumpkin Seed Oil; Seeds; Squash; Squash Seed; Squash, Winter.**

ROASTED PUMPKIN SEEDS

The seeds from pumpkins and other winter squash make a healthy and tasty snack. To hull, crack each seed individually between your teeth, discard the hull, and savor the tender kernel. Or, better yet, crunch and swallow the seeds and hulls together. Whole seeds, incidentally, are a home remedy for expelling pinworms or other intestinal parasites. As the seed passes through your digestive tract, its fibrous, insoluble hull gently scours out unwelcome guests. (Commercially available pumpkin seeds, also known as *pepitas*, are dehulled.)

To roast pumpkin seeds, preheat the oven to 350°F. Remove and discard the stringy membranes from the seeds. Place the seeds in a pan; add a pat of butter and a dash of cinnamon or curry powder and salt. Bake for about 15 minutes, stirring once, until the seeds are aromatic, crisp, and lightly browned.

PUMPKIN SEED OIL

Roasted pumpkin seed oil is green-black and pleasantly flavored. A popular ingredient in Croatian and Styrian (Austrian) cuisine, it has recently become available in the United States. Pumpkin seed is a good source of omega-3 fatty acids; therefore, I cannot recommend this product, as roasting denatures these heat-sensitive fatty acids. Hopefully raw pumpkin seed oil will become available for use in salad dressings.

See **Fat and Oil; Pumpkin Seed.**

PUNTARELLE SEE **CHICORY.**

PURPLE MANGOSTEEN SEE **MANGOSTEEN.**

PURPLE PASSION FRUIT SEE **PASSION FRUIT.**

PURSLANE
Ma Chi Xian, Portulaca, Pussley, Verdolaga
(*Portulaca oleracea*)

A near relative of the garden flower portulaca, or moss rose, purslane is valued in Asia, Central America, and Europe both as a potherb and as a medicinal herb. Purslane leaves and stems have a slightly sour and salty taste. It grows wild throughout the United States. When I taught cookery in New Mexico, my older Latino and Native American students fondly recalled *verdolagas,* as they called purslane, as a staple green from their childhood. This small annual herb with numerous branches and succulent leaves looks something like a jade plant. For my father, this "water weed" is the bane of his garden; it's never reached weed status in my garden, as my and my chickens' appetite for purslane keeps it well trimmed.

Medicinal Benefits Purslane is a cold food that acts upon the bladder, large intestine, and liver. It helps disperse damp and hot conditions as well as toxins. It is used externally to remove toxins from eczema, insect bites, and boils. Internally, purslane is used for dysentery, constipation, urinary infections, hemorrhoids, and postpartum bleeding.

It is an excellent source (and the highest vegetable source) of omega-3 fatty acids, especially alpha-linolenic acid—one cup of fresh purslane leaves contains 400 mg of alpha-linolenic acid. It contains antioxidants (betacyanins and betalain), which have antimutagenic properties. It's also rich in vitamin A, C, and some B vitamins and carotenoids. In moderation, purslane is *tridoshic.*

Use A German friend, Karen Di Giacomo, showed me how to pickle purslane seeds in vinegar as "poor woman's capers." They were smaller than capers but quite tasty. More often,

though, I add purslane flower buds, leaves, and stems—raw or blanched—to salads or simmer or stir-fry them in any vegetable dish. Their mucilaginous quality makes them an excellent addition to a soup or stew.

Buying/Foraging Dried purslane is available in Chinese pharmacies. Fresh purslane is sometimes found in specialty food shops or farmers' markets. Odds are, however, that it's outside your back door. Although you may harvest purslane throughout the summer, its flavor is superior before it flowers.

PUSSLEY SEE **PURSLANE.**

MY CHICKENS AND CHOLESTEROL-REDUCING EGGS

Egg yolks from chickens that were fed purslane contained 10 times the amount of omega-3 fatty acids, which reduce cholesterol, as yolks from supermarket eggs, according to a study done at the National Institute on Alcohol Abuse and Alcoholism in Bethesda, Maryland. Of all leafy green vegetables, purslane is the richest known source of the important omega-3 fatty acid.

After reading this information, I went outside to observe my small clutch of banties scratching through my garden. By far, their favorite entrée is bugs and caterpillars. But of the various leafy greens that they peck at, purslane is a close second to a centipede. How do they "know" about purslane's superior nutrition?

QUINCE
(*Cydonia oblonga*)

 I once inherited an old, unruly bank of quince; I trimmed the trees back, and every fall thereafter they produced a few precious, primitive-looking, furry green fruits. The quince, resembling a misshapen apple or pear, is called "the ugly duckling of the apple family." The dazzling, salmon-pink blossoms, however, are one of the most beautiful spring blooms.

An Asian native, the quince was once a staple in many homes in the Northern Hemisphere. Thanks to its generous amount of pectin, it is unparalleled in preserving jellies and as a confection. When home preserving and candy making became unfashionable, so did quince. Happily, the current interest in so-called exotic produce is bringing it back to market.

Medicinal Benefits The astringent taste of raw quince produces a drying, choking sensation, like an unripe banana or crabapple. Quince treats diarrhea, but an excess may exacerbate constipation, dryness of the mouth, difficulty of speech, and palsy symptoms. Astringent foods in moderation reduce *pitta* and *kapha*.

This high-pectin fruit provides a fair amount of vitamin A and potassium and is a good source of fiber. Pectin helps lower cholesterol.

Use The quince is unusual among fruits in that it is almost always eaten cooked, as most varieties, when raw, are exceedingly astringent, hard, and bland. Some varieties, however, are better raw than others, and in Mexico slices of raw quince are eaten with salt, chile, and lime. Stewing, baking, or braising brings out its unique, perfumed flavor, which complements meat, savory, and sweet dishes. If a quince is on hand and I'm baking apples or making an apple pie, I always include quince slices; their lush flavor, texture, and aroma enhance the apples.

Since the fruit maintains its shape even with long cooking, it encourages experimentation. Remove the quince peel, which tends toward bitterness. For jams or jellies, use the fruit alone or in combination with low-pectin fruits such as berries or grapes. A candy-like fruit leather made of pure quince and sugar is a specialty in Spain, Sicily, Hungary, France, and in Germany, where it is called *Quittenwurst*. With cooking, the quince's flesh turns from yellow-white to a delicate pink or red, a reminder in the fall of their exquisite spring blossoms.

Buying The availability of quince is best in the fall. Select firm fruits that are smooth-skinned. Handle carefully because, despite their hardness, they do bruise easily. The quince has a powerful aroma, which, when the fruit is left at room temperature, will perfume a room for several weeks. Quinces store well and may be refrigerated for a month or more.

See **Apple Family; Fruit.**

QUINOA
(*Chenopodium quinoa*)

Native to the high valleys of the Andes, the grainlike quinoa (pronounced KEEN-whah) was revered by the Inca as their mother grain. The Spanish squelched its cultivation, but, fortunately, it endured in remote locations. The plant flourishes under extreme ecological conditions, including high altitude, thin cold air, hot sun, radiation, drought, frost, and poor soil. Although most quinoa varieties grow best at 10,000 feet and above, some varieties grow as low as sea level.

I've sown, weeded, harvested, and threshed quinoa. It's a beautiful plant. Its boldly colored leaves, stalks, and seeds are as flamboyant and varied as the traditional clothing of the former Inca, the Quechua and Aymara. It's a lovely garden ornamental—and its greens, immature seed heads, and mature seeds are edible.

Quinoa, a member of a goosefoot family, is not a true cereal grain but is used as one. About the size of millet, the periphery of each disk-shaped grain is bound with a narrow germ or embryo. When cooked, the wispy germ separates from the seed, and its delicate—almost crunchy—curlicue makes a great visual and textural contrast to the soft grain.

Medicinal Benefits Quinoa is a warming chi and yang tonic that supports the kidney and heart functions. Because it is easy to digest, quinoa is ideal for the very young and the convalescing, and it makes an ideal endurance and fitness food. It decreases *kapha*. *Vata*- and *pitta*-type people may enjoy it in moderation or seasoned to match their needs.

The United Nations World Health Organization reports that quinoa is at least equal to milk in protein quality. Quinoa has the highest protein of any grain (16 percent) and, unlike other grains, is a complete protein, with an essential amino acid profile similar to that of milk. It contains more calcium than milk and is high in lysine, an amino acid that is scarce in the vegetable kingdom. Quinoa is a rich and balanced source of many other vital nutrients, including iron, phosphorus, B vitamins, and vitamin E.

Use Quinoa is so easy to prepare and quick cooking that it readily becomes a favorite grain staple of people regardless of their culinary preferences. Most quinoa available today has been prewashed. But taste a few grains before using; if they are bitter, then wash quinoa well before cooking to remove the protective saponins that effectively keep the birds from eating it in the field. Because the seeds are so small, it's imperative to use a strainer. Place

---

MOTHER GRAIN STAGES A COMEBACK

When I visited Bolivia and Peru in 1987 to research my book *Quinoa: The Supergrain*, I admired the quinoa sold in the open-air Aymara and Quechua Indian markets (quinoa was not yet available in restaurants or in stores). These gentle people, proud of their other merchandise, were reluctant to speak of their quinoa. The Spanish had denigrated quinoa as chicken feed and as food fit only for the poor. For more than 400 years, these people believed that if they fed quinoa to their children, it would make them stupid. As soon as these indigenous people could afford it, they chose foods of the upper and middle classes, pasta and white bread. And Bolivia, at that time, had the highest rate of infant mortality.

Fortunately, North American interest in quinoa is helping reinstate the status of the mother grain in its homeland. Today quinoa is available in restaurants and stores throughout the Americas.

the quinoa in a bowl, add water to cover, and, using the palms of your hands, lightly scrub for a few seconds. Strain out the washing water and repeat this process. Pour all the quinoa into the strainer and run fresh water over it for 5 seconds, or until the water runs clear.

Imported quinoa takes 2 cups of stock or water per cup of grain. Our smaller domestic quinoa requires 1½ cups of stock or water per cup of grain. Both yield about 3 cups of cooked grain and take about 15 minutes to cook.

As versatile as rice, quinoa can be substituted freely for rice, millet, or couscous in any recipe. It's also good plain as a side dish or as an ingredient in soups, pilafs, and casseroles. For an unusual pudding, substitute quinoa for the rice in your favorite rice pudding recipe.

If you have a garden patch of quinoa, the leaves are edible when the plant is young; so also are the immature seed heads, which are interchangeable with broccoli in many recipes.

Buying Imported quinoa was first marketed in the United States in 1984 and is now available in many supermarkets as well as in natural food stores. Although quinoa will not set seed east of the Rocky Mountains, commercial crops are grown in several western states and Canada. Both black and red quinoa have some availability; they are more robustly flavored than is the white quinoa.

See **Goosefoot Family; Grains; Quinoa Flakes; Quinoa Flour.**

QUINOA FLAKES

Similar in size and use to instant oats, quinoa flakes are an excellent oat substitute for breakfast porridge or in cookies, quick breads, muesli, and granola.

See **Quinoa.**

QUINOA FLOUR

Quinoa flour, used primarily by people with wheat allergies, adds interest to quick breads, cookies, and cakes.

Because quinoa is a soft grain, you can pulverize it to a flourlike consistency in a coffee mill or blender. A grain mill, however, gives superior results. If the quinoa has a bitter taste, then wash it and dry it before grinding. Quinoa flour, which has had its bitter-tasting saponin removed, is available in natural food stores and some supermarkets.

See **Flour; Quinoa.**

RADICCHIO SEE **CHICORY.**

RADISH
(*Raphanus sativus*)

Grown in Egypt since at least 2780 BC and originally black skinned, the radish helped fuel the slave labor on the pyramids. Several centuries later, Asia developed a range of red, green, and white radishes. And what a range—from our petite cherry radish that matures in a mere three weeks to a 40-pound daikon that takes up to three months to mature. Larger radishes inspire culinary artists wielding a sharp knife to carve garnishes as fanciful as radish "butterflies," with wings so delicate that they "flutter" as they are set upon the table. Radishes belong to the cabbage family.

Medicinal Benefits A cooling food, radishes support chi circulation, help remove toxins, and dispel excess heat, mucus, and damp. Radishes act on the lung and stomach meridians; they stimulate the appetite and are an excellent digestive aid. They have antibacterial and antifungal action.

In the West, radishes are commonly used in a salad or as an hors d'oeuvres to arouse the appetite; in Asia, they're served at the end of the meal, especially a fatty meal. European folk medicine recommends eating radishes—several a day—on an empty stomach to help melt gallstones and kidney stones. Radishes reduce *vata* and *kapha*.

Radishes are a good source of ascorbic acid, folic acid, and potassium. They are a good source of vitamin B_6, riboflavin, magnesium, copper, and calcium.

Use The pungent, peppery taste of radishes makes them a popular salad ingredient and snack. Cooking transforms their tangy bite into a delicate sweet kiss. Radish greens add flavor and nutrition to soups, and when tender they may be used as a stir-fry ingredient; they are, however, too coarse for a salad.

Buying Select firm, crisp radishes with bright, fresh-looking greens. Avoid limp or oversize radishes, which tend to be pithy and overly hot. Also avoid those that are split and have leaked their flavor. These are the common varieties:

- **Black Radish** When fresh, this pungent radish is unsurpassable cooked into a stew or stir-fry. The size and shape of a turnip, it has a coarse black skin and a spunky pungent-tasting white flesh. When old, it's overly hot, bitter, and unpleasant.
- **Easter Egg Radish** A rainbow-colored collection of small globe radishes.
- **French Breakfast Radish** Red with a white tip, this small cylindrical radish has a mild flavor.
- **Icicle Radish** White and several inches long, comparable to a red radish in bite and texture.

RADISH SOLITAIRE

Here is a gorgeous but simple soup. The radish color softens to a rich pink, set off by one green leaf nestled in among a few shimmery strands of translucent noodles.

Serves 4

4 small red radishes with greens
5 cups vegetable stock
2 small fresh shiitake mushrooms, thinly sliced
½ ounce fine bean thread noodles
Unrefined salt and freshly ground pepper

Trim away all but the innermost leaf from each radish. Place the stock, mushrooms, and noodles in a soup pot and bring to a boil. Reduce the heat and simmer for 2 minutes, or until the noodles are almost tender. Add the radishes and simmer for 2 minutes, or just until the radish turns from red to pink. Season with salt and pepper.

Divide the soup among individual soup bowls and serve immediately, before the radish color fades.

- **Red Radish** Cherrylike in size and shape, this is the most common radish variety; an elongated red radish is more pungent than a round one.

See **Cabbage Family; Daikon; Vegetable.**

RAISIN

What's great about raisins is that they're still cured the old way, in the sunshine rather than in commercial ovens. As we know, the sun imparts its own energy, and sun-cured foods often taste better than oven-dried foods. Take four pounds of grapes and remove most of their water, and you'll have one pound of raisins. The other components of the grape, most notably the sugar, remain intact. The high sugar content of raisins has made them a popular food since time immemorial. Until the European medieval period, when cane sugar was imported, raisins were second only to honey as a sweetener.

You may be eating more raisins than you imagine, as more than a hundred processed foods use raisin paste or juice. Because of their natural sugars, flavor enhancers (tartaric acid), and preservatives (propionic acids), raisins are a valuable and common ingredient in yogurt, ice cream, and baked goods.

Virtually all our domestic raisins are produced in California's San Joaquin Valley, within a hundred-mile radius of Fresno. Harvested in August, grapes are spread on paper trays and sun-dried for two to three weeks in the vineyard, then the stems are removed and they're sorted and packaged.

Medicinal Benefits Valued as a high-energy food, raisins contain, by weight, about 60 percent sugar. They contain antioxidants, but most of their oxygen-sensitive vitamin C, abundant in grapes, disappears in the drying process. Raisins are comparable to hamburger in iron. Raisins reduce *kapha* and *pitta* and, when soaked or stewed, are least aggravating to *vata*.

Use A popular ingredient in baked goods, stuffings, and chutneys, raisins are also enjoyed out of hand, in trail mixes, with salted nuts, and covered in chocolate.

Before using raisins in baked goods, plump them by soaking them in water, rum, wine, or brandy for 15 minutes, or simmer them for several minutes. A plumped raisin doesn't become overly dry when baked.

Buying A new raisin crop is available each September. Look for plump raisins that show no signs of being overly dried or sugary. Store raisins in a dark, cool cupboard to prolong their shelf life and prevent flavor and texture deterioration. If refrigerated for more than six months, they become sugary. Store raisins away from brick or concrete walls, as raisins can absorb moisture from these surfaces.

- **Golden Raisins** are Thompson grapes that are and dried and either treated with sulfur dioxide to prevent them from darkening or oven dried. (In England, they're called **Sultanas.**)
- **Monukka Raisins** are from an especially large grape; they are an old variety used specifically for drying. It makes a large raisin with a pleasing, mellow sweetness.
- **Muscat Raisins** are made from the large, seed-bearing muscat grape. This raisin is extra sweet with a distinctive fruity flavor; the seeds are mechanically removed. Muscat raisins, about twice the size of other raisins, have limited availability; they are more easily found in the fall and winter months. Muscats are prized for baking, especially in fruitcakes.
- **Thompson Raisins,** are medium size, dark-colored seedless raisins that are sun-dried for several weeks. They have a shriveled appearance and comprise 95 percent of U.S. domestic raisin production.

As grapes are among the top seven fruits highest in pesticide residues, these toxins are more concentrated in raisins. Fortunately, organic raisins are free of toxic residues. Rather than being fumigated with methyl bromide, organic raisins are frozen to −5°F to rid them of insects.

See **Currant (Dried); Dried Fruit; Grape.**

RAMBUTAN
(*Nephelium lappaceum*)

A tropical fruit from Malaysia, rambutan's name aptly means "hair of the head." The

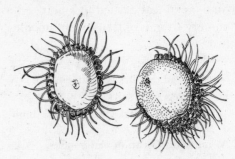

plum-size rambutan is red-orange to green-yellow and covered with soft green spines. A relative of the lychee, the rambutan's inner grayish white, grapelike flesh surrounds a single seed.

Use The soft shell is easy to peel with a small knife or your thumbnail. To remove the seed, cut the fruit in half lengthwise and cut out or pull out the pit. The flesh has an appealing, sweet, slightly acidic taste and is usually eaten raw by itself or in a fruit salad. Rambutans may also be stewed or pureed and used in jams, jellies, or sorbet. The seeds are roasted and eaten as a snack. The fruit is a good source of vitamin C.

Buying When possible, purchase rambutans that are still attached to the branch; as such they remain fresh much longer and are less prone to rot or infestation.

If not on the branch, select fruits without cracks and that show no sign of moisture or mold on them. Spikes should be flexible and look fresh, and the fruit should have a fresh smell. Store at room temperature for a day or two, or refrigerate in a perforated plastic bag for up to a week. Our domestic supply of rambutans is available from October through May.

See **Fruit; Lychee Family.**

Ramon Fruit See **Breadfruit.**

Ramon Nut See **Breadnut.**

RAMP
Wild Leek
(*Allium tricoccum*)

In springtime the wild leek, or ramp, is foraged in the Northeast woodlands; it is occasionally available in farmers' markets. A ramp has a strong onion-garlic taste and may be used as an alternative to a scallion but in smaller quantities due to its stronger flavor. The size of a large scallion, the ramp has broader leaves like a leek; however, unlike leeks, these leaves splay open.

See **Leek; Onion Family; Vegetable.**

Rapadura See **Sugar.**

Rapini See **Broccoli Rabe.**

RASPBERRY
(*Rubus idaeus*)

As fate would have it, the most delicious fruit of the temperate climate is also the worst traveler. The sweet and tart raspberry is so fragile that it turns to pulp if simply held in the hand too long. This makes local raspberries an expensive and rare summer fruit. A raspberry is a cluster of tiny juicy drupelets that surround a hollow core. It is a member of the rubus family.

Medicinal Benefits

A warming food, raspberries support the liver and kidneys and are a blood and yin tonic. In addition, their leaves, as well as the fruit, strengthen both the kidneys and vision. Ripe raspberries cleanse the blood, benefit the liver, and are a good treatment for diarrhea, mucus conditions, and dysentery. Tea made of raspberry leaf is very strengthening to the female system and is a popular herb throughout pregnancy. It eases childbirth by increasing muscle tone in the uterine walls throughout a woman's cycles, and it reduces menstrual cramps. Raspberries are *tridoshic* in moderation; their astringency makes them especially calming for *pitta* and *kapha*.

A raspberry is an aggregate fruit composed of many miniature fruits, each of which contains a protective outer skin. All that protective skin explains why they are extraordinarily high in fiber, 20 percent per total weight. They contain significant amounts of polyphenol antioxidants and are a rich source of vitamin C and vitamins B_1, B_2, and B_3, and they are a good source of copper and iron.

Use My favorite use of raspberries is to cap a toddler's fingertip with one and then savor her wonderment of this jewel-like fruit; repeat for multiple fingertips and multiple sticky refills. A sprinkling of fresh raspberries is an elegant garnish for puddings, cakes, and fruit dishes. Use in fruit salads, smoothies, and pureed sauces. Raspberry salad dressing, raspberry vinegar, chocolate-covered raspberries, raspberry corn muffins . . . these bright berries enliven all types of dishes. Among jam connoisseurs, raspberry remains unsurpassed. If you have extra raspberries, freeze them in a single layer on a jelly-roll pan. Once frozen, store in a plastic freezer bag in the freezer.

Buying Select raspberries that are fresh, brightly colored, plump, and well mounded in the package. If the green cap is intact, a raspberry is immature and will never become sweet. If the color is dull, the package is stained, or the fruits are leaking, the berries are overmature. Lift and tilt the package to see if the berries move freely; if they stick together, they probably are moldy. Refrigerate and use within 24 hours. Most local raspberries ripen in July; some varieties, however, bear also in September.

Due to climate-controlled airfreight, raspberries from as far away as Chile and New Zealand are available year-round. In flavor, these imports are a poor substitute for local berries.

The most common raspberry is red, but there are yellow, golden, and black varieties. The black one is known as a black cap. The yellow variety, called a white raspberry, is more mildly flavored and is rarely available because it is particularly soft and perishable.

The seven fruits highest in pesticide residues according to the FDA are raspberries, strawberries, apples, pears, grapes, peaches, and nectarines. As you are able to do so, favor organic raspberries.

See **Blackberry Family; Fruit.**

RAW SUGAR SEE **SUGAR.**

RED CHICORY SEE **CHICORY.**

RED KURI SQUASH SEE **SQUASH; SQUASH, WINTER.**

RED PALM OIL SEE **PALM OIL.**

HOW MANY FRUITS DOES ONE RASPBERRY CONTAIN?

Raspberries and blackberries are not true berries. Each tiny bump on a raspberry or blackberry is actually a minuscule fruit, or drupelet. A drupelet is a fruit with a soft outside and a single seed within. Thus a peach is a drupelet, while a raspberry is an aggregate, a cluster of 80 drupelets.

RED PEPPER SEE **CHILE PEPPER.**

RED RICE SEE **RICE.**

REISHI
Ling Zhi
(*Ganoderma lucidum*)

Called the "herb of spiritual potency" and the "mushroom of immortality," the reishi outshines many other mushrooms for its well-documented medicinal properties. Although it grows throughout the world, the reishi is best known and valued in China and Japan, where it has been used in folk medicine more than 4,000 years.

Medicinal Benefits Reishi is an adaptogen, and indeed it sounds like a cure-all. It is the only known source of ganoderic acid, which acts as a natural steroid hormone. An immunostimulant, reishi is helpful for people with AIDS, leaky gut syndrome, Epstein-Barr, chronic bronchitis, and other infectious viruses. It is used as an aid to sleep, as a diuretic, as a laxative, and to lower cholesterol. Reishi mushrooms are antioxidants and liver protectants.

Buying Water extracts of reishi are found as an ingredient in herbal preparations. In the past two decades, cultivation has increased the availability of this heretofore wild, priceless, hard-to-come-by fungus. A boletus type of mushroom, the reishi is found wild in various colors. The red reishi, the most potent medicinally, is the one that is now cultivated. It is available dried, in tinctures, in tablets, and in liquid form in natural food stores and from Chinese herb dealers.

See **Mushroom Family; Vegetable.**

RENKON SEE **LOTUS ROOT.**

RHUBARB
(*Rheum rhaponticum*)

Tightly furled, scarlet, primitive-looking rhubarb sprouting up out of the garden heralds spring—and with it, the springtime ritual of strawberry-rhubarb pie. Rhubarb is not ready to eat until its large reddish celerylike stalks are a foot in length and its forest green leaves seem the size of elephant ears. This perennial plant grows throughout temperate regions.

Rhubarb root has remained a prized medicinal herb for thousands of years, but its tart, astringent stalk has been used as a food only for the past 400 years, since the widespread availability of sugar. Today it is primarily a local vegetable that is available fresh when it's in season. Rhubarb, along with its relative buckwheat, is northern Asian in origin.

Medicinal Benefits Rhubarb is a sour, astringent, and cooling food that removes toxins and heat and helps blood circulation. It's an excellent food to cool an inflamed liver and for detoxifying after eating too much rich food. Rhubarb has a long-term heating effect on the digestive system. It also relieves constipation and reduces *vata* when used a little at a time.

High in vitamins C and A and in potassium, rhubarb also contains tannin, the astringent substance responsible for making your mouth pucker up.

Use Trim off the dried stalk ends of the rhubarb, coarsely chop, sweeten to taste, and stew or boil until tender, 10 to 15 minutes. To be edible, this tart vegetable, which is used like a fruit, demands ample added sweetener. Cook it in a nonreactive (stainless-steel or glass) pan. Rhubarb is eaten in a compote and is used in pies, dessert sauces, and jams.

Buying Rhubarb stalks are available in early spring. Select crisp, firm, glossy, plump, stalks; the sweetest stalks are small and brightly colored. The stalks range from deep red to mottled pink to green. Refrigerate, tightly wrapped in plastic, and plan to use within a few days.

Be Mindful Rhubarb leaves are poisonous. Eating them has caused deaths, probably because of the leaves' high oxalic acid content. Even the fleshy stalks are high in oxalic acid, and so rhubarb is a food that should always be eaten in moderation and is *not* recommended for people who form calcium oxalate kidney stones or for those with inadequate calcium absorption.

See **Buckwheat Family; Fruit.**

RIBES FAMILY

A genus of flowering shrubby plants in the family Grossulariaceae that are native through-

---

"IN THE PINK" SPRING TEA TONIC

Rhubarb tea has a fruity, tangy flavor and a lovely pink color. It's an easy-to-make spring cure for liver-related problems. Do not use for more than five consecutive days, and discontinue if it causes diarrhea.

Serves 2

- 1 stalk rhubarb, chopped
- 3 cups water
- 2 teaspoons mint or chamomile leaves (optional)
- Honey

Place the rhubarb and water in a glass or stainless-steel (not aluminum) pot over medium-high heat and bring to a boil. Reduce the heat and simmer for 5 minutes, then remove from the heat. If using mint or chamomile, add it now and let steep for 5 minutes. Add honey to taste.

Drink in the morning at least 20 minutes before breakfast.

out the temperate regions in the Northern Hemisphere, it includes many ornamental plants and several nutritious berries.

See **Currant; Gooseberry.**

RICE
(*Oryza sativa*)

Grain upon grain
Fresh and delightful as frost
A dazzling jewel
To what can I compare this treasure?
—Yang Ji (Ming Dynasty)

Rice is the staple food for more than half the world's population. What an incomprehensible number of people are probably sitting down right now to a bowl of rice. The word "meal" is synonymous with rice in both the Chinese and Japanese languages, just as in English the word "meal" originally referred to our staple food, ground grain. As grain no longer enjoys this prominence in the United States, it is sometimes difficult to appreciate the importance of rice to cultures where it is *the* primary staple.

Americans eat about 25 pounds of rice per person per year, compared to more than 100 pounds per person per year in the Far East. The United States grows about 1 percent of the world's rice and exports about 60 percent of this crop. Less than 2 percent of the U.S. production is brown or whole grain rice.

Medicinal Benefits Rice is a blood and yang tonic that specifically nurtures the spleen and stomach, calms the nervous system, and promotes good digestion. It quenches thirst, relieves mental depression, and stops diarrhea that's caused by spleen deficiency. White rice digests more quickly than brown; but because it is refined, it is not a strengthening food or nutrient dense. However, it takes a robust digestive system to assimilate brown rice, and many people find white rice easier on their system. White rice is *tridoshic*. Brown rice reduces *vata* and may slightly aggravate *kapha* and *pitta*.

Whole or brown rice is the highest of all grains in B vitamins but somewhat lower than others in protein. It contains 85 percent of the grains' fat, 70 percent of its minerals, and most of the B vitamins. Short-grain rice contains less protein than long-grain rice, but more minerals.

Sweet, or glutinous, rice is more warming, higher in protein, and more easily digested than regular rice. It has the medicinal properties of regular rice, plus it supports the lungs and blood and chi circulation.

Use Rice is unlike such cereal grains as barley, corn, rye, and wheat. It is easy to eat whole, day after day, without tiring of it—whereas most other grains are ground into meal or flour to enhance their palatability. Rice fits in with haute cuisine or with its humble partner beans. Serve rice with a protein complement, or plain or fried, or in soup, croquettes, casseroles, salads, sushi, and breads and desserts.

Rice is the basis of the traditional Japanese beverages amasake and sake and a refreshing Mexican drink, *horchata*. There is a 100 percent rice (cellophane) noodle, and rice is used in various gluten-free products, including bread, chips, crackers, cookies, and beer.

No matter the variety, be it long or short, black or red, regular or sweet, rice for consumption has its inedible outer hull removed. A farmer needs an intact hull for germination, but it is too tough to eat and so it is removed for table use. Once hulled, rice is available to consumers in one of the following three ways:

- **Whole (Brown, Black, or Red) Rice** Whole grain rice has its bran layers intact and therefore all its nutrients are present and accounted for. Furthermore, the bran protects the germ's fragile fatty acids. Black and red rice varieties are available only whole or scarified because if their bran is removed, they look like ordinary white rice.
- **Scarified (Partially Milled) Rice** The bran of whole grain rice makes it slow to cook and, for many people, hard to digest. Therefore, historically, most people ate partially milled or scarified (scratched) rice that had some bran scoured off to shorten its cooking time and ease digestion. Depending upon the degree, scarifying compromises some of a grain's nutrients and exposes the essential fatty acids to light (and light instigates rancidity). In the past, this was not a problem since the rice was coarsely milled at the local millers, a week's supply at a time. Today, however, it is problematic due to increased storage times. Smell scarified rice; if it has an acrid or stale aroma, discard it.
- **White (Refined) Rice** The germ and all of the bran layers are removed so that what remains is a white starchy carbohydrate. Extended shelf life is one advantage of such rice. Many manufacturers coat white rice with glucose or tapioca and nutrients to enrich the rice and give it a shiny appearance. This coating is not listed as an ingredient. Imported rice may be coated with talc, a known carcinogen.

Buying I recommend purchasing whole or scarified rice from a store that has a fast turnover—I typically find the broadest and freshest selection in the bulk bins. As the shelf life for white rice is longer, freshness is typically not an issue.

Rice varieties include:

- **Long-Grain Rice** The most popular rice variety in the United States is long and slender, about five times longer than it is wide. Once cooked it remains intact, fluffily, light, and separate due to its starch content—it is high in amylase and contains little of the more sticky amylopectin.
- **Medium-Grain Rice** A popular rice variety in Latin America, medium-grain rice contains enough amylopectin to make it more sticky, moist, and tender when cooked than long-grain rice. It's about twice as long as it is wide.
- **Short-Grain Rice** Compared to medium-grain rice, short-grain rice is highest in amylopectin, enabling it to best retain moisture and making it stickier when cooked. It is oval in shape and is the favored rice in Asia.
- **Sweet (Glutinous) Rice** This variety is more warming, higher in protein, and more easily digested than regular rice. Here the term "glutinous" refers to the grains' stickiness and *not* to the protein gliadin that is common to wheat, rye, and barley. See the **Mochi** entry for a popular Japanese food that is readily available in natural and Asian food stores. A black variety of sticky rice is a popular Thai food.

Types of processed rice include:

- **Germinated Brown Rice (GBR)** For the most protein-rich option, soak rice in tepid water for a day to initiate germination, then cook in fresh water. This activates its enzymes to make a more complete amino acid profile. GBR rice has limited availability but is easy to prepare yourself.

- **Instant (Minute) Rice** This white rice has been fully cooked, then dehydrated. Its texture and nutrients are compromised, and it takes about 5 to 10 minutes to cook. If you're in the habit of making instant rice, make a pot of full-cooking rice and note how much more flavor, pleasure, and energy it imparts.
- **Parboiled (Converted) Rice** This is whole grain rice that is steamed or parboiled, dried, and then milled. This treatment drives the nutrients from the bran into the grain itself and gelatinizes some of the grain's starch and turns the grain from white to yellow. The rice is then refined or used as brown rice. Milled parboiled rice is nutritionally superior to white rice.

These are the various rice cultivars:

- **Arborio Rice** This is a starchy, nearly round rice that absorbs up to five times its weight in liquid to yield a creamy dish with a toothsome texture. This white rice is a featured in the Italian dish risotto.
- **Basmati Rice** This aromatic and premium Indian rice was traditionally aged a year to develop its nutty flavor. Unlike other rice varieties, as basmati cooks it elongates rather than plumps, to yield a flaky and light grain that doesn't clump together. It has an aroma reminiscent of buttered peanuts. Both white and brown varieties are available. **Texmati** and **Calmati** are trademarked basmati hybrid cultivars that are grown in, respectively, Texas and California.
- **Carnaroli Rice** This Italian import is a white, short-grain rice that absorbs more liquid than other grains but still stays firm during cooking. This makes it ideal for risotto and other creamy-but-chewy rice dishes. As a crop, it has a low yield and therefore is the most expensive Italian rice.
- **Jasmine Rice** Imported from Thailand and now also grown in the United States, jasmine rice has a floral aroma and a tender, silky texture. It is a long-grain, crystal-clear white rice that is soft and slightly clingy when cooked.
- **Pecan Rice** This partially scarified rice is pale gold and long-grain. Grown in Louisiana, it has an aroma and flavor reminiscent of pecans.
- **Red Rice** is any rice variety with a red bran layer covering a white endosperm. While most are Asian (*O. sativa*), some are African (*O. glaberrima*). Asian red rice varieties with increasing availability are from southern India, Sri Lanka, Bhutan, and Nepal. They are typically scarified, or coarsely milled, so that only part of their colorful bran layer is removed. Lundberg Family Farms' **Wehani**, a large, plump red rice, is whole rather than scarified.
- **Sushi Rice** A short-grain, glutinous rice that, contrary to many foods, is prized for its neutral flavor. Since sushi rice doesn't overpower the palate, it doesn't detract from the alluring flavors of raw fish. Rather than each cooked grain being fluffy and distinct, cooked sushi rice sticks together; thus, when formed into an artful sushi morsel, it holds its shape.
- **Valencia Rice** A medium-grain Spanish rice that is featured in paella, a rice dish seasoned with saffron that includes fish, chicken, meat, and vegetables. It is available in specialty stores. Valencia rice is similar to Italian Arborio rice.

- **Vialone Nano Rice** A short, round (*nano* means "dwarf" in Italian) white rice that is favored in risotto. Vialone nano is available in specialty shops.

A WONDROUS KITCHEN REMEDY

Rice porridge has been popular throughout Asia for 5,000 years. While it's called congee, jook, or kitchari, gruel is an apt translation, but please don't let that put you off! Western equivalents are the Old English and Native American kitchen remedies barley water and atole. Congee is deeply satisfying. Long cooking makes it easy to assimilate and absorb the ingredients' medicinal properties.

The Buddha, as noted in Vinaya Pitaka [Book of Discipline], praised congee as giving "life and beauty, ease and strength. It dispels hunger, thirst and wind. It cleanses the bladder. It digests food." It is an ideal food for the young, convalescents, people under stress, or those with a weakened digestive or immune system. Congee can be a lifesaving remedy for someone with an inflamed, ulcerated digestive tract or with extreme diarrhea.

The recipe is simple: Simmer 2 tablespoons rice (or another grain) in 2 cups water over the lowest possible heat (or in a slow cooker) for 4 to 6 hours. Add one or more seasonings to taste, such as ghee, nuts, vegetables, meat, spices, or herbs. In *The Book of Jook,* Bob Flaws has translated specific congee recipes from Chinese medical texts for a wide range of ailments. For example, cook a teaspoon each of honey and butter with the rice and water to build energy and blood. This helps counter emaciation, a dry cough, vomiting blood, dried skin, and dry, difficult constipation.

Be Mindful Despite labels advising you not to wash white rice, I advise washing it to remove the glucose, tapioca, starch, or other coating that producers may apply to give the rice a shiny appearance. Imported rice may be dusted with a known carcinogen, talc; washing reduces, but does not entirely remove, talc.

Some organic rice producers do not use additives. Curious about your favorite rice? Find the phone number for your rice grower online; give them a call or e-mail them to find out if they use additives. I consistently find that quality producers and manufacturers are happy to field consumer questions.

See **Grain; Grass Family; Mochi; Rice Bran Oil; Rice Flour.**

RICE BRAN OIL (NOT RECOMMENDED)

This by-product of the rice industry is a highly refined oil.

See **Rice.**

RICE FLOUR

Unlike the bran of wheat, the bran of brown rice is an insignificant colorant; therefore, white and brown rice flour may be used interchangeably in any recipe. Because rice flour is gluten-free, it cannot be used to make a conventional bread dough.

Brown rice flour imparts a lively, seedlike flavor to baked goods. Since brown rice flour, like other whole grain flours, starts to oxidize as soon as it's milled, it should be used fresh. (Whole grain flour is rancid if it tastes or smells strong and acerbic.) White rice flour doesn't become rancid; it has a slightly smoother texture and less flavor and nutrients.

There is a significant performance difference among rice types. Unfortunately, packages do not usually specify which is which; you may assume it is made from multipurpose medium- or short-grain rice unless the package specifies that it is not for use in baked goods. These are the types of rice flour:

- **Long-Grain Rice Flour** Suited to breadings, sauces, and use as a thickener; it is not good for baking, as it yields a wet, soggy product with a large crumb.
- **Medium- and Short-Grain Rice Flour** This flour is multipurpose: It can be used as a thickener and in cookies, crackers, and quick breads. It gives a sandy crumb that is similar to corn flour in its dryness. It is excellent for dusting bread dough when shaping it into loaves because it dries the dough's surface without adhering to it so that any excess may be brushed off.
- **Sweet Rice Flour** Yields a moist, dense texture that's unsurpassable in brownies and Japanese-style dumplings.

Buying Mail-order suppliers and full-scale natural food stores carry the largest selection of rice flours. All-purpose white rice flour is available in many supermarkets and Asian markets.

See **Flour; Rice.**

RICE MILK See **NONDAIRY MILK SUBSTITUTES.**

RICE SYRUP

Rice syrup is a mildly sweet syrup with an almost butterscotch flavor. I've made it from scratch the traditional way, adding 5 percent of sprouted barley as an enzymatic starter to a pot of cooked and still warm—but not hot—rice and then incubating it for several days. The resulting mixture is cooked and run through a food mill to produce a sweet puddinglike cream. It's a much different product from today's high-tech rice syrup, which looks rather like honey but is less cloyingly sweet.

For most palates, rice syrup is not an adequate honey or sugar substitute in baked goods, as its sweetness is easily overpowered by other flavors. It's at its best straight from the jar, as a delicious spread for peanut butter sandwiches, waffles, toast, and crackers.

LEMON-DROP COOKIES

These sunshine-colored cookies have a refreshing lemon flavor. The rice flour gives them an airy, delectable crumb.

Makes 30 cookies

- 3 cups medium- or short-grain brown rice flour
- ½ teaspoon baking soda
- ½ teaspoon freshly grated nutmeg
- ½ teaspoon unrefined salt
- 8 tablespoons (1 stick) unsalted butter, melted
- ½ cup honey or maple syrup
- 1 teaspoon pure vanilla extract
- Juice and grated zest of 1 organic lemon
- 15 blanched almonds, halved

Preheat the oven to 375°F.

Sift the flour, baking soda, nutmeg, and salt into a large bowl.

In a separate bowl, whisk together the butter, honey, vanilla, and lemon zest and juice. Stir the wet ingredients into the flour mixture.

Using your fingers, form the dough into small rounds. Place on a greased cookie sheet and press each cookie down with moistened fork tines (or damp fingers) to 2½ inches in diameter and ½ inch thick. Press an almond half into the center of each cookie.

Place in the oven and bake for 10 to 12 minutes, until the bottoms are lightly browned. Remove to a rack; cool. Store in an airtight container for a week or more.

Rice syrup has a long shelf life and requires no refrigeration. Unlike honey, it does not crystallize. If rice syrup hardens in cold weather, set the jar in warm water until the syrup softens.

See **Sweeteners.**

RICE VINEGAR SEE **VINEGAR.**

ROCAMBOLE GARLIC SEE **GARLIC.**

ROCHA PEAR SEE **PEAR.**

ROCKET SEE **ARUGULA.**

ROCK MOSS SEE **IRISH MOSS.**

ROCKWEED SEE **BLADDER WRACK.**

ROMAINE SEE **LETTUCE.**

ROOIBOS
(*Aspalathus linearis*)

With the 1994 apartheid end in South Africa, export bans were removed and their first food to penetrate our markets was the flavorful herbal tea *rooibos* (pronounced ROY-BOSS). Made from the leaves of a leguminous bush that means "red bush" in Afrikaner, rooibos leaves are finely shredded, bruised, and left in heaps to oxidize and then sun-dried. They color to a deep mahogany red that, when brewed, yields a naturally sweet and nutty-flavored red tea. Of the various herbal teas, rooibos is comparable in flavor to a full-bodied and complex-flavored black tea.

Green or unoxidized rooibos tea is also available but is less popular than the oxidized rooibos; it tastes rather grassy and thin.

Medicinal Benefits Green rooibos is higher in antioxidants than the red, but both are a good antioxidant source. They are low in tannins and are caffeine-free, making rooi-

bos popular among health-conscious consumers. Traditional South African use of rooibos is to alleviate infantile colic, allergies, nervous tension, asthma, skin problems, and digestive complaints. Red rooibos is more warming than the green.

Use Rooibos is available at your local coffeehouse as a hot chai or in an herbal tissan. At the store, you'll also find it as a bulk herb and in numerous herbal blends. Unlike black or green tea, it withstands long brewing and reuse, as it will not become bitter. Serve it hot or cold, with or without milk or added sweetener.

See **Legume Family.**

ROQUETTE SEE **ARUGULA.**

ROSEMARY
(*Rosmarinus officinalis*)

There's rosemary, that's for remembrance.
—William Shakespeare, *Hamlet*

In ancient times, rosemary symbolized both love and death and was a frankincense substitute for the poor. A perennial in mild climates, this Mediterranean region native shrub is often used as a landscape plant as well as a culinary herb. It is a mint relative and its green, silver-tipped leaves look like small pine needles.

The name rosemary comes from "dew" (*L. ros*) "of the sea" (*L. marinus*), as apparently the most delicious rosemary thrives in ocean mist. Its name later came to be associated with the Virgin Mary.

Medicinal Benefits Rosemary is a warming herb and a yang tonic that supports the heart, kidney, liver, lung, and spleen functions. It helps mediate conditions of cold, mucus, and damp. An excellent stimulant, rosemary contains oil of camphor, which gives a pungent flavor and distinctive scent. Rosemary is a potent antioxidant that helps slow the aging process and reduce the risk of heart disease and cancer. It is recommended for headaches, chronic fatigue, poor appetite, low blood pressure, and weak circulation. Rosemary improves poor circulation, lowers cholesterol, eases muscle and rheumatism pains, and treats lung congestion, sore throat, and canker sores. Rosemary stimulates the nervous system, supports mental functions and memory, helps relieve a sluggish gallbladder, and is often used in penetrating liniments and, for lustrous hair, in hair rinses. It is an especially good tonic for the elderly. Rosemary reduces *vata* and *kapha*.

Rosemary tea buffers or alkalinizes an overly acidic stomach. Rosemary tea is also a good aspirin alternative for treating headaches, gas, and fevers. To make the tea, steep 3 tablespoons dried rosemary or 4 springs fresh rosemary in 1 cup just-boiled water for 10 minutes. Strain, sweeten if desired, and drink.

The essential oil of rosemary is used for headaches, fatigue, rheumatism and gout, skin infections, aches and pains, dandruff, and obesity, and as a nerve stimulant, heart tonic, and liver decongestant.

Use With its pinelike camphor flavor, rosemary is more potent than most herbs, and just a little rosemary nicely seasons chicken, lamb, and pork, and it often is added to breads, black olives, biscuits, and seasoned vinegar. Its flavor is not reduced with cooking.

Buying/Growing Rosemary is available fresh and dried. An advantage of purchasing fresh rosemary is that is has a long shelf life and, refrigerated, will slowly dehydrate and will still be usable.

Better yet, one no-fuss rosemary plant in an undisturbed garden spot (or potted and in a sunny kitchen window) will thrive for many years and produce more herbs than you can possibly use.

A "SPA" IN YOUR OWN BATHTUB

For an invigorating and restorative bath, make a big pot of rosemary tea, strain it into your bathwater, slip into the hot water, and how the cares of the world ease away!

Even easier is to add 5 to 10 drops of rosemary essential oil right under the running faucet. This gives a wonderful aroma plus the therapeutic value of the rosemary. For convenience, I keep several bottles of my favorite essential oils right on the tub ledge and mix and match according to my fancy. Rosemary is a favorite, as are lavender, ylang-ylang, geranium, sandalwood, and frankincense.

Be Mindful If pregnant, rosemary is not advised as an herbal remedy or an essential oil; a little as an occasional herbal seasoning is not, however, problematic.

See **Herbs and Spices; Mint Family.**

ROYAL MANDARIN SEE **ORANGE.**

RUBUS FAMILY

This large subgroup of the rose family is typified by woody stems and rose-like spines and is commonly known as brambles. Their better-known fruits are an aggregate of drupelets.

See **Blackberry, Raspberry.**

RUCOLA SEE **ARUGULA.**

RUNNER BEAN SEE **GREEN BEAN.**

RUSSIAN KALE SEE **KALE.**

RUTABAGA
Swede, Swedish Turnip
(*Brassica napus napobrassica*)

The rutabaga is actually a horticultural cross between a turnip and a cabbage; it was created by Swiss botanist Gaspard Bauhin in the seventeenth century. Like a large turnip in shape, a rutabaga has green and purple skin at its top and is golden yellow at the point. Its golden flesh is firmer and sweeter than a turnip, but unlike a turnip, it is not pungent. Rutabagas are a common ingredient in Scandinavian and Scottish cuisine, as this crop thrives in cold climes.

Medicinal Benefits Like other root vegetables, rutabagas are a warming food that strengthen digestion, especially the stomach and spleen; they also help detoxify the liver. They reduce and are thus beneficial for *vata* and *pitta*. As with other cabbage relatives, they contain anticancer, antioxidant properties as well as antibiotic and antiviral properties. Their nutritional profile is comparable to a turnip, but, unlike turnips, they do contain vitamin A.

Use Fresh, young rutabagas make a pleasant-tasting—and beautifully golden colored—puree; they may be substituted for or used alongside carrots, in a salad or soup, or stir-fried, braised, or steamed dish. If old, their flavor develops an assertive and strong flavor. Unless very young, rutabagas are cooked before eating—trim as necessary.

In Scotland they're often mashed and seasoned like mashed potatoes. The dish "tatties and neeps" refers to a side-by-side presentation of mashed (po) "tatties" and "neeps," in reference to the rutabaga's alternate name, Swedish turnip.

Storage Rutabagas have been coated in paraffin to keep them fresh; peel and discard their skin.

Buying In winter, the selection of underutilized root vegetables in some markets may not be worth their purchase price. Turnips become flaccid, hot, and bitter, and parsnips become woody and strong tasting. Whereas even if old, a rutabaga's limitations are workable. Of course, freshly harvested rutabagas are a treat. Select rutabagas that are heavy for their size and firm and that are not withered or overly large. There are also white-fleshed rutabagas.

Rutabagas may cause flatulence in some people who have a similar problem with cabbage.

See **Cabbage Family; Vegetable.**

RYE
(*Secale cereale*)

Unlike other grains, rye appeared quite abruptly in the Bronze Age (1800 to 1500 BCE) of Central Europe as a grain field weed. Rye soon flourished in northern soils and soils that had been depleted by annual crops of wheat. Rye reigned in Western Europe through the Middle Ages, and still flourishes in Central and Eastern Europe and across the Russian plains.

Like a slender wheat in shape, rye has blue-gray overtones and a robust, tangy flavor. The United States produces only 2 percent of the world's rye.

Medicinal Benefits Rye's strong, almost bitter flavor seems to match its strong, weed-like hardiness. It energetically supports the gallbladder, liver, spleen, and heart and helps circulate chi and mitigate problems aggravated by excessive damp or water. Rye is said to build muscles and promote endurance. A broth or congee (see page 303) made of rye is a kitchen remedy for a migraine headache. Rye reduces *kapha*.

Nutritionally rye is similar to wheat, but it contains less gluten. Of the common grains, rye has the highest percentage of the amino acid lysine. It contains eleven B vitamins, vitamin E, protein, iron, and various minerals and trace elements.

Use The main use of rye in the United States is in rye whiskey and, to a lesser extent, in bread. Rye berries are rarely cooked whole by themselves, but for the pleasure of unadulterated rye, I find it a robust dish that makes a tasty treat. One-fourth cup rye berries cooked with a cup of brown rice is also excellent. The secret is to toast the grains first and then to cook them as you would brown rice. Flaked rye is used like rolled oats for a breakfast cereal and in granola; unfortunately, it is not a fast-moving product, so it is apt to be stale.

Be Mindful Rye contains gluten and is an allergen for some people. If you have compulsive eating patterns with gluten-containing products, this is a gluten sensitivity indicator.

See **Grains; Grass Family; Rye Flour.**

RYE FLOUR

Rye flour is available in several different grades. If not made from whole grain rye, it is typically labeled dark, medium, or light (with the darker flour having the most bran) and will have been degermed, giving it an excellent shelf life.

Whole grain rye flour, on the other hand, contains all the bran and germ, is a shade darker than whole wheat flour, and will become rancid with age.

Rye flour is mildly sweet, and I often combine it with another flour to make quick bread, cornbread, muffins, and waffles. The most popular rye bread, sourdough rye, gains its characteristic sour flavor from the starter, not the rye. Pumpernickel bread is colored by something besides rye, usually caramel, to give it its characteristic dark brown color.

Bread containing rye stays moist longer than an all-wheat loaf and slices thinner. Traditional gingerbread desserts were made of rye flour. Today it's easy to find Swedish hardtack crackers made of rye, but it's found in few other products.

See **Flour; Rye.**

SAFFLOWER OIL

Near the rural northern Utah town where I was born grow fields of safflowers with brilliant orange-red flowers; they are a comely crop. The stalks are knee-high and bear multiple blossoms that dry into thistlelike heads and are used in floral arrangements. Their petals are used as a saffronlike food colorant and flavor agent, especially in Mexican cuisine. But it's the oil that this sunflower relative is grown for.

In recent decades, safflower has become a common culinary oil. One variety of safflower seed is high in polyunsaturated fatty acids, predominantly omega-6 fatty acids, and its oil is recommended for use in salad dressings. Another is high in monosaturated fatty acids and typically labeled as a high heat oil. Tradition suggests moderate—if any—use of safflower oil, as it has a reputation in Ayurvedic medicine for not promoting longevity Also, it lacks the historical precedent of the more stable oils olive, sesame, coconut, and palm.

Safflower prefers a semiarid climate; California and Arizona are the principal U.S. safflower growers. Genetically modified safflowers are used in the production of insulin for diabetics.

See **Fat and Oil.**

SAFFRON
(*Crocus sativus*)

Saffron was once used to dye the robes of Buddhist monks because its brilliant golden yellow color signifies illumination. Also valued as a spice, a cosmetic, and a medicine since the tenth century BC, saffron is the stigmas of an autumn-flowering purple crocus, a cousin of our common garden flower.

Top-grade saffron can cost up to $150 per ounce. It has always been almost literally worth its weight in gold both because it must be hand-harvested and because one flower yields but three tiny stigmas. To collect one pound of saffron requires plucking stigmas from 75,000 crocuses, or what will fill a football field. Imagine that.

Medicinal Benefits Saffron is used medicinally as a blood cleanser and to circulate chi. It supports the heart and liver pathways and the digestive system. It eliminates flatulence and eases menstrual problems and depression. Long considered a nerve tonic and an aphrodisiac, saffron is reputed to increase sperm count. I add a few threads to a cup of herbal tea when I'm ready for a soothing, luxuriating respite. Saffron is *tridoshic.*

Use The smallest pinch of saffron gives dishes a brilliant golden yellow color, a deep honey- and haylike aroma, and a unique, rather bitter flavor. To draw out its maximum flavor and color, crumble saffron threads in a small amount of tepid water, soak for at least 20 minutes, then add at the end of cooking (heat destroys some of its properties).

The Pennsylvania Dutch of Lancaster County are called the "Yellow Dutch" because of their generous use of saffron in chicken and egg noodle dishes. Saffron is an indispensable ingredient in French bouillabaisse, Spanish paella, and Swedish Christmas bread. It is used

---

SAFFRON ON A SHOESTRING

Clarke Hess, in the tradition of her Mennonite "Yellow Dutch" grandmother, reports that saffron crocuses are easy to grow, require little garden space, and are a welcome blossom in October when the rest of the garden is in decline. While a first year's harvest might yield a scant tablespoon of saffron, the bulbs quickly multiply.

Be sure to distinguish *C. sativus,* which has three stigmas, from a similar-looking autumn crocus (*Colchicum autumnale*), which is highly poisonous.

---

widely in Indian, Middle Eastern, and North African cuisine.

Buying Saffron threads are about one inch long, wiry, a brick red color, and with tips that are slightly lighter in color. Purchase whole threads, as ground saffron is often adulterated with turmeric, paprika, or another colorant—unless, that is, the ground saffron container includes on the package the saffron's coloring strength and crop year (listed as two years, such as 2010/2011). Quality saffron will have a coloring strength of 190 or more, with 250 being the highest quality. Other cues for quality include: Meets ISO Standards, Category 1, or *Mancha Select.* Store in an airtight container in a dry, cool pantry and saffron will maintain its potency for several years.

Be Mindful Use saffron in *small* amounts, no more than several threads once per day, as larger amounts can be toxic or even lethal.

See **Herbs and Spices.**

SAGE
(*Salvia officinalis*)

A perennial herb with a spicy, sharp, and herby aroma, sage is a universal flavoring agent long valued for its medicinal properties and an earthy taste that is both sweet and bitter. The small bushy plant with downy lance-shaped, two- to three-inch-long green or gray-green leaves has small pink, purple, or white blossoms. A mint relative, it is not to be confused with the larger, similar-smelling sagebrush (*Artemisia tridentata*), which covers much of the high deserts of the western United States and is too overpowering to add to food. If you have a garden or room for potted herbs, consider keeping sage. It grows as easily as thyme and, once established, requires little attention.

Medicinal Benefits Sage is a chi tonic that supports the lungs, liver, heart, kidneys, and uterus. It circulates chi and helps regulate heat, damp, and mucus. Sage is a decongestant whose antimicrobial properties make it an effective gargle, an astringent for abraded or inflamed skin, and a treatment against colds, flu, and fevers. It also increases estrogen and helps treat menopausal sweats. Sage is also a muscle relaxant for nervous disorders such as tics.

Sage stimulates and helps regulate bile flow and so is often combined with fatty meats. Herbalist and author Michael Moore observes that the classical use of sage to decrease lactation "works fine if the tea is drunk cool and the breasts are washed with the tea as well. Several goat keepers I know of use the tea whenever a particular female needs her milk slowed or stopped." Sage reduces *vata* and *kapha.*

In aromatherapy, sage essential oil is used for sores, bacterial infections, bronchitis, catarrh, rheumatism, arthritis, sprains, and fibromyalgia.

Use The bold, almost camphorous aroma of sage becomes even more potent when dried, so use dried sage in small amounts. Young, freshly minced leaves are mild enough to be used in salad. Dried sage goes well with other assertive flavors, such as rosemary, thyme, and bay. It is a traditional flavoring in stuffing and sausage.

Be Mindful If pregnant or epileptic, do not use sage medicinally; occasional use as a culinary ingredient is not considered problematic.

See **Herbs and Spices; Mint Family.**

SAINT JOHN'S BREAD SEE CAROB.

SA KOT SEE JICAMA.

SALAD SAVOY SEE KALE.

SALSIFY
Oyster Plant
(*Tragopogon porrifolius*)

With some imagination, salsify is said to have an oysterlike flavor, which accounts for its alias. My hunch is that the oyster association comes from the milky fluid that oozes from a cut in the fresh greens. To me, salsify tastes like a tame burdock. This long, buff-skinned taproot looks like an undernourished and hairy parsnip, with white, mildly sweet flesh that's similar to burdock but not as flavorful. Salsify is a member of the daisy family and is closely related to scorzonera.

Medicinal Benefits Salsify contains inulin, a natural insulin that supports pancreatic function, which explains why old European kitchen remedies regard salsify as strengthening to the digestion. It also nourishes the kidneys and intestines.

Use Tender young salsify leaves are a good salad ingredient. The purple buds are reminiscent of asparagus in flavor and may be cooked as a potherb. The root can be boiled, sautéed, baked, or simmered in soups and stews. Salsify's flavor is best after a frost, so look for it in the late fall or winter.

Before cooking, give salsify a good scrub and then cut it into the desired shape. Salsify becomes mushy if cooked too long or peeled.

Buying/Foraging Salsify is occasionally available commercially and is readily available wild. Look for it along country lanes and as a sturdy weed in gardens. If you are foraging salsify, dig only the taproots of first-year plants, which have not yet sent up their flower stalk.

In the market, select roots that are firm and crisp rather than soft. The root will be up to eight inches long and will have many tiny rootlets. Large roots tend to be pithy.

See **Daisy Family; Vegetable.**

SALT

Befitting its incalculable value, salt is a traditional housewarming gift in Eastern Europe and Hindu cultures. Though my background is English, if I attend your housewarming party, you can expect a gift of quality salt as a necessary staple. Salt is a life-sustaining ingredient for humans. More essential than currency, salt was wages for Roman soldiers—*salarium*, from *sal*, Latin for salt; thus our term for salary.

Salt is concentrated ocean with its water evaporated and its impurities removed. This is also true for salt mined from the earth, the deposits being remnants of ancient salt lakes and oceans.

Medicinal Benefits Our blood, lymph, and extracellular fluids are like a miniature sea with a composition of 97 percent sodium and chloride and some trace minerals, similar to ocean water. Should the normal saline count in our bodily fluids fall below 1 percent, disorders of the nervous system, glands, and organs would develop.

Because we lose these minerals daily through

normal body processes, they must be replaced. Using quality salt that contains these trace minerals is an easy way to do so.

Sodium, the primary constituent of salt, is one of the three vital electrolyte minerals; it helps convey energy and the spark of life itself. It is this electric charge that enables nerve impulses and muscle contraction; it is vital for every living cell's function.

From an energetic point of view, salt is the most grounding culinary substance and gives foods an earthy, substantial quality. Salt strengthens the kidneys and favorably reduces *vata*.

In mild solutions, salt makes an excellent mouthwash, throat gargle, eyewash, and antiseptic. Straight it is used as a toothpowder.

Use Throughout the world, salt has been and remains the primary flavor additive. When cooked into a food, it heightens, deepens, and unites savory flavors. When added at the end of cooking or sprinkled on a cooked dish, it helps whet the appetite and gives a salty tang. Salt not only aids in the digestion of meat, grains, beans, bread, and vegetables, it also transforms them from flat-tasting to flavorful. Salt also acts as a natural preservative.

Buying Just as with oil, so it is with salt: Once you've tasted an unrefined oil or natural salt, you won't go back to using refined oil or salt. Indeed, your taste is telling. It is reassuring that you can trust your own sensory perceptions over marketing jargon.

For the past five decades the term "sea salt" has been used to designate a quality salt. It was not, however, a federally regulated term and a product's quality depended, ultimately, upon the integrity of the manufacturer. For example, while a highly refined salt mined from the San Francisco Bay is sea salt, it is not a quality salt.

The primary indicator of a quality salt is that it is unrefined and that it contains only one ingredient: salt. When you're seeking quality sea salt (evaporated ocean water), look for ones that are labeled "solar evaporated," "hand-harvested," or "hand-processed."

Mined salt can either be scooped up from surface salt beds or it may be mined from underground deposits. In the latter case, water is funneled into deeply buried salt beds and later a salty brine is pumped out. This brine is then dehydrated. With either type of mined salt, if it contains additives or if it's processed at extreme temperatures, it is not an unrefined salt as your taste will aptly discern.

A salt tinted pink (as with Himalayan or Hawaiian salt), black, or gray contains a small percentage more trace minerals than does white salt. In the case of Hawaiian pink salt, it's "enriched" by some of the pink clay beds in which the ocean water was evaporated.

Maldon and Fleur de Sel are the two most famous unrefined salts. Tasting them confirms the reason for their acclaim and top prices. You can purchase a quality natural salt, be it from the land or sea, for a few dollars a pound—and considering how long a pound will last you, that's cheap.

Storage Since salt draws moisture from the air, store salt covered tightly to retard solidifying or caking. Do not store salt in silver saltshakers or saltcellars because the salt's chlorine reacts with the silver, causing a green discoloration.

Be Mindful Highly processed and chemically altered kosher, table, or iodized salt is not recommended. It is refined at temperatures exceeding 1,200°F to 99.9 percent sodium chloride and then, by FDA standards, may contain up 2 percent additives. This intense heat causes the sodium molecules to split into a cosmetically uniform size with diminished bioavailability. Extreme heat molecularly alters any food and makes it hard to assimilate.

Less than 1 teaspoon of salt per day would satisfy our sodium requirements, but Americans typically consume double that amount; over seventy percent of this excess comes from processed and restaurant foods.

Overuse of salt stresses the kidneys, interferes with calcium and nutrient absorption, causes excessive thirst and edema, and contributes to high blood pressure.

SALT PLUM SEE **UMEBOSHI.**

SAMP SEE **POSOLE.**

KOSHER SALT: A MISINFORMED (AND NASTY) TREND

Because celebrities use kosher salt, it is cool to do the same. Hogwash, I say to them. Let me explain why, and I promise that you can taste the difference between quality and raunchy salt.

As culinary salts are nearly chemically identical, some food authorities claim that you need not bother to distinguish between them. Quality salt is delicious, with a sweet aftertaste, whereas table salt, kosher salt, and other refined salts taste sharp, acrid, and nasty. I've had hundreds of students taste-test salts, and these are consistently the results they report. (Taste straight or dissolve ¼ teaspoon of good salt in ¼ cup water, and do the same with commercial salt; then taste.)

It often happens that I'll take something as ordinary as oatmeal cookies to a party. Invariably someone wants the recipe. I promise her that it's not the recipe. Indeed, the substantive difference between oatmeal cookie recipes is negligible. Then I share my secret: quality ingredients. She'll find this hard to believe, unless—that is—she makes cookies using only quality ingredients, salt included.

SAMPHIRE SEE **GLASSWORT.**

SAND PEAR SEE **ASIAN PEAR.**

SAPODILLA
(*Manilkara zapota*)

The sapodilla, a native Central American fruit, looks like a furry brown kiwi. The sapodilla tree yields a valued hard wood and chicle as well as this tasty fruit. The fragrant and melting flesh of the sapodilla has the subtle malty flavor of pure maple syrup and a grainy texture like a pear. The fruit resembles a smooth-skinned round or oval potato, up to four inches in diameter, with a translucent flesh ranging from light yellow to pink. Commercial crops are now growing in Florida and other subtropical regions.

Use Cut open the sapodilla, remove its multiple flat, large, and barbed and inedible black seeds, and then peel and slice or spoon out the soft flesh. Season with lime juice and serve alone or with other fruits in a fresh fruit salad. When dead ripe, mash the pulpy flesh and use in puddings, sauces, ice cream, custard, or baked goods.

Buying If possible, select a sapodilla that is soft as a peach. The fruit, sharp and astringent when immature, is palatable only when fully ripe. To test for ripening, scratch off some of the fuzz; if the skin shows green, hold at room temperature for another day or two or until the skin is brown. Once ripened, it will hold in the refrigerator for two to three days.

Sapodillas are extensively consumed in Mexico, Central America, the Caribbean, India, and some other Asian countries.

See **Chicle; Fruit; Sapodilla Family.**

SAPODILLA FAMILY
(*Sapotaceae*)

Found throughout tropical regions, the evergreen shrubs and trees of this large family include the fruits mamey sapote (but not white sapote) and sapodilla as well as shea butter and, from the bark of the sapodilla tree, chicle.

See **Chicle; Mamey Sapote; Sapodilla.**

Sapote See **White Sapote.**

SASSAFRAS
Filé
(*Sassafras albidum*)

An old and respected North American herbal tonic and member of the laurel family, the bark of the sassafras tree once flavored root beer. Before that, its dried and ground leaves were used by the Choctaw Indians to make filé powder, a seasoning agent that remains an essential ingredient in the Creole stew gumbo.

Medicinal Benefits Spicy and warm, sassafras bark tea treats the lungs and kidneys; it is a diuretic, an anticoagulant, and an excellent blood purifier. It stimulates the liver to clear toxins from the system. Its ability to cleanse the blood explains its usefulness as a treatment for various skin disorders, colds, flu, arthritis, and gonorrhea. Do not consume more than two cups of sassafras tea per day, as larger quantities may be overstimulating.

Safrole, a component of sassafras oil that was declared carcinogenic by the FDA, is no longer available as a food additive. Safrole is, however, an ingredient in natural unguents used to relieve rheumatic pain and as a natural insect repellent.

Sassafras leaves and bark are now treated to remove their safrole—a process that, unfortunately but understandably, reduces their flavor. Sassafras bark and leaves reduce *vata* and *kapha*.

Use Sassafras leaves are dried and ground to make filé powder, a seasoning and thickening agent in gumbo, sauces, and gravy. If the filé is boiled, it becomes stringy, so it is stirred into a soup or sauce immediately after cook-

---

HOW I LEARNED RESPECT FOR A WHITE SUGAR RECIPE

As a child, soda pop was a rare and exotic treat; homemade root beer was our summer thirst quencher. In the canning kettle mother simmered sassafras root beer extract (available from home brewing suppliers), sugar, and 4 gallons of water. When cooled to tepid, she added yeast, then we funneled it into bottles and capped it with a capping gadget. It was a sticky but fun family task.

Several weeks later, we'd sample a bottle to judge its progress. If not fully aged, root beer tastes "green," or yeasty. When the yeast is spent and sugar fermented—with carbonation as the by-product—the brew is ready to drink.

When my children were young, mother—with the old bottle capper in hand—came to visit and headed up a brewing project. The result was as refreshing as I had remembered. Fermented and aged root beer is more mellow, smooth, and satisfying than commercial root beer that is merely mixed and injected with carbon dioxide. Look for naturally brewed soft drinks in the refrigerated section of your natural food store.

I upgraded our next batch with a natural sweetener; then, not sure of its sucrose content, I added extra yeast to compensate. Two weeks later, from the cellar we started hearing explosions. A second before each glass-shattering blast, there had existed an overcarbonated bottle of naturally sweetened root beer.

ing. Or the gumbo may be ladled into individual bowls, and each person stirs the filé powder into his or her own portion while it's still piping hot. The bark is also used as a seasoning agent in cordials and medicines.

As available, tender young sassafras leaves and winter buds may be added to green salads.

Buying Purchase sassafras leaves and filé in small quantities, as their flavor quickly dissipates.

See **Herbs and Spices; Laurel Family.**

SATSUMA SEE ORANGE.

SAVORY
(*Satureja hortensis, S. montana*)

There are two kinds of savory: summer savory (*Satureja hortensis*) and winter savory (*S. montana*). Both have a peppery taste. Native to the Mediterranean region, winter savory is a hardy perennial low shrub; the leaves have a strong, sharp flavor. Summer savory, an annual plant, is milder tasting; it is the more popular of the two. Savory is a member of the mint family.

Medicinal Benefits Savory is a warming herb with yang tonic properties that aids chi circulation and helps disperse cold conditions and phlegm. It supports the functions of the heart, large intestines, lungs, and stomach. Savory aids digestion, especially of fatty foods, beans, or acidic foods like tomatoes. It reduces *vata* and *kapha*.

Use Almost thymelike in flavor, savory goes with bean, pea, and potato dishes. A few chopped fresh leaves are good in a salad, but more would be overpowering. Dried or fresh, savory is a common ingredient in tomato-based dishes, sausage, dressings, and herb blends such as *herbes de Provence*.

See **Herbs and Spices; Mint Family.**

SCALLION
Green Onion, Spring Onion
(*Allium cepa*)

The mildest of the famed onion family, the scallion is the immature stem and bulb of an onion. The scallion is valued for its bulb and leaves. I go a step further and use the stringy rootlets.

Medicinal Benefits The scallion is a warming yang tonic that supports the heart, large intestine, lung, and stomach organ functions. It eliminates toxins and cold and supports blood circulation. The scallion has antifungal and antimicrobial effects, but to a lesser degree than onions and garlic. Scallions alleviate chest and heart pain, promote urination and sweating, and serve as a digestive aid. Cooked scallions reduce *vata*. A moderate use of scallions, cooked or raw, reduces *kapha*.

The green part of a scallion is high in vitamin A. The bulb contains vitamins A, B-complex, and C; it also has some calcium, magnesium, and potassium.

Use Both the scallion bulb and leaves are used either as a garnish or as an ingredient for salads, soups, and stir-fries. They add lightness, both of flavor and appearance, and make a heavy or fatty dish more digestible. I often use the rootlets, washed well and chopped fine, in soup; they are a concentrated source of minerals and add flavor.

Buying Scallions are available year-round, but they are more perishable than mature onions. Look for firm scallions, preferably with their long rootlets intact, and unblemished leaves that show no signs of withering or slime.

See **Onion Family.**

SCALLOP SQUASH SEE SQUASH.

SCHAV SEE SORREL.

WEAR A SCALLION IN YOUR EAR

A scallion makes an effective kitchen remedy for earache. If the scallion is cold, run hot tap water over it to take off the chill. Slice the base of the bulb at an angle so that it will comfortably fit into your ear and leave enough of the greens attached to use as a handle. Place the bulb in the affected ear. I'm not sure why it's an effective poultice, but my own experience plus ages of grandmothers before me attest to its value.

SCORZONERA
Black Salsify
(*Scorzonera hispanica*)

A native plant of Spain and daisy family member, scorzonera is similar to salsify in size, use, and flavor, but with a chocolate brown skin and broader leaves.

While it is easy to cultivate in a vegetable garden, scorzonera is low in demand and current market supplies are imported from Belgium only during the colder months. Select roots that are firm and smooth.

See **Daisy Family; Salsify; Vegetable.**

SCOTCH KALE SEE **KALE.**

SEA ASPARAGUS SEE **GLASSWORT.**

SEA BEAN SEE **GLASSWORT.**

SEA LETTUCE
(*Ulva lactuca, U. fasciata*)

Emerald green patches of gossamer-thin—literally two cells thick—blades of sea lettuce cover rocks on the intertidal zone. This seaweed, which feels like wax paper, has a flavor similar to nori and is delicious to nibble on as you forage it (from a clean beach). Unless foraged, you're most apt to find it as supplement or an ingredient in cosmetics. Sea lettuce has been a traditional food in coastal areas throughout the Northern Hemisphere.

As its name suggests, sea lettuce may be added raw to salads or sandwiches. Dried, shredded, crumbled, or rehydrated for five minutes and chopped, sea lettuce adds its distinctive flavor to any savory dish, but its color quickly darkens.

See **Seaweed Family; Vegetable.**

SEA MOSS SEE **IRISH MOSS.**

SEA PALM
(*Postelsia palmaeformis*)

One of my students, all fired up about the virtues of sea palm, served it in a stir-fry to her husband and two adolescent children. "Black pasta," she casually replied, when asked its identity—and they've been eating it ever since. The pleasing texture, appearance, and flavor of sea palm fits right into family fare.

Sea palm, which looks like a miniature palm tree, is a brown seaweed that grows on the headlands of the northern Pacific coast of North America. It is unusual among seaweeds in that it remains erect out of the water and is more exposed to the air than to the water.

Unfortunately, sea palm has been overharvested and currently it is illegal to harvest it in British Columbia, Washington, and Oregon. With a permit, California allows commercial harvesting.

Medicinal Benefits A cooling food and a yin tonic, sea palm supports the kidneys and stomach and helps dispel toxins. It helps reduce blood cholesterol, soften hard masses, and support normal thyroid function. Like other brown sea vegetables, it contains algin, which fixes and removes radioactive particles and heavy metals from the body.

Use Mildly sweet, with a pleasing al dente

texture, sea palm comes in long, flat, ribbed strands. Hydrate the strands and use them in sautéed and simmered dishes. Or pulverize them with a pestle (or in a blender) and then strew the dark, confettilike flecks into soups, grain, braised, and stewed dishes, condiments, or any pot of beans that's wanting enhanced flavor, mineral enrichment, and eye appeal.

Buying Purchase sea palm from natural food stores, online, or from farmers' markets in coastal areas.

See **Seaweed Family; Vegetable.**

SEA PICKLE SEE **GLASSWORT.**

SEA SALT SEE **SALT.**

SEA VEGETABLES SEE **SEAWEED.**

SEAWEED FAMILY
Marine Algae, Sea Vegetables

Must be our sensual nature that sends us into the blustery dawn of the full moon's ebb tide to gather our spring salad. . . . Gingerly step over the icy granite rocks. Past the slimy ones, tidal pools lined with frizzy Irish moss, the leafy fluorescence of sea lettuce, the swaying dulse palms, delicate purple laver, down to the fleecy crashing ocean roll: our cup overflows. Bending now. Wrist flick of the stick looses the streaming fronds from their holdfasts. Into the baskets.
—Anne Franklin Harris, seaweed wildcrafter and author

Even if you swear you'll never eat seaweed, you already have. It's a ubiquitous ingredient in ice cream, baked goods, jelly, salad dressing, chocolate milk, beer, wine, and toothpaste. These are earth's first vegetables and have often figured in the human diet, and with good reason. Vegetables from the sea are not only the most singularly nutritious food—they're also delicious. Although they're more popular in Asia—especially Japan—they have been valued by many cultures throughout the world. That the Irish, the Inuit, and other coastal peoples use them makes sense. I was amazed, however, to find new-to-me seaweed varieties in open-air Indian markets in landlocked Bolivia. Foods of exceptional value have remained trade items from time immemorial.

Ranging from microscopic plankton to giant kelp with fronds more than 1,500 feet long, seaweed is one of the world's most underutilized foods. It's also the world's most abundant food. Algae is classified according to color as green, brown, red, or blue-green. The color is determined by the spectrum of light available to the plant for photosynthesis.

Medicinal Benefits Seaweed is a cooling food and both a blood and yin tonic that supports the kidney and stomach functions. It helps to regulate conditions of excess heat, water, phlegm, and damp and to dispel toxins. Many varieties act as natural antibiotics and some, like dulse, have antiviral properties.

The nutritional content of all plants reflects their immediate environment. A carrot grown in deficient soil, for example, is nutritionally deficient compared to one grown in good soil. Seaweed is continuously bathed in the mineral-rich sea brine. These greens are a direct transformation of seawater, and their mineral content is 7 to 38 percent of their dry weight!

The documented medicinal properties of seaweed are voluminous. Benefits include reducing blood cholesterol, removing metallic and radioactive elements from the body, and preventing goiter. Seaweed counteracts obesity; it also strengthens bones, teeth, nerve transmission, and digestion. Seaweed softens hardened masses or tumors, and so it is used to treat lumps, swollen lymph glands, fibroid tumors, and edema. Furthermore, seaweed is a beauty aid, helping maintain glowing, healthy skin and lustrous hair; it is also credited with antiaging properties. The thermal property of seaweed is cooling; its flavor is salty. In Ayurvedic medicine, seaweed reduces *vata*.

Ounce for ounce, seaweed is higher in vitamins and minerals than any other class of food. It supplies all the minerals needed for human health in proportions very similar to those found in human blood. The most significant elements are calcium, iodine, phosphorus, sodium, and iron. Seaweed is an extremely rich protein source, containing up to 38 percent protein. Seaweed is a better than average source of vitamins A and B. It's not surprising that the iodine and iodine compounds in seaweed reduce enlarged thyroid glands (hypothyroidism) caused from insufficient iodine. Eating seaweed also alleviates hyperthyroidism by inhibiting the metabolic rate of the disease.

The brown seaweeds, like bladder wrack and kombu, are an important source of fucoidan. This potent anticarcinogen and anticholesterol are available as a supplement in two forms, U-fucoidan and F-fucoidan.

Use The sea garden contains hundreds of nutritious sea vegetables. These highly versatile foods are easily incorporated into numerous styles of cuisine and complement many dishes, from soup to dessert. Those that invite beginners' use are agar, dulse, kombu, nori, and sea palm.

Buying/Foraging My first choice is seaweed that I've wildcrafted at its prime from clean coastal areas. My second choice is the same quality available in natural food stores

WILDCRAFTING IN WET SUITS

Dressed in a wet suit, I foraged salad greens at dawn. In a low, -8.5-foot tide, while gulls squawked and the full moon dissolved into the Pacific fog, I sloshed through tidal pools, sidestepped starfish, and took care to remain on this side of the crashing surf. I cut and bagged sturdy kombu, elegant sea palm, and satiny, purple nori. I nibbled as I worked—these greens are irresistibly delicious.

For me, a foraging highlight of that summer was harvesting seaweed on the Mendocino coast with the wildcrafters who have supplied North Americans with tasty sea greens for the past 20 years.

Using a grape harvester's knife with a curved blade, I trimmed plants that were at their prime for a sustainable harvest. The trimmings went into woven onion bags (the loose weave holds the weed but not the sea), hauled them to the beach, carted them to the parking lot, filled the back of a small pickup, and then headed to the sunny inland drying racks and lines. There, the small varieties—like sea palm, dulse, and nori—were spread onto mesh trays and the longer strands of kelp, alaria, and sea whip were clothes-pinned onto lines, making a beautiful sea green display. We worked quickly to have it all sun-drying by noon, then we pulled out picnic hampers and took refuge in the shade of the surrounding redwood forest. I napped while the sun dried the harvest. By late afternoon, we bagged this invaluable food and made plans for the next day's foraging (the tide is low enough only for three to four days per lunar cycle). Could they count me in on tomorrow's crew? Yes, unequivocally.

and by mail order. Third is seaweed from reputable natural food distributors that import top grades. Commercial-quality seaweed may be indiscriminately harvested. Some Asian markets offer fresh seaweed. Fresh seaweed will keep, refrigerated, for two to three days. Dried seaweed keeps for several years when stored, tightly covered, in a cool, dry place.

As our seas become more polluted, some people worry that seaweed is contaminated. According to laboratory analysis, seaweed tests zero for pesticides, hydrocarbons, herbicides, and toxins such as E. coli, yeast, mold, and salmonella.

See **Agar; Alaria; Arame; Bladder Wrack; Dulse; Hijiki; Irish Moss; Kanten; Kelp; Kombu; Laver; Mekabu Wakame; Nori; Sea Lettuce; Sea Palm; Sea Whip; Wakame.**

SEA WHIP
Bullwhip Kelp
(*Nereocystis leutkeana*)

When I was a child, at the seaside we played jump rope with a 20-foot-long, greenish brown stipe of sea whip that ended in a large bulb with attached fronds. We never thought to nibble on our rope. It has, I have since discovered, a crispy, celerylike texture and taste. It is the sea whip fronds, however, that I'm wild about.

Sea whip fronds are the reproductive organs of this large seaweed. Each frond, a foot or so in length and several inches wide, contains dark oblong patches of spore that, upon maturation, dissolve into the ocean. When fresh, on the ragged frond ends you can see where the spore has been released. When dried, if you look carefully, you can see these intact patches.

Medicinal Benefits Sea whip is remarkable in that it is delicious to nibble on dried

and therefore a superior source of fluorine. While all seaweed contains this important nutrient, which boosts the immune system and strengthens bones and teeth, even minimal cooking destroys it. Sea whip is especially strengthening to the reproductive system. In other medicinal respects, it is similar to seaweed.

Use Undoubtedly one of the easiest seaweed to use, sea whip is as thin as a layer of phyllo dough and, when crumbled into a soup or grain or vegetable dish, is quickly absorbed. To benefit from its fluorine content, stir it into soups or moist grain or vegetable dishes just prior to serving. As a snack, sea whip is like potato chips in terms of crunch and flavor, but unlike the chips, concentrated essence of sea whip leaves you satisfied after a few nibbles.

Buying Sea whip is available in some coastal natural food stores and online.

See **Seaweed Family; Vegetable.**

SECKEL **S**EE **P**EAR.

FINING BEER AND DETOXING PLUTONIUM

For centuries, beer meisters tossed Irish moss into their vats of beer. The seaweed, which was discarded before kegging the beer, bonded with and held impurities. In a like manner, a serving of seaweed will chelate with toxins and discharge them with normal body waste. Amazing stuff. Seaweed not only detoxifies radioactive elements and heavy metals, it also counters the effects of X-rays. Such established journals as *Radiation Research, Health Physics, Nature*, and the *International Journal of Radiation Biology* are among the many that have published papers on this topic.

SEEDS

A seed, like a fertilized egg, is the self-contained embryonic plant, which holds the potential for propagation of the species. This power is reflected in a seed's superior nutritional and energetic properties. It is no coincidence that seeds are a hiker's favorite trail food.

While technically all grains, beans, and many fruits and nuts are seeds, the seeds considered in this entry are oil-rich seeds used in oil production or similar to nuts in culinary use.

Medicinal Benefits Because of their oil content, seeds are high in calories and are a warming and energizing food. That oil content may also make them a digestive challenge for people with a compromised liver. Seeds are an excellent protein and mineral source and are higher in iron than nuts. They contain vitamins A, B-complex, D, and E and are an outstanding source of calcium. Seeds are high in unsaturated fats; if eaten raw, they are a superior source of fatty acids. Seeds generally reduce *vata*.

Use The seeds most often substituted for nuts and eaten as a snack food are sesame, sunflower, and pumpkin seeds. Other culinary seeds include alfalfa, chia, flax, hemp, poppy, and psyllium.

Buying Select vital-looking, debris-free seeds. With larger seeds like sunflower and pumpkin, you can cull out discolored, broken, or rubbery seeds. Taste is the best way to determine the quality of small seeds like poppy and sesame. The seeds should taste fresh and full bodied, with no off flavor.

See **Alfalfa; Chia Seed; Flaxseed; Lotus Seed; Poppy Seed; Psyllium; Pumpkin Seed; Sesame Seed; Squash Seed; Sunflower Seed.**

SEITAN
Wheat Gluten

Seitan (say-TAN), or wheat gluten, is a chic meat substitute that is versatile, hearty, and wholesome. A traditional Asian food, "wheat meat" is eaten by vegetarians and some religious groups such as the Seventh-Day Adventists.

Medicinal Benefits Seitan supports the spleen-pancreas and kidney functions. High in protein, seitan helps build body mass, strengthen muscles, and it engenders overall strength and vitality. When freshly made with quality wheat, seitan is an energizing food. It calms *vata* and *pitta*.

Use Seitan is easily made at home using water to extract the gluten (protein) from wheat flour. First make flour and water into a dough and then, under running water, knead out the whet starch and bran until only elastic-like gluten remains. This gluten is then seasoned, cooked, and ready for use in a variety of dishes as a meat replacement.

Buying Seitan and seitan products are available in natural food stores, refrigerated or in jars. As *kau fu* it is available in Asian markets.

Be Mindful Seitan is not appropriate for a gluten-free diet.

See **Gluten; Wheat.**

SEMOLINA SEE **WHEAT FLOUR.**

SEREH; SEREI SEE **LEMONGRASS.**

SERRANO SEE **CHILE PEPPER.**

SESAME BUTTER

Sesame butter is made of whole roasted sesame seeds and may be used interchangeably with peanut butter. If differs from the better-known tahini, which is made of hulled raw sesame seeds and is therefore refined and denatured. Of the two, tahini is lighter in flavor and color and has more culinary applications. Sesame butter is typically used as a spread.

Sesame butter is high in vitamin E and

therefore has a longer shelf life than other nut butters. Once opened, sesame butter should be refrigerated, where it will hold for about six months. If it tastes or smells harsh, it is rancid and should be discarded.

See **Nut and Seed Butters; Sesame Seed; Tahini.**

SESAME OIL

In Africa, the Middle East, and Asia, the use of nutrient-dense sesame oil dates back to antiquity, and it remains one of the most valued oils for its inimitable flavor, excellent stability, and resistance to oxidation. Even though sesame contains 41 percent of the unstable—but valuable—polyunsaturated fats, it also contains a natural antioxidant that enhances its stability. Along with extra virgin olive oil, sesame oil remains the most healthful and versatile liquid culinary oil available.

Use Favor unrefined sesame oil and enjoy it in sauces and dressings or for sautéing or baking. It's also used as a massage oil and beauty treatment. It may safely be heated to 240°F.

Toasted sesame oil is a distinctive Asian condiment made from toasted seeds that has a rich dark color and a heady aroma. Use sparingly to flavor a stir-fried dish, soup, or sauce.

See **Fat and Oil; Sesame Seed.**

SESAME SEED
(*Sesamum indicum*)

In the Arabic tale *Ali Baba and the Forty Thieves*, the secret command that opens the door to a treasure trove is "Open sesame!" Indeed, the command makes sense if you've grown sesame seeds. They are densely packed in a tiny one-inch, okra-shaped pod; when mature, the pods burst open, showering out their abundant treasures.

Sesame seeds are tiny, flat oval seeds with a nutty taste and a delicate crunch. These nutrient-dense seeds have remained an impor-

tant food since prehistoric times. It is the oldest known plant grown for its seeds and oil and has been especially valued in Mediterranean, African, and Eastern cultures. All it takes are a few hulled sesame seeds topping a bread crust to lend a lively flavor and visual appeal to your loaf.

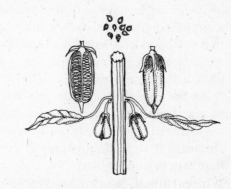

Medicinal Benefits Sesame seeds are a blood and yin tonic that support the kidneys, liver, and large intestine. Sesame seeds have the highest total phytosterol content of any food commonly eaten in the United States and thus help lower cholesterol. They help promote regular bowel movements and lactation for nursing mothers.

Sesame seeds contain more than 35 percent protein, more than any nut; they are about 50 percent oil and are high in vitamin E, giving them excellent antioxidant properties. They protect the liver from oxidative damage and are also a superior source of copper and a very good source of calcium. Sesame seeds reduce *vata*.

Use Whole sesame seeds are used in baking and in condiments, confections, salads, and vegetable dishes. Washing the seeds removes any bitter taste, and toasting them enhances their flavor. To wash, place the seeds in a bowl and fill with water; pour the seeds into a strainer, being careful not to pour out any of the sand or grit (if there is any) that may have settled in the bottom of the bowl. To heighten their flavor, toast until they are a shade darker and start to pop. I find it easiest to toast sesame seeds in a wok, stirring constantly, but some people oven-toast them. These are the common types of sesame seeds:

- **Black Sesame Seeds** This variety, primarily available in Asian food stores, has a stronger flavor, which aptly indicates that it is more nutrient dense and medicinal than the more common tan variety. Black sesame seeds have a dull, matte finish and range in color from coal black to gray black, with an occasional rust-colored seed. If the seeds are a monochromatic shiny black, they are tan seeds that have been dyed black.
- **White (Hulled) Sesame Seeds** Smaller than sesame seeds because their hulls have been removed, these sweetly flavored hulled seeds are white in color and the seed of choice in many commercial food products. They can quickly go rancid because they are hull-less. Favor those that have had their hulls mechanically removed. If the hulled seeds are not organic, you can assume that caustic lye was used to dehull them, thus denaturing nutrients and flavor.
- **Whole (Tan) Sesame Seeds** These seeds have a stronger flavor and more nutrients because of their intact and edible hull.

Be Mindful Sesame seeds and their products are an allergen for some people, typically people who have multiple food sensitivities. Because whole sesame seeds contain a moderate amount of oxalic acid, people prone to developing oxalate kidney stones are advised to use this food moderately.

See **Seeds; Sesame Butter; Tahini.**

SEVILLE ORANGE SEE **BITTER ORANGE.**

SHADDOCK SEE **POMELO.**

SHAKER DRIED CORN SEE **CHICOS.**

SHALLOT
(*Allium cepa*)

The aromatic shallot is sweeter, milder, and more subtly flavored than an onion. It is about the size and shape of a large garlic, only it has two to four large cloves that do not require peeling. The cloves are creamy white and often purple tinged.

Medicinal Benefits Medicinally, shallots are similar to onions but more mild. They reduce *kapha* and, when cooked, *vata.*

Use Considered indispensable for such classic sauces as béarnaise, the shallot cooks down to a creamy, thick consistency. Shallots can also be roasted whole or added, finely chopped, to a salad dressing. When using raw, you may grate a shallot because it has a dry texture.

A shallot bulb, when peeled, divides into two halves. When a recipe calls for one shallot, it refers to both halves. It is an important ingredient in French and New Orleans cuisine.

Buying Yellow, red, and gray shallots are available year-round. Currently, most are imported and therefore pricey, but domestic crops have increasing availability. Look for plump and firm bulbs.

See **Onion Family; Vegetable.**

SHEA BUTTER
Shea Nut Butter
(*Vitellaria paradoxa, Butyrospermum parkii*)

In the West, shea butter is a common ingredient in cosmetics and an occasional cocoa butter substitute or margarine ingredient. It's extracted from the seed of a plumlike fruit of an African tree that thrives in the savannas. It is a member of the sapodilla family. This ivory-colored fat remains a staple ingredient in Uganda, Guinea, Ghana, and multiple other central African countries. Due to its rich nutritional profile and oleic and steric acids, we can hope for it to become more available as a culinary ingredient.

See **Fat and Oil; Sapodilla Family.**

SHEA NUT BUTTER SEE SHEA BUTTER.

SHEEP'S HEAD SEE MAITAKE.

SHIITAKE
Black Forest Mushroom, Chinese Mushroom
(*Lentinus edodes*)

The second most widely produced edible mushroom, the shiitake has a rich, woodsy flavor and a meaty texture when cooked. The shape of a shiitake is similar to that of a common white mushroom—only its brown cap is peaked at the center like an umbrella and its gills are tan.

Medicinal Benefits Shiitakes support the spleen, stomach, and liver functions, and they are a blood and chi tonic. By detoxifying the system and helping to dispel phlegm and mucus, they are a restorative. Shiitake mushrooms contain two potent substances with proven pharmacological effects as immune regulators and antiviral and antitumor agents; they also positively affect the cardiovascular system. Shiitakes treat diseases involving depressed immune function, including cancer, AIDS, environmental allergies, candidiasis infections, and frequent flu and colds. In addition, they soothe bronchial inflammation, regulate urine incontinence, and reduce chronic high cholesterol.

Shiitakes are rich in vitamins D, B_2, and B_{12}, and are a good source of minerals when grown in a mineral-rich medium. They contain about 2.5 percent protein.

Use Shiitakes are widely available both fresh and dried. While the fresh is tender and mild in flavor, the dried is more chewy and has a more intense umami flavor. Cooking, especially roasting, sautéing, or grilling, enhances the flavor of shiitakes. The longer a fresh shiitake is cooked, the more water it loses and the denser and chewier it becomes. In the Radish Solitaire recipe on page 295, the shiitake is simmered just four minutes and is exceptionally tender. Use fresh or reconstituted dried shiitake in soups, stir-fries, pasta sauces, entrées, and side dishes.

To reconstitute dried shiitakes, soak in warm water for at least two to three hours or, preferably, overnight. Use the soaking water for stock and discard the woody portion of the stem.

Buying When purchasing fresh shiitakes, look for firm, fleshy mushrooms with a dry, blemish-free surface. Select thick mushrooms with their peaked caps intact over flat, or broken, mushrooms. The more aroma the mushrooms have, the more flavor.

Dried shiitake are readily available in Asian, natural food, and specialty food markets. Top-quality shiitakes, called donko in Japanese, are costly because they grow outdoors, on hardwood, and take 18 months to mature. Most commercial shiitake grow in a few weeks in warm conditions on artificial substrate.

See **Mushroom Family; Vegetable.**

SHISO SEE PERILLA.

SHOYU SEE SOY SAUCE.

SHUNGIKU SEE CHRYSANTHEMUM GREENS.

SIBERIAN KALE SEE KALE.

SICHUAN PEPPER
Anise Pepper, Ash Pepper, Szechuan Pepper
(*Zanthoxylum piperitum, Z. simulans,* and *Z. schinifolium*)

Nibble on the woody outer pod or husk of the Sichuan pepper, a minuscule citrus family fruit. Initially it has a mild lemonlike aroma and flavor. But hold on. This grows into a pungent, biting, and tingly numbness, an almost anesthetic feeling that memorably overtakes your tongue and mouth.

Sichuan peppers are indispensable for Sichuan and Himalayan cooking and are widely used throughout the rest of Asia. Sichuan pepper is one of the ingredients in the Asian five-spice mix. There are several different varieties that vary in their flavor intensity.

The FDA lifted a ban on their import in 2005, so you may expect to see increasing availability of Sichuan peppers. (The 1968 ban was to prevent spread of a citrus canker; Sichuan peppers are now heated to 158°F to eliminate this plant disease.)

Medicinal Benefits The Sichuan peppercorn is a chi tonic and a warming food that helps circulate blood and chi. It helps purify blood, kill tapeworms, and relieve chronic pain, including toothaches. Rub powdered Sichuan pepper into the areas afflicted by chronic pain (but not over tender body parts or near the eyes). A North American species, *Z. americanum,* is known as "toothache tree," for when the unripe fruits or twigs are chewed, it temporarily suppresses tooth pain.

Use Pick over the spice and discard any stems and tough pointed thorns. Crush and toast the seedpods before adding them to food. The shiny black seeds are always discarded because of their bitter flavor and gritty texture. Add Sichuan pepper at the last moment to retain its flavor.

See **Citrus Family; Herbs and Spices.**

SIU CAI SEE MIZUNA.

SLAKED CORN SEE POSOLE.

SNAP BEAN SEE GREEN BEAN.

SNOW PEA SEE PEA, FRESH.

SNOW PUFF SEE ENOKI.

SOAPBERRY FAMILY
(*Sapindaceae*)

This large family of flowering plants occurs in temperate to tropical regions throughout the world. Many, but not all, of their seeds, leaves, or roots contain a milky sap, some of which have mildly toxic saponins with soap-like qualities.

See **Longan; Lychee; Maple Syrup; Rambutan.**

SORBITOL (NOT RECOMMENDED)

The FDA classifies the artificial sweetener sorbitol as Generally Recognized as Safe. Countless people, however, have direct experience to the contrary as an online search for "sorbitol adverse effects" quickly reveals. Sorbitol causes digestive problems and irritable bowel symptoms including bloating, abdominal cramping, flatulence, and diarrhea. Ten grams of sorbitol can cause severe diarrhea, which explains its effectiveness as the laxative Sorbilax.

Sorbitol, highly processed from corn syrup, is widely used in diet food, beverages, confections, cosmetics, and toothpaste as both a sweetener and softener. It's an artificial sweetener to avoid. But then, your sense of taste will confirm this. Taste—*really* taste—a sorbitol-sweetened candy. While its initial flavor is an intense sweet, its lingering aftertaste is harsh, unpleasant, and metallic.

See **Mannitol; Sweeteners.**

SORGHUM
Jowar
(*Sorghum vulgare*)

Sorghum, a nutritious milletlike grain, has been a staple grain in parts of Africa and Asia since 5,000 BC. The large plant looks like a thin-bladed corn plant, and the seed looks like a buff-colored BB shot, larger than coriander but smaller than a pea. Following wheat, rice, corn, and barley, sorghum is the world's fifth most important cereal crop. It thrives in areas too hot and dry for corn.

Currently in the United States, sorghum is primarily used as animal feed. Its stalks are used for the biofuel ethanol or for the production of sorghum molasses. The most popular Chinese liquor, *maotai*, is made from sorghum.

Medicinal Benefits Sorghum's sweet and slightly astringent flavor make it medicinal for the spleen and stomach. A gluten-free grain, it helps to alleviate diarrhea and to restore a flagging appetite. In addition to protein, fat, and sugars, sorghum contains calcium, phosphorus, iron, and vitamins B_1, B_2, and niacin. Sorghum is nutritionally similar to corn.

Use If you can find a table variety of sorghum, it is delicious with a pleasing mild flavor and it holds its shape without getting soggy or mushy. Its availability is variable, but whenever I can find a supply, I enjoy it as a rice substitute. To prepare whole, add 1 cup sorghum (pre-toasting the grain heightens its flavor) and ¼ teaspoon salt to 2 cups water and simmer, tightly covered, for 40 minutes.

Sorghum, like popcorn and amaranth, may be popped. Sorghum flour makes an excellent flatbread and is added to various gluten-free baked goods.

See **Grains; Grass Family; Sorghum Molasses.**

SORGHUM MOLASSES
Sweet Sorghum Syrup

Sorghum molasses has a smoky, sweet taste and a thick texture, not unlike table molasses made from sugarcane. This delicious syrup was a staple sweetener in American homes in the eighteenth and early nineteenth centuries until being displaced by inexpensive beet sugar. It is made from sorghum stalks.

Medicinal Benefits Sorghum molasses is warming and a blood and chi tonic. It acts upon the kidney, liver, stomach, spleen, and lung meridians. Nutritionally comparable to blackstrap molasses, it has similar effects on body metabolism. Sorghum is high in iron and is a fair source of calcium. It is 65 to 70 percent sucrose. As a sweetener, sorghum calms *pitta* and *vata*.

Use Sorghum molasses may be used as a table sweetener over pancakes, French toast, or waffles or as a substitute for molasses in baking and cooking.

Buying Sorghum molasses is easiest to find in Southeastern states and in some well-stocked natural food stores and specialty shops. As its availability is sporadic, buy it when you find it.

See **Molasses; Sorghum; Sweeteners.**

SORREL
French Sorrel, Garden Sorrel, Schav, Sour Dock
(*Rumex acetosa*)

In the 1885 edition of the classic *Vegetable Garden*, Madame Vilmorin-Andrieux observed that "garden sorrels may be ranked among the plants which have been least modified by cultivation, as most of them are little, if anything, better than wild plants of the same species growing under favorable conditions." The same is true today. There is nothing tame about this sour-tasting perennial potherb, an old favorite in European cuisine. The name "sorrel" comes from a German word for sour.

One of the first spring greens to appear in the garden, the bright triangular leaves of sorrel grow up from a clump; they are like spinach in size but even more tender in texture.

Medicinal Benefits Used as a spring tonic throughout Europe, sorrel stimulates the liver and aids digestion, especially of rich food. It is a rich source of iron and potassium and vitamins A and C. Sorrel reduces *vata*.

Use A few slivered young sorrel leaves perk up any salad or sandwich. Sorrel is very easy to puree, and the puree makes an ideal base for a sauce or soup. Strip the stems, shred the leaves, and simmer in very little water. Within minutes, sorrel melts into a puree. It reduces even more than spinach in volume.

Cream of sorrel soup is a famous Old World dish; salmon with sorrel sauce is popular in France; and a sorrel and egg yolk soup, *schav*, is a favorite Jewish dish.

Buying Sorrel is available in specialty food markets in the spring. Look for bunches of light green arrow-shaped leaves that are firm and not limp. The smaller leaves are less acidic. Plan to use it within a few days.

Be Mindful Due to its high acid content, sorrel discolors if cut with a carbon steel knife, cooked in aluminum or iron pots, or served in a silver dish. Because of its oxalic acid content, moderate use is recommended for people with kidney stones, gallstones, or with rheumatic-type conditions.

See **Buckwheat Family; Vegetable.**

SOUR CHERRY
Montmorency, Pie Cherry, Tart Cherry
(*Prunus cerasus*)

A wild cherry found in both European and American Stone Age sites developed into today's cherry, both sour and sweet. The sour cherry is the smaller and more astringent of the two. It is a member of the prune family. Its color is a bright cherry red compared to the darker sweet cherry. "Acid cherry" would be a more apt name than sour cherry. By any name, it takes just one to reap a serious pucker. Their tangy flavor and bright "cherry" red color is unmistakable. Sour cherries are at their best when cooked.

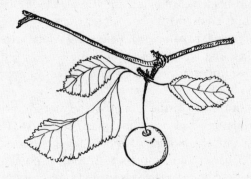

Medicinal Benefits Opposite of the sweet cherries, which are warming, sour cherries are cooling and astringing; they support the stomach, liver, heart, lung, and kidney functions.

While all cherries—sweet and sour—are a remedy for aches and pain, sour cherries are superior to sweet in their medicinal properties. This resonates with common sense. Sweeter fruits are higher in carbohydrates and, therefore, lower in micronutrients with pharmaceutically healing properties.

Sour cherries provide highly effective pain relief and are an excellent source of antioxidant compounds. Their anti-inflammatory compounds, anthocyanins, are at least 10 times more active than aspirin, according to a recent study from Michigan State University.

Lead researcher Muralee Nair, a professor of horticulture, says that 20 tart cherries a day can keep pain related to arthritis and inflammation at bay.

In addition, sour cherries are a potent source of 17 beneficial antioxidants, which are useful in the prevention of cancer and cardiovascular disease and help slow the aging process. Two of these antioxidants, kaempferol and quercetin, are found in supplements used to improve memory, concentration, and vision.

CHERRY BOUNCE FOR CARPAL TUNNEL, ARTHRITIS, OR GOUT

This is an easy-to-make and tasty liqueur that—if you need an excuse—also happens to be an excellent medicinal remedy. Drinking a daily jigger of cherry bounce is an Rx to ease numb extremities, carpal tunnel syndrome, gout, or arthritis.

Makes 2 quarts

- 8 cups fresh sweet or sour cherries, with their pits
- 2 cups sugar
- About 2 cups vodka, port, cognac, brandy, or rum

Remove and discard the cherry stems. Wash and dry the fruit and pack it into two glass quart jars. Add 1 cup sugar to each jar and top with your liquor of choice. Stir, cover tightly, and refrigerate or set in a cool cellar. Over the next few days, stir a few times, until the sugar dissolves.

Let the cherry bounce age for 6 to 8 weeks, then strain and serve as a liqueur. Enjoy the cherries as a garnish or a little nibble.

If you like, you can add 1 teaspoon allspice, 1 teaspoon whole cloves, and/or 1 stick of cinnamon to each jar.

CHERRY PIE BAKING CONTEST

In high school in 1960, I won a cherry pie baking contest that took me to a national competition in Chicago. Each state was represented, and the Sheraton Blackburn Hotel ballroom was fitted with 50 ranges and worktables and several supply tables loaded with lard, sugar, and sour cherries. The winner would travel to the White House kitchen to bake a pie for President Eisenhower. Leading up to the Chicago trip, I practiced my technique, confident that, if given the opportunity, Ike would love my pie. I didn't win—but I sure ate a lot of sour cherries.

Sour cherries are remarkably high in vitamin A and folic acid. They are low in calories. In moderation, sour cherries reduce *vata*.

Use In a pie or chutney, sour cherries become creamy and tender with a bright, refreshing tart flavor and a vividly clear pink juice. Unlike sugary sweet cherries, which often don't require additional sugar in a recipe, sour cherries demand it. Sour cherries are excellent in a cold soup, with game, and in desserts or preserves. They're also available dried.

Buying/Foraging Sour cherries are so meltingly tender and perishable that they bruise at a touch and are thus difficult to market. Look for whole sour cherries the first week in July. Pit and use immediately or freeze for later use.

Hardy sour cherry trees are prolific bearers—one small tree produces more bushels of tart fruit than any one family could use—so pie cherries often fall to the ground for lack of anyone to harvest them. What a waste. Is there an unharvested or underharvested sour cherry tree in your neighborhood? There's no harm in asking to pick a few bags full.

See **Cherry; Dried Fruit; Fruit; Prune Family.**

SOUR DOCK SEE **SORREL.**

SOUR ORANGE SEE **BITTER ORANGE.**

SOYBEAN
(*Glycine max*)

In 5,000-year-old Chinese texts, the soybean was described as one of the most important crops. What's different today is that it's both valued and disparaged worldwide. Whether or not it is healthful depends upon how the product is made.

This versatile Asian pea is the least expensive source of protein in virtually every country. In fact, an acre of soybeans produces more than 20 times more usable protein than if that land were used to raise beef cattle or grow their fodder. The United States produces about 75 percent of the world's soy crop. It is used primarily as animal food.

To skillfully discern how to healthfully enjoy soy, a brief overview is helpful. Soy contains antinutrients such as enzyme inhibitors, which interfere with digestion. More than 3,000 years ago, Asians discovered how to increase soy's digestibility and flavor by soaking, fermenting, and sprouting the beans. This eliminated the antinutrients and increased soy's nutrition. These traditional products include miso, soymilk, soy sauce, tempeh, and tofu. When made traditionally and from whole beans, they're excellent foods. Note, however, that these traditional soy products were used in moderation as condiments rather than as a primary food staple.

Seventy years ago, Western food technologists saw soybeans' potential value as an affordable protein. Bypassing the traditional and time-consuming preparation steps, they created new soy foods. In record time, soy became the least expensive protein and has been widely consumed, with varying health problems. The primary reason is due to how soy is processed. That most nonorganic soy is genetically modified may also be a contributing factor.

Quality soy foods are made with traditional processing techniques and use only organic, whole beans. They are nutritious and medicinal foods.

Modern soy products are made from fractionated soy that is subjected to high temperatures, solvent extraction, alkaline solutions, and acid washing. This process denatures the protein, doesn't remove the antinutrients, and concentrates goitrogens, which depress thyroid function.

Medicinal Benefits Quality soy products are a blood and chi tonic that support the large intestine, spleen, and stomach functions and help regulate heat and remove toxins. (Black soybeans are a yin and blood tonic and support the kidney, spleen, liver, and large intestine meridians.) Both black and yellow soybeans are an excellent source of protein and molybdenum. They're a very good source of iron, calcium, phosphorus, and dietary fiber, and they are a fair source of B vitamins, vitamin E, and folic acid. Isoflavones, a type of plant estrogen usually occurring in soybeans, are credited with slowing osteoporosis, relieving some side effects of menopause, and alleviating many forms of cancer, including breast and prostate cancer, as well as kidney disease and complications from diabetes. Although other plants contain isoflavones, none contain as rich a supply as soybeans do. In addition, soybeans dramatically lower the undesirable low-density lipoprotein blood cholesterol while raising the desirable high-density lipoprotein level. Soybeans reduce *pitta*.

Use If merely boiled, soybeans inhibit the digestive enzyme trypsin; they are a bear to digest. Asian cuisines typically ferment soy to transform it into healthful and flavorful natto, miso, soy sauce, tamari, and tempeh. Traditionally made tofu and soymilk, although not fermented, are also easy to digest and excellent soy foods when made from whole beans and enjoyed in moderation. Other digestible soybeans are available as:

- **Black Soybeans** These beans have a lush, creamy texture and chestnutlike flavor They're available dried and canned from well-supplied natural food stores and Asian markets.
- **Edamame** These are immature soybeans, which are free of antinutrients (see **Edamame** entry).
- **Soy Sprouts** Sprouted soy, primarily available in Asian markets, is easy to digest.

Be Mindful The antinutrients in traditional soy foods are essentially removed, but these toxins remain in processed soy protein and soy flour. The U.S. Food and Drug Administration lists 288 studies on its database showing the toxicity of high-tech soy. Numerous studies show that consumption of nontraditional soy products leads to nutrient deficiencies, digestive disorders, endocrine disruption, and thyroid problems. Soy phytoestrogens disrupt endocrine function and have the potential to cause infertility and to promote breast cancer in adult women.

In infants, consumption of soy formula has been linked to autoimmune thyroid disease. Soy is the highest food in goitrogens; traditional processing removes them, but in modern soy products these substances interfere with iodine uptake and therefore suppress thyroid gland function. This can result in goiter.

Soy allergies are among the top three food allergens. In the United Kingdom, soy allergies increased from 10 to 15 percent following the introduction of genetically engineered soy, as reported by Jeffrey M. Smith in *Seeds of Deception*.

I do not recommend hard-to-digest soy flour or high-tech Western soy products, including soy grits, soy flakes, soy nuts, soy nut butter, soy isolates, soy protein, and TSP (tex-

---

SOY SPLICED WITH HERBICIDES IS PROBABLY ON YOUR PLATE

In 2008, 92 percent of soybeans grown in the United States were Monsanto's genetically engineered Roundup Ready soybeans. We're talking more than tofu. Soy appears in foods ranging from infant formula to meat extenders; it's a primary staple for livestock and found in most pet foods. Furthermore, soy products like soy oil and flour and lecithin are ubiquitous in prepared, packaged, and restaurant foods.

There's only one way to tell whether the soy ingredient in your soup is natural or genetically engineered: Purchase only certified organic foods or products with a manufacturer's statement that it uses *no* GMOs (genetically modified organisms). Otherwise, you're most probably ingesting Roundup Ready soybeans spliced with an herbicide that enables the plant to survive otherwise toxic doses of chemicals. I wish this were a joke. It is not.

Note: Soy oil, lecithin, and soy protein isolates are extracted with hexane, a neurotoxin petrochemical that poses a serious occupational hazard to workers and is an environmental air pollutant. Small amounts of hexane appear in ingredients processed with this toxin.

tured soy protein). I recommend only organic lecithin.

See **Beans and Legumes; Edamame; Lecithin; Miso; Okara; Soy Deli Foods; Soy Flakes and Soy Flour; Soy Isolate; Soy Nuts and Soy Nut Butter; Soy Oil; Soy Sauce; Tempeh; Textured Soy Protein; Tofu; Yuba.**

SOYBEAN CURD SEE **TOFU.**

SOYBEAN PASTE SEE **MISO.**

SOY DELI FOODS (NOT RECOMMENDED)

Be it a soy-based burger, cold cut, bacon, hot dog, or sausage, the familiar fatty and meaty mixture of these soy foods appeals to many people who are reducing their consumption of meat. Made of highly refined soy isolate and textured soy protein, they are not whole foods, and numerous studies implicate them with human health problems. Furthermore, they usually lack savor.

See **Soybean; Soy Isolate; Textured Soy Protein.**

SOY FLAKES AND SOY FLOUR (NOT RECOMMENDED)

The antinutrient trypsin inhibitor is not removed from soy flakes and soy flour, making these ingredients hard to digest and mildly toxic.

See **Soybean.**

SOY ISOLATE (NOT RECOMMENDED)

Whenever soy isolate is an ingredient in a food, *isolate* that food from your diet.

Here's how this toxic ingredient is made. When oil is pressed from soybeans, the dregs or meal is bathed in petrochemical and alcohol solutions to eliminate all the carbohydrates. What remains, soy isolate, is sold as a

protein supplement and is featured in countless energy foods, beverages, and supplements. Chemical contaminants can—and do—remain in these food products. It is also used in imitation meat and cheese, soymilk, salad dressings, whipped toppings, infant formulas, breakfast cereals, pasta, ice cream, and other highly processed products.

See **Soybean; Soy Deli Foods.**

SOYMILK SEE **NONDAIRY MILK SUBSTITUTES.**

SOY NUTS AND SOY NUT BUTTER (NOT RECOMMENDED)

I do not recommend these hard-to-digest bean products. Real nuts or nut butter taste so much better.

See **Soybean.**

SOY OIL (NOT RECOMMENDED)

Soy oil is the most prevalent oil used in commercial food production. Over 95 percent of this by-product of the soy industry is highly refined using the neurotoxin hexane. The exception is organic, unrefined soy oil; it has an intense aroma and flavor and is considered mildly toxic.

See **Fat and Oil; Soybean.**

SOY SAUCE
Shoyu, Tamari

Soy sauce, indispensable to Asian cookery, has a salty, sweet, slightly tart flavor and a rich, fermented fragrance. Even a few drops of quality soy sauce brings out the natural sweetness and subtle hidden flavors of many savory dishes. If soy sauce to you means a cheap, harsh-tasting liquid condiment, then you've never experienced the real thing.

Both soy sauce and tamari are made of soybeans, salt, and water. Soy sauce, however, also contains a wheat koji and so has a milder flavor. Tamari originally referred to the liquid that rises to the surface of aging hatcho miso; today it refers to wheat-free soy sauce. If traditionally made, both sauces are aged for a year or more. In contrast, commercial rot-gut soy sauce is chemically brewed in a 24-hour process.

Medicinal Benefits Soy sauce and tamari act upon the stomach, spleen, and kidney meridians and help regulate excess heat conditions and dispel toxins. They are nutritious natural flavor enhancers and an excellent source of amino acids and glutamic acid. Because they are fermented, they enhance digestion. Plain salt contains 2 grams of sodium per teaspoon, while the same amount of natural soy sauce contains 286 mg of sodium, about a seventh as much.

In low-sodium circles, soy sauce has a bad name because of its high salt content. This reputation would be warranted if it was consumed by the glassful—which of course is not the case. Soy sauce's wide range of flavors allows richer seasoning with less salt than if straight salt were added to a dish. Soy sauce and tamari have more than 20 identified flavor components. Soy sauce and tamari reduce *vata*.

Use Much of the sweet aroma and flavor of soy sauce is lost during long cooking, so it is best to use it to season during the last few minutes of cooking. Do not boil soy sauce. Strongly flavored tamari, on the other hand, holds up to long simmering, which serves to round out its flavor.

Use tamari or soy sauce in place of table salt in soups, stir-fried vegetables, dressings, and marinades. They're also good as a seasoning for grilled and fried foods, be they Asian or Western in flavor.

Buying Excellent soy condiments are made in the United States, but the most flavorful are aged in cedar kegs and imported from Japan. To preserve the flavor of quality soy sauce or tamari, purchase it in small quantities and

STIR ONCE A WEEK FOR 52 WEEKS

I once made soy sauce from scratch using homemade koji and aging the mash in a 20-gallon crock. I loved the ritual of uncovering the mash and stirring it once every week for a year. As the seasons progressed, the aroma became increasingly complex and rich. There's something about incubation—be it a crock of soy sauce or a baby chick—that is fundamentally satisfying. In a year, friends came to assist with the pressing of the mash and then, of course, sampling it. Although it was not as mellow as a premium soy sauce, it had a distinct and enjoyable flavor and I thoroughly enjoyed both using and sharing it.

store it, tightly covered, in glass in the refrigerator.

See **Fermented Food; Soybean.**

Spaghetti Squash See **Squash; Squash, Winter.**

Spanish Onion See **Onion.**

Spearmint See **Mint.**

Spelt See **Wheat.**

Spices See **Herbs and Spices.**

SPINACH
(*Spinacia oleracea*)

Spinach is a popular green vegetable throughout temperate regions. Its thick, juicy leaves, cooked or raw, have a velvety quality and a flavor that's both sharp and bitter. A fast-growing member of the goosefoot family, spinach originated in Southwestern Asia, where wild varieties still grow.

Medicinal Benefits Spinach supports the functions of the large intestine, stomach, and liver. It is a tonic food for building blood and yin. Spinach moistens, quenches thirst, and supports vision; it is especially useful for easing constipation for frail or elderly people.

Spinach is one of the most nutritious greens, being an exceptionally high source of iron and calcium. However, because it contains oxalic acid, these nutrients are not fully bioavailable to us; thus you'll see contradictory reports as to the nutritional value of spinach.

Spinach is one of the richest sources of lutein, the nutrient that supports good vision and helps prevent macular degeneration and cataracts. Its numerous flavonoid compounds have antioxidant and anticancer properties. Spinach is a low-calorie food and an excellent source of vitamin K, carotenes, vitamin C, and folic acid. An Ayurvedic remedy for a chronic cough is to eat spinach soup seasoned with ginger two times a day on an empty stomach. Spinach reduces *kapha*.

Use Surely the bad reputation spinach once had was due to canned or overcooked spinach, which is indeed without savor. Lightly cooked spinach (cooked only until it begins to go limp), on the other hand, is a delicacy that absorbs any seasoning agent and doesn't impart its flavor to other food. Spinach can be eaten raw as a salad green, and it makes a handsome garnish or plate liner upon which to mound or arrange other foods.

Spinach crowns, the top of the plant stalk with multiple immature leaves, are delicious sautéed and seasoned only with garlic and salt and served as a separate side dish.

Spinach grows in sandy soil, so it needs several washings prior to cooking. Avoid cutting spinach with a carbon blade knife, cooking it in aluminum, or serving it in silver, for it dis-

colors these metals. If spinach stems are overly large and coarse, remove them.

Buying Spinach is available throughout the year; in the winter, its taste is stronger than in the summer. Look for crisp bright green leaves with short stems. Avoid spinach that is yellow, wilted, slimy, or with stem ends that show drying.

Savoy spinach (with crinkled leaves) is the most commonly available. There are also flat-leafed varieties. Prewashed baby spinach is available as a salad ingredient.

Be Mindful "More than 60 percent of the nonorganic spinach tested by the FDA contains pesticide residue, including DDT, permethrin, and other highly toxic pesticides . . . including chlorothalonil, a probable human carcinogen," reports researcher Cindy Burke in her informative *To Buy or Not to Buy Organic*. Burke ranks nonorganic spinach as one of the top four vegetables (along with potatoes, sweet peppers, and celery) to avoid. In addition, commercial spinach is one of the vegetables commonly irradiated.

Because spinach contains a large amount of oxalic acid, people prone to kidney stones or gallstones are advised to eat spinach sparingly. Its purine content puts it on the "consume moderately if at all" for individuals suffering a gout attack. Likewise, moderation is recommended for anyone with a tendency toward loose stools or urinary incontinence.

See **Goosefoot Family; Vegetable.**

SPIRULINA
(*Spirulina platensis*)

Spirulina, a microalgae, is a remarkable chlorophyll source with an intense chlorophyll flavor that occurs naturally in lakes with a high acid content. It is free-forming and floats on the water surface. Unlike macroalgae (seaweed), spirulina is microscopic and derives its name from the spiral shape of its filament. One of the most primitive forms of plant life, spirulina was used by the Aztecs and some Africans as an important food staple. One acre of spirulina ponds produces more than 20 times the protein produced by an acre of soybeans, the next best protein crop.

Medicinal Benefits Spirulina is a cooling and detoxifying food that is a chi, blood, and yin tonic. It supports all the organ functions. Spirulina lowers cholesterol, suppresses fatty accumulation in the liver, prevents tumor formation, enhances the immune system, protects kidneys from mercury poisoning, is useful in treating obesity, and aids digestion by increasing the levels of beneficial bacteria in the intestines.

Spirulina is up to 77 percent complete and a readily digestible protein. It is rich in nucleic acids (RNA/DNA), gamma-linolenic acid (GLA), B vitamins, vitamins C, D, and E, iron, selenium, and other trace minerals.

Use The easiest way to consume spirulina is in a capsule or tablet. It's less expensive to purchase it in a flake or powder form and to stir it into a glass of water or juice, but not everyone will enjoy its curious texture and intensely chlorophyll-like flavor. Spirulina is a common "superfood" ingredient in energy beverages and bars and nutritional supplements.

See **Microalgae.**

Splenda (Not Recommended) See **Sucralose.**

Spring Onion See **Scallion.**

SPROUTED WHEAT (OR GRAIN) PRODUCTS

Sprout grains, then grind and bake for a dense and cakelike "Ezekiel" or sprouted wheat bread. Or, alternatively, sprout grains, dry them, and then mill into a flour and use in baked goods. That is, admittedly, a time-consuming process, so you may also purchase ready-made sprouted wheat, rye, Kamut, spelt flours, breads, or muffins.

As sprouting converts the complex carbohydrates of grains into simple sugars, sprouted wheat products are naturally sweet and may be easier to assimilate. Of late, they've gained popularity in the United States as a wheat alternative.

Unfortunately, even when sprouted, wheat, rye, spelt, and Kamut still contain gluten. They are, therefore, not acceptable foods for the gluten-intolerant or for individuals with wheat sensitivities.

Sprouted wheat flour, *harina para panocha*, is used in a traditional Mexican pudding.

SPROUTS

Germinate a seed and it develops into a sprout with a minuscule rootlet and two tiny leaves that, if planted, would reproduce itself. As a food, sprouts burst with easy-to-assimilate nutrients. The tender sproutlets of grains, seeds, and—primarily—beans have been consumed for thousands of years in Asia; in the West they've been commonplace since the 1970s.

Medicinal Benefits A sprouted seed is easier to assimilate than the seed itself. People who have a hard time digesting beans, for example, often can easily digest bean sprouts or even beans that are just starting to sprout.

Sprouts are valued for their cooling properties and their ability to detoxify the body, especially the liver. They support the kidneys, large intestine, spleen, and stomach and are regarded as tonifying for the blood and yin. Sprouts are a cooling food.

Broccoli sprouts have recently made news as a concentrated source of sulforaphane. One ounce of broccoli sprouts contains more of this potent anticancer compound than two pounds of broccoli. In the process of sprouting, seeds attain higher levels of protein, sugar, enzymes, hormones, vitamin C, and some B vitamins. Sprouts are low in fat and calories. Sprouts of all kinds reduce *pitta* and *kapha*.

Use To make sprouts at home, use organic seeds from a natural food store that are whole and preservative-free. Place a tablespoon of seeds in a widemouthed jar, add water to cover, cover the jar's mouth with a piece of cheesecloth, nylon, or fine mesh, and secure with a rubber band or screw-on jar ring. Soak overnight. The next morning, strain out the water, rinse the seeds, and strain again. Repeat as necessary until the water runs clear. Invert the jar, drain, and set out on the counter, as light increases the seeds' chlorophyll. Rinse and drain the seeds twice a day. In five days or so, you'll have a jar full of ready-to-eat sprouts.

Sprouts may be made of legumes, vegetables, herbs, oil seeds, or of wheat, Kamut, spelt, or rye. Any legume will sprout, but unlike other sprouts, legume sprouts (alfalfa excepted) need to be cooked prior to eating. The carbohydrates in grain convert to sugar; they may become alcoholic and develop an unpleasant sweetness if allowed to grow longer than the length of the grain.

Buying Choose fresh and vibrant-looking sprouts that have no signs of brown discoloration, a slimy texture, or a musty aroma. Some of the more common and easy-to-sprout seeds include alfalfa, broccoli, clover, fenugreek, lentil, mung, and radish.

Be Mindful Children, the elderly, and pregnant women and people with weakened immune systems should not eat raw sprouts. Alfalfa sprouts are *not* to be consumed by people suffering from lupus.

When sprouts are grown in contaminated environments, they may contain food borne diseases that put vulnerable consumers at risk. Salmonella-tainted alfalfa sprouts caused a 2009 outbreak of food poisoning, and the FDA currently advises against their consumption. In the meantime, favor cooked sprouts or sprout your own.

See **Alfalfa.**

SQUASH
(*Cucurbita*)

The Narragansett and Iroquois said *askutasquash* and *isquotersquash;* the pilgrims "heard" squash. Squash is the most important American member of the gourd family (cucumbers and melons are Old World gourd family members). Squash are technically a fruit and when fully mature contain seeds in their central cavity.

As a lifelong squash connoisseur, I remember excitedly obtaining some heirloom squash seeds, planting them, and then anticipating feasting on the "real thing." I was naive—the flesh was edible but, essentially, flavorless. I later discovered that Native Americans primarily grew the plant for its seed.

Squash neatly falls into two categories: summer (immature) and winter (fully mature) varieties. But there's less agreement about their names and, because squash rampantly cross-fertilize, hybrids are endlessly created. As the medicinal properties, use, and storage differ greatly between summer and winter squash, I've listed them below in two separate categories.

Pondering the maturation period between a summer and a winter squash helps appreciate their differences. From blossom to table takes a week for a zucchini; from blossom to table for a winter squash takes 60 days or more. The more watery, immature squash is a more cooling and refreshing vegetable, whereas the mature squash is more nutrient dense and filling. *Vive la différence!*

See **Gourd Family; Pumpkin Seed;**

Pumpkin Seed Oil; Squash Blossom; Squash Greens; Squash Seed; Squash, Summer; Squash, Winter; Vegetable.

SQUASH BLOSSOM

If your zucchini plants are churning out more squash than you could possibly eat, here's an easy solution. Eat the blossoms. All squash blossoms are edible. Their sunny orange blooms are mildly flavored and limp as silk. They have a respected culinary history in both Native American and European cuisine.

Use Squash blossoms are tasty when stuffed with savory morsels and sautéed, baked, or batter-coated and deep-fried. Or slice and liberally strew them in a salad or use as a garnish for their spectacular golden color.

If the blossoms are more than several hours old, pinch out and remove the central stamen because it becomes slimy. Likewise, if you are going to stuff the blossom and the stamen is overly large, remove it.

Buying Look for squash blossoms during the summer months at farmers' and specialty markets. Select fresh blossoms with closed buds; expect them to be as soft and limp as silk lingerie. The cost per pound is high, but don't let that put you off; a dozen blossoms weigh only an ounce or two, and a few ounces are probably all you need.

See **Flower Blossoms; Gourd Family; Squash, Summer; Squash, Winter; Vegetable.**

HOW TO TELL THE BOYS FROM THE GIRLS

Does harvesting squash blossoms mean that you'll have less fruit? Nope, you can have your blossoms and your crooknecks, too. All flowers of the gourd family are edible, whether male or female. When gathering squash blossoms from your garden, pick some of the male flowers, but leave a few on each plant for a bee or bug to do its pollinating work.

How to tell male from female? It's easy. The male blossoms are narrow stemmed, while the female blossoms attach to the stem with a large bulge, which is, in fact, the nascent squash.

SQUASH BLOSSOMS STUFFED WITH SUN-DRIED TOMATOES

Squash blossoms as a garnish are mostly for eye appeal, but stuffed and lightly pan-fried, they are surprisingly flavorful and have a pleasant, moist texture. I use a chopped tortilla to absorb the rich juices of the mushrooms and lend a meaty texture. You can also use breadcrumbs or a cooked grain such as rice or quinoa.

Makes 16

- 3 tablespoons extra virgin olive oil or palm oil
- 2 cloves garlic, minced
- ½ cup chopped mushrooms
- 2 tablespoons drained and chopped oil-packed sun-dried tomatoes
- 1 finely chopped tortilla (or ½ cup breadcrumbs or cooked quinoa or rice)
- ½ teaspoon ground coriander

¼ teaspoon ground turmeric

1 cup chopped cilantro

Unrefined salt and freshly ground black pepper

16 squash blossoms

Heat 1 tablespoon oil in a medium sauté pan. Add the garlic and sauté for 1 to 2 minutes, until aromatic. Add the mushrooms and sauté for 3 to 5 minutes, until softened. Add the tomatoes, tortilla, coriander, and turmeric and sauté for 3 to 4 minutes, until warmed through. Add the cilantro and salt and pepper to taste and cook for an additional minute. Remove from the heat and set the filling aside to cool until just warm.

Loosely stuff each squash blossom with the filling. Twist the petals closed to contain the filling; if necessary, secure with a toothpick. Heat the remaining 2 tablespoons oil in a large sauté pan. Add the stuffed blossoms and lightly fry for about 3 minutes or until very lightly browned. Gently turn and brown the other side. Serve hot or cold as an appetizer or side dish.

SQUASH GREENS

The tender young greens of squash, cucumbers, and gourds may be used as a potherb. Destem, cut, and use as you would spinach. I most typically find squash greens from Asian farmers at farmers' markets.

See **Squash; Squash, Summer; Squash, Winter; Vegetable.**

SQUASH SEED

Roasted winter squash seeds are a superior source of fiber and zinc. They are so chewy that some people find them bothersome to eat; others find the succulent kernel well worth the exercise. Depending upon the squash va-

---

A HIGH-FIBER SNACK

Makes 1 cup

1 cup winter squash or pumpkin seeds

½ teaspoon curry powder

Unrefined salt

1 tablespoon melted butter (optional)

Preheat the oven to 350°F. Separate the squash seeds from the stringy pulp. In a medium bowl, toss the seeds with the curry, salt, and butter, if using. Spread in an even layer over a small baking pan. Bake for 10 minutes, or until the seeds are crisp and lightly browned.

---

riety, you may either eat the seed and hull together, or crack a seed between your teeth and use your tongue to extract the nutmeat from the hull. Use seeds from winter squash or pumpkins, or purchase them toasted and seasoned from Latino food markets.

See **Pumpkin Seed; Squash, Winter.**

SQUASH, SUMMER
(*Cucurbita pepo*)

Tender-fleshed summer squash flourish in the summer, and one plant can produce more squash than you can eat or give away. There could very well be truth to the small-town counsel of needing to lock your car in the summertime to prevent a neighbor from filling the front seat with her excess garden zucchini.

Summer squash are harvested when immature and are typically lightly cooked. These brightly colored vegetables are charmingly flavorful—bitter melon excepted—when small and garden fresh. Their flavor rapidly diminishes as their size and/or time past harvest increases.

Medicinal Benefits Summer squash support the stomach, spleen, large intestine, and liver. They are a yin tonic that treats hot conditions, as their 95 percent water content suggests. While not an especially nutrient-dense vegetable, summer squash is easy to digest and does contain anticancer properties and carotenes. Summer squash is *tridoshic*.

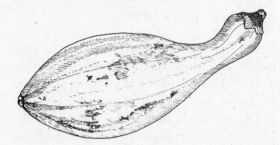

Use Garden-fresh baby summer squash can be served as crudités or finely sliced in salads. Squash longer than three inches is most flavorful when cooked. Size, however, is not always an indication of maturity. An overly mature summer squash has a tough skin, hard seeds, and dry flesh, which makes it best suited to stuffing and baking. When I have an abundance of garden zucchini and yellow squash, I pickle them whole like dill pickles. Summer squash is a popular ingredient in stir-fries, casseroles, and soups, or on their own steamed or sautéed.

Buying The prolific summer squash plants produce continuously throughout the growing season. In the garden, I harvest summer squash just when the blossom withers, for then its flavor is developed but its flesh is still tender.

Even though zucchini and crookneck squash are available from warmer climates during the winter months, they lack flavor. When squash is fresh and seasonal, choose those with brightly colored skin free from discoloration. These are the common varieties:

- **Crookneck Squash** This sunny-yellow summer squash—which averages about six inches long—has a crook neck that can range from a small arch to a decided hook. Its thin skin is either smooth or bumpy. Compared to its near relative zucchini, a crookneck is less efficiently packed and therefore less available or sometimes more expensive than the zucchini. Both may be used interchangeably.
- **Pattypan Squash** Among vegetables with fanciful shapes as well as names, the pattypan ranks high. It looks like a squat pincushion with scalloped edges. The pattypan has a pale green skin when immature, which turns white or cream when the squash ripens. Some varieties are speckled green. Small pattypans, under four inches in diameter, are superior in flavor and texture to larger ones.
- **Yellow Summer Squash** In all respects except that it is yellow in color rather than green, this popular squash is a zucchini variety.
- **Zucchini** The British call it marrow, the French say *courgette*, and in the United States we use the Italian name, *zucchini*. This best-known summer squash is generally dark green when small, but it may develop white stripes as it matures. A newer zucchini variety is circular and about the size of a tennis ball.

Be Mindful Unless you're buying yellow summer squash from a farmers' market, the odds are that it has been genetically modified (GM). In a store, if possible, purchase certified organic or squash that are labeled non-GMO. To a lesser extent commercial zucchini squash may be GM.

See **Bitter Melon; Gourd Family; Squash; Vegetable.**

CALABACITAS (ZUCCHINI, CORN, AND ROASTED CHILES)

Don't let looks deceive you. It's with good reason that this unassuming dish has remained a seasonal favorite in the New Mexico region for hundreds of years.

Rather than slicing nearly intact corn kernels from the cob, I slice them in half, as this frees all the flavor and creamy juice from the hulls.

Serves 4 as a side dish

- 3 to 4 ears corn
- 2 tablespoons butter, extra virgin olive oil, sesame oil, or palm oil
- 1 onion, sliced
- 2 cloves garlic, minced
- 4 medium-small zucchini, sliced into thin rounds
- 2 New Mexico or other fresh chiles, roasted, peeled, seeded, and diced
- Unrefined salt and freshly ground black pepper
- ½ cup chopped cilantro

Holding an ear of corn in an upright position on a cutting board, slice the corn kernels from the cob, shaving off the top half of each kernel until all the kernels are partially removed. Next, shave the cob a second time to remove the kernel remainders. Repeat with each ear of corn to yield about 1½ cups of corn.

Heat the butter in a large skillet over medium heat. Add the onion and garlic and sauté until almost softened, 3 to 4 minutes.

Add the zucchini and sauté for about 4 minutes, until slightly softened. Add the corn and chiles and sauté for 3 to 4 minutes, until the corn is cooked through. Season with salt and pepper to taste, stir in the cilantro, and serve.

SQUASH, WINTER
(*Cucurbita maxima, C. moschata, C. pepo*)

> Go to sleep now, my pumpkin,
> I will cover your toes.
> If you sleep now, my pumpkin,
> You'll turn into a rose.
> —Lullaby

The word "squash" aptly describes this vegetable's cooked texture, but it doesn't hint at its sweetness. A good winter squash packs a wallop of flavor. Winter squashes have dark yellow to orange flesh and a hard rind. The sweetest squashes generally are those with the most deeply colored flesh.

Unlike summer squash, winter squash is eaten when fully matured with a tough, protective rind and fully mature seeds capable of reproducing themselves. A winter squash is superior in flavor if it was harvested after the first frost; with proper storage, it will hold for up to six months.

Medicinal Benefits Squash is considered a chi tonic and a warming food that is medicinal to the spleen, stomach, large intestine, and lungs. It improves energy and blood circulation. Compared to summer squash, winter squash is a better source of natural sugars, carbohydrates, and beta-carotene. Winter squash is exceptionally high in complex carbohydrates and is medicinal for diabetics and those with digestive problems.

It provides vitamins A and C, potassium, and magnesium. It is an excellent source of pre–vitamin A and often carotenoids, and therefore has anticarcinogenic properties; in fact, winter squash, sweet potatoes, and carrots are the vegetables highest in carotenoids. Most winter squash reduces *vata* and *pitta*, while spaghetti squash reduces *kapha*.

Use Cutting a winter squash requires a

sharp knife, or if it's large and unwieldy, drop it onto the floor—it will crack and then you can insert a knife. You may also purchase a small squash, bake it whole, then cut it with a butter knife. If a round squash doesn't rest firmly on the cutting board, trim a wedge to give stability as you cut the rest. Butternut squash are easily cut in half and then stood on end for additional cutting.

Once cut, taste the squash. If it is bland raw, it will be bland cooked—toss it. Winter squash are not eaten raw; they can be baked, stuffed, simmered in a little water, steamed, or fried—but boiling in water to cover leaves it flavorless. Pureed it makes a sweet soup or pie, or raw it may be grated and added to cookies, puddings, and cakes.

Use Regional winter squash is available in the fall and winter. Choose heavy squash with a smooth, hard, richly colored rind. Look for precut pieces of large squash, such as the hubbard or banana. Because a butternut's skin is thinner and lighter in color than most other winter squash, I often cook and puree it with the skin intact. This saves preparation time and increases nutritional value. Also, in some presentations, the rind of a green-skinned squash lends great eye appeal. If using the skin, trim and remove any rough spots.

Buying Select squash that are heavy for their weight, with a firm rind and mottled markings. The rind should be free of soft spots, cracks, and bore holes. An intact stem indicates better storage properties.

If you have a cool, dry storage area, purchase enough to see you through the winter. Arrange squash, uncovered, so as not to touch another and they'll hold into March. Check them periodically and use first any that develop a soft spot. Once cut, refrigerate. Do not store uncut squash in plastic bags, as moisture develops, which encourages spoil-

age. These are the common winter squash varieties:

- **Acorn Squash** Shaped like a deeply ribbed acorn, this tasty squash is a long-time American favorite. Newer varieties are supersweet, whereas the heirloom varieties are mildly sweet. An acorn's hard skin is typically dark green. However, some varieties are orange (golden acorn) or even multicolored with green, orange, and white splotches (carnival). Compared to a buttercup or butternut squash, the acorn flesh is typically pale yellow rather than orange, drier, and less dense. For beautiful flower shapes, slice this squash into thin horizontal rounds. With extended storage, its flesh becomes fibrous.

- **Banana Squash** The banana squash is reminiscent in shape of a banana with a muted orange skin and attractive orange, slightly stringy flesh that is bland in flavor. It grows up to two feet in length and is about six inches in diameter. In some markets it is sold in pieces.

- **Buttercup Squash** This dark green, rounded but squat-shaped squash is crowned with a blue-green "turban" at its blossom end. With bright orange flesh, it ranks just under the kabocha as the sweetest squash. Creamy describes its texture.

- **Butternut Squash** The longest keeper in the squash family, butternut squash is similar in shape and color to a peanut in the shell, and thus its name. Some, however, are more pear shaped. Its sweet, orange flesh is similar to the buttercup squash. If a butternut is too old or was not properly cured and stored, its interior color fades to white, becomes pithy, and lacks flavor.

- **Calabaza Squash** This is a generic Spanish term for a winter squash. It also specifically identifies the bottle-shaped gourd of a *C. foetidissima species.*

- **Delicata Squash** As its name suggests, this squash has a sweetness somewhat reminiscent of sweet corn. This small squash is shaped like a fat yellow cucumber with grooves and orange stripes. Its pale yellow flesh is moist and creamy. It's a type of acorn squash, but unlike acorn squash, its thin skin is edible.

- **Golden Nugget Squash** Ranging in size from a tennis ball to a grapefruit, the golden nugget looks like a tiny pumpkin; when fully ripe, it has a mildly sweet squash flavor. If picked before maturity, the golden nugget has a shiny (rather than dull) rind and is bland and tasteless. It keeps well. The golden nugget is treacherous to cut because of its size and extremely hard shell. Bake it whole, then cut into desired shapes, season, and serve.

- **Hubbard Squash** The thing I remember most about hubbard squash from my childhood is my father chopping it with a hatchet. Hubbard was an autumn standby in our home, but whatever else was baked alongside it was eaten first. This large (often weighing more than 25 pounds) winter squash has dark green or reddish orange pebbly skin. A blue variety can also be found. Today smaller sizes are available. The hubbard looks some-thing like an oversize crookneck squash, or it can be more rounded in shape. A hubbard's flesh is more mustard colored than orange, with a dry texture and mild flavor.

- **Kabocha Squash (Baby Red Hubbard, Hokkaido Pumpkin, Japanese Pumpkin, Red Kuri)** To my palate, kabocha squash is a strong contender for the ultimate sweet vegetable. It's satisfyingly rich, almost nutty, and never cloying like chocolate or sugar. Kabocha's sweetness makes me feel both nurtured and content. It's a good keeper—I store a stash under the spare bed in my basement. Kabocha skin is either slate green or a loud orange-red. Its flesh is mustard yellow and its texture is similar to buttercup squash, but it's drier, flaky (if overbaked), and never stringy. It's delicious baked, sautéed, in a soup, with a grain, beans, or vegetables, or in pie.

- **Pumpkin** The culinary use of pumpkin is primarily limited to pies. Bred for their extra-sweet flavor and silky texture, sugar pumpkins are ideal for pie. While you can turn any pumpkin into a pie, remember that a large pumpkin is stringy and small in flavor. The canned pumpkin is actually made from a yellow-skinned squash. Unlike canned pumpkin, fresh pumpkin tastes more vital, so you can use less sugar for a satisfying rather than cloying sweet taste.

- **Spaghetti Squash** Pale in flesh and flavor, it is like a summer squash but with the storage capabilities of winter squash. Its memorable property is that when it is cooked, the flesh may be coaxed into spaghetti-like strands, which some people adore. Others find the vegetable all texture and no taste.

SOUP TUREENS

Golden nugget squash is the perfect size for an individual soup tureen. Allow one squash per person. Rub the shell with oil and bake at 350°F for 30 minutes. Remove from the oven; cut off and reserve the top to use as a lid. Remove the seeds and fibers. Add hot soup (cream of celery goes especially well) and replace the lids. Bake for another 15 to 20 minutes, until the squash is just cooked through. Watch carefully—overcooked squash loses its shape and eye appeal. Sprinkle the soup with a green garnish such as chives. Serve hot, with or without the lid.

- **Turban Squash** The turbanlike swirl on the blossom end of this vividly orangered squash makes it a contender for the most comely of vegetables. The turban, with its brightly variegated orange-red rind, is shaped rather like a buttercup. Its flavor is fairly mild.

See **Gourd Family; Squash; Vegetable.**

STAR ANISE
Chinese Anise
(*Illicium verum*)

Undoubtedly, the most comely spice is star anise. This fruit, the size of a quarter, grows on a Chinese evergreen and dries into a star shape with six to eight points; each point contains a glossy brown seed. Collected when green, the fruits are sun-dried until the remaining pod is woody and mahogany colored. The pod is more aromatic than the seeds, but both are used as a favorite spice in Vietnamese, Indian, and Chinese cuisine. Star anise contains anethole, the same essential oil found in anise—just stronger.

Medicinally, star anise is a warming herb with stimulant and a diuretic properties; it aids digestion, relieves pain, and has antifungal properties. Star anise tea is soothing for a cough. It is the primary source for shikimic acid, which is used in the production of the antiflu drug Tamiflu.

Star anise is used to flavor anisette and other licorice-flavored liqueurs and is an ingredient in Chinese five-spice powder and Indian garam masala.

See **Herbs and Spices.**

STAR FRUIT
Carambola
(*Averrhoa carambola*)

The banana yellow star fruit is a Disney-like creation that slices into perfectly shaped stars to delight the eye and spirit. A three- to five-inch-long oval fruit, it contains five pronounced lengthwise ribs. The star fruit has a thin, edible waxy skin, and its citrusy, juicy flesh is almost translucent. Rather plumlike or grapelike in flavor, it ranges from tart to fragrantly sweet. Star fruit contains soft white edible seeds.

A native of India, Indonesia, and Sri Lanka, where the fruit still grows wild, the star fruit is now grown in Florida, Hawaii, and other semitropical regions.

Medicinal Benefits Star fruit is cooling and astringent and thus clears excess heat. It allays biliousness and diarrhea. Star fruit is a good source of vitamin C and potassium. It is low in calories.

Use Sweet star fruit can be eaten out of hand, used in salads and desserts, or added as a garnish. Slice into quarter-inch star-shaped pieces and use as a base for an appetizer. Pureed it may be added to sauces, sorbet, soups, and beverages. Or slice and poach in a syrup and use as a topping. Star fruit may also be stir-fried.

The skin is edible but remove any browned, and therefore toughened, ridges or tips. Tart star fruit may be used as a lemon or lime substitute or in jams and chutneys.

Buying Look for star fruits that are evenly colored and without brown spots. Narrow-ribbed fruits are tart, whereas larger and more fleshy-ribbed fruits are sweeter. Leave at room temperature until their full fruity aroma is apparent and they are yellow. When ripe, refrigerate for up to one week. Star fruits are available year-round. Dried star fruit is available in some natural food stores.

See **Fruit.**

STEM GINGER SEE **GINGER.**

STEM LETTUCE SEE **LETTUCE.**

STEVIA
(Stevia rebaudiana)

Imagine a healthful herb that is 30 times sweeter than sugar, nonnutritive, and essentially noncaloric. Stevia, which the Guarani Indians of Paraguay call *caa-hee*, is such a plant. Its leaves and flower buds contain two glucosides that are 200 and 300 times, respectively, sweeter than sucrose, and which cannot be metabolized in the human digestive system. An extract of this leaf, stevia, is used as an alternative sweetener. Stevia is a member of the daisy family.

Medicinal Benefits Stevia has a long history of use in South America and, for the past 30 years, it has widespread use in Japan, where clinical data indicates that it suppresses dental bacteria. Stevia apparently regulates blood sugar and therefore may be of use for people with hypoglycemia and blood sugar imbalances and as a treatment for type 2 diabetes. It assists with weight loss, regulates blood pressure, and reduces mental and physical fatigue. There is currently no evidence of adverse reactions to stevia.

Stevia is the one sweetener people suffering from candidiasis and yeast-type conditions can tolerate. As sweetened foods exacerbate an overly hot and moist internal environment, which fosters yeast overgrowth, people on anticandidiasis diets must forego all sweets. Stevia is the sweet exception. Stevia reduces *pitta* and *vata*.

Use Do not expect stevia-sweetened products to have the same flavor or texture as sugar-sweetened foods, and if you use the dried leaf itself rather than its extract, expect it to imbue light-colored foods with a green tint. Stevia is not affected by heat. Its taste has a slower onset and longer duration than does sugar. To extract the sweetness from the leaves, soak 1 teaspoon of stevia in 1 cup of water overnight and strain. Use to sweeten beverages and desserts. Refined stevia—as a clear liquid or white powder—won't color your food, but it is not as healthful as the whole leaf products. Two drops of stevia liquid extract sweeten 1 cup of liquid. One speck of refined stevia sweetens 1 cup of liquid.

Buying Stevia is available in natural food stores as a cut herb, a liquid extract, a pure powdered extract, and blended with rice syrup powder as a granulated sugar substitute. Store stevia tightly covered in a cool, dry place.

See **Daisy Family; Sweeteners.**

STINGING NETTLE SEE **NETTLE.**

STRAWBERRY
(*Fragaria virginiana, F. vesca, F. moschata*)

> Doubtless God could have made a better berry, but doubtless God never did.
> —William Butler

I hope that everyone knows of at least one wooded path that promises wild strawberries. It takes time, down on the knees, to ferret out these pea-size jewels. The payoff, in volume, is negligible—but that's no deterrent.

The strawberry is an ancient plant and a distant blackberry relative that grows wild throughout Europe and North America. It is an unusual fruit in that its seeds are imbedded on its surface. They vary widely in size, shape, and flavor but, at their best, have a musky floral aroma and are sweet but acidic, almost pineapple-like in flavor. They are vivid red, plump, juicy, and soft as a baby's cheek. California provides 80 percent of the nation's fresh and frozen strawberries.

Medicinal Benefits Research has determined that strawberries have a tranquilizing effect; that's why surgical gloves for dentists and masks for children's anesthesia are often perfumed with a strawberry scent.

Strawberries are an excellent spring tonic, beneficial to the kidneys, liver, lungs, stomach, and spleen. They are a yin tonic and help break down excess toxins in the liver. They increase the appetite and are moistening and lubricating. Strawberries have clinically proven antiviral properties.

Strawberries provide vitamin A, as much vitamin C as oranges, and some B-complex vitamins, as well as silicon, some potassium, and fiber. Strawberries in moderation reduce *vata* and *kapha* and, to a lesser degree, *pitta*.

Buying Buy local strawberries, fully red, unblemished, fragrant, and slightly soft, with hulls intact. Since strawberries do not ripen off the vine, those with green or white tips will never become fully sweet. Local vine-ripened strawberries will be the most aromatic, flavorful, and nutrient dense. Peak season is from late spring through early summer. Do not remove the green caps until after washing the fruit and just before serving.

Use You can dry, pie, jam, or sauce strawberries or dip them into melted (but not hot) chocolate. They're great out of hand or enveloped in whipped cream and topping a shortcake for a classic American dessert.

Be Mindful Nonorganic strawberries are the food that most often exceeds pesticide tolerance levels set forth by the USDA. The "joke" is that you could grind up commercial strawberries and spray them as a pesticide. Commercial strawberries are often irradiated. Strawberries are one of the more common fruit allergens for some people and may cause swelling of the air passages, hay fever, or hives.

See **Fruit.**

A SWEET WAY TO WHITEN TEETH

A kitchen remedy to remove tartar and strengthen teeth is to rub a halved strawberry on the teeth and gums and leave on for 45 minutes. Rinse with warm water.

STRAWBERRY SPINACH SEE **BEETBERRY.**

STRAWBERRY TOMATO SEE **GROUND CHERRY.**

STRING BEAN SEE **GREEN BEAN.**

SUCANAT SEE **SUGAR.**

SUCRALOSE (NOT RECOMMENDED) SPLENDA

Sucralose is a chlorinated artificial sweetener derived from sugar and sold as Splenda or mixed with other artificial sweeteners. Reputable natural food stores do not carry Splenda-sweetened products. Its consumers report weight gain, sleep disruption, sexual dysfunction, increases in cancer, multiple sclerosis, lupus, and diabetes.

SUCROSE SEE **SUGAR.**

SUGAR
Dehydrated Cane Juice, Sucrose, Table Sugar

Just as tasting oil or salt is the best way to determine its quality, so it is with sugar. Table sugar is 99.5 percent pure sucrose and made from either sugar beets, sugarcane, or corn. The flavor is sharp, harsh, one-dimensional, and intensely sweet. For a more enjoyable flavor, favor dehydrated cane juice (also called evaporated cane juice), which contains 2 percent or more trace minerals and has a mellow, round sweet flavor.

Logically it is indeed hard to fathom that your sense of taste can so clearly distinguish such minute chemical differences. As with other foods, it appears that how a food is processed also affects how it tastes and how it is digested and, therefore, how it impacts your health.

Medicinal Benefits Sugar can ease spasms, relieve pain, give a sense of ease and nurture, and, in the short term, boost energy. Sugar acts upon the spleen, stomach, kidney, and liver meridians. It passes quickly into the bloodstream, shocking and weakening the digestive system, to result in a blood sugar imbalance that causes a craving for more sugar.

Use In my grandmother's time, sugar was used sparingly in desserts and preserves. In her grandmother's time, it was a precious treat used primarily by the wealthy. Today it is a ubiquitous ingredient in prepared, packaged, and restaurant foods. Sugar remains a primary ingredient in desserts, preserves, and confections.

Buying If buying table sugar, select 100 percent pure cane sugar, or you'll be purchasing an inferior and more highly refined beet or corn sweetener that will not give the same results in some applications such as candy making. As possible, favor organic sugar, for it is free of pesticide residues and is a cane product.

- **Dehydrated (Evaporated) Cane Juice** Also known as rapadura and sucanat, this is pressed from sugarcane, cooked to reduce its water content, granulated at low temperatures, and sifted. It is composed of small brown grainy crystals and retains all of its trace minerals. This is the least processed of all sugars and the one that I use and recommend.
- **Sugar (Sucrose, Table Sugar)** Chemically refined from cane, beets, or corn, it is 99.5 percent pure sucrose. (To make powdered sugar or confectioners' sugar, this product is more finely ground and mixed with cornstarch, wheat flour, or calcium phosphate to keep it from clumping together.)
- **Sugar with Molasses** There are multiple sugars that are processed like table sugar but still contain some molasses because either the molasses is added back in or because the sugar didn't undergo the final processing steps. The higher the molasses content in a sugar, the darker its color, the stronger its taste, and the greater its moisture-retaining properties. The following molasses-containing sugars may or may not be made from cane:

Brown sugar White sugar with added molasses; it is available as light brown, golden, and dark brown sugar.

Cane crystals A raw sugar derived from cane.

Demerara sugar A large-crystal, light brown, raw sugar.

Granulated cane juice Raw sugar made from cane.

Invert sugar A highly processed granular sugar used commercially because it is sweeter than white sugar.

Milled cane sugar Small-grained cane crystals with a golden color and subtle molasses flavor.

Muscovado sugar A raw, dark brown sugar with small crystals.

Powdered sugar White sugar from any source that is finely ground and blended with cornstarch.

Raw sugar Created from the first stage of sugarcane manufacturing and, therefore, not produced with dyes or chemicals used in subsequent stages of white sugar production.

Turbinado sugar A raw cane sugar with large, light brown crystals.

Unbleached sugarcane White cane sugar that does not undergo the final bleaching process.

Yellow-D sugar Another term for brown sugar.

Be Mindful Sugar consumption is associated with increased incidence of type 2 diabetes, obesity, and tooth decay. It creates an acid condition that consumes the body's minerals and causes calcium loss. Refined sugar use is implicated in all our contemporary degenerative health problems. It may also contribute to gas, fatigue, and PMS. Sugar depresses the immune system and contributes to osteoporosis.

See **Goosefoot Family (sugar beet); Grass Family (sugarcane); Sweeteners.**

SUGAR SNAP PEA SEE **PEA, FRESH.**

SUMAC BERRY
(*Rhus*)

The lemony flavored pea-size red berries of several species of small sumac trees are used in Middle Eastern and Native American cuisine. The small fruits grow in dense clusters called sumac bobs. They are a cashew family relative. They're most commonly available from specialty food stores dried and ground to a purplish powder. If wild harvesting, carefully identify, as some sumac fruits contain an irritant, urushiol, and are toxic.

See **Cashew Family.**

SUMMER SAVORY SEE **SAVORY.**

SUMMER SQUASH SEE **SQUASH, SUMMER.**

SUNBERRY
Garden Huckleberry, Wonderberry
(*Solanum retroflexum*)

Last summer, I planted some sunberry seeds in a rather untended garden corner. At summer's end, I was surprised by an abundance of handsome, three-foot-high bushy sunberry plants. The purple-black fruits of this nightshade family member, about the size of a cherry, were bitter, acidic, and harsh on the tip of the tongue; perhaps they were the near relative *S. nigrum*, which goes by the same common names but is highly toxic. I cooked some up, tasted, and then tossed the mess.

Various references claim that sunberries are bland, but with adequate sugar they make a good pie ingredient. My agronomist friend Duane Johnson at Colorado State University (CSU) told me that their New Food Products Development lab failed to find a commercial application for sunberries. He knows of no domestic commercial use. Johnson warned me—now too late—that after one experimental crop, they've remained a problem weed in CSU gardens.

See **Fruit; Nightshade Family.**

SUNCHOKE SEE JERUSALEM ARTICHOKE.

SUNFLOWER FAMILY SEE DAISY FAMILY.

SUNFLOWER OIL

Unrefined sunflower oil has the heady aroma of the sunny blossom itself. The sweet, nutty oil, pressed from sunflower seeds, is, when unrefined and fresh, a good all-purpose stove-top cooking oil that is popular worldwide.

There are various types of sunflower oil available, including one high in omega-6 fatty acids (linoleic), and one high in omega-9 fatty acids (oleic). As a high consumption of omega-6 fatty acids appears to increase the likelihood of breast and prostate cancer, choose accordingly.

Once a bottle of sunflower seed oil has been opened, refrigerate.

See **Fat and Oil.**

SUNFLOWER SEED
(*Helianthus annuus*)

More than any other flower, the sunflower suggests the glory of the summer sun itself. Wild, it lines roadways and gilds whole fields with its stunning, suncolored mandalas. Cultivated in home gardens, it towers to impressive heights of 20 feet and boasts a flower up to 30 inches in diameter. A showy plant indeed.

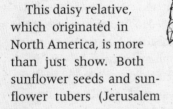

This daisy relative, which originated in North America, is more than just show. Both sunflower seeds and sunflower tubers (Jerusalem artichoke) were important Native American foods. Sunflowers were introduced in Europe in the 1500s and now have spread throughout temperate regions worldwide. Until the popularization of health foods in the United States in the 1960s, its domestic use was primarily for bird feed; hence its once common name "polly seed." Sunflower seeds are also nicknamed "sunnies." The shells may be white, brown, black, or black with white stripes.

Medicinal Benefits Sunflower seeds are a chi tonic and nurturing food that support the spleen and large intestine function; they are used to treat constipation. Sunflower seeds contain more protein than beef and 20 percent fat, most of which is unsaturated. A good source of calcium, phosphorus, and iron, as well as vitamins E and several of the B-complex vitamins, they also contain the amino acid arginine and a trace of fluorine, which may explain the claim that they are good for the teeth. They are rich in the cholesterol-lowering phytosterols. Sunflower seeds are *tridoshic* used in moderation; in larger quantities, they primarily reduce *vata*.

Use Shelled sunflower seeds can be substituted for nuts in many recipes as an ingredient or garnish; for example, they are a flavorful and economical substitute for pine nuts in pesto. Sprouted sunflower seeds are wonderfully flavored and aromatic and excellent in salads or on sandwiches. The seeds may be ground into a butter similar in use to peanut butter. They are a popular snack food and ingredient in trail mixes and energy bars. To heighten their flavor, toast the seeds lightly in a skillet before eating and season them with soy sauce if you like.

In-shell sunflower seeds are, of course, the most fresh. They're easy to hull, one at a time, by cracking the shell between your teeth and then removing the hull. Here's a faster method:

Fill a zip-top bag about a quarter full, place it on a counter, and roll with a rolling pin or wine bottle to break up the shells. Transfer the seeds to a water-filled bowl and stir. The seeds will sink; the shells will float, where they can be skimmed off.

Buying Sunflower seeds are available shelled or unshelled, roasted and salted, or raw. Whole seeds have a good shelf life, but once hulled they need to be refrigerated. Look for unbroken, even-colored seeds. Avoid discolored or rubbery seeds.

Be Mindful Sunflower petals are toxic. If you have a gluten sensitivity, note that in-shell sunflower seeds may be dusted with flour. Sunflower seeds contain a moderate amount of oxalic acid. If you have a proclivity toward forming oxalate-type kidney stones, eat sunflower seeds in moderation.

See **Daisy Family; Jerusalem Artichoke; Seeds.**

SUSHI RICE SEE **RICE.**

SWAMP CABBAGE SEE **HEART OF PALM.**

SWATOW MUSTARD SEE **MUSTARD GREENS.**

SWEDE SEE **RUTABAGA.**

SWEDISH TURNIP SEE **RUTABAGA.**

SWEET BROWN RICE SEE **RICE.**

SWEET CORN
Corn on the Cob
(Zea mays saccharata)

On or off the cob, we think that sweet corn is as American as apple pie—but it's actually a newcomer to the scene. Popular for only the past hundred years, the first recorded sweet corn was collected from the Iroquois in 1779.

The distinguishing characteristic of sweet corn is a defective gene that prevents its sugars from being completely transformed into starch. In other words, sweet corn remains almost sugary sweet and is eaten in its immature (milky) stage. With other corn varieties, their simple sugars become complex carbohydrates at maturity.

Use Sweet corn is enjoyed eaten on the cob (either roasted, grilled, or boiled) or sliced from the cob and eaten as a side dish or used as an ingredient in numerous dishes. Immature or baby corn that's only two to three inches long is eaten cob and all either fresh, canned, or pickled. Corn on the cob is delicious seasoned with butter, salt, Tabasco sauce, lime juice, or the flesh of an umeboshi plum. Corn kernels go well with squash, beans, peppers, tomatoes, and cheese.

Buying Fresh sweet corn has vibrant (rather than dry and matted) silk, dark green, compact, and moist husks, and kernels that are plump and full. Keep the husks intact until just before cooking. For the sweetest and most delicious dish, fresh immature (rather than overmature) corn is best. Even though available year-around, sweet corn is primarily a seasonal food because of the superior taste of local fresh corn.

Be Mindful Genetically modified sweet corn is commercially available in the United States as Bt corn, as the gene *Bacillus thuringiensis* has been inserted into the corn. When consumed by the European corn borer, it perforates the larval digestive tract, causing sepsis and death. There are reports of adverse reactions in humans from Bt corn ingestion. Purchasing organic corn, or corn from a farmers' market, assures against Bt corn, as the gene is only available to large producers.

See **Chicos; Corn; Vegetable.**

PUT THE POT ON . . . THEN HARVEST AND SHUCK THE CORN

Grandma, putting the water on to boil, would then send us out to collect and shuck enough corn for dinner. Corn is best when it's *fresh* and before its sugars have time to convert to starch. With the season's first harvest, ears upon ears of corn are our first and second courses.

New supersweet hybrids are exceptionally tender and, as their name suggests, almost cloyingly sweet, with up to 36 percent sucrose. Their more durable sugar content lasts up to ten days after picking. I prefer the older, less sugary (14 percent sucrose) varieties that are more "corny" in flavor and a little more chewy. Silver queen and golden bantam are two heirloom varieties that you can either grow or sometimes find at the farmers' market.

SWEETENERS

Mother's milk is sweet. Maybe this is where it all starts, for most everyone loves sweets. This doesn't have to be a problem as long as attention is paid to quality and quantity.

It's useful to recall that no sweetener is a whole food; each has had something removed to concentrate its sugars. Nectar is refined by bees into honey, maple sap is concentrated into maple syrup, and cane's fiber and nutrients are removed to make table sugar. Your best option is to avoid artificial and highly refined sweeteners, then delight in the *minimally* refined sweeteners that retain their trace minerals and rich flavor.

Medicinal Benefits The sweetness found in grains, dairy, meat, legumes, and some vegetables like squash, carrots, and yams strengthens the spleen and helps build energy. These foods satisfy the sweet tooth.

The sucrose found in many sweeteners, when highly refined or when used in excess, causes the spleen to secrete more insulin to monitor the amount of sugar going into the blood; extra adrenaline from the adrenal glands is also mobilized to monitor the blood sugar level. Simple sugars provide a few hours of increased energy, which are followed by energy depletion and an emotional low, aptly known as the "sugar blues." Over time, this damages the spleen and stresses the adrenal glands. Excessive use leads to chronic fatigue, bodily weakness, edema, and various digestive problems.

Even though fructose is metabolized differently than sucrose, it is implicated in the current high rates of diabetes, elevated cholesterol and triglycerides, gastrointestinal distress, and obesity.

Unrefined sweeteners reduce *pitta* and *vata*.

Use Today you're hard-pressed to find a prepared or packaged dish that does not contain added sweetener. Furthermore, new fruit and vegetable cultivars are bred to have higher percentages of sugar. This trend seems out of control and it is, undeniably, unhealthful. Fortunately, in your own kitchen, you have choices. Favor heirloom produce, enjoy unsweetened beverages, and frequently cook from scratch.

Be Mindful Excessive consumption of sweeteners is associated with increased incidence of type 2 diabetes, obesity, and tooth decay. It creates an acid condition that consumes the body's minerals and causes calcium loss. Excessive use is implicated in all our contemporary degenerative health problems. It may also contribute to gas, fatigue, and PMS. Sugar depresses the immune system and contributes to osteoporosis.

Artificial sweeteners "trick the body" by delivering a sweet flavor; but as the sweet is noncaloric or not digested as a natural sweetener, it is incapable of satisfying one's sweet tooth. Conversely, consumption of chemical sweeteners typically goads the appetite for more sweets. Artificial sweeteners are implicated in obesity, diabetes, sleep disruption, cancer, and other degenerative illnesses.

See **Agave Syrup; Aspartame; Barley Malt Powder; Barley Malt Syrup; Birch Syrup; Carob; Date Sugar; Dextrose; Fructose; Fruit Juice Concentrate; Glucose; Granular Fruit Sugar; Honey; Mannitol; Maple Sugar; Maple Syrup; Maltodextrin; Molasses; Rice Syrup; Sorbitol; Sorghum Molasses; Stevia; Sucralose; Sugar; Xylitol; Yacón Syrup.**

Sweet Fennel See **Fennel.**

Sweet Imperial Onion See **Onion.**

HOW TO BEAT THE SUGAR BLUES

If you're one of the many people who suffer from sugar cravings (as did I for decades), you can free yourself. I have done so, as have many of my students and clients. Here's what we've discovered.

When a meal is balanced and pleasing, it satisfies, and you don't nibble on carbohydrates between meals. When, however, you scrimp on quality, freshness, protein, or fats, expect the following: You'll be hungry before the next meal and low on energy. Predictably, you'll reach for something to nibble on or a sweet drink, attempting to "fill the hole"—but, of course, it's a cheap fix.

Your first step in freeing yourself from the teeter-tottery sugar blues (and to prevent diabetes) is to, as your mother admonished, eat three good meals a day.

Sweet Laurel See **Bay Leaf.**

Sweet Marjoram See **Marjoram.**

Sweet Neem Leaf See **Curry Leaf.**

SWEET PEPPER
Bell Pepper, Capsicum, Pepper
(*Capsicum annuum*)

During Indian summer, sweet peppers rival all other produce at market displays in terms of their flashy hues. Plump and glossy, the peppers range from delicately sweet and peppery to very sweet in taste. They come in a variety of shapes as well as colors. The pepper is so adept at cross-pollination that we can anticipate many more new colors, shapes, and flavors in the future. Florida, California, and Texas supply most of the peppers except during the winter months, when they are imported from South America. The sweet pepper is a nightshade family member.

Medicinal Benefits Peppers are a warming food that act upon the stomach and kidneys and support blood circulation. They whet the appetite and help treat cold conditions. They are a nutrient-dense vegetable and contain zeaxanthin, which helps prevent cataracts. They are an excellent source of vitamin C, beta-carotene, vitamin K, thiamine, folic acid, and vitamin B_6. Sweet peppers contain capsaicin, but in comparison to chiles, it's in minute quantities. Peppers reduce *pitta* and *kapha*.

Use Sweet peppers can be juiced or served raw in salads and as finger food and are valued for their crisp, juicy texture. They can be roasted, grilled, broiled, sautéed, or stuffed, or they can be added to soups and stews. For stuffed peppers, steam for three minutes to soften, then core and fill with a savory meat or bean filling for a comely and always welcome entrée. This Native American food now figures prominently in ethnic cuisine throughout the world. Sweet peppers go well with basil, garlic, chiles, tomatoes, and onions.

Sweet peppers are also available dried and in flakes, with 1 tablespoon of dried red pepper flakes being equivalent to 3 tablespoons of chopped fresh peppers.

Buying The color of a pepper depends on the variety. Many peppers are green through most of their development but turn red as they reach full maturity. Others are purple, orange, or yellow at maturity, or even white or brown. Green peppers are typically less sweet and a little more bitter than are other peppers. The riper the pepper, the greater its flavor and nutrition. Select firm, glossy peppers with fresh and intact stems. They should feel heavy for their size. Avoid those with soft spots or shriveled, pale skin, signs that they are past their prime. In general, those with thinner skins are more peppery; those with thicker skins are sweeter. Refrigerate for up to a week in a plastic bag. Green peppers have a slightly longer shelf life than yellow and red peppers. These are the common varieties:

- **Banana Pepper** Long and tapered, usually bright yellow but also green or orange-red, with a thin wall. It is preferred by many over the bell pepper. The banana pepper, also called Hungarian pepper, may be fried or served raw.
- **Bell Pepper** Boxy in shape and green, red, yellow, or purple in color, with a thick wall. Crisp with a refreshing taste, the bell pepper is equally good cooked or raw. Red bell pepper, a fully mature green bell, is the sweetest of the bells. The yellow bell pepper is pleasantly sweet but less flavorful than the banana pepper. The purple bell pepper is eggplant colored on the outside and green inside. Cooking may render its purple flesh an unappetizing gray, so it is most often served raw.
- **European Sweet Pepper** Similar to the bell pepper in shape but larger with tapered ends; green, red, yellow, purple, or even brown. It is very thick fleshed.
- **Pimiento** Small to medium, squat, and dark red, with thick flesh that is sweeter than other sweet peppers. Pimiento slivers are used to stuff green olives. It is available primarily in late summer and in farmers' markets or well-supplied greengrocers.

Be Mindful Sweet peppers rank at the top of "buy organic" vegetables list because the commercial crop is one of our most heavily treated with pesticides, herbicides, fungicides, and fumigants. These chemicals cannot be washed off.

Is this also true for chile peppers? Nope. Fortunately for us, bugs are not chile-heads, and even though they are treated with other chemicals, pesticides are not as much of an issue.

Some people suffering from arthritic-type conditions report improvement when they avoid nightshade vegetables.

See **Chile Pepper; Nightshade Family; Peppers; Vegetable.**

SWEET POTATO
Boniato, Yam
(*Ipomoea batatas*)

The sweet potato is sweet. It is native to South America, a member of the morning glory family, and related to that horrible garden nuisance bindweed. The sweet potato is actually not related to the potato or to the yam, though very sweet and dark sweet potatoes are called yams. There are more than 300 sweet potato varieties, and their flesh ranges from white to orange and their skin from every color in the yellow-red spectrum to purple. They may be long with tapered ends or squat and stubby in shape. True yams are native to Africa and are a staple in tropical and subtropical countries.

Medicinal Benefits Higher in sugar than potatoes, sweet potatoes are also an excellent source of carotenoid antioxidants (the varieties with the darkest orange flesh are highest in beta-carotene). Unlike potatoes and other starchy vegetables, sweet potatoes help stabilize blood sugar levels and improve the response to the hormone insulin.

Sweet potatoes are regarded as one of the most nutrient-dense vegetables. In Oriental medicine, this vegetable is valued for tonifying chi, blood, and yin and for nourishing the spleen, stomach, kidney, and large intestine meridians. It helps quench thirst and lubricates dry conditions. Sweet potatoes are high in vitamins A and C, with a fair amount of thiamine. They reduce *pitta* and *vata*.

Use Cooking converts most of the sweet potato's starches and softens it into a sweet and soft or dry vegetable, depending upon the variety. While candied yams are a classic holiday dish, sweet potatoes can be eaten throughout the year; they can be substituted for squash or carrots in soups, salads, pilafs, and baked goods. Sweet potato pie is a Southern classic. One easy way to enjoy a sweet potato is to pierce its skin with a fork and place it in a toaster oven at 350°F for an hour, or until soft.

Couldn't be easier . . . or sweeter. The skin is also edible.

Sweet potatoes may be substituted for potatoes in french fries and potato chips. Their starch is made into a gluten-free flour substitute.

Buying Select smooth-skinned sweet potatoes with no bruises or harvesting scars. Size is of no concern in terms of sweetness or storage capability. Sweet potatoes bruise easily, so handle with care. Store in a cool, dry area. Sweet potatoes are at their peak in late fall. The sweet potato is denser than a potato, so allow a somewhat smaller serving size per person.

Typically sweet potatoes with a light-colored skin, like Jersey or Japanese varieties, have a firm, dry flesh with a delicate sweetness. The deep orange or purple-skinned sweet potato—often called jewel or garnet yam—has a soft, moist flesh colored a flamboyant orange. This sugar-sweet vegetable is suitable for desserts or as a winter squash substitute.

Be Mindful Overconsumption of sweet potatoes may cause abdominal swelling and indigestion. If raw, they are not suitable for people with sensitive digestion.

See **Vegetable**.

SWEET RICE SEE **RICE**.

SWEET RICE WINE SEE **MIRIN**.

SWEET SORGHUM SYRUP SEE **SORGHUM MOLASSES**.

SWEET TOOTH SEE **HEDGEHOG MUSHROOM**.

SWISS CHARD SEE **CHARD**.

SZECHUAN PEPPER SEE **SICHUAN PEPPER**.

TAHINI

Tahini is a creamy smooth paste ground from hulled sesame seeds (as opposed to sesame butter, which is ground from whole, or unhulled, sesame seeds). This high-protein spread is a culinary staple in Middle Eastern and some Asian cultures.

Use Tahini is an oily ingredient used in dressings, sauces, and desserts. In some recipes, tahini serves as an oil replacement. In whole foods recipes, sesame butter may replace tahini. Tahini is an essential ingredient in halvah, hummus, and baba ghanoush.

QUICK AND CREAMY SALAD DRESSING

Makes about ½ cup

- ¼ cup tahini
- ¼ cup water
- ¼ cup minced fresh oregano leaves
- 2 tablespoons freshly squeezed lime juice
- 1 clove garlic, pressed
- Unrefined salt and freshly ground pepper to taste

In a medium bowl, whisk together all the ingredients. As different brands of tahini vary in consistency, you may need to add more water to reach the desired consistency. Use as a vegetable dip or to dress vegetable, grain, or chicken salads or steamed vegetables. The dressing will keep refrigerated for up to 5 days.

Buying The best tahini is made from mechanically hulled seeds and is sweet and nutty tasting. Commercial tahini, made from seeds hulled and processed in caustic chemical baths, tastes bitter and slightly soapy.

See **Nut and Seed Butters; Sesame; Sesame Butter.**

TAI GOO CHOY SEE **TATSOI.**

TAI SAI SEE **BOK CHOY.**

TAMARI SEE **SOY SAUCE.**

TAMARILLO
Tree Tomato
(*Solanum betaceum*)

The attractive tamarillo is a fruit the size and shape of an egg with a patent leather–like red or yellow skin. Its dense, copper-colored, soft flesh is pleasantly bitter and contains a number of soft, small magenta- or yellow-colored seeds. Like a cherry, it grows in clusters on a tree. Not surprisingly, this tomato relative has a tomato-like aroma; its flavor is also similar to tomato but sweeter and more acidic. Yellow tamarillos are sweeter than the red variety.

Medicinal Benefits The tamarillo is a good source of vitamins A and C and is low in calories.

Use The aromatic tamarillo requires peeling, or slice in half lengthwise and scoop out the flesh with a spoon. Its meaty texture is best when cooked in relishes, chutneys, and sweet and savory sauces. Tamarillo may also be sliced and served with other fruits in a salad or cooked in a compote. Add its juice or puree to beverages, salsa, or sauces.

Buying Tamarillos are primarily available as a New Zealand import from early summer through the fall. Choose firm, heavy tamarillos as you would select a tomato, and allow them to soften at room temperature. Then they can be refrigerated for up to four weeks. The more yellow the fruit, the sweeter it is.

Be Mindful Red tamarillos can stain clothing. As a member of the nightshade family, tamarillos contain the toxic alkaloid solanine, and so moderate consumption is advised.

See **Fruit; Nightshade Family.**

TAMARIND
(*Tamarindus indica*)

Cooked tamarind pulp gives a complex tart-sweet flavor that defines many curries and soups in Sri Lanka, India, Mexico, and other tropical regions. Until mandatory labeling, it was the secret ingredient in Worcestershire sauce. This brown fruit from the tamarind tree is a leguminous pod with a tan, papery skin. The five- to eight-inch bean pod surrounds inedible seeds and a sticky pulp that tastes like sour apricots and dates.

Medicinal Benefits Tamarind is astringent and treats both damp and hot conditions. It acts upon both the large and small intestine and the stomach; it aids digestion, lowers fever, and has antiseptic and laxative effects. It reduces nausea in pregnancy and treats jaundice, fever, and dysentery. Tamarind reduces *vata*.

Use The way lemon is used as an acid seasoning agent in the West, tamarind is also used as a curry ingredient and by itself to season meat, vegetable, and bean dishes as well as tropical beverages. Tamarind fruit may be eaten fresh or dried or made into confections or pickles.

To use, remove the hard outer shell and strings from the tamarind pods. Simmer in water to cover for 25 to 30 minutes, adding more water if necessary. Allow to cool. Force the pulp through a sieve and discard the seeds to yield a thick puree. Use as directed in recipes. The extract can be stored in a closed jar in the refrigerator for up to a week.

Buying Tamarind pods are available in the international section of some supermarkets and in Indian, Asian, and Mexican markets. The pods may be stored at room temperature for a year. The pulp is available in an easy-to-use paste form that is sold in jars or that is cellophane wrapped and sold in blocks. The paste may be stored for a year or more. Tamarind is also available powdered.

See **Herbs and Spices; Legume Family.**

TANGELO SEE **ORANGE.**

TANGERINE SEE **ORANGE.**

TANGOR SEE **ORANGE.**

TANNIA SEE **YAUTIA.**

TAPIOCA

Tapioca, a traditional Brazilian food, is extracted from a cassava variety rich in starch but with a bitter and toxic hydrocyanide content. The purified starch, or *tipioca* in the language of the Tupi peoples of the Amazon region, is without flavor, color, or aroma and makes an excellent thickener and pudding. It was widely used in puddings in the United States until displaced by easier-to-use gelatin and agar products.

Medicinal Benefits Tapioca is soothing, nutritious, and easy to digest. It's medicinal for convalescents and anyone with a compromised digestive system. Tapioca reduces *pitta* and *kapha*.

Use When set, the starch in tapioca, amylopectin, is crystal clear and glossy, which makes it an ideal glaze. However, tapioca thins if reheated. With exposure to air, tapioca loses its thickening action over time. Unlike instant tapioca or tapioca flour, pearl tapioca must be soaked for 45 to 75 minutes before being cooked. The flour is an excellent thickener for soups, sauces, and pie filling. Added to bread or cookies, it gives a tender crumb.

Buying When processed from cassava, tapioca forms small pearls, which are graded into varying sizes and available as pearl tapioca. Or tapioca may be precooked and ground, flaked, or granulated into instant tapioca or tapioca flour.

See **Cassava.**

TARO
Albi, Dasheen, Eddo
(*Colocasia esculenta*)

As the potato is to the Irish, so is the taro to the peoples of the Pacific region. A potatolike tuber (corm), it is one of the earliest cultivated vegetables. The taro has a shaggy, barklike brown skin circled with distinct rings. Its crisp white, cream, or almost lilac flesh has a mild flavor, tasting something like chestnuts. Hawaiians ferment the taro to produce their "staff of life," poi.

Medicinal Benefits In Chinese medicine, taro is medicinal for the large intestine, stomach, and spleen, and for loss of appetite and fatigue owing to weak digestion. It has the ability to dissolve masses and is used as an external plaster for the treatment of cysts, tumors, and boils. High in potassium and a fair source of calcium and iron, the taro contains vitamins B_1, B_2, and C. Taro reduces *vata* and *pitta*.

Use As a food, taro may be substituted for potatoes, but expect a drier, sweeter, nuttier flavor. My favorite use for taro is in soups, where it holds its shape nicely and absorbs other flavors. Taro may be baked, steamed, or broiled. It is crisp and delicious when thinly sliced and pan- or deep-fried and is now available as a packaged potato chip. Taro stems and leaves are also edible.

Buying This plant produces two types of tubers. One is a large turnip-shaped and turnip-size "corm," from which the leaf stalks grow. There are also smaller, subsidiary cormels, the size of an egg, which grow attached to the main corm by rootlets. Select corms that are moist and plump and show no sign of withering. Store as you would potatoes—in a cool, well-ventilated place—and use before they start to soften. Taro is available in Asian markets and some large supermarkets.

Be Mindful Raw taro contains minute and exceedingly sharp crystals of various substances including calcium oxalate. Some varieties contain more crystals than others. If eaten raw, these crystals can cause intense irritation of delicate mouth and tongue membranes. Cooking (or soaking in cold water for eight hours prior to use) deactivates the crystals.

See **Arum Family; Vegetable.**

TARRAGON
(*Artemisia dracunculus*)

Believed an antidote for bites of venomous animals, tarragon's name probably comes from the Greek *drakon*, for "little dragon." The aromatic, long, delicate, polished gray-green tarragon leaves are a favorite in French cuisine. It's a multibranch herb with long, narrow, twisted green leaves and a distinctive anise flavor and aroma, but it is more peppery and briskly tart than anise. The only common culinary herb from the important *Artemisia* genus, which gives us sagebrush, mugwort, and wormwood, tarragon originated in Russia. It is a member of the daisy family.

Medicinal Benefits Tarragon is a bitter, warming herb that is a diuretic, supports the digestive system, and helps reduce fever. It may be used to treat constipation or expel intestinal parasites. As a treatment for dysmenorrhea, drink three or four cups a day leading up to a menstrual cycle. It contains the flavonoids quercetin and patuletin. Tarragon reduces *vata* and *kapha*.

Use Along with chervil, chives, and parsley, tarragon is one of the ingredients in the classic French herb blend *herbes fines*. Tarragon is a principle seasoning ingredient in tartar and béarnaise sauces. Fresh tarragon enhances salads and dressings and vegetable and fish dishes. It's exceptional with chicken: Place fresh tarragon leaves under the skin or in the cavity of a fowl before roasting it. Tarragon is especially compatible with beans, mushrooms, squash, and eggs and is, perhaps, the quintessential herb for flavoring vinegar. Use sparingly, as its flavor easily overpowers other ingredients.

Buying There are two tarragon varieties: French and Russian. The French is higher in essential oils, is sweeter and more aromatic, and is most commonly available—both dried and fresh—in our markets. The more astringent Russian tarragon has more narrow leaves and is most commonly grown in home gardens. Even more so than other herbs, dried tarragon does not keep its flavor well.

Look for deep green tarragon sprigs with long, narrow, pointed leaves. Sniff for a peppery scent with anise undertones. Tarragon will keep only a few days, wrapped and refrigerated.

Be Mindful Due to its emmenagogic properties, tarragon is not recommended during pregnancy.

FORMERLY FERTILE

French tarragon flowers are always barren. There is, coincidentally, an ever-increasing number of foods that are incapable of reproducing themselves at all or of reproducing themselves true to form due to hybridization or infertility. If we are what we eat, possibly our rapidly increasing consumption of sterile foods—from eggs and beef to bananas and seedless grapes—may be implicated in the increasing rate of human infertility.

In the case of tarragon, several hundred years ago the plant produced fertile seed, but because cultivars propagated by division or root cuttings were favored, the fertile plants were irretrievably lost.

See **Daisy Family; Herbs and Spices.**

TART CHERRY SEE **SOUR CHERRY.**

TATSOI
Flat Cabbage, Tai Goo Choy
(*Brassica rosularis*)

In my garden, these small, flat nosegays of deep forest green are a favorite crop. As with its near cousin mustard greens, tatsoi is good in almost any cooked preparation, but its young, spoon-shaped leaves are also delicious raw. Those with a mild mustard-like bite are medicinally similar to mustard greens, while sweeter-tasting varieties are more similar to bok choy. Tatsoi leaves

are a common mesclun ingredient. It is primarily available in farmers' markets and Asian markets.

See **Bok Choy; Cabbage Family; Mustard Greens; Vegetable.**

TEA
(*Camellia sinensis*)

According to legend, tea—which has eye-shaped leaves—sprang from the eyelids of the Bodhidharma. This semimythical Indian who introduced Chen Buddhism to China in the first century AD vowed to meditate for nine years straight. Despite his most firm resolve, he dozed. In anger, Bodhidharma cut off his own eyelids and threw them to the ground. From that spot emerged the tea plant, whose leaves help us remain alert.

Second only to water, the world's most widely consumed beverage comes from a small, native Chinese evergreen tree with stiff, shiny, pointed leaves. Its leaves—and, to a much lesser extent, its blossoms and twigs—are used as a refreshing and mildly stimulating infusion.

Just-harvested tea leaves make an insipid, thin, raw-tasting brew, and so must be processed. Tea is grown and processed on large tea plantations throughout China, Japan, Taiwan, Indonesia, India, and Sri Lanka. Tea from the tea bush is not to be confused with herbal drinks or tisanes, also called teas.

Medicinal Benefits The therapeutic benefits of tea are impressive. It supports the heart, lungs, large intestine, stomach, bladder, and liver systems. Tea helps eliminate toxins and it helps dry, damp conditions like edema. Recent research shows that both black and green teas inhibit tumor cells, help prevent heart disease, strengthen the immune system, have antioxidant activity, reduce cavities, and retard atherosclerosis. This broad array of medicinal value is derived from tea's rich supply of polyphenols. Green tea is a better source of polyphenols and is generally considered the more healthful of the two kinds of tea.

Green tea is considered cooling, black tea more warming. Strong tea, in excess, is mucus forming. When milk is added to tea, either green or black, the milk inhibits the tea's antioxidant activity. Tea aids digestion, relieves thirst, and is a diuretic. Tea contains the B vitamin folacin, vitamin C, fluoride, and magnesium. It reduces *kapha*.

Use Tea etiquette ranges from the highly stylized and formal Japanese tea ceremony to a rushed, microwaved, generic orange pekoe in a Styrofoam cup at the local convenience store. Granted, tea bags make brewing a tidy event. If the bag dangles from a plastic strip, however, consider removing that strip, since, as you may well imagine, infused plastic does *not* enhance the flavor of tea.

Buying There are hundreds of tea varieties. They are, however, either fermented or nonfermented (green) and broadly classified accordingly (see page 357).

For tea connoisseurs, in addition to whether the tea is organic, several factors determine quality. These include the leaves' age and the season they were harvested in, as well as the elevation and geographic region they were grown in. The size of the leaf also makes a difference in quality and whether it's whole, broken, or bruised. Brick tea, with leaves that are compressed into a solid mass, is considered inferior to loose tea. Like instant coffee, instant tea is made by spray-drying a tea infusion. De-caffeinated tea is also available.

Any tea may be flavored with floral, spice, fruit, or chemical extracts or agents. Flavored teas are prepared in a range of ways, from adding flower blossoms, such as jasmine, to flavoring with the citrus oil bergamot, as for the classic Earl Grey tea. Making your own house blend is as easy as putting a cinnamon stick, a few cardamom pods, or other flavoring agent in a tea container, closing it, and letting the flavors meld for several weeks or more.

Store tea tightly wrapped or in a covered container in a cool, dry cupboard and it will hold for up to a year; however, try to consume the more delicate teas in a more timely fashion, as storage does compromise their freshness. These are the common varieties of tea:

- **Black Tea** Leaves are fermented through enzymatic oxidation. Leaves darken and release their bitterness, producing a tea that is more robust in body, aroma, flavor, and color. These teas are primarily produced in India and China; they comprise more than 80 percent of world production.
- **Green Tea** Leaves are steam-heated to deactivate their enzymes and dried immediately after harvest. They have a thin, mild, fruity but sometimes astringent flavor and a pale yellow color. China and Japan are the primary producers of green tea.
- **Kukicha Tea** The Japanese word for twig is *kukicha*, and, indeed, this tea is made only from the roasted twigs and stems of the tea plant. It is robustly flavored but lower in caffeine than is green tea, and the roasting process reduces its tannin content. A variation on kukicha is *bancha* tea, which is a blend of green tea

leaves and twigs. Kukicha tea is often simmered for 15 minutes or more and helps neutralize an overly acidic digestive system.
- **Oolong Tea** (also called Yellow or Red) Lighter in color and less fermented than a black tea, oolong tea is lighter in flavor, body, and character than black tea. It is primarily produced in Formosa and China.
- **White Tea** The most subtle tea in flavor and color, only new leaves are dried. They are neither steam-heated nor fermented, resulting in a mild-tasting but slightly sweet, pale yellow tea that is low in caffeine.

Be Mindful Like coffee and chocolate, tea affects the central nervous system with three stimulants: caffeine, theophylline, and theobromine. Caffeine predominates in coffee, theophylline in tea, and theobromine in chocolate. Excessive tea may overstimulate your nervous system and cause anxiety, insomnia, or irritability.

Tea also contains 5 to 20 percent tannin. Tannin, which gives tea its body, is a growth depressant—and therefore tea is not recommended for children. Also, excessive tea consumption can deplete iron, yet another reason children should not drink tea.

With the exception of kukicha, tea is a high source of calcium oxalate, and so moderation is advised for people with a tendency toward forming calcium oxalate kidney stones.

Tea decaffeinated with ethyl acetate is not recommended. Buy only water-processed decaf tea.

TEA FAMILY
(*Camellia*)
This genus of flowering plants native to Asia gives us two popular plants: the aromatic camel-

lia blossom and the tea plant. Seeds from the camellia blossom are pressed for tea seed oil.

See **Tea; Tea Seed Oil.**

WHY A PROPER CUP OF TEA REQUIRES JUST-BOILED WATER AND FAVORS LOWER ELEVATIONS

If made from reheated or overboiled water, which has lost some oxygen, tea tastes flat. To treat yourself to an excellent cup of black tea, use just-boiled water. For green tea, use water that has almost reached the boiling point. At high elevations, the water boils at a lower temperature so getting a full extraction is difficult. Here are tips to making an excellent cup of tea.

Good tea requires quality tea, good water, an enamel or glass pot for boiling the water, a ceramic teapot (but you can make do with a Pyrex measuring cup), and a relaxed atmosphere in which to sip. Use loose tea so the hot water can better circulate, coaxing out the tea's maximum flavor. (Stainless-steel infusing spoons, tea balls, or strainers inhibit adequate water circulation through the leaves.)

Warm the teapot with hot water and then drain it. Bring water to a boil. Add a teaspoon of tea for every cup desired, plus one for the pot, to the warmed pot. Just as the water comes to a full boil, immediately pour it over the tea, cover, and allow to steep for 3 to 5 minutes. If oversteeped, the tea develops a bitter taste. Serve, straining if necessary, as is, or with lemon, honey, or milk. Sit back, relax, sip, and savor.

TEA KVASS SEE **KOMBUCHA.**

TEA MUSHROOM SEE **KOMBUCHA.**

TEA SEED OIL (NOT RECOMMENDED)
Camellia Oil
(*Camellia oleifera*)

A bitter-tasting oil extracted from the seeds of the beautiful camellia flower, a near relative of the tea plant, has been used in Asia in cosmetics, soap making, textile manufacture, and as a lubricant to protect tools from corrosion.

Currently it is highly refined to a tasteless oil and fraudulently marketed as a "virgin" and "cold pressed" healthy product. Note: Tea oil lacks historical precedence as a culinary oil. It is also marketed as camellia oil. Tea seed oil is not to be confused with the medicinal *melaleuca* or tea tree oil.

See **Fat and Oil.**

TEF
T'ef, Teff
(*Eragrostis tef*)

In the rugged Simian Mountains, at the source of the Blue Nile, grows a tiny cereal grain, tef. This prized Ethiopian staple was virtually unknown outside Ethiopia until this century. Tef is so small that 150 grains weigh the same as a single kernel of wheat. For a grain, it has a uniquely sweet and robust flavor. Because tef has little economic value in the world market, the Ethiopian government discouraged its cultivation. In addition, the cultural disruption brought on by the warfare and famine for many recent decades has caused the irretrievable loss of many valuable tef varieties.

Medicinal Benefits Because of the grain's sweet flavor and its high mineral concentration, I find it supportive to kidney, stomach, and spleen function. Tef is a remarkably rich source of calcium and is an excellent source of iron, zinc, and copper. It is, for a grain, high in protein. As an ancient grain like quinoa and amaranth, it is often well tolerated by people with O blood type. Tef is gluten-free. Ayurvedic writer Amadea Morningstar observes that tef is *sattvic* (helps the mind become clear and stay focused). Tef reduces *vata* and *pitta* and in moderation can be used by *kapha*.

Use For people who like small grains like amaranth—and I admit I am one—the texture of tef is enjoyable. Others, who object to the tiny size of the whole grain, will enjoy tef flour. In fact, traditionally tef is used as a flour rather than as a whole grain.

To cook whole tef, lightly toast 1 cup in a dry skillet for about 3 minutes, or until it starts to

---

THANKS TO ONE MAN'S VISION

In the 1970s, Wayne Carlson spent seven years in Ethiopia working as a biologist for the Red Cross; in the process, he developed a taste for their staple, a sourdough pancake-like bread called injera, which is made from tef. When Carlson returned to his Caldwell, Idaho, home, he tried to buy some tef, but there was none available in the United States. He eventually obtained some seed, planted it in his backyard, and soon was growing 200 acres to satisfy both the Ethiopian immigrant market and the natural foods market.

Due to horrific cultural disruption in Ethopia, many tef cultivars have been lost. When a displaced farmer would again be able to farm, obtaining tef seed often was problematic. Carlson provided start-up seed for many such people. I met Carlson in the 1980s and found this friendly Idaho farmer, tef, and injera equally likable.

If you have the chance, ask an Ethiopian about their beloved staple grain. Odds are good that they'll be surprised you even know of it, and odds are that their passion for tef will warm your heart.

---

pop and emits a pleasant aroma. Add 1½ cups boiling seasoned stock or water, cover, and simmer for 15 minutes. Serve with a condiment, as a breakfast cereal, or as a side dish.

Buying Tef is available in various colors, including ivory, red, and a deep chocolate brown. The most flavorful available is the brown. Store tef, tightly wrapped, in a cool, dark cupboard for up to a year. Tef is available in some natural food stores or online.

See **Grains; Grass Family; Tef Flour.**

TEF FLOUR

The Ethiopians use tef flour, which is gluten-free, to make their staple bread, injera. This large—up to two feet in diameter—flatbread is cooked in a concave, woklike vessel. The dough is fermented for three days, and the injera is soft and limp like a crêpe but with a moist spongy texture and a decidedly sour flavor. When ordering injera in an Ethiopian restaurant, request a tef injera if you want the real thing; often a less expensive millet or wheat flour may be used.

Use To my palate, sweet and nutty-flavored tef flour is a superior flour for cookies, cakes, and quick breads. My favorites include spicy banana-nut muffins, waffles, and a gingery cake. I substitute tef flour for part or all of the wheat flour in these recipes.

Please don't add tef flour to a yeast bread, however. Like grapes, tef has its own symbiotic yeast, and the synergy between the two is wild. The dough can run amok (this is from firsthand experience) and create a fetid stench that takes hours to air out of the house.

Buying Tef flour is available online and in many natural food stores. The grains are too small to be ground in a blender but may be pulverized in a coffee or spice grinder or a home flour mill.

See **Flour; Tef.**

TEMPEH

Tempeh is a traditional Indonesian food made by splitting, cooking, and fermenting soybeans. More versatile than tofu, tempeh's hearty texture holds bold flavors and lends itself to vegetarian burgers, kabobs, mock chicken salad, and the like.

Medicinal Benefits With an easily assimilable protein content of 19.5 percent (50 percent more than hamburger), tempeh is an energy-building food, especially good for people with low energy. Homemade tempeh is one of the world's richest sources of vitamin B_{12}. This vitamin is not available in commercial tempeh. Tempeh contains the important omega-3 fatty acids. Tempeh is bound together with a mycelium of branching, threadlike enzymes. This mycelium makes the soy easily digestible, provides many valuable B vitamins, and produces a natural antibiotic that supports immune system function. Tempeh reduces *pitta*.

Use Tempeh is not eaten raw. Baked, grilled, broiled, or fried, tempeh appeals to many palates, especially fried or grilled, when it becomes reminiscent of Southern fried chicken or seafood fillets. Assertive seasonings like garlic, ginger, curry, and coriander complement it; souring agents such as wine, lemon juice, or vinegar enhance it. Seasoned tempeh cutlets that can go directly onto the grill are also available.

Buying Tempeh is available in thin, 8-ounce cakes in the refrigerator or freezer section of many stores, especially natural food stores. Fresh tempeh is preferable to frozen tempeh. Fresh tempeh smells mushroomlike and its cottony mold is either white, gray, or black. Compost tempeh that has an unpleasant ammonia aroma or with any other color of mold.

Grains or other foods, such as rice, wild rice, arame seaweed, coconut, or peanuts, may be fermented with soy to make a variety of tempeh blends.

See **Fermented Food; Soybean.**

TEMPLE ORANGE SEE **ORANGE.**

TEPARY BEAN SEE **BEANS AND LEGUMES.**

TEXAS SWEET ONION SEE **ONION.**

TEXMATI RICE SEE **RICE.**

TEXTURED SOY PROTEIN SEE **TEXTURED VEGETABLE PROTEIN.**

TEXTURED VEGETABLE PROTEIN (NOT RECOMMENDED)
Meat Analog, Meat Extender, Textured Soy Protein, TP, TVP

Textured vegetable protein (TVP), also known as textured soy protein (TSP), is a shoddy, highly refined by-product that's chemically extracted from defatted soy meal. Just as polyester may be spun into various shapes and textures, a TVP slurry is flavored, colored, and extruded into granules, flakes, or chunks, the latter of which looks like dry dog kibble. As an ingredient, TVP is found in countless products, including vegetarian burgers, lasagna, frozen desserts, trail mixes, and breakfast cereal. It is also available as an ingredient, bulk or packaged.

For a healthful and excellent-tasting, low-tech vegetarian protein, consider cooking up a pot of beans.

Be Mindful TVP may cause gastric distress because it contains the hard-to-digest oligosaccharides found in soybeans.

See **Soybean; Soy Isolate; Textured Soy Protein.**

THAI GINGER SEE **GALANGAL.**

THYME
(*Thymus vulgaris*)

> Wind-bit thyme that smells like the
> perfume of the dawn in paradise.
> —Rudyard Kipling

Balmy, aromatic thyme, a native of southern Europe, is a very small undershrub, with slender woody stems and gray-green leaves that are whitish on the underside. There are more than a hundred species of this herb, whose name comes from the Greek for "to burn as incense." Thyme is a member of the mint family.

Thyme was valued by the ancient Greeks and Romans as an aphrodisiac and for instilling bravery and courage. Or, in the words of Euell Gibbons in *Stalking the Healthful Herbs*, "According to ancient tradition, if a girl wears a corsage of wild thyme flowers, it means that she is looking for a sweetheart; and according to another tradition, if a bashful boy drinks enough wild thyme tea, it will give him courage to take her up on it."

Medicinal Benefits Thyme is a warming herb that supports the lungs, spleen, kidneys, bladder, heart, and uterus and that helps with chi circulation. It helps relieve lung congestion, rheumatism, whooping cough, candidiasis, spasms, flatulence, and indigestion. The primary fragrant oil of thyme, thymol, is a powerful antiseptic used in Listerine mouthwash, cough drops, and vapor rubs. It destroys some intestinal hookworms and roundworms. In aromatherapy, thyme is used to relieve mental instability, melancholy, and nightmares and to prevent memory loss and inefficiency. Thyme reduces *vata* and *kapha*.

"Taken before sleeping, it is a remedy against nightmare," according to Michael Tierra in *Planetary Herbology*. "It has both stimulant and relaxant properties so that it tends to regulate the system as needed."

Use Thyme is one of the most popular all-purpose savory herbs for flavoring soups, stews, stuffings, and sauces, either alone or in a bouquet garni. It is a classic ingredient in tomato sauce for pasta and pizza. It performs especially well in slowly cooked dishes, and it doesn't overpower other flavors. Among the many different varieties of thyme are lemon thyme and caraway-scented thyme.

Thyme is available fresh or dried; as possible, favor the fresh. Add thyme toward the end of cooking to preserve its subtle flavor. As the leaves are tiny and their stems are woody, instructions for using the fresh herb range

---

HONEY-THYME COUGH SYRUP

This is so very easy to make and much more soothing than a ready-made cough syrup. One teaspoon taken as needed will relieve a cough.

    2 cups water
    3 tablespoons dried thyme
    1 cup honey

Bring the water to a boil in a small saucepan, then remove from heat. Add the thyme, cover, and steep for 10 minutes, or until cooled. Strain, then whisk in the honey until dissolved. Store in a glass jar; the cough syrup will keep refrigerated for 2 months.

from tying thyme up in a cheesecloth to stripping the leaves through the tines of a fork. Here's my method: Cook thyme springs in the dish, and then discard the sprig as you would a bay leaf.

See **Herbs and Spices; Mint Family.**

TOFU
Bean Curd, Soybean Curd

In four decades tofu, the best-known Western soy food, moved from an obscure curiosity to a staple in American cuisine—but now its popularity is rapidly waning due to concerns about overconsumption of soy. Tofu has a mild, unimposing, delicate flavor and a chameleon-like ability to take on the flavor of whatever food it is cooked with. Tofu has the consistency of a firm custard. It originated in China and is made from curdled soymilk.

Medicinal Benefits Tofu supports the large intestine, stomach, and spleen; it is a yin and chi tonic and a thermally cold food that helps clear heat and toxins. When lightly cooked, it is especially good for people who feel too hot or who have high blood pressure. Tofu is said to neutralize toxins. Used as a poultice, it is excellent to reduce fever or to reduce congestion from a concussion or a bump on the head.

When combined with grains, tofu yields easily digested protein. Tofu is cholesterol-free and low in saturated fats. It can be an excellent source of calcium, depending upon the coagulant used. It also contains essential B vitamins, choline, and fat-soluble vitamin E. Tofu reduces *vata*, *pitta*, and, when well spiced, *kapha*. Depending upon their constitutional type, *vatas* may or may not tolerate tofu well.

Use Drain tofu, and if using it in a dressing or sauce, blanch it in boiling water for one minute. Or cut tofu to desired size and pan-fry, bake, broil, steam, or simmer with ingredients and flavors of choice. For a meatier texture, freeze tofu for at least two weeks. Thaw, squeeze out the water, break into small pieces, and sauté with robustly flavored seasoning agents.

Buying Tofu is available extra firm, firm, or soft, according to the percentage of water contained. Soft tofu is more delicate and is better suited to soups and desserts. Harder tofu holds its shape better in stir-fried and grilled dishes.

Water-packed tofu from the refrigerated section of a supermarket or natural food store has a superior, more delicate flavor if it's made with the traditional Japanese coagulant nigari. Traditional Chinese tofu is coagulated with calcium sulfate and yields a more brittle but calcium-enriched product. An acid coagulant produces an almost jellylike, smooth tofu with a slightly sour flavor.

I do not recommend tofu in shelf-stable (unrefrigerated) packages. This highly processed product lacks palatability. Store water-packed tofu refrigerated in its package until use. Once opened, store unused tofu in a covered plastic tub or glass jar with water to cover. If you change the water every day or two, the tofu will last up to a week. If the tofu develops a sour flavor, discard it.

Be Mindful The U.S. Food and Drug Administration lists 288 studies on its database showing the toxicity of soy. Numerous studies show that overconsumption of soy can lead to nutrient deficiencies, digestive disorders, allergies, endocrine disruption, and thyroid problems.

While the antinutrients, phytates, are significantly reduced in long-fermented miso or soy sauce, they remain in tofu. If tofu is consumed, as it was traditionally in Japan, as an occasional condiment and served with seaweed to counter the antinutrients, this is not problematic. However, today people—especially vegetarians—who have consumed tofu as a primary staple are at risk for being mineral deficient. And that's not all.

TEMPERATURE OF SEX

If you were to describe good sex in terms of temperature, would it be "hot" or "cold"?

Cooling foods, like tofu, tend to temporarily reduce the blood flow to the regenerative organs. This explains why tofu was used by some Buddhist monks to abate their sexual desires.

If it's a cold day and you're feeling cold and in the mood for tofu, then prepare it with warming foods such as onions, ginger, and garlic; it will be more warming. Traditionally, tofu was served as a savory dish rather than (as many do in the West) sweetened (which makes it cooling) as a dessert ingredient or even as an ice cream substitute.

Soy phytoestrogens disrupt endocrine function and have the potential to cause infertility and to promote breast cancer in adult women. They are potent antithyroid agents that cause hypothyroidism and may cause thyroid cancer.

Women with estrogen-sensitive breast tumors should eat soy rarely, if at all. Soy is the highest food in goitrogens, substances that interfere with iodine uptake and therefore suppress the thyroid gland function. This can result in goiter.

See **Okara; Soybean; Tofu.**

TOMATILLO
Husk Tomato
(*Physalis ixocarpa*)

The tomatillo comes wrapped in a fanciful parchmentlike husk, and the enclosed fruit, which ranges in size from a cherry tomato to a small egg, is yellow or green-purple when ripe. Most often it is used green. Although it may also be called a ground cherry, the ground cherry is a related but smaller and different plant.

In texture and flavor, the tomatillo is like a green plum—sweet and sour but with a delightful aroma of fresh-mown hay. Its lemony balm and gelatinous texture lend body and flavor to a variety of sauces.

Use This member of the nightshade family is featured in Southwestern and Mexican cuisine. Cooking enhances its flavor and softens its skin. Tomatillos are primarily used in salsa and sauces, but they may also be added, raw, to salads.

Buying Look for tomatillos throughout the year. If they're not in your supermarket, you'll find them in Latino food stores. Select those that are firm and evenly colored, with intact dry husks. They hold refrigerated for several weeks. Husk just prior to use.

See **Nightshade Family; Vegetable.**

TOMATO
(*Lycopersicon esculentum*)

It's just short of miraculous how a slice of a good tomato can sublimely boost the pleasure of a sandwich. A member of the nightshade family, tomatoes range in size from that of a small cherry to larger than a grapefruit, and their color, though typically red, may be yellow, orange, black, green, purple, or even white. They originated in Central and South America and are now grown throughout the world.

Botanically speaking, tomatoes are a fruit, but technically they're a berry since they are pulpy and contain one or more soft seeds. According to an 1893 U.S. Supreme Court ruling, however, the tomato is legally classified as a vegetable because it is used as a vegetable. Now, there's some logic.

After potatoes and lettuce, tomatoes are the most commonly consumed vegetable in the United States. But tomatoes rank above all produce in terms of popular fervor, which upholds them as a dietary necessity. Tomatoes are produced in all states; our primary sources are Texas, California, Florida, and Ohio.

Medicinal Benefits Tomatoes have both a sweet and sour flavor, are a yin tonic and a cold food, and act on the stomach and liver meridians. They clear heat, promote body fluids, nourish yin, and cool and detoxify the blood.

Even though the tomato is acidic, after digestion it alkalizes the blood and is useful in some cases of gout and rheumatism. When cooked with warming spices like cumin or mustard, they are a more balanced food. The peel and seeds are most aggravating to *vata*.

Tomatoes are second only to gac fruit as a superior source of lycopene, the antioxidant that helps promote healthy vision; for most Westerners, tomatoes are the primary source of lycopene. This nutrient actually is higher in cooked tomato dishes than in raw dishes.

The highest concentration of vitamin C is in the jellylike substance that surrounds each seed. Vine-ripened tomatoes are an excellent source of vitamin C and a good source of vitamins A and B complex and of potassium and phosphorus. A hothouse-grown tomato has half the vitamin C as a field-grown one. Tomatoes are rich in sugar (fructose, glucose, and sucrose) and have a moderate fiber content. They contain flavonoids and other phytochemicals with anticarcinogenic properties.

Use The easiest way to slice a tomato is with a serrated knife. To retain its juice, slice lengthwise from stem to blossom end rather than crosswise. Because tomato seeds are hard to digest, it is best to remove them; because the skin is tough, it can also be removed. To seed a tomato, cut it open, set a strainer over a bowl, and squeeze the tomato firmly enough to push out the seeds. Discard the seeds and reserve the juice.

Buying Because ripe tomatoes are fragile and don't withstand shipping, the commercial crop is picked and shipped when green and then "hard-ripened" with ethylene gas, which turns the skin red by eliminating the chlorophyll. Such a tomato has negligible flavor and aroma. If tomato seeds, or any part of its fleshy interior, are green, then it was picked green, despite its cosmetic red facade.

The best assurance of a delicious tomato is to purchase it from a local grower during tomato harvest season, which is, in temperate regions, roughly from mid-July up to the first frost. Hydroponic and hothouse tomatoes lack the flavor and nutrition of vine-ripened field tomatoes, but at least they may be grown (and in some areas, purchased) locally 12 months of the year.

Purchase tomatoes that are firm but yield slightly to pressure and have an even, bright red color and a rich tomato aroma. Avoid those with bruises, cracks, and dark spots. To ripen immature tomatoes, put them in a closed paper bag or in your fruit bowl for about three days, or until fully ripened. Use fresh. Do not refrigerate tomatoes; refrigeration drains their flavor and gives a mealy texture.

Drying does not enhance the flavor of most vegetables, but it does concentrate and enhance the flavors of fruits, including tomatoes. Dried tomatoes have a sweet, roasted flavor. They are a popular ingredient in Mediterranean cuisine. They are available packed in oil or dry-packed. The former need only to be drained; the latter need to be rehydrated in a two-minute-long boiling water bath.

Be Mindful Never cook tomatoes in aluminum or cast iron; their acid binds with these metals, and this will impart a metallic flavor to the tomatoes.

If purchasing canned tomato products, favor

domestic tomatoes, as the United States has strict standards for lead content in metal containers. White, ceramic-lined cans may release the hormone disrupter bisphenol A (BPA), and acidic foods, like tomatoes, more actively leach this toxin from containers. Consider glass or Tetra Pak tomato products.

Consumption of nightshade family members, tomatoes included, upsets the calcium balance due to their solanine content and exacerbates arthritis or osteoporosis in some individuals. According to Dr. Bernard Jensen, author of the popular *Foods That Heal*, the acids in green tomatoes are especially detrimental to the kidneys.

In the Ayurvedic tradition, tomatoes are problematic for two reasons. First, they are *rajasic*, stimulating outward motion, creativity, aggression, and passion—a food recommended to warriors before battle. Second, their sour *vipak*, or postdigestive effect, makes them stay sour after metabolism, which—with extended or excessive use—irritates the gut, to which any person with an ulcer or an already sensitive stomach will attest.

See **Nightshade Family; Vegetable.**

TOMATOES ON THE VINE PRETENSE

In the market, clusters of tomatoes on their vine look and smell just great and, one easily assumes, they are worth the extra price. Wrong. It's the aromatic vine that you smell, and it does not indicate a tomato's flavor.

TRAILING BLACKBERRY SEE **DEWBERRY.**

TREE EAR MUSHROOM SEE **WOOD EAR.**

TREE TOMATO SEE **TAMARILLO.**

TRITICALE
(*Triticum* × *Secale*)

A laboratory hybrid of wheat and rye, here's a dud that has all but slipped into oblivion. Once touted as "science's gift to the world" because of its high protein content, triticale was developed in the late 1800s in Sweden. Two reasons that consumers have never fully embraced triticale, despite periodic press on its behalf, are that it's tricky to turn it into a good loaf of bread, and, when whole, it's a tough chew.

See **Grains; Grass Family; Wheat.**

TRUFFLE
(*Tuber magnatum, T. melanosporum*)

The most famous fungus of the West, the "diamond" of mushrooms, the magically aromatic truffle is so flavorful and hard to obtain that it sells for upward of $2,000 a pound. When fresh, their unmistakable scent almost instantly fills your kitchen. The white truffles from Piedmont (*T. magnatum*) and the black truffles from Périgord (*T. melanosporum*) are the best known. Truffles had defied cultivation until the 1970s; now 90 percent of the crop is cultivated in oak or hazelnut orchards in France, New Zealand, and North Carolina.

Franklin Garland, of Garland Gourmet Mushrooms and Truffles Company in Hillsborough, North Carolina, favors growing his black Périgord truffles on hazelnut trees. An inoculated hazelnut seedling produces truffles in four to five years (an inoculated oak sapling produces in ten years).

Medicinal Benefits The almost meaty flavor of truffles is due to their high glutamic acid content, which not only enhances the flavor of other foods but also acts as a tenderizer. The truffle has long been considered an aphrodisiac for humans as well as for sows (see sidebar).

Use Truffles are excellent in risottos, grain dishes, or salads, but they are famous with pasta. Their essence is also available in flavored oils, a splash of which magnificently rounds out a pasta dish or salad. Because of their price, they are used sparingly; just few shavings will flavor a dish.

Buying Truffles vary from marble size to as large as an orange. They are a firm, dense, knobby mass, which may be black or white in color. The black are black-skinned with a

---

EUROPEANS USE PIGS, NORTH AMERICANS USE RAKES

Because truffles grow underground, European truffle hunters use a female pig to sniff them out, a practice in use since Greek and Roman times. But why a pig? A truffle emits an aroma that is also found in a male pig's saliva; this musky smell, which makes a sow amorous, propels her through the woods to a truffle site. (The same chemical hormone is also secreted, as it happens, in the underarm sweat of human males.) The more contemporary practice of using a trained dog has an advantage as, unlike a pig, dogs don't devour the truffles if given the chance.

Pat Rawlinson, director of the North American Truffling Society, forages both white and black truffles with a rake. She looks for signs of animal digs under Douglas firs, hemlocks, oaks, alders, or pines that have nothing growing under them, as if the area were burnt out. Rawlinson and her colleagues, who are collecting samples for studies at Oregon State University, rake from three to five inches of the tree's litter from the trunk to the tree's drip line and, in the process, unearth truffles. Rawlinson urges any forager to positively identify truffles before eating them, as they could be mistaken for a poisonous mushroom.

---

jet black or gray marbled interior. In specialty stores, they're available fresh, bottled, or dried. Or plant a truffle-inoculated hazelnut tree available online from Garland Gourmet Mushrooms and Truffles. Wait five years and then harvest your own.

Be Mindful A fairly common truffle-flavored oil is typically composed of olive oil and the synthetic compound 2,4-dithiapentane. Oil that actually contains truffles will be labeled—and priced—accordingly.

See **Mushroom Family; Vegetable.**

TRUMPET MUSHROOM SEE **CHANTERELLE; OYSTER MUSHROOM.**

TSP SEE **TEXTURED VEGETABLE PROTEIN.**

TUNA SEE **PRICKLY PEAR.**

TURBAN SQUASH SEE **SQUASH; SQUASH, WINTER.**

TURMERIC
Indian Saffron, Yellow Ginger
(*Curcuma longa*)

The rhizome, or root, of turmeric is bright orange but otherwise has a similar thin skin as does its relative ginger. It has an astringent flavor that is reminiscent of both ginger and oranges. Turmeric is smaller than ginger, less knobby, and sometimes available fresh. Most turmeric is, however, boiled, peeled, dried, and ground into a powder. This powder is an essential ingredient in Indian cuisine. It is also used as a yellow dye for clothing (in particular the robes of Buddhist monks) and as a dye for margarine and some dairy products. Turmeric originated in India.

Medicinal Benefits Turmeric is a warming herb that supports both blood and chi circulation and tones the spleen and liver. Its yellow pigment, curcumin, makes turmeric one of the highest-known sources of beta-carotene. It is an antioxidant with antibacterial, antiarthritic, antioxidant, and anti-inflammatory properties. Turmeric strengthens the nervous system and helps dissolve uterine tumors, cysts, and gallstones. Turmeric may be used to regulate blood sugar for diabetics.

Turmeric may also be used topically to reduce canker sores and cold sores. Apply the powder directly to the afflicted area or mixed with water to form a paste.

Combined with coriander and cumin, turmeric aids in the digestion of complex carbohydrates. It also aids in the assimilation of protein and so is good combined with milk for very young children. Turmeric is *tridoshic* in moderation; in excess, its astringency can agitate *vata*.

Use In addition to its mustard yellow color, turmeric lends to food a warm, musky aroma and flavor that's slightly astringent. The yellow color may stain clothing, and it will temporarily color counters, wooden spoons, and other kitchen surfaces that it comes in contact with. To improve its flavor and medicinal properties, sauté it briefly in ghee or oil before cooking it with other ingredients. As an essential ingredient in curry, turmeric may be used to add color and flavor to any vegetable or grain dish. It is also a common ingredient in chili powders and blends.

Buying Purchase fresh turmeric rhizomes that are crisp and evenly colored; refrigerate for up to three weeks. With ground turmeric, purchase that with the brightest color and store it tightly covered in a dark glass jar, as exposure to light and oxygen quickly denatures it. Turmeric has, however, excellent heat stability.

See **Ginger Family; Herbs and Spices.**

TURNIP
(*Brassica rapa rapifera*)

The turnip has a rustic character, and—among those people who have not tasted it at its prime—a low reputation. This inexpensive white root grows in impoverished soils and keeps well—features that have endeared it to the poor and given cause for the uninformed to scorn it.

I, on the other hand, am an unabashed fan of the turnip. I love its sweet, tender but crisp flesh, its mild bite, and sweet flavor. I adore a cooked turnip's funky, earthy mustard oil aroma. I also find the dark leafy greens delicious.

The turnip originated in northern Asia and has been used throughout Asia and Europe since prehistoric times. It is a member of the famed cabbage family. The turnip is similar in many respects to its near and typically larger relative the rutabaga. The turnip is white fleshed, shaped like a radish, and has a white skin with a purple collar.

Medicinal Benefits Raw grated turnip serves as a digestive aid, much the same as radish and daikon. Turnips clear heat, dissolve mucus, moisten, and cool and strengthen blood, and they are good for general detoxification. Turnip juice reduces mucus and catarrh.

While the whole cabbage family is valued for its anticarcinogenic glucosinolates, turnips and rutabagas are exceptionally high in these important nutrients. Likewise, they contain mustard oil and, when overcooked, release a sulfurous aroma—but not as intensely as cabbage and Brussels sprouts do. Turnips contain vitamins B and C, potassium, phosphorus, calcium, and other trace nutrients. They have more naturally occurring sodium than most vegetables. Turnips reduce *kapha*.

Use Use fresh young turnips in salads as you would a radish. Cooking further sweetens turnips and mellows their bite. When cooked with other foods, turnips have the remarkable ability to absorb other flavors, which allows them to become particularly succulent and rich. Their starchy properties are somewhat reminiscent of potatoes. Peel turnips only if they are overly large and less than fresh. Turnips can be used in soups and casseroles, steamed on their own, roasted, baked, and pureed.

Buying A turnip past its prime is bitter and pithy and has nothing to recommend it. A fresh, small turnip, no longer than three inches in diameter, grown in the spring or fall, is sweet with a mild bite like radish when raw. Turnips grown in the hot months, or without adequate water, are decidedly more pungent.

Select turnips that have root end and stem base intact. If these parts are trimmed away and yellowed at the incision, the turnip will lack flavor. Look for smooth, firm roots, preferably small or medium-small. Reject flaccid, discolored, or withered turnips.

See **Cabbage Family; Turnip Greens; Vegetable.**

TURNIP GREENS
(*Brassica rapa rapifera*)

Turnip tops are just as delicious as their bottoms. There are even some varieties of turnips grown just for their dark leafy greens, which look like exceedingly large radish leaves.

Medicinal Benefits Turnip greens are similar to collard greens in medicinal properties (see **Collards** entry).

Use Turnip greens have a milder flavor than mustard greens and kale and only a hint of bitterness. They are too coarse for salads, but light cooking (*light* being the operative word) turns them into a succulent green.

Buying Turnip greens are sporadically available in the supermarket, usually near the collards and kale. You sometimes can find turnips with their tops. Purchase those that are a vibrant deep green and show no sign of yellowing. Refrigerate in a plastic bag for up to five days.

See **Cabbage Family; Turnip; Vegetable.**

TUSCAN KALE SEE **KALE.**

TVP SEE **TEXTURED VEGETABLE PROTEIN.**

TWIG TEA SEE **TEA.**

$\mathcal{U}$

UGLI FRUIT
Unique Fruit
(*Citrus paradisi* × *C. reticulata*)

The ugli fruit is a grapefruit and mandarin cross, so named because its skin is, well, ugly: puffy, misshapen, mottled yellow and green, and baggy fitting. The sweet, juicy, and fragrant

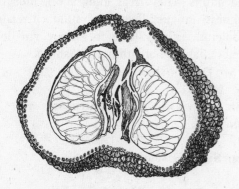

citrus fruit tastes more like a mandarin than a grapefruit; it typically has few seeds. Look for this native Jamaican fruit in the winter and early spring months. Its orange-brown skin blemishes indicate ripeness. The unique fruit is an ugli fruit that is trademarked.

See **Citrus Family; Fruit.**

UMEBOSHI
Salt Plum
(*Prunus mume*)

A Japanese seasoning agent that ranks right under soy sauce and miso in use and versatility is the pickled plum umeboshi. Sour, immature plums are partially sun-dried and then fermented in salt with the herb perilla for a full year. Perilla is high in iron, acts as a natural preservative, and imparts the characteristic pink color to the plums.

Medicinal Benefits A highly alkaline condiment, umeboshi is high in citric acid and antibiotic in action. It eliminates lactic acid (which contributes to fatigue, colds, flu, viruses, diseases, and chronic illness) from the body. It increases hydrochloric acid levels and therefore enhances digestion and helps to strengthen blood quality. It relieves indigestion due to overeating, alcohol overindulgence, or morning sickness. Umeboshi calms *vata* beautifully.

Use When pureed, umeboshi may replace salt and vinegar in salad dressings, spreads, seasonings, and sauces, or it may be cooked with grains and vegetables. It is a signature ingredient in the digestive aid and restorative *ume shoyu kudzu* (see recipe on page 192).

Buying Whole umeboshi plums contain the pit and perilla; remove the pit and crack it, and then savor its sweet-and-sour pickled kernel; chop and use the perilla along with the plum. Umeboshi is also available in a less expensive and more convenient paste form (without the pit and perilla).

I purchase umeboshi from a natural food store to be assured that it is additive-free and traditionally fermented for one year (a chemically induced fermentation period lasts only a few weeks).

In paste form or whole, umeboshi keeps for several years at room temperature. Hold in a glass jar with a tight-fitting lid to prevent de-

PICKLED PLUM WORKSHOP

Some years ago, the beloved Japanese healer the late Sensi Naboru Muramoto gave a plum pickling workshop in my home. As the plum variety used for ume does not grow in the Americas, we used the nearest equivalent—immature apricots. The fruits were partially sun-dried on bamboo mats for several days, then mixed with perilla and Sensi's own hand-harvested sea salt. This mixture was packed into a 20-gallon ceramic crock, topped with a wooden lid, weighted down with heavy stones, and stashed in the basement to ferment for a year. These "apriboshi" and their brine—umeboshi vinegar—were wonderful.

hydration. If old, salt crystals may form; these may be rinsed off prior to use.

See Perilla; **Plum; Umeboshi Vinegar; Ume Plum Extract.**

UMEBOSHI VINEGAR
Ume Plum Vinegar, Ume Su

Umeboshi vinegar is a pink brine with a deep, cherry aroma and fruity sour flavor; it is a by-product of umeboshi making. Technically it is not a vinegar because it contains salt; nevertheless, it may be substituted for vinegar and salt in any recipe. Umeboshi vinegar imparts a light, refreshing citric flavor, which enhances salad dressings and steamed vegetables. Its medicinal properties are comparable to, but less potent than, umeboshi.

See **Umeboshi.**

UME PLUM EXTRACT

A black, almost tarlike extract of sour green plums, ume plum extract is a highly concentrated source of citric acid. This concentrate is also available in convenient pills called ume plum balls, which also contain jinenjo. Both these products are available in natural food stores and by full-service whole foods suppliers.

Ume plum balls and ume extract are highly effective natural medicines for both children and adults. They treat indigestion, morning sickness, fatigue, liver- and stomach-related problems, asthma (due to kidney yin deficiency), labored breathing, and shock.

See **Umeboshi.**

UME PLUM VINEGAR SEE UMEBOSHI VINEGAR.

UME SU SEE UMEBOSHI VINEGAR.

UNIQUE FRUIT SEE UGLI FRUIT.

UNREFINED, EVAPORATED CANE JUICE SEE SUGAR.

UNSULFURED MOLASSES SEE MOLASSES.

URAD SEE BEANS AND LEGUMES; DAL.

VALENCIA ORANGE SEE **ORANGE.**

VALENCIA RICE SEE **RICE.**

VANILLA
(*Vanilla planifolia*)

Of all flower species, the beautiful, delicate orchid is, botanically speaking, the most highly evolved. Of the many orchid varieties, there's only one with an edible fruit: the vanilla orchid. In its natural environment, a very small hummingbird and a tiny bee once pollinated this orchid. Both bird and bee are now extinct. All vanilla is now hand-pollinated, and pollination must occur within a few hours of the flower's opening. The orchid fruit then takes seven months to mature into a long, skinny yellow-green pod.

This vanilla pod has little flavor until it is cured, and then a smidgen of it imbues foods with a rich floral aroma and flavor. A superior-flavored vanilla takes up to six months to cure and ferment; it is cold—rather than heat—extracted. Hand pollination and the lengthy maturation and fermentation period explain why, after saffron, vanilla is the most expensive seasoning agent.

Today vanilla is produced throughout moist tropical areas within 20 degrees of the equator. Vanilla orchids grown north or south of this zone will flower but will not produce pods. Native to southern Mexico, vanilla was used by the Aztecs long before it became popular elsewhere in the world.

Medicinal Benefits Vanilla has tonic, stimulant, antiseptic, and digestive properties. It is especially effective in aiding the digestion of rich foods. There are 36 aromatic compounds in vanilla, and vanillin, the most active component, is mildly toxic in both its natural and synthetic forms. The synthetic form, vanillin, is a wood industry by-product. The FDA, however, considers it safe because such small amounts are used. Workers who daily handle large quantities, however, may be afflicted with vanillism, which causes headaches and allergic skin reactions.

Vanilla is *tridoshic* in action. In aromatherapy, vanilla's consoling aroma is used to support self-confidence, to dissolve pent-up anger and frustration, and to access sensuality.

Use Vanilla is heat sensitive and so, whenever possible, it should be added at the end of cooking. Its most common use is in baked goods, desserts, and fruit dishes, but it also may effectively flavor savory dishes. Vanilla goes well with chocolate, a combination that the Aztecs first used.

Buying Choose dark brown vanilla pods or beans that are supple, plump, and tender, with a strong but round vanilla aroma. Quality beans are covered with a fine white powder, which is crystalline vanillin. Vanilla beans in an airtight glass jar stored in a cool, dark place will keep for about six months.

Pure vanilla extract contains at least 35 percent alcohol. Best-quality vanilla is nothing but vanilla extract and alcohol, and its flavors mature and develop as it ages. Lesser-quality extracts may contain sugar or corn syrup, glycerin, and/or propylene glycol. Vanilla extract in an airtight glass jar will store indefinitely in a cool, dark place.

Be Mindful Many people come home from Mexico with a quart of Mexican vanilla that cost only a few dollars. If it has a coarse aroma and acrid, bitter aftertaste, don't use it. By U.S. law, pure vanilla extract must be derived from *V. planifolia*. If the vanilla label does not say vanilla extract, it's probably a sulfite waste byproduct from the paper industry, a chemically extracted compound known as coumarin. This substance, a potential toxin, was outlawed as a food ingredient by the USDA.

VANILLA PASSION FRUIT SEE **PASSION FRUIT.**

VEGETABLE

Technically the vegetable realm includes any edible part of a plant—leaf, stem, tuber, root, bulb, berry, and seed. So while mushrooms are excluded, it includes grains, legumes, nuts, seeds, fruits, and seaweed. In common usage, the term "vegetable" refers to fleshy, edible plants that typically are more mineral rich and less sugary than fruit and are favored in savory dishes.

An excellent way to attune to their energetic and medicinal properties is to consider how each plant part has a propensity to support the corollary body part (see page xxi).

See **Agar; Agretti; Alaria; Amaranth Greens; Arame; Artichoke; Arugula; Asparagus; Avocado; Beet; Beetberry; Bitter Melon; Bladder Wrack; Bok Choy; Broccoli; Broccolini; Broccoli Rabe; Brussels Sprout; Burdock; Cabbage; Cardoon; Carrot; Cauliflower; Celery; Celery Root; Chard; Chayote; Chicory; Chile Pepper; Chinese Broccoli; Chrysanthemum Greens; Chuño; Collards; Cress; Cucumber; Daikon; Dandelion; Dulse; Eggplant; Fat Hen; Fennel; Flowering Cabbage; Gac; Garlic; Ground Cherry; Hijiki; Horned Water Chestnut; Horseradish; Irish Moss; Jerusalem Artichoke; Kale; Kanten; Kelp; Kohlrabi; Kombu; Laver; Leek; Lettuce; Long Bean; Loofah; Lotus Root; Mâche; Mizuna; Mushroom, Common; Mushroom Family; Mustard Greens; Napa Cabbage; Nasturtium; New Zealand Spinach; Nori; Oca; Okra; Onion; Onion Family; Orach; Parsley Root; Parsnip; Peppers; Potato; Pumpkin; Purslane; Radish; Ramp; Rutabaga; Salsify; Scorzonera; Sea Lettuce; Sea**

HOMEMADE VANILLA

Commercial vanilla, even from a natural food store, is often harsh tasting and adulterated with shoddy ingredients. It's effortless and inexpensive to make your own quality vanilla extract. Here's how:

Vanilla Brandy Extract

2 whole vanilla beans, split and cut into 1-inch pieces

1 cup good-quality brandy (or vodka or rum)

Place the ingredients in an 8-ounce dark bottle, cover, and allow to steep for 1 month before using. As the extract is used, refill with brandy a second time. The third time you make the extract, remove the spent beans and use fresh beans.

To make vanilla sugar, place the spent beans in 2 cups of sugar (use the sugar of your choice; see the **Sugar** entry), cover tightly, and set aside for at least a week.

Palm; Sea Whip; Sorrel; Spinach; Squash; Squash Blossom; Squash, Summer; Squash, Winter; Sweet Pepper; Tatsoi; Tomatillo; Tomato; Turnip; Turnip Greens; Wakame; Wasabi; Water Chestnut; Watercress; Winter Melon; Yacón.

Vegetable Gelatin See **Agar.**

Vegetable Oil See **Fat and Oil.**

Vegetable Pear See **Chayote.**

Verdolaga See **Purslane.**

Vialone Nano Rice See **Rice.**

Vidalia See **Onion.**

VINEGAR

For about 10,000 years throughout the world, vinegar has been an important seasoning agent, preservative, medicine, beauty aid, and antibiotic. The word "vinegar" comes from the French *vin*, meaning "wine," and *aigre*, meaning "sour." Indeed, vinegar may be made from any sugar-containing liquid that can be fermented by acetic acid bacteria to less than 18 percent ethyl alcohol. Vinegar may be made from sweeteners such as honey and maple syrup; fruit and coconut; vegetables such as beets and potatoes; grain and malted grain; and whey.

Traditionally, whatever local sugar-containing food source was in abundance was fermented, in a process taking weeks or even years, into the predominant vinegar of a region: malt in England, grapes in France and Italy, rice throughout Asia, coconut and palm in tropical regions, and apples in North America. Unlike modern vinegar that is quickly made in one to three days, a traditional vinegar is not pasteurized.

Medicinal Benefits Vinegar has a sour and sweet flavor, it energizes the stomach and liver meridians, assists with digestion, and moves blood stagnation. Vinegar is warming and detoxifying; it quickly resolves liver congestion and can significantly reduce mental depression. Vinegar immediately increases circulation and therefore moves blocked energy—be it emotional or physical. In Ayurvedic medicine, vinegar is considered *rajasic* and is best used sparingly. It calms *vata*.

Vinegar is a common ingredient in many kitchen remedies. Applied topically, vinegar relieves sunburn and may ease arthritis and insect bites or stings.

Traditional, unpasteurized, unfiltered vinegar contains as many as 50 different nutrients, amino acids, and trace elements, which contribute to its distinctive taste and also its medicinal properties. The amino acids counter the effect of lactic acid buildup in the blood and help prevent the formation of toxic fat peroxides, which contribute to aging, fatigue, and irritability and to cholesterol formation on blood vessel walls.

The vinegar of a given region is valued as a versatile folk remedy. In the United States, apple cider vinegar is a cure-all according to the perennially popular book *Folk Medicine*, by Dr. D. C. Jarvis. He prescribes an old Vermont kitchen tonic: two teaspoons of apple cider vinegar and a teaspoon of honey in a cup of water to treat chronic fatigue, headache, arthritis, colitis, obesity, food poisoning, kidney inflammation, insomnia, high blood pressure, dizziness, sore throat, and a host of other ailments in humans as well as in farm animals. Several centuries later, the effectiveness of this remedy is still attested to by countless individuals. It is a treatment, however, that may lead to a kind of vinegar dependency, according to Paul Pitchford in *Healing with Whole Foods*. Furthermore, Pitchford advises, it is contraindicated in cases of "weak digestion marked by loose, watery stools; general *deficiency* (frailty); and muscular injury or weakness, including rheumatism."

Use Much of vinegar's volatile pungency is lost when it is heated, so stir in vinegar after removing the dish from the heat.

Buying For eons, delicious and healthful vinegar has been made using slow fermentation over a several-month period. Today the bulk of it—even when organic—is produced in a quick 20- to 72-hour process, resulting in an inferior product. Labeling laws do not require that manufacturing processes be listed. Key words that indicate traditional process include "unpasteurized," "unfiltered," "traditionally brewed," "traditionally fermented," or "aged in wood."

Store quality vinegar in a light-free environment to protect it from free radical activity and the breakdown of vital nutrients. These are the common types of vinegar:

- **Apple Cider Vinegar (or Apple Vinegar)** Raw and unpasteurized apple cider vinegar has a punchy, bright, and crisp flavor. Traditionally made vinegar from cider is nothing but freshly pressed apple juice allowed to ferment over a four- to six-week period at room temperature, and it contains no added clarifiers, enzymes, or preservatives. Rich with sediment and about 5 to 6 percent acetic acid, a quality cider vinegar tastes like the apples from which it was pressed. It is generally used for dressings, condiments, marinades, pickles, and sauces. Unless it's specified as *certified* organic, unfiltered, and unpasteurized, I don't buy cider vinegar. Favor a brand name you trust, and expect to see cloudy sediment at the bottom of the bottle.

- **Balsamic Vinegar** Undoubtedly the best balsamic vinegar is from Modena, Italy, and it has been treasured since at least 1508. It has a dense but flowing texture, a luminous brown color, a penetrating and persistent aroma, and a pleasant but harmonious sweet-sour flavor. Quality balsamic is a minimum of 12 years old but may be 20 years or older. It's labeled "Aceto Balsamico Tradizionale di Modena" and, as guarantee of its authenticity, is sealed with a serially numbered strip. It is used on salads, in desserts, and—provided it has been aged more than 50 years—is a delicious beverage. As the vinegar ages, it is concentrated in a series of casks made from different types of wood, including juniper, oak, chestnut, cherry, ash, and mulberry. The casks flavor the vinegar; no other flavoring agent is added.

  More quickly fermented balsamics from the same region are labeled "Aceto Balsamico di Modena" and don't have a serial number. They lack the flavor depth, concentration, and sweetness of the more expensive traditionally made balsamic but still are a quality ingredient.

  Today many vinegars labeled "balsamic" barely resemble their namesake. They may be made from any grape variety and in any grape-producing country. Ask the producer precisely what he means by the unregulated terms "barrel aged" or "produced in wooden casks," as most vinegar today is quickly produced in fiberglass containers.

- **Distilled (Spirit or White) Vinegar** (Not Recommended) By FDA regulations, distilled vinegar may be synthetic ethanol made by direct chemical oxidation of wood, sugar, or fossil fuels. If the ingredient simply states "vinegar," you may assume it is the least expensive quality. I use—and recommend—distilled vinegar for washing windows.

- **Flavored Vinegar** As vinegar is a preservative, the number of potential flavorings is as vast as one's imagination. Herb and fruit vinegars, especially thyme, oregano, raspberry, and blueberry, are popular. To make, add either a fresh or dried herb or fruit or fruit flavoring to a mild vinegar such as a white wine vinegar, and age for a week or more.

- **Fruit Vinegar** Specialty fruit wines may be made from any fruit. They range from the more common apple and raspberry to the more exotic persimmon, goji berry, and quince.

- **Malt Vinegar** Made of sprouted and fermented barley, malt vinegar, at 5 to 6 percent acetic acid, is too strongly flavored for salad dressings. The English liberally splash it on fish and chips to help cut the oil. Malt vinegar is superb for pickling.

- **Rice Vinegar** The most popular vinegar in East and Southeast Asian cuisines, it is available in white, black, and amber varieties. The white is made from white rice, black from sweet black rice, and the amber from brown rice. My favorite is the latter that contains only organic brown rice, koji, and spring water and that is blended in clay crocks and aged six to eight months; its acidity is 4.5 percent. Some rice vinegar varieties are sweetened with spices or other flavorings, one if which is colored red by red yeast rice.

- **Wine Vinegar** When made from organic ingredients and aged traditionally, without the use of preservatives, wine vinegar is an excellent product with a complex, mellow flavor. Wine vinegar may be made from red or white wine as well as from specific grape varieties, including champagne, sherry, and pinot grigio. Wine vinegar is lower in acidity than cider, malt, or distilled vinegar.

Be Mindful Vinegar is a solvent; its 4 to 6 percent acetic acid is corrosive. Therefore, vinegar stored in plastic or metal becomes enriched with polycarbons or metallic ions. I purchase traditionally made vinegars aged in wood or ceramic and bottled in glass (rather than plastic or cans). When cooking with vinegar, I use nonreactive cookware, such as an enameled pot, as opposed to aluminum, copper, or cast-iron cookware.

In the last 50 years, technology has enabled vinegar to be produced in a 20-hour process. As one producer told me, "Who, today, can afford to keep a product in storage for one year before selling it?"

Commercial and even "natural" or "organic" vinegar by law may be diluted with water and treated with sulfites.

WAKAME
(*Undaria pinnatifida*)

Wakame is a versatile and tasty olive-green sea vegetable that grows in fronds in both deep and shallow water. Most of the North American supply of wakame comes from northern Japan; however, our domestic equivalent, alaria, is harvested in Maine and northern California.

Medicinal Benefits Wakame is a cooling food and both a blood and yin tonic that supports the liver, kidney, and stomach functions. It helps to regulate conditions of excess heat, water, mucus, and damp and to dispel toxins and treat edema. It contains alginic acid, a polysaccharide compound that has the ability to chelate or bind heavy metals like lead and radioactive elements, as well as excessive sodium. It reduces *vata*.

After hijiki, wakame is the seaweed highest in calcium; it is also rich in iodine, protein, iron, and niacin, It contains numerous trace minerals and vitamins A and C.

Use Wakame acts as a tenderizer and so increases the digestibility of beans and any other fibrous foods it is cooked with. A popular soup ingredient, wakame may also be used as a green vegetable in salads and other dishes. When toasted in a 350°F oven for seven minutes or until crisp, then crumbled, it makes a tasty condiment. Or pulverize toasted wakame in a blender and use it as a seasoning agent or salt replacement.

Instant wakame flakes may be crumbled into a broth and simmered for one or two minutes before serving. Wakame fronds should be soaked in cold water to hydrate and the fibrous stipe cut out and discarded (or reserved for soup stock). Once hydrated, wakame should be cooked for about seven minutes, or until softened.

Buying Except for seasonal fresh wakame from an Asian market, most wakame is available dried. Ita wakame is an exceptionally fine quality wakame. Wakame may or may not be precooked; the latter is usually available as wakame flakes. When purchasing wakame in fronds, note that the younger, more tender plants have a thin rather than a wide stipe. When dried, it is impossible to determine the stipe size, so purchasing a reputable brand is the best way to obtain quality wakame. Fresh wakame requires refrigeration and prompt use. These are the wakame varieties:

- **Ita Wakame** An exceptionally fine quality wakame that comes in thin sheets.
- **Mekabu Wakame** This is the reproductive part of the plant that bears the plant's spore; it grows in a spiral fashion on a thick stipe. Mekabu wakame is highly mucilaginous and rich in the valuable nutraceutical fucoidan and is considered a superior female tonic. For many people, mekabu is an acquired taste—or, rather, texture, as it is mucilaginous. It requires longer cooking than wakame.
- **Wakame Flakes** Precooked wakame in small pieces makes for very convenient use. Add at the last minute or so to a soup, or toss into a salad.

See **Alaria; Kelp; Seaweed Family; Vegetable.**

WALLA WALLA ONION SEE **ONION.**

BLOOD ORANGE, WAKAME, AND CUCUMBER SALAD

Crisp cucumber, juicy-sweet orange, and succulent wakame make this an unusually beautiful and refreshing salad. As wakame aids the digestion of fat, it's an excellent side dish to serve alongside a fatty meal. The unique perfume and bold garnet color of blood oranges is unbeatable, but if they're not available, substitute navel oranges or mineola tangerines.

Serves 4

1 cucumber
2 tablespoons wakame flakes
2 medium blood oranges
2 teaspoons finely grated ginger
Unrefined salt

Slice the cucumber in half lengthwise; scoop out and discard the seeds. Chop the cucumber and place it in a small bowl with the wakame.

Peel 1 of the oranges, chop it into small chunks, remove the seeds, and add it to the cucumber mixture.

Juice the remaining orange into a small bowl and strain out the seeds. Using your fingertips, squeeze the ginger to extract ½ teaspoon ginger juice. Add the ginger juice to the orange juice and season with salt to taste. Pour over the salad and toss to combine. Allow to marinate for 5 minutes. This salad is best when eaten within an hour of making it.

WALNUT
(*Juglans regia*)

The most popular and widely used nut throughout the world is the Persian walnut, which, in America, is called the English walnut because of who shipped it here during the Colonial period. Unlike the American native black walnut, the English walnut is easy to shell and does not stain. Walnut kernels are plump, meaty, and crisp, with a sweet flavor that has bitter aftertones because of the tannic acid in the nut's skin. Most of the U.S. domestic supply—and a significant percentage of the world's supply—of English walnuts come from California. Walnuts are a member of the hickory family.

Walnuts are said to tonify the kidneys, strengthen the back and knees, warm and hold chi in the lungs, help kidneys to grasp the chi, moisten the intestines, and move stool. They are believed to stop asthma and are prescribed to be taken between bouts of asthma, but not for acute asthma. They are used for elderly as a constipation cure.

Medicinal Benefits The walnut is a warming food and is used as a kitchen remedy to strengthen the kidneys and lungs and to lubricate the large intestines and help regulate the bowels; it is a chi and yang tonic and sweet in flavor. Walnuts help reduce inflammation and alleviate asthma and pain. After fish, walnuts are the highest food in omega-3 fatty acids; they're an excellent source of antioxidants, especially ellagic acid, and vitamin E. The English walnut contains fair amounts of protein, zinc, calcium, and potassium as well as the amino acid arginine. The walnut balances *vata*.

Use To minimize the tannin in the skin and to concentrate the flavors, toast walnuts just prior to use. I prefer toasting them in a dry wok while stirring constantly rather than toasting them in the oven. Walnuts are excellent in savory dishes such as casseroles, stir-fries, stuffings, and salads, and they're a classic ingredient in cakes, confections, and cookies.

Buying For the freshest nut with the most flavor, purchase walnuts in the shell and crack just prior to use. For convenience, purchase shelled whole walnut halves, but only if they are refrigerated and if their flesh is white rather than yellowed, which would indicate rancidity. Broken, chopped, and/or unrefrigerated walnuts quickly become rancid and bitter tasting.

Commercial walnuts sold in the shell are washed, bleached, and polished to a uniform tan color. Organic walnuts have darker brown shells, and their color varies depending upon how shaded or sunny the branch they grew on was.

Shelled commercial walnuts frequently are treated with ethylene gas, fumigated with methyl bromide, blanched in hot dye or glycerin and sodium carbonate, rinsed in citric acid, and dried to increase shelf life. The result is a uniform nut with reduced flavor and tannic acid. A less processed and therefore "lower," baking grade commercial walnut has more flavor than the bleached nuts.

See **Black Walnut; Hickory Family; Nuts; Walnut Oil.**

WALNUT, BLACK SEE **BLACK WALNUT.**

WALNUT OIL

A richly scented and flavored delicacy with a fragile shelf life, walnut oil is best bought in small quantities with its manufactured date on the label. Keep refrigerated. Use walnut oil in salad dressings or over steamed foods. Do not heat it. Use only unrefined walnut oil.

See **Fat and Oil; Walnut.**

WARREN TURBAN SQUASH SEE **SQUASH; SQUASH, WINTER.**

WARTED HUBBARD SQUASH SEE **SQUASH; SQUASH, WINTER.**

WASABI
Japanese Horseradish
(*Wasabia japonica*)

Eat just a speck of wasabi and immediately it feels as if smoke is pouring from your nostrils. Some stuff. Its mustardlike heat memorably—but briefly—burns both your mouth and nasal passages. (Whereas the capsaicin of a chile burns longer and primarily your mouth.)

Wasabi is the gnarled and warty root of a plant that is unique to the Japanese islands and highly valued in Japanese cuisine. Its pale green flesh packs a furious wallop. Although it is called Japanese horseradish, wasabi is more fragrant than horseradish and has a cleansing taste. Wasabi is a cabbage family member.

BRAIN FOOD

According to the Doctrine of Signature used in traditional, plant-based medical systems, the walnut looks like the human brain and, therefore, is used to treat brain injuries and to enhance cognition. The thin, fleshy, outer green husk, which is removed before the walnuts are marketed, is likened to the scalp. The walnut's hard shell is like a skull. The thin envelope inside, with its paperlike partitions between the two halves of the nut, is like the covering membrane. The convoluted nut itself represents the human brain's two hemispheres.

Eating a handful of walnuts would not cure a concussion. However, walnuts freshly cooked in a rice congee (see page 303) and eaten daily for a week or more will energetically support the brain's function.

Medicinal Benefits Wasabi contains protein-digesting enzymes, which make it a digestive aid. It is also used as a kitchen remedy to antidote fish poisoning. It is a heating food. Wasabi is balancing to *kapha*.

Use Wasabi is available as a root, dry powder or constituted in a paste form. The digestive enzymes in wasabi quickly dissipate; therefore, grate fresh wasabi, or reconstitute powdered wasabi, just prior to use. Prior to grating, remove the "eyes" and pare away the tough skin. To use the powder, mix with an equal portion of tepid water to form a paste and allow to stand, covered, for about 10 minutes to develop flavor.

Serve wasabi in half-teaspoon amounts as an accompaniment to fatty foods or raw fish dishes. Because it stimulates the palate, it is a useful ingredient in hors d'oeuvres, barbecue sauces, dressings, dips, and condiments.

Buying Fresh wasabi is occasionally found in Asian markets in water-filled pans. Select a plump, fresh-looking root, preferably not sprouting.

Powdered wasabi is available in both Asian markets and natural food stores in convenient tiny tins or envelopes. Note that if reconstituted, the "wasabi" is bright green (rather than a greenish gray), and it is powdered horseradish or daikon with green coloring. Most of what is referred to as wasabi—be it at the market or served alongside sushi—is in fact derived from horseradish rather than the costly and often hard-to-find wasabi root.

See **Cabbage Family; Herbs and Spices; Vegetable.**

WATER

Pure water is critical for maintaining or regaining health. Human embryos are 95 percent water, newborns are about 75 percent water, and most elderly people are about 50 percent water. Whatever your age, I do hope you're consuming good-quality water.

Medicinal Benefits I disagree with the common Western mantra "hydrate, hydrate, hydrate . . ." Traditional medical systems more wisely advise to drink when you are thirsty. What is important is to gauge what works best for you; some people need less water than others, and too much water may "dampen" your spirits. If you're sedentary, you'll need less water than if you're physically active; on a cold day you'll often need less than on a hot day.

One sign of not getting enough liquid is strong-smelling, dark yellow—or even brownish—urine. (Note: Taking B vitamins causes the urine to turn bright yellow.) Some signs of potential overhydration include pale or clear-colored urine and needing to get up to urinate at night (unless you're pregnant). Unfortunately, some people, in an effort to remain slim, drink excessively in an attempt to "fill the hole."

Pay attention to your own body signs, and your common sense will help you discern your liquid requirements.

Use If you have a sunny countertop, here's an easy way to reenergize water before using it. Decant into a glass jug, loosely cover, and expose it to natural light—preferably sunlight—for several hours.

If you are consuming demineralized (reverse osmosis or distilled) water, add a scant ⅛ teaspoon unrefined salt per gallon of purified water.

Buying Feel fortunate if you have a natural source of deep underground water that tests free of contaminants. Otherwise purchase pure water. Or install an activated charcoal home purification unit (unless, that is, your water contains water-soluble toxins that cannot be removed by a filter, such as nitrates, nitrites, and sodium fluoride). Under-the-counter or countertop water filters are effective when the filters are replaced as necessary; in a year's time, their price per gallon is considerably less expensive than are the popular freestanding units like Brita or PUR. These are some terms to be familiar with:

- **Artesian Water** From a free-flowing well that taps a confined aquifer; it doesn't require pumping.
- **Mineral Water** From an underground source that is naturally rich in flavor-enhancing minerals; no minerals can be added. Mineral water is often named for its place of origin.
- **Purified Water** Many bottled waters are no more than filtered municipal tap water. They may be dechlorinated, purified using ultraviolet light, and have minerals either added or subtracted. They may also be carbonated.
- **Sparkling Water** Naturally contains carbon dioxide, which makes it bubbly. Carbon dioxide may be added to equal but not exceed the amount of carbonization the water contains as its emergence from the source. (Soda water, seltzer, and tonic water are not considered sparkling water.)
- **Spring Water** From an underground source that flows naturally to the earth's surface.
- **Well Water** Water pumped from a man-made hole in the ground that taps an aquifer.

Be Mindful I do not recommend processed waters, including distilled or reverse osmosis (RO) water. Food cooked in demineralized water loses a much higher percentage of minerals to the water as a result of osmosis. It is the minerals in water that provide taste and character. To remineralize RO and distilled water, add a scant ⅛ teaspoon unrefined salt per gallon of purified water. Furthermore, RO water is hard to justify from an environmental vantage point, as it wastes two to five gallons of water for every gallon produced.

Store water in glass or inert plastic. Most plastic water jugs actually "enrich" water with toxic polycarbons; both heat and time accelerate the leaching rate. Thin and flexible plastic containers contaminate water faster than do heavier-weight plastic bottles. In addition, a cancer-causing chemical, methylene chloride, has been found in water stored in polycarbonate resin bottles.

More than 40 percent of American faucets deliver water that's been recycled through a sewer or industrial conduit. Moreover, the

---

WATCHING GRANDPA WASH HIS HANDS

I remember my grandfather coming in from the garden carrying a bouquet of beets and greens in his soil-encrusted hands. He would fill the bathroom basin with 1½ inches of water, wet his hands, lather them well, rinse in the now-darkened washing water, and then dry his spotlessly clean hands. To my young eyes, his ablutions were a magic show—that a smidgen of water could clean such dirty hands.

But then Grandpa understood the value of water. The well on his dry farm near Blue Creek, Utah, had brackish water, and so he hauled drinking water for his family and livestock. He'd hitch a double team of draft horses to the buckboard and, during the summer months, leave well before dawn to miss the heat of the day. He'd go up over and then down Rattlesnake Pass, fill the water barrels, recross the pass, and head back home. On a sweltering day, Grandpa's spent teams would drink more than a third of the just-fetched water.

water supplies of an increasing number of communities are contaminated by the waterborne giardia parasite. Other water contaminants include radon, which makes water radioactive; old pipes and soldered joints, which contaminate water with lead; agricultural toxins such as nitrates and pesticides; chemical additives such as chlorine and sodium fluoride; and numerous industrial pollutants, including trichloroethylene.

WATER CALTROP SEE **HORNED WATER CHESTNUT.**

WATER CHESTNUT
(*Eleocharis tuberosa*)

The most memorable property of the water chestnut is its applelike crunch. Although jicama and the Asian pear come close in texture, they do not match its refreshing delicacy or its juicy, buttery sweet flavor. The water chestnut, which looks like a grubby chestnut in size and shape, actually grows in the mud. It has a black outer peel and a slightly peaked, tufted top. It has been a food staple in Asia since Neolithic times.

Medicinal Benefits The water chestnut is a cold and sweet bulb that disperses excess heat from the body. It acts upon the lung, large intestine, stomach, spleen, bladder, and liver systems and helps dispel mucus. The water chestnut treats diabetes and jaundice and inhibits infectious diseases such as staphylococcus and E. coli. It is also said to aid vision. It calms *pitta* and in moderation reduces *kapha*.

The water chestnut is a low-calorie food, containing ample protein, calcium, phosphorus, iron, and vitamins B and C.

Use Wash well and pare the top and bottom ends to expose the white flesh. Peel and discard the skin. Slice or used whole the water chestnut, like a tree chestnut, may be boiled,

roasted, or made into flour; water chestnuts may also be stir-fried, braised, or steamed. Cooking enhances its flavor, does not detract from its texture, and eliminates the possibility of contamination by waterborne pathogens.

Buying Currently water chestnuts are not grown commercially in the United States despite several attempts to do so. They are readily available canned but as such have little flavor and a compromised crunch. Look for fresh water chestnuts exported from China and Taiwan in Asian markets and some supermarkets. Select those that are rock-hard and free of withered, wrinkled, or soft spots. Expect them to have some encrusted dirt as, when washed, they deteriorate.

See **Horned Water Chestnut; Vegetable.**

WATERCRESS
(*Nasturtium officinale*)

One of my favorite pastimes as a child was gathering peppery and pungent watercress, which forms a deep green carpet along creek sides and can even cover most of a pond. Because of giardia and other waterborne contaminants, however, it is no longer safe to eat wild watercress. What a loss.

Eurasian in origin, watercress probably was introduced in America in the 1600s and now thrives in all 50 states. A cabbage family member, watercress—be it cultivated or wild—comes in only one variety. This aquatic plant has hollow stems; when mature it bears small white flowers. Commercial supplies are grown hydroponically.

Medicinal Benefits Watercress is a pungent, stimulating, and cooling herb that treats the lung, large intestine, spleen, stomach, bladder, and kidney systems. It is a blood and chi tonic that clears toxins, aids digestion, and is useful for gallbladder complaints, bronchitis, and rheumatism. It is a diuretic and digestive aid and contains antioxidant properties that help protect against cancer, especially lung cancer. Raw watercress is not recommended for the young, the elderly, or anyone with compromised health, a propensity for yeast infections, or with a history of internal parasites. Watercress balances *kapha*.

Use Watercress has a mustardlike bite and aroma but surprises the palate with a cooling, refreshing effect rather than a fiery one. Cooking eliminates its bite and leaves a sweet vegetable. When cooked, its volume is reduced by three-quarters, so plan accordingly. Raw, it is delicious in salads or on sandwiches and makes an attractive garnish. For a tasty herb butter, mince and mix with butter.

Buying Purchase vibrantly green watercress with no yellowed leaves. Store it in cold water up to the leaves, but do not soak the leaves. It is highly perishable, so plan to use within a day or two. Wash watercress with extra care.

See **Cabbage Family; Vegetable.**

WATERMELON
(*Citrullus lanatus, C. vulgaris*)

How perfect that our most watery fruit originated in Africa's hot and arid Kalahari region. There is indeed some logic in favoring your region's native foods; and, when you're not in the Kalahari but it feels like it, then cool down and rehydrate with watermelon. Technically a vegetable, and a member of the gourd family, this fruit of a vine is more closely related to a cucumber than to a cantaloupe. It's a classic picnic food, enjoyed out-of-doors, especially by children

and participants in seed-spitting contests. Some new varieties have yellow instead of red flesh, and some, due to genetic engineering, are seedless. Watermelons typically range from under a pound in weight to as large as 10 pounds.

Medicinal Benefits Watermelon is a cold food that treats the bladder, heart, and stomach meridians. Surprisingly, it has only half the sugar (5 to 6 percent) of an apple. It tastes much sweeter, though, because sugar is its main taste-producing element—the rest is primarily water. This makes it a popular detoxifying and diet food and an unexcelled cooling food; it's even more cooling than cantaloupe. Watermelon relieves thirst, mental depression, and edema, and it induces urination. Watermelon, especially bright red-fleshed watermelon, is a good source of lycopene and therefore supports healthy vision. It contains vitamins C and A and potassium.

Use Watermelon flesh is enjoyed in fruit salads, smoothies, and fruit punch, and just by itself. Its seeds may be seasoned, toasted, and eaten as a snack food like squash or pumpkin seeds; and its rind (both the green skin and the white layer) makes a delicious pickle. To make watermelon juice, remove the seeds and process the flesh in a blender or processor to create a uniform pulp, which may be diluted with water or another juice.

Watermelon doesn't stand up to cooking or mincing, so use large chunks in combination with other fruit salad ingredients.

Buying As the melon ripens, the white spot where it rests on the ground turns to yellow, and this will indicate its maturity. A dry, brown stem, rounded ends, and a smooth rind that is neither shiny nor dull are other signs of ripeness. Heft several melons and choose one that is heavy for its size and symmetrical in shape. Also hold the melon in one hand and thump it with the other. If it sounds hollow with a slight ring, it is ripe.

If purchasing a cut watermelon, avoid one with immature white seeds, pale flesh, or white streaks. If overmature, its flesh is mealy and either dry or watery.

Be Mindful Watermelon is not recommended for someone with weak digestion, and it can inhibit semen production. It balances *pitta*.

See **Fruit; Gourd Family; Melon.**

WAX BEAN SEE **GREEN BEAN.**

WAX GOURD SEE **WINTER MELON.**

WEHANI RICE SEE **RED RICE.**

WEST INDIAN LIME SEE **LIME.**

WHEAT
(*Triticum aestivum*)

The common ancestor of all wheat is einkorn, first cultivated in 8500 BC in what is now Iraq. In world trade, wheat is the world's most important carbohydrate crop and the most widely distributed cereal grain; it is grown in nearly every country and in 42 states in America. In many cultures, wheat is now the staple grain, having replaced amaranth, barley, buckwheat, corn, millet, oats, quinoa, rye, and wild rice.

Wheat is decidedly the most versatile cereal grain, and more food products contain wheat than any other grain. Its primary use is in flour form and its popularity is because of gluten, a protein that gives wheat dough elasticity and enables it to be shaped into pizza crust, pasta, croissants, and an endless variety of products.

Thousands of wheat varieties exist, but three types are commonly used for human consumption: hard, soft, and durum. There is also spelt, a wheat variety that is growing in popularity.

- **Durum Wheat** Used primarily for pasta because its hard starch granules hold together even in boiling water. Semolina is refined, or white, durum flour. Most types of pasta and couscous are made from semolina; in the natural food trade, however, excellent whole grain durum products are also available. Two durum wheat varieties newer to our market are:

  Kamut Large, plump, and blond, this heirloom and trademarked durum wheat has a buttery flavor due to its high percentage of lipids. Cooked whole, it is the most tasty wheat berry; when ground, it makes rich-tasting breads, pasta, and baked goods. It makes a delicious Sicilian-style bread and is the traditional flour used in chapatis. For homemade pasta, I favor Kamut flour.

  Khorasan Named after a region in ancient Persia where it originated, this ancient wheat has lacked widespread use for many centuries. Khorasan is more closely related to durum wheat than to bread wheat. A trademarked variety of khorasan, Kamut, is in numerous health products. Khorasan products are newly marketed in the United States; hopefully it's not to garner an "allergy-free" niche (as we've seen with Kamut and spelt), for indeed khorasan contains gluten.

- **Hard Wheat** Has a higher protein (gluten) content. It is used for bread. It is usually rust colored with plump kernels; there are, however, some white (actually buff colored) varieties. Hard wheat is also defined by the season it is sown in.

Hard Spring Wheat is a fast-growing crop that is sown in the spring and harvested in the fall. Because it generally has the highest protein content, it is preferred for bread making.

Hard Winter Wheat is sown in the fall; it germinates, lies dormant through the winter, starts growing again in the spring, and is ready for harvest in June. It is grown where winters are mild. Because it has a longer growing season, it establishes a more extensive root system and is therefore higher in minerals.

Spelt, also known as **Farro,** is an ancient hard wheat that thrived in the Middle East and Mediterranean more than 9,000 years ago. It is mentioned by name in both Exodus and Ezekiel in the Bible. Spelt became available in America in the 1980s as it erroneously appeared to be a wheat substitute for people sensitive to common wheat. In some cases, wheat-sensitive people could initially consume spelt (or Kamut or sprouted wheat) with no side effects, but repeated use leads to adverse reactions.

- **Soft Wheat** Contains more carbohydrates and less gluten than hard wheat. It is not suited to bread making. Also called white wheat, because of its light, golden color, or cracker wheat, it is mainly used for crackers, cakes, and pastries.

Medicinal Benefits Wheat nurtures the heart and, as a cooling food and yin tonic, calms and focuses the mind and treats a wide range of stress and mental health symptoms. It also supports the spleen, liver, and kidney meridians. Whole wheat contains 12 B vitamins, vitamin E, protein, essential fatty acids, and important trace minerals such as zinc, iron, copper, manganese, magnesium, and phosphorus. Like rye, wheat is good for the musculature. Wheat balances *vata* and *pitta.*

A bushel of ground wheat yields 60 pounds of whole wheat flour, or 42 pounds of white flour. Imagine dishing up a bowl of soup for dinner and then throwing out 30 percent of it—that's the percentage of invaluable wheat nutrients that are lost when it is refined. Refined wheat is proportionally higher in carbohydrates but much lower in all other nutrients. For example, the iron in whole wheat and white flour is 26 and 8 percent, respectively. Favor whole grain wheat and wheat products.

The more refined a wheat product is, the higher it is on the glycemic index and the more unfavorably it affects the blood sugar balance.

Use Wheat berry is the term applied to the whole wheat grain with just its outer and inedible hull removed. Because cooked wheat berries are so chewy, they are rarely eaten whole. Wheat is most often milled into a versatile flour, but it may also be germinated and malted, crushed into cracked wheat, or processed into the products listed below.

- **Bulgur** Steam, dry, crush, and debran whole wheat berries and you've got bulgur. Why did Middle Eastern peoples devise this dish? Whole wheat is a long and hard chew, and cracked wheat is but a slight improvement. Bulgur, however, is light textured, has a tasty, nutty flavor, and needs considerably less cooking—and in some cases, none at all. Dark bulgur is made from hard red wheat. White bulgur, made from soft white wheat, has a more delicate flavor. As bulgur is a whole grain product, it can become rancid. Purchase bulgur that smells fresh and nutty. Store airtight in the refrigerator or freezer.

- **Couscous** Feather-light couscous is a delectable refined grain product. Indigenous to North Africa, it is essentially a minuscule pasta. Traditionally Berber women made it from a mixture of coarse and fine granules of moistened semolina that they rolled together using their palms and fingers. These granules were then sun-dried. How I would love to see their hands at work—and then to taste their couscous. Today couscous is mechanically mixed (agglomerated) with water, shaped in a rotating drum roller, steamed, and then oven-dried. Our domestic couscous is manufactured in the United States. In North Africa, couscous may also be made of millet. Traditionally couscous is steamed in a *couscousiere* and served with a stew that is also called couscous. For a quick-cooking cereal, stir 1 cup of couscous into 1½ cups of seasoned boiling water and simmer for 1 minute, then let stand, covered, for 10 minutes. As a complement to a heavy meal or for a refreshing hot-weather grain, couscous is a hit. A tan-colored whole wheat couscous has some availability; however, because it contains the germ, this product can become rancid and should be stored in the refrigerator. Select couscous, especially whole wheat couscous, that looks fresh and that has a fresh aroma and taste.
- **Cracked Wheat** Coarsely ground wheat is called cracked wheat and is used primarily as a hot breakfast cereal.
- **Cream of Wheat** A trademarked hot breakfast cereal consisting of farina (see below).
- **Farina** "Middlings," or small hard bits of wheat, are sold as a hot breakfast cereal. In the past, after the germ and bran were removed from wheat, it was ground and then bolted, or sifted, through a coarsely woven fabric for the end product, flour. The middle product was farina, granular nubbins, too coarse to go through the cloth. Farina is the Italian word for "meal" or "flour."
- **Gluten** Chew a teaspoon of wheat berries for several minutes or until all that remains is the water-insoluble, gumlike endosperm protein—that's gluten. Without gluten, yeast cannot perform its leavening function. When wheat flour is made into a dough, this protein becomes elastic and traps gas bubbles released from yeast. Gluten, the protein that enables bread to rise, is made up of gliadin and glutelin. While gliadin is specific to the wheat family, all grains contain glutelin proteins.
- **Green Wheat Berries** Immature wheat kernels harvested while still green and then dried. This grassy-tasting traditional Middle Eastern food is featured in pilafs, soups, and casseroles; it may be ground into a flour.
- **Israeli Couscous** This almost pea-size cereal product is extruded from refined hard wheat flour and then toasted in an open-flame oven to heighten its flavor and color. It is not really couscous, but it is from Israel; a rice shortage in the 1950s inspired its creation.
- **Malt** While malted barley is the most common sprouted and then extracted grain, wheat malt is also available for beer making and other commercial uses.
- **Seitan** A meat substitute made of wheat gluten. (See **Seitan** entry.)
- **Wheat Bran** Six fibrous protective layers of the wheat berry are resistant to digestion and thus are an effective bowel regulator because they add bulk and fiber to the diet. For those eating refined wheat products, it makes sense to supplement

with wheat bran. However, a more commonsense response is to eat the whole grain, which has more vitality and flavor. Bran accounts for 15 percent of the wheat kernel. In addition to its indigestible cellulose, it is also a rich reserve of nutrients, including niacin, pyridoxine, pantothenic acid, riboflavin, thiamine, and protein.

Be Mindful Wheat is the primary source of gluten, and there's an increasing epidemic of people who are intolerant of gluten (technically gliadin); 1 in 133 Americans have allergic reactions to wheat, according to the Celiac Disease Foundation. In its advanced stages, gluten allergies appear as celiac sprue or colitis but may present earlier as food sensitivity with symptoms like bloating, fatigue, bowel irregularity, and digestive complaints.

Unfortunately for gluten-sensitive people, wheat is a common additive in the majority of processed foods and products, ranging from potato chips to the glue on postage stamps.

See **Gliadin; Grain; Glutelin; Grass Family; Wheat Flour; Wheat Germ.**

WHEAT FLOUR

The most universally consumed cereal grain, wheat is most commonly milled into flour and is a primary ingredient in bread, crackers, pasta, quick breads, snack foods, baked goods, and many breakfast cereals—hot or cold. Wheat is a secondary ingredient in countless processed foods in such seemingly unlike foods as ketchup, prepared mustard, candy, and cheese. These are the common forms:

- **Bleached All-Purpose Flour** Made of refined hard and soft wheat and processed with up to 30 chemicals. By law, all refined flour must be enriched with four synthetic nutrients. Self-rising all-purpose flour also contains leavening and salt.
- **Bolted Wheat Flour** Flour sifted through a bolt of coarsely woven cloth to remove hulls and a large portion of the bran and germ, a refining technique developed by the Romans. Bolted flour retains 20 percent of its bran and all the germ but has limited availability today. It yields a bread with a higher volume than a 100 percent whole wheat flour does.
- **Bread Flour** A high-gluten blend of 98 percent refined hard wheat flour, which contains malted barley to improve yeast activity. It may or may not contain potassium bromate to increase the gluten's elasticity.
- **Cake Flour** A fine-textured, soft wheat

THE ULTIMATE BULGUR EXPERIENCE

Just as fresh pasta is incomparable to dry pasta, fresh bulgur gives a marvelously heightened taste experience compared to purchased bulgur, and it's surprisingly easy to make. Soak 2 cups of wheat berries in 3 cups of water overnight. Drain and discard soaking water. Place the berries and 4 cups fresh water in a saucepan, cover, and bring to a boil. Reduce the heat and simmer for 1 hour, or until the wheat is slightly tender. Drain and reserve the cooking liquid for soup stock. Spread the wheat in a thin layer on a cookie sheet and place out in the sun to dry for about 5 hours, or until it is completely dry, stirring occasionally. Or oven-dry at 250°F for 45 to 60 minutes. When the wheat is completely dry, coarsely grind it in a grain mill, food processor, or blender and store in a glass container until ready to use.

flour that is low in gluten. Makes light and airy cakes and pastries. A cup of self-rising cake flour contains 1½ teaspoons baking powder, ½ teaspoon salt, and cornstarch as an anticaking agent.

- **Durum Flour** Made of 100 percent durum wheat. Used primarily for whole wheat pasta.
- **Gluten Flour** A high-protein hard wheat flour with a reduced starch content and a gluten content of at least 55 percent. Bakers often add a small amount of gluten flour to bread dough to produce a lighter loaf. I don't recommend gluten flour because it is highly processed and it toughens bread.
- *Panocha* **Flour** Flour made from sprouted wheat and used, most typically, in a pudding called *panocha* that is a traditional Lent food in New Mexico and southern Colorado.
- **Semolina** Ground from refined durum wheat. Used primarily for pasta, but it makes an excellent traditional Sicilian bread and, until recent times, was the primary flour used in chapati.
- **Unbleached All-Purpose Flour** Made from wheat refined of its bran and germ. By law, it must be chemically enriched, but at least it is a less processed food than bleached flour. For people who find 100 percent whole wheat products too heavy, including some unbleached white flour yields a lighter product.
- **Whole Wheat Flour** Made from whole hard wheat berries. This flour contains all of the 40-plus nutrients of wheat and has a rich, full taste. Once milled, however, the fatty acids in the wheat germ start to oxidize and become rancid. Therefore, purchase whole wheat flour in small quantities from a store with a brisk turnover or, better yet, purchase it from a natural food store that refrigerates its whole grain flours. At home, wrap tightly and refrigerate or freeze until use.
- **Whole Wheat Pastry Flour** Made from whole soft wheat berries. Preferred for pastries, crackers, cakes, cookies, pie crusts, and other delicate baked goods. Because it is low in gluten, it is unsuitable for bread. This flour requires the same care as whole wheat flour.

See **Flour; Wheat.**

WHEAT GERM

Wheat germ is the heart or the embryo of the wheat. It comprises only 2 to 3 percent of the whole wheat berry but is nutritionally the richest part. Rich in insoluble fiber, B vitamins, vitamin E, and calories, wheat germ also contains octacosanol, which promotes oxygen utilization and therefore reduces fatigue and enhances overall stamina and endurance. Octacosanol extracted from wheat

---

CORN DOLLY MADE OF WHEAT

An Old World folk tradition is to weave grain shafts into a talisman, referred to as a corn dolly. She hangs in the kitchen through deep winter as promise of harvest to come. After frost has left the ground, the corn dolly is undone to sow her precious grains.

In Europe, the generic term for all grain is corn, which is derived from the word "kernel" and means "small particle." Thus, for example, biblical references to corn are not about Native American maize but about the cereal crops of the region—barley and spelt. This explains why Christopher Columbus named America's native grain Indian corn.

germ is available as a supplement. Wheat germ is highly susceptible to rancidity. Some people maintain that wheat germ must be used immediately after milling to obtain its vitamin E. Toasted wheat germ has a delicious nutty flavor, although some nutrients are destroyed by toasting.

See **Wheat; Wheat Germ Oil.**

WHEAT GERM OIL

A dietary supplement extracted from the germ of wheat. It is nutrient dense but highly susceptible to rancidity.

See **Wheat Germ.**

WHEAT GRASS JUICE

Available fresh in some natural food stores, the juice from young, seven-inch-long wheat grass is high in chlorophyll, potassium, calcium, and magnesium. Imagine a flavor so aggressively sweet that it borders on astringency. Few people claim to enjoy this flavor and so wheat grass juice is generally mixed with another juice. Wheat grass is also available powdered and in tablet form. It is a potent detoxifier, especially for the liver and gallbladder.

WHITE GOOSEFOOT SEE **FAT HEN.**

WHITE MUSHROOM SEE **MUSHROOM, COMMON.**

WHITE SAPOTE
Zapote, Zapote Blanco
(*Casimiroa edulis*)

This lush fruit, actually a distant citrus relative, is not related to a mamey sapote but is indeed a soft sweet fruit, which is what the Aztec word *zapotl* means. The semitropical white sapote looks like a large pointed but green peach. A coreless fruit, it has an ambrosial mango-vanilla-and-peach aroma, a sugary taste, and a crisp, pearlike flesh and juicy texture.

Commercial crops are being developed in California and Florida, and of the many new and exotic fruits, this seems destined to gain in popularity as the "peach of the tropics."

Medicinal Benefits White sapote has soporific properties that can make one drowsy. Recent studies indicate its effectiveness against colon cancer. The skin is edible but sour, and the seeds have narcotic properties and can be fatally toxic. It is a significant source of vitamin A and a good source of vitamin C.

Use Cut in half, discard seeds, and spoon out its creamy flesh with a spoon or use in preserves, beverages, frozen desserts, or fruit sauces. It is delicious alone or in combination with other fruits. A squeeze of lime enhances its flavor.

Buying Choose firm fruits that are free of bruises and green or yellowish green in color. Allow sapote to ripen and soften at room temperature until it is softer than a ripe avocado, then refrigerate; it may be refrigerated for up to 10 days in the crisper drawer.

See **Citrus Family; Fruit.**

WILD BLUE-GREEN ALGAE
(*Aphanizomenon flos-aquae*)

In the summer, if you drive through the small farming and ranching town of Klamath Lake in southern Oregon, you'll see what looks like a green carpet covering Upper Klamath Lake. Some would say "scum," which prevents the lake from being used for recreational purposes. This green cover consists of several bacteria varieties that thrive because the lake is oxygen deficient due, in part, to agricultural runoff.

One of these bacteria, known as wild blue-green algae, is a potent superfood that is available as a supplement and in protein beverages and products. It reduces *kapha*.

Medicinal Benefits Cooling, drying, and a neurostimulant, antidepressant, and relaxant, wild blue-green algae is of special medicinal benefit to people who have robust energy.

Be Mindful Blue-green algae is not advised for people who are cold or weak, have trouble gaining weight, and/or who have chronic diarrhea. Note: Do not attempt to collect pond algae, as some varieties of *Aphanizomenon flos-aquae* are toxic to both humans and animals.

See **Microalgae**.

WILD LEEK SEE **RAMP**.

WILD LIME SEE **KAFFIR LIME**.

WILD RICE
(*Zizania aquatica*)

All that is around us is animate. As such it has spirit. I'm very careful when I harvest [wild rice] because I must reckon with that spirit. I must reckon with an aspiration to harvest. Because you are respectful when you harvest, this ensures that you are able to continue harvesting. It is not because you're smart or clever; it's because you're respectful. The value of eating and harvesting the same way that our ancestors have done cannot be quantified. Both spiritually and culturally, it reaffirms those things which are ours and those things which make us strong as a community. We're not a wealthy people in terms of monetary income. We are wealthy in terms of our culture.

—Winona La Duke

Winona La Duke of the Anishinabe Ojibwa, who lives on the White Earth reservation in Minnesota, harvests 150 pounds of rice a year. "We eat it plain and I put it in everything—omelets, muffins, and casseroles," she says. "Rice has always been a staple on the reservation. And I'm not talking Uncle Ben's."

A staple food for the Ojibwa, Chippewa, and Algonquian tribes, who called it *manomin*, wild rice has a wondrous flavor that is a complex blend of nutty sweet with a hint of spice. Although closely related to rice, wild rice is a separate species and native to North America. It grows in shallow water in small lakes and slow-flowing streams primarily in the Great Lakes region. This gorgeous, six-foot-tall plant is also grown as an ornamental.

Heirloom wild rice is unique in that it is the only foraged cereal grain with commercial availability. All other cereal crops throughout the world have been cultivated and selectively bred for thousands of years and therefore have a limited gene pool. Wild foods are energetically more robust, nutritious, and flavorful.

Today more than 80 percent of all wild rice is commercially grown; fortunately, traditionally harvested *wild* wild rice is available. By tribal decree, this rice may be harvested only in a canoe and with two "knocker" sticks. The harvester bends the rice stems over the rim of the canoe and across her lap with one knocker and with the second one knocks the grass so that the ripe grains fall into the canoe. About four to six days following the first harvest, the patch is gone over a second time to reap the newly ripened grains. One patch may be harvested as many as six or seven times because the seeds on the same stalk ripen over a span of several weeks. This is nature's guarantee for the continuation of the species and protection against a late spring or early frost. During the harvesting, some grain falls into the water, thus assuring a crop for the following year.

Tame wild rice is one of four hybrid varieties

selected for responsiveness to petrochemical fertilizers, herbicides, insecticides, and fungicides, as well as for ease of mechanical harvesting and factory production. Cultivated wild rice is typically an inch long and is ebony black in color. It is farmed mainly in California paddies but also in northern Idaho, Saskatchewan, Manitoba, and Ontario. In some lakes it is harvested by airboat. Wild rice is also commercially grown in Hungary and Australia.

Medicinal Benefits Wild rice is a cooling and drying food that strengthens the spleen, stomach, kidneys, and bladder. It is mildly astringent and helps treat excessive urination and diarrhea. Wild rice is an excellent source of zinc and, among the grains, is high in protein. Wild rice balances *vata*.

Use Even a small amount of this black grain imparts its distinctive character to other ingredients. Most commercial wild rice is used sparingly as a flavoring agent in rice pilafs, soups, dressings, casseroles, and in quick breads like pancakes, muffins, and cookies; most home cooks also use it sparingly. I invite you to use it neat, on its own, or as a wild rice entrée or side dish. The bounteous flour of wild rice is something to savor again and again. The heirloom rice is scarified (to remove part of its bran and so is mottled brown, gray, and black). This scarification does, however, make its fats more quickly subject to oxidization; store refrigerated or in the freezer.

The cooking time and water measurement for foraged and commercial wild rice is different because foraged wild rice has its bran layer partially removed (scarified). Cook 1 cup of foraged wild rice in 1¾ cups of water for 45 minutes. One cup of commercial wild rice requires 60 minutes (sometimes 70 minutes) cooking in 2½ cups of water. Because the cooking times vary, wild rice recipes usually suggest cooking with extra water and draining off the

excess liquid—but this drains off flavor and nutrients. Instead, prepare the grain without extra water. It is cooked when it is tender but not mushy and when some of the grains have "butterflied" or burst open. Ideally, at this point, the liquid will be totally absorbed. If liquid remains, drain it, measure it (reserving it for stock), and next time add that much less liquid.

Buying Foraged wild rice from the rivers and lakes of the Great Lakes region comprises less than 20 percent of the market share. Pur-

---

WILD WILD RICE

This morning I put on a pot of hand-harvested wild rice and headed out to the garden for soup ingredients. When I stepped back inside with a basket of thinnings, my kitchen smelled like wild rice country, and for a moment I imagined I was in fragrant wetlands edged by deep green forests. The heady aroma of this aquatic grass, a complex blend of nutty sweet with a hint of spice, kindles an ancient memory of the movement of water, the change of seasons, and the freshness of a breeze through tall grasses, of something wild and free.

I recently had four samples of rice from Leech Lake Band of Ojibwe—three were lake-harvested and one stream-harvested. I cooked the four varieties and had my cooking class sample them. They were astonished that such a range of subtle flavor differences could exist from lake to lake. While the rice from Tamarack Lake was the general favorite, all four were winners.

Favor *wild* wild rice. It will state on its label "hand-harvested." I find it substantively different from domesticated wild rice that is paddy grown or mechanically harvested by airboat.

chasing this natural, organic rice supports the traditional folkways of Native Americans. It's available as a pricey boutique item from several online sources. Over the decades, I've watched various foraged wild rice suppliers come and go; the one consistent—and most economical—source I've found is from the Leech Lake Indian Band of Ojibwe, Division of Resource Management.

See **Grains; Grass Family.**

WILD SPINACH SEE **FAT HEN.**

WINE VINEGAR SEE **VINEGAR.**

WINGED BEAN
Asparagus Pea, Goa Bean
(*Psophocarpus tetragonolobus*)

Tropical in origin, the winged bean is billed as a "new soybean" because it's an excellent and inexpensive food source. The bean is like a plump, long green bean up to nine inches long with four ridges, or wings, running lengthwise down the pod. Thus, when cut in cross sections, the bean pieces are square. It, along with the long bean, is also called an asparagus pea, as their flavor is reminiscent of asparagus. Winged beans are widely consumed in Southeast Asia and Papua New Guinea.

Medicinal Benefits Winged beans contain an impressive 30 to 39 percent protein, similar to the protein content of soybeans.

Use Unlike other beans, the whole winged bean plant is edible. The pods are eaten in their immature stage when about an inch long. Cook them as you would green beans; they're pleasantly flavored with a texture that's almost meaty. The tubers are protein rich and make an excellent potato substitute; the young leaves and shoots are eaten as a potherb. The mature and dried seeds may be made into flour or roasted and used as a beverage.

Buying As cold-resistant varieties are developed, expect to see greater availability of this bean. Currently their availability is erratic in the United States.

See **Beans and Legumes; Legume Family.**

WINTER MELON
Ash Pumpkin, Chinese Winter Melon, Don Qua, Fuzzy Melon, Wax Gourd
(*Benincasa hispida*)

Crunch, rather than flavor, is what this bland-tasting, basketball-size squash is about. Winter melon takes on the flavors of other foods it is cooked with yet retains its pleasing crispiness. The name "winter" refers to its lengthy storage abilities and not its growing season, which requires five months of warm temperatures. This member of the gourd family has a pale green skin with a thick and waxy bloom, which looks like frost or ashes, thus its other names ash pumpkin or wax gourd. This wax (*petha*) is actually a wax source for candles in Asia. Its flesh is white.

Medicinal Benefits A winter melon is cold in nature and supports the lung, stomach, and bladder meridians. It helps clear heat, dissolve mucus, relieve thirst and edema, and induce urination. Like a watermelon, a winter melon is 95 percent water. It has anti-inflammatory properties and anticancer terpenes. It is popularly used in China in reducing diets and as a diuretic. In Ayurvedic medicine, it is used for lung ailments, coughs, and water retention.

Use When immature, winter melon is a favorite soup ingredient in Asian cuisine, especially in hot weather because of its cooling properties. It is also found in savory concoctions, candied, and pickled. The seeds may be roasted and eaten.

Buying/Storing Winter melon is available year-round, primarily in Asian markets. Select one that is firm and unblemished. A whole melon, when stored in a cool, dark, and dry place, will keep for many months. This large vegetable is often sold cut into slices, which should be used within several days of purchase. When buying by the slice, look for a firm-fleshed, evenly colored piece.

See **Gourd Family; Vegetable.**

WINTER SAVORY SEE **SAVORY.**

WINTER SQUASH SEE **SQUASH, WINTER.**

WITLOOF SEE **CHICORY.**

WOLFBERRY SEE **GOJI BERRY.**

WONDERBERRY SEE **SUNBERRY.**

WOOD EAR
Cloud Ear, Dried Black Fungus, Tree Ear Mushroom
(Auricularia auricula)

When foraged or fresh, wood ear has a rubbery texture with a shape that's decidedly ear-like. This dark purple, brown-black fungus is typically found on dead elder or elm trees. When dried, its texture is like a piece of black shoe leather. This relatively tasteless mushroom has a very short stalk. Wood ear grows throughout Asia, Europe, and the Americas.

Medicinal Benefits Wood ears are a yin tonic that support the lung, stomach, and liver meridians. They lubricate and so help relieve a dry cough, dry throat, dry eyes, constipation, and hemorrhoids. They are an effective immune and blood tonic and help increase energy. They lower cholesterol, clear the body of free radicals, and support brain function. As a poultice for eye inflammation, place a fresh or rehydrated wood ear directly over the afflicted eye for 15 minutes.

Use Wood ear is a classic ingredient in an Asian hot and sour soup, as it soaks up the flavor of other ingredients and has a pleasing but unusual texture that is a bit like a gummy bear. To rehydrate a dry wood ear, soak it until supple, for at least 20 minutes, or as long as overnight. It will almost quadruple in size when hydrated. Pick it over to remove any bits of bark or debris. Chop and simmer in a soup, stew, or any Asian vegetable or meat dish.

Buying Wood ear mushrooms are occasionally available fresh in Asian markets. Dried, they can be found in supermarkets, natural food stores, and in Asian markets.

Be Mindful There is some evidence that wood ear mushrooms inhibit egg implantation in animals. Do not use when pregnant or when wishing to conceive.

See **Mushroom Family; Vegetable.**

WORMSEED SEE **EPAZOTE.**

WRAPPED HEART MUSTARD CABBAGE SEE **MUSTARD GREENS.**

XYLITOL (NOT RECOMMENDED)

A by-product of the plywood industry, xylitol is extracted from cellulose by an energy-intensive chemical process. This low-calorie artificial sweetener may also be made from other hardwood chips, almond shells, pecan shells, cornstalks, or corncobs. Xylitol is used in sugar-free gum, candy, and jam. The FDA permits xylitol-based products to make the medical claim that they do not promote dental cavities; it is also advertised as "safe for diabetics and individuals with hyperglycemia."

Our common sense indicates otherwise; xylitol is a chemical and not a food.

Be Mindful Dogs ingesting significant amounts of xylitol-containing gum or candy may develop a sudden drop in blood glucose levels, resulting in depression, loss of consciousness, or seizures. It is possible that it causes liver failure in dogs, but this remains to be proved. In animal studies, xylitol is linked to cancer, kidney stones, and bladder inflammation.

See **Mannitol; Sorbitol; Sweeteners.**

𝒴

YACÓN
(*Smallanthus sonchifolius*)

The seven-foot-tall yacón growing in my garden is a handsome green perennial with daisylike orange flowers. Following the first hard frost, clumped about its roots it will yield up to 20 fleshly tan-colored carrot-size tubers that turn dark brown or purple upon exposure to air.

Crisp and juicy, these tubers have a delicate flavor reminiscent of apple, jicama, or melon and a surprising sweetness that increases with storage. They're a sunflower relative and member of the daisy family, native to the Peruvian Andes.

Medicinal Benefits In the Andes, yacón leaves, stems, and tubers have a venerable history as a diuretic for kidney and bladder problems. Their roots are high, up to 50 percent, in fructooligosaccharides (FOS), a type of fructose that cannot be assimilated by the human digestive system but that helps establish beneficial bacteria in the colon and therefore supports healthy immune function. Both yacón leaves and roots also have antioxidant properties.

Use To increase their sweet flavor, dry the tubers in sunlight until their skin is slightly wrinkled. The skin has a bitter taste; peel it or scrub it off with a stiff brush. Eat yacón out of hand, juice, or chop and add to salads; or stir-fry, steam, or boil and mash. When baking yacón, remove the skin after cooking. Both the leaves and the root are available as a dietary supplement.

Buying In the United States, yacón are found in farmers' markets and some natural food stores. A sweet syrup made from the roots is quickly growing in the worldwide health market (see below).

See **Daisy Family; Vegetable; Yacón Syrup**.

YACÓN SYRUP

The newest natural sweetener to the market is extracted at 140°F from yacón tubers. The tubers are juiced and then concentrated primarily into a low-calorie honeylike sweetener. It is glucose-free and a suitable sweetener for diabetics; unlike sugar, animal products are not used in its production and so it is appropriate for vegans.

Yacón syrup has a deep, rich, and sweet flavor that's likened to molasses and honey. Use it to sweeten beverages or baked goods, or spread it directly on toast. At this time, it costs about $24 a pound. This syrup may be further concentrated to yield a solid dark brown sweet block of sweetener.

See **Yacón**.

YAM
(*Dioscorea rotundata, D. cayenensis, D. composita*)

One of the most widely consumed foods in the world, the yam was first cultivated more than 10,000 years ago in Africa. It is the tuber of a climbing plant that today grows throughout tropical and subtropical regions and, in the United States, in the Deep South.

Yams are round or oblong with a thick, often coarse, skin and their starchy flesh may be white, ivory, cream, pink, or purple. The vegetables called yams in supermarkets are, in fact, sweet potatoes and are small enough to be handheld. There are more than 6,000 species of yams, some of which weigh well over 100 pounds.

Medicinal Benefits Yams are a cooling food that treat the kidney, large intestine, lung, and spleen meridians and have both yin and chi tonifying properties. They treat arthritis, asthma, spasms, and both diarrhea and constipation. Their plant estrogens ease many low estrogen symptoms, help regulate menses, increase milk in lactating women, and work as an agent to prevent miscarriages. Yams are also useful for people who want to gain weight. Their simple peptide substances bind with heavy metals like cadmium, copper, mercury, and lead and thus assist in metal detoxification of body tissues. Yams that contain diosgenin are used for treating fatigue, inflammation, spasms, stress, and colitis. Yams are high in vitamin C, dietary fiber, vitamin B_6, potassium, and manganese.

Use Yams have more starch than potatoes, but they are like a mealy potato, with a coarse, dry, and rather bland flavor and texture. Also like a potato, yams must be cooked to convert their indigestible starches into sugar. They absorb flavors of other ingredients they are cooked with, and they are tasty boiled, roasted, mashed, and fried. Unlike a potato or sweet potato, however, the skin is not edible. In countries where yams are a staple, they are most frequently seasoned with spices, served with a sauce, or combined with other foods.

Buying Select yams that are firm and intact with no signs of mold or soft, shrunken spots. Smaller yams have more flavor than larger yams. They are most often available in Latino and Asian markets. As with potatoes, do not refrigerate, but store in a cool, dry, dark place for up to six months.

Yam powder is similar in use to potato flour; however, it forms lumps more easily, and when reconstituted, yields a dense dish similar to mashed potatoes in texture. In the West it has some online availability as a gluten-free substitute.

Be Mindful Raw yams must be cooked to remove a toxin. In fact, even handling raw yam can cause the skin to itch. Should this happen to you, flush the area with cold water.

See **Jinenjo.**

YAMAIMO See JINENJO.

YAM BEAN See JICAMA.

YAM FAMILY
(Dioscoreaceae)

The yam is the most economically important food crop in this large family of primarily tropical, herbaceous plants. Their starchy tuber are staples in the Southern Hemisphere.

See **Jinenjo; Yam.**

YARD-LONG BEAN See LONG BEAN.

YAUTIA
Cocoyam, Malanga, Tannia
(*Xanthosoma*)

A root crop that food experts believe holds great promise as a nutritious food of the future is the funny-looking, potatolike yautia. When cooked, this tropical tuber has an earthy, almost nutty flavor and a lush, creamy texture. It originated in the Americas in both dry and swampy soils. Like taro, the yautia is thin-skinned and shaggy, but it tends to be larger and is frequently club shaped. Its yellowish or pinkish flesh is visible through its splotchy skin.

Medicinal Benefits As a kitchen remedy, the yautia may be used to regulate energy, support digestion, and disperse congestion. The size of its starch is small, making it easy to digest and therefore an excellent hypoallergenic food. It has a moderate amount of thiamine and riboflavin and a modest amount of vitamin C and iron. It is high in calories.

Use Do not eat yautia raw; cook this tuber as you would taro or potato. It has an earthy and nutty flavor and makes an excellent sweet potato substitute. A common Caribbean use of yautia is to peel it, boil it like a potato, and serve it with savory dishes. It is also baked, fried, grilled, pureed, and ground into flour. In a stew, yautia flavors, thickens, and adds creaminess. If overcooked, however, it tends to disintegrate.

Buying Many supermarkets as well as Latino markets now carry yautia. Select fresh-smelling, firm specimens. Store at room temperature and try to use within a few days of purchase.

See **Arum Family.**

YEAST

I recommend purchasing bulk dry bakers' yeast from the refrigerated section of your natural food store rather than the rapid-action, preservative-containing yeast sold in individual packets or fresh cakes in the supermarket. And buying in bulk from the natural food store yeast is more economical. Store it in a closed glass jar in the refrigerator for six months or more.

Be Mindful Yeast is a common allergen.

YEAST, NUTRITIONAL SEE **NUTRITIONAL YEAST.**

YELLOW CHIVE SEE **GARLIC CHIVE.**

YELLOW-EYE BEAN SEE **BEANS AND LEGUMES.**

YELLOW GINGER SEE **TURMERIC.**

YELLOW WAX BEAN SEE **GREEN BEAN.**

YERBA MATÉ SEE **MATÉ.**

YI YI REN SEE **JOB'S TEARS.**

YOUNGBERRY SEE **BLACKBERRY.**

YUBA

Yuba is an intriguing soy product that looks like sheets of yellow taffy. It is the skin that forms on the top of hot soymilk when soymilk is being made. This skin is layered, pressed into slabs or cakes, and dried. To use, soak yuba and add it to stews and braised vegetable dishes for its excellent flavor and pleasing texture. It is high in protein and easy to digest. Yuba is available in Asian markets and occasionally in natural food stores.

See **Soybean.**

YUCA SEE **CASSAVA.**

YUZU SEE **BITTER ORANGE; CITRUS FAMILY.**

Z

ZANTE CURRANT SEE CURRANT (DRIED).

ZAPOTE SEE WHITE SAPOTE.

ZAPOTE BLANCO SEE WHITE SAPOTE.

ZEST SEE CITRUS PEEL.

ZUCCHINI SEE SQUASH; SQUASH, SUMMER.

ZUCCHINI BLOSSOMS SEE SQUASH BLOSSOM.

GLOSSARY OF TERMS

ACRID Unpleasantly pungent or caustic.

ADAPTOGEN Improves resistance to stress and thus supports homeostasis.

AIDS A severe immunological disorder resulting in increased susceptibility to opportunistic infections and certain rare cancers. AIDS stands for acquired immuno deficiency syndrome.

ALKALOID A plant-based, nitrogen-containing compound that has a potent effect on body function.

ALLERGEN Any substance that produces an allergic reaction.

ALTERATIVE Improves vitality, primarily by enhancing the breakdown and elimination of waste products.

ANALGESIC A natural or synthetic substance that removes or relieves pain.

ANTIBACTERIAL Destroys or inhibits the growth of bacteria.

ANTIBIOTIC Destroys or inhibits growth of microorganisms.

ANTICOAGULANT Prevents or slows clotting of the blood.

ANTIFUNGAL Destroys or inhibits the growth of fungi.

ANTI-INFLAMMATORY Reduces inflammation.

ANTIOXIDANT Inhibits oxidation and thus slows or prevents cell deterioration.

ANTISPASMODIC Reduces muscle spasms and tension.

ANTIVIRAL Inhibits a virus.

ASTRINGENT Firms and contracts tissues (by precipitating proteins from cell surfaces); forms a protective coating; and reduces bleeding and discharges.

AYURVEDA The ancient Indian science of life and self-healing.

BETA-CAROTENE The orange-yellow plant pigment that the body converts to vitamin A.

BILE A thick, bitter fluid stored in the gallbladder and secreted by the liver; it aids fat digestion.

BIOENGINEERED Genetic material of an animal or plant that is manipulated, altered, or added to. The industry term is genetically modified organism (GMO).

BIOFLAVONOID A plant glycoside that improves circulation and has diuretic, antispasmodic, and anti-inflammatory effects.

BITTER One of the five tastes in Chinese medicine. It is a yin, cooling taste, which clears, improves appetite, detoxifies, and stimulates secretion of digestive juices. It supports heart and small intestine functions.

BLOOD SUGAR The concentration of glucose in the blood.

BLOOD TONIC Improves and maintains the quality of immediate nourishment available to the body; includes foods such as beans, beets, and dark leafy greens.

CARMINATIVE A food, usually an herb or spice, that reduces intestinal gas, pain, and distention; promotes peristalsis.

CATARRH An inflammation of the mucous membrane, most often affecting the nose and throat.

CATHARTIC Strong laxative that initiates rapid elimination.

CHI A Chinese term for the vital energy, or life force, of an organism. Pronounced *chee* and sometimes spelled *qi*. It is called *prana* in India and *ki* in Japan.

CHI TONIC Improves and maintains the quality and quantity of available energy in the body. Beef, ginseng, and sweet potatoes are examples.

CHINESE MEDICINE Traditional Oriental medicine based upon thermal property, five flavors, four directions, and the twelve meridians.

CLEANSING The property of improving excretion of waste products from the body.

COOLING The property of clearing toxins and reducing internal heat.

CYSTITIS Inflammation of the urinary bladder.

DAIDZEIN Along with genistein, a plant estrogen and isoflavone uniquely abundant in soy foods; it is an anticarcinogen. In addition, daidzein relieves menopausal symptoms and reduces cholesterol levels.

DECONGESTANT A substance that relieves congestion, especially from nasal passages.

DEMULCENT The property of soothing and protecting damaged or inflamed internal membranes.

DEPRESSANT The property of lowering the rate of vital physiological activities.

DIAPHORETIC A substance that induces perspiration and increases elimination through the skin.

DIURETIC The property of increasing urination by acting upon the kidney and bladder.

DNA A nucleic acid found in all living cells that is important in protein synthesis and the transmission of genetic information. Nutritional sources of DNA and RNA, such as those found in microalgae, are known to benefit cellular renewal.

DOSHA An essential biological energy or structure in Ayurveda. The balance of our three primary doshas, *vata*, *pitta*, and *kapha*, determines our health.

EDEMA Abnormal accumulation of serum fluid in an organ or body cavity.

EMOLLIENT The property of softening the skin.

ENTERITIS Inflammation of the small intestine.

ESTROGENIC A plant substance similar in effect to the hormone estrogen.

EXPECTORANT A substance that promotes the discharge of phlegm from the respiratory tract.

FDA Food and Drug Administration, a regulatory branch of the U.S. government.

FIVE TASTES The five tastes in Chinese medicine: sour, bitter, sweet (also bland), pungent, and salty.

GENETICALLY MODIFIED (GM) An organism that contains altered, manipulated, or added genetic material. Also known as bioengineered or genetically modified organism (GMO).

GENISTEIN See Daidzein.

GLUTATHIONE An enzyme, a deficiency of which is associated with hemolytic anemia.

GRIT A broken cereal grain, especially buckwheat and corn. Unless degerminated, it oxidizes faster than a whole grain.

GROAT Refers to any hulled grain, most often oats and buckwheat.

HEIRLOOM SEEDS Cultivated seeds that are handed down from generation to generation and valued for characteristics such as flavor, hardiness, natural pest resilience, or ability to thrive in a specific area. Unlike hybrid and bioengineered foods, use of heirloom foods helps preserve genetic diversity.

HERBOLOGY The study of herbs and their use as medicinal and culinary agents.

HORMONE A substance produced in the endocrine glands and transported by the blood to another site to affect a physiological activity such as growth.

HYBRID SEED A cross between different varieties designed to achieve desired cosmetic, nutritional, or harvesting properties. Not capable of reproducing like heirloom seed. With hybrids, the natural integrity and viability of the original seed is lost.

HYDROGENATION A process of treating liquid oil with hydrogen gas to change its molecular structure. This process saturates the fatty acids to render a solid or semisolid product like margarine and shortening. Most processed cheeses and commercial peanut butters also contain hydrogenated oil. Avoid all hydrogenated products.

HYPERTENSION High blood pressure.

HYPOGLYCEMIA A lack of sugar in the blood that causes muscle weakness, sweating, and mental confusion.

IMMUNE SYSTEM The body's system that recognizes and defends against foreign materials such as allergens and infectious organisms.

INDOLE-3-CARBINOL An indole (an anticarcinogen found in cabbage family members) that helps protect against hormone-related cancers such as breast cancer.

INULIN A polysaccharide found in the roots of various sunflower family members that is medicinal for diabetics.

ISOFLAVONE A class of flavonoids that may help prevent hormone-related cancers such as breast cancer.

ISOTHIOCYANATES Sulfur compounds that are among the most effective cancer prevention agents; they are partially responsible for the pungency of some cabbage family vegetables.

KAPHA Ayurvedic term for a waterlike biological energy and constitution that is cold, wet, slow moving, heavy, solid, stable, and enduring. Foods that reduce *kapha* are drying, warm, and eliminative with pungent, bitter, and astringent flavors.

LACTATION Milk secretion from the mammary glands.

LAXATIVE A substance that promotes bowel movements.

LIPIDS Fatty compounds present in most tissues and especially in the blood.

LUTEIN Lutein and zeaxanthin are two antioxidants and yellow carotenoids found in the eye; they filter out harmful blue light and protect against macular degeneration, the leading cause of blindness in people over 65 years of age.

MERIDIAN One of the twelve vital organs and pathways of Chinese medicine. The heart meridian, for example, includes not only the physical heart but blood and circulation throughout the body and the heart's interrelationship with all other systems.

MUCUS A slippery, sticky, thick secretion produced by, and covering, the internal organs and various body cavities that are exposed to the external environment.

NERVE TONIC A substance that supports the normal functioning of the nervous system.

NUTRACEUTICAL A phytochemical with pharmaceutically recognized healing properties.

NUTRITIVE A food that nourishes the body.

PERISTALSIS Involuntary, wavelike muscle contractions of the digestive tract that move its contents.

PHLEGM Thick mucus secreted by the respiratory tract lining.

PHYTIC ACID A heat- and acid-stable astringent acid found in cereals, nuts, and seeds (especially in sesame seeds and soybeans) that protects against some cancers and may help control blood sugar, cholesterol, and triglycerides.

PHYTOCHEMICAL A biologically active substance in plants (phyto) responsible for giving them characteristics such as color, flavor, and natural disease resistance. Our common foods contain millions of phytochemicals.

PHYTONUTRIENT A nutrient found in plants (phyto), which includes vitamins, minerals, essential fatty acids, phytochemicals, and nutraceuticals.

PHYTOSTEROL Plant sterols that can lower cholesterol and that show anticancer activity.

PITTA Ayurvedic term for firelike biological energy and constitution, typified as hot, light, clear, sharp, and oily. Foods that reduce excess *pitta* are drying and cooling, with bitter, astringent, and sweet flavors.

PROPHYLACTIC An agent that protects or defends against disease.

PUNGENT (Spicy) One of the fives tastes in Chinese medicine; it is yang (warming, dispersing, and drying). Also called spicy, it moves energy from the interior to the surface; it supports the lung and colon.

PURGATIVE A strong laxative.

RAJASIC Ayurvedic term for fiery foods that excite the appetite and stimulate outward motion, creativity, passion, and aggression; in Ayurveda, they are best avoided unless you are seeking these experiences.

REJUVENATE Restore vitality.

RELAXANT A substance that relaxes overactive, tense muscles and tissues.

RESTORATIVE A substance that revives strength.

RNA A nucleic acid found in all living cells that is important in protein synthesis and in the transmission of genetic information. Nutritional sources of DNA and RNA, such as those found in microalgae, are known to benefit cellular renewal.

RUTIN A bioflavonoid obtained from buckwheat and used in the treatment of capillary fragility.

SALTY One of the five tastes in Chinese medicine; it is yin (cooling and moistening) and supports the kidney and bladder system.

SAPONIN A plant substance similar to soap.

SATTVIC Ayurvedic term for foods that are pure and fresh and clear the mind. They are to be favored.

SEDATIVE A substance that reduces tension by lowering the functional activity of an organ or body part.

SOPORIFIC A substance that induces drowsiness or sleep.

SOUR One of the five tastes in Chinese medicine; it is yin (cooling and refreshing) and promotes digestion, enzyme secretion, and liver and gallbladder function.

STIMULANT Increases physiological activity, circulation, and heat; dispels internal chill.

SUSTAINABLE Dietary habits and food production that meet our present needs without compromising the ability of future generations to meet their own needs.

SWEET One of the five tastes in Chinese medicine; it is yang (warming, soothing, building, and nourishing) and supports the stomach and spleen-pancreas functions.

SYSTEMIC Affecting the entire system or body.

THERMAL PROPERTY The ability of a food to help regulate body temperature, either up or down. All foods are cooling, neutral, or warming by nature. For example, watermelon is cooling and garlic is warming.

TONE The property of strengthening and restoring an organ or muscle to normal fitness.

TONIC A substance that stimulates and increases body tone, chi, or energy in the absence of illness. See Blood Tonic; Chi Tonic; Yang Tonic; Yin Tonic.

TONIFY To invigorate, refresh, build, and strengthen.

TOPICAL A skin remedy applied directly to the afflicted area.

TOXIC Harmful or poisonous.

TRIDOSHIC A food that ameliorates all three body types. See *vata, pitta,* and *kapha.*

USDA United States Department of Agriculture.

VATA Ayurvedic term for airlike, corresponding to biological energy- and constitutional-type movement. It is dry, cold, light, mobile, rough, and clear. Foods that reduce excess *vata* are demulcent, nutritive tonics with a sweet taste and warm energy; they also calm the nervous system.

VERMIFUGE A substance that expels intestinal worms.

WARMING A substance that increases the body's temperature by dispelling cold or hypoactivity and increasing vitality, circulation, and digestion.

YANG Complementary to yin in Chinese philosophy. Yang is the male element associated with the sun, day, dry, hot, exterior, and ascending.

YANG TONIC Maintains and improves our ability to generate warmth and stimulate our system; examples include cinnamon, garlic, and quinoa.

YIN Complementary to yang in Chinese philosophy. Yin is the female element and associated with moon, night, damp, cold, interior, and descending.

YIN TONIC Improves and maintains our deepest reserves of subtle nourishment and soothes our system; examples include apples, honey, and watermelon.

ZEAXANTHIN Antioxidant and carotenoid associated with decreased lung cancer risk. In addition, it helps prevent macular degeneration (see Lutein).

APPENDIX I: STORAGE

All foods deteriorate to some extent during storage, with a diminishing of flavor, color, aroma, and weight. While a raspberry goes in hours, it takes years to lose a chickpea. To minimize deterioration, store foods in a closed, nonreactive container away from light, heat, and moisture and at the temperature appropriate to them.

BEANS
Dried beans have the longest shelf life of our common whole foods. Whole beans are much harder than grains and generally do not become infested unless they are more than several years old. Split beans are more prone to infestation. For convenience—as well as for the delight of seeing their beautiful colors and shapes—store beans in closed glass jars in a cool cupboard.

DRIED FRUIT
To extend the shelf life of dried fruit, refrigerate it in a glass jar or tightly wrapped in plastic.

FAT AND OIL
Olive, palm, and coconut oil need no refrigeration; store them in a dark cupboard. All other unrefined oils must be refrigerated, preferably in opaque glass or inert plastic containers. Unlike other oils, flax oil remains liquid when stored in the freezer—thus freezing flax oil extends its shelf life (it is a fragile oil), and even frozen it is easy to pour.

FRUIT
When fruits are not fully ripened, place them in a closed, roomy paper bag at room temperature and out of direct sunlight. Turn the fruits daily to assure even ripening. Placing an apple or banana in the bag facilitates ripening.

Remove any fruit that shows sign of leaks, bruises, mold, or spoilage, as one bad fruit quickly taints surrounding fruit. Wash fruit just prior to using. Once a fruit is cut or peeled, refrigerate it in a tightly covered container, and use quickly.

- **Apples, Grapes, Loquats, Mangos, Nectarines, Passion Fruit, Peaches, Pears, Pineapple, Plums, Pomegranates, Prickly Pears, Quince, Rhubarb, Star Fruit** Refrigerate in a perforated plastic bag in the crisper drawer. Apples, pears, and quince are excellent keepers and may also be held in a cold (32 to 40°F), dry place.
- **Berries, Cherries, Figs** Layer between paper towels, refrigerate, and use as quickly as possible.
- **Kiwis** Refrigerate ripened kiwis, tightly covered in plastic and away from other fruits, as the ethylene gas emitted by other fruits will oversoften kiwis.
- **Bananas, Citrus Fruits, Melons, Pineapple** These fruits are compromised by refrigeration; store them in a dark, cool (50 to 65°F) pantry. Use orange-fleshed melons within a few days. Whole, green-fleshed melons may be stored for a month. Once cut, wrap melons tightly in plastic or their aroma will taint

other foods; refrigerate and use within three days.

- **Watermelon** Store watermelon in a dark, dry, cool (50 to 65°F) place for a week. Once cut, cover, refrigerate, and use within five days.

GRAINS

Store whole grains in closed glass jars in a cool, dry place. (If you live in a hot, humid area, refrigerate them.) Except for millet, most grains can be stored for a year or more. A prevention to retard insects from hatching is to tuck a bay leaf in the jar.

For optimum flavor, buy small quantities of whole grain products that contain the germ, and keep them refrigerated. These include rolled oats, steel-cut oats, rye and quinoa flakes, bulgur made from whole wheat, and whole wheat pasta and couscous. If they have little aroma or flavor or if they have a bitter taste, they're stale. Toss them out.

Grain products that have had their germ removed, like couscous and white bulgur, are best stored tightly wrapped in a cool cupboard. Whole wheat pasta has a shorter shelf life than pasta made from refined flour.

To retard oxidization, refrigerate all whole grain flours, tightly covered, and use within a few weeks. Or freeze and use within six months. Flour with a bitter taste is rancid; discard it.

HERBS AND SPICES

To extend their life, immerse stem ends of fresh herbs in water, loosely cover with a plastic bag, and refrigerate. Every other day trim the stem ends.

A rack of spices over the stove may look attractive, but heat and light diminish their essence. Keep spices in dark-colored closed glass containers in a cool, dark place.

Fresh, quality dried herbs are resilient and have a vibrant look. I routinely compost leaf herbs that are more than a year old or that are stale, brittle, and flat-looking. Whole spices have a long shelf life; once ground, their vitality diminishes.

MUSHROOMS

Mushrooms respire more actively after harvest than other vegetables and lose nearly half their sugar and starch within a few days. Refrigerate and use as quickly as possible. Refrigeration in airtight wrapping will slow down respiration, but it will also cause moisture condensation, which speeds spoilage.

Refrigerate mushrooms in the container they were purchased in, in a paper bag or paper towels, or in a small cotton bag. Should they become dehydrated, place damp paper towels over paper- or cloth-wrapped mushrooms to keep them moist but to permit air circulation.

Store dried mushrooms in an airtight container in a cool cupboard.

NUTS

If you have refrigerator or freezer space, consider purchasing a year's supply of the unshelled new crop in the late fall. Shelled nuts keep in the freezer for up to a year. If rubbery, hollow, moldy, or acrid tasting or smelling, they are rancid and should not be eaten.

Avoid dry-roasted nuts, which often contain sugar, salt, starch, monosodium glutamate, vegetable gums, spices, and preservatives. Also avoid packaged shelled nuts, as they are often coated with a preservative and contain excessive salt and the packaging typically is chemically treated.

Nut and seed butters easily become rancid, so purchase in small quantities and keep refrigerated. A stale, foul aroma and a sharp, burning taste indicate rancidity.

SEAWEED

Seaweed stores well for a year or more. Keep it tightly wrapped in a dark, cool, dry cupboard.

SEEDS

Hulled seeds like sunflower and pumpkin seeds require refrigeration. Whole seeds like sesame, poppy, and flax should be stored in a closed container in a dark, cool cupboard.

VEGETABLES

Most vegetables should be stored in the vegetable drawer of the refrigerator. Tomatoes, avocados, garlic, potatoes, and sweet potatoes, however, are damaged by the 30 to 40°F temperatures that other vegetables thrive in. Store these as follows:

Avocados

A ripe avocado holds best at 40 to 50°F. If storage at this temperature is not possible, refrigerate a ripe avocado for up to three days. Once cut, sprinkle with lemon juice to prevent discoloration, tightly wrap in plastic, and store refrigerated for a day or two.

Garlic

Stored in a cool, dry, well-ventilated area, garlic will keep for several months. Do not refrigerate, as garlic's flavor will taint other foods. If stored in a damp, warm environment, garlic will sprout or become moldy.

Onions

Onions are dormant after harvest and so can be stored without sprouting for, in the case of sharp yellow onions, two to three months. Sweet, moist, and/or red onions have a shorter shelf life and may be stored from two to four weeks. Hang onions in an aerated basket or bag in a cool (ideally 30 to 40°F), dry, well-ventilated place. Do not store onions near potatoes, as onions absorb moisture, which causes potatoes to sprout and rot. Do not refrigerate onions. Once cut, onions oxidize and quickly lose their flavor.

Potatoes

Keep mature potatoes and sweet potatoes in a cool (ideally between 41 and 48°F), dry, ventilated, dark area and they will keep up to two months; use new potatoes within a few days. Store in an aerated basket, paper bag, or recycled clean pantyhose. The higher the temperature, the shorter their storage life. Refrigeration causes their starches to convert to sugar. Do not store potatoes near strongly flavored foods, apples, or onions, as they absorb moisture and flavor.

Roots

Most roots store best in the refrigerator, where they'll keep for several weeks, but they are best within a few days of harvest. Packed in sand, roots hold in a root cellar for several months. Bright greens attached to a turnip or other root vegetable are a welcome sign of freshness. Home from the store, separate greens from roots at the leaf base, but do not cut into the root itself. Leaves left attached to a root draw moisture and flavor from it.

Tomatoes

Store tomatoes in a cool area (ideally 50°F) for up to a week. Do not store in direct sun. If overripe, then refrigerate tomatoes for up to three days; however, refrigeration compromises their flavor and makes their texture mealy.

Winter Squash

Squash harvested after the first frost typically keeps until March when stored in a dry, cool, dark, well-ventilated place. Store each squash individually on a shelf; if in a box, wrap each in paper, as direct contact with another squash diminishes shelf life. Butternut is the best keeper, with kabocha, buttercup, and hubbard lasting almost as along. If you do not have a cool storage area, hold the squash at room temperature rather than refrigerate, and use within a few weeks. Once cut, the unused portion should be refrigerated, wrapped in plastic, for up to five days.

APPENDIX II: NUTRITIONAL SOURCES

The following is a list of the primary macronutrients and micronutrients required for optimum health and superior plant sources in which they can be found.

MACRONUTRIENTS

Air Consumed more than any other element. Regular exercise, which helps fully oxygenate the system, is vital for all people, and especially those with sedentary jobs. For all of us who breathe in less than pristine environments, consider an air purifier for your home, office, and automobile. Houseplants are remarkable detoxifiers (see box on page 9).

Water The second most important element by volume, it accounts for most of our body weight. To support optimum health, drink and cook with pure water (see pages 379–380).

Carbohydrates The next most important nutrient by volume, carbohydrates are found almost exclusively in plant foods (dairy products are the primary exception). Carbohydrates can be either simple or complex. Carbohydrates with a simple molecular structure are quickly assimilated and cause a rapid fluctuation in blood sugar; they are primarily found in fruits and sweeteners. Because complex carbohydrates take longer to digest, they help stabilize blood sugar; unless, that is, they are eaten in excess. When eaten in moderation, complex carbohydrates help stabilize blood sugar; thus they help prevent hypoglycemia and diabetes. Complex carbohydrates are found abundantly in vegetables, whole grains, and beans and legumes.

Fiber A form of carbohydrate, abundantly found in all whole vegetable foods. When a vegetable or fruit is juiced, its fiber is removed. Peeling produce and refining grains significantly reduces their fiber content. By favoring a varied whole foods diet, one obtains ample complex carbohydrates, including fiber.

Protein Meat, dairy, and eggs are regarded as superior protein sources due to their amino acid profile. However, whole grains, legumes, vegetables, nuts, and seeds also provide human protein needs. Quinoa and amaranth are unique in the plant realm, as their amino acid profile makes their protein equal or superior to milk.

Fat The most concentrated source of energy; it is vital for human health. Oil is fat in a liquid form. Most of Americans' fat-related health problems are due to the consumption of highly refined fats and oils. Consider switching over to unrefined fats and oils—they satisfy both our nutritional needs and our hunger.

SOURCES OF MICRONUTRIENTS IN VEGETAL FOODS

Vitamins

Biotin Soybeans, nutritional yeast, and whole grains.

Choline Soybeans, whole grains, and beans and legumes.

Coenzyme Q10 Peanuts and spinach.

Folic Acid Microalgae, sprouts, leafy green

vegetables, whole grains, nutritional yeast, dates, beans and legumes, mushrooms, oranges, beets, fenugreek, and root vegetables.

Inositol Fruits, vegetables, whole grains, molasses, nutritional yeast, and beans and legumes (especially soybeans).

Para-Aminobenzoic Acid (PABA) Whole grains, spinach, molasses, and mushrooms.

Vitamin A Microalgae, alaria, barley grass/wheat grass juice, and deep green or orange vegetables.

Vitamin B$_1$ (Thiamine) Whole grains (especially brown, red, and black rice), nori, wakame, and beans and legumes.

Vitamin B$_2$ (Riboflavin) Whole grains, beans and legumes, spinach, nutritional yeast, and hijiki.

Vitamin B$_3$ (Niacin, Niacinamide, Nicotinic Acid) Whole grains, especially brown, red, and black rice (but not corn), posole, masa, nori, wakame, alaria, peanuts, and nutritional yeast.

Vitamin B$_5$ (Pantothenic Acid) Whole grains, fresh vegetables, beans and legumes, mushrooms, nuts, and nutritional yeast.

Vitamin B$_6$ (Pyridoxine) Whole grains, leafy green vegetables, dulse, nori, laver, nutritional yeast, carrots, peas, sunflower seeds, and walnuts.

Vitamin B$_{12}$ (Cyanocobalamin) Nutritional yeast, unpasteurized fermented vegetables, and microalgae.

Vitamin C (Ascorbic Acid) Citrus fruits, bell peppers, chiles, amaranth, berries, cabbage, parsley, potatoes, sprouts, and tomatoes.

Vitamin D The "sunshine" vitamin we obtain from exposure to sunlight. Sunflower sprouts contain vitamin D, and chlorophyll-rich foods perform like vitamin D in the body.

Vitamin E Nuts, seeds, whole grains (especially wheat, oats, quinoa, and brown, red, and black rice), the dark green leaves of cabbage, broccoli, and cauliflower, dandelion greens, sprouts (especially sprouted wheat), asparagus, cucumbers, and spinach.

Vitamin K Alfalfa sprouts, natto, asparagus, blackstrap molasses, dark leafy green vegetables, green tea, kelp, soybeans, oats, rye, and wheat.

Vitamin P (Bioflavonoids) The white pith of citrus fruits, peppers, buckwheat, and black currants.

Vitamin U Cabbage, alfalfa, unpasteurized sauerkraut.

Minerals

Boron Seaweed, alfalfa, and unrefined salt. To a lesser extent, grains, nuts, leafy green vegetables, grapes, pears, apples, and carrots.

Calcium Seaweed (especially wakame and hijiki, followed by kelp, kombu, and alaria), amaranth, quinoa, oats, beans and legumes, microalgae, leafy green vegetables, almonds, nutritional yeast, sesame seeds, sunflower seeds, figs, dandelion greens, and unrefined salt.

Calcium is abundantly provided in a varied whole foods diet. However, our calcium reserves can be depleted by overconsumption of dairy and meat, consumption of refined flours, grains, salt, and sweeteners, and a sedentary lifestyle.

Chromium Seaweed (especially kelp and alaria), whole grains (especially wheat), mushrooms, beets, nutritional yeast, beans and legumes, and unrefined salt.

Copper Seaweed, whole grains, beans and legumes, raisins, apricots, beets, garlic, nuts, mushrooms, leafy green vegetables, and unrefined salt.

Fluorine Seaweed, rye, rice, parsley, avocados, cabbage, and unrefined salt.

Germanium Seaweed, garlic, shiitake mushrooms, onions, ginseng, aloe vera, and unrefined salt.

Iodine Seaweed and unrefined salt. Also, when grown in iodine-rich soil, garlic, asparagus, lima beans, sesame seeds, soybeans, and turnip greens. Similarly, if microalgae is grown in iodine-rich water, it provides iodine.

Iron Seaweed, molasses, whole grains, beans and legumes, nuts, beets, nutritional yeast, sesame seeds, prunes, raisins, dates, and unrefined salt.

Magnesium Seaweed (especially kelp and alaria), whole grains (especially amaranth), microalgae, beans and legumes, seeds, chlorophyll-rich foods such as leafy greens, and unrefined salt.

Manganese Seaweed, whole grains, nuts and seeds, blueberries, green tea, alfalfa leaf, avocados, and unrefined salt.

Molybdenum Seaweed, whole grains, beans and legumes, dark green leafy vegetables, and unrefined salt.

Phosphorus Seaweed, whole grains, beans and legumes, dried fruit, garlic, nuts, seeds, and unrefined salt.

Potassium Seaweed (especially kelp and dulse), carrot juice, whole grains, beans and legumes, fruit, vegetables, and unrefined salt.

Selenium Seaweed, whole grains, beans and legumes, organic garlic, mushrooms, and unrefined salt.

Silicon Seaweed, whole grains, lettuce (especially bib lettuce), parsnips, dandelion greens, strawberries, celery, cucumbers, apricots, carrots, and unrefined salt.

Sodium Seaweed (especially kelp and alaria), celery, unrefined salt, and virtually all foods.

Sulfur Seaweed, cabbage family, beans and legumes, onions, garlic, nettles, soybeans, and unrefined salt.

Vanadium Seaweed, whole grains, vegetable oils, dill, radishes, green beans, and unrefined salt.

Zinc Seaweed, whole grains, legumes and beans, nuts, seeds (especially alfalfa and pumpkin), mushrooms, nettles, soybeans, and unrefined salt.

Nutraceuticals

Biologically active substances in plants that have pharmaceutically recognized healing properties. Beta-carotene is one example of a nutraceutical. There are potentially millions of nutrients with pharmaceutical properties. To obtain adequate nutrients, eat a varied diet of whole foods that, ideally, are sustainably grown, seasonal, and freshly prepared.

APPENDIX III:
AYURVEDIC FOOD GUIDELINES

To follow Ayurvedic food guidelines, you must first discern which of the three elements (*vata*, *pitta*, or *kapha*) you predominately are. By recalling what foods make you feel good and matching them to the elemental types below, you may correctly ascertain your predominant type. Or you may consult one of the many popular Ayurvedic books that provide self-identification guides. A third choice is to visit a qualified Ayurvedic practitioner, who will assess your elemental type plus provide a diagnosis, medicinal herbs, and a recommended treatment plan. Note: Some people are a combination of types, and one's type(s) may vary over time or even with the season.

These guidelines are just that—guidelines. They are not law. Please bypass them when you choose, but then pay attention to any emotional, mental, or physical impact. Better yet, when hungry for a food from the "Not Recommended" category, balance it with other ingredients or dishes that better suit your type.

Rather than limiting your diet and enjoyment of food, these guidelines will help you discern those foods that you most readily digest and that help you feel balanced and at your best.

VATA (AIR TYPE)

Vata people flourish with a warming, grounding diet composed of strengthening, substantial foods that are moistening and lubricating. For example, a bowl of warm oatmeal with ghee and cinnamon balances *vata*, whereas a granola bar or a bowl of granola with cold milk does the opposite. It is important for *vata* types to eat freshly prepared warm foods that, ideally, contain digestion-enhancing herbs and spices such as ginger or cumin. Thus soups are much more calming to this air type than are salads.

Note that even a food that is "good" for *vata* is upsetting if it is cold, stale, undercooked, eaten with too many other dishes, overeaten, or eaten when stressed. Flavors that benefit *vata* are sweet, salty, and sour. For example, sour umeboshi plums considerably help *vata* digestion.

Beans and Legumes challenge *vata*, tend to cause gas, and are drying. *Vata* responses to beans and legumes vary widely. Tofu, mung, urad dal, and, in small quantities, aduki beans, are generally easy to assimilate. Some *vatas* do well with lentils, others with split peas, and others with neither of these. To aid bean digestion, soak beans thoroughly and cook them until they are well done, moist, and tender. In addition, cook beans with seaweed, warming herbs and spices, and ghee or a quality fat. Beans are easier to digest when served in modest quantities, or in soup, or when combined with vegetables.

Beverages are important for *vata*. Water may not be substantial enough for *vata* people, although adequate water is necessary to keep *vata* hydrated. To support *vata*, drink warm herbal teas, preferably noncaffeinated chai (warming spices with milk) or room-temperature milk, buttermilk, or kefir. In hot weather, enjoy sour fruit juice or water with lemon or lime juice. Small quantities of beer or wine sometimes are helpful.

Fats and Oils moisten, warm, lubricate, and help ground *vata*, providing they are unrefined. Ghee and sesame oil are the most balancing, followed by almond oil, extra virgin olive oil, butter, and coconut oil.

Fruits moisten and harmonize *vata*; however, they are generally too light to have a grounding effect. Favor regional and seasonal fruits; enjoy them separately rather than combined with other ingredients. Dried fruits, however, challenge *vata* unless they are rehydrated. Watermelon, raw apples, and cranberries are unbalancing.

Grains that are most balancing to *vata* are wheat, oats, and rice. While barley, buckwheat, corn, millet, quinoa, and rye are mildly unbalancing, they can be ameliorated with ghee or sesame oil and digestion-enhancing spices, herbs, or condiments. In addition, favor one-grain dishes (rather than multiple grain combinations like mixed-grain bread or cereal). Avoid granola, cold breakfast cereals, crackers, rice cakes, crusty bread, yeast bread, and dried grains.

Herbs and Spices benefit *vata*, as they aid digestion and help dispel gas. They are especially beneficial added to sweet or heavy foods and include asafetida, basil, bay leaf, cardamom, cinnamon, cloves, coriander, cumin, epazote, fennel, fenugreek, fresh ginger, mace, marjoram, mustard seeds (in moderation), nutmeg, oregano, savory, thyme, and turmeric. Very hot spices, such as dried ginger, chiles, or mustard, may aggravate *vata*, especially in hot, windy, or dry climates.

Nuts and Seeds are moistening, heavy, and warming and so nourish *vata* as long as they're taken in small, easy-to-digest quantities. Enjoy them raw or lightly roasted. Avoid nuts and seeds that are dry-roasted, fried, stale, or overly salted.

Sweeteners nurture *vata* when they are natural and used in moderation. Dehydrated cane juice is especially beneficial. Strive to completely avoid white sugar.

Vegetables cooked support *vata*. While well-cooked onions and garlic are superior *vata* tonics, raw onions are best avoided, as are most other raw vegetables. To make salads more digestible, favor them in hot weather and with an oil-rich dressing and digestion-enhancing herbs or a small amount of garlic. Celery, eggplant, mushrooms, tomatoes, and potatoes unbalance *vata*; to ameliorate their effects, cook, season, and combine them with cheese.

Vata responses to the cabbage family vary widely. The more tender and watery the cabbage relative, the easier for *vata* to digest. Thus, Chinese cabbage is usually preferred over other types of cabbage. For some *vata* types, cabbage family vegetables with a high mustard oil content, such as broccoli, cabbage, and mustard greens, will be more challenging than broccoli rabe, cauliflower, or Chinese cabbage.

PITTA (FIRE TYPE)

Fiery *pittas* thrive with a diet that is cool, slightly dry, and a little heavy. Typically their digestion is good and they seemingly better tolerate poor eating habits than other types (but indiscretions typically manifest as infectious disease or other toxic blood-related problems). *Pitta* does best with bland, mild-tasting foods and with flavors that are sweet, bitter, and/or astringent.

Beans and Legumes are easily assimilated by *pittas*, with the exception of lentils and peanuts. Add herbs and spices to aid digestion, favoring ground coriander seeds and fresh cilantro leaves. Go easy on any added fat or oil cooked with beans and legumes.

Beverages are especially needed by *pittas*. Favor spring water, black or green tea, astringent herbal teas (such as alfalfa or raspberry leaf), or astringent fruit juices (such as pomegranate), milk, vegetable juices, green drinks (such as wheat grass juice or spirulina). Avoid coffee, spicy tea, alcohol, beer, and wine.

Fats and Oils are warming and therefore best used discreetly by *pittas*. Ghee and butter are less warming and more harmonious. Favor the more cooling vegetable oils: coconut and sunflower. Minimize the more warming oils: sesame, peanut, almond, olive, and safflower.

Fruits tend to cool, calm, and harmonize *pitta* as well as relieve thirst. The fruits to favor are sweet-flavored ones. Fruits to minimize are those with a sour flavor: grapefruits, lemons, limes, sour cherries, sour plums, peaches, papayas, and apricots.

Grains are well tolerated by *pitta*, as they strengthen, but do not overeat. This includes quality bread and pasta. When suffering from an acute condition, it is best not to use brown rice, buckwheat, corn, or rye as a primary staple.

Herbs and Spices are best avoided by *pitta*, except those that are not too heating (cardamom, cilantro, cinnamon, coriander, cumin, fennel, mint, parsley, turmeric, and, in small quantities, black pepper). Saffron and rose petals calm the *pitta* mind as well as body. Generally, *pitta* does best with a low-salt diet except during the summer heat.

Nuts and Seeds are warming and oily and therefore best used in moderation. Favor coconut and sunflower seeds, and less frequently sesame seeds, pine nuts, and pumpkin seeds. Avoid Brazil and macadamia nuts, and use other nuts rarely.

Sweeteners are cooling and more soothing to *pitta* than any other constitution. Dehydrated cane juice, maple, syrup, and fruit-based sweeteners (such as fruit juice, apple butter, or date sugar) are especially recommended.

Vegetables cooked or raw support *pitta*. (But raw vegetables are not recommended in cold weather or when convalescing.) Avoid deep-fried foods, chiles, raw onions, garlic, tomatoes, and avocados. Also minimize acidic vegetable such as eggplant, potatoes, chard, and spinach.

KAPHA (WATER TYPE)

Kapha is the water type but with a strong earth influence. It is slow moving, heavy, wet, cold, and enduring and so does best with foods that are light, dry, and warming. The best tastes for *kapha* are pungent, bitter, and astringent. It is important for this type to eat less food and less frequently.

Beans and Legumes support *kapha*, as they are drying and increase air. Adukis are particularly diuretic. Chickpeas, however, imbalance *kapha*, as does processed soy or excessive soy.

Beverages in moderation is the guideline for *kapha*. Avoid all iced and chilled beverages. Green and black tea, and occasionally coffee, are acceptable. Pungent, astringent herbal teas such as ginger, chicory, or dandelion are balancing. Drink milk moderately, if at all.

Fats and Oils are heavy and dampproducing and therefore best used in small amounts. Sunflower, sesame, and olive oils and ghee are best tolerated.

Fruits increase water, a feature not needed by *kapha* people; however, as fruit is light it often ameliorates *kapha's* heaviness. Small amounts of dried fruits (dates excepted) balance *kapha*. All fruit is best tolerated alone, rather than in combination with other foods. Sweet fruits such as ripe bananas and watery fruits exacerbate *kapha*, as do fatty fruits such as avocados and coconut. Favor apples, underripe bananas, berries, cranberries, cherries, peaches, pears, pomegranates, and persimmons.

Grains that are drying with diuretic properties, such as amaranth, barley, buckwheat, corn, millet, dry oats, and tef, support *kapha*. Puffed or popped grains are drying. Basmati rice is favored over other types of rice. Oats and all wheat products are heavy and increase *kapha*'s tendency to retain fluid.

Herbs and Spices warm and dry *kapha*, increase metabolism, and help prevent fat and water from accumulating. Use salt (preferably unrefined) in moderation. *Kapha*'s slow steady digestion can benefit from digestion-enhancing herbs and spices such as asafetida, basil, black pepper, black mustard seeds, chiles, coriander, cumin, fennel, fenugreek, galangal, and fresh and dried ginger. *Kaphas* who are not fond of these pungent spices may find themselves better tolerating allspice, cardamom, cinnamon, and nutmeg, which will also support their metabolism.

Nuts and Seeds are heavy, mucus-forming, and fatty in nature and therefore best used moderately by *kapha*. Seeds (especially chia, flax, pumpkin, and sunflower) are preferable to nuts. Occasional use of coconut and almonds is acceptable.

Sweeteners such as carob are drying to *kapha*, and, curiously enough, so is raw honey, which has warming, drying, and expectorant properties. As much as possible, avoid other sweeteners or only use them occasionally.

Vegetables are mostly dry and light and therefore aid *kapha*, especially when they are cooked (except in hot weather) and prepared with little oil. Indulge in arugula, artichokes, asparagus, bitter melon, dark leafy cabbage family greens, endive, mâche, fresh peas, and peppers. When craving starchy foods, *kaphas* do well with the following root vegetables: beets, carrots, Jerusalem artichokes, potatoes, and rutabagas.

The few vegetables to use in moderation include sweet and juicy vegetables such as cucumbers, seaweed, squash, sweet corn, sweet potatoes, tomatoes, and zucchini.

APPENDIX IV: FAMILY (OR GENUS) CLASSIFICATION

ALGAE FAMILY (*Algae*) Chlorella; Seaweed Family; Spirulina; Wild Blue-Green Algae.

AMARANTH FAMILY (*Amaranthu*) Amaranth; Beet; Chard; Epazote; Fat Hen; Orach; Quinoa; Spinach; Sugar (beets).

APPLE FAMILY (*Maloideae*) Apple; Asian Pear; Loquat; Pear; Quince.

ARUM FAMILY (*Araceae*) Arrowroot; Taro; Yautia.

BEECH FAMILY (*Fagaceae*) Acorn; Chestnut.

BIRCH FAMILY (*Betulaceae*) Hazelnut.

BLACKBERRY FAMILY (*Rubus*) Blackberry (includes hybrids: Boysenberry, Dewberry, Loganberry, Youngberry); Raspberry.

BLUEBERRY FAMILY (*Vaccinium*) Bilberry; Blueberry; Cranberry; Huckleberry; Lingonberry.

BRAZIL NUT FAMILY (*Lecythidaceae*) Brazil Nut.

BUCKWHEAT FAMILY (*Polygonaceae*) Buckwheat; Rhubarb; Sorrel.

CABBAGE FAMILY (*Crucifer* or *Brassica*) Arugula; Bok Choy; Broccoli; Broccolini; Broccoli Rabe; Brussels Sprout; Cabbage; Cauliflower; Chinese Broccoli; Chinese Cabbage; Collards; Cress; Daikon; Flowering Cabbage; Horseradish; Kale; Kohlrabi; Mizuna; Mustard Greens; Nasturtium; Radish; Rutabaga; Tatsoi; Turnip; Vegetable; Wasabi; Watercress.

CARROT FAMILY (*Umbelliferae*) Ajowan; Angelica; Anise; Asafetida; Caraway; Carrot; Celery; Celery Root; Chervil; Cilantro; Cumin; Dill; Fennel; Lovage; Nigella; Parsley; Parsley Root; Parsnip.

CASHEW FAMILY (*Anacardiaceae*) Ambarella; Cashew; Mango; Mastic; Pistachio; Sumac Berry.

CHERIMOYA FAMILY (*Annonaceae*) Atemoya; Cherimoya; Pawpaw.

CITRUS FAMILY (*Rutaceae*) Bitter Orange; Citron; Curry Leaf; Grapefruit; Kumquat; Lemon; Lime; Mandarin; Orange; Pomelo; Sichuan Pepper.

COFFEE FAMILY (*Rubiaceae*) Coffee; Noni.

DAISY FAMILY (*Composite*) Artichoke; Burdock; Cardoon; Celtuce; Chamomile; Chicory; Chrysanthemum Greens; Dahlia; Dandelion; Echinacea; Jerusalem Artichoke; Lettuce; Salsify; Scorzonera; Stevia; Sunflower Seed; Tarragon; Yacón.

FIG FAMILY (*Moraceae*) Breadfruit; Breadnut; Fig; Jackfruit; Mulberry.

GINGER FAMILY (*Zingiberaceae*) Cardamom; Galangal; Ginger; Turmeric.

GINSENG FAMILY (*Araliaceae*) Ginseng.

GOOSEFOOT FAMILY (*Chenopodium*) Agretti; Amaranth; Beet; Beetberry; Chard; Epazote; Fat Hen; Orach; Quinoa; Spinach.

GOURD FAMILY (*Cucurbitaceae*) Bitter Melon; Chayote; Cucumber; Gac; Kiwano; Loofah; Melon; Pumpkin; Squash, Summer; Squash, Winter; Watermelon; Winter Melon.

GRASS FAMILY (*Poaceae* or *Gramineae*) Bamboo Shoot; Barley; Corn; Job's Tears;

Lemongrass; Millet; Oats; Rice; Rye; Sorghum; Sprouted Wheat (or Grain) Products; Sugar (Cane); Triticale; Wheat; Wild Rice.

HEMP FAMILY (*Cannabis*) Hemp; Hops.

HICKORY FAMILY (*Juglandaceae*) Black Walnut; Pecan; Walnut.

LAUREL FAMILY (*Lauraceae*) Avocado; Bay; Cinnamon; Sassafras.

LEGUME FAMILY (*Leguminosus*) Alfalfa; Beans and Legumes; Dal; Fava; Fenugreek; Green Bean; Honeybush; Jicama; Kudzu; Licorice Root; Long Bean; Lotus; Lupin; Mesquite; Pea, Dried; Pea, Fresh; Peanut; Rooibos; Tamarind; Winged Bean.

LYCHEE FAMILY (*Sapindaceae*) Longan; Lychee; Rambutan.

MALLOW FAMILY (*Malva*) Cocoa; Cotton (Seed Oil).

MANGOSTEEN FAMILY (*Clusiaceae*) Mangosteen; St. John's Wort.

MINT FAMILY (*Lamiaceae*) Basil; Chia; Crosne; Lavender; Lemon Balm; Marjoram; Mint; Oregano; Perilla; Rosemary; Sage; Savory; Thyme.

MUSHROOM FAMILY (*Agaricaceae*) Bolete; Cauliflower Mushroom; Chanterelle; Enoki; Hedgehog; Maitake; Matsutake; Morel; Mushroom, Common; Oyster Mushroom; Reishi; Shiitake; Truffle; Wood Ear.

MYRTLE FAMILY (*Myrtaceae*) Allspice; Clove; Feijoa; Guava; Jabuticaba.

NIGHTSHADE FAMILY (*Solanaceae*) Chile Pepper; Eggplant; Goji Berry; Ground Cherry; Paprika; Pepino; Peppers; Potato; Sweet Pepper; Sunberry; Tamarillo; Tomatillo; Tomato.

NUTMEG FAMILY (*Myristicaceae*) Mace; Nutmeg.

OLIVE FAMILY (*Oleaceae*) Jasmine, Olive.

ONION FAMILY (*Allium*) Chive; Garlic; Garlic Chive; Leek; Onion; Ramp; Scallion; Shallot.

PALM FAMILY (*Arecaceae*) Açaí; Coconut; Date; Palm Kernel Oil; Palm Oil.

PEPPER FAMILY (*Piperaceae*) Black Pepper; Kava; Long Pepper.

PRUNE FAMILY (*Prunus*) Almond; Apricot; Cherry; Nectarine; Peach; Plum; Prune; Sour Cherry.

RIBES FAMILY Currant; Gooseberry.

SAPODILLA FAMILY (*Sapotaceae*) Chicle; Mamey Sapote; Sapodilla; Shea Nut Butter.

SEAWEED FAMILY (*Algae*) Agar; Alaria; Arame; Bladder Wrack; Dulse; Hijiki; Irish Moss; Kanten; Kelp; Kombu; Laver; Nori; Sea Lettuce; Sea Palm; Sea Whip; Wakame.

SESAME FAMILY (*Pedaliaceae*) Sesame Seed.

SOAPBERRY FAMILY (*Sapindaceae*) Guarana; Longan; Lychee; Maple (Syrup); Rambutan.

TEA FAMILY (*Camellia*) Tea; Tea Seed Oil.

YAM FAMILY (*Dioscoreaceae*) Jinenjo; Yam.

SELECTED BIBLIOGRAPHY

Allgeier, R. J., et al. "Vinegar: History and Development. Part One and Part Two." *Food Products Development* (June/July/August 1974), U.S. Industrial Chemicals Co., Cincinnati.

Anderson, Jean, and Barbara Deskins. *The Nutrition Bible: A Comprehensive, No-Nonsense Guide to Foods, Nutrients, Additives, Preservatives, Pollutants, and Everything Else We Eat and Drink.* New York: William Morrow, 1997.

Arasaki, Seibin, and Teruko Arasaki. *Vegetables from the Sea: To Help You Look and Feel Better.* Tokyo: Japan Publications, 1983.

Barnett, Robert A. *Tonics: More Than 100 Recipes That Improve the Body and the Mind.* New York: Harper-Collins, 1997.

Belleme, John, and Jan Belleme. *Culinary Treasures of Japan: The Art of Making and Using Traditional Japanese Foods.* Garden City Park, NY: Avery Publishing Group, 1992.

———. *Cooking with Japanese Foods: A Guide to the Traditional Natural Foods of Japan.* Garden City Park, New York: Avery Publishing Group, 1992.

Boyles, Peg. "Dandelion Season." *The Gardener's Companion Newsletter*, P.O. Box 420296, Palm Coast, FL 32142. March 1997.

Brennan, Georgeanne, Isaac Cronin, and Charlotte Glenn. *The New American Vegetable Cookbook: The Definitive Guide to America's Exotic and Traditional Vegetables.* Berkeley, CA: Aris Books, 1985.

Brown, Deni. *Encyclopedia of Herbs and Their Uses.* New York: Dorling Kindersley, 1995.

Brown, Tom, Jr. *Tom Brown's Guide to Wild Edible and Medicinal Plants.* New York: Berkley Publishing Group, 1985.

Burke, Cindy. *To Buy or Not to Buy Organic: What You Need to Know to Choose the Healthiest, Safest, Most Earth-Friendly Food.* New York: Marlowe and Company, 2007.

Carter, Jean. *The Food Pharmacy: Dramatic New Evidence That Food Is Your Best Medicine.* New York: Bantam Books, 1988.

Castelvetro, Giacomo. *The Fruit, Herbs, and Vegetables of Italy.* New York: Viking, Penguin, 1990.

Chalmers, Irena. *The Great Food Almanac: A Feast of Facts from A to Z.* San Francisco, CA: Harper Collins World Publishers San Francisco, 1994.

Chao-liang, Chang, Cao Qing-rong, and Li Baozhen. Translated by Ron Edwards and Gong Zhimei. *Vegetables as Medicine: A Safe and Cheap Form of Traditional Chinese Food Therapy.* Selangor Darul Ehsan, Malaysia: Pelanduk Publications (M) Sdn. Bhd., 1999.

Colbin, Annemarie. *Food and Healing.* New York: Ballantine, 1986.

Corriher, Shirley O. *CookWise: The Hows and Whys of Successful Cooking.* New York: William Morrow, 1998.

Creasy, Rosalind. *Cooking from the Garden.* San Francisco, CA: Sierra Club Books, 1988.

Cusumano, Camille. *The New Foods: A Shopper's Guide with Recipes.* New York: Henry Holt, 1989.

Devi, Yamuna. *Lord Krishna's Cuisine: The Art of Indian Vegetarian Cooking.* New York: E. P. Dutton, 1987.

DeWitt, Dave, and Nancy Gerlach. *The Whole Chile Pepper Book.* Boston, MA: Little, Brown and Company, 1990.

Elias, Thomas S. *The Complete Trees of North America: Field Guide and Natural History.* New York: Van Nostrand Reinhold Company, 1980.

Elias, Thomas S., and Peter A. Dykeman. *Edible Wild Plants: A North American Field Guide.* New York: Sterling Publishing Co., 1990.

Enig, Mary, and Sally Fallon. *Eat Fat, Lose Fat: Lose Weight and Feel Great with Three Delicious, Science-Based Coconut Diets.* New York: Hudson Street Press, 2004.

Erasmus, Udo. *Fats That Heal, Fats That Kill: The Complete Guide to Fats, Oils, Cholesterol, and Human Health.* Vancouver, BC: Alive Books, 1986.

Eterson, Emily. "Dried Fruit Labels May Not Tell the Whole Story." *Natural Foods Merchandiser* (February 1995), p. 26.

Fitzgibbon, Theodora. *The Food of the Western World: An Encyclopedia of Food from North America and Europe.* New York: Quadrangle/The New York Times Book Co., 1976.

Flaws, Bob. *The Book of Jook: Chinese Medicinal Porridges.* Boulder, CO: Blue Poppy Press, 1995.

———. *The Tao of Healthy Eating: Dietary Wisdom According to Chinese Medicine.* Boulder, CO: Blue Poppy Press, 1998.

Flaws, Bob, and Honora Wolfe. *Prince Wen Hui's Cook: Chinese Dietary Therapy.* Brookline, MA, Paradigm Publications, 1995.

Frawley, David, and Vasant Lad. *The Yoga of Herbs (An Ayurvedic Guide to Herbal Medicine).* Twin Lakes, WI: Lotus, 1990.

Fussell, Betty. *The Story of Corn.* New York: Alfred A. Knopf, 1992.

Gagné, Steve. *Energetics of Food: Encounters with Your Most Intimate Relationship.* Santa Fe, NM: Spiral Sciences, 1990.

Gates, Donna. *The Body Ecology Diet: Recovering Your Health and Rebuilding Your Immunity.* Atlanta, GA: BED Publications, 1996.

Gould, John. "The Home Forum," *Christian Science Monitor,* February 13, 1988, p. 17.

Gutman, Robert L., and Ruy Beung-Ho. "Rediscovering Tea" *HerbalGram,* No. 37, pp. 33–48.

Hamerstrom, Frances. *Wild Food Cookbook.* Amherst, MA: Amherst Press, 1994.

Harrington, H. D. *Edible Native Plants of the Rocky Mountains.* Albuquerque, NM: University of New Mexico Press, 1967.

Harris, Lloyd J. *The Book of Garlic.* Berkeley, CA: Aris Books, 1980.

Hausman, Patricia, and Judith Benn Hurley. *The Healing Foods: The Ultimate Authority on the Curative Power of Nutrition.* Emmaus, PA: Rodale Press, 1989.

Herbst, Sharon Tyler. *The Food Lover's Tiptionary.* New York: Hearst Books, 1994.

Hess, Clarke. "Saffron on a Shoestring." *The Kitchen Garden,* #12, January 1998, pp. 32–35.

Hobbs, Christopher. *Foundations of Health: The Liver and Digestive Herbal.* Capitola, CA: Botanica Press, 1992.

———. *Herbal Remedies for Dummies.* New York: Hungry Minds, 1998.

———. *Medicinal Mushrooms: An Exploration of Tradition, Healing, and Culture.* Santa Cruz, CA: Botanica Press, 1995.

Jacobi, Dana. *Natural Kitchen: Soy!* Rocklin, CA: Prima Publishing, 1996.

Jensen, Bernard. *Foods That Heal: A Guide to Understanding and Using the Healing Powers of Natural Foods.* Garden City Park, NY: Avery Publishing Group, 1988.

Jilin, Liu. *Chinese Dietary Therapy.* New York: Churchill Livingstone, English edition, 1995.

Kamman, Madeleine. *The New Making of a Cook.* New York: William Morrow, 1997.

Katz, Sandor Ellix. *Wild Fermentation: The Flavor, Nutrition, and Craft of Live-Culture Foods.* Chelsea Green, 2003.

Lad, Usha, and Vasant Lad. *Ayurvedic Cooking for Self-Healing.* Albuquerque, NM: The Ayurvedic Press, 1997.

London, Sheryl, and Mel London. *The Versatile Grain and the Elegant Bean: A Celebration of the World's Most Healthful Foods.* New York: Simon and Schuster, 1992.

Lu, Henry C. *Chinese Natural Cures.* New York: Black Dog and Leventhal Publishers, 1994.

Madlener, Judith Cooper. *The Sea Vegetable Book: Foraging and Cooking Seaweed.* New York: Clarkson N. Potter Inc., 1977.

Mars, Brigitte. "Calm Down with Chamomile." *Delicious! magazine* (November 1995), pp. 52–53.

McGee, Harold. *On Food and Cooking: The Science and Lore of the Kitchen.* Charles Scribner's Sons, 1984, 2004.

———. *The Curious Cook: More Kitchen Science and Lore.* San Francisco: North Point Press, 1990.

Moore, Michael. *Medicinal Plants of the Desert and Canyon West.* Santa Fe, NM: Museum of New Mexico Press, 1989.

———. *Medicinal Plants of the Mountain West.* Santa Fe, NM: Museum of New Mexico Press, 1979.

Morningstar, Amadea. *Ayurvedic Cooking for Westerners: Familiar Western Food Prepared with Ayurvedic Principles.* Twin Lakes, WI: Lotus Press, 1995.

Murray, Michael, and Pizzorno, Joseph. *The Condensed Encyclopedia of Healing Foods.* New York: Pocket Books, 2006.

Nadkarni, M. *Indian Materia Medica.* Bombay: South Asia, 1988.

National Research Council Staff. *Lost Crops of the Incas: Little Known Plants of the Andes with Promise for Worldwide Cultivation.* Washington, DC: National Academy Press, 1989.

Ortiz, Elisabeth Lambert. *The Encyclopedia of Herbs,*

Spices and Flavorings: A Cook's Compendium. New York: Dorling Kindersley, 1992.

Phillips, Robert, and Martyn Rix. *The Random House Book of Vegetables.* New York: Random House, 1994.

Pitchford, Paul. *Healing with Whole Foods: Oriental Traditions and Modern Nutrition.* Berkeley, CA: North Atlantic Books, 1996.

Reich, Lee. "Upstart American Persimmons Add to Fall Colors." *New York Times,* November 5, 1998, pp. D1, D8.

Rhoads, Sharon Ann. *Cooking with Sea Vegetables.* Brookline, MA: Autumn Press, 1978.

Rinzler, Carol Ann. *The Complete Book of Food: A Nutritional, Medical, and Culinary Guide.* New York: World Almanac, 1987.

Root, Waverley. *Food.* New York: Simon and Schuster, 1980.

Ross, Rosa Lo San. *Beyond Bok Choy: A Cook's Guide to Asian Vegetables.* New York: Artisan, 1996.

Ryman, Daniele. *Aromatherapy in Your Diet.* New York: Berkley Books, 1997.

Saltzman, Joanne. *Amazing Grains: Creating Vegetarian Main Dishes with Whole Grains.* Tiburon, CA: H. J. Kramer Inc. 1990.

Sass, Lorna J. *To the King's Taste: Richard II's Book of Feasts and Recipes Adapted for Modern Cooking.* New York: Metropolitan Museum of Art, 1975.

Schechter, Steven R., and Tom Monte. *Fighting Radiation with Foods, Herbs, and Vitamins.* Brookline, MA: East West Health Books, 1988.

Schneider, Elizabeth. *Uncommon Fruits and Vegetables: A Commonsense Guide.* New York: HarperCollins, 1986.

Shannon, Sara. *Diet For the Atomic Age: How to Protect Yourself from Low-Level Radiation.* Wayne, NJ: Avery Publishing Group, 1987.

Shurtleff, William, and Akiko Aoyagi. *The Book of Kudzu: A Culinary and Healing Guide.* Brookline, MA: Autumn Press, 1997.

Singh, Yadhu N., and Mark Blumenthal. "Kava: Distribution, Mythology, Botany, Culture, Chemistry and Pharmacology of the South Pacific's Most Revered Herb." *Herbalgram* (No. 39), pp. 33–56.

Sokolov, Raymond. "America's First Food Writer." *Natural History,* October 1992.

Susser, Allen. *The Great Citrus Book: A Guide with Recipes.* Berkeley, CA: Ten Speed Press, 1997.

Thomas, Cathy. *Melissa's Great Book of Produce.* Hoboken, NJ: John Wiley and Sons, 2006.

Tierra, Michael. *Planetary Herbology.* Twin Lakes, WI: Lotus Press, 1988.

Toussaint-Samat, Maguelonne. Translated by Anthea Bell. *History of Food.* Cambridge, MA: Blackwell Publishers, 1994.

Travers, Rachel. "The Wild and Whorly Fiddlehead." *Christian Science Monitor,* May 2, 1996, p. 14.

Tropp, Barbara. *The Modern Art of Chinese Cooking.* New York: William Morrow, 1982.

Underhill, Ruth. *Autobiography of a Papago Woman.* New York: Holt, Rinehart, and Winston, 1979.

———. *Papago Woman.* Reprint, Prospect Heights, IL: Waveland Press, 1985.

U.S. Department of Health, Education, and Welfare et al. *Food Composition Table for Use in East Asia.* Washington, DC: DHEW Publication No. (NIH) 79-465, 1978.

Van Aken, Norman. *The Great Exotic Fruit Book.* Berkeley, CA: Ten Speed Press, 1995.

Vaughan, John G., and Catherine Geissler. *The New Oxford Book of Food Plants.* New York: Oxford University Press, 1997.

Vilmorin-Andrieux, M. *The Vegetable Garden.* English Edition. Berkeley, CA: Ten Speed Press, 1981.

Weil, Andrew. *Spontaneous Healing.* New York: Alfred A. Knopf, 1996.

———. "Therapeutic Hemp Oil." *Natural Health,* March/April 1993, pp. 10–12.

Williamson, Darcy. *The Rocky Mountain Wild Foods Cookbook.* Caldwell, ID: Caxton Printers, 1995.

Wittenberg, Margaret M. *Good Food: The Complete Guide to Eating Well.* Freedom, CA: Crossing Press, 1995.

Wolverton, B. C. *How to Grow Fresh Air: 50 Houseplants That Purify Your Home or Office.* New York: Penguin, 1997.

Wood, Rebecca. *Quinoa: The Supergrain.* Tokyo: Japan Publications, 1989.

———. *The Splendid Grain.* New York: William Morrow, 1997.

Worwood, Valarie Ann. *The Complete Book of Essential Oils and Aromatherapy.* San Rafael, CA: New World Library, 1991.

Yin-Fang, Dia, and Liu Cheng-Jun. Translated by Ron Edwards and Gong Zhi-Mei. *Fruits as Medicine: A Safe and Cheap Form of Traditional Chinese Food Therapy.* Selangor Darul Ehsan, Malaysia: Pelanduk Publications (M) Sdn. Bhd., 1999.

Young, Kay. *Wild Seasons: Gathering and Cooking Wild Plants of the Great Plains.* Lincoln, NE: University of Nebraska Press, 1993.

INDEX

NOTE: Medical conditions, organ systems, and micronutrients are listed in ALL CAPS. *Unless otherwise specified*, subentries for medical conditions and organ systems are presumed to help the condition or organ. When there are multiple entries for a food item, the main entry is in **bold type**. Index entries for medical conditions are meant to be pointers to information in the text; please be sure to consult the text referenced.

RECIPE INDEX